AROP M~~~~~~~~~~~

SUDAN'S PAINFUL ROAD TO PEACE

A FULL STORY OF THE FOUNDING AND DEVELOPMENT OF SPLM/SPLA

2006

To order additional copies, please contact us.
BookSurge, LLC
www.booksurge.com
1-866-308-6235 ·
orders@booksurge.com

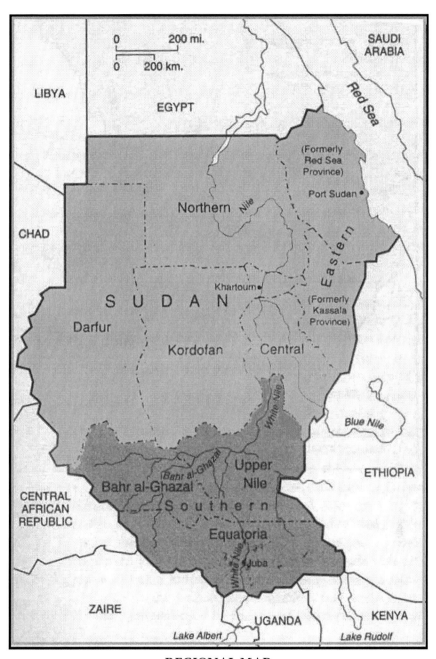

REGIONAL MAP

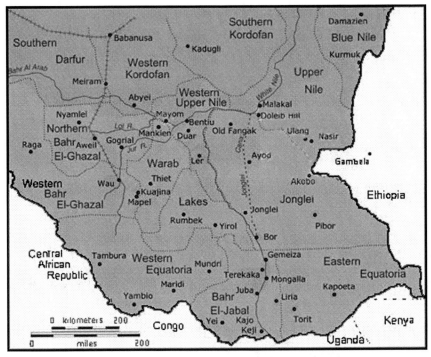

SOUTHERN SUDAN

Photo: Sudan.Net Website

General Dr John Garang de Mabior.
Sudan's First Vice President and historic President of South Sudan—first
SPLM Chairman and Commander-in-Chief of the SPLA July 1983—July
2005.

Photo: Gurtong.Net Website

Lt. General Salva Kiir Mayardit.
Sudan's First Vice President—succeeded Dr Garang as President of South
Sudan
Chairman of SPLM and Commander-in-Chief of SPLA.

This Book Is Dedicated To My Nephew, Captain Arop Ring Madut-arop. Arop Ring Met His Tragic Death During The Spla Infighting In Bor, 1992. Because Arop Ring Was Not Given The Honourable Burial He Deserved, This Book Is Therefore Dedicated To Him And His Fallen Colleagues: Wuor Jook Abyei And Kuol-thuuk Deng Kuol, Who Were Savagely Slain In Cold Blood In Nasir During The Same Period. Also Captains Deng Bul Dengluak And Laal Longo, Whom I Met Briefly In Addis Ababa Shortly Before They Fell. May Those Who Read This Book Remember Arop Ring Madut And His Fallen Colleagues.

CONTENTS

Part II

Chapter 6

SPLA Fighting And Talking Strategy   117

Chapter 7

The Third Democratic Experiment And Prospects For Peace   143

Chapter 8

SPLA Bright Star Campaign Takes Firm Grip On The South   189

Chapter 9

The Islamists Military Iron Fist Regime   223

Chapter 10

The Nif Stratagem And Split In SPLM/SPLA   259

Part III

Chapter 11

Nif Launches Operation' Seif Obuur Against SPLA   301

Chapter 16

Conclusion: Final Road To Peace 391

ABBREVIATIONS

AACC	=	All African Conference of Churches
AI	=	Amnesty International
APF	=	Anya Nya Patriotic Front
ALF	=	Abyei Liberation Front
AU	=	African Unity
BOSS	=	Bank of South Sudan
CAR	=	Central Africa Republic
CCI	=	Compagnie Centrale internationale
Cdr	=	Commander
CPA	=	Comprehensive Peace Agreement
DDF	=	Darfur Development Front
DOP	=	Declaration Of Principles
DUP	=	Democratic Unionist Party
EPDRF	=	Ethiopian People Democratic Revolutionary Front
ELI	=	Egyptian Libyan Initiative
EICC	=	Equatoria Intellectual Central Committee
CUSS	=	Council for Unity of South Sudan
DUP	=	Democratic Unionist Party
GOS	=	Government Of Sudan
GOSS	=	Government Of South Sudan
GUN	=	General Union Of Nubas
HEC	=	High Executive Council
IARA	=	Islamic African Relief Agency
IFP	=	Internal Front for Peace
ICF	=	Islamic Charter Front
IGADD	=	Inter-Governmental Authority for Desertification and Drought
IGAD	=	Inter-Governmental Authority for Development
MP	=	Member of Parliament
MTLSS	=	Movement for Total Liberation of South Sudan
NANS	=	National Alliance for National Salvation
NAM	=	National Action Movement
NIF	=	National Islamic Front
NCP	=	National Congress Party

NCO	=	Non Commissioned Officer
NDA	=	National Democratic Alliance
NIF	=	National Islamic Front
NPG	=	Nile Provisional Government
NUP	=	National Unionist Party
OAU	=	Organisation of Africa Unity
OLF	=	Oromo Liberation Front
PDP	=	People Democratic Party
PDF	=	Popular Defence Force
PMHC	=	Politico-Military High Command
PPP	=	People Progressive Party
PCP	=	Popular Congress Party
PR	=	Public Relations
RASS	=	Relief Agency for South Sudan
RCC	=	Revolution Command Council
SAC	=	Sudan African Congress
SAF	=	Sudan Alliance Forces/Sudan Armed Forces
SANU	=	Sudan Africa National Union
SAPCO	=	Sudan African People Congress
SCC	=	Sudan Council of Churches
SCIS	=	Strategic Centre for International Studies
SCP	=	Sudan Communist Party
SDF	=	Sudan Defence Force
SF	=	Southern Front
SIFP	=	Southern Islamic Front for Peace
SPAF	=	Sudan People Armed Forces
SSLM	=	South Sudan Liberation Movement
SSPA	=	South Sudan Political Association
SSPG	=	South Sudan Provisional Government
SSIM	=	South Sudan Independent Movement
SSIA	=	South Sudan Independent Army
SSRM	=	South Sudan Revolutionary Movement
SNP	=	Sudan National Party
SPLA	=	Sudan People Liberation Army
SPLM	=	Sudan People Liberation Movement
SRRA	=	Sudan Relief and Rehabilitation Agency
SSU	=	Sudan Socialist Union
TMC	=	Transitional Military Council
UNHCR	=	United Nations High Commissioner for Refugees
UNPG	=	Upper Nile Provisional Government
UDSF	=	United Democratic Salvation Front

UDSSF	=	United Democratic South Sudan Forces
USAP	=	Union of African Parties
WCC	=	World Council of Churches
WUN	=	Western Upper Nile

ACKNOWLEDGEMENTS

This book would have not seen the light of the day without the assistance and the encouragement of Dr. Douglas H. Johnson, who not only supported the initial idea, but afforded me financial assistance. I am particularly grateful to Professor William Beinart, Rhodes Race Relation Chair Professor, St. Antony's College, University of Oxford, who offered me the scholarship for the part of Academic year 1999-2000. Thanks are also due to Professor Wendy James, Head of the Social and Cultural Anthropology Institute, St. Antony's College, University of Oxford, for affording me the necessary academic environment for compiling the book. Gratefully, I appreciate the efforts of the following SPLA Officers: Stephen Madut Baak, Dominic Diim Deng, Dr. Richard K. Mulla; Captain Mayom Kuoac Malek, Bol Wek Agoth for availing useful inside knowledge about the administration and the structure of the SPLM/SPLA. Thanks also go to one of the SPLA pioneering officers, Captain Wadang Biong Kuol, who enlightened me about the SPLA first military Campaign in Eastern Equatoria. Without this inside knowledge, I might have missed much of what has made this book what it is. Thanks are also due to Uncle Gordon Muortat Mayen, veteran southern politician, former President of the rebel Nile Provisional Government of the defunct Anya Nya Movement for giving me the background and particularly about the demise of the first liberation struggle. Muortant was a good source because he has keenly been watching events as they unfolded at his exile home in London.

My gratitude also goes to the late Hilary Paul Logali for educating me about much of the information about the defunct regional government in which he was a key figure. I am also obliged to Dr. Zachariah Bol Deng for his repeated encouragement not to despair, but tell the story to its successful end. Thanks are due to Aldo Ajou Deng, former adviser to the Regime, and John Angol (member of the regime) for throwing more light about the Salvation Regime's Policies on the South. I am also obliged to Major General Hassan Ahmedein Suleiman who, in an unofficial capacity, discussed with me about the strategies of the Salvation Revolution. The General, though one of the top coup makers and the Junta strategist and its First Secretary General of the Ruling National Congress Party, he was finally sent into the dustbin of history for being a non NIF insider. His strategic position made him a formidable and an authoritative source about the basic policies of the regime.

I am very grateful also to the following persons: General Dominic Kassiano (former RCC member) General Gissmallah Abdalla Rassass, General Robert Mayuk Deng, Justice Wilson Aryamba and Oliver Albino Battali with whom I cross checked the information contained in my plan before I left the country to write this book. I would like also to thank my long time friend Joseph Dut Wuor Abyei who first advised me to keep the records of my interviews. "Who knows, these interviews could provide basis for writing books in foreseeable future" he often remarked. I am deeply indebted to the following: The Avenue Charitable Trust, The Gordon Memorial College Trust and The Window for Southern Sudan Development Project for giving me the initial financial assistance which enabled me to visit various libraries in search of material to cross check my work.

I am very much indebted to Jeremy Herklots who not only offered me a computer but also helped me to learn computer skills. Without these skills I would have not have been able to make the book ready for publication. My gratitude goes to my friend David Nailo Mayo for typing the first part of the manuscript and Isabella Birkin of the Institute of Social Anthropology, St. Antony's College, for completing typing the last part of the first manuscript. There are countless people who deserve thanks but who may not have been mentioned by name. This is not because I am ungrateful for their valuable contributions but because it is not always practicable to put everything down in a book of this nature.

I thank all members of my family for enduring all sorts of discomforts during my absence to compile the book, especially during my previous arrests and long detention. I am obliged to my sons Madut Arop and Jeiel Arop who suspended their studies in order to support the family. Last but not least I am particularly grateful to my nephew Deng Akol Kuot Leng (Deng Nyanngok Madut-Arop) for his financial contribution toward the completion of the book.

AMA

PREFACE

At the heat of fighting between the government army and the rebels of the Sudan People Liberation Army in 1986 and as the editor of the *Heritage Weekly Newspaper*, it was natural that I should conduct interviews with key players in the country's civil war.

The aim behind these interviews was basically to sound out opinions of various people beginning from the grassroots to the top government officials and political echelons about the possibility of halting the war in favour of permanent peace.

These interviews were conducted under the theme "Sudan Quest for Peace: Who is Telling the Truth?" With that in mind, I travelled extensively in the country making a wide range of contacts, gauging the general feeling about the attainment of peace. I was struck by the general feeling that the whole nation was yearning for peace and against the continuation of the war that was at that time increasingly galvanising into widespread civil strife.

To put the plan into practice, I ventured into the field to talk to the rank and file of the SPLM/SLA cadres. I also had the chance to talk to the underground cells inside the country.

I also discussed peace issues with the government's security personnel who were ready to give me the general trend of thinking in the country about the need to re-establish peace and stability in the country.

At the centre of this war game, there were accusations and counter accusations with the two neighbourly states trying to denigrate each other. The Sudan Government was accusing the Ethiopian Government for allegedly supporting the SPLA rebels materially and logistically and the Ethiopian Government was accusing the Sudan Government for aiding the Eritrean and the Tigrinyan guerrillas in a tit for tat venture.

This trading of accusations was bound to affect relations not only between the two states, but their respective people caught up between the battle lines. There was, therefore, a dire need to interview authorities in both countries as well as their respective rebel groups on the issues of war and peace.

Thus in December, 1986, I travelled to Addis Ababa where I met with the Ethiopian Incumbent President Colonel Mengistu Haile Mariame who generously offered his views and discussed at length the issues involved.

Back home I interviewed the then Sudanese Prime Minister Sadig al

Mahdi who also told me his part of the story about what he thought could be done about the war and how best it could be halted.

Following my interview with al Mahdi and some of his ministers, I met and discussed issues of war and peace with a number of leading northern and southern politicians. Among the northern elite I frequently discussed the northern viewpoint with Dr. Taiseer Mohamed Ahmed Ali who, since the overthrow of the Nimeiri Regime in 1985, had devoted much of his time in the search of peace.

Dr. Taieseer was then shuttling between authorities inside the Sudan and the SPLM officials in the Ethiopian Capital Addis Ababa. He was indeed very central in the later rapprochement between the northern elite and the SPLM leadership, which led to the signing of the Koka Dam and Ambo accords. He was therefore a good source for my purpose.

On the southern spectrum, I continuously discussed the issues at stake with Hilary Paul Logali, the most respected and seasoned of southern leaders. Late Hilary Logali was always handy, even at the small hours of the night, to offer me his views and analysis on my plan.

Having ascertained the general trends of events inside the country, I travelled once more to Ethiopia where I talked with senior commanders of the SPLA.

The top officers I interviewed included an all-weather southern politician, Uncle Joseph Oduho; William Nyuon Bany, SPLA Chief of General Staff, Kerubino Kuanyin Bol, SPLM/SPLA Deputy Chairman and Deputy Commander in Chief; Arok Thon Arok, Deputy Chief of Staff for Administrations and Logistics, Dr Lam Akol Ajawin, SPLM representative for peace and external relations; SPLA Commanders: Lual Diing Wuol; Yousif Kua Meki and Alfred Lado Gore. I also talked with Captains Bary Wanji, Simon Mori Didumo and many others in the rank and file of the Movement. Indeed the list was long. Some of those interviews were later published in the *Heritage Newspaper* in Khartoum, The Africa Events in London and Nigrizia in Verona/ Rome, Italy.

My later work with the Sudan Council of Churches (SCC) at the Advocacy and Communications Desk (1988 and 1994) offered me a golden chance to follow up closely the issues of war and peace.

At the SCC Advocacy Desk, I was able to shuttle between Khartoum and Addis Ababa in an effort to follow up peace negotiations between the Sudanese officials and the rebel leaders at various stages and fora.

Having assessed the opinion inside and outside the country, I travelled to Kenya to cover the meetings between the parliamentary delegation of the Union of Sudan African Parties (USAP) from Khartoum and the SPLM leaders. The USAP and the SPLM meetings were aimed, among others, at efforts to compare their agendas on the peace process.

In Nairobi, I managed to conduct a lengthy interview with the SPLM/ SPLA leader, Dr John Garang de Mabior, who elaborately gave me an inside story about the birth and policies of the SPLM/SPLA. Besides this basic information, Dr. Garang talked at length on the issues of war and peace in the Sudan.

These interviews however, were continued between 1986 and 1989. But before I could put my ideas together, the Islamists seized power in a military coup. The period that followed witnessed the intensification of the war and the resultant mutual destruction in lives and materials not only in the southern Sudan where much of the fighting took place, but throughout the country.

Predictably, the military regime that took power in 1989 scrapped all the previous peace initiatives and imposed its own Orwellian peace overtures. Not only that, I was arrested and detained for the next fourteen months from March to September (1990) at Kobar Prison and September (1990) to May (1991) at New Halfa. Apparently, the military Junta may have designed this in order to curb my activities which they looked at with suspicion.

Sadly to say, my long detention brought my plan to a halt, albeit temporarily. Nonetheless, I continued discussing my plan with the political inmates, some of whom were senior cadres of their respective parties or former ministers in the defunct democratic regime.

Following my release from detention in 1991, I came over to London to recuperate in 1992. It was during this time that I was able to put my ideas together and then laid down the main theme of the book.

Yet these writings remained on paper till January 1994 when I paid a visit to Oxford where I discussed my plan with old friend Dr. Douglas H. Johnson. He suggested that the material could provide basis for a book.

I immediately started making the structure of the book. I returned to the Sudan to gather more materials in order to come back to the UK in 1995 to put my plan into practice.

Unfortunately, I could not get back in time because of a visa problem. Hence another delay to start my programme. However, with the assistance of Dr. Johnson, I managed to get a fellowship at St. Antony's College, University of Oxford.

Dr. Johnson was at this time a Senior Fellow at St. Antony's College, University of Oxford. Dr. Johnson and I had worked together in the regional ministry of Culture and Information in Juba 1977 to 1980. He was therefore not alien to my plan.

Thus under the Rhodes Race Relations Chair Fund, in April 1999, serious work began. Eighteen months later the book started to take shape. It took another two years to complete the final manuscript. Basically, the work is a collection of interviews compiled in the course of time about the Sudanese conflict in general and the SPLA military campaign. It starts with the winding up of the first Anya Nya War (1969/1972), through the ten years of the regional self rule, to the emergence of the SPLM/SPLA in 1983. The book then discusses in details the military campaign and efforts exerted to bring the warring parties to the negotiating table in addition to the conclusion and the signing of the Naivasha Comprehensive Peace Agreement.

In brief, the book could be described as an inside story of the rise and development of the Sudan People Liberation Movement and Liberation Army (SPLM/SPLA): Its subsequent military campaign which eventually galvanised into large scale civil war and the final attainment of a permanent peace.

INTRODUCTION

Sudan, a former British colony and the largest country in Africa, two million square kilometres with an estimated population of about 35 million people, according to population growth estimates, emerged into nationhood in 1956 with a predicament. Since it came into existence as a geographic expression in the early part of the 19th Century, Sudan had never been ruled as one country.

Throughout its colonial and post colonial period, Sudan had never been brought up to feel as one nation. The reason was simple: Its two distinct parts were kept rigidly apart as two separate entities, with two different official languages, Arabic in the north and English in the south.

Islam predominated in the north, Christianity in the south. There were even two different days of rest in the week, namely Friday in the north, and Sunday in the south. There were also two different sets of public holidays. The mentalities of the two people were therefore different.

To make things worse, the dawn of independence in January, 1956, triggered off a civil war that took much of the first seventeen years of its political life.

With the civil war escalating by the day, years of independence started with suspicion between the two antagonistic parts of the country. Consequently, bitterness was created, nursed and nurtured between the two peoples.

All along the south felt betrayed, firstly by the British, the principal ruler in the condominium rule (1899-1956) and secondly hoodwinked by the north in the immediate years after independence.

The subsequent attempts by the successive national regimes to make the two parts of the country grow together in order to mould them into one nation was, unfortunately, slowed down and brought with it a built in time bomb.

With the differences widening year by year, it was natural that such a country could not possibly draw together to become a homogenous nation state.

To guide such a country into unity of purpose may have needed much more insight and good imagination from the founding fathers. But unfortunately, those who took over power immediately from the colonial administration failed miserably to live up to the country's expectations.

Instead of introducing a slow, purposeful, well-designed, good process and system to integrate the two alien and antagonistic parts of their country into one nation state, the post independence leaders behaved as if they had inherited a homogenous country which had been kept apart by a malicious ruler.

Furthermore, without giving themselves time to bring the two parts of their country to pull together and build unity in diversity, the Sudanese, who assumed power at the onset, hurriedly rushed in many measures intended at creating homogeneity. These were sudanisation of all the posts from the colonial administration to the exclusion of southerners and the integration of the army.

The later move to transfer southern military units to the north, a part of the country totally alien to the soldiers of those units recruited mainly from the southern village warriors, created a friction that triggered off the first explosion which led to the first conflict (1956-1972).

The subsequent solutions offered by the post independence authorities to crush the rebellion and contain the south, after which it could quickly be integrated into an Arab Islamic entity, dismally led to more resentment from the aggrieved people of the region when discovering that those solutions hankered on the slogan that Sudan was unquestionably one country.

Additionally, any southerner wanting differentiation or diversification was taken as a separatist, a move that was tantamount to treason. Even the genuine attempts by the south to be left alone as a young child that would naturally grow to maturity by its own after which it could finally join the rest of the country, was rudely denied.

So as years wound by, things began to drift from bad to worse. Instead of achieving the ultimate goal of creating homogeneity in which Islam and Arabism predominated and of reaching a national consensus, the gap between the two parts of this vast country began to widen more and more.

As efforts to enforce a military solution continued, the country was dragged into a devastating civil war. To stem out the civil war, the army was brought in for a purpose by the north in 1958.

The new military Junta immediately suspended the nascent parliamentary democracy. It then agitated and prepared the young nation in order to crush the rebellion that was rapidly galvanising into a civil strife.

With the Army making more blunders in its execution of the war in October 1964, the Military Junta was overthrown by a popular uprising which became known as the October Revolution.

The overthrow of the military Junta was followed by a brief period of second experiment with the parliamentary democracy between 1964 and 1969.

During this period it was assumed that the leaders of the October regime had learned lessons that may have prepared them as to how best they might deal with the rebellion that was by then gaining momentum.

From the examination of the records of the political and historical developments of the times, it would appear that no clear lessons were learned by the October authorities.

Once back on the high ground of politics after six years out of power, it was assumed that those authorities would attend to the crucial issues that brought about the civil war and the overthrow of the military regime.

Regrettably in 1964, the northern political parties, refused to accept the fact about the reality of the situation. Instead they began, in earnest, with their political bickering; holding the reins of power while continuing to rule the country in the same manner as they had done immediately after independence (1956-1958).

Since the days of the self-government in 1954, it would appear that the principled aim of the north had, all along, been to enforce the axiom of one religion, Islam, and one language, Arabic. Unfortunately, due to their insistence to implement this axiom, the writing of a permanent constitution was not made possible.

Basically, the insistence of the northern politicians to adopt an Islamic constitution, a move which the southerners opposed vigorously in the 1965, 1966 and 1968 parliamentary sessions, and at the all party constitutional conferences, fuelled the insurgency.

Because of the above political bickering over the writing of the constitution as well as the escalation of the war in the south, the Army once more took over the reins of power in May 1969. This move ushered in the May Regime Era which was to remain in office for the next 16 years (1969-1985).

The leaders of the May Regime, however, fared better in that they behaved and acted as if they had drawn good lessons from the previous experiences of the successive governments that preceded them.

In order to satisfy the southern Sudanese grievances, the leaders of the May Regime recognised the futility in the centralism philosophy and adopted a more pragmatic approach to the country endemic problems in general, and the southern question in particular. Indeed the May Regime recognised that the problem of the south was basically responsible for the country predicament.

The May Regime leaders scored some measure of successes. These successes were crowned when they took further positive steps to halt the war in 1972 and conceded and gave the south some form of self rule which ushered in a period of relative calm for the next ten years (1972-1982).

Indeed the period between the signing of the Addis Ababa accord, March 1972 and June 1983, when this accord was scrapped, can be described as the only period that witnessed a restoration of confidence lost between the south and the north in the previous years.

There was, at this time, an apparent urge to move forward in order to take the country toward a sustainable socio-economic and political development which the country badly needed.

Those hopes were soon dashed when the same leader, President Nimeiri, who brought peace, with a stroke of a pen, abrogated the Accord, thereby ending the special status of the south as a self governing region, a move which was to plunge the country headlong into a civil war.

Essentially, the abrogation of the Addis Ababa Agreement and the subsequent introduction of the ever harsh and discriminatory Sharia (Islamic Laws) in September, 1983, brought a clandestine revolutionary movement in the south onto the surface; very highly organised, and led by sophisticated and well-educated young men and women.

The launching of the people's revolution, the Sudan People Liberation Movement and the Liberation Army plunged the entire country into worse bloodshed than had hitherto been known. Unlike the previous ones, the SPLM/SPLA and the Khartoum Army used modern weapons. That situation regrettably led to mutual destruction, not only to the warring parties, but also to civil population caught up between the battles.

It is in this light that the re-emergence of the civil war in the southern Sudan for the second time in 1983 could at best be explained; as a continued expression and desire by the people of that region to identify themselves as a different people from their northern counterparts.

They should therefore be recognised as a people with inalienable rights capable of ruling themselves by themselves. They could at the same time participate and contribute as a partner on equal footing with their counter partners in the building of the nation that they have come to wittingly or unwittingly, claim as their country.

In contrast to the previous rebellion, the leaders of the SPLM/SPLA brought about changes in the country as a whole. The rebels' agenda was basically aimed at the creation of a new country founded on new basis that included the restructuring of the power base in Khartoum in favour of the age long marginalised people of the rural Sudan.

This book, therefore, intends to put together the records of those sad events highlighted above for the benefit of students of political history of Southern Sudan and future researchers of this important period.

Throughout the book, the reader is guided through, highlighting in the process, the inside story of the second southern revolt scene by scene from the beginning to the end. The reader is reminded again and again throughout the book about the crux of the crisis that has been holding the national advancement hostage for decades.

The author believes that the true story of the Sudan People Liberation

Movement (SPLM) and the Sudan People Liberation Army (SPLA) has yet to be thoroughly documented.

It is the opinion of this author that the full story of the SPLM/SPLA war, as told by various contemporary writers, has insufficiently been recorded. Hence the need to narrate the whole story of the emergence and development of the Sudan People Liberation Movement and Liberation Army in which this author has been an observer and sometimes an activist, having had access to all the key players in this war game in a professional capacity. Basically, the book can be divided up into three parts.

PART ONE

Part one of the book commences with a brief revisit of the Anya Nya Movement and its subsequent winding up when south Sudan was given a regional self rule in accordance to the Addis Ababa Peace Agreement of 1972. The advent of the May Regime in 1969 and its approach to the problem of the south is re-examined.

The ten year period of the regional self-rule (1972-1982) ushered in by the agreement between the May Regime and the rebels of the Southern Sudan Liberation Movement (SSLM) will adequately be highlighted. This will give the reader the actual background of the war.

The problematic absorption of the Anya Nya freedom fighters into the national Army and the difficulties that accrued therefrom and which would give rise to the Underground Resistance and the birth of the SPLM/SPLA (Chapter 1) is discussed in more detail.

The political climate in the south and between the north and the south before the re-emergence of the civil strife in May 1983 and SPLA initial military campaign and politics embroiled in the leadership contest at the onset are discussed thoroughly. The scene is set for the next stage, eruption of war.

The vital question: whether there was a dire need for the people of Southern Sudan to take up arms once more after ten years of relative calm during which time they had tested the fruits of political and socio-economic developments, is highlighted sufficiently.

Furthermore, discussion of politics leading to the resumption of the war that has now reshaped the Sudanese political landscape, is important because it will disprove the Sudan military establishment theory that the SPLA war was triggered because of a dispute over the salaries of the soldiers of 105 Battalion stationed in Bor District in March 1983.

Equally important to note at this point in time is the claim that the fragmentation of the South in 1983 and the imposition of the Sharia Islamic Laws in September of the same year had any direct bearing in the re-emergence of the civil war in the Southern Sudan. They were rather complementary factors to say the least.

The emergence of the Anya Nya Two and its political wing, the Nya Patriotic Front, formed by Southern politicians in exile in response to the prevailing political situation at home is thoroughly discussed.

Precisely, the prevailing political situation between 1981 to 1983 can be said to have only laid down fertile ground for the return to armed struggle suspended by the conclusion of the Addis Ababa Peace Accord in 1972 (Chapter 2).

The formation and launch of SPLM/SPLA in Western Ethiopia between July and August 1983, in addition to the events that triggered off the first split of the Movement and the effective start of the military campaign, is discussed at some greater length scene by scene (Chapter 3).

The Movement, instead of fighting the one enemy that set the entire region on a painful road to peace and which they must now confront vigorously, began to fight against itself; SPLA against Anya Nya Two. This was unfortunate because it led to the unnecessary death of some of the southern nationalists who agitated for the resumption of the war of liberation like Benjamin Bol Akok, Samuel Gai Tut and Akuot Atem in addition to thousands of innocent freedom fighters delaying the war of liberation.

Ideologically and strategically, the two factions of the Movement could not agree to form one movement. While the SPLA wanted to fight for a united democratic secular, New Sudan, the Anya Nya Two had wanted to fight for total liberation of Southern Sudan from the Arab Islamic North. This became a bone of contention throughout the war and extended into the interim period. It would also be reflected in the choice during the referendum.

Consequently, the infighting within what should have been one Southern movement fighting one enemy became responsible for the delay in the recruitment, training and procurement of military logistics by the SPLA. In the process, thousands of southern recruits were confused. They could not comprehend which side of the movement was the right one for each of them to join. Thus it became extremely difficult for the infant movement to get sufficient recruits to begin the war.

This can explain the reason the SPLA was forced to send military expeditions deep into Bahr al Ghazal, the region that had vehemently opposed the suspension of the liberation struggle in 1972, and the re-division of the South into mini-regions in 1983 so as to get recruits through direct contact with the local population (Chapter 4).

It was in this light that the execution of the war was marred with tragedies, agonies and ruins left at its wake once a comprehensive peace agreement was signed.

President Nimeiri's last days in office and the desperate attempts he made in effort to reverse the crisis he had helped create is well documented because it was the beginning of the bloody war that nearly plunged the country into total abyss.

SPLA attempts to counteract vigorously a move that brought about the demise of the May Regime giving rise to the Transitional Military Council (1985) and the running of general elections (1986) are also illuminated at the conclusion of part one.

PART TWO

The second part of the book begins with a brief analysis about the serious search for peace when northern opposition parties and university lecturers and trade unions approached SPLA/SPLM leadership and held peace talks which culminated with the signing of Koka Dam and Ambo Declarations (Chapter 6).

SPLA responded to the northern opposition peace overtures and adopted a fighting and talking strategy (1985-1989). From there things began to move past. The combined rebels and opposition agitation brought the public onto the streets in popular uprising which brought down Nimeiri's 16 year autocratic rule ushering in the emergence of Sudan Third Parliamentary Democratic Experiment under Prime Minister Sadig al Mahdi (Chapter 7).

Additionally, the later intensification of war by the democratic regime of al Mahdi and continued search for peace led to the signing of the DUP-SPLM Sudan Peace Initiative signed in Addis Ababa on November 16, 1988.

The DUP/SPLM peace initiative eventually led to the formation of a pro peace party government in March 1989. As a consequence, all the pro peace political parties were agreed to meet on July 4, 1989 to set the agenda rolling for the convening of the National Constitutional Conference scheduled for September 18, 1989. By May 1989, it became quite apparent that peace was on the horizon.

But the anti-peace group, consisting of the Pan-Arab political parties led by the National Islamic Front (NIF), opposed these peace overtures. It was in this light that while the whole nation was awaiting for the descent of peace, hopes were soon dashed by the emergence of another military take over on June 30, 1989.

The military coup coincided with intensification of the war in the south by the SPLA Bright Star Campaign. Between 1988 and 1989, SPLA reorganised its military structures. Fighting forces all over the region were recalled, retrained and re-equipped. One Mobile Division code-named Bright Star Campaign was unleashed. The activities of the SPLA Bright Star Campaign in 1988 and 1989 sent shock waves to Khartoum. It made it crystal clear that the SPLA was controlling nearly ninety per cent of the Southern Sudan.

While these developments were welcome signs of hope for south Sudanese that the end of the war was in sight in their favour, they were very worrying to northerners as some of them began to speculate the possibility that the south may break away sooner than later.

The National Islamic Front Seizure of power on June 30, 1989 is attributed to the Bright Star Campaign military might that brought ninety per cent of the southern rural territories as well as controlling the southern Sudan main cities.

NIF seizure of power in June 1989 (Chapter 9) was apparently welcome by the entire north because the new rulers had promised they would reverse the situation in the south.

The new Junta, calling itself the Salvation Revolution, took effective control of the country. It immediately mobilised the entire north for war to end wars in the south.

For the north, it was the first time since Sudan attained independence in 1956 that a real determined government had come to power; a government that launched direct conventional confrontation between the north and the south.

The NIF policies brought untold disasters to the nation. These policies were orchestrated with the regime launching a two tiered agenda for a peaceful resolution of the war: the Peace From Within (internal peace) and the Peace From Without (external peace (Chapter 10). Each of the two agendas was directed and manned by an inner circle cadre.

The internal peace process was intended to win over the southern population in order to support the government policies through financial inducements or political incentives. However, the external peace process was a propaganda machinery aimed at diverting the attention of international communities away from their fundamentalist agenda.

PART THREE

Part Three discusses the declaration of an all out war—the jihaad—or the Holy Islamic War Campaign between 1992 and 1995 (Chapter 11). The massive military campaign code-named "The Operation Seif al Obuur" (the dry season offensive) was unleashed against the southern infidel rebels at the beginning of 1992. The dry season offensive in fact was an invading force intended to wipe out the rebellion in the south.

This massive military operation executed with the assistance and guidance of the SPLA dissident groups and almost brought the SPLA down to its knees. The Army managed to overwhelm the rebels and regained almost all the areas previously taken from the government.

At first instant it appeared as if the Islamic regime could crush the rebellion. It became true when the SPLA was split in 1991 into two factions, each fighting the other. But, the situation soon changed in favour of the SPLA (Chapter 12) forces which did not only re-occupy the south, but took the war to eastern Sudan.

The two-tiered desperate peace policies the NIF adopted as far back as the 1990s were aimed at attempts to win the war by declaring an all out war against the rebels. At the same time, NIF kept painting false picture that it was embarking on a genuine peaceful engagement with the rebels.

The NIF policies which were essentially designed and directed at an effort to crush the rebellion in the south of the country once and for all also resulted in the making of the short-lived Khartoum Peace Agreement (Chapter 13).

The dissident rebels tricked into signing this "fake" agreement soon discovered the truth. Although some of the rebels managed to walk back and rejoined the Movement they had left in 1991, others could not make it; as they were caught up in a web of no return.

They could not abandon the internal peace process because of the financial inducements or because they were too blackmailed to extract themselves from the complex social situations they have found themselves in.

Essentially, the NIF policies were being implemented at the time that the international communities were clamouring for peace in order to bring about an end to the untold human disasters created by the continued war in the Southern Sudan and particularly in the Nuba Mountains.

The international clamour described above came as a result of human rights and humanitarian organisation that have vigorously been campaigning against the continuation of the Jihaad War which has devastated much of the Nuba region.

Regrettably, the consequences of those jihaad wars also brought untold sufferings to the people of South Sudan and led to the total devastation of the main theatre of war, Southern Sudan, and threatened the existence of Sudan as a nation state.

The later intensification of the war included eastern Sudan and the polarisation of the conflict (1995-2001) was a natural reaction from the National Democratic Alliance (NDA). This was a concerted attempt by all opposition forces posing as "the government in waiting" to get rid of the NIF regime from power once and for all.

During this period described by watchers of Sudan's politics as a watershed, the war was no longer fought as the south against the north, but the government and the southern dissident groups versus the SPLA collaborating with the forces of Northern Opposition Parties in exile.

Unfortunately, the polarisation and the contradictions that ensued, the schisms in the NIF leadership in addition to multinational competition in Sudan oil, became complicating factors that almost hindered the achievement of peace.

The war then entered the crucial stage in 2002 that put to test the SPLM/SPLA manifesto of July 1983 that called for the restructuring of power base in Khartoum. This manifesto would devolve most of the powers to the long marginalised regions in the South, West and the East.

A troika bringing together USA, UK, Norway (later joined by Italy) headed the international peace campaign and financed and facilitated the IGAD peace process which had continued steadily due to reluctance of the warring parties to make adequate concessions necessary for midway solution of the conflict.

With the change of guard in the US administration in 2000, the Bush Administration took Sudan to the top of its agenda of priorities. The appointment of Senator Danforth as special envoy to Sudan accelerated the quest for peace. Pressure was successfully exerted on both sides to abandon war and accept peace. The troika's efforts were rewarded when the two parties were finally goaded into negotiating seriously and in good faith.

Between the signing of the Machakos (July 20th 2002), the Naivasha Protocol (May 26 2005), and the Nairobi Declaration (June 5th 2004), the clock of the Sudanese conflict suddenly turned back full cycle. The war was being fought once again in the traditional manner of the north versus the south.

The SPLA, apparently reading the message on the wall and without losing sight of its main objective of creating a new Sudan in favour of the marginalised rural Sudan, adopted the South Sudan as its traditional constituency and began to negotiate as a southern movement.

The reason that the SPLA took such action, according to observers, has to do with the fact that the international communities who were their backers and the Southern Sudan (its constituency) were desparate for a permanent peace. It was a fact SPLA could not disregard.

The political development created by the Machakos Protocol and political polarisation (Chapter 16) convinced those concerned with the resolution of the conflict that it was possible to reconstruct a scene that could, in the short term, help the Sudan to come out of its chronic predicament.

The international communities were able to exert maximum efforts and indeed successfully pressured the warring parties to agree and reached a compromise through a number of protocols including; security, power sharing, wealth sharing and modalities for implementing the Peace Agreement which they signed on January 9, 2005.

While the CPA has brought the war to a final halt and promised the South Sudan a vote for independence in a referendum to be held in six years time, it has also promised for devolution of more security and political and socio-economic powers to the marginalised regions in the north.

In summary, "Sudan's Painful Road to Peace" is basically an elaborate detailed study of the Sudanese conflict in its entirety. It is an inside story of the Sudan's bloody war that had pitted the Arab Muslim north against the African-Christian-Animinst south using unity as a strategic slogan that won the SPLA respect as a genuine nationalist movement rather than a regional one with a parochial agenda.

The book is precisely an eye witness account of what has been going on behind the scene unknown to the outside world about how successive Arab regimes in Khartoum were able to declare the jihaad war with resultant atrocities and agonies on the south with one principled aim: to defeat the south, Arabicisize and Islamise its people after which it would then be integrated into the Arab Family of God. (See the book by Dr. Abdel Wahab el Effendi, "Sudanese Dilemma about the spread of Islam in Africa.")

As the Book comes to a close, readers are once again reminded that the agreement has raised guarded hopes that following many years of strife and political isolation, Sudan could once again join the ranks of civilised nations of the world as a proud, stable, nation state. Readers are cautioned to take note of one vital fact. The fact is that it is too early to celebrate because the final fate about the future of South Sudan's demand, now hinging between interim unity and creation of a separate independent state, remains to be decided. We may now read the book.

CHAPTER 1
THE ANYA NYA MOVEMENT REVISITED

1.0. THE SETTING

In 1969, two important events happened in the Sudan which were to re-chart the political landscape in the country. The first of these events was the appearance in the Southern Sudan of an effective organised political and military movements, the South Sudan Liberation Movement (SSLM) and its military wing, the Anya Nya (cobra's venom) guerrilla force.

From the onset, the SSLM's main task was to reorganise the Anya Nya freedom fighters scattered throughout the South Sudan and to drill them into an effective fighting force capable of facing the better organised and equipped Sudan Defence Force (SDF).

The new movement and its military wing were led by a young officer, Joseph Lagu, a graduate of the Sudan Military College. Lagu defected from the SDF and joined the rebels in 1963 in order to fight for the liberation of the South Sudan from the domination of the Arab-Muslim north.

The second event was when a group of young military officers under the command of Colonel Jaafar Mohamed Nimeiri, took over the reins of power on May 25, 1969.

These two episodes, many people believe, may go down on the anal of Sudanese history because they ushered in a period in which both the south and the north agreed to experiment with how to live together peacefully, though seemingly temporarily, as events subsequently proved.

Others are able to advance that the ten years of peace (1972-1982) may also mark the end for the two antagonistic parts of the Sudan to coexist under a unified political entity.

However, and in view of the importance of the changes they engendered, it will be instructive and appropriate to treat each of these episodes in their rightful perspective.

1.1. EXPULSION OF FOREIGN MISSIONARIES AND CHURCH ADVOCACY

The Military regime of General Abboud expelled, in 1964, foreign

Christian missionaries from South Sudan. The allegation was that they were responsible for arming the rebels as well as facilitating their movements.

Back in Rome, the Verona Fathers, headed by Bishop Edward Mason, launched an unprecedented propaganda against the Sudanese government, accusing it of persecuting the Christians in Southern Sudan.

In their book *The Black Book of Sudan,* the Verona Fathers denied the allegations heaped against them that they were helping the rebellion. Instead they disclosed details of widespread atrocities the government soldiers inflicted on the Christians in the region.

Fr Renato Bresciani, former Rector of the Roman Catholic Major Seminary Tore, Yei District, in Equatoria, led the Verona Fathers' anti-Sudan Government campaign in Italy.

The Roman Catholic campaign was picked up and reinforced by the World Council of Churches in Geneva and the Church Missionary Societies in Salisbury, headed by former Anglican Bishop of Sudan, Oliver Alison.

The anti-Sudan propaganda rhetoric depicted Khartoum regimes as terrorists to the extent that all that was preached in the Churches and reported in the press in the west against Khartoum was taken as naked truth.

The Roman Catholic propaganda and that of the Anglican Missionaries sent electric shock throughout the Christian World. It was particularly strong in the Scandinavian countries, France, and Italy.

Subsequently, both the government and humanitarian organisations all over Europe accused the governments of Mohamed Ahmed Mahjoub (1965-66), al-Sadig al-Mahdi (1966-67), and Mahjoub again (1967-1969) for unleashing terror against Christians and non-Christians of African origin in South Sudan.

The Christian world immediately responded to the call to save the people of the Southern Sudan from the state sponsored terrorism, the crusading anti-Christian regimes in Khartoum, and by extension from Arabicisation and Islamisation of the non-Arab people of the Sudan.

During the colonial bygone days that ended in 1956, the provinces of Bahr al-Ghazal, Equatoria and Upper Nile, were kept as preserves for the proselytization of the Christian faith under the Closed Districts Ordinance of 1922[1]. In Bahr al Ghazal, the Catholics had the upper hand.

Christian lobby groups in America and Europe and other sympathisers of the southern predicament were relieved by the formation of the SSPG in 1967 replacing the defunct SANU. SSPG was indeed accepted as a genuine movement that would manage to bring both the political and the military wings under one leadership in the south.

Immediately, some Church organisations like the Catholic Relief Agency, CARITAS, and the World Council of Churches were reported to have sent some relief assistance to the Anya Nya rebels.

Additionally, other sympathetic organisations in Europe, America, and Britain recommended that a number of officers be sent for training before sending arms and ammunition to the Southern rebels. Besides training, those officers were expected to study military sciences and guerrilla tactics before they could launch an effective war of liberation in the South Sudan.

Following the Six Day war in 1967, Israel, the age-long enemy of the Arab world, thought it opportune to come to the aid of the Southern Sudan.

To the Israelis, it was an excellent opportunity to counteract the anti-Zionist propaganda in the Arab world.

Thus between 1967 and 1968, Colonel Joseph Lagu Yanga was selected, along with forty officers, and sent to Israel for military training. The first batch included: Frederick Brian Maggot, Paul Awel, Emanuel Abuur Nhial, Alison Manani, Magaya, William Yanga, Bartholomew, Matthew Pagan, Stephen Ogut, John Okwak, Edward Peter, Escopas Juma, and Edward Lumodi, among others.

The second batch to go for effective training in the art of war were: John Okech, Peter Cyrillo, Dominic Diim Deng, Isaiah Paul, Ambrose Monyteeng, Kenneth Simone, Bona Baang, Gordon Muortat Mabei, Francis Ngor (Makiec) Ngoong, Abraham Hilel, and others.

The third batch that was sent in 1970 included John Garang de Mabior (the only university graduate), Stephen Madut Baak, Salva Mathok Beny, Caesar Ayok Deng Kuol, Simone Ayom, Francis Malek, Simone Makuach, and Amos Agook.

Earlier on, three of the officers—Stephen Madut Baak, Caesar Ayok Deng and Samuel Jeiel—were sent to France for training. But the French government under President George Pompidou changed its mind. The three officers were sent back to South Sudan with a promise that the French government would send thirty tons of arms and ammunition to the southern rebels through Israel.

Upon their arrival in South Sudan, they were also sent to Israel to join the rest already in the training. Other training camps were established at various spots under the Nile Provisional Government control.

1.2. THE LEADERSHIP QUESTION IN THE ANYA NYA MOVEMENT

Following the split of Sudan African National Union (SANU) into two factions in 1965, (SANU inside under William Deng and SANU outside under Joseph Oduho) Southerners who decried the split held a convention at Agundri on the Congo border, in June 1967. They then formed what became known as South Sudan Provisional Government (SSPG).

Aggrey Jaden, the first southern Sudanese University graduate was unanimously elected President in order to bring together all southerners under one liberation movement. The structure of the SSPG was as follows:

1. Aggrey Jaden President (Equatoria)
2. Camilo Dhol Kuaac, Vice President (Bahr al Ghazal)
3. Akuot Atem de Mayan (Upper Nile) Minister of Defence
4. Gordon Muortat Mayen (Bahr al Ghazal) Minister of Foreign Affairs
5. Elia Lupe (Equatoria) Minister of Interior
6. Clement Moses (Equatoria) Minister of Finance
7. Balieth Kuak (Upper Nile) Minister of Cabinet Affairs
8. Gabriel Kaau Ater Minister of Justice
9. and others.

In order to keep the balance of equal representation, a move which apparently plagued SANU, other senior and junior posts were also distributed equitably among the members of the three southern provinces of Bahr al Ghazal, Equatoria and Upper Nile.

On the military front the structure was as follows:

1. General Emilio Taffeng, (a veteran of the Torit Uprising), Commander in Chief
2. Ali Gbattala (also a veteran of Torit Uprising) Deputy Commander in Chief
3. Joseph Lagu Yanga (graduate from Sudan Military College) Chief of Staff (Equatoria)
4. Paul Awel Deputy Chief for Upper Nile Province
5. Emmanuel Abuur Nhial, Deputy Chief of Staff for Bahr al Ghazal Province
6. Frederick Brian Maggot Deputy Chief of Staff for Equatoria Province

Having formed his cabinet, Aggrey Jaden and his Foreign Minister Gordon Muortat led a delegation to Nairobi in order to meet and discuss with the Israelis a possible logistics support for the SSPG rag tag Anya Nya military wing.

Jaden's delegation duly met the Israelis and military support was pledged. It would be a matter of time and the war would effectively start.

But while Jaden was away in Nairobi, many things happened which are worth discussing because they were to plague the SSPG and brought its early demise.

The first incident involved the minister of defence Akuot Atem de Mayen. As a minister of defence, Akuot executed commander Nanga without the sanction of the president and the court martial that may have been formed to try the officer involved.

Having executed Nanga, Akuot, on the pretext that he was going to open a new front in Upper Nile, left for Bor where he went and created his own movement. This event disappointed Jaden immensely.

The second event involved the minister of Justice Kau Ater who went to the Rumbek area and also established his own empire.

The third event was that the Chief of Staff, Joseph Lagu, did not only refuse to take up his post, he had been seen in constant touch with the Israelis. As the military man responsible for logistics, Lagu may have convinced the Israelis to channel the logistics to his command posts. All attempts exerted to make Lagu take up his posts or cooperate failed dismally. Lagu was a lord unto himself.

Meanwhile Jaden's Commander in Chief, Emilio Tafeng, deserted his post. He went and established the Anyidi Republic, named after Anyidi post they had occupied as his headquarters on the Ethiopian border. Tafeng Deputy Commander Ali Gbattala also deserted and went to his home in Yei District.

In Western Equatoria, there was existing a rudimentary government named "the Sue Republic" under Samuel Abu John, an ex-officer of the Sudan Army.

The Anya Nya guerrillas force, launched as early as 1964, had, by 1969, degenerated into a seemingly tribally based bush governments under various warlords, each threatening to do away with the others.

On the whole, deserted by nearly all the politicians who joined the mushrooming splinter groups of their choice in Kampala and Nairobi, and apparently out of frustration, Aggrey Jaden left the bush and went and lived in Kampala, Uganda.

To fill the vacuum created by Jaden's abdication, the Southerners, in April 1969, held a convention inside the South Sudan and elected Gordon Muortat Mayen as President.

Muortat, a former Minister in the October Revolutionary Government of Sirr al-Khartim al-Khalifa, former Vice President of the Khartoum-based Southern Front Party, defected in 1967 to join the SANU in exile, in protest against William Deng's[2] decision to go back to Sudan to struggle within. After his election, Muortat formed the Nile Provisional Government (NPG) and a splinter group of Anya Nya as its military wing.

Following the convention, the following persons were appointed into the Nile Provisional Government:

1. Gordon Muortat (Bahr al Ghazal) President
2. Marko Rume, (Equatoria) Vice President
3. David Kwak, (Upper Nile) Secretary for Defence
4. Bari Wanji, Secretary for Foreign Affairs
5. Camilo Dhol Kuaac, Secretary for Interior

On the military Front Muortat confirmed in office the following officers:

1. Emilio Tafeng (Commander in Chief)
2. Ali Gbattala (Deputy Commander in Chief)
3. Joseph Lagu (Chief of Staff)
4. Frederick Brian Maggot (Deputy Chief of Staff—Equatoria)
5. Paul Awel (Deputy Chief of Staff—Upper Nile)
6. Emmanuel Abuur (Deputy Chief of Staff—Bahr al Ghazal)

But many of them were not available to hold the posts as mentioned elsewhere in the narrative. Emilio Tafeng had established his own movement. Ali Gbattala retired to his home county in Yei. Brian Maggot decided to do his own private business.

Paul Awel, Deputy Chief of Staff for Upper Nile and Emmanuel Abuur, continued in their position. Thus the Nile Provisional Government started in a precarious situation without a coherent military wing.

However, as the NPG was putting things in order, the supporters of Jaden, mostly from central Equatoria, and who had refused to recognise the NPG under Gordon Muortat, launched an attack on the Anya Nya supporting Muortat. Consequently, a fratricidal war broke out between the two groups.

Although the crisis between the two factions started in June 1969, it was resolved in June 1970. But even then, much damage had been done to discredit the Anya Nya as an effective fighting force to face the might of the Sudan government's army.

Whether it was because of the fighting between Jaden and Muortat forces or some hidden agenda, the lobby groups and supporters in the west stopped giving assistance to the NPG. They were reportedly sending assistance to Joseph Lagu who was already discreetly organising his own movement.

Lagu's early education in Malek near Bor under Archdeacon Shaw of the Anglican Church Missionary Society had perhaps provided him with an opportunity to interact more intimately with other groups like the Dinka.

Undoubtedly, his strong Christian background, charismatic personality, his flamboyant appearance and his military training made Lagu the right choice of the lobby groups; a move apparently intended to bring the Anya Nya forces together under one single command.

The new leader was not only expected to liberate the South from the North, but to put a halt to an apparent spread of Islam far beyond the confines of the South Sudan, especially the central and southern African regions which had not previously effectively been affected by Islam.

It was in the light of these changes that Colonel Joseph Lagu established his headquarters at Owiny Kibul[3] in Acholi area in Eastern Equatoria. Thus Lagu asserted his command as the leader of an independent movement.

Soon it transpired that all the logistics and financial support that were apparently intended for the NPG were now being channelled to Owiny

Kibul, Lagu Command Post. To the Muortat NPG, it was clear that external supporters, mostly Christian organisations, had thrown their support on the new leadership.

In the Meantime, Lagu made it be known to the Anya Nya factions all over the South Sudan that consignments of military hardware and relief supplies would not reach them unless they pledge their allegiance to his leadership.

In response, the Anya Nya forces in Upper Nile and Western Equatoria sent their envoys to Owiny Kibul to negotiate for their supplies. Lagu told them that he would authorise for each of their share only if they stopped fighting each other and pledged their allegiance to him. That was easily obtained and supplies were subsequently provided.

The Israeli experts who had been training the Anya Nya freedom fighters flew to Kampala, Uganda. From there they sent a letter to *Teet-Adol*, the Anya Nya secret command post in Bahr al-Ghazal[4].

Among others, the letter contained an order to the local commander to send his representative to them in Kampala. Colonel Emmanuel Abuur and his adjutant Stephen Madut Baak immediately left for Kampala to meet the Israelis.

The Israeli envoys told Colonel Abuur, in no uncertain terms, that the decision had been reached that all the Anya Nya forces all over the southern provinces should pledge their allegiance to Joseph Lagu, now Major General. Only then could they receive their fair share of supplies from Owiny Kibul.

Colonel Abuur was convinced that any military and non-military aid was conditional upon loyalty to Major General Joseph Lagu. Any further move to cling to the defunct NPG would mean the needed military and other material aid would not reach them.

"You support Lagu, you get all the supplies," Abuur briefed his forces at Teet-Adol. He urged the Anya Nya rebels in Bahr al Ghazal to support Lagu in order to get their necessary supplies.

A military delegation was sent to Chairman Gordon Muortat to brief him about the sour turn of events. The delegation pleaded to him to stand down and leave for exile. Muortat was assured that they would always seek his political advice while the war was going on.

Surrounded by a force supporting Abuur Nhial, and heeding the advice of his commanders, Muortat lowered the NPG's flag, dissolved his government and stepped down peacefully. He was then escorted to the Congo border where he was to live in exile.

In an interview, Muortat told this author, " I went to the bush in order to fight for the liberation of the South Sudan. And since Lagu had managed to secure arms for the liberation of our people, I did not see any reason to continue with a parallel struggle.

So, I decided to stand down. Because it is my belief that South Sudan cannot be liberated from the Arabs unless all the Africans in the south are united and fight as one people and for one goal, the independence of the South Sudan."[5]

After the dissolution and the submission of the Anya Nya forces at Teet Adol to Lagu leadership, the whole fighting force in the three provinces of Bahr al-Ghazal, Equatoria and Upper Nile came effectively under one command. Henceforth, military logistics were dispensed accordingly.

Having secured the full support of the fighting forces from all over the south and assuming an effective command of the Anya Nya forces, General Lagu appointed himself Commander-in-Chief of the Anya Nya forces and Chairman of the newly created South Sudan Liberation Movement (SSLM). Other appointments were :

1. Frederick Brian Maggot, Chief of General Staff
2. Joseph Akuon, Deputy Chief of Staff for Upper Nile
3. Habbakuk Soro, Deputy Chief of Staff for Equatoria
4. Emmanuel Abuur, Deputy Chief of Staff for Bahr al-Ghazal

Forthwith, the arms and ammunitions that had been stockpiled at Owiny Kibul were distributed as follows: Bahr al Ghazal 1,OOO, Upper Nile 2,000, and Equatoria 5,000.[6]

By 1970, the Anya Nya, now well armed and well officered, became a formidable fighting force to be reckoned with. Indeed, the Anya Nya scored a number of victories by attacking and overrunning the government's outposts and garrisons in southern Sudan.

The news about the coming of the Israeli military trainers and arms to the South Sudan and the increasing number of casualties on its forces greatly traumatised and demoralised the Sudan government. Previous to the reorganisation of the Anya Nya, the government had dismissed them as a mere marauding band of bandits without any political motives.

The continuous rebel harassment dealt a heavy psychological blow on the Sudanese army. In response, the government began to look elsewhere for friends to rearm its forces. Within weeks, modern arms began to pour into Sudan from West Germany.

Thus the period between 1969 and 1970 witnessed an escalation of the Sudanese conflict. Military clashes between the Sudan government's troops and the Anya Nya rebel army became rampant.

1.3. THE MAY REGIME POLICY ON THE SOUTH

Unlike General Ibrahim Abboud's Military Junta (1958), who came to maintain the status quo, and unlike the elected regime of Mohamed Ahmed Mahjoub (1965-69), Colonel Jafaar Mohamed Nimeiri's seizure of power on

May 25th, 1969, ushered in a great deal of political change on the Sudan political landscape.

The Military Command Council, headed by officers of the free officers movement, a kin to Gamal Abdel Nasir's Free Officers Movement of Egypt that overthrew King Faroug in 1952, declared that it came to power with one aim in mind: to change the political landscape of Sudan.

In its first policy statement, the May regime unequivocally declared its commitment to complete the unfinished agenda of the October Revolution of 1964: the agenda that adopted a conciliatory approach to the southern problem.

Aware of the serious political and military development in the south, the mounting anti-Sudan government pro-Communist leanings in Western Europe and the United States, where it was assumed, the Anya Nya got its logistics and financial support and; conscious that the effective military campaign in the south could pose a real threat to the policies and objectives of the young Regime, the Revolutionary Command Council put on the top of its agenda a peaceful solution and resolution of the southern problem.

To implement its political objectives about urgent settlement of the Southern problem, the Revolution Command Council Chairman on 9 June, 1969, declared an interim policy statement designed to promise the south some measure of regional autonomy within a united Sudan.

The 9 June 1969 Declaration—though it appeared at first as a propaganda rhetoric and a ploy typical of a desperate regime—in effect led to the creation of the Ministry of Southern Affairs headed by a southern member in the new regime, Joseph Ukel Garang.

This development represented a significant progress. It was reassuring to Southerners, at least those in the Khartoum, who greeted the pronouncements with huge demonstrations in support of the new government policy on the south.

The response of many Southerners in the south and abroad was that the May regime was the first northern government to give the southern problem the recognition they had fought to achieve. Hence the need to support it.

However, little progress was made in fulfilling what the declaration promised. Apparently, there were two reasons responsible for this delay. The first was the internal political wrangling within the regime's Revolutionary Command Council; the Communists versus the Pan Arab Socialists. Each one of the two antagonists had seized the opportunity to implement the party radical policies to change the nature of things in the country in its favour.

Second was Joseph Garang, a committed Southern Sudanese Communist. Instead of drawing up a workable programme on the peace process that could be used as basis to conduct peace negotiations with the rebels, he dismissed the

Anya Nya organisation as an imperialist and Zionist agent. He did not see any reason to discuss peace with its leaders.

However, Joseph Garang spent most of his two years in the office of the Ministry for Southern Affairs (1969-1971), devoting his time and energies in attempts to create Communist cadres in the south.

And as he always reminded the people of the south, the aim of his ministry was to create a progressive cadre that he hoped would provide the badly needed power base for his party, the Sudan Communist Party (SCP). Apparently, Garang had hoped that it would be by then that a regional autonomy could be implemented in the south.

Throughout the 1969-1971 period, Garang with that agenda in mind, toured the south and preached

his approach to peace. To the Anya Nya rebels he said: "You destroy the south, and I will reconstruct it."

The government's policy on the south was thus put in suspense. It remained only a promise on paper until the July 1971 Communist coup attempt led by Hashim Mohamed al-Atta.

The purges that followed the coup attempt led to the execution of Joseph Garang and his Communist comrades. It was only then that the issue of regional autonomy for the south was put forward among the top priorities of the regime.

Abel Alier, another Southern Sudanese politician—a former district judge and the Secretary General of the defunct Southern Front (SF) party—had been in the cabinet since 1969 and was not affected by the coup attempt. Alier was then appointed as the Minister for Southern Affairs, replacing Joseph Garang.

Following a referendum hammered out in September 1971, Nimeiri had become the President of the Republic. He dissolved the Revolution Command Council and appointed a cabinet and three vice presidents.

Former Chief Justice Babiker Awadallah became the First Vice President and Major General Khalid Hassan Abbass and Abel Alier as Second and Third Vice Presidents respectively.

However, Alier's appointment as a Vice President of the Republic brought him nearer to the President. He used that position to press for peace talks with the rebels.

He drew up a peace programme to reflect the Twelve Men Committee of the Round Table Conference of 1965, and the recommendations of the All-Political Party Charter of 1966. The latter had recommended, among others, a regional autonomy for the south.

From Alier's peace proposals, Dr. Jaafar Mohamed Ali Bakheit, the then Minister of Local Government, drew up a draft of administrative set up. Dr. Bakheit's document was circulated among the government and the Northern

Sudanese circles and the press. Alier's proposal was apparently communicated to the rebels for their consumption.

1.4. MAY REGIME FIRST CONTACT WITH REBELS

In March 1970, Abel Alier was asked by President Nimeiri, to visit Europe on a fund raising mission for the support the Southern Sudanese refugees in Ethiopia, Kenya, Uganda and Congo (Zaire). Alier used that opportunity and made direct contacts with the countries supposedly supporting the rebels and with the rebels living in those countries.

The countries Alier visited included Italy, France, Britain, Switzerland and the Scandinavia. He also had the opportunity to visit the Vatican and the Headquarters of the World Council of Churches in Geneva.

At the headquarters of the World Council of Churches, Alier held meetings with Dr. Nilius Leopoldo, the General Secretary of International Affairs in the WCC and Dr. Kwado Ankarah, the General Secretary of the All-African Conference of Churches.

Dr. Ankarah and Dr. Nilius had been working among the Sudanese refugee communities in Africa and undoubtedly had an immense influence on refugee matters. Besides discussing issues of relief with the two Church officials, Alier also discussed the possibility of mediation and holding a peace negotiation between the Sudanese government and the Anya Nya rebels.

Alier meeting with the two top Church officials apparently provided a window of opportunity that peace could be secured in the Sudan. Dr. Leopoldo and Ankrah were attracted by Alier's programme on the peace process. The two Churchmen promised that they would make further contacts within the World Council of Churches and the circles affiliated to it.

In Rome, Abel Alier met the officials of the Verona Fathers Missionaries, many of whom had been expelled from South Sudan. Among these was Rev. Fr. Bresciani, who was responsible for Sudanese refugee affairs. After a lengthy discussion on relief and peace issues with the Verona Fathers, Alier managed to have an audience with the Holy Father, Pope Paul VI at the Vatican.

Throughout his contacts and discussions with world leaders, Alier stressed that the Sudan government was serious and genuine about its policies to allow Southern Sudan to manage its own regional affairs within a united country. That the peace move was going to be exchanged with a regional autonomy for the Christian southern provinces was very intriguing and attractive. It undoubtedly won support from the governments and organisations contacted.

It was particularly convincing to the churches whose interests laid squarely on being allowed back to the country to carry out the gospel without hindrance.

Before flying home to Khartoum, Alier made another crucial contact.

He met Enoch Mading de Garang, the editor of the *Grass Curtain Magazine*, mouthpiece of the South Sudan Liberation Movement (SSLM) believed to have been financed and published with the support of the Church organisations in Britain.

Mading de Garang was also the spokesman and representative of the SSLM in the United Kingdom, a position that made him an important contact person for the rebel movement.

Although de Garang was cautious about meeting officials of the Sudanese government, he and Alier came from the same county of Bor, where they were raised, grew, and went to school together; and both as members of Anglican Communion, perhaps made it easier to arrange a meeting with him.

These long relationships, undoubtedly, removed the official restraint of the political organisations they represented. The meeting was more successful than was envisioned by those who arranged it.

Alier's position to realise peace through negotiation with the rebels was apparently strengthened by the contacts made in 1970 by the then Sudanese Ambassador to London, Abdin Ismael, with Mading de Garang.

Those contacts were reportedly arranged through some British citizens, Barrister Dingle Foot, Barbara, and Ruth who were members of a left wing organisation known as the Friends of Sudan.

These earlier contacts had apparently worked effectively on de Garang by putting some pressure on him to bring the SSLM to the negotiating table with the Sudanese government.

It was through these contacts that Mading de Garang had written to the Sudanese government, making assurances that the rebels would be willing to start peace talks with the government.

It is believed that Mading de Garang's letter was dismissed by Joseph Garang, the then Minister for Southern Affairs who described Mading de Garang as an imperialist agent.

Another important contact Alier made which contributed much to the success of his mission to sell the government's programme for peace was the meeting with Dr. Lawrence Wol Wol, the SSLM Representative in France.

Wol Wol was the only Roman Catholic, young politician from Bahr al-Ghazal, who had accepted Joseph Lagu's leadership, while the rest remained loyal to the defunct Nile Provisional Government of Gordon Muortat and reluctant to align themselves with the SSLM.

It was, therefore, important for Alier to meet Dr. Wol Wol, who could be utilised to influence the Catholics in France and Italy and henceforth be acceptable to the Verona Fathers who educated him at Kuajok Mission Primary School in Gogrial District and Bussere Intermediate School, both in Bahr al Ghazal province.

Back in Khartoum, Alier briefed President Nimeiri about the results of his European tour and particularly the contacts and the discussions he held with various Church leaders and representatives of the rebel organisation.

After the discussion with the President, Alier was assured of the government's commitment to peace. He was then given further instructions to proceed for substantive contacts with those who would matter in the search for peace.

But as serious talks must begin with immediate effect, Alier was able to sent delegates outside the country one after another. His choice for delegates sent outside the country included politicians, influential elders, students, civil servants, and clergymen who had some connections with influential people in exile.

Alier also sent peace committees deep into the countryside in South Sudan to make informal contacts with the Anya Nya fighters and their administrators.

1.5. THE ROLE OF CHURCHES IN THE PEACE PROCESS

As the Sudan government was busy making contacts with regional and international communities and selling its peace package, Alier's proposals were drafted in what became known as Dr. Bakheit's draft document on regional autonomy that became a reference point. The Sudan's diplomatic missions abroad were then asked to disseminate Dr. Bakheit's draft document and sell it as the Government peace package.

The Christian organisations in Europe in the meantime also sent fact—finding missions to Sudan where they were accorded opportunities to visit the three war affected southern provinces in order to review the situation there.

A Church delegation composed of the members of the World Council of Churches and the All-African Conference of Churches (AACC) headed by Dr. Nilius Leopoldo and Dr. Kwado Ankarah, visited Khartoum to a welcome reception by the government. During their presence in the country, the two Church leaders visited the Southern Sudanese towns of Wau, Juba and Malakal where they met directly with church leaders and citizens. This was the first visit by foreign Churchmen since the foreign missionaries who were expelled in 1964 visited the Southern Sudan. The high level Church's visit to the war zone was taken seriously as confirming that the Sudan government was genuine to allow peace to have a chance.

The Sudan Council of Churches and the Ministry of Southern Affairs impressed the visiting Church delegation that there was nothing to fear anymore, and that the refugees could now return back home. The visitors were told further that the government was serious and would be ready to put its policies on the south into practice once peace and stability prevails throughout the south. The Churches were convinced and accepted that contacts on the peace process should begin immediately.

Notwithstanding, the Church representatives were unwittingly dragged into a role the Churches were least qualified to undertake: mediating between the two warring parties in which emotions had been hardened by the dirty war and prolonged period of animosity.

It was against this background that the Sudan government pushed into the hand of the South Sudanese leaders and their arch-supporters issues related to winding up the war and return back to the fold where their fate would ultimately be decided and sealed with their own signatures.

Precisely, within a matter of weeks following the Church delegation visit to the war affected capitals of the Southern provinces, it transpired that the Churches all over Europe and America were preaching peace.

Back in Geneva, Dr. Nilius Leopoldo wrote a letter to Enoch Mading de Garang urging him and his Movement to make their position clear on the peace process.

He pointed out that there were no reasons why negotiation between the Sudan government and the rebels in the south should not begin immediately.

Dr. Nilius hinted that the church would be the contact point, and that the Sudan Council of Churches would be involved when and where necessary.

On 28 July 1971, Mading de Garang responded in favour of starting the negotiations. He stated that the Movement was willing to enter into a direct negotiation with the Sudan government under the auspices of the church. Here are extracts of de Garang comments:

(a) The idea of negotiation is very much welcome, so long as its aim is to take into account the particular interest of the south and the general interest of other regions of Sudan. We welcome the use of your good offices in attempting to establish contacts between the representatives of the Sudan government and the South Sudan with a view of holding talks on negotiations;

(b) The question of groups to be represented in the proposed talks is naturally a matter for Southerners themselves to decide…the only competent and organised body which you can contact and which will eventually nominate a delegation to the proposed talks is the Southern Sudan Liberation Movement (SSLM);

(c) The willingness expressed by the Sudan government that the proposed talks can take place anywhere is both acceptable and appreciated. We proposed either the OAU Headquarters in Addis Ababa or the Zambian capital, Lusaka… The choice must be made jointly by both sides;

(d) The conditional proposal made the Sudan government that they "agree to a cooling period taking place" if there is no danger to security should be clarified;

(e) Discussion of the details or regional autonomy within one Sudan as a proposal of the Sudan government for solving the southern problem is welcome. We feel the Sudan government offer…is a good starting point for discussion of other problems;

(f) We agree that the question of under whose auspices the talks are to be held should be made jointly by both sides.

Whether Mading de Garang's reply represented an official viewpoint of the SSLM leadership in the field and the military wing is of little importance for the purpose here. What is interesting to note and to remember at this point is that de Garang's letter to the World Council of Churches in Geneva was sufficient enough for the WCC to start making contacts with the parties concerned in the dispute.

In August 1971, another church delegation visited Khartoum for peace talks. This time the delegation was given official reception by the Sudan government. The delegates were also afforded a chance to visit Juba, Wau, and Malakal before returning to Europe.

Within weeks of the delegation's arrival back from Khartoum, the church organisations throughout the world announced their acceptance of the Sudan government's peace overtures. They made it clear to the rebels in the south that they should start negotiations with the Sudan government.

Sadly enough, the Churches were not only putting pressure on the SSLM to start talks, but were intermediaries making the necessary arrangements on its behalf and footing SSLM's travel and lodging expenses.

1.6. THE MAKING OF THE ADDIS ABABA PEACE AGREEMENT

Assured by the leaders of the SSLM and the Sudan government's commitment and acceptance to the peace process, the AACC and the WCC began official contacts and made arrangements for talks to start.

By November 1971, the preliminary secret talks between the Sudan government and the SSLM were underway in Addis Ababa under the auspices of the Ethiopian government. Dr. Kwado and Canon Burges Carr of the WCC mediated the initial talks.

To the embarrassment of the mediators and the South Sudan Liberation Movement, the heads of the delegations on both sides fell into the hands of southerners. In that way, the objective of the Sudan government to make it a south-south war was then fulfilled: It was Abel Alier who led the government's delegation, while Ezboni Mundiri headed the SSLM's side. Added to embarrassment was the fact that the leaders of the two delegations were members of the executive committee of the defunct Southern Front Party, the main mass organisation inside the country.

Founded in 1965 at the Round Table Conference, the South Front party was led by veteran Southern politicians: Clement Mboro, President, Gordon Muortat Mayen, Vice President and Hilary Paul Logali, General Secretary.

The Southern Front Party was considered the most critical and outspoken southern party. This position led the successive governments in Khartoum to single it out as a separatist organisation.

Now that two prominent members of the Southern Front Party were negotiating the end of the war, one representing the government and the other representing the rebels, was very embarrassing enough in the eye of the people they had led.

Ezboni Mundiri, now leading the rebel delegation, had represented the Southern Front in the All-Party government that took over power in October 1964 following the overthrow of General Abboud's regime.

The presence of Ezboni Mondiri, a well-known Southern extremist leader who spent most of his time in jail before becoming a government minister, intrigued many Northerners. Some took it that the talks would fail because of his presence. For the northern party leaders, they were of the opinion that if the talks were to succeed, a Southerner known to him and well respected by him should lead the government's side.

Perhaps because of this or other motives, the government decided that Abel Alier should lead the government's delegation. According to observers at the talks, the negotiations would probably have collapsed at the initial stages if the government's side was led by a person other than Alier—a cool-headed personality who always remained calm during crisis.

By the beginning of the third week of February, all groundwork had been completed and ready for signature. On 27 February 1972, the world awoke to hear that an agreement had been reached between the Sudan government and the rebels of the Southern Sudan Liberation Movement under the aegis of His Imperial Majesty Emperor Haile Selasie of Ethiopia.

Precisely, the speed in which the talks were hurried up and signed, the mere seven days of the 17-year war, rooted in its history and orchestrated by mutual mistrust, will continue to remain a riddle not only to students of politics, but to historians alike.

Looking at the documents after they were signed and enacted into law, it was discovered that they contained many loopholes which any party to that agreement could exploit to its own advantage.

Dr. Mansour Khalid, then the Minister of Foreign Affairs and a scholar on international law, was a senior member of the Sudanese delegation.

Some years later when he published his book, *The Government They Deserve*, Dr. Khalid was amused and surprised to note: "The misreading of those provisions by Nimeiri led to a curious situation. The president of the HEC though recommended by the national president is elected by and answerable to the Regional Assembly; he could not therefore be appointed or relieved of office by the unelected national president over the head of the assembly members."

There were further loopholes, Dr. Khalid wrote, "...the national president's right to veto any bill which he deems contrary to the provisions of the national constitution was regrettable."

In a public address at Wad Nubawi Square in Omdurman, March 3rd, 1972, President Nimeiri enacted the Agreement into law. The Agreement was officially ratified on March 27th, 1972 by President Nimeiri and Joseph Lagu.

According to legal experts like Justice Wilson Aryamba, former member of Sudan's Supreme Court, the Addis Ababa Agreement was not a legal document backed by international law.

Who was to be the custodian of the Accord when the leader of the SSLM was already appointed into the army and the President with whom he signed a peace accord with is his Commander-in-Chief?

"What was actually the point to ratify it again when it had already been enacted into law by the President on March the 3rd, 1972?" Justice Wilson Aryamba recalled.

More curious is why the Church organisations that had been agitating for the interest of the south, supporting the insurgency against the Arab Muslim north, could all of a sudden turn and come to be the very people to urge southerners to accept an agreement without sufficient safeguards for them. This too would remain a mystery, said Justice Aryamba.

Aryamba lamented the fact that it appeared that the Church personnel who took it upon themselves to mediate the peace process did not even bother to consult with people experienced in making agreements, international protocols and conventions.

However, such were the loopholes and many more that are not part of our purpose here to cite. Suffice it to state that the Agreement was ill-conceived and mishandled to make it a permanent protocol that would be binding on the people who were signatory to it.

1.7. PUBLIC REACTIONS TO THE ADDIS ABABA PEACE AGREEMENT

The news that an agreement had been signed between the Sudan government and the Any Nya rebels was received with mixed feelings nationally, regionally and internationally.

In the south, the news was received with euphoria and outpouring jubilation. All the messages of support poured into the palace in Khartoum, praising President Nimeiri and General Lagu for ending the long-drawn war.

This support enhanced the position of the May Revolution, a position that had a few months earlier been shaken by the failed Communist-backed coup attempt. Immediately, Southerners in the south and in the north staged huge demonstrations in support of the Agreement and the May Regime.

In the Northern Sudan, the news was received with mixed feelings. Although the majority welcomed the Agreement, others called it a sell-out to the south and swore to wreck it at any first opportunity.

The Africans in the north and particularly in the Nuba Mountains, Darfur and in the Beja areas, received the news with dismay, apathy and disappointment.

These areas, as might be expected, remained equally backward and marginalised. They had hoped that liberation of the Southern Sudan by the Anya Nya might have brought freedom and dignity to all the marginalised areas, even in the far north.

Reverend Philip Abbass Ghaboush, leader of the General Union of Nuba (GUN), felt that Agreement betrayed the cause of the African people of the Western Sudan that he represented.

Regionally and internationally, the Agreement was welcomed and described as a rare experiment of how two antagonistic people can reconcile and live once again in harmony. It was assumed by many that the Addis Ababa Agreement would serve as a model for the resolution of some regional and national conflicts in future. And President Nimeiri, in the eyes of the international community, was qualified for a peace prize award.

In brief, while many were gullible enough to accept the Agreement in its entirety, there were others, who after analysing the terms contained in the Agreement were cautious and warned that Southerners were cheated and swindled over to accept the Agreement without proper safeguards.

Such voices of dissent were expressed by, for instance, Maria Sander, a member of Comitod Sud-Sudan in Geneva—who accused those who accepted the Agreement, of ignorance about the contents of the Agreement. Maria Sander said:

> "We have thoroughly studied the said document and are not optimistic about the wide powers granted to the Southern Region in the Agreement...The Addis Ababa Agreement is giving nothing vital to the South Sudan....because the Agreement is more restricted than that of the regions of Italy...The true liberty of the Southern Sudan, the liberty to think, to speak, liberty of exploitation from want and ignorance is very very far away"

In the Anya Nya camps, the reaction was also varied. There were groups who immediately responded to the order of their commander in Chief and assembled in camps ready for further orders.

In Bahr el-Ghazal, the Anya Nya headquarters at Teet-Adol received the news with a great deal of surprise. Commander Emmanuel Abuur, on hearing the news that an Agreement had been signed, left immediately for Kampala to go and inquire from their Commander-in-Chief the minute details about the Agreement and to meet the Bahr el-Ghazal politicians—among them, their former leader Gordon Muortat—in order to gauge their reactions.

Upon his arrival in Kampala, Abuur discovered to his surprise and shock that Lagu had already left for Khartoum and declared a cease-fire and general demobilisation of the Anya Nya. Not only that, he had already ratified the Agreement, appointed representatives of Anya Nya into various organisations, and had been promoted to the rank of Major General in the Sudanese national army. He was due to leave Khartoum for Juba.

After conferring with the Bahr el-Ghazal group: Gordon Muortat, Francis Mayar Akoon, Elia Duang Arop, Dominic Muorwell Malou Agolong Chol Agolong, and others, Abuur was informed that the group had already rejected the Agreement as a sell-out to the Arabs.

Commander Abuur left for Lobone, the Anya Nya headquarters, in the hope of meeting Joseph Lagu. But that was too late an attempt, as the Anya Nya had already been ordered to demobilise and assemble at given places waiting to be absorbed into the national army.

At Lobone, the Anya Nya officers at the headquarters met secretly to discuss whether they should and how to react to the Agreement. Those who met included Emmanuel Abuur Nhial, Alfred Deng Aluk, Alison Manani Magaya, Habakkuk Soro, Stephen Madut Baak, Disan Ojwe Olweny, Kamilo Odongi, Paul Awel, Albino Akol Akol and John Garang de Mabior.

The first reaction was to reject the Agreement in favour of continuing with the war. A letter was written. It was circulated to all the Anya Nya camps in order to reject the Agreement and to resist any attempt to implement it. Lagu was to be arrested and a new commander appointed to lead the Movement.

But before they could strike, the letter was allegedly betrayed by Saturnino Arika, who was a commander of Eastern Equatoria. It was alleged that Arika surrendered it to Lagu. Through the help of Lagu supporters, Camilo Odongi and Disan Ojwe Olweny were arrested.[7]

Discovering that the plan was discovered and aware of the fact that the public opinion in the south was for peace, the plan to resist and continue with the war was discarded. .

In an interview with John Garang de Mabior, he said:

"We tried to oppose it. But realising that it was not going to be successful and opportune because the masses of the people in South Sudan were not prepared to support our move to continue with the war, we stopped the opposition. We thought that it was going to be a futile opposition because the south, the springboard of our opposition was not prepared to back us. We realised that the people badly needed peace and not war. We thus suspended our activities and knowing the character of the Agreement after close analysis, we accepted to be absorbed into the Sudan Army. Of course we were aware that the contradictions and conflict that brought the war situation would continue and could be exacerbated during the course of time. We calculated that the clique in Khartoum would erode the government in Juba because its basis for the Agreement was first to absorb the Anya Nya into the National Army, second to integrate it after absorption and third to destroy it. So you have the process of achieving a cheap victory over the Anya Nya Forces."

However, the discovery of the plot to sabotage the Peace Agreement sped up the assembling of the Anya Nya forces faster than it was expected. Convinced that there would be nothing to persuade their leader to abandon the Agreement and aware that their constituency in the south wanted peace, the plotters left for their respective areas and provinces to go and await their absorption into the national army.

Dr John Garang, in an interview in 1987 cited above, gave reasons why they had wanted to continue with the war and why at the later stage reconsidered their original plan and accepted to be absorbed in the Sudanese Army. He said that: "We were opposed to the agreement. We also accepted to be absorbed because we knew that the North would dishonour the Agreement, and the south would be ready for the war. Then we would be ready to launch a genuine movement, the people's revolution."

The circumstances surrounding the negotiations and the conclusion of a peace pact in 1972 is reminiscent of the 1947 Juba Conference. In both scenarios, the Southerners were caught unprepared for a deal they could not comprehend or were made to regret long afterwards.

In both conferences, southern representatives were herded into the conference rooms by those they took were their protectors and had some amount of sympathy for their situations.

In 1947, it was the British colonial administrators who were responsible for the affairs of the south. They had lived and worked among the Southern Sudanese people and were led at one stage or another to sympathise with them. They were prepared to help them if only they could convince the British government to understand the situation in which the two parts of their colony were at the beginning of the Anglo-Egyptian rule.

Despite the southern policy of the 1930s, unfortunately, British colonial officials in the end failed in their mission to protect the Southern interests. The Christian missionaries also made matters worse by agitating for spiritual salvation without accompanying socio-economic progress and civic participation. Even their lobby in favour of Southern Sudan in the 1960s was not sufficient consolation to the country long battered by successive rulers from Sudan.

In the early 1970s, it was the same Christian organisations such as the World Council of Churches and the All African Conference of Churches, who were intrigued by the Khartoum government to recognise and accept a peace agreement that fell short of meeting the southern interests.

What is common in the two agreements is that Southerners were not educated about the deal they were being asked to enter into or given sufficient time to consult among themselves. What if they were given the chance to comprehend the mechanics of the deal about to be imposed on them?

What is more common in both scenarios and perhaps many to come is that southerners were caught between two choices. To go back to the Devil; their supposed enemy, or plunge into the deep blue sea—the denial of the material support in case they refuse being herded back into the enemy camp.

Such was the situation when the Sudan Liberation Movement (SSLM) delegates were asked to sign the Agreement that granted regional form of government to that part of the Sudan in 1972. According to Ezboni Mundiri Gwanza, the head of the SSLM delegation to the Addis Peace Talks, He told the author in an interview that the peace deal was imposed on the Southerners.

In any case, what happened between 27 February 1972 when the Agreement was signed, and 27 March when the Agreement was ratified, cannot and may not be explained in few lines. Rather it has to be left to the students of Sudanese politics or keen observers of the south-north relations to gauge for themselves!

Suffice it to state that the leaders of the SSLM, the Anya Nya fighters, and General Lagu were overtaken by events of their own making, especially as General Lagu has been kept out of the scene.

Lagu had apparently kept himself away from the public glare throughout the talks, making some people to mistakenly believe that Lagu was not interested in the peace deal. Others took it that the deal was being forced on him.

Whatever the case may have been, Lagu appeared to have been convinced that the peace was genuine. He flew down to Khartoum only to discover the real situation was a little obtuse. If Lagu did not know the mechanics of realpolitick, this was his first lesson.

In the morning of his second day since his arrival to Khartoum, Lagu was summoned with his delegation to meet President Nimeiri. After courteous exchanges regarding the ratification of the peace, Nimeiri congratulated him that he had been re-instated back into the Sudanese Army with the rank of a Major General, two ranks above his batch in the military college.

He disclosed further that Vice President Abel Alier was appointed President of the Interim High Executive Council for the Southern Region. Tension arose immediately! While General Nimeiri had the feeling of victorious commander, Lagu had the feeling of a vanquished commander unwittingly lured into the enemy camp! Lagu looked at his delegation expecting the members to protest against this twist of events. But the delegation was equally stunned and unable to protest.

Leaving the Presidential Palace, Lagu could not talk to members of his delegation for the next 24 hours. He was thoroughly devastated! Perhaps his only consolation to this humiliating episode was his betrothal to the daughter of Sheikh Abd el-Rahman al Tahir, a trader who was killed during the Torit Uprising in August 1955. She was brought from Juba in a party of girls to serve the guests on the first day of their arrival. He later married her. A sign of goodwill!

Speaking to the author in London, 2002, Lagu disclosed that before he left Addis Ababa for Khartoum, he was promised that he would be appointed to the post of Vice President of the Republic.

In that position, he would recommend to the President of the Republic a candidate of his choice to be appointed President of the Interim High Executive Council with the consultation of Southern Sudanese leaders inside and outside the country.

Thus when Nimeiri told him that Abel Alier was going to take his position, Lagu was so bitter with Alier. He accused him for conniving with Nimeiri. This bitterness remained unabated to the extent that it contributed negatively dragging the south in the process into two hostile opposing camps which, unfortunately, were instrumental in policies of dismantling the Addis Ababa Agreement. And as will be discussed in the next chapter, these policies that orchestrated the re-division issue, and plunged the Sudan back to war in 1983.

What is more intriguing in Lagu's personality is that he did not change his mind when he left Khartoum for Juba and then to his former Headquarters at Lobone. Instead of undoing the Agreement, he felt cheated; nevertheless he helped implement the peace process. Perhaps a simmering opposition to peace in Lobone by junior officers could have been instrumental in his decision to continue with the peace process.

However, on 4 April 1972, President Nimeiri issued presidential decrees appointing the Chairman and members of the Provisional High Executive Council. On 22 April, the Chairman and the members of the new regional government moved to Juba, the new capital.

In translating the Agreement into practice, many loopholes that would in the end wreck the Peace Accord began to appear. Some of them were legal and others technical.

1.8. ABSORPTION AND INTEGRATION OF ANYA NYA FORCES INTO THE NATIONAL ARMY

As stated earlier, the Anya Nya forces were hurriedly ordered to assemble at various spots in the three provinces in the south waiting to be absorbed in their respective provinces at the conclusion of the peace Accord.

In Bahr al-Ghazal, for instance, the Anya Nya forces from Aweil assembled at Mathiang 3 miles west of Aweil town. Anya Nya from Gogrial, Tonj, Raga, and Abyei assembled at Bussere 12 miles south of Wau; Anya Nya forces from Lakes (Yirol and Rumbek) assembled at Malou, 12 miles east of Rumbek town.

In Eastern Equatoria, the Anya Nya forces were first assembled in Lobone, but later on moved to Torit District headquarters. After absorption they were moved to another camp for training near Juba.

In Upper Nile, the Anya Nya assembled at Lelo outside Malakal and at Malek near Bor. It was at Malek camp where the absorption was first to begin but was abandoned when a young officer, Captain John Garang de Mabior, put forward a request before the Technical Committee for Absorption to suspend the process of reintegration in Upper Nile for the time being until such a time that it was conducive to make the absorption work.

The head of absorption team, Brigadier Mirghani Suleiman, was stunned that a junior officer could speak on behalf of his senior commanders. He took the request seriously, but as emotions were still running high during this time, nothing could be done. This was a peculiar matter and not a normal military situation. And since the Agreement was political, political considerations were of paramount importance in such situations. To this effect, the absorption in Upper Nile was suspended and Brigadier Suleiman and his team first moved to Equatoria. Nevertheless, he returned later on in August 1972 to finish the absorption process.

In the end of the process, 6,000 Anya Nya men were absorbed into the national army (including 203 officers and 2,000 men from each of the three provinces). Major General Joseph Lagu was the highest ranking ex-Anya Nya officer, followed by 4 colonels: Emmanuel Abuur (Bahr al-Ghazal) Samuel Abu John (Equatoria) Paul Awl (Upper Nile) and Frederick Brian Maggot for the headquarters.

In addition, there were 7 lieutenant colonels; 18 majors; 48 captains; 58 first lieutenants; and 67 second lieutenants. This was in accordance with the Security Protocol of the Addis Ababa Agreement which provided for the First

Infantry Division composed of 12,000 men divided equally between the north and the south.

A further 4,500 Anya Nya personnel were absorbed into the police, prisons, and wildlife forces. The rest of the Anya Nya fighters were disarmed and assigned non-military duties such as road construction, veterinary, and agricultural occupations.

Their services were paid through a special fund for resettlement and rehabilitation of the former rebels. However, a great deal of best Anya Nya fighters were dumped into these non-military assignments or absorbed in a lower non-commission soldiery or demotion: the cases of Commander William Nyuon Bany; Kwenen, Kaffu are cases to cite.

Meanwhile maximum efforts were exerted through the cooperation of both regional and national authorities to avert the breakdown of the Agreement at its initial stage of the ten-year period. This was the longest period the two parts of the Sudan lived together in relative peace. After the absorption the next move was to train and commission the new forces and organise them into platoons, companies, battalions and brigades.

By September 1972, the Anya Nya forces, now already absorbed forces, were being sorted out and were being organised into the said classifications. But as soon as the absorption was completed and the new forces were being commissioned, the central government began to exploit the loopholes inherent in the Agreement.

As the Anya Nya forces were disbanded and their Commander-in-Chief no longer in charge, there was no longer anybody to refer to for the necessary arbitration. One such loophole came to the notice of the absorbed forces when an order came for the most senior former Anya Nya officers to report to the General Command Headquarters in Khartoum for training abroad in India, Pakistan and Britain.

Who could resist such a well-designed move? The officers mentioned did report to Khartoum and went for training. Upon their return abroad, they were posted elsewhere in the north. Similarly, some Anya Nya officers were transferred to other departments such as the airforce, mechanised artillery units, logistics, signals and others. These were unfortunately not expressly mentioned in the Agreement.

But all these technical fields in the military require some training, and promotions were tied to such training. The ex-Anya Nya became far vulnerable to be moved here and there and mostly away from the south. Some were taken to the Republican Palace as Presidential Guards to protect President Nimeiri, the apostle of peace, from possibly being overthrown by some perfidious man.

By 1973, the Anya Nya absorbed forces were all too aware about the danger awaiting them. Things, at times, appeared desperate for the ex-Anya

Nya because their former Commander-in-Chief was not approachable and no one dared to speak since they, as soldiers in the national army, were subject to transfer.

Captain John Garang de Mabior, who had put the request before the Technical Military Committee for Absorption of the Anya Nya forces to postpone the absorption process in Upper Nile, all of a sudden appeared in Bussere where resistance to absorption was first manifested.

He joined officers who tacitly were opposed to the agreement. Among them were Lt. Colonel Alfred Deng; Lt. Colonel Joseph Kuol Amuom; Major Stephen Madut Baak; Major Albino Akol Akol; Major Thomas Dhol; Major Santino Ajing Dau, and a number of junior officers.

Captain Garang de Mabior was now among comrades! Being the only college graduate, he was certainly the brains behind this resistance since the Lobone attempt to hijack the peace process. He organised the officers and taught classes on economics and radical sociology and political theories.

The Security/Safeguards of the Agreement were radically analysed and interpreted by this group as hollow and a palliative use to disarm the Anya Nya through a facade peace Agreement.

According to the terms of the agreement, which were not explicitly explained to the absorbed forces, the Anya Nya forces would remain in their separate camps for five years. After that they would automatically be incorporated into the national army where they would be subject to transfer to any part of the country by the order of the Commander-in-Chief, who according to the prevalent system was the President of the Republic.

Why the Army General Headquarters in Khartoum was not patient enough to wait for five years before making attempts to transfer the former Anya Nya to the north would become clear as we go deeper into the next chapters of the book.

However, the absorbed forces got rumours that were circulated day after day about the impending transfers. Each order or attempt to transfer some of the newly absorbed forces, even for genuine reasons, was received with suspicion and therefore turned down with threats of returning to the bush if pressed to obey such orders.

The actual terms of the agreement governing the absorbed forces were as follows. That the Anya Nya forces would: (1) remain with their arms they brought from the bush for five years; (2) the absorbed forces would be reintegrated first among themselves area by area, district by district, and a province by province transfer. After these processes, they would then be integrated regionally into the 12,000 army of the Southern Command (3) the movement of troops would come from President Nimeiri, in his capacity as the Supreme Commander of the Sudanese Armed Forces. He would only do so through the advice of the Regional President.

These points were not explained to the newly absorbed forces and there was no one ready to address these sensitive issues which in the main were political in nature.

It suffices to state that things dragged on, and the General Headquarters kept sending instructions to transfer some of the ex-Anya Nya to the north. And repeatedly these instructions were not well received in the south. One may recall that the mutiny in Bor in 1983 precisely was triggered by an attempt to transfer that battalion by force to the north.

As time went on, the discontent of the absorbed officers became too obvious to be ignored. Garrisons in the South were at the verge of revolt, defying the initial integrationist hypothesis that the spirit and culture of the guerrilla war ethic would wear out with the passage of time.

In Bahr El-Ghazal, for instance, the absorbed forces increasingly became defiant. When they were asked to go to Wau for shopping and refreshments, they insisted on going in a convoy. On the way, they sang Anya Nya war songs depicting the Arabs as the enemies at the door.

Matters came to a head when security reports alleged that these incidences were originating from the Anya Nya forces while at the same time they were enjoying being members of the Sudanese army. It was these series of contentions that the January 1974 grenade incidents in Wau could be explained.

In the end, the Regional government sent a report to General Lagu to come and ease matters with the Bussere forces. Lagu and Brigadier Mohamed Yahya Monawra, Commander Southern Division, did visit Bussere.

While they were trying to address the officers, General Lagu was jeered, calling him traitor and other sorts of names. Offended by this act of indiscipline, Lagu left the camp calling the garrison a tribal army, since 90 percent were from Dinka ethnic group.

Two weeks following General Lagu's visit, a delegation was sent from the High Command Headquarters in Khartoum to arrest Captain John Garang de Mabior—apparently accused as being the ring leader of the underground resistance. The officers present in the meeting threatened to revolt if Captain de Mabior was arrested. After a meeting which dragged on from 9.30 p.m. to 3.30 a.m., the delegation left for Khartoum without making any arrest.

Apparently to avoid a possible repeat and defiance as shown in Bussere, the Anya Nya forces all over the south were sorted into platoons, companies and battalions: Aweil, battalion 110; Rumbek, 111; Wau, 103; Malakal 104; Bor 105; Juba 116; Torit and Kapoeta 117.

The resisting Bussere forces were integrated into battalion 103 and 110. Captain John Garang de Mabior was subsequently transferred to Bor and to

Khartoum. He was later given a scholarship for further studies in military science in the United States and later on joined Iowa State University where he graduated with a doctorate degree in Agricultural economics in 1981.

Other recalcitrant officers with Garang de Mabior were also transferred. Lieutenant Colonel Stephen Madut Baak was transferred to Jebeit in Port Sudan to train non-commissioned officers. Others were scattered into various battalions where it was assumed they would pose no threat to security.

1.9. DISENCHANTMENT AMONG THE ABSORBED FORCES AND START OF THE MOBILISATION FOR WAR

The Bor incident which ignited the return to the conflict in the Sudan in 1983 was not, in reality, caused and staged by dissatisfied elements within the rank and file of Battalion 105. Nor did the two-month salary delay of March and April of that year prompt the insurrection, as many in the official in the northern Sudan circles persistently assert. Rather, the discontent with the peace Agreement expressed throughout the ten years of peace and the persistent reluctance of the former Anya Nya officers to fully integrate with their troops into the national army as required by the Agreement were the main causes.

Basically, the immediate cause, which ignited the insurgency, has more to do with the government's reaction to the Anya Nya refusal to transfer to the North where they would integrate into the national army.

In the effort to restore law and order, General Sidig al-Banna, commanding officer of Southern Division in Juba, made a grave mistake. Instead of using other tactics to calm down the imminent mutiny, he sent down an ex-Anya Nya Officer, Lt. Colonel Dominic Kassiano, to storm the headquarters of the rebellious garrison of Battalion 105 in Bor, on 16 May, 1983.

As will appear in the subsequent paragraphs, the Bor Mutiny not only prompted the return to war, but in reality, it was a part and parcel of an overall plot to return to the conflict which had started in Bussere in the early years of the Agreement.

Another factor worth mentioning is that Khartoum was not happy to see the south remained a united "strong Region." It would therefore be plausible to argue that such an insurrection in the course of time became impossible to prevent.

The most important point to make as we go through this delicate period is that since 1972, the absorbed forces continued with their underground resistance making discreet contacts among themselves. This soon became evident with the passage of time. Every move made by Khartoum to transfer the former Anya Nya forces to the north pushed the looming insurrection ever closer, a move that would eventually wreck the hard won peace Agreement.

Throughout the ten-year period of experimenting with the Regional

Autonomy, the ex-Anya Nya forces had given themselves the label that empowered them as "protectors" of Southern Sudan's interests against any imminent sign of Arab domination. Hence the custodians of the Addis Ababa Peace Agreement. Both of these points are hard to dispute.

From these perspectives, however, the absorbed forces had from the beginning jealously but carefully watched the implementation of the peace accord. They were all along on the lookout for possible reversals of things by the north.

One such suspicion was the possibility that a coup d'etat against the Nimeiri's regime would return the south to the status quo ante, the 1955-1972 situation. The Anya Nya were therefore prepared to the tune that in the event of sudden overthrow of the May Regime, they would be in a position to return to the bush and resume the armed-struggle without any serious problems.

The first ever attempt in 1973 to transfer one battalion of the absorbed forces from their initial assembly point outside Juba city to a new location on the bank of the River Nile demonstrated the prevalent suspicion among the absorbed forces throughout South Sudan.

The former Anya Nya forces were convinced that their old location at the western outskirts of Juba was more secure than the new place between the Army General Headquarters and the River Nile.

Speaking to this author, the officer commanding Anya Nya forces noted that their new place would put them at a disadvantage militarily, adding that if the Army Main Garrison (still an enemy garrison) could rise against their Battalion, opposite the River. In the event of a war they could easily be pinned against the River with disastrous results. The OC asserted that his troops would not move to the new location. Thus any advice given to them by the regional authorities was viewed as not nationalistic, a guise to disarm them in the name of keeping law and order.

When Commander Peter Cyrillo, himself an ex-Anya Nya officer, came to order the execution of the orders to move Battalion 116 to the new place, he was arrested and beaten by his own troops until diplomatic moves prevailed over the former rebels much later.

The same experience was encountered again in 1974, when members of the same Battalion, this time under Commander Habakkuk Soro, gave orders to his troops to occupy Juba airport, sealing off all outlets and inlets into Juba City.

Commander Habbakuk Soro was responding to a rumour circulated by two students from the University of Khartoum Walter Kunijwok Ayoker and Lual Acuek[8] to all Anya Nya officers in Juba including prisons, police, and wildlife to be on full alert because a coup against President Nimeiri, the apostle of peace, was in the making in Khartoum. The letter urged the former Anya

Nya forces in Juba to be on full alert and to strike with impunity should such a conspiracy surface.

Diplomacy again prevailed on Commander Habakkuk Soro, and the troops were reassured that no conspiracy of such nature existed. Hence, the troops were ordered back to barracks peacefully.

Another incident occurred in the same year at Wau Cinema area, when unknown culprits threw Chinese-made hand grenades into the crowded cinema, killing and wounding many innocent civilians. The accusing fingers were undoubtedly pointed at the Bussere camp as potential suspects.

This later incident apparently sped up the integration of the Bussere camp to the following Battalions 111 stationed at Rumbek, 110 at Aweil, and 113 to remain in Wau. A subsequent transfer of ringleaders to remote areas followed the closing down of Bussere Camp.

In the same year, Battalion 111 in Rumbek was asked again to transfer to replace Battalion 117 in Kapoeta, which was also to transfer to Rumbek. The troops involved in the transfer defied the orders. These orders would have led to a widespread mutiny, thereby wrecking the uneasy peace.

A similar incident happened also when some troops were to be transferred from Aweil to Rumbek. But this was also contained.

In March 1975, while the whole nation was celebrating the third anniversary of the Addis Ababa Peace Agreement, this time round, a unit of the former Anya Nya mutinied in Akobo, eastern Upper Nile, killing their commanding officer, Colonel Abel Chol, and sealed off the town.

The Akobo troops were reportedly acting on the rumour that a contingent of Northern Sudanese troops was on its way to disarm them before they would subsequently be transferred to Northern Sudan.

According to reports to this author, the mutineers were hoping that their move would have sparked a mutiny all over the south to mark the return to the war for total independence of the South Sudan from the north put to a halt by the Addis Ababa Peace Accord.

The situation was delicate enough to the extent that both the regional and the national governments were forced to response with diplomatic tact. The mutiny was successfully contained and many mutineers surrendered to the authorities. Those who surrendered in their weapons were subsequently arrested and executed later on.

The ringleaders, who astutely refused to surrender, included Lieutenant Vincent Kuany and Corporal James Bol Kur Alangjok and scores of soldiers, who crossed over to Ethiopia.

In 1976, another drama occurred in Wau when Captain Alfred Agwet Awan, a company commander, mutinied with his troops. He had just been transferred from Battalion 111 at Rumbek to Battalion 103 in Wau. He took his company to the bush in the expectation that the former Anya Nya in the army, police, prisons, and wildlife not only in Wau, but elsewhere in the south, would defect en masse to join him.

After Captain Agwet's departure to the bush, his former Commander, Emmanuel Abuur, now Brigadier, was ordered by Isaiah Kulang Mabor, the Commissioner of Bahr al-Ghazal, to pursue and persuade him to come back to Wau.

But instead of taking a large force with him, Brigadier Abuur and two officers, Captain Bullen Kucha and Gabriel Abdalla Mabok, followed Captain Agwet. Unfortunately, Brigadier Abuur and his fellow companions were instantly shot and killed in the shower of bullets fired by the mutineers.

Captain Lawrence Aleu and some NCOs in Agwet's company escaped back to Wau. A few troops loyal to Captain Agwet followed him across the border to Central African Republic. He was later apprehended by the CAR forces and extradited back to Sudan where he was court-marshaled and executed.

During the execution of Captain Agwet, the absorbed forces in Aweil and Rumbek were in restive mood, but were contained by regional authorities who appealed for calm using various means and methods.

According to reports to the author, Captain Agwet's mutiny was allegedly triggered by a letter written by Deputy Speaker in the Regional Assembly in Juba, Benjamin Bol Akok to Joseph Oduho, then a Regional Minister, and Malath Joseph Lueth[9].

The letter was allegedly informing Oduho and Lueth that time was opportune to start the war for total liberation of the South Sudan. The letter is said to have disclosed, among other things, that all the former Anya Nya forces were to be put on alert to stand by for the zero hour in effort to resume the unfinished war of total liberation.

The author of the letter, writing from Wau, told the receivers that he was on his way to Aweil to meet Kawac Makwei, an ex-Anya Nya Major, who was now serving as a Regional Member of Parliament in Juba. Makweit was on vacation in his Aweil constituency—as Parliament was on recess. So when this letter was leaked to the former Anya Nya officers, Captain Agwet executed the plan prematurely.

An important question to ask is: What were the purposes of these constant attempts to move the troops from one Battalion to another, and each time, against their will? Meanwhile, major incidences of Akobo and Wau were threatening enough for the government to institute discipline among the ex-guerrillas?

The President of the High Executive Council, Abel Alier, had been aware of the gravity of the situation. He had recommended to the national authorities that the best way was to integrate first, the absorbed forces among themselves.

They would then be integrated and transfer within the Southern Division before an attempt to transfer these units and battalions outside the southern region in accordance with the provisions stated in the security arrangements protocols of the Addis Ababa Agreement.

Apparently, Alier's recommendations were ignored by the National Authorities for strategic reasons. Instead, the Army General Headquarters in Khartoum planned the transfer of all the former Anya Nya units to the North in an attempt to neutralise the Anya Nya restiveness. This would render them ineffective in the event of the apparent looming insurrection.

Ring leaders in the Battalions still manned and officered by the former Anya Nya were targeted for liquidation through either professional or physical processes. Indeed, many retirements among the former Anya Nya officers became frequent.

Despite these measures, which in effect were myopic, the government had to tiptoe touching sensitive battalions and indeed Battalions 103, 104, 105, 111, 116 and 117 were left intact. Nevertheless a contingent plan was made to contain other forces in the police, prisons and wildlife.

In a related development, one more important revelation was made in 1979. Colonel Andrew Makur Thaou, a senior officer from the former Anya Nya forces, was transferred from Wau to Juba to take over the "operations room" from his Northern colleague, Colonel Umar, who was going for El-Hajj in Mecca.

During the handover, the outgoing officer forgot a copy of a secret letter which contained a contingent plan—"How to deal with the absorbed forces in the Army, police, prisons, and wildlife forces in the Southern Region" in the event of any rebellion[10].

Colonel Makur could only take the letter to General Joseph Lagu in his dual role as the leader of the Anya Nya and also the incumbent Regional President of the High Executive Council. He trusted that General Lagu was the only person that could warn the north not to tamper with the provisions of the Accord that regulates the military movement in the south and also the modalities of Regional Administration. Upon reading the "secret letter," General Lagu asked Colonel Makur:

"Why do you bring this letter to me when you know that I'm no longer the Commander-in-Chief of the Anya Nya? I am the President of the High Executive Council, a political role, not military. You are a military officer. If I were you, I would make a counter-plan and alert the former Anya Nya officers...according to the military rules of the game, an officer who discovered the enemy's plans to annihilate his forces is expected to take an immediate counter plan to preempt the enemy's move," Lagu commented.

Colonel Makur undoubtedly took the message to the concerned officers in their underground cells. Within months, the underground resistance became much more active. Hitherto, attempts to transfer senior officers to the north were vigorously resisted.

However, the results of the investigations to all the violations in the south revealed an existence of a strong underground movement (Alier 1991). The investigation further revealed that the ex Anya Nya forces were in constant contact with one another. From then on, the central government began to draw up plans how to transfer the new forces away from the south to the north without igniting a widespread rebellion as was the case in 1955.

Meanwhile, when General Gismalla Abdalla Rassass[11] replaced Abel Alier in 1981 as the President of the High Executive Council, Makur—who was part of the rebellious group—was appointed Rassass's Vice President of the HEC. He was expected to help Rassass divide the south into three regions. But Makur put a great deal of resistance against re-division. It was then that Makur, now Brigadier, was made a prime suspect of anti re-division, thus highly suspected as a member of the underground movement.[12]

The most serious violations of the Addis Ababa Agreement which strengthened the underground movement was a policy initiative made by President Nimeiri himself on 5 October 1981.

Apparently without consulting with his most senior advisers, not even referring to the provisions of the Self-Government Act, President Nimeiri issued a presidential decree dissolving the elected Government of the High Executive Council under Abel Alier. He replaced him with General Gismalla Abdalla Rassass, commander of the Sudan Military College as interim President. The President also dissolved both the National and Regional Assemblies and called for new elections within a six month period.

The appointment of General Rassass, a Muslim, to lead the south was received with mixed reactions from the southern intelligentsia. Some saw a Muslim leader as part and parcel of dismantling the Addis Ababa Agreement itself. While others, especially in Equatoria, who did not benefit materially during the ten-years of peace, were inclined to welcome the re-division and even campaigned for such an eventuality.

General Rassass's assignment was, therefore, to prepare the region for elections and a new form of regional government similar to the new regions in the North[13].

Undoubtedly, Rassass's task was not going to be a smooth running of affairs, as he took over at the time the south was badly bruised by a re-division issue. For instance, the leaders from Bahr al-Ghazal and Upper Nile outrightly rejected the re-division of the south into three regions.

There was a sizable number of opponents of re-division in Equatoria as well, who rightly expressed fears that re-division was intended, not only to dismantle the Addis Ababa Agreement, but to weaken the south as a whole.

But the majority in Equatoria, including General Joseph Lagu, naively supported re-division in a bid to get rid of an allegedly Dinka domination of the regional government.

What is important to stress at this juncture is that the interim administration was composed of the most senior former Anya Nya officers who had shown, beyond doubt, their capabilities and responsibilities throughout their service in the Sudanese Army.

Some of these officers included: Brigadier Andrew Makur Thaou, appointed Vice President of the High Executive Council and Minister of Commerce and Industry; Brigadier Joseph Kuol Amuom, appointed Minister of Administration and Local Government; Colonel Habbakuk Soro, Minister of Wildlife Conservation; Colonel Alison Manana Magaya, Commissioner of Western Equatoria; Colonel Saturnino Arika, Commissioner of Eastern Equatoria; Colonel John Kaong Nyuon, Commissioner of Jonglei Province; Colonel Peter Mabil, Commissioner of Upper Nile; Colonel Alfred Deng Aluk, Commissioner of Bahr al-Ghazal; and Major General Samuel Mabor Malek, Commissioner for Lakes Province.

On the night before these officers were sworn into office, they met in the officers' mess at Hillat al-Taiyeb, a suburb east of Khartoum, to consider their appointment. On the agenda of the meeting were two items: whether to accept their appointments and join the government that was intended to violate the Addis Ababa Agreement and divide the south against the wishes of the majority of the Southern Sudanese people; or to reject and turn down their appointments. At the end of the lengthy meeting, which went throughout the night, a consensus was reached that:

1. They would join the government on condition that the President of the Republic in his capacity as the Commander-in-Chief of the Sudanese Armed Forces make a ruling to the effect that all officers appointed into respective posts without their expressed consent would be reinstated back into their military ranks when the transitional period ended in April 1982.

2. That if their requests for reinstatement were rejected and prematurely retired from the military in accordance with the existing Sudan's military regulations and laws, they would return to the bush.

Nevertheless, they went to the palace the following day and were sworn into their respective positions. They were then flown to Juba where they served their full term as regional ministers till the end of the transitional period.

However, the regional elections were held as scheduled in April 1982. Two groups emerged to contest these elections. These were: the unity group headed by Clement Mboro; and the re-division group, backed by Joseph Lagu who campaigned for decentralization of South Sudan. The former group won 68 seats, thus sweeping all the seats from Bahr al-Ghazal and Upper Nile, while the latter won 35 seats, mostly from Equatoria.

During the campaign, which went throughout the whole of May 1982, many members from the Unity Group were swayed over to the Re-division Group when they were secretly told that the President did not intend to proceed with the division of the south.

Engineer Joseph James Tombura, the divisionist candidate, managed to beat the unionist candidate Clement Mboro, amidst accusations that northern hand was behind the electoral process and had influenced the outcome of the elections, in favour of Joseph James Tombura, the divisionist candidate.

When in June, the interim administration handed over power to the newly elected Regional Administration; all the military officers serving in the interim administration were retired with immediate effect.

And since most of these officers were senior officers of the former Anya Nya forces, their retirement led to a widespread discontent in the south. It was seen as an attempt to increasingly weed out the former Anya Nya in the senior ranks of the Sudanese Army.

By 1982, the number of the senior Anya Nya officers had dropped from 203 in 1972, to a mere 100; an average of 10 officers retired every year without any reciprocal recruitment into the Sudan Military College.

Similarly, the number of the former Anya Nya fighters dwindled in 1982 to one third of the original number of 6,000 in 1972. All went without replacement because there was no provision in the Addis Ababa Agreement regarding the replacement of the Anya Nya upon death or old age retirement.

As stated earlier on, the former Anya Nya were seen in the southern psyche as the protectors of the south, and custodians of Addis Ababa Agreement against the scrupulous northern domination. Hence their exit from the national army in large numbers was bound to influence the later events in favour of the return to the civil war.

In brief, the removal of many senior Anya Nya officers in the military, police, prisons and wildlife services, and simultaneous violation of the Addis Ababa Agreement, undoubtedly opened doors for the former Anya Nya underground movement to agitate and ring the bells of the resumption of insurrection in the south.

Indeed, the government's policies and reactionary propensities of the Southerners naturally synchronized the rhythm towards war that was gaining momentum day by day.

CHAPTER 2
POLITICS LEADING TO RENEWED ARMED STRUGGLE

2.0. THE SETTING

The politics of the 1972-1982 period were the politics of implementing and maintaining the peace agreement on one hand, and attempting to subvert it and thus returning the country back to the pre-1972 status quo ante. Hence, the bickering between the Northern and Southern Sudanese political forces that had already started right after the Addis Ababa Agreement heightened in the early 1980s.

Two important but delicate military and political (re-division) issues came to the fore between 1980 and 1982. First, the Army General Headquarters in Khartoum specifically gave orders to finally integrate Battalions 103, 104, 105, 110, 111, 116, and 117 still manned by the former Anya-Nya to fully become part of the National Army.

It was hoped that these battalions would effectively be transferred to any part of the Sudan without involving major risks by President Nimeiri who, until then, was considered by the whole south, an apostle of peace.

But the insistence of transferring and dispersing these troops from their units may have been an outright subversion of the agreement under Article 27(ii) of the Addis Ababa Agreement.

Second, in the Sudan Socialist Union (SSU) Congress in January 1980, the President of the Republic put forward a proposal to divide the south into three regions. As stated earlier, this brought a direct confrontation between the President and the southern political forces that accused him of contravening the Addis Ababa Agreement.

These issues have been meticulously discussed in the previous chapter. Suffice it to state that there has been a wide discontent in the political and military circles in the south on Nimeiri's policies toward the south, particularly his tactics in dismantling the Addis Ababa Agreement piecemeal since the day it was enacted into law of the land.

An attempt to transfer the Battalions composed mainly of the former Anya Nya personnel, as discussed before, was to start in Bor, regardless of the former Anya Nya soldiers' unwillingness to go to the north where they would be more vulnerable.

Seen by common Southern Sudanese citizens, the Anya-Nya were their protectors as well as custodians of the Addis Ababa Peace Agreement that had enabled them to enjoy relative calm.

Instead of averting possible risks that could jeopardize the peace agreement, as always advised against such action by the then President of the High Executive Council, the Army General Command Headquarters in Khartoum disregarded the implications of these two issues.

Since 1980, the former Anya-Nya forces in various military support units, such as the medical, engineering, signals corps, were increasingly, transferred to the north. This was followed by an unscheduled transfer of most of the senior officers, some of whom were suspected for being involved in the underground movement.

Some of the senior officers stationed in Bor, Ayod, Rumbek, Torit, and Kapoeta who may have escaped transfer, were being discreetly watched, and their movements closely monitored..

According to reports, the reasons given for not having been affected by the mass transfer was that each time they were ordered to go on transfer to the north, they would threaten to revolt against such orders.

As for the issue of redivision, it was picked up and played out of proportion by the Equatorian intellectuals, and especially by those who had just arrived from Uganda after the fall of General Idi Amin regime. Most of these new arrivals, it was reported, had held very high senior positions in Uganda during the Amin rule.

Back in the South, they could not listen to their better-informed elders—like the late Hillary Paul Logali, Ezboni Mundiri, Joseph Oduho, Venansio Loro, Zakariah Wani Yugusuk, and Archbishop Paulino Lokudu—who told them the reality of the situation.

The decentralization policy that was gaining momentum by the hour began to take different connotations altogether among the populace in Equatoria and western Bahr al Ghazal.

To many, it was a chance to get rid of what they imagined and were led to believe as the Dinka domination of the Regional Government machinery in Juba. To others it was a genuine move to have the part of their region developed.

There is no doubt that some corrupt officials may have practiced nepotism before the re-division issue came to the fore. For instance, it was common for some officials to favour some of their tribesmen when filling some positions that would have genuinely been offered for public competition through merit in accordance to the existing public service regulations.

Some of these examples were reported, especially in the recruitment of police, local government, and wildlife departments; the recruitment process was controlled by Dinka or Nuer officers.

The Equatorian intellectuals who agitated for the division of the south were genuinely intrigued by the idea that dividing up the south could create job opportunities and socioeconomic development which was badly needed.

Under the Regional Government, the south remained stagnant in all aspects of social development. Projects that have been initiated were not even functioning, let alone producing desired production levels.

What these compatriots did not apparently realize, fail to analyze or have no time to put it into right perspective, was what the devolution programme was all about. It was indeed the May Regime tacit agenda apparently created as a wedge against a united strong Southern Region. The May Regime agenda to dismantle the south became very obvious following the discovery of oil in large commercial quantities in western Upper Nile Province.

The other two regions of Bahr al-Ghazal and Upper Nile regrettably reacted unscrupulously against the re-division policies by staging what amounted to a call to crush the rebellious Equatoria region.

To them, the people who called for the division were taken as unpatriotic, and therefore should be subdued, and, if need be, punished severely. Such attitude was bound to widen the gap of understanding between the division and the unionist lobbyists. The end result was that it created political bickering among the leading southern politicians.

The above political bickering unfortunately divided up the southern region into two hostile camps—the divisionists, under the Equatoria Central Committee (EICC) and the unionists, led by the Council for the Unity of the South Sudan (CUSS). In the process, each side began exerting extreme measures aimed at swaying President Nimeiri into the merits of their own position.

This was the genesis of the south-south conflict that led to the renewed armed struggle. It is in this context that one can logically explain why the Equatorian youth hesitated long before they joined en masse the Sudan People Liberation Army in the early years.

For the Equatoria youth, according to interviews, they saw it as a Dinka Movement instead of a legitimate struggle against the Northern Sudan domination which all the people of the South Sudan abhorred.

Nonetheless, President Nimeiri, for whatever reason, called off the division programme and assured the southern populace that he would not divide up the south against the will of the majority of the South Sudanese people.

The President added, "The proposal to divide the South Sudan must be carried through by making reference to the clauses of the 1972 Self-Government Act that stipulated that the amendment of that Act must be done with the approval of three fourths of the majority of the members of the sitting National

Assembly. It would be endorsed thereafter by two-thirds of the entire Southern Sudanese citizens in a referendum carried out in that region."

This was reassuring to the unionist lobby. But the divisionist lobby was outraged and intensified its campaign for "Equatoria region now," as some T-Shirt logos showed.

In April, elections were conducted as scheduled. But when the election results were announced, it was expected that the contest for the post of the President of the High Executive Council would revolve around the EICC standing on one side and CUSS on the other side. It was not to be. Abel Alier's(CUSS Candidate) opponent was Samuel Aru Bol, a CUSS member too.

Alier defeated Aru by 68 to 35 seats in the Regional Parliament. Alier was then appointed President of the HEC for the second time (the first was in 1973). For the time being it appeared that the division issue was dead and buried. It was not, as discussed in the following chapter.

Aware of the reasons that led him to lose his seat to Lagu in 1978, and conscious of real issues of sustainable socioeconomic development in the south, including the discovery of Oil deposits in commercial quantity Bentiu, Alier took these challenges seriously.

During his time as an interim President of the HEC between 1972 to 1973 and as an elected President 1973 to 1977, Alier recognized and gave peace and stability a priority. According to him in his public speeches, this was necessary as the seventeen-year war had hardened the feelings between the Northerners and the Southerners against each other.

The former Anya-Nya threats to revolt discussed in Chapter One made Alier assume the role of a peace-maker all around; and many would, indeed, recognize that without the efforts of this uniquely cool-minded character, the two parts of the Sudan would have rushed back to war much earlier.

2.1. ABEL ALIER SECOND TERM OF OFFICE

Alier's second term in office was characterized, unfortunately, with deteriorating relations between the north and the south because of the government's policies referred to above. Attempts to redraw the map of the adjoining areas between the south and the north where oil deposits are largely located to become a unity province; and the decision to put a refinery in Port Sudan instead of Bentiu in the oil area were bound to escalate hostilities than harmony.

To the greatest disappointment of the south people, President Nimeiri, who brought peace to their region in 1972, was now a different person. They saw him as a northern Sudanese Arab Muslim working for the interest of the north. There was no joke about that. It soon became increasingly clear that

Nimeiri was leading the crusade to divide the south altogether. These were really bad days for the south.

Upon the discovery of oil deposits in commercial quantity by the American Chevron Oil Company in 1978, the opinion all over South Sudan was that the oil would at last help alleviate the badly needed funds for socio-economic development.

The refinery was expected to be built in Bentiu where the by-products—especially tar—could be used for the constructions of roads; the finished products, exported for hard currency and the revenue shared fairly to reflect the backwardness of the Southern Region, in particular, and the national development in general.

But to the dismay of South Sudanese leaders, this was not the case, but a total swing to Islamic fundamentalism in the Northern Sudan that was bound to complicate matters further.

This development on the part of the north could be traced back to the 1977 Port Sudan Reconciliation with the northern opposition parties: the DUP, the Islamists and Umma. It was during this Islamic fervor that President Nimeiri published his book, *Why the Islamic Path?*

Meanwhile, in attempts to implement his divisive policies in the South, Nimeiri realized that his long time aide, Abel Alier, was now a leader in his own right. He has been honored twice by his constituency, the south, by electing him President of the High Executive Council.

Could he possibly be made to lead his people downwards? This was impossible, as Alier's second cabinet was composed of the most able and influential ministers including Bona Malwal, Hilary Paul Logali, Peter Gatkuoth Gwal, Ezboni Mondiri, Natale Olwak Okalawin, Andrew Wiew Riaak, Toby Maduot and Joseph Oduho. These were highly respectable personalities ever visible in the Sudanese politics since 1960s. It was fit for Alier to deal with this volatile period.

Additionally, two of Alier's cabinet colleagues; Bona Malwal, Mining and Industry Minister, and Peter Gatkuoth, finance and economic minister, were shuttling between Khartoum and Juba pressuring the President to take off his hands of the southern problems and particularly southern oil.

Nimeiri was alarmed! He had come to the conclusion that the South was an uncontrollable region. He began to plan how to teach Alier and his team a lesson that he would not forget. For the South, there was no doubt that Nimeiri was no longer its once benevolent, a protector of the south, but a northern Arab-Muslim patriot; the experiment of harmonious co-existence between the north and the south had sadly failed abysmally.

The above political wrangling was heightened again in early 1981 when some anonymous members of the National Assembly and some students from the University of Khartoum wrote a booklet in which they, among other things, criticized the central government policies in the south, and President Nimeiri in person.

The booklet stressed the role the southern officers played to keep President Nimeiri in power. Incidences such as the 1975 Hassan Hussein coup and the 1976 Libyan-back invasion by the "Murtazeka" against the May Regime.

Without the southern officers like Chol Aywaak Gwiny, Nikonora Magar Aciek, just to mention a couple, President Nimeiri would have been ousted from power then. The booklet concluded with a warning to President Nimeiri not to tamper with the south and to let it run and manage its own affairs and to let the region exploit its own resources for its regional development.

The north took the last point of the booklet as tantamount to the declaration of war against its authority. It also helped to create a consensus in the north that the Southern Region had become so strong that, if allowed to grow stronger, it would be detrimental to the national interests. The booklet in general angered Nimeiri in person. It was natural that such a region must be dismembered.

In the south, instead of focusing on issues of social development in the region, the two antagonistic groups (unionists and divisionists) escalated the dispute. The Equatorians threatening to revolt if their demand for devolution was not accepted, and the members of other two regions, Bahr al Ghazal and Upper Nile preparing to go to war if the south was divided.

When Nimeiri visited Juba, a huge demonstration in support of Equatoria region outpoured into the streets, and some lives were lost as well. Abel Alier was able to address the region via Radio Juba, admonishing the demonstrators and the citizens in general to be orderly in their move to press forward their viewpoint or else it's easy "to lose freedom very quickly."

But the pro-division lobby took this address as provocation and thereafter relations between the two groups went from bad to worse instead.

On 5 October 1981, President Nimeiri—apparently worried about the worsening situation between the two groups and angered by the solidarity booklet—sacked Abel Alier and his cabinet.

A Provisional Military Government, headed by General Gismallah Abdalla Rassass, Commander of the Sudan Military college, as discussed earlier, was installed in office.

Nimeiri also dissolved the National and Regional Assemblies and forced the nation to run new elections in April 1982. But Rassass' cabinet, as Nimeiri came to realise, was composed of the former senior Anya-Nya officers (the majority of whom were also members of the underground Resistance).

Most of these individuals who composed General Rassass' administration were not inclined to implement the division of the Southern Region into three regions. The electoral officers who supervised these elections had to be ferried from the north.

2.2. THE DISMANTLING OF ADDIS ABABA ACCORD

Before the election results were announced, Joseph James Tombura was returned unopposed by the Cooperative Union constituency of Western Equatoria. Somehow the public, being busy with electoral politics, did not notice the politics behind returning Tombura unopposed.

Tombura was apparently tipped by President Nimeiri and Joseph Lagu as a likely candidate for the High Executive Council to implement the division of the Southern Region.

Back in Juba, after winning the seat of the Cooperative Constituency, Western Equatoria, a ring of security officers was standing at Tombura's residence at Kator township.

In an interview with the author as to why there was security personnel at his residence when he was only an MP elect, the soft-spoken politician smiled and said: "Why not call me President elect (of the High Executive Council)?"

That was a scoop for the author to digest, and when he was declared a winner later on in June, his election victory was the cover story of the *Sudanow Magazine*[1] confirming that he had been, indeed, the President of the High Executive Council in waiting.

Tombura, who stood on the division ticket against Clement Mboro, who contested the election on the unionist ticket, triumphed over his opponent. Tombura's cabinet was expected to carry out Nimeiri's task to divide the Southern Region. What was hard earned as a result of the seventeen-year war was pitifully being given up to appease a heedless president, as Dr. Mansour Khalid puts it.[2]

In December 1981 President Nimeiri, on his tour of the Southern Region, visited Wau. Instead of being greeted with the usual welcoming ululation, as has always been the case during his earlier visits, the President was received by huge angry demonstrations, mostly students of Bussere Senior Secondary School, and school children of various levels.

Although the police managed to disperse the demonstrators with some casualties, the embarrassment was clear to the President.

A similar demonstration in Rumbek was equally symbolic. Students from Rumbek Senior Secondary School staged a demonstration against the President for trying to re-divide the Southern Region into three regions.

For the President whose authority has never been challenged so openly, it was too much for him to bear, especially as some slogans were directed to his personality rather than the office.

Acting on the impulses of such insults, the President ordered Rumbek

Secondary School to close down. Other politicians who gave speeches pleading to the President to drop the division proposal and maintain the unity of the Southern Region were also arrested and detained.

Back in Khartoum, still breathing fire against the demonstrators, the President ordered for the arrest of all the leading members of the Council for the Unity of South Sudan (CUSS), including the elderly statesmen Clement Mboro, Samuel Aru Bol and Joseph Oduho.

Members of the National Assembly and students of the University of Khartoum who co-authored the *Solidarity Booklet* discussed before, were also arrested and detained.

Meanwhile, these mass arrests undoubtedly clarified the President's position in the division of the Southern Region into three regions against the will of the majority of Southerners.

In January 1983, President Nimeiri ordered the convening of the SSU congresses in the Southern Region in order to discuss the division issue. The majority of the conveners recommended that the division issue be dropped since it was bound to divide the people of the Southern Region more than any other issue.

The congress argued that imposing division against the will of the majority of southern people was not in the interest of peace and stability in the country. But to the dismay of those who attended the convention, the President announced that the recommendations were in favour of division.

Reacting against this misrepresentation and forgery about the results of the Congress, Dhol Acuil Aleu, the Vice President of the High Executive Council, and Matthew Obur, the Speaker of the Regional Assembly, flew to Khartoum and held a rally at the students' club in the University of Khartoum.

Addressing the students, the two regional officials accused Tombura and central ministers who supervised the congress of misrepresenting the wishes of the majority of Southern Sudanese.

They pointed out that the SSU congresses had rejected the division of Southern Region. They added that the results were altered in the plane between Juba and Khartoum.

At the end of the rally the two leaders were arrested at the gates of the University and taken to Kobar (maximum security prison) to join those of Bona Malwal, Dr. Justin Yac, Ambrose Ring, Ezekiel Kodi, William Ajal Deng Gai, and members of the CUSS. In the same month, the security forces had arrested members of Abyei Central Committee[3] on allegations that they were behind the Anya-Nya II uprising in Northern Bahr el-Ghazal.

According to security reports, the activities of Anya-Nya II had claimed the lives of twelve merchants from the North in Ariath Rural Council north of Aweil town. The chiefs of Abyei had just been to Juba in a bid to push for a referendum of the area to join the south in accordance with Article 3 (iii) of the Self-Government Act of 1972. They too were arrested and sent to Kobar.

It was in this light that the underground resistance, which had been in gestation throughout the peace time, surfaced at the time the political climate was conducive.

2.3. EMERGENCE OF JOHN GARANG de MABIOR

In 1981, Colonel John Garang de Mabior was back from abroad. As one of the chief architects of the underground movement, it is believed that he had been purposely kept out of the country by granting him one scholarship after another throughout the ten years.

Garang was granted a scholarship for a Master's Degree in Military Science, and later a doctorate in Agricultural Economics at Iowa State University in the United States.

Upon his return home, Dr Garang was appointed assistant researcher in the Military Research Unit. He was also a visiting lecturer in the Faculty of Agriculture in the University of Khartoum. Dr Garang's return coincided with the turbulent political environment in the country. But that made him connect quickly with his underground Resistance.

As the central government discreetly but cautiously planned to transfer the former Anya-Nya from the south into the north and divide the Southern Region, the Underground Resistance was clearly at work. It gained momentum at each government's political blunder, such as the political mass arrests.

The armed organization, calling itself Anya-Nya II, was already engaged in hit-and-run tactics in eastern Upper Nile, from a base at Bilpam village inside Ethiopia which many Southern youths were going to for training.

Samuel Gai Tut, who was one of the former Anya-Nya officers opposed to the 1972 truce and later a prominent politician in the south (he was the Regional Minister of Wildlife and Tourism during Lagu's tenure), had been sending recruits to Bilbam secretly. The recruits were mostly from the Nuer Nationality.

Meanwhile, Dr. Garang, had started in earnest to canvass for support among the Southern Sudanese in the armed forces, politicians and professionals, and among students to articulate the turn of events.

Dr. Garang got a house at Hajj Yousif residential area, on the outskirts east of Khartoum North in 1983. He also got himself a nice second-hand car from an American diplomat, which was definitely necessary for transport in Khartoum.

At lunch parties Colonel Garang would tell his guests that he needed the car for the transport of his children at Comboni School. It would also facilitate his research work in the Military Research Unit and lectures at the University of Khartoum.

As an agriculturalist, he had also brought a tractor with him from the United States for his farm project in the Jonglei area, Bor County.

Nonetheless, Hajj Yousif's location was perfect for underground meetings and brainstorming. In one of the meetings with members of the underground cells in Khartoum, it was decided that war must start without any delay.

While engaged in some of these clandestine activities, Colonel Garang tactifully camouflaged his activities through regular association with the top brass in the Army General Headquarters. As an academic he was also in contact with the professional class without difficulty.

To keep security agents at bay from his footmarks, Colonel Garang was constantly seen with Major Arok Thon Arok[4], a highly respected and popular security officer in the military. Major Arok was also a tutor at Wad Saidna Military College in Omdurman.

Following the Fourth Regional elections in April 1982, Arok Thon was appointed a member of the Regional Assembly representing the military constituency, a position which made him free from the routine military duties.

Colonel Garang was also made regular contacts with members of the underground officers in the security like Salva Kiir Mayardit in Malakal and in other garrisons in the south.

William Abdalla Chuol was directed by the underground movement to coordinate with Anya-Nya II in Bilpam on the Ethiopian border. He was also shuttling between Malakal and Khartoum to report to Colonel Garang, an apparent leader of the underground movement.

Chagai Atem, who was coordinating between Bor-Juba-Malakal-Khartoum, also came to Khartoum to report to Colonel Garang.

In February 1983, a meeting was held in Khartoum in the house of a prominent politician from the south. After a lengthy discussion, it was concluded with a consensus that the political development was ripped for launching the revolution long in gestation.

August 1983 was chosen as the right month to strike, just as the Torit Mutineers chose August 1955 to start their rebellion. It was also agreed that all battalions in the south, especially Battalions 116 in Juba, 117 in Torit and Kapoeta, 110 in Aweil; 111 in Rumbek; 105 in Bor, Pibor and Pochalla; 104 in Ayod, Waat and Akobo were to be put on full alert in early August 1983.

The aim was to strike a deadly blow to the northern segments in the army, capture Juba the capital city in the south, and all the major southern towns of Wau and Malakal in the shortest time possible and at minimum cost to the Southern Sudanese revolutionaries.

After this meeting, Chagai Atem left for the south, and upon arrival in Malakal, he briefed Salva Kiir and Francis Ngor Makiec, William Abdalla Chol, and Salva Mathok. The group sent a telegram to Colonel Garang to visit Malakal immediately. The telegram stated that Garang's brother was too ill and needed his immediate attention.

Immediately Garang took leave and flew to Malakal supposedly to attend to his brother's illness. Garang had no brother in Malakal, let alone a sick one, and he was invited to set ground for the revolution in Upper Nile.

While in Malakal, he was briefed about the Anya-Nya II activities in eastern Upper Nile, and training conditions in Bilpam in Ethiopia. Instructions were given to William Abdalla Chol and Chagai Atem to proceed to Bilpam and meet Gordon Kong, who was already commanding the recruits in Bilpam to stay put and ready to give support in the planned August D-Day. The events were starting to run so fast that August seemed like decades away.

Back in Khartoum, Colonel Garang was informed that the General Army Headquarters, as a part of the overall plan to transfer recalcitrant units in the south, had succeeded to transfer Battalion 110 in Aweil to El-Fasher in Darfur region of Western Sudan. It was reported that the transfer was carried out with the connivance of one of their former commanders, Albino Akol Akol[5], the former Anya-Nya officer and active member of the underground movement.

As they were listening to their former commander, the post was immediately occupied by a contingent of northern Arab troops.

Without arms and outside their command post, the battalion had no choice and reluctantly left for El-Fasher without resistance. According to the underground Resistance, this was a missed opportunity to strike before the August D-Day.

General Albino Akol Akol confirmed this in an interview that he was in Aweil at the time of the transfer of Battalion 110. But he denied the charge that he connived in the transfer of the said Battalion. He disclosed that Battalion 110 was no longer composed of members of absorbed forces at the time of their transfer.

Long before the transfer was effected, General Akol alluded two companies were already in Khartoum on transfer. The third company was stationed in Raga. What was left in Aweil was one service company. What could one service company do to resist the transfer effectively? General Akol Akol asked.

In March 1983, a dispute erupted in Bor over the unpaid salaries of Battalion 105. According to Army Headquarters in Juba, there were some discrepancies in the salaries for the soldiers of Bor garrison. It was reported that the pay-sheet of the salary for the month of March was sent back to Bor for correction and subsequent adjustment.

It was further reported that the acting commander of 105, Captain Bullen

Alier, resented the order to redo the payroll and adamantly refused to cooperate. In early April 1983, the upaid soldiers in Bor grew restive. Rumours about eminent war were also in the air.

Nathaniel Anai Kur, the Commissioner of Jonglei Province, intervened by forming a committee to investigate the dispute as to whether it was purely an accounting problem or a political sabotage.

The committee's efforts to convince the Army Headquarters in Juba to pay the salaries and look into the matter administratively when calm could return to Bor was simply ignored.

In Bor, in the meantime, the Army went on a rampage. Major Kerubino Kwanyin Bol, commander of Pachalla garrison and member of the underground movement, appeared in Bor. And because the commanding officer in Bor was out of town, Kerubino took over the command, permitting him to combine Bor and Pachalla garrisons.

A personal friend to General Siddig al-Banna, the O.C. First Infantry Division for Southern Region, Major Kerubino Kwanyin Bol was able to shuttle freely between Bor and Juba for some few weeks. He had managed to secure necessary logistics, food and non-food items for the whole rainy season (May to October). These items were unwittingly dispatched by Juba to Foshalla troops timely.

To the disappointment of the underground resistance, Major Bol's flamboyant and transparent character betrayed the whole plan to organize successfully the launch of the revolution scheduled for August.

The Bor garrison was entirely composed of the former Anya-Nya fighters: its headquarters was at Malualchat outside the town. A platoon that was stationed at the airport was composed entirely of Northern-Arab troops.

There was a company at Langbar suburb, south of Bor town, which was meant to guard the Jonglei Canal Project and the Dutch DeGroot Road Project facilities. The latter was constructing an all-weather Juba-Malakal highway.

2.4. GARANG GOES TO BOR AMIDST SECURITY COMMOTION

The tension in Bor forced the underground movement to change its plans for August D-Day. A contingent plan was promptly adopted in order to preempt a possible attack by the Army Headquarters in Juba to cordon Bor. It was here that Colonel John Garang moved to Juba and Bor in order to organize and plan the operations there.

On May 9, 1983, Garang arrived to Juba and put up with Major General Peter Cyrillo. The latter, it should be recalled, was a former Anya-Nya officer and a member of the underground Resistance. Speaking to the author on why he made that decision, Colonel Garang said:

"Of course when you're planning an illegal or underground activities, it is always best to be close to the authorities. So in Khartoum, I was very close to the army top brass like General Yousif Ahmed Yousif and General Sowar el-Dhahab. I was also close to General Abu Kodok, the Chief of Staff in the Sudanese army. We used to have dinners together. My calculation was that if there were intelligence reports about my activities...These generals would dismiss the reports saying: 'John Walled Kuez wa ma mumkin yamoul hajjat zeidi', John is a good boy, and it's not possible for him to do such things."

In Juba, Colonel Garang made a number of contacts with representatives of the underground Resistance, including members of the outlawed Council for the Unity of the South (CUSS), Members of Parliament in the Regional Assembly, police, prisons, wildlife, and student unions leaders. He also held discussions with Major Arok Thon Arok, his confidante and representative, who was also in the Security Committee set up to mediate between Bor and Juba over the issue of salaries.

Colonel Garang also held long discussions with Elijah Malok and Martin Majer Gai—members of the Regional Assembly representing Bor north and south constituencies respectively.

In his contacts, Colonel Garang made it clear that due to the growing tensions and the government's apparent plans to preempt their move, in case such a move had already been discovered, the August deadline to launch the Revolution had to be abandoned.

Colonel Garang was also planning to visit Torit and Kapoeta to meet soldiers and officers of Battalion 117in order to put them on full alert to defy orders of their transfer to the north. They were told to be ready and to back up Battalion 105 in Bor in the event of a sudden insurrection in the midst of resisting an attack from the government forces from Juba.

Garang was also kept abreast with events in Bor. He was told that Major Kerubino Kwanyin Bol had left his command post in Pachalla, where he was a company commander. He had moved to Bor and had assumed the command of the rebellious Battalion 105. Garang also learned that the authorities in Bor were accusing Major Bol for inflating the figures of salaries of Bor soldiers in order to provoke the standoff.

Elijah Malok had informed Garang that Bol had inflated the salaries for his own personal gain. Malok[6] added that he thought Kerubino could have inflated the salaries in order to have sufficient money in the treasury to pay the troops in Bor in case the war did break out suddenly.

It was also known that Kerubino had managed to convince the Command

Headquarters in Juba and had got all the logistics and financial requirements for his command in Pachalla for the whole rainy season from May to October when the territory is usually over flooded.

In an interview with Nathaniel Anai Kur, the then Commissioner of Jonglei Province (1984), he said that 'the Army Headquarters in Juba was looking for a scapegoat so as to force the soldiers concerned to accept transfer to the north.'

Speaking to the author in Khartoum (1998), General Gismallah Abdalla Rassas, former President of the Provisional High Executive Council for Southern Region (1981 and 1982), remarked: "Assuming the amount in question (£107,000) was inflated, it was not a significant sum of money to push the country to the brink of war. The government had a hidden agenda; otherwise, a political decision could have been made to divert this catastrophe that was gasping at the threshold."

It is very regrettable that General al-Banna saw things solely in terms of disobedience against the military orders and not the fateful consequences of his refusal to pay the mere £107,000 to silence the soldiers—as rebellious as they were.

General Rassass's remarks are shared by concerned Sudanese public that a political decision should have been made to avert the developments toward conflict. However, given the circumstance described elsewhere in the literature, it would appear that General al-Banna was just executing the orders of his senior commanders at the General Command Headquarters in Khartoum.

Meanwhile, the drama created by the salary issue had already created a dangerous commotion in Bor town. The Province Commissioner's desperate attempt to diffuse the situation was thwarted by General al-Banna's hardline stance.

But in the meantime, General al-Banna organized a meeting which brought all the MPs of Jonglei Province and other senior military officers including: Major General James Loro Siricio; Major General Musaad al-Nueri; and Major Arok Thon Arok and four other members of the Security.

In the meeting which was held in Juba General Headquarters in late April 1983, General al-Banna disclosed that the commotion in Bor had become a security concern to the authorities. He warned the MPs from Jonglei that unless they convince the soldiers in Bor to obey the lawful orders from their commander, they would be held responsible.

In response to the threat, the MPs told General al-Banna that the administration of the national army was the responsibility of the President of the Republic in his capacity as Supreme Commander of the Armed Forces in the country.

According to the security, safeguards' protocols embodied in the Addis

Ababa Agreement, the movement of troops in the Southern Region is regulated by the President in consultation with the Head of the Southern Regional Government," the MPs told General al-Banna.

After a heated argument the meeting resolved that a committee handled the stand off to be chaired by Dhol Acuil Aleu, Vice President of the High Executive Council and in the membership of: Philip Obang, Minister of Education; Abdel Latif Chaul Lom (MP); Elijah Malok (MP); Michael Wal Duany (MP); Samuel Gai Tut; Akuot Atem de Mayen; General James Loro; Brigadier Musaad Nueri; and Major Arok Thon Arok.

The Committee immediately went to Bor to meet with the soldiers. The troops were told that their transfer to the north was cancelled and that their salaries for April which were unpaid, would be released with immediate effect. The delegation also assured the soldiers that their dismissed comrades would be re-instated back to their jobs.

Upon re-assuring the troops in Bor about the government's pledges, the Committee returned to Juba and reported to the authorities about its mission. Unfortunately, nothing dramatic was done to ease the situation that was worsening by the hour.

It was in the light of these circumstances that Colonel Garang paid a courtesy call to General Siddiq al-Banna in the Juba Army General Headquarters tacitly to gauge the true situation and to see whether it would be feasible and safe to travel to Bor.

Colonel Garang was expected to spend his annual leave in his Agricultural Project outside Bor town. A conversation between General Siddiq al-Banna and Colonel John Garang is hereby reproduced to highlight the situation.

"General al-Banna: John, when did you come to Juba?
What do you want here, and where are you going?
John Garang: Three days ago, Sir. I am going on leave [to Bor], Sir.
General al-Banna: Where do you come from?
John Garang: From Bor, Sir.
General al-Banna: John, if I were you, I would not go to Bor.
John Garang: Why Sir? I am an officer on leave and Bor is my home.
I have taken my annual leave and the General Headquarters knew about it Sir. Moreover, I have my Agricultural Project in Bor that I intend to organize.
General al-Banna: If I were you John, I would not go to Bor. To be frank with you John, those of Kerubino have revolted and as far as the Sudanese army is concerned, Bor, Pibor, and Pachalla are no

longer part of the Sudanese Army. They are rebels. If you go there and if they do not kill you it means that you are with them.

John Garang: I am very happy with your advice, Sir. But what you have told me has made it very necessary for me to go to Bor.

General al-Banna: Why?

John Garang: I have sent my family to Bor four days ago. My family has gone ahead of me. They are now in Bor. So, with your permission sir, if I leave tomorrow for Bor, collect my family and come back the following day, will that be acceptable to you sir?

General al-Banna: If you stick to that programme, if you go tomorrow and come back the next day, there will be no problem.

John Garang: Thank you very much Sir. You're really a senior officer...this is an advice a senior officer can give to his junior officers. But sir, I am unhappy because I am a senior officer in the Sudanese Army.` I am also a Deputy Director of the Military Research Unit. If there is something of that nature, I should have not been given my leave in the first place.

In the second place, I should have been briefed in Khartoum of what is going on in Bor. I do not blame you anyway but those in Khartoum who gave me leave without briefing me. I should have been allowed to go to Bor where there are military operations. This is unbecoming. But nevertheless, you have saved the situation sir. That is why it is always necessary to have a good commander. You have briefed me about the situation in Bor. I will go to collect my family tomorrow. Thank you Sir.

I gave General al-Banna a salute and left the office. "General Siddiq al-Banna might have been a 'big fool'," remarked John Garang, rather amused for having tricked his superior. "He [General al-Banna] knew the exact situation. As a veteran soldier, he should have not allowed me to go to Bor...However, I left for Bor the following day[7]."

2.5. THE BOR UPRISING

On May 1983 13, having been given permission to bring back his family from Bor according to General al-Banna's instruction, Colonel Garang left for Bor. With him were Major Arok Thon Arok, Elijah Malok Alaeng, and Chagai Atem. Except of Elijah Malok, the individuals accompanying Colonel Garang were members of the underground Resistance.

On the way, Colonel Garang briefed Elijah Malok, who knew nothing about the on-going strategies of the underground movement (as these were purely military plans). He convinced him to abandon his grudges and quarrels against Kerubino, whom Malok had accused for creating the state of lawlessness in his hometown constituency, Bor.

Elijah Malok was also informed that what Major Kerubino had been doing was a part of the underground plan to create a climate conducive for lauching the Revolution that had been in the making for the previous ten years.

Colonel Garang appealed to Malok to cooperate and to treat Kerubino kindly. At 11:00 p.m. Colonel Garang and his companions arrived at the outskirts of Bor.

The Garang and his team was met by Major Kerubino, then on patrol on the outskirts of Bor Town. The team learned that Kerubino had already lynched a secret agent sent from Juba to monitor and report on John Garang's activities.

When Major Kerubino Kwanyin Bol saw the the leader of the Revolution arrived on time, he was delighted and said to him:

"Garang, the son of my mother, have you come? Take over the command from here, now. Chagai, my work is finished: give me something to drink and celebrate the start of the Revolution. Chagai Atem, I said my work is finished here. Let the wise man, Garang of my mother assume the responsibility. Chagai, where is your AK47? Garang will show us how to shoot the enemy."[8]

On May 14, 1983, Major Arok and Elijah Malok briefed the members of the Security Committee. They disclosed that they were in Bor to take the details of the salaries of the troops in Bor. That wanted to take along with them to Juba, a properly adjusted payroll for the April salaries. That was done, and the members returned to Juba the following day.

On May 15, the Army Command Headquarters in Juba told Arok that Khartoum had already given orders for the invasion of the rebellious Battalion 105 in Bor.

As the events were moving fast, Colonel Garang received an urgent message from Captain Salva Kiir Mayardit in Malakal on 14 May.

The message stated that the Army General Headquarters in Malakal was already airlifting troops to Akobo in eastern Upper Nile, with instructions to attack Pibor and Pachalla (both posts were closer to Ethiopian border) and that Bor would be attacked from Juba. From Captain Kiir's message, it became crystal clear that the attack on Bor was emminent.

After receiving the message, Colonel Garang called his cohorts immediately and met at the house of Dr. Leuth, which was made into an operation room for planning strategies of resisting the armies being sent against them. The members included: Major Kerubino Kwanyin Bol, Captain Bullen Alier, and other members of the underground movement. Preparations were made without delay.

There were three army posts in Bor town: the Headquarters of Battalion 105 was at Malualchat, south of Bor town. This was ordered to face Juba. The Platoon at the Airstrip east of Bor town was not considered a threat since it was commanded by a southerner.

A third Company was at Langbar north of Bor, commanded by a Lieutenant Colonel who was a northerner. This was seen as a threat.

According to Garang's calculation, if an attack came from Juba with Langbar supporting from the rear, that would dislodge the defenders completely.

Major Kerubino and Captain Bullen Alier were instructed to take over the command of the Battalion 105 Headquarters at Malualchat. John Garang was to go and put up with the Commander of Langbar Company. As a senior military officer, he would automatically take over the command there.

Langbar was the headquarters of the CCI French Company digging the Jonglei Canal. The Dutch Engineers of DeGroot Company constructing the Malakal-Juba Highway had also moved to Langbar for protection.

Former Vice President Abel Alier, after removal from office and replaced by his archrival Joseph Lagu, for unknown reasons had moved to Bor area.

After his removal from Office of Vice President, Alier had moved to Bor. There he had collected hundreds of youth for a self-help project, an embankment of Bol Achiek estuary, which used to impede the movement of the locals and their animals during the rainy season. With instructions from Khartoum, the Security in Bor brought Alier to Langbar for protection.

On May 16, 1983, an assault was launched on Bor at dawn by the government's forces under the command of Lt. Colonel Dominic Kassiano, an ex-Anya-Nya officer. Battalion 105 counter attacked, and for the next five hours the war raged.

At 10:00 a.m., Major Kerubino was wounded. He was taken to the hospital for treatment and then escorted to Ajuong village, outside Bor town. Captain Bullen Alier was to take over the command and maintained the momentum.

The Deputy Commander of the invading force and a number of soldiers were killed in the first day of battle. The next three days witnessed the fiercest battle ever experienced in Bor town.

At Langbar, Colonel Garang had virtually taken over the command of the company. Twice, the Commander of Langbar, a northerner, attempted to attack Bor from the rear; a move that would have been disastrous against the defenders. But Colonel Garang advised him against doing that.

However, Colonel John Garang made use of Abel Alier, though no longer the Vice President, he was still a member of the Sudan Socialist Union political

Bureau, the highest party organs of the state. He asked the Commander of Langbar to protect him and the expatriates.

The presence of many expatriate engineers in Langbar made it extremely important that they needed proper protection and security. The commander of Langbar knew it was his responsibility. Hence he could not spare forces to attack Bor from the rear. Colonel Garang described the situation vividly in an interview[9]:

> "I told Kerubino to take over Battalion 105 and since I was on leave I would go to Langbar to tie down the company there. I told him that if we were attacked from the rear at Langbar and attacked from Juba, it would be a disaster, as it would dislodge us altogether. So, I went to Langbar to be around as a senior officer. And in order to control the situation, I made friends with the company commander of Langbar. We used to play cards with him and other officers."

On the morning of May 18, 1983 the rebellious forces in Bor were already outnumbered, outgunned, and overwhelmed by continues reinforcements from the government forces from Juba. So they pulled out and marched into the bush.

Similarly, Pibor and Pohalla forces also pulled out from the towns and marched into the bush after emptying all stores of equipment and ammunition.

When the news of Bor mutiny reached Ayod garrison (part of Battalion 104) north of Bor, its commander Major William Nyuon Bany intercepted an army convoy from Malakal outside his command post.

The convoy was, possibly sent to prevent the spread of Bor rebellion into many neighboring garrisons. Major William Nyuon Bany invited the officers into his residence and ordered the troops to spend the night outside his command post.

The officers (all northerners), though aware of the danger that awaited them, grudgingly accepted the invitation. During the night, Major William Nyuon Bany killed all the officers and had their bodies dumped into a disused well outside the post.

In the morning, the soldiers camping outside the barracks, unaware of what had befallen their officers at night, were allowed to enter the barracks. William Nyuon had them sorted out, separating the northerners from the southerners. The former were all killed. Their bodies too, were dumped into the same well.

Having executed his merciless plot successfully, William Nyuon and his troops emptied Ayod garrison's stores and ammunition and left for the border with Ethiopia to join the rebellious troops from the other garrisons already camping there.

Similarly, a company in Waat also revolted, joining forces with those already in the bush. In June-July 1983, all the mutineers from the above garrisons converged in the Ethiopian border. They were a standing rebel army.

After making sure that the mutineers were already marching toward the Ethiopian border, Colonel John Garang and family slipped out of Langbar and went straight to the Ethiopian border. An Ethiopian area commander directed him to Adura village that he eventually used as his command post.

2.6. DIVISION OF THE SOUTH FUELS INSURGENCY

Having witnessed terrible bloodshed for the first time in ten years, and despite the imminent serious threat poised by the mutineers for long confrontation with the government, President Nimeiri did not reassess the course of his policies.

Regardless to the insurgencies in Bor and the surrounding garrison towns, Nimeiri took a more radical policy. He decided to divide the south into three mini-regions. This decision was bound to augur a great deal of discontent among the people of the south as well as gaining sympathy for the cause which the mutineers were already destined to execute.

In May 1983, Joseph Lagu, then the Vice President of the Republic, led a delegation to meet President Nimeiri to "persuade him to divide the south" into three regions immediately.

The delegation was composed of both northerners and southerners, including: Philip Obang; Luigi Adwok Bong; Othwon Dak; Oliver Albino Battali; Dr. Abdel-Hameed Saleh; and the Speaker of the National Parliament, Ezz El din al Saeed.

In the meeting, President Nimeiri was told that the incumbent President of the High Executive Council, Joseph James Tombura, was not very enthusiastic about the division of the south. They added that being a Zande, Tombura would keep dodging the division of the south nicely without angering the President, nor provoking the pro-division lobby until his time expired as President of the HEC. He would then exit without blame for having divided the south. The delegates powered a great deal of scorn over Tombura's leadership.

Joseph Lagu, who had a great backing and sympathy in Equatoria, has been championing the re-division of the south for the previous two years. Lagu believed that the redivision of the south into small units would eliminate the influence of Abel Alier (his arch-rival) and the Dinka hegemony once and for all.

President Nimeiri, who had already been badly hurt by what was happening in Bor, sent an urgent message to Tombura to report to Khartoum immediately. Tombura arrived on 4 June 1983 and met the President the next day.

Tombura was told that Presidential decrees dissolving the Regional Government and dividing the south into three mini regions were already out and would be announced that evening.

In the meeting, Nimeiri congratulated Tombura as the new Governor of Equatoria Region. He was also told that Daniel Kuot Matthews would be the Governor of Upper Nile Region, and Dr. Lawrence Wol Wol, the Governor of Bahr el-Ghazal Region.

Tombura was apparently dumbfounded and embarrassed by President Nimeiri's unilateral decision. He was unable to say anything. Reluctantly he accepted the post as Governor of Equatoria Region, a modest demotion from being the governor of a united south.

Instead of commenting on the President's decision to divide the south without seeking his consent and the use of proper channels, Tombura only warned President Nimeiri to drop Dr. Lawrence Wol Wol from his lists for Governors. He told the President that Wol Wol was not the right candidate for the post of governor of Bahr el-Ghazal. He suggested to President Nimeiri to reverse his decision and replace Dr. Wol Wol with a person he would recommend.

President Nimeiri politely took note of Tombura's suggestion but did not change Dr Wol Wol's nomination when the names of new governors were announced that evening. Thus on June 5, 1983, the Presidential Decree No. 1, dividing the south into three regions and appointing new governors, was announced. Other decrees transferring the members of the defunct Regional Assembly, the Regional Public Service, and so forth to respective new regions were also announced.

The subsequent sorting out of workers and officials in the former Southern Regional Public Service and members of the organised forces such as the police, prisons, wildlife and local government according to regions of origin created untold confusion and suffering never experienced before. In the process, the people lost sight of the aim that was supposed to be achieved in decentralization of administration in the south for sustainable social development. Even the people who had been married and settled in particular areas were sadly uprooted and sent away—tearing families apart—in the most crude and humiliating manner foreign to the Southern Sudanese ethics and cultures.

The people who hesitated in the belief that the new administration would consider allowing them to be absorbed into its service found themselves rudely thrown out and evicted from their own houses and made to dwell homeless under the trees during the rainy season.

In addition to the suffering described above, the regime—instead of releasing sufficient funds to help people going to the new regions transport and rehabilitate themselves—did not provide any money to facilitate his new policies. The central government just told the regional authorities to divide the assets that were jointly held in the former Southern Region.

Movable assets such as cars, furniture, and cash might have been easy to move around. But fixed assets such as plots of land, houses, public buildings and offices were definitely hard to divide.

However, heads of departments and their officials found themselves shamelessly fighting over these things! There was no doubt that President Nimeiri was out to destroy the south, and the resentments were meted against the north through mass exodus to Ethiopian border to join the new rebellious forces, then already launching the revolution.

After dividing the South, Nimeiri proceeded to decree the September Laws (Islamic Shari'a Laws). The implementation of these laws further pushed an exodus of Southerners to swell the training camps in Ethiopia.

Furthermore, the release of the members of the Abyei Liberation Front from the Cooper maximum Prison on the assumption that they had promised to relinquish their demand to join the Bahr al Ghazal region caused another exodus to Ethiopia.

Meanwhile, Joseph James Tombura, after making consultations with President Nimeiri about the formation of a new cabinet in Equatoria Region, finally flew to Juba. At Juba Airport, a huge crowd had turned up to receive the new Governor of Equatoria Region.

The members of Equatoria Intellectuals Committee, a pro-division group, were visibly jubilant and somehow forgot that they had seen Tombura take off to Khartoum some few days ago as the President of the High Executive Council. Some from other provinces joined the crowd at the airport, more or less in curiousity to see what was going on.

Descending from the Sudan Airways Boeing 737, Tombura waved to the cheering crowd, and he addressed the people that: "I have brought you, your demand (Kokora)."

In response, the crowd thundered: Kokora! Kokora! And Sheikh Abd el-Rahman Sule, a veteran southern politician since the colonial days and who was considered one of the staunchest anti-northern, was served with a guard of water to sprinkle at the new governor in accordance to African tradition of cleansing sacrifice. He said: "Let all the dirt go with those aligned with them." After the sacrifice, Governor Tombura was ushered through the crowd waving his way to his residence.

But when he announced his cabinet, Tombura left out all the senior members of the division lobby group who had been pestering him to divide the south. Among those left out were: Oliver Albino Battali; Eliaba James

Surur; Luka Monoja; Samson Kwaje and Jino Gama. These people were not silenced though. They felt that the distribution of ministerial jobs in the new Equatoria regional government was not equitable. Instead they called for further decentralization. This was, however, overtaken by events, as we shall see in the following chapters.

The bitterness created by those left out of the Equatoria Region new order was clearly reflected later in the formation of two political parties after the fall of Nimeiri. The two parties were: the Sudan African People's Congress (SAPCO) under Joseph James Tombura, and the People's Progressive Party (PPP) under Eliaba James Surur, the Chairman of the EICC (the pro-division lobby).

These divisions were only removed as the war dragged on engulfing the whole South, and after many realised Khartoum's games. Indeed, many of the EICC members later on joined the SPLM/SPLA and now are its ardent supporters.

2.7. IMPOSITION OF ISLAMIC LAWS GALVANIZES INSURGENCY

The division of the South, as described above, had help to escalate dissent against Nimeiri's policies on one hand, and promoting the new liberation movement in the South.

But as if those policies were not sufficient enough, Nimeiri made yet another unpopular divisive policy by imposing Islamic Shari'a Laws in September 1983. This latest move pushed almost the whole Southern people into wide scale rebellion as it provided them with genuine reasons to join the liberation struggle.

Within weeks following the declaration of Shari'a Laws, leaflets were being distributed all over the three regions by the students, especially in Equatoria. Although some of these students were in favour of dividing up the South into small administrative homelands, which have been instrumental in providing President Nimeiri the courage to take the ill-fated decisions referred to above, these students became agents against the Islamisation of the country.

These leaflets were distributed by different student groups such as: the National Action Movement (NAM); the Southern Sudan Revolutionary Movement (SSRM); and the Movement for the Total Liberation of Southern Sudan (MTLSS). All these groups were agitating and appealing for Southern populace to join the insurgency.

Furthermore, a week after the imposition of the Islamic Shari'a Law, which according to the students' slogans, were discriminatory against the Christians in the South Sudan and African time-honored-cultures, a huge demonstration was staged in Juba against the new Islamic policies.

The demonstrators started from Malakia and marched peacefully to the former seat of the Regional Government, now offices of the Governor of Equatoria Region.

On the way, a rabbit sprang out of the bush into the crowd and was caught and crucified. According to the BBC correspondent monitoring the event in Nairobi, the poor rabbit became the first victim of the Shari'a Laws in the South.

The crucifixion of the rabbit was an indication that whatever policies the government enacted in conjunction with the Islamic Laws, would be rejected as unacceptable by the entire Southern people.

However, if the division issue had escalated the rebellion, the imposition of the Shari'a Law further galvanized the insurgency into full-blown rebellion.

Thus after ten years of an uneasy peace, the two parts of the Sudan were plunged back into another war. And as shall be discussed in the subsequent chapters, the South, for the second time in three decades, was embroiled in an armedstruggle.

CHAPTER 3
THE LAUNCHING OF SUDAN PEOPLE'S LIBERATION ARMY AND MOVEMENT

3.0. THE SETTING

Before describing the launching of Sudan People Liberation Movement/ Army there have been growing insurrections in many parts of the South since 1972. This fact that often escapes attention of many scholars and the central government authorities when taking stock into the causes of the Bor Uprising in May 1983.

For instance, the National Action Movement (NAM); the Movement for the Total Liberation of Southern Sudan (MTLSS); the Absorbed Forces Underground Movement within the southern military officers, and finally the Anya-Nya II were veritably the forerunners of the Bor Uprising. These prior movements were, undoubtedly, instrumental in spiralling dissent against the Nimeiri's regime.

But as the Sudanese government was attempting to respond to the situation in Bor, members of those movements were already moving to Ethiopia to launch a revolution. But what was not clear was whether each movement was going to be an independent organisation or unite into a single and stronger organisation and leadership.

However, what was seemingly clear was that most of the hard line Southern politicians had already started marking time.

With the arrival in Ethiopia of the mutineers from Bor, Ayod, Waat, Pibor and Pachalla, there was reason to join the Anya-Nya II forces who were already in the field in order to unify the rebellion. Hence the reason to describe the situation prior to the formation of the Sudan People's Liberation Movement in July.

3.1. THE BILPAM VILLAGE IN WESTERN ETHIOPIA

Following the crushing defeat of the Akobo uprising and subsequent execution of the soldiers involved in it in 1975, those who refused to surrender to the authorities crossed over the border into Ethiopia. The insurgents were under the command of Lieutenant Vincent Kuany and his deputy Corporal James Bol Kur Alangjok.

Apart from sporadic skirmishes with the government forces, little was known about their activities. But since Sudan-Ethiopian relations during this time were somehow precarious, it would appear that the insurgents have reached some agreement with the authorities in western Ethiopia.

The Regime in Ethiopia has been keen to use any opposition groups in the Sudan for its tit for tat operations against the Sudanese government whom it believed was giving sanctuary to the rebels operating in Eritrea, Tigray and Wollo against the Ethiopian state.

The mutineers were also joined by the ex-members of the Anya-Nya I, most of whom were already discontented with the state of affairs in the post-Addis Ababa Agreement. In the end, the Sudanese rebels, as the Ethiopians began to call them, were given a centre at Bilpam village in Gambella district of western Ethiopia.

Gambella District is inhabited by the Gajaak section of Nuer and Anyuak tribes who are also across the border with Sudan. It therefore provided a cultural consanguinity from eastern Upper Nile to western Ethiopia.

In addition, Gambella has some historical significance—as it was just transferred to Ethiopia in exchange for Kassala Province in eastern Sudan as part of the settlement of the Italo-Abyssinian War (1936-1941). Hence, Gambella, apart from providing a perfect environment to conceal the rebel activity, was also conducive to wage guerrilla activity against the Sudanese government's military targets and disappear into the Ethiopian Nuer villages for refreshments.

Ill equipped and poorly organised militarily, as they were, the rebels could only inflict a psychological blow on the Sudanese authorities who were clearly, and with good reasons, scared about possible guerrilla activity in the Southern Sudan. Khartoum authorities were conscious of a wide scale state of insecurity that could arise if the political wrangling that was already gaining momentum, especially after the discovery of oil in commercial quantities in Bentiu.

Thus, the news about rebel activity in Bilpam spread rapidly among the Southern Sudanese circles to an extent that it soon became a catch word if not a word of warning to the authorities to behave appropriately: "If you do not stop doing this, I will go to Bilpam...or the only thing that can save us from this mess is Bilpam." So Bilpam was seen as a place where many people would go to come and change the order of things in South Sudan.

3.2. THE APPEARANCE OF ANYA NYA PATRIOTIC FRONT

The Akobo uprising encouraged South Sudanese exiles to reassert their presence as a separatist movement to be reckoned with. After a careful consultation among themselves, the exiles launched a new movement in 1975 called the Anya-Nya Patriotic Front (APF). The aim of the APF was to liberate the South Sudan from the rest of the Sudan, with separation as its main aim.

The exiles, therefore, elected Gordon Muortat Mayen (who lived in the United Kingdom) as their leader. The members included: Elia Duaang Arop, Francis Mayar Akoon, Agolong Chol and many others who had disapproved of the Addis Ababa Agreement of 1972[1].

The members of the APF were also members of the Nile Provisional Government that was dissolved in 1970. From their literature, it became apparent that war for a total liberation of Southern Sudan was at the threshold.

The appearance of APF boosted the morale of the South Sudanese people who became defiant and openly aired their grievances against the central government.

The appearance of a separatist group in addition to an armed rebel group in Bilpam encouraged the former Anya-Nya officers to resist vigorously their transfer to the north.

While it was being expected that the APF would provide all the discontented groups in the south with genuine reasons to restart the war, the movement was immediately confronted with hosts of difficulties and problems.

Launched as a genuine separatist movement to liberate the South Sudan and establish an independent African state, the politicians heading it were not ready to entertain any ambiguous directives to the contrary from the host Ethiopian government.

But this uncompromising attitude throttled the APF and starved it right at inception of badly needed logistics and training ground. The Ethiopian government dismissed the APF leaders as a group of petty bourgeoisie—a product of western imperialism[1]. As the financial and logistical support was not forthcoming from anywhere, the APF abysmally dissolved itself. Rather than being dragged into the Communist demagoguery, Chairman Gordon Muortat and most of his group chose to remain in exile instead.

The exception was Elia Duaang Arop, the Secretary General of APF, who chose to return to Sudan. He was subsequently elected as a Member of Parliament (1980-82) representing his Gogrial North constituency. But while an MP, Arop was still interested in the activities of the underground movement then brewing in the south. He became involved in organising ex Anya Nya Underground cells in the south.

3.3. THE ANYA NYA II EMERGED

In early 1977, a new development in the Sudan took place: the Akobo mutineers so described above met on 20 February 1977 and founded the Anya-Nya II Movement. Bilpam Village was its operational base.

Immediately they sent representatives deep into Southern Sudan to canvass for support and agitate the youth to join the resumption of armed struggle for an independent south.

Apart from the military prowess the dissidents exhibited, most of its supporters were illiterate or poorly educated to launch a meaningful military campaign with a set of articulated political objectives against the powerful Sudanese State.

Furthermore, the host country, Ethiopia, was being run by a military regime (the Derg) that was avowedly Marxist-Leninist in its ideology. It was assumed that the less educated dissidents from Southern Sudan would be aware or interested in the kind of sophisticated system of the Derg.

But in the meantime, they could just be welcomed as bandits that could be utilised when necessity arises against the Sudanese government under the slogan: "Watch out. You use our dissidents against us, we too, will use yours against you."

Moreover, tribal divisions were also thwarting the Anya-Nya II efforts to move forward from the formative stage to operational stage of military campaign. The majority of the Anya-Nya II hailed from Nuer ethnic group.

Although other ethnic groups included the Anyuak, Dinka Shilluk, and Nuba members, political power was in the hands of the Nuer. Yet this leadership was scared of new non-Nuer recruits, believing that they may spy for the Sudan government.

While this was obviously expected, the new recruits were subjected to severe screening before being admitted into the Anya-Nya II. Many of the suspects were scared to the extent that some of them simply fled and returned to Sudaa. Others were killed in the process.

As a consequence the movement splintered into two factions. One continued as Anya-Nya II led by Vincent Kuany (Nuer); and the other by Corporal James Bol Kur (Shilluk), Bernard Bakam (Anyuak), Thaan Nyibil, (Shilluk) and Joseph Mubarak (Nuba) who adopted a Revolutionary Committee which was a more comprehensive vision following the Libyan model.

Despite their desire to move forward, the Revolutionary Committee could not write a convincing document that could win them support and sympathy—even from Libya that tenuously gave them support. The only meaningful appeal appears to have been the forays it sent deep inside the Southern Sudan, the Nuba Mountains, and even Khartoum to persuade the youth to join them.

The Revolutionary Committee's mission appeared to have been successful, as that coincided with *Kasha* (eviction) policy in Khartoum. *Kasha* was an order by the Khartoum's authorities to evict the unemployed lot allegedly accused for criminal activities. Under this policy, the target group was citizens from Western Sudan (Kordofan, Darfur, Nuba Mountains) and Southerners. They were sorted out and sent back to their areas of origins.

Hence, many Nuba and southern Sudanese were easily attracted by the new movement and managed to march to Bilpam through hostile environments where they either joined the Revolutionary Committee or the Anya-Nya II.

3.4. THE DINKA MESSIRYIA CONFLICT

Another thing that is worth describing before turning to the formation of the SPLA was the appearance of another armed group in Bahr el-Ghazal calling itself Anya-Nya II of Northern Bahr el-Ghazal.

This movement consisted mainly by citizens from Ngok Dinka of Abyei and the Malwal Dinka of Aweil who had perennial problems with their northern Arab neighbours since time immemorial.

The Anya-Nya II of Northern Bahr el-Ghazal, which became a part of the overall Southern Sudan movement at later stage, was born out of and orchestrated by local grievance against the Rezeigat people of Southern Darfur and Misserya people scattered around Kordofan. These groups have been sending raiding expeditions into the lands taking along with them booties in cattle and slaves.

Although the Rek Dinka of Aweil and the Ngok Dinka of Abyei had lived in relative peace with the Rizeigat and the Misserya people for a over sixty years (1900-1965), relations started to deteriorate in 1965 when these ethnic groups were embroiled in what appeared to have been an ethnic and racial conflict. This continued to engulf the neighbours concerned and the nation as a whole.

Hence, as the relations between the Dinka and the Arab ethnic groups have taken a national dimension in the current crisis, it will be instructive to narrate the genesis of what appeared at the first instance as a tribal affair and how it intertwined itself into the national politics.

The story started when Misserya Arabs at their annual grazing grounds in northern Bahr el-Ghazal in search of water and pasture for their animals, got embroiled into a local quarrel that led to a wide scale intertribal war.

In the pitched battle that ensued, the Arabs killed four Dinka warriors cutting off their limbs and withdrawing into Ngokland in Abyei area where they began to use them to beat their drums, a sign of victory over the Dinka people. To the Misserya, the limbs of their Dinka victims were being paraded during the dancing ceremony marking the victory to enable their women to compose songs praising their heroes. For the Dinka, it was a provocation, a declaration of war against them. The incident was reported to the local police who were all from the Misserya tribes. They did not undertake any investigation or legal action against the Misserya.

But when no action was taken, the Ngok Dinka youth took the law into their own hands and invaded the Misserya [dry season] camps in Abyei district. The Dinka on foot while the Misserya were on horses back fought savage battles for three successive days before the police intervened and restored order.

In Muglad town Babo Nimir, the paramount chief of the Misserya wept bitterly after returning from the Abyei fighting grounds and announced that the war was a disaster for his people. Seeing their chief helpless, the Misserya sought revenge by killing innocent Dinka in Muglad town. Some Dinka were burnt alive in the police station while the police authorities looked on. These atrocities which shocked the nation were also repeated at Babanousa, some 30 miles north of Muglad. These two incidences led to intermittent conflicts between the Misserya and the Dinka where the former was supported by the government against the latter.

Between 1965 and 1972, the Ngok Dinka youth from Abyei and Aweil joined the Anya-Nya ranks in great numbers to secure arms to resist the Misserya and the government forces as well.

It is from this perspective that the Ngok Dinka asked to be administratively part of Bahr el-Ghazal instead of being administered as part of Kordofan. Article 3 (iii) of the 1972 Addis Ababa Agreement, provided for a referendum to be conducted in Abyei Area in order to determine whether it reverts to Bahr al-Ghazal where the Ngok Dinka culturally and geographically belong.

However, the politics of the post-Addis Ababa Agreement were hostile to the conduct of a referendum for Abyei District.

Whereas every year the Misserya kept entering into the Dinkaland, they were always supported by the government's mobile militia force known as "Quaat al-Marheel" whose purpose was tacitly to ensure that the Misserya rights to graze their cattle in Dinkaland should not be denied.

The ex-servicemen among the Misserya were soon to command this mobile militia force. This force has been indeed responsible for many cases of slave abductions in the region. It is from this source that militia policy gained prominence.

In 1977, the worst Misserya-Dinka conflict took place. Between Muglad and Abyei, the Misserya intercepted and killed a group of Dinka youth that were returning from their seasonal work from the northern Sudanese towns.

Among hundreds of Dinka men who were killed was Mark Majak Abiem Bagat, a PhD student in the University of London who was on his research. Matthew Mithiang Deng Akonon, a primary school headmaster in Abyei, and Barnaba Mijok Kueth Ayom, a naval sergeant on leave were also killed in front of the police security guards who did nothing to stop the slaughter.

As the Anya-Nya II activities were already reported at the Ethiopian borders, the Ngok Dinka sold many of their cattle and used that money for arms acquisition. By 1978 they also formed Anya-Nya II in northern Bahr el-Ghazal under the command of Michael Miokol Deng Majok. Twic and Rek Dinka of Gogrial and other neighbours also joined the Anya-Nya II ranks.

The Aweil people action to join the Anya-Nya Two, was apparently precipitated by an urge to settle accounts with the Rezeigat Arab tribe in Darfur Region, their traditional enemies, over the 1974 incident in which over 1,000 Dinka children and women were abducted and kept in captivity.

After the intervention of the authorities, which led to their return, nearly 700 women were found pregnant by the Rezeigat Arab scums. For the Dinka male youth, it was a permanent injury to their manhood—as they were unable to protect their future wives from the Rezeigat. The male youth could only find solitude by joining the Anya-Nya II, where they composed a song appealing to the Dinka youth to rise up and defend the nation:

"You Dinka people, you Dinka people
The world will not be peaceful again
You Dinka people, you Dinka people
The world will not see peace again
A terrible tragedy had befallen our nation
You Dinka people, you Dinka people
We're caught in the middle of forces
The forces are divided into three
There's the Murahael force
There's the southern force, and the red Arab force
You Dinka people, a disaster has befallen us: we're doomed."

Thus traumatised by continued Misserya incursion into their area and snatching children and young women whenever possible, the Aweil youth sought alternative ways to defend their country. Again, the Anya-Nya II insurrection was the only alternative visible.

In 1982, for instance, some Ngok Dinka in the national Sudan Defence Force took early retirement from the service to go home and train their brethren in the Anya-Nya II. For instance, Luk Yowe, Bagat Agwek in addition to Michael Deng Majok trained many Dinka youth.

In December 1982, another incident took place in the area: twelve Arab merchants were killed at Ariath Rural Council in Northern Bahr al Ghazal. It is believe that this incident was instrumental in the government pressure to transfer Battalion 110 in Aweil with tacit connivance of their former Commander Albino Akol Akol[2,] a member of the underground movement discussed earlier, to el-Fasher.

Some observers believe that had Battalion 110 refused to move during this time, perhaps the war could have started much earlier. This might have given credence to why Bol Madut single-handedly shot his way into the bush hoping that the rest of Battalion 110 would have followed suit. Moreover, when no one followed Bol Madut, he went to Tonj area and recruited the Anya-Nya II there.

3.5. SOUTH SUDAN UPROOTED-THE ROAD TO BILPAM

Having described the Bor uprising earlier on and the simmering underground movements, it is, perhaps, timely to describe how the South Sudan nation was uprooted and followed by unprecedented migration and immigration.

The period between the Bor incident and the launching of the SPLM in August 1983 can rightly be described as the most devastating and pan-demonic era in the history of the South Sudan since the end of British wars of pacification in the 1920s.

This period is indeed very crucial in that it widened the vision of the South Sudan people about themselves and their future relations with their competitors in the north in the context of a series of events in 1983.

I believe[3] this period would be written down as the period in which the north, rightly or wrongly, set the entire southern people into an unprecedented commotion; and the north stood by, gloating over the suffering of the southern population, a suffering of their own making.

Indeed, the period under scrutiny was very crucial in that it was marked by massive displacement and migration of the entire Southern Sudanese people, some moving away from the cities to the borders as was the case in Jonglei province where the war started. Others were moving from one region to another and still others had to move across international borders to escape from Shari'a laws which southerners particularly resented.

In these episodes of migration and immigration, the division of the south would be remembered, at least by the generation that witnessed it, for the psychological effect and impact it left on the people of the South Sudan. This was because it divided the Southern Sudanese people to the extent that they could not stand together and face one common enemy in accordance to their time-honoured tradition of collective resistance against the Arab aggression. Hence, their survival as a people with one common destiny was cast in a shadow of oblivion.

It is therefore an undisputed fact that in the past, the people of Southern Sudan could easily forget their local feuds and quarrels and were able to forge temporary alliances, however ephemeral such alliances were, as in international system where "an injury to one, is an injury to all."

It is to be noted that in African customary norms, it was enough for the whole tribe to mobilise at short notice and assemble to resist any approaching danger. Perhaps the Northern Sudanese Arabs had discovered this and used it effectively. The southern leaders were somehow unaware that the evil deeds that had been planned by the Arabs were finally entrusted into their own hands to implement them upon their own people.

But this was not going to go unnoticed. Upon discovering the truth, many joined the Movement en masse as discussed in the subsequent chapters. The northerners, on the other hand, discovering their own mistakes, were able to come to terms with their own actions and attempted to rectify their mistakes; but that was veritably too late.

3.6. THE LEADERSHIP QUESTION: ADURA VERSUS BUKTENG AND BILPAM CAMPS

After the withdrawal of forces of Battalion 105 from Bor following the mutiny, Colonel John Garang de Mabior, his family and some close associates involved in the underground movement left for Kongor District. Thereafter, they proceeded to the Ethiopian borders.

The members of the underground movement who were still in Khartoum immediately informed the Ethiopian Embassy in Khartoum to notify the Ethiopian government that the leader of the underground movement, as it had no name then, was on his way to Ethiopia. Forthwith, the Ethiopian government instructed the commander of the western Ethiopian area to stand by and locate the whereabouts of the Sudanese rebel colonel once he arrived in the Ethiopian territory.

The commander[4] of Gambella region sent his troops stretched out along the Sudan-Ethiopian border to monitor the colonel's movement and he was soon allocated.

Meanwhile, Samuel Gai Tut and Akuot Atem de Mayen, two of the leaders of the National Action Movement (NAM) that had been notoriously active throughout the ten years of self-rule in the South Sudan, had also arrived in Ethiopia. Gai and Akuot were ministers of the Anya-Nya dominated government under Joseph Lagu in 1978-1980.

Instead of joining the Anya-Nya in which they were in league, Gai Tut and Akuot de Mayen set up their own camp at Bukteng Village inside Sudan. It is to be recalled that Gai Tut had assumed that since he had been instrumental in the formation of the Anya-Nya II and subsequently recruiting forces to join it, he would, upon arrival, automatically become its leader.

It was in that spirit that he approached Gordon Kong, the chief of Anya-Nya II, in his headquarters in Bilpam camp and gauged his opinion, or possibly made a deal before other rebel groups could arrive.

Gai suggested that he himself, de Mayen and William Abdalla Chuol could form a political wing of the movement to be launched while Gordon Kong would maintain the military wing. This offer seemed attractive, but Gordon Kong who had been the sole rebel leader was not pleased with the idea of becoming a chief commander and taking orders from politicians. After all, he was certainly aware that Colonel John Garang was coming soon as well.

Hence, he turned down the offer. He had a good reason to do so; after all, he had been the warlord with lots of resources including money, cattle and wives. He also knew that the Ethiopians would not take anybody for granted, there must be conditions to be fulfilled before starting a movement.

The former Anya-Nya rebels that had not been integrated into the Sudanese regular army rushed to Bukteng and Bilpam camps in great numbers. They were veritably a standing army; hence upon the sound of a gun, they had no moment to waste. Most of those who swelled the Bukteng camp were from Nuer ethnic group under Gai Tut and Akuot Atem de Mayen.

By the end of May, Colonel John Garang and his supporters were spotted by the Ethiopian government at the borders and were taken to Adura where he set up a camp. Lt. Colonel Francis Ngor and Salva Kiir joined Garang. Ngor had unsuccessfully attempted to take over Malakal with Captain Salva Kiir Mayardit, second in command before leaving for Ethiopia to join the insurgents.

The two men arrived with a mere platoon of 37 soldiers who stood with them in the uprising. Needless to say, the two officers were part of the underground movement in the Upper Nile Region.

However, Gai Tut and Akuot Atem de Mayen made a move to contact the Adura camp. They were well received but no subsequent views were expressed or exchanged between Adura and Bukteng.

Concurrently, a large group of the Abyei Liberation Front (ALF) had just arrived and joined Adura Camp. The ALF group, indeed, did not only swell the number of the Adura camps, but increased the number of the members of the underground in any contest for leadership. Two of the members of this group were Chol Deng Alak and Deng Alor Kuol who had been deputy and general secretary of the ALF.

Deng Alor left Khartoum suddenly where he was a third secretary in the Ministry of Foreign Affairs. Alor and Alak's defected following the arrest of the top members of the ALF executive central committee and head chiefs of Abyei area and got detained at Kober maximum prison from January to May 1983[5].

The other group on the scene was the Revolutionary Front composed of progressive Southern Sudanese students from various universities. The prominent student bodies included: Ladu Lokurnyang, Nyachigag Nyachiluk, and Pagan Amum. These student leaders arrived in Ethiopia early on.

However, they found Bilpam was embroiled in tribal politics and instead decided to set up their own camp in Boma Plateau. However, the Student Front immediately made a direct contact with Colonel Garang's group and established good working relations. The group soon dissolved itself and most joined the Adura group.

When the news reached Addis Ababa that Colonel Garang and his group were already camping at Adura, General Tesfy Masfin, an Ethiopian Chairman of General Joint-Chiefs of Staff, visited Gambella. There he ordered the area commander to send for a helicopter to pick John Garang to meet and exchange views with him regarding his movement. At this time, several southern politicians were increasingly arriving in Ethiopia to join the movement. These included Joseph Oduho, a veteran politician, and Martin Majier Gai, a lawyer and former minister.

The hundreds of thousands of new arrivals were directed by the Ethiopian authorities and each one of them joined the camp of their choice: Bilpam, Bukteng, and Adura. Oduho and Majier joined the latter camp.

When news reached both camps (Adura and Bukteng) that the Ethiopian Chief of Staff had sent for Colonel Garang to meet him, Akuot Atem de Mayen and Gai Tut reacted against that meeting immediately. They question: "Why would an Ethiopian General choose a leader for us?" Nevertheless, they were assured that it was the first contact made and that there was no objection if the Sudanese wanted to meet the Ethiopian official as a group.

The Sudanese rebels met, and a delegation headed by Akuot Atem de Mayen was formed; and in the membership were Joseph Oduho, Colonel Dr. John Garang, Samuel Gai Tut and Captain Salva Kiir Mayardit. The meeting was then arranged and the team consequently met General Masfin.

General Mesfin asked the Sudanese rebels to go back and draft a document stating their objectives so that they could be considering whether they deserve assistance at all. Of course the Ethiopian authorities were not aware of the looming leadership crisis.

When the team arrived back at the camps, Akuot Atem (as the leader of the delegation) was asked to write the position paper. This was because Akuot Atem had already shown some suspicion against John Garang. A document was hurriedly done. The most crucial aspects of the document included that:

1. The group should adopt and be guided by socialist ideology.

2. Financial and logistical resources to wage a guerrilla movement were needed.

3. The war was to liberate South Sudan into an independent entity.

The document was passed over to the Ethiopian authorities without critical comments for fear that such discussion could end up in a quarrel that could jeopardise the launching of the movement.

When the document was shown to General Masfin, he told the team that the document was badly written and did not contain any substance. The

General also added that the Socialist Ethiopia would not support any separatist organisation.

So the group met again immediately upon their return from Gambella, and finally agreed that Colonel Dr. John Garang de Mabior draft the position paper. At first, Dr. Garang—being aware of the feelings already expressed—declined to write the document. But the elderly and respected Joseph Oduho made a rare and emotional appeal to Dr. Garang to help the group out so that they could meet the conditions that would meet the interests of the Ethiopian authorities.

Garang accepted to write but put forward three conditions that would allow him to write a meaningful document. He stated that the movement we are about to form must:

1. Fight for the creation of a new united Sudan that would give the marginalised areas of the Sudan equality and justice

2. Adopt a Socialist system of rule.

3. The fighting forces scattered all over the south, including Anya-Nya II, be regrouped, trained and then start the war.

Some critics could certainly argue that Colonel Garang extracted these objectives from the manifesto of the long-planned underground movement. Nevertheless, the three points were unanimously accepted and Colonel Dr. Garang selected members of his team to write a document.

When it was presented to the group, it was adopted with some slight modification. Issued in July 1983, the document was proclaimed as the manifesto of the Sudan People's Liberation Movement. The highlights of the manifesto follow.

The movement was committed to:

1. Radical restructuring of the power of the central government in a manner that will end, once and for all, the monopoly of power by any group of self-seeking individuals whatever their background, whether they come in the uniform of political parties, family dynasties, religious sects or army officers.

2. Firmly stand for putting an end the circumstances and policies that led to the present uneven development of the Sudan, a state of affairs in which vast regions of the east, south, west and the far north, find themselves underdeveloped peripheries to the relatively developed central regions of our country.

3. Fight against racism in which various minority regimes have found useful to institutionalise a thing reflected in various forms and colours such as the apartheid-like kasha; a policy that drove many poor and unemployed people out of northern cities en masse back to their regions of origin. (This policy affected mainly western and southern parts of the country for the simple reason that they do not "belong" to Khartoum which the ruling clique think is their home alone and not for all the Sudanese people)

4. Fight against similar obnoxious attitude of the ruling clique when they describe any attempted coup by soldiers from Western and/or Southern Sudan as racist, while similar action by members of the regular armed forces who originate from other areas is never so described!

5. Eradication of tribalism, sectionalism and provincialism, which have lately been fanned by the regime and other self-seeking politicians to divide and weaken the Sudanese struggle.

6. Rapid transformation of our country from its present state of helplessness, backwardness, underdevelopment, bankruptcy, dependency and retrogression to an industrial and agro-industrial society where the Sudan shall never again be the sickly and degenerate dwarf of the Arab World nor the bastard child of Africa. We have sufficient natural resources, bountiful agricultural lands, water and minerals, skilled manpower and national will to realize this socio-economic transformation of our society[5].

Following the adoption of the movement's manifesto, the Sudan People's Liberation Movement (SPLM), and the Sudan People's Liberation Army (SPLA) was officially accepted as the sole organisation that was to fight the war. There was harmony and each member was calling the other brother, struggler, or comrade.

Before the group, now calling itself SPLM/SPLA, left for Addis Ababa to meet Chairman Mengistu Haile Mariam something strange happened. Akuot Atem de Mayen, enthusiastic to prove the point that he was leader of the movement who had been suspicious of Colonel Garang's relation with Ethiopians, during June and July, suggested that a government be formed first.

Akuot collected his supporters and he was declared the Chairman of the SPLM/SPLA and immediately formed his cabinet. Gai Tut was made the Minister of Defence; Joseph Oduho, Minister of Foreign Affairs; Martin Majier, Minister of Legal Affairs; Colonel Dr. Garang, Commander in Chief.

De Mayen's approach was reminiscent of his style of politicking in the 1960s during the Anya-Nya I. For instance, in 1969, General Joseph Lagu removed him from responsibility for his corrupt practices and instigation of change.

At the time de Mayen hurried to form a government, many commanders of Bor and Ayod uprisings, including Major Kerubino Kwanyin Bol and Major William Nyuon Bany, were still on their way to Ethiopia. Kerubino was still in the hospital owing to the wounds he sustained in Bor, and William Nyuon was reportedly amassing cattle and money for himself. He appeared to have not been in any hurry to get to Ethiopia, nor seemingly pondered whether the movement should be launched sooner or later.

However, the elderly Joseph Oduho mediated through this leadership crisis and advised that a delegation be sent to Mengistu Haile Mariam and that the leadership issue would be settled later on when the movement had secured some support.

Up to that point, the new movement had not yet received any support from the Ethiopian authorities. So the team left and met Chairman Mengistu in the town of Nazareth outside Addis Ababa.

When the SPLM's document was handed over to General Masfin, he told the group that the document was well written and that he would present it to the Chairman. The group was subsequently allowed to go and meet the Chairman at Nazareth.

During the meeting, Chairman Mengistu told the group that their manifesto had been accepted and that he had given instructions to allow the Sudanese groups to launch their Movement. But, Ethiopia, he said, would not allow a separatist movement to operate within its territory. He cited three reasons for his objection to separation that:

1. Ethiopia is the seat of OAU and must abide by its charter.

2. The 1972 Addis Ababa Agreement which granted the Southern Region self rule was signed in Addis Ababa.

3. The world community in general, Africa and Sudan in particular, looked to Addis Ababa as a city of peace.

4. The one point Mengistu did not explain left us to insinuate that Ethiopia too had its regional problems in Eritrea, Tigray and Wollo Provinces. Hence secession is simply an unacceptable way of resolving regional disputes.

5. He asserted that his country would support any liberation movement that fights for social justice and equity in the distribution of wealth and power.

6. The young Movement, Mengistu pointed out, was in line with the policies of social justice that his government was pursuing.

7. Finally he assured the group that his government would share with the group whatever is available.

At the end of the meeting, General Mesfin in his capacity as the Chief of Staff told the group that Colonel Garang as Chief of Staff would be the only point of contact with him, particularly in the things connected with military assistance.

Colonel Garang was left behind to work out military details for guerrilla operations. The rest of the group went back to the camps to brief the rest of the comrades about the fruitful meeting with the Chairman, Mengistu Haile Mariam.

Soon after meeting the Ethiopian Authorities, the rebel delegation went to Itang, a village selected purposely as a new centre for the Movement inside Ethiopia. At this time, Kerubino Kwanyin Bol and William Nyuon Bany, heroes of Bor and Ayod, arrived at Itang. The two officers, upon arrival, joined Colonel John Garang's group (which they had been a part at its underground stage).

The arrival of these two officers (Bol and Bany) was hailed by Garang's group as one that would enhance the group's voting capacity in the eventual leadership contest. Apart from that, their arrival brought together more members of the underground movement, thus unifying the group before the Movement was launched. Others expressed fears that their arrival may spoil matters. This was much owing to the single-mindedness of the two officers approach to sensitive issues, such as the pending leadership contest.

When Kerubino and William were informed that Akuot Atem had made himself Chairman of the new movement (SPLM/SPLA) and that he had already appointed his long time friend, Samuel Gai Tut, Minister of Defence and Colonel Garang Chief of Staff, they reacted indignantly.

The report about the reactions of the two officers to Akuot and Gai group heightened tension between the two groups that had been simmering since their return from Addis Ababa.

Meanwhile, despite the sensitivities created as a result of a leadership contest, the two groups continued to discuss how to come out of the deteriorating situation. To that effect, a committee of ten was formed to thrash out the differences.

The Committee was, among others, composed of Joseph H. Oduho, Martin Majer Gai, Chol Deng Alak, Salva Kiir Mayardit, Francis Ngor Makiec, Garjiek, Ganyjuj, William Abdalla Chuol, Kerubino Kuanyin Bol, William Nyuan Bany and Elijah Hon.

But as the dialogue was going on, Major Kerubino shot dead a young man called Marial Alek, who he accused of insubordination and impudent behaviour toward his most respectable senior leader. The death of this recruit set the fire ablaze.

As if this was what the group had wanted, Akuot and Gai assembled all their supporters and told them that the incident was a plain conspiracy by Garang's group against them. Tension rose further as the two groups traded with charges and counter-charges between them.

Fearing that the situation might go out of control, the Ethiopian security forces had been sent in order to keep peace and stability while the two groups sought to organise themselves. The presence of the Ethiopian Security complicated the matters further.

In a meeting with his group, Akuot accused the Ethiopian authorities of an attempt to install John Garang as the leader above all the Sudanese groups. He alleged that John Garang had been sent by Khartoum and with the help of Ethiopian authorities to come and wreck the Movement about to be launched.

He told the soldiers and the refugees who supported him to move back to the Sudan and to launch the Movement on the Sudanese soil.

In response the refugees took all their belongings and walked across the Sobat River to the Sudanese side of the Bukteng village.

To make things worse, Major William Nyuon Bany, with a force that had come along with him from Ayod and Waat, stormed Bilpam and successfully disloged Gordon Kong and his Anya-Nya II.

Following these skirmishes, Gordon Kong and his forces retreated from Bilpam camp and joined Akuot/Gai Tut's forces at Bukteng. In an interview with Dr. Garang, he stated that they had actually started as two movements:

"Our objective was therefore to influence the Anya-Nya II and to have them join us. The Anya-Nya II, on the other hand, was trying to influence us to join them. Thus at the start...we had two movements with different objectives. While the SPLM was for the unity of the Sudan, the Anya-Nya II was for the separation of the Southern Sudan."

Following the departures of Akuot's group, and the Anya-Nya II forces back into the Sudan, the remainder of the Anya-Nya II forces and other refugees who disagreed with Akuot went to Itang and joined John Garang's group.

3.7. THE FOUNDING AND DEVELOPMENT OF SPLA/SPLM REVOLUTION

In July 1983, after two months of leadership dispute, Colonel Dr. John Garang de Mabior was elected Chairman of the SPLM and Commander-in-Chief of the SPLA. Immediately, the following arrangements were also promulgated: Major Kerubino Kwanyin Bol and William Nyuon Bany were promoted as lieutenant Colonels to bring them closer to Dr. Garang in military rank and in the military chain of command.

Kerubino was made Deputy Chairman and Deputy Commander-in-Chief; while Lt. Colonel William Nyuon Bany was made Chief of Staff for Security Operations; Major Salva Kiir Mayardit, Deputy Chief of Staff for Security Operations and Nyachigag Nyachiluk, as an Alternate Member.

Joseph Oduho and Martin Majier were appointed members of the SPLM (political wing) in their capacities as Secretary for foreign and legal affairs respectively.

Colonel Francis Ngor-Makiech, a well-trained officer and a long-time member of the underground movement since Bussere days, remained one of the commanders (because he and Kerubino and Salva come from the same area and for fairness-sake could not be given an equal senior position). Forthwith the new organisation endorsed the Movement's manifesto embodied in the Draft Document presented to General Masfin as stated before.

John Garang acknowledges, in his book, that the birth of the SPLA/SPLM was not easy:

"From June to November 1983, we engaged in an extensive and intensive debate concerning the direction of the newly formed Movement. Ardent separatists, reactionaries and opportunists gave us a very hard time. People like Akuot Atem, Gai Tut, Gabriel Gany, Abdellah Chuol and others stood for the forces of reaction. They wanted a Movement similar to Anyanya I, a Movement connected with international reaction and calling for a separate and independent Southern Sudan. It took us six months of bitter struggle to resolve the correct direction of the Movement. The principles proclaimed in our revolutionary Manifesto prevailed. The forces of reaction and separatism were defeated."

The struggle, whose manifestations were to haunt the South Sudan liberation struggle throughout the campaign, thus started as Two Movements[6]. There was no initial split as purported by other writers of this crucial period in the history of the South Sudan. Rather, the two organisations failed to absorb each to its own side.

At the launch of the Sudan people liberation Movement and Liberation Army, only the following members of the Underground Movement attended: Colonel John Garang de Mabior, Lt. Colonel Francis Ngor-Makiec, Lt. Colonel Stephen Madut Baak and Major Salva Kiir Mayardit.

Colonel Baak had just arrived from England where he had been in self-imposed exile after his dismissal from the Sudan Army following his continuous defiance against the system. The most senior member of the clandestine underground movement, Brigadier Emmanuel Abuur Nhial, died in the 1976 incident in Wau, killed by the mutineers under Captain Alfred Agwet Awan.

Meanwhile, the bulk of the underground movement members remained inside the Sudan, either on retirement, serving as ministers in Nimeiri's government or, still in active service.

The senior ones among others, included: Major General Andrew Makur Thaou; Major General Albino Akol Akol; Major General Alison Manani Magaya; Major General Peter Cirillo, Brigadier General Robert Mayuk Deng, and Brigadier Scopas Juma.

I now turn to discuss the Movement's recruitment, training, logistics and the military activities against the Sudanese government in the next chapter.

CHAPTER 4
SPLA'S MILITARY RECRUITMENT CAMPAIGN

4.0. THE SETTING

Having described the formation of the Movement and the setting up of the military hierarchy of the leadership, the next move expected was the launch of guerrilla activities against the Sudan government. Hence, the soldiers and refugees who had flocked to Ethiopia in thousands in the wake of Bor Uprising provided the first source of manpower for the nascent liberation movement. The soldiers and refugees were immediately sorted out according to their skills and abilities.

The manpower required at that time for a conventional guerrilla warfare against a strong military regime still posed a great deal of worry, especially that the SPLA was born during the time where the south was divided into three regions. The politics of re-division were particularly not welcoming to the Movement that was bent on liberating the whole country.

4.1. THE START OF RECRUITMENT CAMPAIGN

The twin worries of the SPLM/SPLA were, undoubtedly, two factors: how to find adequate military support (an external factor) and a sustained supply of man-power (an internal factor) that would enable it to launch a military campaign that was in the making.

Meanwhile, the troops of the former Sudanese army Battalions 105 and 104 came together under Lt. Colonel William Nyuon Bany, the hero of Battalion 104, Ayod uprising.

The soldiers who defected from various sectors of the South Sudan were heaped together under Jamus (Buffalo) Battalion, under Lt. Colonel Kerubino Kwanyin Bol, hero of the Battalion 105 that triggered the Bor Uprising.

Those with no military background but were physically able men were sent to Bonga Training camp. The rest of the eunuchs, women and children were sent to the refugee camps in Itang, Panyudo, Dima and Gambella under the UNHCR care.

As the military wing of the Movement was being put together, news began to filter out of eastern Upper Nile. This news indicated that, Akuot Atem de Mayen and Samuel Gai Tut group (also calling itself the SPLM/SPLA) was causing havoc on the various people coming from Bahr al-Ghazal and other areas affected by the uprising.

After leaving Ethiopia during the leadership crisis, Akuot and Gai regrouped at Bukteng village (between Akobo and Nasir) and carried on with recruitment for their separate movements. The Anya Nya Two that had its headquarters at Bilpam before and during the leadership crisis aligned itself to Gai and Akuot group.

Most of the new recruits arriving from Bahr al Ghazal, unaware of the existence of two antagonistic movements, with two different ideologies and strategies, were killed in cold blood by the Anya-Nya II, on discovering that they were intending to join the Garang group of SPLM/SPLA.

To reach the SPLA training camps in Ethiopia, the recruits must pass through eastern Upper Nile, a territory under the Anya-Nya II control. As it was trying to sabotage the SPLA from gaining more recruits, the Anya-Nya perpetrated these wanton killings throughout the first five years of the armed struggle.

The biggest group that fell into the Akuot/Gai trap was the Ngok Dinka of Abyei led by Bagat Agwek Acaak. Bagat was a sergeant from the first Infantry Division Headquarters in Juba. He was on leave and training the recruits of the Abyei Anya Nya Two at the time the war broke out in 1983.

On receiving the news that the rebellion had started in eastern Upper Nile, and that all the mutineers from Bor, Ayod and Pibor were on their way to Ethiopia, Bagat Agwek hurriedly assembled over a thousand recruits and led them toward Ethiopia. As he got to eastern Upper Nile, the Akuot/Gai Tut group fell upon them killing nearly two thirds of the recruits. Bagat bravely fought his way through with the remnants of his soldiers and joined a group that was receptive to him, the Adura Group. The captured recruits also left one by one later on to join their comrades in Ethiopia[1].

The splinter group of the SPLA set up check—points. Any body or group of people who were moving toward the Ethiopian frontier for any reason was suspected of intent to join the Adura of the SPLA. In the process, many people were intercepted and interrogated.

Individuals willing to join their group were treated as their recruits. Whereas those who declined to join them and who had preferred to join the Garang's group were detained, tortured or killed.

Under this duress, many innocent recruits became victims of torture, long detention or possibly death unless they could prove beyond reasonable doubt that they did not intend to join John Garang's SPLA. Throughout the day and night, Akuot was seen addressing new arrivals from Bahr al-Ghazal saying:

"You're welcome to the SPLM/SPLA, a movement bent for the total liberation of Southern Sudan into an independent state. And be aware of John Garang. He's a traitor sent by Arab-Khartoum government through the connivance of the Ethiopian government to come and wreck the people's movement."

The second group that fell into Gai/Akuot's trap was recruits from Aweil, led by Lual Diing Wuol, a veteran politician who became a senior SPLM leader. Before he left for the bush to join the SPLA in 1983, Lual Ding was one of the anti-division hard line members in the Regional Assembly in Juba.

During one of the debates about the division of the south in the Regional Assembly, one of the pro-divisionist MPs carelessly remarked that the division was intended to bring the Dinka to their proper size. Lual Diing is quoted to have warned that: "Stop your anti-Dinka venom...the Dinka by arithmetic are capable of raising an army of 100,000 strong to fight the divisionists and the central government effectively." That was in 1982.

It was in this light that following the Bor uprising in 1983, Lual led a force of over 10,000 recruits from Aweil on their way to join the movement in Ethiopia. The Aweil Dinka group too, like the Ngok Dinka group who came before them, fell into Akuot's headquarters mistaking it for the authentic SPLA.

Upon discovering that they were not in the main group, Lual Diing, well known for his rare diplomatic way of manoeuvring things and being a seasoned politician who knew the group well, secretly told his force to join the group whom he described as the "Real" SPLM/SPLA. To disguise his feelings, Lual congratulated the group and began to tell them how to organise an effective Movement to counteract the false SPLA Adura Group[2]. He secretly told all his recruits that each one of them must go back home to sell his cows and report back to join the people's revolution.

The people's revolution was thus a catchword to escape Akuot Gai group and detour to Ethiopia. One by one the Aweil recruits left the camp on pretext that they were going to sell their cows and would be back within a couple of weeks in order to join the launch of the people's revolution. It was a matter of weeks and Lual himself left the camp clandestinely and reported to Itang, the Headquarters of the SPLM/SPLA, in Ethiopia.

After attending officers training, Lual was appointed Alternate Commander in the SPLM/SPLA Political Military High Command. At the time of writing was Secretary for Civil Societies and religious affairs advising the Chairman on political matters.

Between 1983 and 1984, the havoc they encountered on the way to Ethiopia continued to haunt new recruits. Fears of being intercepted by the Akuot/Gai group intensified as the contest between the two groups escalated over the leadership question. Most of the recruits who fell victims came from Tonj, Aweil, Gogrial and Abyei. Similarly, thousands of innocent citizens who were either moving to Ethiopia or moving with their cattle in search of pastures were sighted as Garang's supporters. They too were harassed, apprehended and perished at the hands of Anya-Nya II.

In those difficult times, bodies of victims were seen floating on the Nile River at Malakal and far beyond. Nevertheless, despite these horrors, many recruits chose to go through Rumbek, Yirol and Bor and, indeed, managed to get to Bilpam safely.

4.2. THE DEATH OF GAI TUT AND AKUOT ATEM

In April 1984, it was reported that the two factions were making contacts in the hope of reconciling and merging into one movement. But while Samuel Gai Tut and the forces under his command was on the way to a supposed place of talks, he fell into an ambush and was fatally wounded near Adura by the SPLA Jamus Battalion forces under the Command of Lt. Colonel Kerubino Kwanyin Bol.

Opinions regarding the circumstances surrounding Gai Tut's death differed greatly. One opinion has it that Gai Tut's acceptance for peace talks, in order to resolve the leadership question and bring hostility to an end between the two factions, was an ostensibly tacit opportunity to lure the SPLA. Gai would than overwhelm the camp and take all the military supplies that have been pouring at Adura camp.

The plan was said to have been unearthed and proper arrangements were made to pre-empt his moves and punish him for the atrocities he had inflicted upon the recruits. Thus, he was killed in a fair combat, the fate that could have befallen officers of the opposing side[3].

The other opinion, mostly from Gai Tut's supporters, stressed that Gai Tut had genuinely gone to Adura in order to make peace and if possible to persuade the other side to accept merger of the two groups. Gai Tut, though a Dinka by ethnic origin, had a great deal of Nuer following.

Therefore, they saw him as their hero. Hence the fateful revenges and avenges over Gai Tut's death. His death was to haunt the Movement for many years to come.

But, whatever were the reasons for these avenges, the death of a Southern Sudanese nationalist who has been committed throughout his life for the separation of the South Sudan from the Arab domination, was regretted.

Many recruits who chose to associate with the Anya-Nya II, throughout the struggle, however, used Gai Tut's death as an excuse for not supporting the main SPLM/SPLA. After Gai Tut's death, Akuot Atem appointed William Abdalla Chuol, his Minister of Defence and Commander-in-Chief. But the two men disagreed some time later. The latter killed the former over the dispute whether to get logistical support from the Sudan government (that they had rebelled against) in order to relieve their hard-pressed forces in the eastern Upper Nile.

Akuot Atem de Mayen has all along exhibited the South Sudanese nationalism of separatism. He was veritably opposed to any collaboration with the Arab governments in Khartoum. He paid that with his dear life.

Throughout his lifetime Akuot Atem had travelled to the north and to Khartoum only twice. He first went to Khartoum on a training course in the fifties as an administrator. Akuot was also forced to go to Khartoum for the second time for a swearing-in ceremony as Minister of Public Service in Lagu's government in 1978. Regardless of his leadership struggle with Dr. Garang, Akuot Atem de Mayen was just executed as a Dinka, believed to have been planted by Garang in order to wreck the Nuer's movement from within. William Abdalla Chuol, who assumed power upon the death of Akuot Atem, changed the name of his Movement from SPLM/SPLA to Anya-Nya II.

Apparently for fear of an imminent attack by the SPLA and due for the dwindling of his military hard wares, Chuol immediately decided to cooperate with the successive governments in Khartoum until he was killed in 1986 by the SPLA forces under Commander Kulang Puott. The Anya-Nya II leadership then reverted to the command of Gordon Kong.

Regrettably, the death of Gai Tut and Akuot Atem de Mayen and subsequent ethnic tensions generally contributed immensely to the delay in the recruitment process of the SPLM/SPLA.

4.3. THE MYSTERIOUS DEATH OF BENJAMIN BOL AKOK

The mysterious death of Benjamin Bol Akok in Addis Ababa jail in August 1984 also led to a certain degree delayed in recruiting the political class from South Sudan in general, and the citizens of his Aweil central constituency in particular, that elected him twice in the 1973-77 and 1978-1980.

Bol, a graduate of Makerere University College in Kampala Uganda, was well-groomed, articulate and an astute politician. He was veritably an outspoken critic of the Arab domination in the Sudan.

Bol won the respect and admiration of most Southern Sudanese intellectuals when he was a member of Regional Assembly (1973 to 1980). His secessionist inclinations, however, angered the Arab rulers in Khartoum and led to his detention (1975/1977) and dismissal from the Regional Cabinet (1979). He was among Bahr al Ghazalians opposed to the Addis Peace Accord.

Bol had decided to wait till such a time that political atmosphere was ripe for the resumption of the war of total liberation of South Sudan. His high profile led to his arrest suspected of master minding the Wau incident in 1976 involving Captain Agwet Awan (described in chapter Three), who apparently was intending to start the liberation struggle brought to a halt in 1972. His sudden death in the Ethiopian's custody was very much suspect. His close political associates and supporters were quick to act and allegedly accused the SPLA for his death. "But why could that have been the case at the time the infant movement needed all the nursing?"—asked a South Sudanese nationalist on hearing of Bol's death in 1984.

According to reports, Benjamin Bol's permission to leave for London was refused by Vice-Chairman Cdr Kerubino Kuanyin who told him that he would leave for London after he (Bol) had met the SPLM/SPLA Chairman. According to reports, a misunderstanding thus ensued and Benjamin defiantly left for Addis Ababa on his way to London.

At Addis Ababa Airport, Bol was seized by the Ethiopian Security and taken to an unknown location. His coffin was later handed over to the SPLA for burial. In fact there are many theories about Bol Akok's sudden death. The official explanation of his death was that he died of liver failure. There was no mentioned of any medical report to confirm this assertion.

In an interview with an ex-SPLA soldier in London who was in Ethiopia at the time of the incident, he believed that Kuanyin had ordered the Ethiopian Security to prevent Benjamin leaving for London without his orders. The Ethiopian Security may, acting on the orders of SPLM/SPLA vice Chairman, have arrested Benjamin to stop him from leaving.

But what followed his arrest remained a mystery the source said. One source interviewed by the author in Addis Ababa (1987) believed that Bol died in the hands of the Ethiopian Security personnel in connivance with some SPLA officers. Another source alleged that the Sudan government used the Eritreans in the Ethiopian Security to eliminate Benjamin in order to embarrass the Ethiopian government for its support of the SPLA. By extension it would hurt the SPLA for the loss of such a popular personality and effective spokesman.

A further theory which may have alienated Bol from some SPLA commanders has to do with his attempt to persuade the rebels to set free foreign aid hostages so that the world community would not take them (rebels) as terrorists. Another source interviewed, strongly believed that the circumstances surrounding Bol's death might never be known, but suggested that any future investigation to find out the truth must also look into Bol's alleged plan to marry a daughter of a certain Ethiopian Security personnel. The source withheld any further details of the alleged plan. He only confirmed that Bol died in the hands of the head of the Ethiopian Security Desk that was responsible for Sudanese affairs and who investigated Bol after his arrest at the Addis Ababa Airport.

Whatever the circumstances surrounding Bol's sudden death and whoever was behind it, the death of a beloved, popular leader without clear cause was bound to have serious consequences with far reaching effects on the

SPLA mission to recruit capable leaders among the South Sudanese old guard politicians, particularly from Aweil District, Bol's constituency.

Between 1984 to 1986, many South Sudan politicians who claimed they were inclined to join the SPLA naturally started dragging their feet, if not cautiously shunning the Movement altogether. Even as leaders in their own right they failed to leave the country and join the movement in order to fight for the cause of the south they claimed was their constituency.

To many Southerners, Benjamin Bol, is a martyr. He died in the field fighting against the one enemy all the Southern Sudanese have been fighting and are fighting to defeat.

The arrests and subsequent detentions of Joseph Oduho, Judge Martin Majer Gai and Malath Joseph Lueth heightened the fear and suspicion held by most politicians in the south about SPLA's effort to attract and work with leading political leaders. Some old politician took the death of Bol as a pretext for not identifying with and sympathising with the Movement. Let alone making further attempts or gestures that they were part of the Movement. Most of this group of politicians had the guts to collaborate with the successive regimes in Khartoum apparently using Bol death as a trump card for job security.

4.4. RECRUITMENT ORGANISATIONAL HURDLES

As mentioned earlier, the most important factor that affected the political and the military wings of the Movement as an organisation and which delayed the recruitment drive to enrol suitable and qualified cadres was possibly its abrupt formation and militaristic domination. The militaristic domination of the Movement, added to all the constraints pointed out earlier, appeared to have slowed down the recruitment of political cadre.

However, the national fervour to take the liberation struggle to its logical conclusion appeared to have made many to forget personal differences and joined the Movement regardless.

As time went by, it became evident that the military campaign gained momentum at the expense of political wing. Naturally, this scenario was inevitable. The troops who mutinied in Bor and from other garrisons withdrew orderly with their commanders and reached the Ethiopian borders with all their equipment.

Some critics of the Movement interviewed may think that the Movement should have declared itself an ad hoc council to start work and later dissolve itself to set up a capable organisation to face the imminent problems ahead.

Perhaps this could have been possible once highly qualified members of the underground movement came, or new qualified officers were recruited and brought into the leadership council, the critics alleged. It would have also enabled many committed liberators who were marking time to join the

Movement. This would have been the time to form what became known as the Politico-Military High Command.

In fact the situation on the ground at the time, May, June and July 1983, demanded that there was no way but to form the first Politico-Military Command and for practical purposes, limited to a few individuals available. Obviously critics of the Movement were people who have all along claimed are the god-given leaders of the south. "Before the outbreak of the war in 1983, many of our best politicians were agitating and making fuss that they would go to war with the north if the south was divided. But when the war did break out they did not only hesitate to join struggle, they kept on blaming the Movement for not waiting for them."—argued an ardent SPLA supporter.

The SPLA political critics did not have sufficient grounds to convince their constituents why they waited too long and why they were not fulfilling their long-preached desire to launch a liberation struggle, continued the SPLA supporter.

One constraint that must not be taken lightly and which may have been the reason behind the SPLA difficulties in recruiting political cadres at the onset, unfortunately, may have been this one fact. That is that Kerubino Kwanyin Bol and William Nyuon Bany, the actual field commanders the SPLA depended upon for its military operations, were quite different characters altogether to manage such huge military operations efficiently, Cmdr Dim[5]. Despite their nationalistic zeal and apparent military wits, the two were defiant, singled-minded, flamboyant, wreckless characters, quite frightening when added with an air of such authority, Commander Dim Deng who knew them well maintained. For instance, right from the beginning, Kerubino Bol outrightly objected the inclusion of Colonel Francis Ngor-Makiec into the Politico-Military High Command and, indeed, successfully kept him out. He did not like him. Kuanyin dislike of Ngor may have been the reason why he was accused for being responsible for the failed operation that led to Ngor death, Dim added. Kerubino's objection for the inclusion of Ngor in the High Command was that Ngor did not bring enough forces and equipment when he defected from the Sudanese army in Malakal, said Commander Dim. However, the real crux of the matter, according to SPLA officers interviewed, was that Colonel Francis Ngor, being a Lieutenant Colonel in the Sudanese Army, would have been the second person in seniority to Colonel Garang in the military and political hierarchy of the Movement. Colonel Francis was a long time member of the underground movement since the Bussere days until his revolt in Malakal in 1983. He would have rightly been deputy to Garang. He was definitely qualified in many ways to be a member of the High Command. But since both Kerubino and Ngor hailed from the same area of Gogrial in Bahr al Ghazal, the choice of deputy could have actually gone to Lt. Colonel Francis Ngor which Bol would have not countenanced. It would have been unlikely to leave Kerubino Kuanyin out because he commanded the 105 Battalion force that triggered the uprising that formed the nucleus of the New SPLA army. Similarly, Major Salva Kiir Mayardit, also a fellow citizen from Gogrial, would have been excluded. But this too would have been unlikely because Kiir was central in the underground resistance success in the planning process that led to the Bor Uprising described in Chapter two. Speaking to the author in London 2000, Commander Dim Deng made it clear that the presence of two wreckless officers in positions of responsibility could have destroyed the movement from the start. But due to Dr. Garang's power of perseverance, the Movement prevailed.

"William Nyuon and Kerubino Kuanyin, in an effort to push their ideas through in the High Command meetings, would often threaten to use their fists. The Chairman, dumbfounded, would sit back and wait until the two decided to reconcile their differences and resume normal relations. The two would then appear as if they have not had the slightest quarrel. It was indeed a tragedy to have had them in the Military High Command which desperately needed seasoned military cadre." Commander Dim told the author.

Nevertheless, the exclusion of Francis Ngor has also been cited throughout the campaign by members of the underground movement still in active service in the Sudan as the stumbling block for them to join the Movement. They saw these two officers as junior to them because in 1972, they were absorbed into the national army in the ranks of non-commissioned officers. It was only due to their skilful way of manipulating things; the manipulation that they did with great skill and courage, and it seemed, they always succeeded.

Commander Dim agreed that the two officers had contributed in one way or another in the delay in the recruitment process to the SPLA. He added that William Nyuon and Kerubino Kuanyin were a problem even inside the Sudanese Army. The Army had tolerated them until they reached the rank of major.

"But this was not a convincing reason for my colleagues in the Sudanese Army not to have joined the Movement. I was an officer in the Sudanese Army. I had just been promoted to the rank of a colonel. I knew the shortcomings of the SPLA's two senior Officers. But because I was committed for the Liberation of my people, I left my family behind without knowing what would happen to them and joined the Movement in order at least to share the experiences I have gained in the Military Academy with SPLA young recruits.

Thanking God on my arrival, I was given the task of training many
SPLA recruits which I did with confidence", said Commander Dim.

Despite recruitment constraints and lack of highly qualified military field
commanders, added to the fact that majority of the SPLA rank and file was
composed mainly of poorly educated and ill-trained cadres, the Movement
miraculously managed to launch an effective military campaign, as discussed
in the next paragraphs.

What actually prevented many experienced southern officers, especially
the former Anya Nya officers, from joining the war at its various stages was
one single fact.

The Sudan government had, following the upsurge of fighting in the
South Sudan, made discreet plans as to how it could prevent the suspected
former Anya-Nya officers from joining the insurgency that was threateningly
engulfing most of the countryside. After all, most of them were in senior
positions in the public service, and accordingly, many were put under strict
surveillance.

It was in accordance to those plans that some of the senior Anya-Nya
One Officers alluded to in Chapters 1 and 2 were appointed into political posts
at different stages and times. Many of the officers who were the most senior
at the time of their absorption into the Sudanese army in 1972 were retired
prematurely in 1984 and 1986.

Although many of the former Anya-Nya 1 Officers in the Sudanese army
had chosen to distance themselves from the new rebellion spearheaded by
the SPLM/SPLA, it should be recalled that most of them were inwardly and
emotionally sympathetic with the cause of the rebellion.

But in front of their Northern Sudanese superiors, the southern generals
in active service were able to express a great deal of reservation against the
SPLA, for instance. They would openly criticise John Garang as a person, but
shied away from condemning the Movement as such. In personal conversations
and interviews with the author, General Akol Akol disclosed that once Garang
had parted with William Nyuon and Kerubino Kwanyin he would join the
Movement[6]. But when Kerubino and William died, the General saw no
particular reason to go and join the Movement.

It was in this light that one could explain why many highly qualified
South Sudanese Officers were caught up in such dilemma, the dilemma to
join the Movement or stick to personal glory, satisfaction and rising in senior
positions, putting personal interests above the people's interests.

To be fair, one would sympathise with them. Because the incentives of
ministerial, political posts and large families, as well as other social pressures,
kept many of such southern nationalists officers away from actually marching

into the bush to join the rebellion, according to an SPLA officer in an interview with this author.

As time wound by it became abundantly clear to the Movement that the officers mentioned above were not practically a pool by which the SPLA could draw personnel, but useful public PRO if not useful political sympathisers.

In the event, the Movement stopped wooing the old comrades at armed inside the Sudan payroll, but pinned hopes upon the young officers who were more bound to continue with the struggle until the objectives of the Movement were attained. The dividends were high.

4.5. SPLA LAUNCHES INITIAL MILITARY RECRUITMENT EXPEDITIONS

When it became clear that senior members of the underground were not forthcoming, and as the SPLA leadership was experiencing a series of obstacles in obtaining further recruits, a decision was made to send expeditions deep into the interior of the South Sudan.

To do so effectively, the expeditions were sent to the Dinka areas of Aweil, Tonj, Gogrial, Bor and the Lakes districts. New routes to take the recruits to Ethiopia were adopted. These routes included, bypassing the Nuer territories that were controlled by the Anya-Nya II.

All the recruits from Bahr al-Ghazal were re-routed via Lakes districts and across the Nile River to Bor and then directly to Ethiopia. The expeditions were under the command of the following officers: Kawac Makuei Mayar, Deng Alor Kuol, Pagan Amum and Victor Bol Yol.

Despite such careful arrangements, a number of difficulties were still being encountered. First, the SPLA must guard its recruits through guerrilla tact or fighting their way through if intercepted by the national army or militia of the Anya-Nya II. Within a couple of years the SPLA became not just a hit and run guerrilla force, but a rebel group capable of withstanding a conventional warfare.

In the early days of these expeditions, the SPLA forces fought fierce battles with the government forces in Yirol, Rumbek, Tonj and Gogrial. The expeditions later on marched on Aweil town—where a railway line was interrupted for some time.

Such aggressive attacks on the national army meant that the SPLA was able to pin down and immobilise the government forces while it was gaining more recruits in the highly populated areas of Bahr al Ghazal.

Within a short time, thousands of recruits trekked over land across the Nile River into Ethiopia. It was not an easy task. Many of the recruits were not armed and could not defend themselves successfully when ambushed by the national army or by government aligned militias.

In one instance, a fierce battle between the SPLA and the Sudanese Army, not very far from Aweil, left behind Captain Deng Alor[7] who was wounded during their withdrawal.

It was only after a night long search by his comrades that Captain Alor was found bleeding almost to death. Similarly, such battles also forced some recruits, mostly students, to retreat back to their homes. But still, many of them risked their way through and reinforced the SPLA.

A visitor from the former East Germany who was visiting the Bonga refugee camp in 1984-85 wept when he saw thousands and thousands of peasant armies of volunteers marching past the guard and showing a "V" shape (a sign that victory is ours).

In a short subdued speech, the team leader remarked that he had never seen such a massive and huge response from citizens in support of a revolutionary leader. These recruits were to form the Tiger and Tuek Tuek (wood pecker) Battalions.

4.6. PROCUREMENT OF MILITARY LOGISTICS

Having assembled enough recruits, the other aspect the Movement had to attend to was how to obtain sufficient logistics and military supplies to arm such a huge army, awaiting orders to go into combat against the better-equipped Sudanese Army.

Though the Ethiopian regime had provided sanctuary and support for the SPLA to operate in its territory, the Socialist Government in Addis Ababa lived and survived by the 'skin of its teeth' as the saying goes. Hence, little was expected from Addis Ababa.

Disappointingly, the Socialist Block nations, including the Soviet Union, were not forthcoming in pouring in military support as had been anticipated; apparently because to them John Garang was still an unknown entity, ideologically speaking.

Regardless to the Ethiopian regime's insistence that the SPLM/SPLA was a progressive Movement worth supporting, the Soviets and their Socialists allies in Eastern Europe were not easily convinced.

Additionally, the Sudanese Communist Party wrote to the Communist nations that the SPLA was not really Communist, but a separatist group seeking to break up the country.

John Garang, having just completed his doctoral studies in Agricultural Economics at Iowa State University in the United States, was probably a cause for concern of most Communist groups. The Soviets definitely doubted his Socialist inclinations or credentials. In fact, none of the members of the Politico-Military Command in the SPLA was a known Communist.

However, John Garang's early socialisation and education in Tanzania with his associates, Yoweri Museveni of Uganda, Paul Kagame of Rwanda, and Laurent Kabilla of the Congo, adding to his upbringing in the oppressed Southern Sudan, provided him with a convincing revolutionary spirit to liberate his people. Communists or no communists, Garang was committed and bent to rearrange the politics of his country, the Sudan.

There was some ray of hope in the SPLA vision to procure military logistics from the Communist nations. Hopes were raised when delegate after delegate from Communist countries frequently visited Bilpam and Bonga, the SPLA's main command posts. These visitors were there perhaps to observe for themselves and finally report their findings about the 'so-called progressive Movement' and its leader John Garang.

Whatever happened to those reports are, unfortunately, outside the scope of this book. Suffice it to say that the Movement's manifesto, in spite of its Communistic phraseology, did not say much about ideology being strictly scientifically socialist, nor did its leadership exhibit a deep-rooted Communistic orientation or acculturation in the dialects of Karl Marx or Lenin.

Hence, constant visits to Bilpam and Bonga by officials from the Soviet Bloc countries appeared to have been somewhat of a bit of homework. Attempts were made to penetrate into the ranks and file of the Movement. The impression gained by these visitors may have been by then apparent.

Although the Movement was lacking communist flavour, the choice appeared to indicate that a move to inject into it some Communist blood was necessary, after which some aid may flow to water, the germinating seeds of Communism in the Nile Valley.

Chol Deng Alak[8], one of the pioneering cadres and the first Commander of SPLA/SPLM Political School at Bonga, was probably the only one qualified socialist cadre. He was at best aware of the cultural orientation of a Communist Movement and state. Chol had studied Marine Engineering in the Soviet Republic of Ukraine. He had also lived in the Soviet Union.

Amon Mon Wantok had been an associate of late Joseph Garang, the first ever Southern Sudanese leader who was avowedly Communist, could also have been counted as a Communist cadre. The Soviets and allies however found some comfort in the Movement in that it was open to the Socialist orientation. Through individuals like Chol Deng Alak, Amon Mon Wantok and Bary Wanji, there was a reason for consideration as whether it could be included in the list of Communist Parties.

While the Soviets and their allies were considering whether to recognise the SPLM and send military supplies to it, SPLA in the meantime depended on the Ethiopian regime. In the words of Chairman Mengistu, when he first met the SPLA delegation before it was launched—"We will share with you whatever little Ethiopia can afford."

Between 1983 and 1984, the SPLA was relying entirely on much of its arms and ammunition brought from Sudan during the uprisings. Only the relief supplies did come from the UNHCR and other humanitarian agencies, sympathetic with the cause of Southern Sudan Christians.

Suffice to state that in many months to come, the SPLA's main source of logistics was from the battle ground with the Sudanese Army in addition to the little handouts from the Ethiopian regime, but only supplementary.

Hard pressed by lack of military supplies, the SPLA Leadership must look elsewhere for assistance. It was decided that Libya was a soft touch. Libyan Muamar al-Ghaddafi, who had qualms with President Nimeiri, must be won over in order to be a potential main supplier of arms to the SPLA.

Taking the philosophy that 'the enemy of your enemy is your friend,' the SPLA dispatched a delegation to Tripoli on a weapons shopping mission. In an interview with John Garang in Nairobi, September 1987, he had this to say:

"We reached a good understanding with Gaddafi and so he gave us lots of arms and ammunition, including anti-aircraft missiles. We knew, of course, that this would be a temporary support because once Nimeiri was overthrown, this support would come to an end. So, we stockpiled a lot of arms and ammunitions. Having received these arms, we became very strong and began overrunning enemy camps; making ambushes and virtually annihilating military convoys and taking over all of their equipment,'"

the SPLA Chief told the author.

For years, Colonel Muamar al-Ghaddafi of Libya had wanted to punish Nimeiri. He had looked for an appropriate tool to inflict a deadly blow upon him, but did not succeed. Here was time to punish Nimeiri.

Understandably, the Libyan leader turned against his one time friend in the Arab-unity during the tripartite meeting in the 1970s in which Gamal Abd al-Nasir of Egypt, President Nimeiri of Sudan, and Colonel Muamar al-Ghaddafi had agreed to merge their countries together to form the United Arab States (UAS).

In the spirit of Arab unity, Ghaddafi gave support to President Nimeiri to foil the 1971 Communist backed coup attempt. For instance, the leaders of the coup had their plane hijacked in mid air from London and extradited to Khartoum for execution. Inspite of this goodwill, the two men soon fell apart. After the death of President Nasir, unity dissipated.

By the mid-1970s, Ghaddafi housed the anti-Nimeiri opponents composed of Umma, the Islamists and DUP. On June 6th, 1976 the group that had infiltrated Khartoum from Libya launched street fighting. As they were not a match to the well-organised Sudanese Army, they were soon routed out after six days of fighting.

The Anya-Nya II discussed earlier had also visited Libya to seek some military help. Although al-Ghaddafi did give them some assistance, he was, however, disappointed with the Anya-Nya II movement's poor leadership quality.

In Gaddaffi's calculation, the Anya Nya Two was not in a position to withstand nor inflict a deadly blow on Nimeiri's regime. Since Ghaddafi did not succeed to topple his archenemy, he kept on looking for other ways and means to harm him.

Soon after the launch of the SPLM/SPLA, Dr. John Garang de Mabior, the SPLA leader, was invited by Gaddaffi to visit Tripoli. After the SPLM delegation visted Tripoli and proved to be a strong movement founded and organised parallel to the Libyan system (where states are supposed to be run by popular committees and congresses) al Gaddaffi immediately embraced them as true allies. Gaddiffi hoped that they would be the ones to inflict a deadly blow on Nimeiri's regime.

Speaking to the author in the African Hotel in Addis Ababa December 1986, shortly after coming back from Tripoli where he was the SPLM representative, Commander Lual Ding Wuol had this to say, "We explained to al Gaddaffi that 'central in SPLA ideology was the Third World Theory expounded in al-Ghaddafi's Green Book.".. Gaddaffi was impressed.

Once al Ghaddafi was satisfied with the SPLA's ideology logistical support was pledged. The delegation came back to Addis Ababa to break the good news to the Movement's leadership. According to Commander Lual Ding, the delegation members had studied al-Ghaddafi's green book on "third world theory" and had used many quotations which impressed the Libyan leader.

Subsequently, arms and ammunition were ferried daily to Bilpam and Bonga training camps.

When the Libyan commitment to supply logistics became evidently clear, the SPLA adopted a strategy: to graduate one battalion every month and each time the head of the popular bureau (ambassador) in Addis Ababa was invited to attend the passing out of new recruits celebration. Each time a battalion was graduating, the Libyan office in Addis Ababa sent large quantities of arms and ammunitions equal in number to the new graduates.

What the Libyans did not know or expect to know was that it was actually the same battalion that was graduating every month, just to secure more arms quickly, said Cdr Lual Diing Wuol[10]. After a full year of this game, the SPLA had stockpiled enough to recruit and train a whole division to start a military campaign.

In the past, any military action, be it a coup d'etat or uprising in the

Sudanese Army and supported by the soldiers from the Southern or Western Sudan, was dismissed by the authorities in Khartoum as racist attempts to destabilise the country.

The new insurgency in the south, already spreading to all the backward areas in the Sudan, was taken seriously. Without delay, Nimeiri and his generals began to make contacts and preparations in attempts to rectify the causes of rebellion. But this was too late.

4.7. THE IMPACT AND EFFECT OF SPLA RADIO

Meanwhile, the appearance of SPLA radio, clandestinely broadcasting at Naru outside Addis Ababa in Ethiopia, was as powerful as al-Ghaddafi's weapons.

It was a useful propaganda tool intended to divert Khartoum's misrepresentation of the Movement as a southern Movement rather than a national one. The radio also served as a means to mobilise recruits and political sympathy—including the former members of underground Resistance, many of whom immediately came to join the SPLA.

Among the useful national leaders from the backward areas in the geographical north who came to join the SPLA were: Yusuf Kuwo Mekki of the Nuba Mountains; Mahmoud Bazarra from the Beja region; Malik Agar from the Ingessana, and Boladi from Darfur.

Other leading personalities from the north also included Dr. Khalil Osman, a textile tycoon in Khartoum and Dr. Mansour Khalid, a diplomat of renowned international standing. Dr. Khalid, it will be recalled, negotiated the 1972 Addis Ababa Agreement with the southerners (when he was Minister of Foreign Affairs) on behalf of the Sudan Government. With these northern nationalist leaders, the SPLM/SPLA mission to liberate the whole Sudan was given much more credence.

Indeed, there was unity of purpose behind the policy of creating a new Sudan, most of which were expressed in war songs and poems over Radio SPLA. One Dinka song could be translated as follows:

"If the regional autonomy is offered again, we shall not accept it
If a small government is offered, we shall not accept it too
Why accept a small government?
To whom shall we leave the Sudan?
You students, leave the schools
pen can no longer liberate the Sudan
But with guns, such as Klashnikov
The government of Garang will liberate the country with blood."

4.8. TRAINING AND START OF ALL OUT MILITARY CAMPAIGN

After the SPLM had triumphed in acquiring assortments of weaponry from Libya and other countries, the main attention was now focused on training thousands of recruits streaming daily from Sudan. This was in preparation for a major confrontation with the Sudanese troops. A politico-military college was also opened at Bonga in Gambella region to train the officer corps in the art of military science, tactics, and more fundamentally the politicisation process.

The latter was the basis of ideological transition from peasant politics to a sophisticated Socialist ideology embodied in the Movement's Manifesto. Deng-Alak, a soviet trained Principal of SPLM/SPLA Military College, was therefore viewed in the socialist camp as a committed Communist who would impart such Socialist foundation upon the recruits which the Movement needed. This would attract military aid from Socialist nations as well as influencing the civil administration in future liberated areas. Other training centres for training the non-commissioned recruits were also established mainly at Bilpam, and in some camps elsewhere.

The art of military science required various areas of expertise in the training of cadets. Experts,mostly from the former East Germany, and a score of Ethiopian experts in various fields were employed. Also a few Southern Sudanese with Socialist backgrounds were also appointed to assist.

The heterogeneity of training was necessary as the future successes and failures in the Movement depended largely on the level of training in both military and political disciplines. But how did the Military College at Bonga meet this ideal?

Before the establishment of the Sudan People's Liberation Movement, Chairman Mengistu Haile Mariam who had become convinced that this Sudanese Movement was quite different from the opposition groups that preceded them, made a prophetic warning to the new leadership not to paint their organisation "red." Mengistu added: "Given the circumstances and the geopolitics in the region and the world at large, your Movement would be frustrated and nipped in the bud!"

Though the training at Bonga Military academy was probably meant to guard the Movement against painting, the organisation red, unfortunately, the staff of the Military College, particularly the principal and his Sudanese Socialist colleagues, embarked in an emotional and hectic programmes that knew no bound.

Instead of teaching basic principles of Socialism, some of the "pseudo-Socialists trainers" as many began to call them, commenced the training with dialectic drills of "Socialist phraseology" unknown to the huge collection of Sudanese of varied backgrounds. The latter included students, peasants, soldiers and the "old-guard politicians." To cement these differences turning them into members of effective Movement to fight an effective war was the most difficult undertaking that needed very highly trained, educated and sophisticated staff.

The situation, as complex as it was, suggested that the staff of the college started with a wrong "tone and tune." This was because injecting the Socialist phraseology of armed-struggle of the Che Guevara Type into the minds and souls of the recruits without analysing properly and identifying what were suitable or unsuitable for the recruits from such diverse backgrounds was heavily laden with irrelevant commodities.

Within a short period of time, the Socialist phraseology of petty bourgeoisie, reactionaries, revolutionaries, anti-revolutionaries and comrades, became common in the drills. The recruits soon became bored with these terminologies to the extent that some of them were frustrated. Naturally, western educated politicians and particularly those who had held positions in the Sudan found themselves ill-fitted into the demagoguery being preached to them at Military College.

Some of the western educated recruits did sometimes walk out from the lecture rooms. But where would they go? Nowhere! So they were brought back to complete the course—which was often hectic, harsh and difficult in comparison to their previous occupations.

According to Dr. Peter Nyaba: The SPLA, by its definition, is a peasant army made of volunteers. To train them into effective soldiers needed careful approach that would season them into professional freedom fighters.

Apart from the initial tribal and other contradictions, the members of the SPLM/A were propelled into action by nationalist and patriotic sentiments. Its training was rigorous and the conditions in the training camps severe and harsh to say the least. Nevertheless, the soldiers and men persevered till the end of the training sessions, when they were deployed[11].

Indeed, it would be necessary to point out that the staff given to the recruits widened the gap between them and the leadership. On the top, the experiences from the College and other training camps created unnecessary animosity among the different groups as they were being commissioned and given assignments in the field and in the administration of the SPLM.

The most important aspect to be noted when dealing with this background of the SPLA recruits was that the Socialist staff should have known two facts: that many southerners who went to Ethiopia had different reasons of joining the armed-struggle (as described in earlier chapters).

The politicians and the former government officials, who were educated in the mission schools, had come there to gain training and go back to the Sudan to fight first to liberate the south from the north and to form an independent state in Southern Sudan.

Second, the majority of the new recruits join the SPLA simply to fight against their traditional enemies, the Arabs, and nothing else. Hence, to be heavily laden with Marxist dialectics was assumed to be an unnecessary burden.

By and large, the College created two categories of cadres: those who benefited from the new ideological orientation, and those who were veritably alienated by it. The former group may have actually met the intentions of the authorities who sent them there.

They came out with rare revolutionary zeal and ardent supporters and fighters till the time of writing (21 years later). For the latter group who found themselves alienated by the system, they became reactionaries and turned against the Movement to its detriment and demise.

Dr. Peter Adwok Nyaba, in his sentimental book *The Politics of Liberation* had this to say: "The assiduous reactionaries in the SPLA were those who passed out of that political training school"

Furthermore, Mayom told the author that those politicians and officials who joined the Movement and claimed that they were ignored or marginalised, and the bad administration in the refugee camps under the command of the pseudo-socialist officers, earned those grudges from Bonga Military College [12].

4.9. COLONEL MANYIEL AYUEL AND MAJOR AROK THON JOIN SPLA

In the early days, just before serious confrontation with the Sudanese government commenced in earnest (1984), two interesting personalities joined the Movement. Lt. Colonel Martin Manyiel Ayuel defected with all of his entire unit and equipment into the SPLA.

Colonel Manyiel had been a member of the underground resistance described previously. His defection at that critical moment was hailed as a patriotic move indeed.

The second new arrival was Major Arok Thon Arok. He had been arrested and detained for almost a year following the Bor mutiny and his connection with John Garang during the planning stages of the revolution.

Upon his release, Major Arok Thon left for the bush and arrived at Bonga in good health. The two men boosted the position of John Garang who had been puzzled by Kerubino Kwanyin Bol and William Nyuon Bany's fortuitous and parochial performances in the SPLA.

Upon arrival, Arok Thon was appointed Deputy Chief of Staff for logistics and administration. Colonel Martin Manyiel was appointed the Director in the Office of Chairman and Commander-in-Chief.

Having acquired sufficient logistics and trained guerrilla forces, the SPLA started the military campaign. In a speech marking the Movement's first anniversary in March 1984, the leader of SPLM/SPLM Colonel/ Dr John Garang de Mabior stated[13]:

In pursuance of protracted revolutionary armed-struggle, the SPLA has been organised and has already achieved significant victories. In the first offensive after May 16, 1983, the SPLA attacked and captured Malual Gahoth on November 17, 1983.

In the battle, the enemy (Sudan Army) suffered 120 killed, 60 wounded and one helicopter shot down with SPLA losing 12 killed and 30 wounded. The second attack on Nasir was on December 12, 1983.

In the attack, the enemy lost 267 killed 173 wounded, 3 helicopters shot down, 3 boats destroyed on River Sobat, one armoured personnel carrier and the Commander's Land Rover knocked out. The SPLA lost 4 killed and 9 wounded. The SPLA withdrew after holding part of the Nasir town for seven days.

In its second offensive, February 8,1984, ending with the bombardment of Malakal, February 22, 1984, the SPLA units under Lt. Colonel Kerubino Kwanyin Bol, Lt. Colonel William Nyuon Bany, and Lt. Colonel Kawac Makuei attacked and overran Ayod, CCI Camp at Kilo 215 on the Jonglei Canal Company Project) at the Sobat Mouth, and a Nile Post Boat steamer at Wathkec.

In its second new year, two week offensive, the SPLA inflicted the following casualties on the enemy: 1,069 killed, 480 wounded to the SPLA, 30 killed and 59 wounded.

In material terms, the SPLA managed to destroy nine T55 tanks, 8 anti-personnel carriers, 8 Magirus army trucks, 1 civilian CCI truck, 2 small chesna planes, two bulldozers, two steamers, two fuel stations, 1 big winch, a large quantity of medicine and 2 long-range signal sets. The magnitude of those operations led to the closing down of the CCI operations digging the Jonglei Canal and the Chevron Company.

In related attacks, SPLA captured Jebel Boma and took hostages; Pochalla and Yirol towns were also captured. There was no doubt for the Nimeiri regime that the SPLA campaign had successfully started. The regime must be in panic now. The SPLA military campaign as discussed in the book has thus begun.

CHAPTER 5
NIMEIRI REACTS TO MOUNTING INSURGENCY

5.0. THE SETTING

In the short period of its life (1983-1985) the Sudan People's Liberation Army managed to assemble a huge and formidable force capable of conventional confrontation with the Sudanese army.

The tactics it employed to acquire sufficient logistical supplies in addition to the sudden involvement of external players, e.g. Ethiopia and Libya, frightened President Jaafar Mohamed Nimeiri and his generals in Khartoum.

At the onset, it appeared as if Nimeiri was taking the matter lightly as he had done in the past fifteen years of his autocratic rule. This was evidenced in his numerous contradictory press statements in which he admitted the seriousness of the situation. At other times he described the uprising as a storm in a teacup.

Moreover, the manner in which he had handled the division of the south, the subsequent imposition of the Islamic Shar'ia Laws without seeking informed advice from his lieutenants, not considering the apparent consequences the events would bear on his regime, baffled everybody and the nation as a whole.

As the security reports started filtering out of Ethiopia and eastern Upper Nile indicating the seriousness of the situation, the dictator began to panic, behaving in the process like a wounded giant.

Recognising that the tide was increasingly coming against him day by day, Nimeiri decided to face the insurgency. But how was he to react in order to avert the crisis he had helped create and what methods would he use?

This Chapter will detail Nimeiri's response to insurgency through the invigoration of the State Security apparatus, declaration of the state of emergency that permitted unlawful detention and torture, the declaration of Jihad (holy war) upon the south, and many attempts to win back the opponents.

5.1. NIMEIRI'S ATTEMPTS TO WIN NORTHERN PUBLIC

As a military officer who had fought in the south against the Anya-Nya in the 1960s, Nimeiri was very aware of the magnitude of the insurgency he was about to face. He decided to strike while the iron was still hot, and indeed the iron was getting hotter.

In a desperate but well-calculated move, Nimeiri decided he should rally behind him the northern public opinion (his constituency) before turning around with vigour and rigour to face the insurgency in the south. Mansour Khalid, Nimeiri's Foreign Affairs Minister and Assistant President (1971-1976) writes[1]:

> "Having destroyed his institutions in the south and the north and emaciated the army, Nimeiri's tricks caught up with him. So he resorted to religion, the last resort of scoundrels. In the course of his sixteen-year rule, Nimeiri has used and abused all ideologies; only religion was left for him. He thus conjured up his so-called Islamic laws and ambushed the unsuspecting nation with the September Decrees. In those laws, there was nothing but terror."[2]

Since the 1977 Port Sudan National Reconciliation between the regime and a coalition of Northern opposition group (Umma, DUP, and the Islamic Front), Nimeiri had realised the potency of religion in taming the religiously rooted polity in the Northern Sudan.

So, by imposing the Islamic Laws, Nimeiri cowed down the Northern Sudanese people and made them gullible to stand solidly behind his ailing regime.

This enabled him to turn against the insurgency in the south. Nimeiri, henceforth, declared the state of emergency throughout the country. He finally declared a Jihad against the rebellious south.

5.2. NIMEIRI DECLARES JIHAAD AGAINST SPLA

As President of the Republic and the Commander-in-Chief of the Armed Forces, and now the Imam of the Faithful Muslims, Nimeiri decreed that the Sudanese army has become the 'Army of God.'

"From now on," Nimeiri told the nation in a televised and radio broadcast: "there will be no longer any death for a soldier in the holy war in the south but martyrdom."

With that pronouncement, Nimeiri toured the length and breadth of the country appealing for support. Addressing officers and men in the armed forces in their respective units and garrisons, Nimeiri said: "You have now become the Holy Warriors of God. Those of you who will fall martyrs in the war against the infidels in the southern part of our beloved nation will go straight to Heaven, the eternal Home of Martyrs."

At the end of all his speeches, Nimeiri invoked the Islamic cry: Allahu Akber, Allah wu Akber, and the soldiers reciprocated. He was their Commander in Chief.

To go straight to heaven, the home for everlasting peace and comfort for a simple soldier recruited from the property-less society of the rural Sudan was a very attractive and intriguing proposition indeed.

Nimeiri's appeal was attentively listened to and embraced by the majority of the military with rare zeal. The exception were the southern soldiers who might have nonetheless, been inflamed by these speeches.

Within a couple of months following Nimeiri's decrees converting the national army into the *Army of God*, the entire army in the country responded favourably by pledging unconditional allegiance to their Commander-in-Chief, the one time architect of secularism and now turned an Imam overnight.

To conform to the new Islamic codes, judges in the country's judicial system and the legal counsellors in the Attorney General Chambers were reshuffled or dismissed with immediate effect. They were replaced with Shari'a Judges. Zealous Islamic Legal Counsellors were also appointed.

A new Islamic system naturally needed an effective and conforming head of the Judiciary. In conformity, a notorious Shari'a Judge, Fouad al-Amin Abdel Rahman, was named the country's new Chief Justice. He replaced Daffallah Hajj Yousif who had been holding the post since 1982.

Without delay "Al Adalla al-Najiza" or "prompt justice system," was introduced in order to guide the Shari'a Laws. Prompt justice system was subsequently set up with prompt courts to try suspects according to Sharia jurisprudence. Hard-line Islamists were appointed to head the prompt courts. Among them were two ruthless Islamist judges, Mohamed Mohjoub Abdalla Hajj Nour and al-Makashiffi Taha al-Kabashi.

In these decisive prompt courts, suspects of all classes and grades were rushed to these courts daily. The suspects charged of civil and criminal offences were hurriedly tried. These sentences were executed immediately and with impunity.

By August 1984, fifty-eight amputations including 12 cross-limb amputations had already been carried out. The victims, not surprisingly, were mainly the non-Muslims[3]. Besides, citizens accused of minor charges that could have previously merited lesser sentences ranging from three to four months imprisonment were included in capital crimes and amputations.

The nation, unaware of the harshness and the strictness of the Shari'a Laws, was thrown into utter confusion. Example was the case of Michael. Though a Christian, he was accused of theft and punished as a Muslim.

However, in efforts to put some Islamic flavour on his discredited and seemingly decaying regime, Nimeiri brought into his cabinet two prominent members of the Ansar al-Sunna sect. Awad al-Jeed Mohamed Ahmed, a legal counsel from the Attorney General's Chambers was appointed the Attorney General to replace Dr. Hassan Abdalla al-Turabi. The latter had held the post since the National Reconciliation of 1977. Al-Turabi was then named the

Assistant President. The second Islamist appointee was al-Neil Abu Gurun who became Presidential Chief Legal Advisor.

It was an ironic turn of events that the President who took over power in 1969, who had wanted to transform the country into the "Cuba of Africa," had overnight become an absolute right wing Islamist. He continued to push the country from abyss to abyss. His former aid, Dr. Mansour Khalid writes: "The harsh application of Muslim penal code (hudud), particularly amputations and floggings for such crimes as petty theft, was unjust and unreasonable by any standards of religious ethics when inflicted on a population (both Muslim and non-Muslim) that was predominantly impoverished.[4]"

To frighten off other potential opponents, Nimeiri picked the 75-year old Sheikh, Mahmoud Mohamed Taha, leader of a small but influential Republican Brotherhood Islamic Sect, and executed him for a crime of apostasy.

Taha had been known for his moderate Islamic approach and teachings to conform to the changing world. This was unacceptable to the authorities that took this as offence against orthodox Islam. The execution of Taha was condemned world wide as an abuse of justice. Appeals for clemency even at the last moment could not change Nimeiri's mind.

5.3. NIMEIRI'S NATIONAL MOBILISATION AND PROPAGANDA WAR

Having traumatised the northern public through the harsh use of Islamic Laws and other dictatorial methods, Nimeiri then found himself safe to confront the insurgency in the south. To begin with, Nimeiri called for the unity of the north to enable him to defeat the enemies of God whom he described as *"al-Khauona"* or treacheries. Thereupon, Nimeiri ordered that all the national material and human resources be used in the defeat of the rebels.

For that purpose, Nimeiri and his propagandist apparatuses conjured the terms that when matched together defeat the very purpose that it was meant to accomplish.

Nimeiri depicted the SPLA as a Communist inspired Movement. On other instances, he labelled it a Dinka tribal movement formed in protest against the loss of power under the defunct Southern Region regime.

Nimeiri also described the SPLA leader as a crusading Christian detractor. And As though those name-callings did not suffice, Nimeiri declared the SPLA a separatist Movement.

Indeed Nimeiri manoeuvres were apparently targeted to separate audiences from within an international community in order to isolate the SPLA, denying it the support that it was in need of.

The period that followed the adoption of this policy of propaganda rhetoric clearly marked the start of the subsequent intensive propaganda war against the rebel Sudan People's Liberation Army.

Throughout, all the national media (newspapers, radio, and television) coverage was devoted toward one main objective: the destruction and discrediting of the SPLA.

In the event, Radio Omdurman and Radio Juba embarked on the campaign of hate against the SPLA in general and the Dinka nationality in particular.

This campaign went to near hysteria where the authorities sometimes could not comprehend what they were telling their audience or populace in the country. One such example was Mohamed Khojali Saleheen, a broadcaster by training, the incumbent Minister of Information.

Salaheen was addressing the press about the visit of the SPLA leader, Colonel John Garang to Libya in 1984. He had this to say: "Gentlemen of the Press. Of course, all of you are aware that Garang is a well known Communist." The minister was apparently referring to late Joseph Garang, a southern Communist executed by Nimeiri following the Communist-backed coup attempt in July 1971.

In the Northern Sudan, anti-SPLA and anti-Dinka hate campaign was well tailored and disseminated, not only by the media, but also in the mosques.

During the Friday Prayers, for instance, in the main cities in Khartoum, Omdurman and Khartoum North, and many more, the greater part of the sermons were devoted to the anti-SPLA and anti-Dinka hate campaigns. Dr Mansour Khalid writes:

> "The intimidation and the hate campaign was so permeating that even those who seemed to be addressing the real issue in Khartoum did not feel comfortable enough to make their position known on the issue without first enumerating the wrong doings of the SPLA leader Dr. John Garang. If anything, this only went to show that it was Garang who was uppermost in the people's thinking rather than the situation that made Garang a rebel.[5]"

In some parts of Equatoria, where the division of the south fervour was deeply rooted, Nimeiri's hate campaign to depict the SPLA as a tribal Movement of the Dinka people who revolted for the loss of their hegemony over other tribes was taken up very seriously.

In Juba, the main base of the pro-division lobby, slogans to depict the Dinka nationality were abundantly shown everywhere. Such as Dormander Actien Bauerai Or DAB (a German beer label) was taken as an acronym of 'Dinka Are Bad.' The label of J.B. Whisky was also taken to mean Jienge Bor

(Dinka Bor). Other demeaning labels against the Dinka like "the Dinka Are Born to Rule!!" were concocted so as to fan the anti-Dinka sentiment.

Prominent leading Equatorian politicians like the late Hillary Paul Logali, Joseph Oduho, Ezboni Mundiri, Gamma Hassan and Church leaders such as Archbishop Paulino Lokudu and Elanana Ngalamu, Justice Wilson Aryamba and a good number of Equatoria students rejected the campaign.

They warned their fellow country folks, particularly in Equatoria, against the adverse consequences such hate campaign would bring to bear in the future relations among the people of South Sudan.

Some self-made politicians who had good reasons to believe that they could have very little to gain under one Southern Sudan Regional administration seized the opportunity and responded very fast to the Nimeiri campaign of hate. Such personalities included Francis Wajo, the Deputy Governor of Equatoria Region, and Gajuk Wurnyang Lupai, Commissioner of Eastern Equatoria Province.

Wajo—a trained paramedic and a long time advocate of an independent South Sudan, a move that had brought him during the Anya-Nya I long detention, torture and prison sentences—seized the campaign very effectively against the cautious advice of Governor Tombura.

Although Wajo failed to convince his own Moru constituency to bandwagon with him, he managed, nevertheless, to win Gajuk to his side. Gajuk Wurnyang Lupai, a graduate of Makerere University College in Uganda, was a self—claimed leader of the Mundari ethnic community.

The Mundari and the Dinka nationalities share common borders. They had a long tradition where their people have been mixing freely, intermarrying and had lived in harmony. Nevertheless, traditional battles did occur over intermarriages and grazing lands. These were at times, translated into political rivalry as well.

In a public address to the Sudanese people in March 1984, one year following the launch of the SPLM and SPLA, Colonel Garang had this to say about the hate campaign:

"Seeing that the north-south divide crumbled, the regime found another weapon: 'tribalism'. The regime openly conducted a morbid campaign of hate and distortion...projecting the SPLM/SPLA not only as a separatist southern movement, but a tribal organisation of the Dinka. Proceeding from this obnoxious reasoning, the regime has tried all means to play tribes against one another with the hope of destroying the Movement. [6]"

However, the end result of the Nimeiri's unscrupulous hate campaign throughout the country between 1983-85, paid dearly against his regime.

Responding to the hate campaign against them, the Dinka people, seeing it was a matter of death or life, officials, politicians, organised forces, local government officials, students and workers, left the country en masse to join the SPLA.

It was from these groups that the SPLA got the best pool of educated officers, who subsequently became top commanders in the Movement.

In a nutshell, the unbridled and ill thought policy focused on a single tribe had a counter-effect as it forced thousands—some of whom might have not conceived the idea of joining the Movement. A Dinka gentlefolk, Minyiel Aywaak Guiny, once puts it tersely: *"Nimeiri has unwittingly disturbed the bee-hives. The bees are out! How could he collect the bees back into the hives?"*

5.4. SPLA COUNTERS NIMEIRI'S PROPAGANDA CAMPAIGN

Countering the Nimeiri's hate propaganda, the SPLA set up a clandestine Radio Station in Ethiopia. The radio became known as 'Radio SPLA: The Voice of the Revolutionary Armed Struggle. It operated everyday at Naru station outside Addis Ababa starting at 15 hours Sudan local time.

Radio SPLA became the main voice of the Movement, which had a wider audience and broadcasting news in English, Arabic and local languages about the battles fought with the Sudanese Government Army.

Besides the news, the Radio filled the airwaves with politically charged commentaries, war songs and poems that depicted the heroism of the revolutionary army, the SPLA. These were further translated into other Southern Sudanese languages, Nuba and Southern Blue Nile. It was a welcomed move, in fact a relief against incessant Arab propaganda in Khartoum.

Radio SPLA also became the main medium by which the SPLA leadership could address the people from the marginalised regions in the north, east, west and the south to correct or repulse any hostile propaganda exercise by the Movement.

By 1985, it became abundantly clear to Nimeiri and his regime that the SPLA meant business. It was no longer the so-called racist or tribal Movement he had assumed he could nip in the bud, but a Movement with a national character that was there to stay. As the SPLA ideological orientation was unfolding, dictator Nimeiri was forced to act, and he acted fast.

But as soon as it became clear that the SPLA propaganda was winning the northern public opinion, Nimeiri summoned up his previous dictatorial methods and tactics. He declared the SPLA as a racist and crusading Movement that was against the Arab and Muslim interests in the Sudan.

To that effect he appealed to the Arab and the Muslim worlds to come and rescue the Arabland of the Sudan and the Arab Muslim interests in the region.

Nimeiri's sudden call to protect the Arab interests in the Sudan was immediately condemned by the Movement's leadership, calling it a "racist attitude." Captain Marhoum Dut Kat and Captain Chau-Mayol Jok-Chau of Radio SPLA picked it up and effectively exposed the regime's racist attitude in a daily Radio SPLA commentary.

Encouraged by the strong Radio propaganda and despite the Sudanese Army's superior capacity in training and equipment, the SPLA continued scoring strings of victories after victories.

Recognising the effectiveness of Radio SPLA in exposing the regimes racist attitude and lies attached to it, John Garang, at the conclusion of his speech marking the passing out of the Locust Division (Kaoryaom) said: "Finally I must mention an unconventional Battalion, Radio SPLA. I congratulate Atem Yaak Atem and his staff for effectively combating the enemy's obnoxious lies and propaganda, and for correctly informing the Sudanese people and educating them in the realities of the new Sudan we (SPLM) aim to build."

The Northern Sudanese racist attitude upon the southerners, and particularly the policy of "divide and rule" using one tribe against the other as was the case taking the Dinka versus smaller tribes in the current civil war, is at best described and reflected in Mansour Khalid's remarks:

"Charitably, one could blame all this on the ignorance of those outdated people of the socio-economic dynamics of human settlements in a developing country. However, when those very narrow-minded elements bewail the injustices suffered by southern tribes at the hands of Dinka...at the very times they are taking for granted the mastery of one region over the whole country, one sensed something rotten in the State of Denmark. This bewailing is nothing but to sow discord among tribes to divide and rule [7]."

5.5. THE USE OF TRIBAL MILITIAS AND SOUTH-SOUTH WAR

Before discussing Nimeiri's policy of forming and arming tribal militias in the south to counteract the insurgency, it would be appropriate to analyse the pre-existing traditional discord and animosity among various ethnic groups in Southern Sudan.

The traditional animosities among ethnic groups, when exploited by a state or a politicised group can rekindle and transform the level of conflict into a state of total war of one ethnic group against another.

Since time immemorial, some ethnic groups in Southern Sudan, especially among the cattle owning people, inherited a culture of warfare. Such warfare did involve cattle rustling feuds or fighting over traditional pastures and water. Examples include the Dinka-Dinka, Nuer-Dinka, and Nuer-Nuer; Dinka-Murle and Dinka-Mundari; Toposa-Didinga; Longarim-Lotuho; and much more. Those feuds were relatively less destructive because traditional weapons; spears, knives were used.

But the acquisition of modern weaponry from the fall of Idi Amin Dada in Uganda and the rise of the Sudan People's Liberation Army have flooded the region with modern automatic weapons which were, in turn, employed in traditional warfare.

Thus the well-armed traditional warriors could wilfully wipe out sections of their enemies with impunity or inflicting immeasurable amounts of disaster on their foes. Others may regroup and wage a revenge and so forth. This has been one stumbling block to sustaining peace in the region.

President Nimeiri might have been contemplating the exploitation of traditional animosities to wreck havoc to the rebellious Southern Sudan when, for instance, he summoned the three governors of the divided Southern Region: James Tombura (Equatoria), Daniel Koat Matthews (Upper Nile), and Lawrence Wol Wol (Bahr al-Ghazal).

The aim was to discuss how to respond to and counteract the insurgency that was already threatening not only his May Regime, but the very fabric of the Sudan as a nation-state.

In the meeting, Nimeiri told the governors that he had divided the Southern Region in order to remove the mechanical majority of the Dinka people from dominating other smaller tribes. He then instructed the governors to form tribal militias among the smaller tribes to protect themselves against the master tribe and its rebel organisation. To that effect, a huge sum of money was availed to enable them recruit and train militiamen to prevent the insurgents from spreading into other areas.

Back in Southern Sudan, the three governors immediately embarked on arrival, upon the government programme to defeat the SPLA forces that were already visibly seen and heard everywhere in the countryside of the Southern Sudan.

For some time following the governor's arrival to the south, it appeared as if the governors would not implement the dreadful policy. As such a policy would only complicate matters in the region that had already seen a great deal of instability.

However, as time went on and the SPLA taking grip on the Region day by day, the governors were forced into taking some drastic actions to prove their worth before President Nimeiri could take drastic measures against them. Each of the governors knew very well how to butter his bread in the Nimeiri's kitchen. Soon the policy was put into practice, each marking his time cautiously.

However the policy could only succeed when the tribes, which the division was taken to mean freedom from domination of the so-called master tribe, were ready to embrace it.

Deputy Governor Francis Wajo wanted to prove his salt agitated effectively for the formation of the anti-SPLA militias. In collaboration with Gajuk Lupai Commissioner of Eastern Equatoria Province, the formation of the militias was successfully put into effect.

An auspicious environment created by Joseph Lagu, the incumbent Vice President of the Republic and chief architect of the divisionist policy and a protagonist of tribal militiamen, had encouraged these politicians.

Within a matter of months, hundreds of Mundari who feared reprisals from the SPLA were assembled and trained as militiamen. On the onset of the SPLA formation, many Mundari started moving toward Juba District for fear of reprisals. This prompted the Mundari youths to join the militia ranks to secure arms which they could protect their cattle and people with.

Upon receiving some training, the militiamen were instructed to guard their cattle and themselves against the SPLA rebels. However, the consequences of delegating security to individual citizens became evidently clear.

Instead of using the weapons solely against the SPLA, the weapons were used to raid the Dinka people who had moved and settled in the Mundariland following the floods in Jonglei region in the 1970s.

Dinka cattle camps were attacked and the cattle seized; the process which resulted in the deaths of thousands of Dinka people, especially women and children. The authorities, as expected, continued to remain unconcerned.

The climate also warranted the Mundari to loot Dinka cattle around Juba City. Even the Dinka inside the city who were either professionals or petty merchants were also harassed and had their property taken away from them.

In an interview,[8] Ngor Ayuel Kuocgor, a Dinka trader married to a Bari woman and who stayed in Juba throughout the crisis, stated that the Dinka who remained in Juba town following the division of the south were hunted down and killed randomly like rats and rabbits.

In our African war ethics, Ngor Ayuel stressed, women and children are not generally molested or killed. But in the recent Dinka-Mundari clashes, unlike the traditional warfare, all sundry were killed, including merchants.

Indeed, Many of the Dinka who survived those sad episodes have their own tales to tell. It was against this background that all the Dinka youth who witnessed those events left for Ethiopia where they joined the Zindia Battalion of the SPLA. The Zindia Battalion was later deployed around Juba during the Bright Star Campaign described in Chapter Eight. As a result of the policy to arm all tribes against the Dinka, many tribal militias sprung up in many parts of Equatoria owing to intensive anti-SPLA campaign by the government.

Unfortunately, instead of fighting the SPLA forces in their respective areas, the militiamen used the guns to settle their old inter-communal feuds of cattle rustling and trade.

In Equatoria, only the Bari and the Moru ethnic groups were spared the pains and agonies of killing their own kin and kith. The exception was attributed to the great role exerted by the leading politicians and church leaders in dissuading their fellow compatriots not to become involved in the Arab game to hatch and orchestrate fratricidal wars.

In Upper Nile Region, Governor Daniel Kuot Matthews—an old-time anti-north, anti-Islam and anti-Arab—was won over out of sheer political expedience and accepted the principle of "unity of the country."

DK, as he is well known, had never entertained in his life the idea of uniting with the Arabs. In an interview with the author in 1984, DK said he favoured the independence of Southern Sudan, but not under the leadership of "Jaang Bor" (Dinka from Bor).

Garang also confirmed this attitude when he labelled William Abdalla Chuol and others as separatists who became friends of the successive regimes in Khartoum for expediency[9].

However, Daniel Kuot Matthews did not succeed to form the proposed militias in his region until the split between Gai Tut and Garang came to the surface. When this happened, Mathew immediately wrote a letter to President Nimeiri recommending that Gai Tut rebel wing be supported and armed in order to fight the SPLA to prevent it from advancing into the interior of Upper Nile.

Governor DK's proposal was immediately endorsed, but it took some time before it was put into practice. He was assured, however, that Chuol's rebels would be given material support, but only if the forces in question were demobilised and turned into a government militia.

With this green light, DK (though his mother is from Dinka Ngok) unleashed an anti-Dinka campaign. This was unprecedented when considering close consanguinity between Dinka and Nuer.

His propaganda coincided with the death of Samuel Gai Tut in April 1984 and that of Akuot Atem de Mayen a few months later. Chuol, who took over from the latter, contacted DK and asked him for assistance (military and food) as his forces were being hard-pressed by the SPLA.

Nevertheless, when William Chuol got DK's pledge for financial and logistical support, he immediately dropped the name of SPLA and renamed his movement 'Anya-Nya II, ' the name Gordon Kong and his friends have been using at different times and stages before the launch of the Sudan People's Liberation Army.

Chuol, henceforth, reinforced the hindsight policy of liberating the South Sudan just as Akuot Atem and Gai Tut had preached. He regrouped his scattered forces and established his headquarters at the Zeraf Valley in Fangak District.

It was there that Chuol began to resist the SPLA forces and precluded them from advancing into the area under his control while at the same time intercepting and killing the SPLA recruits from Bahr al-Ghazal from crossing over to Ethiopia for training.

According to various reports, it was during this time (1984-86) that witnessed a great deal of destruction of thousands of recruits from Bahr al-Ghazal. Almost weekly, bodies were seen floating on the Nile River at Malakal.

Although Chuol might have been genuine in pursuing the policies of his predecessors (to fight for an independent south), reality might have also persuaded him that that was unattainable given the circumstances facing him. Hence, he turned and adopted a unionist approach in order to secure the necessary support.

Chuol then announced new tactics of fighting for a federal system of government for the south. He stated that federalism was the most suitable system of government in the Sudan.

These new tactics more or less intrigued the authorities in Khartoum and began to send large quantities of arms, ammunition, and cash through Governor Daniel Koat Matthews.

Unfortunately for Chuol, Khartoum attached aid with a condition that the support send to him was on conditional that he transform the Anya-Nya II into a government's militia whose aim would be to assist the national army to defeat the SPLA. Chuol was assured that when his forces had defeated the SPLA, his request for a federal form of government for the south could then be given "full consideration."

With the government insisting on transforming the Anya-Nya II into government's militia, Chuol responded by declaring that his forces would only lay down their weapons only after a negotiated settlement. For months in a row, William Chuol and his team entered into a long and tedious negotiation with the Khartoum authorities.

In November, barely seven months since Gai Tut's death, Chuol held a series of meetings with the Sudan government's authorities. Chuol believed that if Khartoum wished to negotiate with the south, he could as well negotiate for a political settlement for the south with Anya-Nya II acting on behalf of the whole Southern Sudanese people.

What was not clear on the side of the Sudanese government was whether the intended settlement with members of one tribe would bring a comprehensive peace between the south and the north. Or was it a hoax?

Though the Nuer constitutes a sizeable portion of Upper Nile population, and also the second largest of tribes in the South Sudan after the Dinka, it appeared very unlikely that any agreement it concluded with Khartoum authorities would bring an end to the war in the South Sudan.

No doubt, the representatives of the Sudanese government in the talks with Anya Nya Two might have been keenly aware of Chuol's façade. Even so they continued to meet and discuss with him for weeks.

Despite uncertainty about Chuol intentions, in the meantime, Khartoum seized the opportunity of enticing him in the belief that he had become a genuine anti-SPLA and government supported militia. A great deal of logistical and financial support poured to him in great quantities until the fall of Nimeiri's rule.

To secure the support of Anya-Nya II, Khartoum played up the nineteenth century Nuer-Dinka antagonism successfully. It declared that the SPLA was a Dinka Movement. The Government used its propaganda machine and depicted the Dinka as a belligerent group as opposed to the law abiding Nuer people.

William Churl's tactics, moreover, were synchronised by a deep-seated sense of nationalism as well. For instance, in the last days of negotiations, he laid down a proposal for a confederate plan, which in his view was intended to be the final and comprehensive solution.

When the results of the Anya-Nya II-Sudan government negotiations were presented to Khartoum, President Nimeiri and his advisors were shocked, as they were not happy with Chuol's peace plan.

Despite rejecting Chuol's peace package, the Sudan government, nevertheless, continued to support Anya-Nya II on the basis of being a lesser evil than the mightier SPLA. For some time, Chuol's peace plan remained in suspense.

Having secured a cease-fire with the government as well as receiving the logistical support he needed from the government, he nevertheless launched a vigorous attack against the SPLA.

In some of these intractable fights, William Chuol was ambushed and killed by the SPLA forces under Commander John Kulang Puot in 1986. The new Leader of the Anya Nya Two was no other person than Gordon Kong Chol, its original leader.

But this changeover from Chuol to Gordon Koang was to lead to the Anya-Nya II-SPLA reconciliation later that year. The reconciliation was mediated by DK, who this time had been deprived of his position as Governor of Upper Nile after the fall of Nimeiri in 1985. DK had joined the SPLA in 1986. The SPLA used him to bring his Anya-Nya II back into the Movement.

In Bahr al-Ghazal, Governor Lawrence Wol Wol found it very difficult to implement the militia policy for many reasons. First, it was in Bahr al-Ghazal that the Underground Movement started. It was also there that the Anya-Nya II of northern Bahr al-Ghazal was first formed. In addition, the majority of the natives who went to Ethiopia were victims of Arab and Anya-Nya II disruptions.

Second, the leadership of the SPLA and the new regional government in Bahr al-Ghazal were incidentally composed mostly by members of the Solidarity Committee and the Council for the Unity of the South who had been against re-division of the Southern Region into three regions.

Under such situation, Governor Wol Wol could not move freely—even though he had to prove to Nimeiri that he was doing something to defeat the SPLA. He did this by encouraging Darius Beshir, the Deputy Speaker in the Regional Assembly, to form the Fertit ethnic group militia.

Deputy Speaker Darious had been one of the founding fathers of the Southern Front Party (1964-69). He got himself marginalised in the Southern Regional Government of 1972-82. Nevertheless, he had fought hard to gain a province for his people in western Bahr al-Ghazal. Even though Darious was in a better position to organise the Fertit Militia, yet the Fertit comprises only five percent of the population of Bahr al-Ghazal. Hence it cannot effectively cause any threat to an overwhelming support for the SPLA in the Region.

Fertit intellectuals like Clement Mboro, the veteran all time South Sudan politician, was opposed to the militia policy. Indeed, the attacks against the SPLA by Fertit militiamen were minimal in comparison with those of Equatoria.

Governor Wol Wol, however, was increasingly showing hostility to the SPLA. To prove to Nimeiri that he meant business, he—at one point—took the picture of John Garang to the Freedom Square in Wau Town and shot at it. This caused arousing amusement of the entire population of Wau. Although satisfied that he had proven beyond doubt his anti-SPLA stance, the incident embarrassed him and his government. Throughout the rest of his term as governor of Bahr al-Ghazal, he was continuously ridiculed when passing by.

It is to be recalled that Bahr al-Ghazal had a regular contact with the Arab tribes who have been at war with the Dinka in Abyei and northern Bahr al-Ghazal since pre-colonial days. Hence, the government's attempt to teach the Dinka (who form the bulk of SPLA) some lesson only proved counterproductive.

The militiamen who were at first a mobile force intended to assist the nomadic Arab tribes of southern Darfur and Kordofan (the Misserya and

Rezeigat) to gain water and pasture without difficulties from the Dinka of Bahr al-Ghazal and Abyei, were reorganised into popular defence forces. The latter meted horrible scorched earth terror against the civilian population in the guise of fighting the SPLA rebels.

These atrocities also introduced another dimension in the war: children and women trafficking in the classical slave-trade became a norm which even embarrassed successive governments in Khartoum, but which they were at least willing to admit or stop the practice.

Meanwhile, the militia policy and the creation of militiamen everywhere meant that the SPLA had to fight on two fronts: The Sudan government regular forces and South Sudan militiamen.

The latter was instrumental in transforming a north-south conflict into a south-south conflict. Thus Nimeiri's dream of fighting the SPLA might have been realised. But that policy only complicated the war to his own detriment and which eventually led to his final demise.

5.6. SPLA LAUNCHES FULL-SCALE MILITARY CAMPAIGN

Throughout 1984, the SPLA was undoubtedly in preparatory stage: to move away from the hectic situation and to find a positive atmosphere to consolidate itself by adopting structural policies on political and military arenas. This was simply an expedient move. As stated earlier, the mutiny among the garrisons were to mark the first wave of resistance against the Sudanese government forces in the south.

Recruiting missions mentioned in Chapter 4 were sent to various provinces in order to engage the government troops when and where possible.

When the SPLA graduated the Timsah (Crocodile) and Tiger battalions it became necessary that the new well-charged batches must be put into action. They were now in the position of possessing sophisticated anti-aircraft Surface to Air Missiles (SAM) 6 and 7, capable of keeping off the Sudan airforce.

The Timsah Crocodile Battalion was put under the command of Major Arok Thon Arok and the Tiger Battalion led by Major Salva Kiir Mayardit. The two battalions went into action, swept and captured Pacholla and Pibor, and inflicted a devastating destruction upon the government troops including the shooting down of the two Soviet-made F5 fighter crafts.

The two armies crossed over the Nile to Bentiu Oil-fields where another Oil Battalion was already operating. The guerrilla activity in the Bentiu Oilfields terrorised the country a great deal. Soon after the SPLA graduated a whole division code-named "Kaoryaom" (locusts). It was so named to reflect the locust capacity and power to devour out plants and vegetation, thus making areas they passed through barren.

Koryaom Division may have been a turning point in the SPLA military operations. Just like locusts always do, Kaoryom armies swept the countryside much more extensively to the extent that Nimeiri's regime was shocked and became weary.

Kaoryom was divided into many battalions. The southern axis composed of Zindia, Cobra, and Raad (lightning) battalions.

These battalions were sent to the southern Upper Nile and areas adjacent to Equatoria. They were under the command of Major Arok Thon Arok and assisted by Bona Baang, Benjamin Nyankot, Gatwec Dual, Peter Panhom Thanypiny and Benjamin Makur.

The Zindia and Cobra went into action and wiped out two companies of the government paratroopers sent against them at Gemeiza, just 50 miles south of Bor Town. They also fought pitched battles with the Sudanese armed forces at Lokiliri near Torit.

Koryom's southern axis also destroyed one enemy battalion at Owiny-Kibul in Acholi area. It also attacked Terekeka just 50 miles north of Juba.

Another sector of Kaoryom Division, the "Central Command," consisted of Bilpam, Lion, Elephant, and Hippo battalions that came directly under the command of Colonel John Garang. He was assisted Kerubino Kwanyin Bol, Kuol Manyang Juuk, Daniel Deng Alony, Captain Alfred Akuoc, Captain Francis Tago, Captain Deng Alor Kuol, Captain Chol Deng Alak, Captain James Jok Muon, and Captain John Lem.

The Central Command went on the offensive and on the 3rd of March 1985 it captured Jekou garrison and killed many troops including Colonel Balaa. The remnants were taken prisoners of war.

The other sector of Kaoryom Division, the "Northern Axis" under the command of Lt. Colonel Francis Ngor-Makiech was sent to the Southern Blue Nile region. It engaged the Sudanese government troops and captured Dago, Padigli and Maban.

The fourth sector of Kaoryom Agrab (scorpion) Battalion "The Eastern Axis" was under the command of Major Nyachigag Nyachiluk. The Agrab Battalion overran the government forces in Boma plateau, and other posts east of Bor town with relative ease.

Finally, the fifth column of Kaoryom was the Rhino Battalion under the command of Lt. Colonel Martin Makur Aleiyou and Pagan Amum. This battalion was sent to Bahr al-Ghazal where it paralysed the transport system in the whole province. It overran the towns of Yirol, Aluakluak, Tonj, and isolated Wau and Rumbek towns.

With these operations, SPLA was now in a full-scale conventional warfare. President Nimeiri became exceedingly restless; to the extent that he started a shuttle diplomacy going around the world looking for effective means of halting the ever-powerful insurgency.

In his famous speech of 22 March 1985, Colonel John Garang stated that:

"The Movement's great ability and political achievements within a relatively short period of twenty-two months of revolutionary armed-struggle have thrown the oppressor in Khartoum into complete disarray. Nimeiri's May Regime has lost its bearings, is tottering, senile and is moving towards its final collapse. The Regime is like a patient at a terminal stage of illness[10]."

Surprisingly, Garang's prophecy was soon to prove true. In barely two weeks from this speech, Nimeiri's Regime was overthrown by popular uprising in Khartoum.

With these sweeping operations in the south and some parts of Southern Blue Nile, northern public opinion, for the first time, began to go against President Nimeiri. The also became aware about the vulnerability of the May Regime.

These operations also emboldened the northern opposition leaders who immediately began contacting the SPLA offices in Europe, especially in the United Kingdom and other African countries.

Earlier, the northern Sudanese opposition groups had dismissed the SPLA as a separatist Movement, as they put it, fighting in order to divide the country into Sudan Arab and African states.

But seeing that the SPLA was increasingly becoming effective as the war intensified and spread northward, northern opposition leaders became convinced that there was no reason to stand by when the SPLA objectives were to topple Nimeiri as well.

After holding several meetings with the SPLM/SPLA representatives in London, the northern opposition groups agreed to cooperate with the Movement. Dr Barnaba Marial Benjamin and John Luk Jok represented the SPLM side in the subsequent talks with representatives of northern opposition.

The opposition groups from the north were represented by the following people: Mohammed Ibrahim Khalil and Sarah al-Fadl, Sadig al-Mahdi's Umma Party wing, Mohamed al-Hassan Yasin for the DUP while Dr Ezz al-Din Ali Amer and Mustafa Khogali for the Sudan Communist Party.

The purpose of the London Meeting was to speculate what could be done in the event President Nimeiri was overthrown, which was becoming more eminent. A charter was then drawn up spelling out the policies of how Sudan must be administered in the post Nimeiri era.

Unfortunately, the charter could not be endorsed because the northern groups were divided among themselves.

It would appear that some in the northern opposition groups were not sure whether it would be possible to overthrow Nimeiri, who had tyrannised the country for about 16 years.

In the past, attempts to topple Nimeiri were ruthlessly and mercilessly put down with disastrous consequences. Hence, none appeared ready to take such risks.

Despite lack of resources to defeat or harness the Sudanese army in the first two years (1983-85), SPLA managed to inflict immeasurable damages on them. Even so, it was not without difficulties. The costs of fighting an established regime were enormous, as the SPLA was fighting on two fronts.

The first difficulty was that the SPLA confronted the well-equipped government troops with conventional warfare instead of the expected guerrilla tactics. Consequently it cost the SPLA dearly in terms of men and material. For instance, the SPLA captured the garrison towns of Jekou, Pibor and Nasir with great loss of life.

The second difficulty, which was more worrying for the SPLA, was the government's policy of arming tribal militias to fight against the SPLA and operating within the SPLA lines of defence. These attacks by scores of militiamen worried the SPLA most. However it was easy to contain these heavily laden government troops by laying sieges around the garrisons.

The SPLA efforts to disperse the militia groups, eight of which were operating within the SPLA-controlled territories, posed serious security risks. The most effective tribal militias were the Mundari, Murle, Zande, Madi, Fertit, Toposa, Acholi, the Anya-Nya II, and the Misseriya/Murhalin.

In such hostile terrain, SPLA forces that carelessly ventured into the rural areas (where the militias were very active) ostensibly in search of food were frequently ambushed and killed by these militiamen.

There were many instances when the SPLA fighters were wiped out altogether with their officers and men. Nyaba writes[11]:

"During the capture of Bukteng, the Headquarters of the SPLA Battalions 104 and 105, manned mostly by Nuer officers and men, many lives including those of Lt. Colonel Francis Ngor-Makiech and twenty four officers were lost...in 1984." Nyaba continues, "... the capture of Bukteng turned out later to have been a conspiracy hatched by the Nuer officers out of sympathy and solidarity with their fellow Nuer in the Anya-Nya Two, the militia force friendly to the Sudan government."

From the above analysis, one can safely say the SPLA failure to win all the Southern Sudanese tribes into one rebel organisation led to the infighting on two fronts: the tribal militias (the enemy from within) and the government army (the enemy from without). In such a situation, the casualties were bound to be enormous.

CHAPTER 6
SPLA FIGHTING AND TALKING STRATEGY

6.0. THE SETTING

Following intensive and extensive military operations in the south against the Sudanese Government Army in the previous two years, it soon became abundantly clear to President Nimeiri that the SPLA had transcended its opposition.

Unlike the expected guerrilla force, intending to put pressure on the government to make it realise the seriousness of the situation on the ground, the SPLA went into full conventional warfare.

This was evidently proven during the running battles contested in many towns in the south. Therefore, this chapter describes how the SPLA contributed to the overthrow of the May Regime, how the Transitional Military Council (1985-86) grapples about the situation in the south and the SPLA adopting new tactics; the fighting and talking strategies.

6.1. THE LAST DAYS OF THE MAY REGIME

By the beginning of 1985, President Nimeiri, having clearly recognised the dangerous situation in the country, began to undertake damage control. This second thought led him to desperate attempts to contain the situation, if not reverse it, to his favour. Forthwith, Nimeiri summoned his previous policies, methods, and tactics responsible for his miraculous survival in power for the past sixteen years of his rule.

First, Nimeiri and his new team of Islamist advisors admitted that the defunct Addis Ababa Agreement with the South was the only tangible achievement of his tottered regime and must, therefore, be resurrected.

To that effect, Nimeiri maintained his 1984 negotiations with William Abdalla Chuol of Anya-Nya II, where Governor D.K. Matthews had been Nimeiri's representative on the ground all along.

He also ordered Koat Chatim, the Commissioner of Unity Province (Bentiu Oilfields), to make contact with the Anya Nya II factions in the area and persuade them to reach a peaceful settlement with the regime.

This meeting, however, ended up in a fiasco. The Commissioner and his delegation were captured and put in chains as prisoners of war by the rebels. A few days later the prisoners of war ended up in the SPLA Headquarters.

Second, the President sought to reach the SPLA and negotiate with it directly. This may have been owing to the American pressure. Washington had apparently realised that Nimeiri had committed blunder by revoking the Addis Ababa Agreement and instituting a strict Islamic state ruled by Shari'a.

On 29 September 1984, President Nimeiri announced the lifting of the state of emergency which he had imposed in September 1983. He also rescinded Decree Number I that had divided the south into three regions on 5 June 1983. Nimeiri also suspended the infamous *Adala al-Nagiza* (prompt justice).

The prompt justice courts were "Islamic kangaroo courts" which were responsible, among others, for the notorious amputation of limbs for petty theft; flogging of people who consume alcohol, women believed to be immodestly dressed and much more.

It appeared that these gestures were meant to placate and sway international public opinion than intentions to back down from the Islamic route that had plunged the nation into deep crisis.

Despite Nimeiri's pronouncements, the SPLA did not cease its hostilities against the regime (as discussed in the graduation of Koryom's Division in Chapter 5).

When Nimeiri realised that the SPLA would not respond to his gambit, he asked business tycoons, the Saudi Adnan Kashoogi and the British Tiny Rowland of the London-based Lonrho, to approach the SPLA on behalf of the government. Nimeiri once more set the ball of negotiation with the rebels once more rolling.

For weeks, the two tycoons shuttled between Khartoum and the capitals of the neighbouring countries, particularly Ethiopia and Kenya. The aim of the shuttle diplomacy was to convince the rebel leader Colonel John Garang to abandon war in favour of a peace package based on the 1972 Addis Ababa Agreement.

In response to the peace initiative, the SPLM-SPLA refused to be intrigued into it. John Garang, the SPLA leader, in a Radio speech said, "Nimeiri's slogans for final solution for the Southern Problem were hollow and despicable attempts to win foreign friends and to divide the Sudanese into those who want peace and those who allegedly do not want peace."

Nevertheless, what was new in that proposal was that Nimeiri conceded to appoint the SPLA leader, Dr. Garang, as First Vice President of the Republic, the number two in the country. Since independence in 1956, the number two positions in the country had always been reserved for a Muslim-Arab northerner.

Besides this, Colonel Garang was promised to have an absolute free hand in the administration of the south on behalf of the President of the Republic. This move was viewed by many observers as a great concession and thought that

Colonel Garang would respond more favourably to Nimeiri's unprecedented gesture of "political generosity."

Mansour Khalid writes: "Nimeiri was desperate and it seems he was ready to give to the SPLM/SPLA anything that was short of the Presidency itself."

On December 29, Garang responded saying 'the war in the south was not started to make me Vice President.' Garang assured the nation that the SPLA would never betray the Sudanese people by negotiating with their oppressor.

Southerners inside the country had responded to Nimeiri's 1984 appeal to stage a dialogue with the government with the view of reaching a political settlement to the raging war in the south.

But the response to enter peace negotiations with the regime was soon abandoned on realising that the attempt to convince them to negotiate was simply a palliative venture typical of the northern Arabs desperate approach to certain issues when they seem to be in favour of the south.

Two leading southerners, Abel Alier and Joseph Lagu, wrote a joint letter to the then visiting U.S. Vice President, George Bush. In their letter, the two leaders condemned Nimeiri's latest amendments to Article 80 of the Sudan's Constitution.

Article 80 stipulated that the President of the Republic would no longer be the Head of State chosen by the people in a plebiscite, but rather the "Qaaid al-Muominiin" (leader of the faithful), and the Shepherd of the Sudanese Nation. The letter, among others, told Nimeiri that his constitutional amendment had unmade the Addis Ababa Agreement of 1972 and the Sudan Permanent Organic Constitution of 1973. The two leading personalities and one time Nimeiri aide outrightly condemned Nimeiri's tactics.

While Nimeiri was continuing with his blunders, the May Regime was speeding downhill. The SPLA was at work attacking the government garrisons; cutting the main supply routes between cities in the south and destroying convoys to and from beleaguered garrisons.

It also sank steamers on the White Nile (December 1984), and dismantled the communication network. More important to note was the stoppage of major projects in the south including the CCI—a French Company digging the Jonglei Canal Project—and the American Chevron Oil Exploration Project in Bentiu. These latest disruptions deeply hurt the regime.

In a desperate effort to salvage his tattered regime, President Nimeiri decreed the appointment of a 30-man high-level committee on 13 March 1985. The Committee was headed by Sirr al-Khatim al-Khalifa, the former Sudanese Prime Minister during the Interim Period (1964-65) and included six leading southern politicians.

Abel Alier; Isaiah Kulang Mabor; Dr. Peter Nyot Kok; and Dr. Lam Akol Ajawin, among others, were the southern members on the Committee. The

Committee was expected to look into the possibility of reversing Nimeiri's previous policy on the south.

The southern representatives on the committee declined to take that responsibility. They had not attended any session on the Committee when President Nimeiri was overthrown in April 1985 while on his return journey from USA.

Surprisingly, northern Sudanese groups opposed to Nimeiri had mobilised Sudanese public opinion and exerted rare diplomatic and political contacts to discredit the May Regime. Some of the opposition was done in collaboration and solidarity with the SPLM/SPLA action in battle.

So while Nimeiri was pedalling and grasping with events against his regime rolling downhill and taking every step aimed at ending the war, the northern Sudanese opposition struggled to find a common ground for cooperation with the SPLM/SPLA.

On 31 December 1984, the opposition groups in exile met in Tripoli to decide to form a united front, which might have been the forerunner of the National Democratic Alliance cooperating with the SPLA.

Martin Majer Gai, the head The SPLA of SPLM legal affairs and administration, and Commanders Lual Diing Wol and Nyang Chol attended the meeting on behalf of the SPLA. Colonel Muamar Ghaddafi, Nimeiri's arch-enemy then addressed the meeting.

Though agreeing to work together, the members of the northern opposition failed to reach a consensus on the possibility of a joint front to confront the May Regime.

On 3 March 1985, during the Unity Day celebration marking the thirteenth anniversary of the Addis Ababa Agreement of 1972, Nimeiri, seeing the whirlwind tornadoes about to uproot him out of office, utilised the occasion to win over the public and once more appeared a peacemaker.

Coinciding with the arrival of the U.S. Vice President George Bush to Khartoum, Nimeiri announced a unilateral cease-fire in the south. He stressed that the army would shoot only in self-defence against any possible aggression, offered an amnesty to rebels fighting his government and invited the rebels for a peace negotiation. The SPLA rejected the offers and refused to be duped into accepting a compromise with the dictator.

In his famous speech of 22 March 1985, the SPLA leader Colonel John Garang utterly dismissed Nimeiri's peace gestures as mere slogans. "Nimeiri's slogans of dialogue, negotiations, cease-fire, the so-called High Committee for peace and a final solution to southern problem are hollow and despicable attempts to win foreign friends and to divide the Sudanese people into those who want peace and those who allegedly do not want peace."

The last episode against the regime was the economic crisis brought about by the 1983-84 drought that had resulted in severe famine and decline in the nation's flagging economy. For some time, the regime tried to conceal the magnitude of the famine.

But in order to alleviate "economic crisis," Nimeiri continued to reduce government subsidies, especially on food stuffs like sorghum (dura) the staple food for the rural population in most parts of Sudan.

In the two years duration, many people and livestock in western and southern Sudan regions ravaged by drought, perished, as there was no sufficient food to alleviate the suffering.

By early 1985, the situation became very critical and tragic as the harvest of 1984-85 was short of its target of 1.9 million tons of national requirements.

It was in the light of these backgrounds that Nimeiri, instead of addressing the situation, permitted the situation to worsen further. It was unfortunate that Nimeiri, amidst the public clamour to reverse the situation, paid a desperate visit to the United States where he was said to go for medical reasons. Nevertheless, he met President Reagan.

But while he was still in Washington, D.C., the events he left behind in Khartoum were changing rapidly. Popular uprising and turmoil was witnessed everywhere.

On 26 March 1985, the cities of Khartoum, Khartoum North and Omdurman were paralysed by huge demonstrations staged by the agitated masses led by the Workers and Professional Trade Unions in addition to students and teachers unions of various educational institutions.

At the background was the Opposition Alliance Front, a combination of various political parties. By early April, it became clear that there was going to be a bloody confrontation between Nimeiri's notorious State Security and the demonstrators.

Predictably, confrontation of unarmed masses with armed and desperate Security Organs would have been disastrous. This was averted only when the Minister of Defence, Field Marshall Abdel Rahman Mohamed Hassan Sowar al-Dahab, announced on April 6[th,] 1985 that the dictatorial regime had been overthrown and that the army had taken over power. The announcement thus ended 16 years of one-man dictatorship under General Jaafar Mohamed Nimeiri.

Commenting on the riots that brought down the May Regime (26 March to 6 April), Mansour Khalid[2] writes:

"This was truly a popular uprising in the combined forces of political activists: white and blue collar-workers, students and teachers brought Nimeirism and Nimeiri to his knees. If the dictum that history does repeat itself, it was true, indeed, that the history that was made in October 1964 when the first military dictator General Abboud was overthrown in the like manner by a popular uprising, it was repeated again in April 1985."

6.2. THE INTERIM MILITARY JUNTA

Unlike the 1964 Revolution where the popular uprising managed to oust a strong military man, General Ibrahim Abboud, and handed over power to a civilian transitional government to prepare the country for a democratic rule, the generals of 6 April 1985 uprising acted differently.

On April 9, 1985 the generals formed a 15-Man Transitional Military Council, (TMC), collective head of state with Field Marshall Abdel Rahman Muhammad Hassan Sowar al-Dhahab as the council Chairman. The generals pledged that they would remain in office for a year in order to gear the country toward democratic rule.

Immediately Field Marshall Sowar al-Dhahab appointed General Osman Abdalla, the former chief of operations under Nimeiri, as Minister of Defence, and General Abbas Medani, the former Commissioner General of Police, as Minister of the Interior. The other members of the Junta included: General Taj Eldin Osman, Deputy Chairman; in addition to all the respective Commanders of all the military units: Infantry, Navy, Airforce, Engineering Corps, Signals, Medical and Equipment.

Having consolidated its power, the junta announced that it would maintain the status quo and would hand over power to an elected government within twelve months.

The TMC, in its first move, ordered the release of all political prisoners and dismantled Nimeiri's notorious and ruthless state security that has been so much associated with the hated Nimeiri's administration, especially after his shift to 'Al-Nahaj al-Islami' in the early 1980s.

Increasingly, as Nimeiri's power appeared to be tottering, suspected opponents faced torture, arbitrary and incommunicado detention, murder, and other ranges of human rights violations became rampant.

The political, professional and the trade union leaders who had agitated the masses for a series of strikes that eventually brought down Nimeiri's regime met on April 10th and formed an alliance that became known as the National Alliance for National Salvation (NANS).

With the exception of the National Islamic Front (NIF) which was closely associated with Nimeiri's Islamisation since 1977 and somehow cooperated with the Junta, the NANS became instrumental in unifying various political opinions in the country.

The NANS leaders seemed to have been overtaken by the unexpected exit of President Nimeiri to an extent that they could not notice the obvious thing. It was the former Nimeiri's commanders who had been central all along for the survival of his regime who were now their rulers.

Although the generals were interested in returning the country to a civilian rule, there was no doubt that the maintenance of status quo was much an acquiescence to Nimeiri's policies. The controversial Sharia Law, for example, was not abrogated as demanded by the insurgents in the south.

However, meetings between the Junta and the NANS prompted the inclusion of a parallel civilian government headed by Prime Minister Dr. Gizzouli Dafallah, to prepare the nation towards a democratic civilian rule in the future. Dr. Dafallah had been the leader of the Sudan Medical Association, one of the most active pressure groups against Nimeiri's regime.

While the NANS members dominated the civilian cabinet supposed to exercise executive powers, the TMC made it known that it was the Junta which possessed both political and legislative powers and would be the Head of State during the interim period. The TMC, in that sense, was the sole policy-maker and legislator.

The Sudan People's Liberation Army (SPLA), though supportive of the masses for removing Nimeiri from power, was not enthusiastic about the fact that Nimeiri's close generals were now in control; suggesting that there was no real departure from Nimeiri's policies. In SPLA's view, the interim government—like that of 1964—should have been formed by the civilian administration under the Alliance, perhaps in coalition with itself.

Speaking on the Radio SPLA, Colonel Dr. John Garang[3] stated: "While welcoming the April Uprising with open arms, SPLA is alarmed by the fact that it is the same army officers who pledged holy oath of allegiance to Nimeiri in 1983 and later conducted the unholy war in the south with the orders of Nimeiri, are the ones now who have assumed power."

However, in solidarity with the masses who brought down Nimeiri, the SPLA ordered a unilateral seven-day cease-fire within which the generals were expected to hand over power to the NANS.

But when the generals did not accept Garang's ultimatum, and instead created the 15-Men Junta, Colonel Garang denounced the Junta over Radio SPLA calling it "May Regime II without Nimeiri." He stated that the Movement manifestly viewed itself as the objective ally of those who took to the streets to topple Nimeiri's regime and expected to assume the mantle of power, not the generals who kept him in power.

The same day, the Alliance issued a statement in support and praise of the role of the generals in handling the April popular uprising. It also distanced itself from what it regarded as 'an extreme position' the SPLM/SPLA has taken.

In the words of Dr Mansour Khalid, the Alliance had assumed that the generals sided with the people against Nimeiri because they "bowed down to the will of the streets."

The TMC, in response, accused the SPLA of intransigence and continuation of the war when the common enemy (Nimeiri) was no longer in power. The TMC further called upon the SPLA to stop fighting. It invited the SPLM leadership to return from the bushes to Khartoum to participate in the shaping of the country's future.

Essentially, it would appear that the basis of such invitation was not matched by any policy to resolve the root causes of the conflict and which might have persuaded the Movement to respond positively.

During the celebrations marking the Bor and Fashalla resistance of 1983, a resistance that ignited the return to the civil strife, the SPLM/SPLA leader Colonel Dr. Garang de Mabior declared the following six point statement:

1. As of today May 27 1985, I put all SPLA forces on full alert and declare for general mobilisation in War Zone Number 1 [South Sudan].

2. All SPLA leaves are cancelled with the immediate effect and all SPLA soldiers on leave are to report to the nearest SPLA unit.

3. During this limited phase when the enemy intended to make a show of force by moving in large convoys, SPLA battalion commanders are advised to shift to the tactics of classical guerrilla warfare in order to paralyse and annihilate the enemy.

4. SPLA battalion commanders are to organise command units to apprehend opportunists and collaborators with the enemy in War Zone and escort them to SPLA Headquarters.

5. Call on the officers and men in the Sudanese army to disobey the orders of their commanders and stay in their barracks and start talking with the SPLA in the area in accordance to the SPLA Commander-in-Chief speech of March 22, 1985 before Nimeiri's fall.

6. Ringing the bell for round two of the popular uprising in the streets of our cities and the SPLA's revolutionary armed struggle in the bushes and sands of the Sudan...against the May Regime II (TMC).

In conclusion, the SPLA leader added: "We believe that May II is weaker than May I. Hence we would bring it down in less than one week of street demonstrations with the few blows of SPLA here and there."

The SPLA fears that the TMC had come to power to fight the war in the south rigorously and vigorously and to the finish were increased to breaking point when in July 1985, the military Junta sent its Defence Minister, General Osman Abdalla, to Tripoli, Libya, to seek military hardware in order to re-equip the Sudanese demoralised army.

The TMC was emboldened further by the speech delivered by Colonel

Muamar al-Ghadafi earlier, following the overthrow of his archenemy Nimeiri when he stopped supplying the SPLA forces with logistics. Al-Ghadafi was very delighted and happy to receive the Sudanese envoy; for one thing, he would have strong foothold in Sudan now that Nimeiri was gone into the dustbin of history.

On July 8th, 1985, a Sudanese-Libyan Joint Military Pact was concluded. As a result of this pact, Libya, which had been the most important foreign power supplying the SPLA with logistics since its inception in 1983, made a dramatic shift and staunchly supported the 'regime of the generals' in Khartoum.

Just as the Egyptian airforce helped Khartoum against the Anya Nya I insurgents, the Libyan air power was now utilised to regularly bombard the SPLA positions in the south. For instance, when the SPLA captured Rumbek that year, the Libyan airforce was busy dropping bombs on the town.

But as the generals were wrestling with political issues in Khartoum, the war was escalating seriously in the south. In the words of Mansour Khalid: "Channels of communications between the government and the movement were severely hampered in view of the crisis of confidence."[4]

6.3. SPLA FIGHTING AND TALKING STRATEGY

As the SPLA had managed to deploy one division of troops (Kaoryom) or locust described in Chapter 5, it was expected, naturally, that it could graduate and deploy another similar division sooner than later.

In response to the order of the Commander-in-Chief in May 1985, the SPLA indeed deployed a second division known as Muor Muor (river ants usually pink in colour). It was so named because of its tireless trailing to reach the target.

Muor Muor—which was graduated together with Koryom but was delayed due to lack of sufficient logistics—was targeted for eastern Equatoria, the Nuba Mountains, and other areas of Bahr al-Ghazal and Upper Nile.

As expected, taking the war effectively to cover eastern Equatoria amidst the regime anti-SPLA and anti-Dinka hate campaign was not going to be a smooth-running drive for the following reasons:

1. The hate campaign has turned the majority of the citizens of that area against the Movement, and against the Dinka for that matter.

2. The division-lobbyists in Juba were still at work, trying to move heaven and earth to frustrate the SPLA efforts to bring eastern Equatoria under its control.

These two issues had to be addressed first before a military campaign could start in Equatoria. On the credit side, the Movement was encouraged by the report that there were a large number of enthusiasts, especially among the students ready to embrace the Movement in eastern Equatoria. There were favourable reasons for the success of a military campaign in the area. These were:

First, the SPLA attempt in 1984 to establish a command post at Owiny Kibul, the former Anya Nya I Headquarters near Nimule, had provided easy routes by which the natives of Equatoria could connect easily with the Movement in Ethiopia. Since late 1983 and early 1984 many students, workers, and the former Anya Nya fighters in Equatoria had clandestinely marched toward Ethiopia to join the Movement.

Among them included leaders like James Wani Igga, Alfred Lado Gore, and in early 1986, the American-educated Loki Lincoln. Many of these officers became instrumental in planting the SPLA in eastern and central Equatoria. Nevertheless, these officers were not immediately deployed in their region before forces could effectively move to Equatoria.

Second, the cattle owning tribes of Eastern Equatoria: Boya Didinga, Toposa, Longarim, Lotuho, and others who had been told that the Dinka were coming to rob them of their cattle had been couched through political mobilisation.

Equally, the movement was convinced that the Military Campaign would be welcomed because it was in Equatoria that 'Southern Nationalism' had been strongest and well pronounced since the Torit Mutiny of 1955. Leaders like Paul Logali, Abdel-Rahman Sule, Aggrey Jaden, Ferdinand Adyang, Marko Rume, Pancrasio Ochieng, Natale Oyet, Fr. Saturnino Lohure, Joseph Oduho, Hillary Paul Logali, Ezboni Mundiri, and many more, have stood against the Arab domination throughout their lives.

Joseph H. Oduho, one of the most respected seasoned veteran southern leaders, became one of the founding fathers of the SPLA and Head of its Foreign Affairs strategy. The SPLA officials did not have to read a lot of history to undertake the Equatoria campaign seriously.

It was also recognised that the pastoralist tribes in Eastern Equatoria were the best warriors that the Movement must impress upon in order to win a good deal of its recruits.

The Equatorian herdsmen are well known for self-esteem and pride. They could be relied upon and would fight effectively only if nothing affecting their beloved cattle was brought to the doorsteps of their homes. Consequently, after weighing all these carefully, the eastern Equatoria military campaign was launched immediately.

The first battalions of Muor Muor destined for Eastern Equatoria were, therefore, called into action. An Agrab Battalion (one of Koryom's Battalions) under the command of Major Nyachigak Nyachiluk, and additional forces, was hurriedly put together as Eastern Equatoria Axis.

Nyachigak was deputised by Commander Joseph Kuol Amuom, an

experienced officer who had just defected to the SPLA. Commander Kuol Amuom was, indeed, helpful in the operations.

The Eastern Equatoria Axis and the Bee Battalion went into action and encamped at Riwoto (nine miles north-west of Kapoeta town) under the command of Lt. Colonel Martin Manyiel Ayuel also went into action.

The Niraan Battalion commanded by Major Tahir Bior Abdalla Ajak attacked and occupied Boma Plateau and established the Axis's command headquarters there. With three battalions well co-ordinated, the war was finally taken to Eastern Equatoria. Political commissars were dispatched with the military campaign.

Within a matter of weeks as predicted, over 10,000 Toposa tribesmen were recruited into the SPLA. The SPLA Political Orientation Unit that preceded the campaign managed to establish a base in Didinga, Acholi, and Lotuho areas. Thereafter, the whole eastern Equatoria was occupied. The Towns of Kapoeta and Torit were soon isolated and besieged. Juba was also threatened.

Despite the SPLA triumphant entry into eastern Equatoria, the SPLA Campaign met a lot of predictable disappointing encounters and reverses both militarily and politically.

The Sudanese government forces in the area under the overall command of Military Governor of Equatoria, Major General Peter Cirrilo, were actively engaged in assaulting the SPLA positions in attempts to halt, if possible, its encroachment into Equatoria.

Colonel John Maluk, the regime operational commander, met the SPLA forces at Mogoth, some 40 kilometres outside Kapoeta town but failed to keep off the SPLA incursion until they encamped at Riwoto, 9 miles north-west of Kapoeta Town. It was from Riwoto that the government forces, with the help of the native of Toposa, managed to storm the SPLA forces—killing Commander Nyachigak Nyachiluk. Commander Nyachigak Nyachiluk was one of the early groups of university students who joined the SPLA and had established a base in Buma Plateau.

Although sweeping SPLA advances were somehow halted for the time being, the reverses in Kapoeta were not permanent. Major Galerio Modi Hurnyang, an Anya Nya I veteran, was soon appointed to lead the command of the Eastern Equatoria, replacing Martin Manyiel Ayuel who had taken over the command after the death of Nyachigak. Major Galerio was to keep the Torit-Kapoeta road unsafe for the enemy advance, thereby limiting transport to large government convoys.

Another SPLA battalion, Gaol (wolf) Battalion, was deployed and sent to western Upper Nile region. The wolf Battalion was commanded by Major Dr Riek Machar Teny Dhurgon, one of the first waves of student academics who joined the SPLA in December 1983. Commander Machar, who had just been commissioned, took the war to the Oil Fields of Bentiu, his own district.

After establishing his Gaol Battalion Headquarters in Leer, south of Malakal town, within a short period of time, Machar put the Oil Fields under the complete SPLA control. The American Chevron Oil Company, the main oil prospecting company in Bentiu area, found its operations at stake. The enemy forces confronting Machar Force were commanded by Colonel Omar Hassan Ahmed al-Beshir, who later became President of the NIF regime in Khartoum.

The Mosquito Battalion, commanded by Yousif Kuwo Mekki, was sent to western Upper Nile en route to the Nuba Mountains. After some reconnoitring mission in the area, the Mosquito Battalion finally entered the Nuba Mountains. Mosquito went into action and had its first encounters with the Sudanese army at Gardud in the southern foothills of the Nuba Mountains where it established a command post.

The establishment of SPLA command post in the Nuba Mountains, Southern Kordofan Region, meant that SPLA had effectively exported the war to War Zone II (northern Sudan), a thing which appeared like a dream when it appeared in the SPLM manifesto in 1983. The presence of SPLA in southern Kordofan sent an electric shock to Khartoum's authorities.

Tuek Tuek (wood cutter) Battalion under the command of Daniel Awet Akot stormed western Bahr al Ghazal and soon established its base east of Gogrial. The government forces in the area were effectively confined to Gogrial town.

Tuek Tuek successfully connected with Abu-Shok (porcupine) Battalion a round Malakal area under the command of Major Daniel Deng Alony. Also under Bona Baang, Zaalan Battalion joined operation with Rhino Battalion, commanded by Martin Makur Aleiyou, attacked and occupied the Lakes District countryside, thereby isolating Rumbek from the rest of the district.

The Eagle Battalion, under Major Kerubino Kwanyin Bol, went and established bases in Southern Blue Nile and besieged Kurmuk Town. Before the elections of 1986, Eagle Battalion attacked and captured Kurmuk and Geisan. Thus by 1987, the whole of Southern Sudan and Southern Blue Nile were technically speaking under the effective SPLA control.

6.4. SPLM—TMC CONSTITUTIONAL MANOEUVRES

In October 1985, the TMC promulgated a transitional constitution designed to prepare the country for a democratic rule when the transitional period came to an end by a committee appointed by the TMC and the council of ministers.

The Provisional Constitution was based on the 1951 transitional constitution drawn up by the outgoing colonial authorities under Justice Stanley Baker. According to the new constitution (amended 1985), election for a democratic parliament would be held throughout the country in April 1986.

The SPLM/SPLA did not welcome it because it was silent on the September Shar'ia Laws, one of the major causes that contributed negatively to the re-emergence of conflict.

The SPLA demanded that the Shari'a Laws be rescinded forthwith. In fact, all attempts and efforts exerted by the National Alliance and the SPLM/SPLA could not convince the TMC or its civilian Council of Ministers to repeal the controversial laws.

The TMC instead chose to maintain the status quo approach on the future of the Islamic legislation. The members of the National Alliance were embarrassed when they discovered that Premier Dr. Al-Gizouli Dafallah and the Attorney General, Omar Al-Atti, were both advocates of the Shari'a. This was evidently clear from the earlier letters when the two pledged allegiance to Nimeiri in 1983, following the enactment of September Shari'a Laws.

For convenience sake, the Alliance could not do anything that would divide the coalition in their effort to take the country back to democratic rule. The Alliance, despite lack of clear response from the cabinet and the TMC to repeal the September laws, though frustrated, resorted to a wait and see mode.

It soon became evident that some fascists in the TMC were bent on making things even more difficult in the country already riddled with fears and tensions about the Nimeiri's three fold legacy: the escalating civil war in the south, heavy foreign debts, and perennial famine.

The fascists in the TMC had apparently wanted to keep on holding to power indefinitely as a military junta by delaying the democratic process.

The Alliance could do nothing in such circumstances except to co-operate with the SPLA as the only force that could bring about the two forces to come to terms with the real situation on the ground.

The latter rumour about a coup plot allegedly hatched by officers and men from the western and southern Sudan made cooperation between the Alliance and the SPLM/SPLA on the one hand, and the TMC and the Council of Ministers, on the other, to increase their contacts.

The Prime Minister Al-Gizzouli Dafallah, instead of dismissing the rumour as storm in the tea cup, thereby allaying the fears of northerners, made an irresponsible statement which aroused much hatred and suspicion among the Arab population against the African population.

Tactlessly, the Premier's move almost strengthened the hand of the TMC fascist group. His behaviour alarmed the Arabs in the north that the coup was intended against them and their interests. Worst still, the Prime Minister's actions raised tension higher between the two camps: southerners and northerners. This move was instrumental in the SPLA intransigence to continue with the war.

Having been emboldened by the support of the Alliance, the TMC in the meantime began its own peace initiatives. First, it invited Dr. Garang to come to Khartoum to participate in the rehabilitation of the country now that Nimeiri was gone.

This shallow propaganda bluff was emphasised to an extent that General Sowar al-Dhahab told reporters at a press briefing on 10 April 1985. He stated that he had sent some TMC members to meet with the SPLA leader, and that the talks had reached some delicate stages.

But John Garang refuted that no such talks or contacts had been made or taken place at all. In a similar propaganda ploy, the TMC General Osman Abdalla sent a letter to Colonel John Garang on 27 May. The letter invited Colonel Garang for talks.

Obviously, General Abdalla's letter was not replied to because the Movement did not recognise the TMC as a legitimate government to hold political dialogue or do business with. Colonel Garang described the TMC as Nimeirism without Nimeiri.

In June 1985, Prime Minister Dr. Al-Gizzouli wrote a letter to Colonel John Garang inviting him to accept the holding of talks. This was probably a clear reference to the government's increasing willingness to seek a peaceful end to stop the war by starting negotiations with the SPLA.

The SPLA leader replied to Dr. Gizzouli's letter, not as Prime Minister, but because he was appointed to such a post through the recommendation of the Alliance. In his letter, Colonel Garang pressed a point home that the Movement did not recognise the TMC and therefore could not negotiate with it (Garang 1992). The correspondence between the two was inconclusive.

In the last bid to convince Dr. Garang to hold talks, the TMC sent General Yousif Mohamed Yousif to Addis Ababa carrying a letter to Garang. General Yousif was told that he would only meet Colonel Garang only as a former colleague and friend and not as the TMC commissioner.

After the meeting, General Yousif went back to Khartoum with only one message: that the TMC should step down and allow the genuine forces of the uprising to take over the power.

The Deputy Chairman of the TMC, General Taj Eddin Abdallah, dismissed Garang's call as not very serious. While the TMC was trying diplomaticly to convince Garang to hold talks about talks, the war was increasingly intensifying to all parts of the South Sudan and the War Zone II (Northern Sudan).

6.5. THE KOKA DAM DECLARATION

The SPLA for some time had been speculating how to respond to the national pressure to talk peace with the government or at least with the

National Alliance. At first it appeared as if the SPLA was warmongering. This was made clear in the way the Movement responded to the government's peace overtures. The SPLA's refusal to recognise the TMC and rejection to negotiate with it had provided the government and the Alliance with tools to depict the Movement as a warmonger.

The SPLM's cool response to invitations by the workers conference, better known as the Medani Forum, was also taken to mean that the SPLA's call for unity was just a rhetorical ploy to buy time and to implement its real agenda to separate the south from the north.

The Prime Minister Dr. Gizzouli had also been at work. He had written two letters to Garang appealing to him to come to his senses and talk with the Transitional Military Council.

The SPLM finally responded but only to the call by the Alliance to meet and chart out the future of the country. Admittedly, it was the SPLA and the National Alliance for Salvation that brought down the Nimeiri Regime.

Dr Taiseer Mohamed Ali, the Alliance envoy, came back from Addis Ababa with news of great joy that the SPLA was now ready to meet the Alliance. The venue for such a meeting was soon faxed in. On March 19th 1986, the Alliance/ SPLA conference was convened at a small village town of Koka Dam, outside Addis Ababa.

The Koka Dam Meeting however ended with an important breakthrough in the north-south discord. There was something to celebrate on both sides. To the SPLA, the meeting had achieved recognition. It was now recognised as a National Liberation Movement as opposed to the "southern rebels" stigma it often received from the north. For the Alliance, it prided itself as a legitimate popular organisation that could secure peace for the Sudan.

Earlier on, Nimeiri's regime, Sowar al-Dhahab's TMC and Dr. Gizzouli's rubber stamped Council of Ministers, had tried to depict the SPLM/SPLA just as a southern separatist movement that could have been cornered or bribed into succumbing to the local autonomy within a united Sudan.

The question worth asking is that: What did the Koka Dam Declaration really offer? Was it not another Northern Sudanese ploy to arrest the south when events seemed to be out of their hand? Or was this a landmark meeting to talk peace? The significance of Koka Dam Declaration was follows:

First, it was truly a forum that brought together diverse groups and interests in the Sudan. The National Alliance was a coalition of Trade Unions and the professional organisations including the Umma and the Sudan Communist parties.

Second, with exception of DUP and the NIF, the congress was indeed popular assembly. It agreed on a number of crucial issues that would naturally pave the way for a realisation of a genuine peace in the Sudan.

At the end of the four day meeting (19th to 24th March 19th—24th 1986) the Congress called for:

1. Commitment to peaceful resolution of the Sudanese conflict.

2. Establishment of parliamentary democracy and the convening of the national constitutional conference to chart out the path for the future of the country.

3. The Conference also resolved, among others, that the 1964 Constitution be reinstated in the place of the TMC Charter.

4. The abolition of the September [Sharia] Laws and the abrogation of Military Pacts with other foreign countries (Libya and Egypt) which impinged on national sovereignty.

5. Section 3 of the Koka Dam Declaration, SPLM/SPLA demands a public commitment by all the political forces and the government of the day.

6. That the said government shall dissolve itself and be replaced by a new interim government of National Unity representing all the political forces was an essential prerequisite for the convening of the proposed National Constitutional Conference[5].

The Koka Dam Declaration was in many respects a watershed in the south-north future relations. In a sense, the word "commitment" was enough to convince all, that the Koka Dam Declaration was not another window dressing conference to sway the southerners into the Arab bluff that the local autonomy of 1972 turned out to be.

As the nation was still waiting for the convening of the proposed National Constitutional Conference, elections were soon held in many parts of the country except in SPLA held-towns and districts of which only 37 out of 68 constituencies in the south went to polls.

The government that was going to be formed in the advent of a hung parliament was going to be disabled by the absence of some of the very parliamentarians mandated to write a permanent constitution.

However, the results of the general elections were the only hope for the Southerners—at least those non-combatants who longed that the south could get something through persuasion as opposed to SPLA arm-twisting approach.

6.6. TMC SCORCHED EARTH POLICY ON THE SOUTH

After the collapse of the May Regime in April 1985, it was expected that the government that inherited the reins of power in the country would automatically turn the national resources towards peace. This was a natural expectation as the war had already drained a great deal of national resources and caused untold suffering to the people of the south and had seriously bruised the Sudan image abroad.

The TMC's promise to organise elections for democratic rule after one year was viewed by all the Sudanese people with some hope towards this end.

However, The TMC had the following options to:

1. Organise election for a democratic government, organise the political parties that would contest the elections, be prepared to hand over power to an elected government and retire honourably.

2. Reinforce the state of emergency declared by its predecessor, reorganise and re-equip the demoralised army to fight and defeat the SPLA rebels.

3. Convene the National Constitutional Conference with all the political forces in the country participating.

Regrettably, Field Marshall Sowar al-Dhahab opted for option (b) by bending to the wishes of the TMC and the Council of Ministers composed mainly from technocrats and politicians with obscured backgrounds with little to offer towards the resolution of the civil strife and the nation's multi-faceted problems.

The military solution to the problem of the south, in this respect, appeared to be a palatable course of action. Hence, Sowar al-Dhahab's Administration initiated draconian policies towards the south. These policies: the re-invigoration of the state of emergency that had been in force since September 1983, the mobilisation of the armed forces using Islamic rhetoric and the declaration of Jihad (holy war) against the south, necessitated the re-launch of military operations during the summer months of 1985.

And as if that was not enough, Sowar al-Dhahab revived the south-south war policy; the re-organisation of the Nine Tribal Militias described in the previous chapters. Top on the list of the militias included the Anya-Nya II, the Fertit Militia, the Murle Militia and the Arab Muraheelin forces in southern Kordofan

The SPLA, responded with vigour, as described in Chapter 5, and the country was put back on the road to real disaster. With the new re-invigorated army confronting the SPLA and the tribal militias harassing it from the rear, the war situation was brought back to where it was when Nimeiri was forced out of office.

Dr. Mansour Khalid [6]observes:

"The war has, thus, become one of attrition between the two sides determined to wear each other into submission. And since the SPLA has received much tacit sympathy from several tribal groups in the south, the government has resorted to the much criticised use of tribal militias: these are loosely organised anti-Dinka and anti-SPLA tribes armed by the government in order to subvert the SPLA insurrection. The result has been extremely detrimental to future ethnic cohabitation; so, by its action, the government has sanctioned and promoted wide-scale inter-tribal warfare."

One of the sinister results of the use of the tribal militias, initiated by General Nimeiri and promoted by Sowar al-Dhahab, was the revival of the age-long phenomenon of taking people from the Southern Sudan into slavery by the northern Arab groups.

According to documented report by Amnesty International, slavery became quite rampant and widely practised in areas adjacent to the government sponsored-Arab militia territories. In Bahr al-Ghazal for instance, the Fertit Militia of Tom al-Nour caused havoc among the Dinka and Jur-Luo population in Wau. This led to a clandestine Dinka organisation known as "The 'Survivors' of the 1985-86."

Apart from the slave practices, other untold human rights abuses ranging from lynching and confiscation of Dinka properties and torture of the alleged SPLA sympathisers were rampant in the government controlled areas and cities.

This was in sharp contrast with other southern-based militiamen who, although equally inflicted deadly blows on the Dinka groups, hardly resort to enslaving those whom they subdued in war.

On the administration of the south, Field Marshall Sowar al-Dhahab re-instated the 1972 autonomy act. He also adopted the three mini-regional-system created by General Nimeiri in 1983 to be under the umbrella of his TMC's High Executive Council, mimicking the 1972 Self-government rule.

In line with interim arrangement in the central government, Sowar al-Dhahab appointed Major General James Loro, former Anya Nya I officer and one of the southern members in the TMC, to set up the Regional TMC with a parallel civilian administration. Governors and commissioners were appointed to fill these posts from among the southern officers in the military. Former Anya Nya I officers were specifically targeted and appointed to carry on the policy of administration in the south.

Major General Albino Akol Akol became the Governor of Bahr al-Ghazal, Major General Peter Cyrillo for Equatoria and Major General Peter Mabil Riak for Upper Nile. Provincial posts in the south were also filled by former Anya Nya officers.

Bahr al-Ghazal: Major General Joseph Kuol Amuom, Commissioner Northern Bahr al-Ghazal, Colonel John Fuad, Commissioner Western Bahr al-Ghazal, and Brigadier Martin Makur Chigger, Commissioner of Lakes Province.

Equatoria: Colonel Dominic Dabi Commissioner of Western Equatoria, Colonel Saturnino Arikka, Eastern Equatoria.

Upper Nile: Gordon Kaong Nyuon, Commissioner of Jonglei Pio Yukwan Deng, Commissioner Upper Nile, and Colonel Simon Manyang, Commissioner Unity Province.

In the central government in Khartoum, General Fabian Agamlong and Major General James Loro were appointed members of the TMC. Whereas in the civil administration, Samuel Aru Bol became Deputy Prime Minister, Peter Gatkuoth Gwal and Oliver Albino Battali were appointed cabinet ministers.

All these attempts to impress on southerners to abandon war in the belief that their rights to self-government have been restored, unfortunately, brought no relief to the government of Field Marshall Sowar al-Dhahab.

To the contrary, all those attempts were taken by southerners inside the country and the SPLM/SPLA as half-hearted efforts aimed at impressing the SPLA backers and deceiving the southerners in the main.

In the minds of southerners, serious efforts towards the attainment of peace should have been more emphasised. Such attempts could have made power sharing meaningful. Consequently, the Field Marshall efforts to win the south thus failed miserably.

Hopes to help bring about peace to the south as indicated in the Koka Dam Declaration were now pinned on the elections scheduled for April 1986.

6.7.1. SUDAN'S FOURTH MULTI-PARTY GENERAL ELECTIONS

After consolidating its grip on political power and in realisation of the turbulence facing the Sudan, Transitional Military Council (TMC) decided to honour its pledge to hand over political power to an elected government.

On October 10, 1985, the TMC promulgated a provisional constitution based on universal adult suffrage of one-man one-vote. This Constitution permitted and empowered party formation and guided electoral laws. This round of multi-party practice regarded the fourth such exercise in 30 years, severed the long 16 years of Nimeiri's dictatorship.

It was in 1958 that the Sudanese citizens, in an independent nation, were first able to make decisions on the people they wished to vote for in a multi-party political system. There were then three major parties: Umma Party, the National Unionist Party (NUP), and the People's Democratic Party (PDP). These were the major players.

But that democratic experiment was cut short in 1958 by a military takeover that put the country under the military dictatorship until 1964 when it was overthrown by popular uprising that ushered the October Revolution. After the overthrow of the first military dictatorship of General Abboud, elections were once more conducted in early 1965 and in 1968.

During these elections, the old political forces, the founding fathers of the Sudanese nation, were returned to power but with unstable coalitions. Ismail al-

Azhari's post colonial first prime minister; Mohamed Ahmed Mahjoub; Sheikh Ali Abdel Rahman; Mubarak Zarouq; Mirghani Hamza; Sherrif al-Hindi, and the like were active throughout this period.

Political analysts suggest that the activity of the old-guard politicians who ruled the country throughout that period were owing to their sectarian backgrounds.

Since they had no direct association with the defunct military rule, the traditional parties and their leaders were spared the association with the crimes of the uniformed soldiers.

Although some of them were rounded up and detained for some time by the military, their party assets and political bases were not destroyed. Therefore, when the elections were run, many of the old politicians managed to organise themselves and regained their constituencies easily.

In the 1986 elections, however, the situation was totally different. Nimeiri and his groups of Free Officers Movement came to power with a new vision to transform the Sudan into a modern nation-state free from traditional/sectarian politics based on religious affiliation. On assuming power, Nimeiri immediately banned all political parties and imposed a single-party state under his Sudan Socialist Union (SSU) as the Ruling Party. Most of the party leaders were arrested and detained, their party's assets confiscated, a move that drove many of them into exile.

In few years time, the traditional leaders were infirm, irresolute or dead. Those who died include: leader of the National Unionist Party, Ismail al-Azhari; the spiritual leader of the Umma Party, al-Hadi al-Mahdi, the General Secretary of the Sudanese Communist Party, Abdel Khaliq Mahjoub, and the leader of Trade Union of the Sudan Workers Federation, al-Shafie Ahmed Al-Sheikh.

The people who died in exile in the later years included, Mohamed Ahmed Mahjoub, a long standing Umma Party experienced politician and former Prime Minister (1965-66 and 1967-69), and Sherif Hussein al-Hindi, the NUP (DUP) strongman and former Minister of Finance (1965-69) who went into exile and opposed the Nimeiri's regime till the time of his death in 1980. Thus Nimeiri's regime successfully kept out experienced statesmen and made them under utilised or wasted until death took them away.

However, as Nimeiri's rule became deeply rooted and repressive, the remaining political leaders inside the country—mostly members of the traditional parties—reluctantly joined the ruling SSU one by one. This became especially true after the 1977 Port Sudan Reconciliation where Sadig al-Mahdi, former Prime Minister 1966-67 and the leader of the Ansaar's Umma Party, and Dr. Hassan Abdalla al-Turabi, the leader of the Islamist groups, agreed to enter the government.

The banned Sudan Communist Party leaders like Badr Eddin Sulleiman, Dr. Ahmed Abdel Halim and Ahmed Sulleiman and last but not least, Dr. Hamad al-Seed Hamed of the People's Democratic Party, just to name a few, also joined the government following their self-clearance.

Although some of the leaders mentioned in this scenario left the May Regime either by resigning their posts or on being disgracefully dismissed, they had done much damage to the images of their parties.

Essentially their alliance with Nimeiri's one-man's rule was considered by the former party supporters as sheer abandonment of the parties which they themselves had been the founders.

The politicians were aware of this political environment and could not take it for granted that their former political basis and supporters might vote for them. They had to be won over once more, back to the fold.

Some leaders of the ancient regime who had showed some tendency to resist the May Regime or refused to join the SSU and affiliated institutions were made to languish in jails by Nimeiri's notorious State Security apparatuses. Upon being released they have to recuperate before joining politics.

As a consequence to eliminating the old sectarian leadership and in addition to the establishment of the SSU cadres from the village to the national levels throughout Sudan, the traditional parties seemed to have lost some of their former power bases.

The introduction of regionalism in the 1980 Regional Government Act may have removed SSU influence in some regions, but there was yet no alternative party. According to this Act, Sudan was divided into nine regions replacing the old provinces. This Act finally broke the backbone of the old traditional party power base.

The period between the enactment of the election laws and the general elections scheduled for April the following year marked the start of the return to democracy. It was a critical period for re-organisation before the start of political campaigning.

6.7.2. ELECTIONS AND REGIONALISM PHENOMENA

In accordance to the new election law (October 1985) general elections were scheduled to run in April 1986. Accordingly, Sudan was divided into 257 territorial constituencies in addition to the 26 seats reserved for university graduates, apparently in recognition of their role in the struggle for the realisation of democratic change in the country. No seats were reserved for youth, women, farmers or workers, as was the case during the defunct May Regime.

The regional leaders in the predominantly Arabic regions of the central Sudan (Blue Nile, Kordofan, Northern and Khartoum regions) were against the inherent misallocation of the territorial constituencies in favour of a new design that excluded their interests. They launched a complaint against the proposed changes.

In response, the TMC amended the election laws in December 1985 and the country was divided into 283 territorial constituencies and 28 graduate seats. The new additional seats were redistributed in the following order:

Darfur region, one of the recusant complainants, had its constituencies raised from 29 to 39; Bahr al-Ghazal got 28 to 29, Equatoria 22 instead of 20, Upper Nile from 18 to 21, Central Region from 49 to 51, Eastern Region 18 to 20 constituencies.

The following regions maintained their original number of constituencies: Khartoum (31), Kordofan (39), Northern (18). Thus the Sudanese old territorial constituencies were restructured to suit the new regionalist phenomenon that had been brought about by the May Regime.

In regard to the political party law, it was welcomed without reservation by Umma, DUP, Islamic Front; Southern Sudan Political Association (SSPA) and the SANU (Sudan African National Union) parties. The pro-Libyan Revolutionary Committee, the pro-Iraqi Baath Al-Arabi, the Nasserite and the African Congress parties were opposed to the political party law.

6.7.3. PARTY POLITICS: THE OLD AND THE NEW

During the 1958 general elections, there were four main political parties in the Sudanese political arena: the National Unionist Party (NUP) led by Ismail al-Azhari; Umma Party led by Abdullahi Khalil (with the patronage of Sayyed Abd el-Rahman al-Mahdi); and People's Democratic Party (PDP) led by Sheikh Ali Abd el-Rahman (with the patronage of the Khatmiyya Sect under Sayyed Ali al-Mirgani). These parties are considered in the north as the founding fathers of Sudan as a nation state.

Other parties such as the Communist Party—though registered—did not poise much on the political arena. Smaller but important was the Southern-based Liberal Party led by Stanslau A. Paysama.

In the 1968 elections there were five registered big parties: the NUP merged with PDP forming the Democratic Unionist Party (DUP), the Umma, Sudan Communist Party, the Islamic Charter Front (ICF), Sudan African National Union (SANU) and the Southern Front Party (SFP).

But in the 1986 general elections there were registered an amorphous proliferation of 40 political parties in the Sudanese political scene. All of them were officially registered with full-pledged party structures and all contested the general elections.

But the traditional parties: Umma, DUP, and now the National Islamic Front (NIF) predominated. The Sudan Communist Party (SCP). The

SSPA (amalgam of SANU and SFP), the Sudan African Congress (SAC), the Revolutionary Committee, the Baathist Arab Party, Sudan National Party (former GUN), the Darfur Development Front (DDF), the Beja Congress, the Nasserite Party, SAPCO and PPP were quite active parties in the minority. The rest of the parties were either affiliates or appendages of the main traditional parties.

Unlike the post-independence political parties, which were sectarian in formation and origin, the mushrooming political new parties claimed national character. The parties of the post-Nimeiri era were mostly organised on sectarian (Umma, DUP), racial (Arab Socialist Baath Party), religious (NIF), regional (SSPA), and ethnic-based (SNP, DDF, Beja Congress).

Among all the 40 political parties registered in 1986, only the Communist Party could boast as truly a national party by virtue of its universalistic ideology. The above change in political structure could only hit the two major parties—Umma and DUP.

The most important public concern that was facing the Sudanese voter in 1986 was the lack of dynamic national leaders within the Sudanese political spectrum that could pull the country out of its serious problems: The ethno-regionalist inclinations and the economic mess, the quagmire caused by the war. These were the legacies of dictator Nimeiri's autocratic rule.

However, the only leaders the Sudanese voters were expecting to salvage the country happened to be Sadig al-Mahdi and Dr. Hassan al-Turabi. Even though no one had hope in either of these leaders.

Sadig al-Mahdi's political naivety and incompetence was tested in the 1966-67 period when he was the Prime Minister, while Turabi had been instrumental in creating the quagmire the country faced through his Islamisation Programme.

Besides, the two men were—apart from their flamboyant appearance, fanatical, and demagogic pursuance of religious bigotry—a public distaste, were unlikely to present national image. They did not possess the temperament that could make them command undisputed national leadership in a multi-racial, multi-religious, multi-ethnic society like the Sudan, whose non-Muslim population in the south constitutes a large proposition of the country.

The TMC's decision to run elections in the country and partial elections in the Southern Sudan with the war increasingly raging and spreading between the government and the Sudan People's Liberation Army (SPLA) forces made the whole affair just a mockery.

In the south, the southern leaders saw partial elections as an unpalatable move to bring the war to an end. It could have been reasonable enough to hold elections for an all-nation parliament in order to come and write a new constitution for the country.

It was in that light that the partial elected parliament, without the mandate of southern representatives, was incapable of writing a permanent constitution to restructure the power of the central government as demanded by the SPLA.

Despite warnings to suspend the elections for a later date, the TMC, nevertheless, called for general elections as scheduled—as it could not wait for peace to come to the south. In addition, the peaceful parts of the country were ready to go to the polls on 12 April 1986.

Commenting on the 1986 elections, Mansour Khalid[7], writes:

"These elections bode well neither for the creation of a secular liberal democracy in Sudan, nor for the country's stability.....The northern political parties, impatient for power, went ahead with the elections against the protests of Southerners, who at that time had achieved some measure of rapprochement with the north via Koka Dam Conference.

The traditional parties of the Umma and the DUP wanted a quick end to the transitional period in accordance with the Alliance Charter and saw no linking the departure of the Transitional Government with the holding of the proposed Constitutional Conference."

The elections—as expected—only produced a hung parliament. The seats were distributed as follows: Umma winning 101 seats; DUP, 62; the NIF, 51; the Communists 3; and none for the other numerous northern parties.

Among the regional parties, Nuba's SNP gained 7 seats, all from Southern Kordofan and one, won by Rev Philip Abbas Ghaboush in Hajj Yousif suburb east of Khartoum, SSPA gained 8 seats, SAC gained only 2 seats, SAPCO gained 7 seats, PPP gained 10 seats, SFP gained only 1 seat. The independents gained 6 seats. In sum, only 10 out of 40 registered parties gained seats in the National Assembly (Parliament).

An interesting casualty of democratic elections was Dr. Hassan al-Turabi: he lost in his own constituency (al-Sahafa and Jebra suburbs south of Khartoum) to his challenger[8].

As expected, the peripheral areas scattered their votes and thus were not represented to enable the National Assembly to write a permanent constitution. Peter Nyot Kok[9] noted that the 1986 elections had, as usual, not done justice to other social forces in the country.

The social forces of the marginalised Sudan were not fairly represented either because of the war in the south or because of unfairness in the distributions of seats. The modern forces feel their uprising or revolution has been stolen.

General Sowar al-Dhahab's TMC honoured the results of the elections and left office in June 1986. But the situation in the country had never improved from what he found when he took over power in April 1985. War was escalating by the day, foreign debtors were at Sudan's doors demanding payment, and annual famines crippled many parts of the country.

Unfortunately the third experiment in the democratic system did not provide sufficient hope for salvaging the country unless the leaders had political will to resolve the conflict itself. This was not to be as discussed in the subsequent chapters.

CHAPTER 7
THE THIRD DEMOCRATIC EXPERIMENT AND PROSPECTS FOR PEACE

7.0. THE SETTING

In the wake of the third democratic elections in April 1986, the Parliament was deemed to convene its official session in June of the same year. Before the opening session, nearly all the citizens in the triple cities (Omdurman, Khartoum, and Khartoum North) came out to the streets in thousands to witness the official opening of Parliament.

A year before, these citizens had been to the streets demonstrating as an expression of their anger against the repressive regime of Jaafar Mohamed Nimeiri.

On June 12, the citizens took to the streets again for a different purpose. They were there this time in jubilation just to exercise their "freedom" of assembly and expression; to see their newly elected members chose a Prime Minister, apparently from among the members of the Party that had won the elections.

From all walks of life came citizens flocking to the Parliament Building standing majestically at the confluence of the two Niles—the White and the Blue.

For the past decade and half, this Building had been a symbol of misuse and abuse of democratic process and practices. It was from here that unjust and repressive laws had been promulgated, enacted and abused in the next instance when the authorities found it expedient.

As flags were flapping aloft the Parliament Building and surrounding streets, the citizens clapped their hands and women ululated as the parliamentarians began to arrive singly or in groups; the party supporters and sympathisers trailing behind them.

At the ninth hour, amidst elections' euphoric victory, Sayed Sadig al-Mahdi and followers finally arrived from his official residence in Omdurman to the Parliament Building.

It was indeed a triumphant entry and the Ansar leader was aware of its implications as well. He was about to take over a country in ruins! Yet Sadig's face glittered with smiles of election victory.

Evidently his smiles had a different expression. Besides being a hopeful

Prime Minister, there was an expression of triumph on his face considering the long battles he fought with President Nimeiri's dictatorship.

Al-Mahdi's family had fought battles against the regime of President Nimeiri in many incidences: at Wad Nubawi, 1969; at Aba Island, 1970; and the alleged Libyan Invasion of Sudan in 1976. In one incidence Sadig's uncle Imam al-Mahdi and thousands of the Ansar supporters were killed.

In the opposite direction, from Khartoum South, another procession brought Sayyed Mohamed Uthman al-Mirghani, the spiritual leader of the Khatmiyya Sect and the official patron of the Democratic Unionist Party (DUP). Sayyed Mirgahani had come across the White Nile Bridge accompanied by thousands of his supporters.

He too, entered the Parliament Building with his members of Parliament, his supporters chanting with triumph. But since his DUP did not win many seats in the elections, his display must somehow countenance that embarrassment with subdued emotions.

The third party on the scene, apparently with large following, was Hassan al-Turabi, the National Islamic Front (NIF) leader. His sudden appearance, with a sizeable procession following their Parliamentarians, attracted thousands of onlookers who received them with applause.

As he marched to the Parliament Building, his flamboyant appearance, grin on his face, his usual trademark, Dr. al Turabi was for all practical purposes, grim and astute. Though his party had emerged third in the polls, he had lost his own constituency to a candidate supported by an anti-NIF coalition. Solemnly, Dr. al Turabi and supporters disappeared into the corridors of the Parliament Building.

A few minutes later, an elderly figure emerged from the middle of nowhere with seven members of his party. This was Rev. Philip Abbas Ghaboush, leader of the Nuba Mountains-based Sudan National Party (SNP).

Catching the breath, Rev. Philip Ghabboush and his Parliamentarians, dressing in African Kenneth Kaunda Safari suits chosen for the occasion but in sharp contrast to the loose white ropes of the Arabs, headed toward the Parliament Building.

The African procession was given a standing ovation by the crowds of several thousand members of the Black Rural Solidarity organisations that had come to the surface as a result of the Nimeiri's regionalism policies of the early 1980s. It was clear that Rev. Ghaboush had stolen the show.

Among the huge crowd giving Rev. Ghaboush a standing ovation were his own supporters who had voted him into Parliament. In the words of Dr. Peter Nyot Kok[1]: "They were the shoe-shine boys, the car washers, the seasonally unemployed labourers, the lumpen proletariat, in addition to the unskilled workers who were the controllers of the streets between March, 26th and April

6th, 1985, when they accelerated the demise of the May Regime through riots."

Like a high priest entering the holy of holies, Ghaboush, gasping for breath, turned and waved to the crowd in appreciation, and finally joined the rest in the Building.

As expected, the three members of the Sudan Communist Party (SCP) arrived with their followers. They too were given a standing ovation. The members of the Southern Sudanese Parties came unnoticed by the public as they arrived one by one or in small groups, also entered the Building.

The officialdom was crowned when General Abdel Rahman Mohamed Hassan Suwar al-Dhahab's motorcade arrived followed by the 15 Military Generals, members of the outgoing Transitional Military Council.

Soon Prime Minister Dr. al-Gizouli Daffalah and members of his outgoing cabinet, diplomatic corps and notables also appeared and went direct to the Parliament Building.

Amidst euphoric but subdued emotions, as the MPs, apparently lobbying or consulting among themselves took their seats. The scene was soon interrupted when General Suwar al-Dhahab announced the end of the TMC and the start of a new dawn of democracy and civilian rule. With a quotation from the Holy Qur'an, the official business of the day began.

It was rather a paradox that out of the 40 political parties registered and contested in the general elections, only 10 parties managed to bring members to the National Assembly. Not only that, most seats in the southern constituencies were not contested because they were under the control of the SPLA.

Apart from being a hung parliament, the absence of large members from the southern part of the country made it a partial parliament. We may now turn to discuss the dawn of the third liberal democratic experiment.

7.1.1 SADIG AL MAHDI BECOMES PRIME MINISTER

Before the House could elect the speaker and its deputy, the Prime Minister and five members of head of state council, an event happened worth discussing. This was the appearance, for the first time in Sudanese parliamentary practice, of a combined democratic voice of the marginalised nationalities that constitute the greater part of the Sudanese population. This was an historic event in the life of the Liberal Democratic experiment in the Sudan.

The combined voice, undoubtedly, warned the northern Sudanese leaders about the magnitude of the question of long neglected nationalities and the continuation of regional underdevelopment.

Unless these issues were properly addressed, they were bound to tear this feeble democracy apart and so return the country to the pre-Turco-Egyptian rule where numerous sheikhdoms, kingdoms and chieftaincies ruled the day.

The event could only have proven right John Garang, the leader of the SPLM/SPLA, when, in his numerous speeches, charged that the traditional forces of hegemony, who have held power since independence (1956-1986) were incapable of holding the country together. Hence his vision of New Sudan to create basis for equal opportunity for all citizens irrespective of religion, race or ethnicity must be the answer.

However the combined voice of the rural solidarity became evident when two of their newly elected members; Rev Philip Abbas Ghaboush of the SNP and Mr Eliaba James Surur of the PPP, rose to announce that they were boycotting the session in progress:

"Mr. Speaker Sir, said Eliaba Surur, on behalf of the marginalised people of rural Sudan, the people we represent in this House, we rise Sir, to announce that we are boycotting this session of Parliament. This House, Mr. Speaker, is unrepresentative, illegal, and undemocratic as it is composed mainly of members of northern Sudan. We therefore call upon all the members who identify with what we stand for, in this august House, to follow us. With your leave Sir, we bow and leave the House."

With these words, Surur and Rev. Ghaboush bowed to the chair and walked out. Forthwith all members of the Southern Sudan and the Nuba Mountains who now called themselves the "African Group" left the House[2].

It was a move that was reminiscent to the 1958 move when the southern MPs, led by Father Saturnino Lohure, walked out of the House and continued boycotting the rest of the Parliamentary sessions till November when the Army siezed power and dissolved Parliament.

"Democracy is now nailed to a coffin and buried," Rev. Ghaboush told pressmen. While Eliaba Surur scathingly stated: "We have tolerated the Arabs for all these years and called this Afro-Arab country! But from now on, it is [only] an African country."[3]

Without adjourning the session to try at least to reach some compromise and make concessions with the "African" members of Parliament (as this group of MPs began to identify themselves in the House) the Speaker ignored the "African walk-outs." The House continued (as if nothing had happened) with the schedule with the conduct of business of the day. Dr. Lesch observed[4]: "Those northern politicians did not seem concerned that voting in the absence of important ethnic and regional political forces could weaken their legitimacy. She added: al-Mahdi even called the "African walk-out" as "a deceptive rather than genuine move that proved the boycotters hate democracy and attempt to distort its image." [3](ibid).

Nevertheless, the business in the House proceeded as scheduled. Professor Mohamed Ibrahim Khalil, one of the Umma Party's core pillars, was elected Speaker of the House along with deputy speakers and other officers of the House.

Professor Khalil was a Foreign Minister during Sadig al-Mahdi's first tenure as Premier in the 1966-67 period. Khalil was the Umma's key contact person in London with the Sudan People Liberation Movement. He was also instrumental in the 1983 Tripoli and 1984 London all parties meeting that drew up the charter providing bases for the post-Nimeiri administration in the Sudan.

There were hopes that electing Professor Khalil's Speaker would make him use his extensive experiences and influences to bring pressure to bear on the government in order to salvage the country from the mass left behind by the defunct May regime.

He was also expected to work for the Convening of the National Constitutional Conference agreed upon between the SPLA and the Alliance in the Koka Dam Declaration in which his party was signatory.

The Constitutional Conference was proposed to have taken place in June 1986 under an elected government. It had not been convened at the time of writing in 2004.

After the election of the Speaker, Sayyed Ahmed Ali al-Mirghani of the DUP was elected Chairman of the Council of State, and Idris al-Banna of the Umma Party elected his deputy. Others members included: Dr. Ali Hassan Taj-Eddin (Umma member from Darfur); Mohamed Hassan Abdalla Yasin (DUP); and Dr. Pacifico Lado Lolik (SAPCO). Finally, as expected, Sayyed Sadig al-Mahdi, the leader of the Umma Party that won the elections, was elected Prime Minister of Sudan.

With the democratic processes completed, Field Marshal Suwar al-Dhahab and his TMC Team rose and stepped aside ceremoniously to the applause of the public in the gallery and the members of the House.

Thus after twelve months of speculation and waiting for the restoration of democracy, that promise was finally fulfilled in the spring of 1986 with the change of guards. The Sudan had a democratically elected parliament and a government for the third time in its turbulent history. There was hope that the new leaders would make the hard-won democracy work.

7.1.2. UMMA—DUP FORM COALITION GOVERNMENT

As stated in the previous chapter, the general elections in the Sudan of 1986, like the previous ones 1958, 1965, 1968, had produced a hung parliament. There was, therefore, a dire need for the new Prime Minister to make contact with members of other parties to form a coalition government. As expected,

Sadig al-Mahdi could make contact with two major parties, the DUP and the NIF, in order to form a cabinet.

But as evident in the election of the five-man State Council, the coalition was already between the Umma and DUP. Sadig al-Mahdi also knew that DUP and NIF did not obtain enough members to form a government. He could either negotiate with the NIF and other small parties or with the DUP and some regional parties. Ultimately the Umma Party formed a coalition government with the DUP and three regional parties: The SNP, PPP, and SSPA.

In the distribution of ministerial portfolios, which were [surprisingly] divided equally between the two parties instead of proportionally according to their parliamentary seats (Umma had 101 and DUP 62). The posts of Deputy Premier, Foreign Affairs, Interior and Information went to the DUP in addition to the Chairmanship of the head of State Council.

The Umma on the one hand kept the portfolios of Defence, Legal, Finance, Energy and Mining, Commerce and National Economy. The remaining ministerial portfolios such as Agriculture, Irrigation, and Industry, and Public Utilities were equally distributed among the coalition partners.

As usual, the less important ministries were distributed to the regional parties in the coalition. Suffice to state that no significant ministerial posts were given to these regional parties as a gesture of goodwill. Mansour Khalid [5] writes:

Not even for the sake of form were they [Northern elite] ready to make a gesture to the south and the west [Nuba Mts] by placing one of their numbers in any of the high places.>

Having formed his government, Premier al-Mahdi was immediately expected to translate the policies embodied in his election manifesto into action. The Premier was also expected that he would implement the Koka Dam Declaration that had been charted by political forces in the country, including his Umma Party.

As discussed in Chapter Six, important items were emphasised and accepted by all those involved in the making of the Koka Dam Declaration as prerequisites for cessation of hostilities and the dawn of peace in the country. These items embodied in the Koka Dam Declaration were to:

1. Scrap Islamic Sharia Laws.

2. Abrogate the defence pacts (believed to impinge national sovereignty) with Libya and Egypt concluded between 1970s and during the TMC.

3. Convene the National Constitutional Conference.

4. Declare a cease-fire with the rebels in the south, followed by the writing of a permanent constitution.

These prerequisites should have been on the top priority list of the new Prime Minister.

Unfortunately, as soon as he assumed office, al-Mahdi embarked on a totally different agenda, an agenda tailored to suit his own personal style of rule and thought.

Throughout his first year in office, al-Mahdi's main preoccupation centred on a search for the killers of his uncle Imam al-Hadi Abdel Rahman al-Mahdi—murdered during President Nimeiri's rule in 1970.

Immediately al-Mahdi sent a team of forensic scientists to exhume the remains of his uncle Al Hadi al Mahdi. His remains were brought to the Abba Island where he was accorded an honourable funeral befitting the head of state.

Additionally, the Premier allocated a sum of £s.35 million (Sudanese pounds) compensation for the family's property (fixed and moveable assets) lost during the defunct May Regime.

7.1.3. AL MAHDI ON HOME POLICIES

Upon assuming office, al-Mahdi increasingly distanced himself from the policies listed on his campaign manifesto. Generally, democratic campaign slogans are riddled with promises politicians made to their voters that "I would implement this and that if you elect me." Al-Mahdi was no exception.

Political analysts, who observed this Oxford educated Premier, were quick to conclude that subsequent policies adopted by his government were meant to maximise power than to find solutions to the grave problems facing the country. In order to clear the air, al-Mahdi had this to say [6]:

"I do not think that any declared policy can fully be implemented at the face value. You take as an example: in an architect's blue print, there is often a discrepancy between what has actually been planned and what is actually being implemented; that is to say what you can do when the construction process actually begins. When we come to implement policies, there will always be some discrepancy about what you want to do and what you actually say. The discrepancy is always the result of conflicting interests that arise during the course of implementation. New problems do crop up and so you have to find ways and means of resolving these discrepancies—to improve those policies in order to make them work....It is natural that there can be discrepancies between the declared policies and the actual policies being implemented. In brief, I think that the lack of consistency in my policies which people talk about is due to the discrepancy between idealism and realism."

Though al-Mahdi knew that the actual priorities listed in his election manifesto were not the ones his government was implementing, he volunteered and enumerated some of the priorities agreed upon by the coalition partners. He said on the agenda of priorities we are trying to do the following:

1. Liquidation of the May Regime institutions, laws, and regulations

2. Consolidation of general national conduct of policies—regulating ministers' work of the Coalition Government by not playing up the policies of their respective parties in disregard of the policies agreed upon by the Coalition partners

3. Salvaging the Sudanese economy and clearing economic mess left behind by the defunct military regimes

4. Convening the National Constitutional Conference (apparently outside the Koka Dam Declaration)

5. Restoration of stability and attainment of peace in the south

Presently, we're trying to reconcile points of differences over the Koka Dam Declaration, the Prime Minister concluded.

As seen in the order of the list above, the Prime Minister placed the halting of the war in the south at the bottom line of his priorities. The war, as much as he was aware, had been responsible for the nation's political, social, economic, and security problems the country had been facing. It should have been the utmost concern for a new government to tackle it forthwith.

Perhaps this tells much more about al-Mahdi's attitudes toward the war in the south than his interest to resolve it in the first place.

As it would appear in the discussion, his second time in office was not in any way different from his first term in office (1966-67). His problem then was his inability to act towards peace. What else could he have maintained in the people's mandate in 1986 when the very problems that confronted the people daily were not being resolved?

Like his predecessors, Nimeiri and Suwar al-Dhahab, Prime Minister al-Mahdi, in the eyes of Southerners, was an Arab and a Northerner. That combination could have easily made him take the south for granted; a lost brother that must be won over and rehabilitated. The war in the south was to him a storm in a teacup and the rebels, terrorists.

What was needed in al Mahdi's thinking was a well-designed policy and a determined strong government to defeat the rebels in the south once and for all. To that effect, apparently, al-Mahdi's policies were largely directed toward that goal; to wipe out the rebellion and to restore the Sudan's tarnished image and prestige scarred by the outlaws. That attained, the credit would automatically go to him and the Umma Party. In that way, he would have been regarded as the ablest Sudanese politician.

Al-Mahdi too, had always rated himself and his Ansar Sect as representing the true face of Islam. With that historical nostalgia of Mahdism, the Prime

Minister al Mahdi was ready enough to confront the insurgency in the south with vigour regardless.

7.1.4. AL MAHDI ON FOREIGN POLICIES

Al-Mahdi's Machiavellian approach to realpolitick plunged his Government into executing the war against the SPLA instead of utilising the tacit protocol of amity at Koka Dam Declaration to his benefit.

His radical approach to the war was soon to prove a fiasco of grave magnitude which weakened the Coalition Government making it, in the process, very unstable, and it finally fell apart.

Basically the Prime Minister al Mahdi started his southern Policy by attempting to isolate the SPLA politically and diplomatically at home and abroad. Scathing attacks and propaganda in Khartoum aimed at reducing the SPLA to a mere bandit were common.

Often the SPLA was referred to as "warring party" or "Garang's border war" denoting that he was an isolated guerrilla leader skirting his forces around the borders only. With immediate effect, al-Mahdi started his shuttled diplomacy by touring Europe, USA, and the Arab and Islamic World.

On the first leg of those tours, he visited USA, Libya, Egypt, Syria, Iraq, Iran, and the Kingdom of Saudi Arabia, in that order. In all his tours, the Prime Minister did not consult with the officials in the Ministry of Foreign Affairs, let alone the Minister or the Technical Staff who could have advised him on the international protocols and conventions governing bilateral and multi-lateral relations.

It was necessary for the Premier to seek such advice from the technical staff on how to arrange foreign tours. The aim of which was to shrewdly avoid the expected diplomatic rows and embarrassment such visits would cause in order to achieve the aims the visits were undertaken for.

Perhaps this can explain why his Minister of Foreign Affairs, Mohammed Tawfik—a DUP member—had to resign his post in protest and frustration against the Premier's disregard of his Ministry and officials in matters related to external relations.

Before he tendered his resignation, Tawfik declared that Sudan has failed to have any impact at the external front in view of the contradictory statements by the Government officials. Tawfik's letter of resignation states:

> "Sudan has failed to have any credible foreign policy. Foreign policy is not the sum total of individual foreign policy measures; it is an inter-play between internal and external factors aimed at achieving well-defined objectives and goals. To that end, diplomacy must be orchestrated in such a manner that those measures be they actions or

statements do not clash with each other and certainly do not offend the nation's set goals and objectives." [4]

Regrettably, Prime Minister al-Mahdi's ill-defined internal and foreign policies and his belittling of the magnitude and gravity of war in the south, apart from his ceaseless demagoguery and perilous rhetoric over matters of extreme importance, indeed, alarmed the nation and the neighbours affected by the war.

The author was able to gauge this in an interview with the Ethiopian leader, Mengistu Haile Mariam (26 December 1986). Haile Mariam deplored al-Mahdi's extensive foreign tours. He also ridiculed Sadig's foreign policies as "utterly jumbled" and baseless missions that would serve neither national nor international interests." Mengistu [7] stated:

> "I think your Prime Minister is giving too much time and energy to foreign tours instead of settling down and putting his house in order. He could then blame others for not being complacent to his affairs. The issues of war and hunger afflicting his people should have been top on his list of priorities. Look, your Prime Minister does not seem to differentiate friends from enemies. He does not seem to know or care to differentiate between the enemies of his enemies and friends of his friends. How could he dare to visit Libya after completing his tour of U.S.A and Iran after Iraq and Saudi Arabia soon after visiting Iran? I think your Prime Minister will sooner, rather than later, end up here in Addis Ababa in John Garang's office—a refugee."

Such an impression from a neighbour was eccentrically sharp and cutting. It was more or less descriptive of Sadig al-Mahdi's ineptitude and naïvety.

The former Sudanese Foreign Minister Dr. Mansour Khalid [7] analysing al-Mahdi's foreign policy in a similar vein said: "Two things are to be noted in his foreign policy; one is the contradiction that characterised initiatives in this area; the other is the complete oblivion of the regime to Sudan's role in Africa. Sadig in this respect acted as if Arab co-operation and African solidarity are mutually exclusive."

Explaining the reasons behind his tottering tours, Prime Minister Sadig al-Mahdi told this author:

> "Tours are aimed, among others, at efforts to restore Sudan's position in international affairs and politics that had been lost under the defunct military regime of the immediate past. In the field of foreign affairs, we have committed ourselves to total change in Sudan's

foreign policy. Sudan is now firmly established as a non-aligned state. It has also reactivated its policy towards its neighbours. It is taking positive steps towards the neighbouring states—in short, Sudan has abandoned both alignment and axis policies and is now gearing its policies of friendship and good neighbourliness to all states in the region and the world at large."

Alfred Logune Taban, a Sudanese journalist and BBC Correspondent based in Khartoum, disagreed with al-Mahdi's exposition[8]. He writes:

"Despite the fact that the country's Prime Minister Sadig professes the maintenance of friendly relations with all the countries and our neighbours, this is hardly the case. The unfriendly countries among Sudan neighbours have visibly increased in the past years. Uganda and Chad, for instance, are no longer as friendly as they used to be. They are yet to join the hostile camp where some of our neighbours are already in. Egypt and Libya are suspicious of Sudan. The government is trying to do the almost impossible task to win all and maintain good relations with all the countries of the world. This is ridiculous and unfair on the part of the Prime Minister."

As the Prime Minister continued wooing friends and losing others in efforts to isolate the SPLA, in the hope that it would eventually be forced to accept his terms of peace, the DUP—a junior coalition partner—was at variance with him. Softly DUP began to distance itself from some of the policy bluffs and perhaps caveat for power. After all, it (DUP) had been out of power for more than 18 years. It could therefore hope to gain an absolute majority in the next elections.

In essence, DUP was not in hurry nor interested in the immediate issues of peace, let alone the convening of the often spoken National Constitutional Conference. Dr. Peter Nyot Kok [9]writes: "The other Coalition Partner, the Democratic Unionist Party (DUP) was not noticeably keen on the peace process. Having opposed the Koka Dam Declaration and having committed itself to the retention of the Sharia Laws in the Coalition Charter and being organisationally in disarray, the DUP did not contribute much to the search for peace."

7.2.1. AL MAHDI MEETS JOHN GARANG

On July 31, 1986 while attending the OAU Annual Summit Conference in Addis Ababa, Ethiopia, Prime Minister al-Mahdi met Colonel Dr. John Garang de Mabior, the leader of the SPLM/SPLA and discussed with him for nine torturous hours with no break or breakthrough. This meeting was made possible by the necessity that forced al-Mahdi to disregard his previous insolence against the SPLA and its leadership. Now he had no choice but to meet and talk with him.

According to political observers who attended the meeting or read the minutes of that meeting, there were no real substantive issues raised and resolved worth noting. Essentially the meeting resolved nothing apart from the fact that it offered an opportunity for the two leaders to assess each other's position and strength.

Nevertheless, during the meeting Prime Minister al-Mahdi attempted, in numerous instances, to bypass crucial issues such as the cancellation of Sharia Laws, the convening of the National Constitutional Conference and other issues contained in the Koka Dam Declaration. He narrowed the basic issues down to what he regarded as the "Southern Problem."

In the discussion, for instance, Sadig al-Mahdi hinted that the Koka Dam Declaration has been already overtaken by new realities: the realities he failed to qualify. His opponent, Colonel Garang, remarked:

> "Attainment of peace in the Sudan requires taking bold steps. If you take bold steps in that direction Mr. Prime Minister, we (SPLA) shall take bold steps too and the situation will change radically. But, if you go, Mr. Prime Minister, and declare war on us, if you go and recruit 100,000 soldiers to come out and fight us, you would have increased the number of our recruits as half of those you would recruit would defect to join us."—the SPLA leader sternly warned.

However, the talks that were expected to result in serious search for peace ended up in a hopeless impasse. [10]Dr Mansour Khalid notes, "The meeting between al-Mahdi and Garang could have broken new ground...There were several reasons for that failure. Not only were the objectives of the two parties discrepant; also their premises were antithetical and their personalities irreconcilable."

Commenting further on the al-Mahdi and Garang's encounter, Khalid states: "The meeting had its beneficial side effects. For one thing, it had dispelled the image and exploded the myths northern politicians had of southern leadership. Particularly, the comfortable assumptions that they could always be tantalised by 'political gifts' or pleased with an innocuous constitutional password." [11]

Sadig al-Mahdi and Colonel John Garang's meeting was also seen by many as a positive step because the Umma Party and SPLM leadership had been represented in the Koka Dam Declaration and both have major backing from their respective followers.

Apart, the meeting was also a political muscle testing because in the previous month Sadig al-Mahdi had declared that he would wipe out the rebellion in the south. That stance was probably eased down by the nine hours of heated discussion.

The meeting was also taken as a change of heart (certainly not of policy) for Sadig al-Mahdi, assuming that it would be a matter of time and he may agree to implement the provisions of the Koka Dam Declaration. This would include, among others, the cancellation of Islamic Sharia Laws and the convening of National Constitutional Conference.

But as the Sudanese people were expecting further contacts between the SPLA and the Sudan Government to resume the peace process, a sad incident occurred which apparently slammed the doors of the peace process.

The SPLA shot down a Sudan Airways airliner over Malakal killing 60 people on board including the children and family of a provincial commissioner, Timothy Tot Tut.

Sadig al-Mahdi reacted to the incident angrily, and warned the SPLA that his government would not negotiate with the "terrorists." He also warned that he would punish severely those who were in league or in cooperation with the rebels. He labelled the "would-be SPLA sympathisers" like members of the National Alliance for National Salvation, as "Fifth Columnists."

Addressing the Constituent Assembly, the Prime Minister told the House that his government would negotiate again with the rebels if only they showed some kind of seriousness in their policies.

For the next few months to come, it appeared as if all doors for peace had been irredeemably closed. Thus the peace process which was put on the Prime Minister's agenda in July was once more removed from the list of priorities.

7.2.2. AL MAHDI ON ADMINISTRATION OF THE SOUTH

When the Sudan attained her political independence from Britain in 1956, it was already faced with a revolt staged by Torit Mutineers in August. The Commission of Inquiry that followed had noted clearly the main reasons why Southerners rebelled against the incoming Arab-Islamic administration in the Sudan.

Power-imbalance between the north and the south's ethnic and cultural factors were predominant in the minds and hearts of Southerners. The Torit Mutiny only sparked a long history of animosity, which eventually led to a long drawn political instability in the country.

In 1972, President Nimeiri made concessions by granting Southern Sudan the Regional Government. This move disarmed the hearts of many Southerners.

Some relative peace and stability was restored not only in the south, but in the rest of the country. Sadly, the same President who brought peace in1972 rescinded it in 1983 and the country slowly drifted back to war.

Upon the overthrow of Nimeiri in April 1985, it was hoped that the status quo ante would have been restored. The TMC recognised that fact that the denial of the south to handle its own affairs as one entity had been one of the main causes which had brought ruins to the country.

The TMC therefore attempted to revive, albeit half-heartedly, the 1972 Regional Self-Government Act and appointed a Southern Transitional High Executive Council (Regional Council of Ministers).

Unfortunately, the HEC could not move back to its supposed Headquarters in Juba and remained in Khartoum till it was dissolved after the elections in June 1986.

On taking over as Prime Minister, al-Mahdi acted strangely enough to the disappointment of Southerners. The general opinion in the south was that the new government must revive the 1972 Self-Government Act by reuniting the south as one Regional Government instead of the three mini-regions established under Presidential Decree No. 1 of 1983.

As soon as new Premier assumed office, he dissolved the Provisional High Executive Council established by the TMC. But he retained the three military governors in the south without governments.

In October 1986, the Prime Minister came up with a policy for the Administration of the Southern Sudan. He told the Southerners to agree among themselves whether to reunite the south as one region or retain the three mini regions.

A controversy ensued. Southerners were divided into two opposing camps; those who wanted a united Southern Region and those opposed the return to the 1972. This group instead preferred to maintain three regions in Southern Sudan.

The southern political wrangling based on the 1982 alignments came to the fore again; some supporting division of the south while others opposed it.

The Prime Minster, acting as an honest broker, could not reconcile the two groups. The division itself weakened the southern resolve in pushing for peace from within the country.

The Prime Minister's defence that he was an elected leader and must, therefore, go through democratic processes only added fuel to the feuding southern groups.

To resolve the issue al-Mahdi adopted a new approach. He recognised that he should cooperate with all political parties in the Coalition Government in accordance to the all-party charter that included all the southern parties: SSPA, SAC, SAPCO, SPFP, PPP, and SANU.

The Prime Minister told the southern leaders that they should stop bickering and instead agree on one issue: the formation of either one united Southern Region or three regional governments.

With no solution insight, Southern Sudanese politics began to grind deeper into their divisions. The Southerners too, became resentful at the Prime Minister's wait and watch tactics.

They soon realised that al Mahdi was turning the whole debate into a south-south affair. The skilful Prime Minister at last intervened. He decided to resolve the issue but under a different guise.

In a memorandum intended to resolve the issue, he abandoned the term "High Executive Council" and replaced it with a new label, "The High Council for the South. He then appealed to all the southern parties to endorse his proposal; arguing that the High Council for the south was a mere transitional measure under which the south could be governed till the convening of the National Constitutional Conference.

It would be then that the final administrative arrangement for the south could be decided upon. Again, in the Prime Minister's memo, the High Council for the South was to be chaired by a non-party person and in the membership of three other neutral persons with the governors of the three Southern Regions as ex-officio members.

The Charter did not even specify what the relations between the central government and the High Council for the South would be and the relations between the Council and the three regions. The southern parties were thrown into utter confusion.

What the southern parties did not know, or perhaps knew but purposely shrugged it aside, was that the Prime Minister did not intend to revive a united regional government. It was just the use of public relations exercise as a matter of common democratic practices. Dr. Nyot Kok [12] observes:

> "While the southern parties were embroiled over the oneness of the south or its tripartite regional arrangement, the Prime Minister issued a seven-point scheme in form of a memo to the Council of Ministers seeking its enactment into law. Accordingly, the law would be called an interim administrative arrangement for the south and would remain enforced till final decision would be reached at the Constitutional Conference."

The PM's memo on the regional scheme in the south was apparently leaked separately to the southern parties groupings to see their reactions. The result of that leakage was that the southern parties started intensive political bickering: some in support; others opposing; and a third group dismissing it outright.

Pretending to defuse the situation, al-Mahdi underwent a number of long, tedious consultations with the two main groups.

On January 19, 1987 the Prime Minister signed a charter with one group that consisted of SAPCO, PPP, and SPFP (divisionist group). To this group the Prime Minister promised that the Chairmanship of the Council for the South would come from them. This group nominated for the Chair of the council Eliaba James Surur.

On January 31, 1987, the Prime Minister signed another charter with the other group, SSPA and SAC (unionist group). The nominee of this group was Peter Gatkuoth Gwal.

In February, to much surprise of everybody, the Prime Minister appointed Mathew Obur Ayang, his long time friend since the two met in prison during the May Regime era, as the Chairman for the Council of the South. He appointed nine ministers, including three governors of the south and their deputies. The appointees were all the same as those nominated earlier by the Prime Minister.

On the charge that he did not adhere to the provisions of the self government act of 1972 when he appointed the Council for the South; that he too, did violate the Charter signed between him and the southern parties, and that his decision was unconstitutional, al-Mahdi[13] remarked:

"There are two developments that must be looked into when talking about violating the 1972 Self-Government Act. The point is that the legal institutions referred to no longer exist. Secondly, there is a new political reality that involves the rejection of the HEC by some segments in the south. Moreover, when the HEC was appointed by the TMC in 1985, the 1972 Self-Government Act was not consulted. The absence of the legal institutions embodied in the 1972 protocol and the presence of the new political realities mean that we cannot proceed to do anything about the south unless there was an agreement among the Southerners themselves."

The PM's apparent inconclusive and elusive politics forced the southern parties to accept grudgingly, the unconditional formation of the Council for the South. Each party lobbying for its share of the southern cake!

Contrary to what the parties agreed in the Charter with the Prime Minister, the Council for the South was given the damaging mandate to normalise the war situation in the south. But how the Council without powers and based in Khartoum, could normalise the war situation in the south was not challenged or taken as a serious task worth undertaking for obvious reasons which are out of the scope of this Chapter. As Eliaba James Surur, the leader of PPP told the author in an interview: "The Prime Minister al-Mahdi wanted a man he could control while he implements his ill-intentioned war policies on the south. The Prime Minister had successfully had his war via divide and rule tactics." Surrur was proven right as discussed in the subsequent part of this Chapter.

7.2.3. AL MAHDI'S SCORCHED-EARTH SOUTHERN POLICY

As discussed, Prime Minister al-Mahdi's policy toward the war in the south since June 1986, centred round one main objective, defeating the southern rebels before settling down to consolidate his power.

From his public statements, it was clear the Prime Minister meant business. Consequently, al-Mahdi visited various countries he considered friendly to him. The purpose of his shuttled diplomatic tour was to seek military support and financial assistance.

While visiting European countries, al-Mahdi stressed that he needed help to consolidate democracy. In the Arab and Islamic countries, he said, he needed aid to defend Arabism and Islam in the Sudan. These contradictory statements made some countries he visited reserved about the Premier's jumbled policies. Nonetheless, his visits aimed at efforts to win all did pay him handsomely. He achieved his objective in the following areas: He was given a sum of $400 million U.S. dollars for famine relief. He also received an amount of $30 million U.S. dollars from Libya in addition to assistance from other Muslim countries.

Having obtained sufficient financial and logistic support, Premier al-Mahdi re-equipped and re-organised the army. This move would have won him great respect from the weary army so demoralised by constant defeats in battles with the SPLA.

By then the SPLA had overrun and occupied a number of towns and military garrisons in the South, including Yirol (1985), Lainya (1986), Pibor, Jekou and Kapoeta (1988). But instead of depending entirely on the army to confront the SPLA, the Prime Minister also reorganised and re-equipped his Ansar militias and ordered them to fight alongside the army. In order to use the two forces effectively, al Mahdi appointed more pro-Umma Ansar officers to senior and key positions in the army units. Immediately he appointed retired Major General Fadhallah Burma Nasir, an intelligence military officer and former member of the TMC, to the position of State Minister for Defence, apparently to oversee the army and the Ansaar Militias. He kept the defence portfolio. A number of pro-Umma officers were also appointed to sensitive key positions in security and intelligence units. Al Mahdi,'s nephew, Mahdi Babo Nimr, was appointed Chief of General Staff and Abdel Rahman Farah appointed Chief of Special Security Branch.

As a Minister of Defence, al Mahdi ordered the formation of a crack force charged with the responsibility to move fast whenever necessary to check the rebels advance and contain them. The deterrent force was a special task force resembling the rapid deployment force in some of the sophisticated countries like Britain and the United States. The crack force was then launched and used effectively against the rebels.

The Prime Minster was also encouraged by the efficiency of the crack force and became more militant. He began to call the rebels "terrorists and secessionists," notoriously active and bent to sabotage Sudan's nascent democracy. The Task force immediately went into action and made a breakthrough in its operation against the SPLA for the first time since the fall of Nimeiri 1985.

Moving discreetly through eastern Upper Nile, the Task Force managed to reach Juba undetected to the surprise of the SPLA. Despite al-Mahdi's crack force harassing the SPLA forces in Upper Nile, the war was already galvanising into a full-blown national insurgency contrary to what the Prime Minister had thought.

By this time (1986-87), the SPLA had increasingly grown in numbers and strength. It was spreading northward into southern Kordofan and southern Blue Nile. Commander Kerubino Kuanyin Bol, the Deputy Chairman SPLM and Deputy Commander-in-Chief of the SPLA, had been posted as the overall commander of the forces in War Zone No.2 (northern Sudan) and Commander Yousif Kuwa Mekki appointed to command southern Kordofan forces.

The posting of the two commanders sent chilling messages to the Prime Minister and his generals in Khartoum. The appearance of SPLA in large numbers inflicted fear on the Sudan Army.

It sent a clear message to them that the war was no longer "Garang's border war," a foreign inspired guerrilla force using hit and run tactics and then withdrawing to a base across the frontier, as described by their minister of Defence. Rather it was a conventional force. Both the government and its army began panicking. Something, therefore, had to be done and must be done without delay.

In a desperate move to contain the situation al-Mahdi ordered that tribal militias in the Southern Sudan, started by President Nimeiri in 1983-1984 and used by General Suwar al-Dhahab, be revived and made effective to fight alongside the regular army.

The Misserya Militia, associated with Ansar, *al-Quaat al-Marahael* (mobile force) was reorganised as Home Guards. The intention, apparently, was to relieve the army to fight the rebels in the south while the Home Guards protected the government from possible coup plots against the *Mahdist democratic regime in the capital.*

The marahael militias were also given another assignment. The sacred role to teach the Dinka nationality where SPLA leader John Garang and most of his commanders hailed, a lesson that they would not forget.

After short well charged political, religious, orientation and military training, the Misserya Marahaellin was unleashed. Their first target, as expected, was the Dinka territory in northern Bahr al-Ghazal, northern Upper Nile and Abyei area.

Within a short time following their graduation, the Arab militiamen went on rampage in the said areas. They were dispersed: some on foot, some in lorries, and others on horseback. In the process they made the Dinkaland clean of cattle, grain, and whatever valuable they could lay hands on. The scale of destruction was reminiscent of the Mahdist Dervish destruction of the 1880s.

During the Arab militia campaign (1986-1989), the native Dinka life was assumed the cheapest and worthless. Whenever a Dinka village or cattle camp was on sight, it was declared a rebel camp and targeted for devastation.

It was then that large areas of the Dinka populations were displaced forcing them into big cities in the south and the north.

The young, however, responded to these masquerading militias by trekking with their cattle southwards into more secured areas in Tonj, Rumbek, southern Gogrial and Yirol Districts where they sought the SPLA protection. In the process, tens of thousands of these youth, swelled the ranks of SPLA guerrilla forces.

The Sudan Council of Churches, Relief Department" reporting in 1988 stated:...about 1.2 million Dinka had entered Khartoum, 800,000 to other northern regions of Darfur and Kordofan. Over a million were displaced to the southern towns of Aweil, Tonj and Wau. And a further 500,000 into the neighbouring countries of Ethiopia and Kenya."

Despite international and national condemnation and appeal to the government to halt the carnage, nothing was done to relieve the situation. Instead, northern Bahr al Ghazal, and northern Upper Nile were ethnically cleansed.

The most impeccable of these ethnic cleansing practices was the Dhaein Massacre of 1987[14] where crowds of displaced Dinka people were mercilessly killed by the militia and tribesmen while the national police and authorities looked on.

The massacre was even made more medieval when those Dinka, who ran into some houses for sanctuary, were dragged out and killed. The Rezeigatt Arab militiamen took advantage by capturing many Dinka children and young women into slavery.

The public and international outcry and condemnation against the Dhaein massacre forced the government to issue statements that denied its knowledge and participation.

But Professor Mahmoud Ushari and Professor Suleiman Baldo, both lecturers at the University of Khartoum, took the matter seriously, and investigated that inhuman tragedy and made it public in their famous book *The Dhaein Massacre* to the government's embarrassment.

Without Ushari and Baldo's investigation, the government would have successfully smothered the massacre completely.

Embarrassed by the revelation, the Government turned against the two professors with impunity and locked them up as traitors writing damaging lies against the state and the government.

However, Ushari and Baldo's testimony and useful revelation of the massacre undoubtedly would go down in history that not all northern Sudanese share the same brutality against their southern counterparts.

Writing about the Dhaein Massacre, Dr. Mansour Khalid observes: "Recent reports have claimed that enslavement in the aftermath of those tribal wars was extensively practised in some areas. The slavery, one piece of research has shown, was explicitly linked to the government's practice during recent years of arming the Dinka traditional enemies."[15]

In the south, tribal militias were unleashed upon the Dinka population on the displaced camps in Wau and Juba. The Dinka persecution was more acute in these cities due to the existence of two anti-Dinka militias, the Mundari in Juba, and the Fertit in Wau. The two forces were supported heavily by security organs, with the tacit approval of both the regional and central governments. Dr Khalid states:

"Referring to a recent case of harassment of Dinka people in Juba by government forces in February 1987, Radio SPLA accused the Governor of Equatoria Major General Peter Cyrillo, as the man behind the Government's Nazi-style pogrom. Beneath the obvious propagandist rhetoric, however, there is the hard kernel of truth of the government's deliberate 'divide and rule' tactics and murderous policies."

As the Sudanese were coming to terms with what became known as the Dhaein Massacre of Displaced Dinka, another inhuman tragedy took place in Abyei Area. This time in was the pan-demonic destruction and annihilation of the Ngok Dinka which reached its peak in 1988 when the entire Ngok Dinka people were either killed or displaced.

Aware that no help would come to them from any direction, those with cattle managed to cross over to northern and eastern Gogrial. The majority that had lost all their belongings tracked all the way to far north of Sudan where they continued to live in squalor throughout the war.

Following the intensification of the war in 1988 and 1990, the Ngok Dinka people who had walked with their cattle to Twic and Rek territories in Northern Bahr al Ghazal province, were once again forced to move away further south to seek protection in the areas under the SPLA control.

Those who remained behind in northern Gogrial and Aweil District became victims of the Messiryia cattle raiding and child trafficking operations. It was during this period that hundreds of Ngok children were taken into slavery.

The Messiriya cattle raids into the Dinka Ngok territories and the child trafficking incidents, though again condemned by international community and by men of goodwill among the northerners and particularly the members of the National Alliance for National Salvation, were never investigated and may never be investigated.

7.2.4. AL MAHDI CONSCRIPTS TRIBAL MILITIAS TO CONFRONT THE MOUNTING INSURGENCY IN THE SOUTH

According to interviews with well-placed people in the authority who were genuinely honest in their statements, the unleashing of the Arab militias against the Dinka people was aimed at achieving the basic objectives:

1.To deny the SPLA morale; logistics and manpower support as most of the SPLA recruits come from Dinka districts of Aweil, Gogrial, Abyei and northern Bentiu.

2. The rural south in general and the Dinka country, in particular, must be disturbed for the following factors:

1. The Dinka nationality is a human barrier for the spread of Islam southward and further afield into central African territories.

2. Dinka is an obstacle to the spread of Arab culture not only to the South Sudan but also to the rest of central African countries.

According to this perspective, the British colonialism is blamed for having created barriers for Islamisation and Arabicisation processes through series of ordinances that culminated into the enactment of the Closed District Ordinances after World War I.

The colonial Ordinances had saved Southern Sudan from the ravages of Arab-Islamic devastation during the Turco-Egyptian and Mahdist interregnum. In other words, it had prevented a cultural assimilation under the Arab-Islamic influences.

For the government of the Umma Party, destroying any resistance in the south was a noble mission worth undertaking. The displacement of the Dinka population between 1986 and 1988 was directed toward this principled objective.

In the opinion of Prime Minister al-Mahdi, and perhaps to many of his supporters, the people displaced by the war in the South Sudan and Nuba

Mountains were considered new arrivals from the human zoos into the civilising world of superior Arab culture and Islamic religion.

The displaced people were therefore subjected to extensive and intensive re-education in order to embrace Islamic culture (Nubas in peace camps in to Umruaba Camps).

African nationalism, as professed by Southerners, was described as foreign inspired; negative and repugnant against the superior Arab race in the Northern Sudan. To that effect, national efforts and Islamic resources were directed towards Islamisation, Arabicisation of non-Muslims and non-Arabs in the displaced camps.

Abdel Wahab al-Affendi,[16] an Islamist scholar, vividly described the displacement of the entire population in the South Sudan. He writes:

"With hundreds of thousands [Southerners] killed, over two million displaced mostly to the north [regions and cities], and with the infrastructure (in the south) destroyed and the traditional life styles irretrievably disturbed, a radically novel situation had been brought about. Thus a situation for a change was therefore to be made... Once in the north Islamisation and Arabisation was stepped up (al-Affendi)."

For people who read about the displacement from a distance, like Dr. Abdel Wahab al-Affendi, who spent most of his time in London, a novel situation was being created. But to those who were on the scene and knew the truth, a novel situation for Arabicisation and Islamisation did not work. It was tried using all resources, but failed miserably for one simple reason; to give food upon the pledges to adhere to Islam was unacceptable to the displaced population. If anything it only added more injury to the displaced who took such an approach as not only humiliating to adhere to, it was very insulting and a challenge to their African personality. Ustaz Tarticio Ahmed Morgan, a veteran politician, in an interview with the author remarked:

"What was carried out in the displaced camps around the cities could have angered the god who created Northern Sudanese and made them Arabs and Muslims. I think giving food to the hungry, the displaced people in exchange for conversion into Islamic faith, does not, I think, *augur well in front of God. This unscrupulous approach to the faith is not something to be proud of.*"

In contrast to the Islamic approach, however, the western Christian relief organisations in the Sudan provided relief to all displaced persons irrespective of their religion.

Perhaps this may explain why the Sudanese government was suspecting relief organisations for being sympathetic to the displaced African populations in Khartoum and elsewhere in the north.

Fearing that the foreign relief agencies were being smart trying to convert the southern animists to Christianity, they were kept out from observing and exposing the government's policies to the external world.

Foreign relief workers were therefore targeted, scorned and subjected to all sorts of restrictions including denial of visas and licences. There were even cases where relief workers who failed to commit themselves to unnecessary requirements were simply denied access to places where the government scorched earth policies and flagrant human rights abuses remained preposterous.

Despite protests from western Embassies in Khartoum, nothing could deter the concerned authorities to back down and show the best face of their Islamic religious faith. They became even more aggressive when pressed harder to relent some of the obvious unnecessary restrictions. In the final analysis, the displaced people could not find in the north, existence of 'Islamic tolerance, nor did they find 'Arab Hospitality' that was much publicised by the authorities. They could only find solace in the Church. Those who had not been christened freely adopted Christianity as their religion of identity.

Within a matter of years all the Churches of all Christian denominations in the three towns were filled to the brim on Sundays and other days of rest by thousands of worshippers. To the extent that the Catholic Archbishop of Khartoum, His Grace Gabriel Wako, was forced to admit in one of his Christmas Day sermons at St. Matthew's Cathedral Khartoum that "Indeed 'the harvest is great and there are few labourers.'" He apologised to the faithful that the Church could not take all the attendants despite the three masses celebrated that day. Some years before, only a few hundred worshippers attended the mass at his Cathedral. "Now there are thousands!" Archbishop Wako remarked.

In an exclusive interview with the author over the reports that the Misseriya Arabs were killing the Dinka in northern Gogrial, Aweil, Bentiu, and Abyei , Al Mahdi said[17]:

"I am aware of the Messirya-Dinka acrimonious relations...This is a by-product of violence being escalated by Garang. Moreover, some of the Dinka people have attacked the Arab tribes, especially the Messirya. This has resulted in the Messirya making a counter attack...you see, this is another by-product of Garang's aggression. That is why many Dinka people are suffering, although they are not necessarily against the government or other tribes. But the fact that Garang movement has a tribal overtone has led to the deteriorating relations between the Dinka and non-Dinka in both the south and north. I also think that Garang's Movement has greatly deprived the Dinka of their great wealth and has caused them great social upheavals in history. It is a sad thing because I have seen Dinka people uprooted all over the country."

From the above statement, one can allude that, Al Mahdi's policy of uprooting the Dinka; displacing them and destroying their infrastructure; was a punitive measure, a calculated plan, directed and geared toward one main goal. To force the Dinka people to abandon their homes and flee to the north, where they would be exposed to Arab and Islamic culture.

Another by-product of al-Mahdi's system of wiping out the Dinka reawakened the bitter memories of remote past, the history of slave trade in the previous century.

Equally important to narrate were Mohammed Ushari and Suleiman Baldo's investigation revelation that at least 1,500 displaced Dinka from Aweil, northern Bahr al-Ghazal, had perished in the hands of their Arab-Muslim counterparts in the Dhaein Massacre described earlier. This revelation did have damaging effect upon the al-Mahdi's regime.

More embarrassing to al Mahdi regime was another sad incident involving two innocent Dinka herders who were on their way from Aweil to Muglad through Meirem Village[18].

At Meirem, the two Dinka, Deng Deng Akot and Deng Anei were arrested by the security on the allegations that they were rebel infiltrates. The two men were arrested, hands tied behind their backs and placed to lie in a baking sun from 9:00 am to about 4:00pm.

When this ordeal was over, the ropes, apparently having done their job, made the hands of the victims swollen. No medical help was administered. By the time the victims were taken to Babanusa and by train to Khartoum, four days had already lapsed without medical attention.

On arrival to Khartoum, the victims had already developed gangrene—severe tetanus—and their lives were at serious risk. The doctor could only recommend amputation as the way to save their lives.

Regrettably, neither the central government nor the regional government of Bahr al Ghazal undertook any inquiry into such inhumane and callous acts of torture. The amputation of these two victims sparked a great deal of attention as political activists took this gruesome act up as an opportunity to display the victims who were visited by thousands of people in order to embarrass the Government.

Atrocities like this, including the Dhaein Massacre, and the Meirem Incident, simply forced many Dinka youth across the border to join the SPLA insurgency in order to revenge these atrocities.

If al Mahdi's intensification of the war through the use of local tribal militias had brought problems upon his regime, it had, to a certain degree, also worked against the SPLA policies where its forces were not allowed to fight in their respective areas to counter attack the militias.

One such instance was when a whole SPLA battalion attempted to defect from Jonglei Province in effort to go back to defend their homeland in northern Bahr al Ghazal against the marauding Arab militias.

But the Brigade Commander Arok Thon Arok was reported to have executed the leaders of that company, spearheading the escape to Bahr al-Ghazal.

The SPLA policy of not allowing fighters who hailed from Bahr al Ghazal to defend their own people against the Misseriya militias' incursion into their areas became a bone of contention throughout the rest of the struggle between them and the SPLA leadership. It was used by Kerubino Kuanyin Bol against the SPLA leadership before his arrest.

Precisely, al Mahdi's policies aimed at efforts to defeat the SPLA through the excessive use of local militias against the Dinka population, away from the Army General Command, in addition to the political guises and gambles he adopted in handling the national issues, worked negatively against his government.

In the final analysis. these factors alienated the Army from supporting him and disabled the functioning of his government, leading to his failure to deliver goods.

Equally damaging, al Mahdi's racist attitude in which he prosecuted the war worked effectively against his regime in two ways. It enabled the people affected to mobilise and join the SPLA en masse to fight for their own survival. It also prolonged the war, which was increasingly spreading to include areas which were outside the main theatre of war in Southern Sudan.

7.3. AL MAHDI REASSESSES HIS POLICIES

Prime Minister Sadig al-Mahdi's jumbled policies and warmongering, which brought a great deal of condemnation within and also in external circles, forced him to reassess his policies. He had to start to tackle the economic problems, foreign debts, and how to win the northern Sudanese populace that he was the ruler who had something to offer.

On the war front, he had come to recognise John Garang as someone worth negotiating with. To that effect, Sadig al-Mahdi summoned his Council of Ministers and religious leaders in November 1986 to inform them about his new peace initiative. He stated that he had declared 1987 as the year of peace in Sudan.

This was the time the rebels would have either been defeated or been forced to accept peace within a united Sudan in exchange of a regional autonomy similar to the 1972 Peace Accord.

Without much hesitation, the religious leaders endorsed the Prime Minister's peace proposal without further details. They also pledged their full cooperation to achieve peace. An in Inter-religious Dialogue Committee was set up under the patronage of Idris al-Banna, a prominent member of the Umma Party Executive Committee and Deputy Chairman of the Head of the State Council.

Meanwhile, the religious leaders were expected, in the thinking of the Prime Minister, to mobilise the nation for peace through their sermons in the Mosques and Churches. The faithful would then support the government's peace deal and bring pressure to bear on the rebels to co-operate and join the democratic institutions that were being created.

This Inter-religious Committee was henceforth renamed the Mercy Council, which immediately went into operation within a matter of weeks. A delegation headed by Rev. Ezekiel Kutjok, the Secretary General of Sudan Council of Churches (SCC) visited Addis Ababa to meet with the Ethiopian leader Mengistu Haile Mariam and Col. John Garang, the SPLA leader.

But when the delegation returned and wanted to brief Prime Minister Sadig al-Mahdi about their peace mission and what they had discussed, the clergy were stunned that the Premier was not ready to meet them.

Undoubtedly, the church leaders realised that they had fallen into Sadig al-Mahdi's political bluff. There was no peace in the Mercy Council and in May 1988, it was simply trashed into the dustbin of history.

In regards to the cooperation on matters of national conduct of business, the coalition partners apparently did not have sustainable socio-economic development vision or plans.

What was apparent was that the coalition partners were too busy in efforts to rehabilitate their party structures and policies directed at reasserting their political power bases they had lost during the 17 years they had been out of power.

Thus all talks about peace or lack of it did not concern them much, nor did the suggestions made at the Koka Dam to convene the National Constitutional Conference top their agenda. To say the least, such things were non-issues to the UMMA and DUP leadership cadres.

The two coalition partners were visibly seen straddling the world with no clear cut national policies; neither co-operating nor breaking up the coalition, and perhaps called for fresh elections.

This move, many believed, would have bailed the Prime Minister out of the confusion of socio-economic development, mounting foreign debts, and a series of conferences which brought no peace at all.

Earlier in the year, Sadig al-Mahdi had attempted to amend the draft constitution on the pretext that there were some articles that had tied the hands of his government to take drastic measures against the elements of the defunct May Regime.

But the Parliament countered the Prime Minister's request. Even some of the members in the DUP and Umma party hierarchies did not bless the proposed amendment.

As Dr. Mansour Khalid described, the general feeling in Parliament was that the Prime Minister "...wanted to strengthen his own hand and reinforce his style of personal rule: Nimeirism without Nimeiri."

Although the amendments did take place subsequently, it was apparent that it did not add anything new to enable the government to function as an effective executive.

On April 6, 1987, while the nation was celebrating the second anniversary of the April uprising that brought down Nimeiri's regime, Sadig al-Mahdi, instead of announcing the cancellation of the September Laws as he had promised in numerous occasions to rescind these laws, instead embarked on a fresh peace initiative.

In his speech, the Premier declared a one month-cease-fire, which he said would be followed by peace talks on the modalities on the convening of the National Constitutional Conference. He also promised relief assistance to southern Sudan as well as disclosing his long term plan for a cease fire.

Commenting on Sadig al-Mahdi's latest peace initiative, Dr. Peter Kok noted[19]: "...al-Mahdi played stunts with peace initiatives to deflect attention from other serious issues.

Indeed, many serious issues were at stake and were coming in droves as we shall see later on. Regrettably, as the Prime Minster continued with his jumbled policies, discarding some and creating more problems, public talks about scandals, corrupt practices and too much rampant inefficiency in his government could no longer be ignored.

However, things, came to the open when Mohamed Abu-Harira, Sadig al-Mahdi's Minister of Commerce, heaped charges of corrupt practices against some of his colleagues in the cabinet, finger pointing some of the charges tacitly at his boss.

To prove his point rightly, Abu Harira submitted his resignation to the Prime Minister. Instead of ordering full investigation about the charges surrounding his government, Prime Minister al-Mahdi chose a different approach the public could not adequately comprehend.

On May 13, 1987 al-Mahdi asked the Head of State Council to relieve all his ministers both the accused and the innocent. The Head of State Council immediately dismissed the ministers. Strangely, al Mahdi continued as a Prime Minister without a cabinet.

Speaking to the pressmen, al-Mahdi admitted and said he was forced to take that step because his ministers were inefficient and there were recurrent accusations and counter accusations labelled against most of his colleagues in the cabinet.

Sadig al-Mahdi had thus evaded the normal practice that once the government had reached a stage where it cannot function as a government, the Head of State relieved the cabinet of their function. The Head of State could thereby ask a new person to put together a new cabinet or asked the outgoing Prime Minister to form a new one. Sadig al-Mahdi was not in a mood to wait for that.

The Prime Minister's action is explicitly outlined by Mansour Khalid. He writes that: 'The Prime Minister had thus refused to own up to his own responsibility as head of that team for the mess the government was in. Nonetheless, the Prime Minister himself descended to a debilitating cycle of recriminations and counter recrimination with his resigning ministry."[20].

Another adverse comment on the Prime Minister Sadig al-Mahdi's disregard to the norms and practices regulating the formation and dissolution of governments came from Peter Kok. He writes: "Barely after a year in office, he (PM) dismissed his cabinet in a presidential manner of a questionable constitutionality and proposed that he wanted a more cohesive and cooperative cabinet."

And a bemused Aldo Ajou, former Cabinet Minister and a close friend of the Prime Minister said: "What was obvious was that the Prime Minister, after one year in office, did neither produce a stable cabinet nor bring peace nearer to an achievable stage."

In addition, Sadig could not even rehabilitate the battered national economy or make available essential commodities badly needed by the people. He did not at least manage to liquidate the May Regime structures and institutions which were the public's number one demand, concluded al-Mahdi's former aide.

7.4. AL MAHDI SECOND COALITION GOVERNMENT

When Premier al-Mahdi was asked by the State Council to put together a new cabinet, the second in one year, he surprisingly brought back all of his previous allegedly discredited ministers whom the Prime Minister himself had admittedly described as corrupt and inefficient. And as Mansour Khalid put it,[21]. "Sadig al-Mahdi's second cabinet was a replica of the one accused of inefficiency and the contradictions...that neither helped the credibility of the

Prime Minster, nor the standing of the government which was publicly lashed by its own chief."

The second challenge to Sadig al-Mahdi's second coalition government was the resignation of his Minister of Foreign Affairs, Mohamed Tawfik (DUP). Following his resignation, Tawfik told the press that the coalition was politically baseless and that any future coalition before agreement on ways and means to resolve the problem facing the nation would be condemned to failure.

In August, a more serious challenge came up; a challenge which was to shake the coalition almost to its foundation. This was the resignation of another (DUP) member in the State Council,Mohamed Hassan Abdalla Yassin.

As natural, the DUP nominated another candidate in the person of Hamed al-Sayed Hamed, a veteran and long standing party cadre. This was logical because the post vacated was a DUP quota according to the charter reached by the two partners as bases to form a coalition in 1986.

But Sadig al-Mahdi resisted the nomination of Hamed al-Sayed Hamed. Sadig al-Mahdi instead nominated a neutral candidate, Mirghani al-Nasri, a former Chairman of Sudan Bar Association to fill the post. Sadig's rejection to the DUP's charismatic candidate and one of the party founding fathers was taken seriously as a violation of the coalition agreement.

Instead of breaking up the coalition or giving a vote of no confidence to al-Mahdi, a move which could have brought the coalition to a quick end, the DUP chose to continue in the government,no longer as an active partner. As Ann M. Lesch put it:

"An executive opposition in the sense that the DUP ministers continued in their offices while at the same times opposing the Umma party government policies. The result of lack of cooperation between the two partners of the coalition paralysed the government's machinery: This result in paralysis was reflected in the absence of any significant movement in search of peace and improvement of international relations."[22].

Regardless to party differences and aware of al-Mahdi's arm-twisting policies aimed at the destruction of their constituencies, the southern parties consisting of SSPA, PPP, SAPCO, SAC, SPFP, SANU and the Nuba Mountain based SNP, in July 1987, united and formed an African Bloc, the Union of the African Parties (USAP). Reverend Philip Abbas Ghaboush became the bloc patron and Eliaba James Surur becoming its Chairman.

Immediately the USAP launched a quest for a peace move. Early in July USAP sent a peace mission to East Africa to discuss the issues pertaining to the attainment of peace in their region. The USAP peace mission, led by its

Chairman Eliaba James Surur, met with the leadership of the SPLA Addis Ababa.

The delegation also met with the former Ethiopian President, Mengistu Haile Mariam, and discussed with him peace in the Sudan. Between July 5-7, 1987, USAP and the SPLM met in Addis Ababa and discussed the positions of the two parties in the ongoing peace process.

In a statement highlighting what was discussed at the Addis Ababa peace forum, USAP and the SPLA/SPLM agreed to support the Koka Dam Declaration; adding that, the two parties would work for its implementation. Similar meetings were held between the SPLM and USAP in Kampala in August 1987 and in Nairobi in September 1987.

In a joint Communiques, the two parties reiterated their commitment to:

1. The convening of the National Constitutional Conference.

2. The holding of a preliminary conference to discuss the modalities of the proposed constitutional conference.

3. Possibility of a declaration of long-term cease-fire.

On July 28, 1987, Prime Minister al-Mahdi issued a statement in which he condemned USAP/SPLM peace dialogues and the peace approach.

In the statement, al-Mahdi accused USAP for discussing and holding meetings with rebels. He described USAP delegates to the peace talks as fifth columnists, and the SPLM traitors.

In response USAP members insisted that by meeting the SPLA/SPLM, they were acting as loyal citizens and patriots, adding that they met the SPLA in order to seek and tackle the central ideological issues that would enable the SPLM to participate in the proposed constitutional conference.

The USAP accused the Prime Minister for his lack of commitment to the Koka Dam Declaration. USAP concluded that it did not have faith in the Prime Minister any longer. Though condemned by Khartoum, SPLM/USAP meetings were described by the East African leaders as watershed and a turning point in the history of Sudan's search for peace operation.

7.5. SPLA CAPTURES KURMUK AND GEISAN

As stated earlier, Sadig al-Mahdi's Government remained seemingly in limbo until the SPLA attacked and occupied two strategic towns in Southern Blue Nile, Kurmuk and Geisan in November 1987.

By occupying Kurmuk and Geissan and a number of other small garrison towns, SPLA intended to achieve two important objectives. First to establish presence in the war zone number II (Northern Sudan) so as to divert the government's attention from the main military theatre of war in zone number I (Southern Sudan). Second, to enlist recruits from this most neglected and marginalised part of the Sudan. They would be trained and sent back to control their area.

The occupation of these strategic towns became very worrying to the government. The SPLA intended to bring the war nearer to its doorstep in Khartoum. It was a challenge that must be countered with vigour. The public was made aware of the impending danger.

In order to confront this ominous challenge, the two of the coalition partners (Umma—DUP), abandoned, albeit temporarily, their previous quarrels that had been the main cause of government instability, to deal adequately with the national problems and embarked on a joint campaign to confront the rebel offensive.

Seizing the opportunity to outshine his archrival, Sadig al-Mahdi, DUP leader, Mohamed Osman al-Mirghani, who had hitherto been passive but watchful about the political developments in the country, went on arms and fundraising missions abroad. His mission took him to Iraq, the Arab Gulf states, Egypt (his traditional backer) and Saudi Arabia.

By the will of Allah, al-Mirghani's Mission to secure arms and funds to come home and defend the Arab land and Islam against an imaginary anti-Arab and anti-Islam ominously from the south was taken seriously. And as his political and spiritual constituency is predominantly in the Arab and Muslim northern part of the Sudan, al-Mirghani was very successful. He obtained both military and financial support from the Muslim brethren for the defence of Arabism and Islam.

The Umma party leader, Sadig al-Mahdi, still breathing fire against the rebel advance into the northern fringes, also went on arms and fund-raising sprees to friendly countries. Though his operations were discreet and well managed, it soon became evident that al-Mahdi too, had obtained funds and arms mainly from Libya, Egypt, and Jordan.

The NIF, the third partner in the coalition, had also seized the opportunity and embarked its anti-south, anti-rebels intensive campaign that surpassed the other two Islamic parties.

In its propaganda campaign 'Himayat al-Aagida wal Watan' ("To protect the faith and the Arab land") became the main slogan which the NIF cadre and its media played up successfully.

Precisely SPLA intention to bring the war to the northern Sudan revealed the really racist and hegemonic attitude of the war by the entire northern elite including even the most non-sectarian groups. Even the Sudan Communist Party and the Alliance for the National Salvation which for the previous three years had played unparalleled diplomacy to convince the south that the hyena had signed a true charter committing itself never again to eat meat, unwittingly joined the campaign.

In short, the SPLA's advance to the northern territories thus intrigued the Arab political north into taking a racial posture against the South. Important lessons were undoubtedly learned. The racist attitude, turning the war into a racist war, the Arab north versus the African south is best described by Peter Kok'[23]. He observes:

"The war was made to sound as if it was a war of independence by beleaguered Arab tribes from African oppressors....Kurmuk and Geissan episodes have precipitated important lessons in the social psychology of the ruling classes in Khartoum and their capacity to use racism and religion for mass mobilisation...in normal times they (northern elite) would declare that the present war was not a racial one but a conflict of socio-economic, cultural and political causes."[24]

Similarly, Mansour Khalid, commenting on the Kurmuk and Gessan episode states: "The political king makers and the moulders of the public opinion in the north, more than anybody else, are the ones to blame for turning genuine regional claims into a racial conflict."

Prime Minister al-Mahdi, who had adamantly been on records that the army was doing its sacred job to defend the country against the rebels in the south showed his frustration about the escalation of the war and its eminent spread to the north.

In an exclusive interview with the author about the war that was becoming increasingly destructive following the fall of Kurmuk and other towns such as Kapoeta, al-Mahdi had this to say [25]:

"We have been telling the people clearly that whoever is behind this war or encouraging it should ponder over the following issues: Does this war aim at dividing the north? It does not. The North is being made more militant by this challenge. If it is not dividing the north, does it unite the south? No, it does not. The south, in fact, was better united behind the Anya-Nya Movement. It is not united behind this present warring party. So, it is therefore dividing the south. Furthermore, is the war stopping the north from developing? Of course, it is not. On the contrary, it has stopped the south from developing: Therefore, is it doing anything for the south? No, it is not, because the southern population is being exterminated by internal wars and by diseases. So what is the sense of continuing with the war that is not achieving any military objective and whose possible end result is to make the north more militant to the point of exterminating the south?"

Two months later the Sudanese army succeeded to retake Kurmuk and Geissan from the SPLA after a fierce fighting. But as the threat that united them earlier had just receded, the traditional political parties picked up once again their old quarrels.

For sometime it appeared as if they would make use of their new—found cooperation and unity of purpose to defeat the rebels or make peace with them.

But as time went on, Sadig al-Mahdi went back on his *hide and seek* approach to politics. He began to court all the political parties both in and outside the government. Earlier that January, some parties in the north, with the NIF excepted, had managed to sign 'The Sudan Transitional Charter of a brief programme of political restructuring of power in the Sudan.

Later, the NIF also signed the Charter after being assured by the Prime Minister that its demand for an Islamic constitution would be considered after two months. The Charter was a joint commitment to multi-party democracy in the Sudan and an autonomy for the south with fair distribution of economic resources and the amendments of the September Laws.

The NIF immediately promised to cooperate and joined the government on the strength of that undertaking. The Islamic overtures of the Charter precipitated the withdrawal and alienation of the African parties.

To many political observers and analysts, this was a lost opportunity. In the sense that all the political forces in the country with their different political colours and orientation both in the north and the south, including the SPLM/A, had agreed on a common agenda; and were all at the verge of reaching a political consensus for the first time on the type of system suitable for the country.

But the NIF' insistence on Islamic constitution, and the Prime Minister remaining embarrassingly ambiguous about his position on Islamic constitution, unfortunately, made the country to squander this slight opportunity. This golden chance was lost, and perhaps, forever.

As the war was escalating in the South day by day, the Prime Minister was busy in futile attempts to consolidate power by attempting to bring all parties, including the NIF, into a 'Government of National Conciliation' which would replace the Umma-DUP Coalition.

Experiences in Sudanese unstable coalitions could have advised the Premier that this was an unattainable dream. Nevertheless, he exerted much effort to this end, which dragged on for months. As Dr. Nyot Kok described: [26] "Sadig al-Mahdi wanted to have the parties in his new government and was therefore prepared to sign (and did sign) various agreements with various political groups." Aldo Ajou Deng, a long time associate to Sadig al-Mahdi, explicitly put it in an interview with the author:

"Sadig, in his effort and great urge to bring all into his government, would meet, for instance, with the NIF leader Dr. Hassan Abdalla al-Turabi, and reached and signed an agreement of understanding with him. But the very time that the Communist leader Mohamed Ibrahim Nugud arrived without prior knowledge of al-Turabi, Sadig would have already thrown al-Turabi's charter into the dustbin and signed another one. So, his meetings with all the party leaders signing and de-signing documents ended up in dustbins."

7.6. AL MAHDI FORMS COALITION WITH NORTHERN PARTIES

Prime Minister Sadig al-Mahdi finally reached his target when he, on May 15, announced the formation of a new government of National Conciliation, the third in less than two years. Except for the USAP parties, Sadig al-Mahdi, indeed, brought in all the parties into his Third Coalition Government.

Alienated by al Mahdi's support of the NIF's Islamic Sharia, all the African parties refused to participate. Eliaba James Surur became the official leader of the opposition.

By a sheer twist of events, the African representation in the central government was conspicuously absent, and this was the second time in a row. The first was when they boycotted the opening session of Parliament described at the beginning of this Chapter. However the Africans had made their point to leave the Arabs alone to form their all-Arab government without the participation of the African members of Parliament.

In his speech launching the opposition, Eliaba James Surur said: "Now thanks to Sadig and the NIF, polarisation is now complete. The north versus south. Arab versus African and Muslim versus Christian."

Perhaps unaware of the unprecedented nature of such a role, Surur told Parliament that the issue of Sharia threatened to divide the Sudan between Christian-African and Arab-Muslim. Surrur added: "...this was not our dream and I hope it would not be the dream of our children. I hope this will not be the beginning of the division of our country."[27]

When the new Third Coalition Government was formed, it brought in, for the first time, the three major parties in Northern Sudan: Umma, DUP, and the NIF. In the new coalition:

1. Sadig al-Mahdi (Umma) maintained his position as Prime Minister;
2. Hussein Suleiman Abu Saleh (DUP'), became Foreign Affairs;

3. General Abdel Majid Hamed Khalil (Independent), Minister of Defence;

4. Abass Abu Shama (Independent) Minister of Interior;

5. Dr Hassan Abdalla al-Turabi (NIF), Attorney General and Minister of Justice;

6. Omar Nur al-Daeim (Umma), Finance and Economic Planning;

7. Mubarak al-Fadil al-Mahdi (Umma) Economy and Trade;

8. Bakri Ahmed Adil (Umma), Energy and Mining;

9. Ali al-Hajj Mohamed (NIF), Internal Trade;

10. Abdel Wahab Osman (NIF) Industry;

11. Al-Fatih al-Tigani (DUP) Agriculture;

12. Beshir Jamma (Umma), Irrigation;

13. Ahmed Abdel Rahman Mohamed (NIF), Social Welfare and Zakat;

14. Saleh Abdel Salam al-Khalifa (Umma), Cabinet Affairs;

15. Al-Sheikh Mahjoub Jaafar (Umma), Education and Scientific Research;

16. Fadhallah Ali (DUP, Public Works and Administrative Reform;

17. Taj al-Sirr Mustafa (NIF), Public Communication;

18. Ismail Abaker (Umma), Animal Resources,

19. Ali Mohamed Shummo (independent), Culture and Information;

20. Joshua Dei Wol (pro Umma SPFP) Youth and Sports;

21. Aldo Ajou Deng (pro Umma SANU) Transport;

22. Richard Makobe (SAPCO) Local Government;

23. Mathew Obur Ayang (al Mahdi's friend) Labour;

In response to the tripartite arrangements of the Third Coalition Government, John Garang, the SPLA leader, ridiculed the Coalition, described it as "Unholy Trinity."

However, the DUP was not happy with the way the Prime Minister distributed the ministerial portfolios. Except for Foreign Affairs portfolio, four senior portfolios occupied by DUP in the previous cabinets: Culture and Information; Interior; Commerce and Trade were taken away.

Seen by many as a Coalition between Umma and the NIF and what the Prime Minister called "co-operative Southern Parties, the DUP found itself marginalised in favour of the NIF in the coalition government.

Finding itself marginalised, though second largest party in the country, and its popularity seemingly shrinking, the DUP made contacts with the SPLA with the aim of talking peace.

The DUP move surprised many. First, DUP has always been very evasive about talking peace, let alone meeting with the rebels.

Second, it did not sign the popularly supported Koka Dam Declaration nor did it attempt to make any peace initiative since the overthrow of President Nimeiri's autocratic rule in 1985.

Nevertheless, DUP contacts with the SPLA, for the time being, were very discreet and confined to a few close allies to the spiritual leader Mohamed Uthman al-Mirghani. The initial contacts were apparently aimed at preparing the possible grounds whereby the SPLA leader could meet al-Mirghani personally. Peter Nyot Kok[28] observed: "al-Mirghani or DUP contacts with the SPLA was very surprising because the DUP with its Pan-Arabist sectarian orientation and its strong support from the merchant class has been and still is an enemy of the Southern Sudanese nationalism."

Meanwhile, Hassan al-Turabi, in his capacity as the Attorney General and Minister of Justice, had submitted the Draft Constitution of the Substitute Laws in July 1988. In essence, the revised laws were the same September Laws of 1983 only painted to appear new and for a new political environment.

Al-Turabi's Draft Constitution of the Substitute Laws was criticised and attacked by Abdallah al-Hassan, the Chairman of the Sudan Bar Association, who challenged the constitutionality of the law as the law of the land. The Bar Chairman argued that the Draft laws were illegal and repugnant to the principles of legislation within the unitary state. The Chairman of the Council for the South Angelo Beda expressed similar opinion. He said: "...the laws made the separation of the south a foregone conclusion." The leader of the opposition, Eliaba James Surur, added: "'...if those laws were passed, Sudan shall be divided. God saves my country, the Sudan."

Mohamed Uthman al-Mirghani, the DUP patron, described Turabi's stance as "a venture of play on the emotions of the Muslims."

However on the surface, it might have appeared that the members opposed to Umma and the NIF were the only ones appalled by the Draft Constitution of Substitute Laws. Rather a great majority of opponents were also within the Umma Party who opposed the laws right at the initial stage.

Realising that the Prime Minister was tacitly behind the al-Turabi's Substitute Laws, Professor Mohamed Ibrahim Khalil, the Speaker of Parliament, came out openly against the 'Alternative Laws' and the inclusion of the NIF in the Third Coalition Government.

Without delay, Professor Khalil, who had for years been the closest friend of Sadig al-Mahdi and, a well-respected lawyer and educator, tendered in his resignation. As if that was what the Prime Minister had wanted, the post vacated by Professor Khalil was immediately allocated to NIF cadre.

Commenting on al-Mahdi's gambit and behaviour during this imbroglio, Professor Khalil told the press that: "the Umma Party was suffering from both lack of democracy and leadership."

Mansour Khalid[29] writes: "...what was also not self-evident to the Prime

Minister was that in less than two years, he had squandered all his political assets; if his closest supporters could no longer suffer gladly, why should he expect the rest of humanity to do so?"

However, for all intents and purposes, it appeared that Sadig al-Mahdi was in favour of the Sharia Laws. But as a democrat he wanted to blackmail all the Sudanese into accepting the Sharia Laws.

Perhaps this was one reason why he advocated for a Government of Conciliation. There is no doubt that this statement bears credence when viewing the Prime Minister's reply to this author in an interview about the difficulties in scrapping the Sharia Laws. Sadig al-Mahdi stated[30]:

"The most difficult thing has been that the September Laws were forced on the Sudanese people in a very high handed and repulsive way. However, despite the controversies over these laws, they have raised some additional issues for us in authority. These issues are: do we implement the Sharia or don't we? If we do, what about the non-Muslims? Would the Sharia guarantee one citizenship for all? Such are the issues Sharia has failed to address itself. As this government is concerned, it's committed to the repeal of these laws. But again, if we repeal the Sharia, it also raises the issue of what to do with the Muslims who want to have Sharia and what

to do with the non-Muslims who are opposed to the Sharia? This has been the main problem in the scrapping of the Sharia and which we have been trying to tackle."

7.7. EFFECTS AND IMPACT OF DUP—SPLM PEACE INITIATIVE

In November 1988, the DUP delegation, led by Mohamed Uthman al-Mirghani—its patron and spiritual leader of the Khatmiyya Sect—left for Addis Ababa to meet with the SPLM/A leadership to discuss the possibilities of holding a peace conference. This was in fulfilment of DUP's interest to search for peace in the country, Sid Ahmed Hussein told the author.

The DUP-SPLM meeting in Addis Ababa, a courageous effort indeed, nonetheless discussed many issues pertaining to Sudan's political instability. On November 16, 1988, the two parties issued a joint communique that became known as the 'Addis Ababa Sudan Peace Initiative' and which was to shake the liberal democracy to its foundation as discussed below.

However, the communique outlined the positions of the SPLM and the DUP in regard to the Koka Dam Declaration and particularly the Sharia Laws and the holding of National Constitutional Conference. The highlights of the Communique were:

1. The temporary cessation of hostilities.

2. The lifting of the state of emergency that had been in force since 1983 and setting up working groups to prepare the country for the convening of the National Constitutional Conference which the two parties had agreed tentatively to take place at the end of the year.

3. The abrogation of military defence pacts the two parties considered impinging on the Sudanese national sovereignty.

4. The freezing of Islamic Sharia Law.

This concession by the DUP to freeze the Sharia Laws was a remarkable achievement in the Sudan Peace Initiative as it showed and proved how serious DUP was.

The DUP, in its roots from the Khatmiyya Sect, is deeply rooted in Islamic tradition. Thus removing Islamic Sharia from the Sudanese laws meant that the Sudan was going to revert to a secular constitution—the major demand for the rebels and a fundamental threshold for pluralism in a unitary state.

Upon his arrival at Khartoum Airport on November 24, al-Mirghani received an outpouring heroic welcome by citizens from the three cities of Khartoum, Khartoum North and Omdurman. He was seen as the Apostle of Peace.

Placing carefully the accord within the context of his party and his Khatmiyya Sect, al-Mirghani stated:

> "Sudan embraces differing views and different nationalities, but all people must live in amity and peace. The majority must have its status in matters affecting it but without making an impact on the rights of the minorities. This will lead us to a long debate and a great deal of arguments at the national constitutional conference but in the end we believe in the democratic practice we shall be able to build a modern Sudan." (Lesch 1998).

The SPLA Radio, (The Voice of the Revolutionary Armed Struggle), addressed the Umma and NIF leadership calling directly on Sadig al-Mahdi and al-Turabi to: "Shift from the high gear of intransigence and war hysteria to the low gear of tolerance and peace."

The Umma and NIF felt overtaken by DUP-SPLM's peace gesture. How were they to react to this peace agreement which was of paramount importance to the nation? The reaction was silent for the time being.

Meanwhile, the Alliance for National Salvation that had been party to the Koka Dam Declaration immediately endorsed the Al-Mirghani peace gesture.

General Abdel Majid Hamid Khalil, the Minister of Defence, issued a statement expressing that the Sudanese Army was behind the DUP-SPLM peace initiative. The Council of Ministers subsequently also endorsed this peace initiative.

But the Prime Minister remained unconvinced whether to endorse it himself or not. Nonetheless, he summoned Parliament and asked if it could grant him a mandate to launch his own peace or support the DUP-SPLM initiative. He also made it clear that the NIF should also support the peace initiative.

In a meeting with al-Mirghani, who called upon him to brief him about his mission, Sadig al-Mahdi attempted to convince him to abandon his peace initiative, as [John] Garang was not to be trusted. Al-Mirghani, however, resisted such an attempt and he made his view public in the press.

Al-Mahdi felt that he had been sidelined by this peace initiative, especially as the peace initiative was getting more popular among Sudanese people. But how could he react? He must give himself time to plan if he has to outwit the rest.

The NIF outrightly condemned the Mirghani-Garang peace initiative as a hostile surrender against the Arab-Islamic character of the Sudan. It veritably regarded the freezing of the Sharia Laws as unacceptable. The NIF leadership called upon its followers in the army, among the students and working forces, to oppose the Mirghani venture. It also urged for the intensification of the war and to defeat the rebels.

When the Southern Sudanese went to the streets to express their support for the peace process and the Migrhani-Garang truce, they were confronted violently by agitated NIF supporters.

This politically charged environment forced al-Mahdi to make a clear choice: whether to follow and support the national consensus for peace or the Umma-NIF aligning as anti-peace. He chose the later.

In December, the Prime Minister decided and took the peace initiative before Parliament to have it hopefully, killed democratically.

The Sharia became the centre-stage issue provoking religious sentiments, while the war raging in the country only took a fragment of the government's business as the economy continued to spiral in its downward plunge destined for total ruin.

It was obvious to all that the government was no longer an administration comprising and influenced by a multi-faceted coalition. It appeared like a dominion controlled by a duumvirate Sadig al-Mahdi. [31]

As expected, the highly agitated Umma-NIF dominated Parliament failed to endorse the DUP-SPLM peace initiative. During the session, the Umma-NIF members blocked the DUP motion for peace.

Subsequently, finding itself outnumbered and outvoted in the Council of

Ministers and in Parliament, the DUP pulled out of the Coalition Government on December 28, 1988. The Third Coalition Government had fallen apart.

At the threshold of the rarest opportunity for peacemaking, it was clear that the Sudan lacked leaders with Nehru's or Nelson Mandela's statesmanship.

7.8. THE UMMA-NIF COALITION GOVERNMENT

Following the DUP pull out, the Umma and NIF pulled together and formed a Coalition Government, the fourth in three years of indecision and head on wrong policies. In the new coalition government, ministerial portfolios distributed as follows: Sadig al-Mahdi, (Umma) Prime Minister; Dr. Hassan al-Turabi, (NIF) Deputy Prime Minister and Foreign Affairs Minister. The NIF also took other significant ministries including Attorney General, Internal Trade, Industry, Health and Social Affairs and Zakat. The rest went to Umma members.

Upon being sworn into office, Hassan al-Turabi stated that the DUP-SPLM 1988 accord was no longer a relevant issue to bother about. He instead appealed to the armed forces to intensify military offensive against the rebels in the Southern Sudan. He renewed his insistence on the application of comprehensive Islamic laws, the so-called 'alternative laws.'

By the beginning of the New Year, it became abundantly clear that if peace was not achieved, things might go out of hand in favour of another military adventurer taking over the reins of power in the country. It almost became a possibility, particularly when the country's political parties were aligned into two main camps; each threatening to outwit the other into accepting its position.

In the event, Parliament was divided into two camps. On the one side was the NIF vehemently opposing the DUP-SPLM peace initiative and thereby favouring the re-introduction of the Islamic laws by the incumbent Parliament.

On the other side hung the majority of DUP, (Umma wavering), SCP, The Alliance and Trade Unionists, the African parties, and the military. These groups favoured the DUP-SPLM peace initiative and the Convening of the National Conference that would finally decide on the fate of Sharia which had become the main issue blocking the termination of war.

Meanwhile, some Sudanese intellectuals—mostly university scholars and USAP members—had gone to Ethiopia and held a symposium with the SPLM at Ambo village on February 9, 1989. It was too obvious then that two things might happen. The military would make a coup against the Umma-NIF coalition or the nation would go to the polls sooner than later to have new parliament with a new mandate to face a seemingly insurmountable issue of war or peace.

The aim of the Ambo symposium was an attempt to rescue the DUP-SPLM peace initiative, said Dr. Taiseer Mohamed Ahmed in an interview with the author. Ambo's encounter succeeded to come up with a number of important resolutions:

1. Reaffirmation of their commitment to the DUP-SPLM Sudan Peace Initiative.

2. Urging all democratic forces to unite and bring about the government of national salvation to be composed mainly of all the political forces committed to peace.

3. The future government should include the SPLM.

Reaction from Khartoum to the Ambo symposium and its resolutions was violent. The Prime Minister condemned the Ambo Encounter claiming that it was tantamount to a revolution.

Upon their arrival in Khartoum, the delegates to Ambo were detained at the airport, subjecting them to embarrassing interrogations by the National Security.

As the Umma-NIF government was struggling to re-impose the Sharia, the SPLA was intensifying the war in the South. On January 11, 1989 SPLA took Kapoeta town enabling it to control the border zones from Ethiopia-Kenya-Uganda borders.

On January 26, the SPLA took Nasir and later in February, the strategic town of Torit. A string of smaller army posts were either overrun by the SPLA or demoralised and evacuated before the SPLA arrival—thus bringing the entire east Nile under the SPLA control. This latest SPLA offensive frightened the government and al-Mahdi in particular.

7.9. MILITARY SENDS ULTIMATUM TO PRIME MINISTER AL MAHDI

Responding to the SPLA offensive in February 1989, the military sent a memorandum to the Prime Minister. The memo, which was signed by 300 officers of different ranks, contained the following demands. That Prime Minister should:

1. Reorganise a genuinely broad-based government.

2. Make a drastic reappraisal of his foreign policy.

3. Supply the army with modern weaponry to fight the SPLA.

4. End hostilities in the south.

Earlier on, the Prime Minister had received a letter from the Military High Command in the south requesting that the government should support the DUP-SPLM peace initiative.

With the war escalating in every front, and threatening Juba, the southern capital city, al-Mahdi's Fourth Coalition Government began to lose both moral and political support. Signs of the government's collapse were visible. To make things worse still, General Abdel Majid Hamed Khalil resigned in February.

Before tendering his resignation, General Khalil had some hard times in efforts to convince the Prime Minister to consider resolving a number of important issues he considered were of paramount importance. These were: either the Prime Minister strengthens the army to fight effectively enough and confront the rebels in the battlefronts, or alternatively accept the peace initiative.

General Khalil had requested that the tribal militia be brought directly under direct control of the National Army. General Khalil was opposed to the use of tribal militias as part of the popular defence force. But these seemed to have led to confrontation between the General and the Prime Minister.

In addition, al-Mahdi had brought in his Ansar supporters to positions of authority both in the army and national security apparatus, like his cousin Babo Nimr, the son of the Chief of Baggara Arab tribes of Kordofan. The Chief was well known for his close links with the Mahdi family.

Nevertheless what is important to note at this juncture is that the memorandum to the Prime Minister by army officers squarely put blame upon the government for a series of failures to confront the rebels. The memo finally pressed on the Prime Minister to implement steps necessary for the convening of the National Constitutional Conference.

Prime Minister al-Mahdi, aware of the mounting pressure exerted by the military and from all directions of the national spectrum, and realising that the whole nation was in dire need for peace, he dissolved his Fourth Coalition Government in March 1989. He enticed DUP to join Umma in order to form another coalition government.

By all accounts it became abundantly clear that al-Mahdi had proved the most inept politician, lacking the flexibility and manoeuvrability of Nimeiri; and above all, the statesmanship needed to hold a pluralistic society together.

7.10. THE THIRD DEMOCRATIC EXPERIMENT AND PROSPECTS FOR PEACE

The new coalition government, the fifth and the last government in the three years of the 'Third Democratic Experiment,' was duly formed under a great deal of uncertainty. All the pro-peace parties—the DUP, African parties, the Alliance and Trade Unionists, and the Communist Party—joined with Umma and formed the government with the aim to implement the DUP/SPLM Peace package.

During the formation of the new government, Sid Ahmed Hussein, DUP strong man and negotiator in the DUP-SPLM peace initiative, was granted the portfolio of a Foreign Minister. Hussein immediately placed peace on the top of the new government's agenda. He made final arrangements for the convening of the National Constitutional Conference, which meant he would have to go back and meet with the SPLM about the modalities of the National Conference.

On April 3, 1989, the Parliament sat and endorsed the DUP-SPLM Peace Initiative. The nation was poised for peace.

After the Parliament's endorsement of the peace initiative, the government began to take legal procedures to remove the stumbling blocks on the road to peace. These include Cancellation of the Defence Pacts with Egypt (1976) and Libya (1985). The Parliament was also asked to shelve the entire debate on Islamic Laws until such a time that the question of religious versus secular constitutions are tackled and resolved. The latter was expected to be resolved in the proposed National Constitution Conference.

The SPLM welcomed the Parliamentary decisions but pointed out that Parliament should go a long way to freeze Sharia penal codes 'Hudud' since the September Laws and Decrees were still in the country's statute books. The SPLM needed assurance and guarantees in the sense that no similar laws would be passed before the proposed National Constitutional Conference.

On May 1, 1989, as a matter of goodwill, the SPLM/SPLA Politico-Military High Command declared a one-month cease-fire during the Islamic holy month of *Ramadan*. SPLM also made it known that it was willing to extend the cease-fire beyond June to enable the compilation for the necessary preparations for the holding of the proposed Conference and dialogue.

On May 14, peace talks were held in Addis Ababa between the government delegation and the SPLM representatives. The next round of talks was held on June 9. They were further adjourned to reconvene on July 4, 1989.

At the June meeting, the government and the SPLM Representatives agreed that, if all went well in the July meeting, the National Constitutional Conference could convene on September 18, 1989. This was conditional only if all the modalities were completed before that time.

During the interim period preceding the Conference day, it was expected that the government of Sudan would show its own gesture for peace by freezing the September Laws and annul all the military pacts with other foreign countries as stated earlier. This was expected to pave the way for a formal meeting between Prime Minister Sadig al-Mahdi and Colonel John Garang, Leader of the SPLM/SPLA before the National Constitutional Conference was due to convene ceremoniously blessed by both sides.

Unfortunately, these hopeful signs for resolving the Sudanese conflict were overtaken by many intervening factors including the National Islamic Front (NIF) *coup d'etat* described here below.

7.11. THE ISLAMISTS SEIZE POWER IN A MILITARY COUP D'ETAT

Following the dissolution of the Fourth Coalition Government in March 1989, the NIF was left out and thrown into the opposition. Ali Osman Mohamed Taha, the NIF's strongman, became leader of the Opposition.

As discussed, the NIF was strongly opposed to the kind of society which the SPLM espoused i.e. the creation and establishment of a non-racial, non-religious, and non-ethnic system of government in which all diverse Sudanese people would undoubtedly have equal opportunities and rights at all levels in the national life.

The SPLM/SPLA demand to create a pluralistic society in the Sudan was just simply unacceptable to the NIF. In the event it tirelessly worked to frustrate any progress towards attaining such a society.

The NIF argued that a secular and pluralistic polity would compromise the vital interests of the Arabs and Muslims in the Sudan.

As the Nation was seeking peaceful ways out towards the National Constitutional Conference, the NIF was campaigning for the intensification of the war. It also attempted to win all the different political forces in the north to see the looming danger posed by Africans against the Arab race in the Sudan.

For three consecutive months, the leader of the Opposition Ali Osman Mohamed Taha, with his team of die hard Islamists, campaigned vigorously to rally the north behind the NIF as the sole force that was fighting for the realisation of their vested interest—To keep the Sudan an Arab-Muslim nation.

Threatening rumours of coups and counter coups followed NIF rhetoric and appeal. These rumours were cited to have originated from the supporters of the former Sudanese dictator, General Jaafar Mohamed Nimeiri, who was then in exile in Egypt. At other times, it was rumoured that it was being orchestrated by the NIF cadres in the Army.

As part of the campaign to rally the north behind the NIF, and as leader of the opposition, Taha, went on a marathon tour of South Sudan. During his tour he was reported to have met and discussed problems of war and peace with the officers and men of the Sudan Armed Forces at their various units and garrisons stationed in the South Sudan.

Ali Osman was also reported to have donated large sums of money to the army personnel there. Not only that, Taha was said to have made emotional appeal to the soldiers who, according to him, "bore the brunt of the war casualties in the south."

Undoubtedly referring to the generals who signed the February Memo to the PM, Taha warned the junior officers to distance themselves from the secularist generals. Taha accused the 300 officers who signed the Memorandum as having refused to condemn the SPLA's slow response to peaceful negotiations within the context of national interest.

Throughout the Third Democratic Experiment period (1986-89), NIF had been at work infiltrating institutions of the state including military, trade unions, teachers, workers, farmers, banking and other financial institutions[32].

Foremost, the NIF infiltrated the students unions at different levels of education with a neo-fundamentalist missionary zeal. The NIF's recruitment message to every group was clear and convincing. The message states that reaching a political settlement with the southern rebels in accordance to the DUP-SPLM peace initiative of November 1988 would mean surrendering the Arab-Muslim political and economic hegemony. The expected compromise would also allow the two major parties (DUP and Umma) to reassert their political strength and ascendancy, thereby becoming the largest and most popular parties at the expense of the NIF.

The NIF realised that it would be relegated to an insignificant minority party in the post war Sudan had acted fast and pre-empted such danger. As a party it decided to fight tooth and nail to protect what it regarded as 'Arab-Muslim' interests. Basically, the NIF success in its campaign from March through to June was attributed much to its well-coached and informed crusading political cadres in the Media.

For instance, after the signing of the DUP-SPLM peace initiative, the NIF newspapers *Al-Raya, Alwan*, and *Al-Sudani* were the first to condemn it, calling it the 'Surrender Accord.'

The NIF Media interpreted John Garang's 'equality of justice' based on a secular system of government as a direct attempt to dilute the Arab-Muslim cultural identity in the country. The North, the NIF Media men insisted, must not take a junior position in the country and be dominated by Africans.

Other NIF cadres joining the Media Campaign also picked it up with rare zeal and vigour and the message was driven home.

By March 1989, the NIF had comfortably established itself as the Principal carrier of the Arab-Muslim nationalism and the 'Lord Protector' of Islam and Arab land in the Sudan.

Earlier in February, just before the Fourth Coalition Government collapsed, the NIF had flexed its muscle and a staged a test of strength and demonstrated against the peace initiative.

Demonstrations were organised in all the trio-metropolitan Omdurman, Khartoum, and Khartoum North against the government's ban, regarding demonstrations.

The Pro-Peace Parties groups—Umma, DUP, USAP and Communists— told their supporters not to join the NIF inspired propaganda.

Despite this, the Islamist demonstration against the peace initiative attracted thousands into the streets, the case which lent credence to the NIF's quick manufacture of populist leadership as the party standing for the vital interests of Arab-Muslim interests in the Sudan.

Fearing that the NIF was about to take over power, at least through a popular uprising or a military take over, the coalition partners rallied and pulled their ranks together.

On June 29, 1989, a Committee to prepare a Draft Legislation to freeze the Islamic Sharia Laws and rescind Defence Pacts with other foreign countries was set.

Sid Ahmed Hussein, as the government's negotiator, was expected to lead the peace delegation to Addis Ababa on July 4, carrying the Parliament's Acts of freezing the Sharia and the rescind of Defence Pacts to the peace talks. Hussein was also expected to put the last few touches to the modalities of reconvening of the National Constitutional Conference in September 1989 with the SPLM/SPLA.

As the whole nation was on the vigil as peace was just around the corner, unfortunately all the tables for peace were upside down. On the morning of June 30, 1989, The Islamist troops from the Army General Command Headquarters in Khartoum, supported by a tank unit from Shajera Armour Unit and a number of civilians in military uniforms, occupied the Army Headquarters, the Airport and Omdurman Radio Station.

With striking success, the Islamists had seized power in a bloodless coup. Later in the day, Brigadier Omar Hassan Ahmed al-Bashir announced that the Army had taken over power in the country.

As to why the Islamists rejected the peace overture and took over power instead, how they did it, and whether they would easily relinquish power through democratic processes or remain as the country most powerful party, are questions we will attempt to answer in the subsequent chapters.

Suffice it to say that the NIF's coup, the third military takeover since independence set a long and windy journey in the most difficult period in the Sudanese history whose ultimate end is yet a matter of one guessing.

CHAPTER 8
SPLA BRIGHT STAR CAMPAIGN TAKES FIRM GRIP ON THE SOUTH

8.0. THE SETTING

In this Chapter, attempts will be made to discuss the contradictions and disenchantment in the SPLA leadership and how these contradictions adversely hampered the progress of the Movement in order to realise its desired goals within the given span of time.

We will also survey other issues, such as attempts to restructure the SPLA Military High Command, a move that was aimed at easing the stumbling blocks and difficulties in order to enable the Movement to proceed adequately with the military campaign.

Perhaps the Politico-Military High Command composition was probably the source of SPLA political troubles which finally resulted in its split on August 28, 1991. Whether the split was a result of the power struggle or brought about by external forces is nevertheless a matter of controversy.

8.1. INTERNAL CONTRADICTIONS AND DISENCHANTMENT IN THE SPLA LEADERSHIP

While the SPLA exhibited triumph militarily, it was soon evident that its constituents and cadres were composed of incongruous, unmatchable, and uncompromising groups. On the one hand were the Socialists.

This group was composed of people who wanted to use the socialist ideology for their own ends and the people who had been in close association with the Sudan Communist Party or through their early connection with the Southern Communist leader, late Joseph Ukel Garang, executed in July 1971.

Having embraced Socialist orientation, these groups were among the first to go to Ethiopia for recruitment at the time when the SPLA/SPLM was launched. Many of them were trained and absorbed as officers and were given strategic positions in the Movement's hierarchy.

Among the early trained commissioned officers were Chol Deng Alak and Amon Mon Wantok. Deng Alak was appointed Commander of the Military Training Centre at Bonga, and Amon Wantok, the over all commander of the Main Refugee Camp at Itang.

The two officers and others of their kind, instead of giving the recruits military training and political orientation as assigned to them by the Movement, got involved in efforts to implement the Marxist-Leninist dialectics[1].

Thus instead of the Movement benefiting from the Socialist democratic orientation, the officers imposed stringent training aimed at turning the recruits overnight into Communist cadres. Reportedly many of the recruits resisted some of the 'culturally loaded' Communist ways.

Opposed to the socialist camp was the second group, the anti-Arab group, quite disenchanted and very angry against the Arab domination of the political life in the Sudan. This was the bulk of the recruits, the majority of whom were extracted from numerous Ethiopian border camps where the Southern Sudanese refugees had taken refuge. It was also a mixed group, comprising of peasants, workers, and former government officials who had held various positions during the defunct Regional Administration.

For the second group, what was paramount was how and where to acquire weapons and military skills to take back and liberate South Sudan. They had no interest in Communism or Socialist ideology nor did they need to be in any way oriented to it.

However, the SPLM/SPLA manifesto was accepted by all as a matter of strategy. The socialist ideology was only regarded as a matter of tactics in order to obtain support, but not anything that they would import into South Sudan.

This may probably explain why abuses and torture meted by some pseudo-Socialist cadres (as the recruits used to call them) in the SPLA did not prevent the SPLA from executing military campaigns with a rare zeal.

For some time, the SPLA string of victories between 1983 and 1985 was able to shield hordes of difficulties experienced by the bulk of men in the army. The abuses, especially by the zone commanders in their respective areas, started to mature with the passage of time as habitual modalities of administration.

Reported allegations by sources who claimed they were eye witnesses suggest that some commanders behaved as though the soldiers were their serfs, and they, the self-styled lords in their own serfdom.

At their distant localities of control, these commanders would allegedly exercise rough justice: punishing, persecuting, and executing some of their own soldiers charged with petty crimes such as acts of insubordination, defection to other garrisons and staying back at their villages longer than the time allowed. Such cases were frequently reportedly mushrooming at different times and stages.

In one classical example, it was alleged that Kerubino Bol, the Deputy Commander-in-Chief, while visiting the General Headquarters at Bilpam Camp, ordered the execution of a group of eight detained recruits waiting for confirmation of their sentences, sentences ranging from six months to a few years imprisonment.

A similar episode was the alleged report that Commander Arok Thon Arok, a member of the High Command and Zone Commander of Southern Upper Nile, ordered the execution of the leaders of an SPLA company. Their crime, according to report, was an alleged attempt to escape to their homeland in Bahr al-Ghazal to protect their people from the Arab Murhaleen perennial threats.

According to reports, there was no legal way to prove the intention of those men, nor was their case referred to the General Headquarters where the 'Court Martial' would have been able to try them as their crimes were allegedly of military nature[2].

A further allegation was brought against Dr. Lam Akol Ajawin, an Alternate Member of Politico-Military High Command, and the Zonal Commander of Northern Upper Nile. Dr. Akol was reported to have been involved in the execution of seven Shilluk soldiers under his command. The alleged crime was an attempted 'mutiny.' These allegations were not investigated [3].

Whereas the SPLA disciplinary and penal code of laws of 1984 provided for remedies against such crimes, some senior SPLA officers did not consult such a law and oft were law givers and executors. Such behaviour by senior SPLA officers was bound to cast a dark shadow on the Movement, especially the kind of state they were going to construct once war was over.

It was apparently in this light that some Officers who disapproved of such behaviour in the Movement later emerged and came up with a political programme which they started debating at Itang Main Refugee Camp. In due course, voices demanding reorganisation and restructuring of the SPLM/SPLA began to be audible.

According to Dr. Peter Adwok Nyaba, "...the discussions and the debates attracted many intellectuals and officers of the SPLA. Some of them began to agitate for a genuine realisation of justice and equality of all the members of the Movement. That agitation led in the end to the arrest and subsequent detention of many of the progressive officers who overplayed it.

However, despite internal contradictions in the Movement hierarchy, and regardless to the agitation and awareness it created among the rank and file, many in the SPLA were convinced that taking the war to its logical conclusion should take paramount importance than many of the difficulties confronting them. It will only be then that many of the atrocities committed in the name of liberation would be resolved. In the meantime, all people should continue with their revolutionary struggle with resolve, unperturbed and undeterred. Dr. Nyaba observes:

"There were so many incidents and contradictions that would have caused splits, and worse still, bloody confrontation like what happened in August 1991 when three commanders revolted; a move that led to the deaths of hundreds of thousands of innocent people. The SPLM-SPLA internal cohesion, Nyaba stressed, was stronger not because of political and ideological awareness, but rather because the contradictions between the south and the north of Sudan was stronger than the internal contradictions."

What plagued the SPLA was that, while it was at work trying to tighten the noose around the successive governments in Khartoum, it received many signals suggesting that a power struggle in the High Command was inevitable. These came in forms of secrets that in the end became the core of disenchantment inside the Movement. [4]

The first of these signs was publicly noticed when in 1984, Commander Kerubino Bol drew his pistol and threatened to kill Dr. John Garang. His charge was that Dr. Garang had refused to include some of the non-commissioned officers (who he had recommended) in the list of those to be promoted to the rank of officers. The scuffle was quickly resolved and put aside, but not totally forgotten [5].

The second was the rumour which emanated from Khartoum that Dr. Lam Akol Ajawin, the zonal commander of Northern Upper Nile and the Alternate Member of the Politico-Military High Command, had shot and seriously wounded Dr. John Garang de Mabior, the SPLM/SPLA Chairman and Commander-In-Chief. It was further reported that Dr. Garang was flown to the Republic of Romania for an emergency operation. When this rumour began to die down, another one surfaced.

Sources pointed also at Khartoum orchestrated bluff that Dr. Garang had arrested and detained Dr. Lam Akol on the charge that he had criticised the Movement, calling it 'a one man show.'

Although the majority of the people inside the country dismissed the rumours as the usual enemy propaganda ploy, they continued to haunt the Southern Sudanese public opinion to an extent that a sizeable number accepted the rumours at face value as truth.

Some justified that Dr. Lam Akol was not such a person, a character to accept a junior position for long. The group cited that Dr. Lam Akol was instrumental in the split of the Southern Sudanese political caucus in 1985 when Southern Sudanese young and old guard politicians wanted to launch one southern political party following the fall of Nimeiri in 1985.

It was alluded that the influence of Dr. Akol on the youth led to the formation of two political Parties for the south. Whereas the old politicians congregated around the Southern Sudan Political Association (SSPA), an amalgam of the defunct Southern Front and the Sudan African National Union (SANU) Parties, the new breed of politicians and academics joined the Southerners in Khartoum (SSK), which later became Sudan Africa Congress (SAC).

This reconstruction of Dr. Akol's past was dismissed by many as devoid of any rationality. How and why should have Dr. Akol, a nationalist who had been in the liberation Movement for just only six months, start to differ with the leadership to the extent of shooting Dr. Garang, the leader of the Movement?

While this rumour was not easily comprehended at home and abroad, it became more disturbing because it coincided with John Garang's long silence and absence from the scene. That absence added credibility to the stories in circulation that there is always 'no smoke without fire.'

To clear the smoke, the author as the Editor of the **Heritage Newspaper** in Khartoum flew to Ethiopia and sought truth of the rumour from Dr. Lam Akol[5,] who incidentally was in Addis Ababa.

In an exclusive interview, Dr. Akol dismissed the rumour with rare sarcasm and spite. He stated: "It is not surprising because many leaders who posed threats to entrenched dictatorships have often been claimed to have died and risen many times...so I pooh-poohed the rumour and just went on with my revolutionary work."

On the allegations that he was arrested and detained for describing the Movement as a 'one man show,' Dr. Akol stated: "If the SPLM/SPLA has been a one man show, it would have not achieved what it had achieved so far.

In a matter of three years (1983-86), the SPLM/SPLA had asserted its grip on the country. It now controls about 90 percent of war zone number one (south Sudan) and some areas of War Zone number two (northern Sudan). "Even now," Dr Akol added "the government of Sudan and its media propaganda is not talking about the SPLM/SPLA as a one man show, but many men show [6]."

However, the rumour continued to hang on in the air until Dr. Garang personally appeared at a press conference at the Hotel Intercontinental, Nairobi, in September 1987.

Addressing the press, Dr. Garang amused the conferees when he jokingly stated;" I have just resurrected from the grave in the bushes of the South Sudan in order to come and deny my death."

The SPLM/SPLA leader accused the government of Sadig al-Mahdi for concocting the rumour in order to divert the Sudanese public attention away from the demise of his ancient regime. "The rumour was intended as a disinformation and propaganda ploy," Garang concluded.

8.2.1. SPLA DRAWS UP NEW MILITARY STRUCTURES AND STRATEGIES

Despite the disenchantment in the SPLM/SPLA leadership and a hoard of rumours attached to it discussed above, the High Command convened a meeting in Gambela in March 1987. The meeting was attended by the five permanent members of the PMHC—Dr. John Garang Commander Kerubino Kwanyin Bol, Commander William Nyuon Bany, and Commander Salva Kiir. It passed a number of resolutions. These were:

1. The creation of five military axes charged with the responsibilities to plan strategies which were to achieve certain strategic objectives.

2. Creation of independent military commands in War Zones I and II, the purpose of which was for each of the commands to pursue specific objectives and to implement those objectives for a successful execution of the war. Emphasis was placed on the fact that guerrilla activities are to be stepped up in areas where the SPLA has lightweight presence and otherwise conventional war tactics and operations should be applied.

3. The creation of alternate members of the High Command to enable the Movement benefit from a range of experienced and professional officers who have just joined the Movement, some of whom had been members of the underground movement for many years.

It was therefore resolved that in order to rectify the shortcomings both at the High Command and Field Command Levels, positions of alternate members must be created. Also the movement should benefit from the intellectuals and academics who had just joined the Movement.

After the meeting, Dr. Garang asked each of the four permanent members to make a list of people they thought could fill the posts created in the High Command. But when the final list of the new alternate members was announced, it did not contain the nominees presented by Commanders William Nyuon Bany and Kerubino Kwanyin Bol.

According to reports, the lists presented by Nyuon and Kerubino contained only non-commissioned officers, mostly sergeants and corporals.

In the opinion of the two commanders, the High Command should contain NCOs as it was in the Ethiopian Provisional Military Committee, the then ruling Military Council of the Ethiopian Revolution or the Derg,

Commander Kerubino was reportedly terribly hurt and told Nyuon that Garang was trying to fill the High Command with the so-called 'intellectuals,' the intention of which was to get rid of us (Kerubino and Nyuon) who were the founding fathers of the People's Revolutionary Movement. Kerubino Kwanyin Bol was particularly angry for the inclusion of Dr. Lam Akol Ajawin, James Wani Igga, and Yousif Kuwa Mekki who were still new comers then. Kwanyin argued that better put NCOs in the High Command than intellectuals with little experience and training in the art of war[7].

He may certainly have been correct in that he saw the High Command as purely military. Perhaps the conflict was really about the mixing of military with the political in the High Command, and which would have required the separation of the two.

However, the rejection of William Nyuon and Kerubino Kwanyin Bol's lists created a sufficient tension in the High Command, a tension that could have possibly led to the break up of the Movement. But with persuasion of Nyuon, Kerubino backed down and the following appointments were enacted in a new structure[8].

8.2.2. SPLA/SPLM POLITICO-MILITARY HIGH COMMAND

A. PERMANENT MEMBERS:

1. Colonel Dr. John Garang de Mabior, Chairman and Commander-in-Chief

2. Kerubino Kwanyin Bol, Deputy Chairman and Deputy Commander-in-Chief

3. William Nyuon Bany, Chief of General Staff

4. Arok Thon Arok, Deputy Chief of General Staff for Logistics and Administration

5. Salva Kiir Mayardit, Deputy Chief of General Staff for Security and Operations

B. ALTERNATE MEMBERS:

1. Commander James Wani Igga

2. Commander Martin Manyiel Ayuel

3. Commander Riek Machar Teny Dhurgon

4. Commander Dr. Lam Akol Ajawin

5. Commander Yousuf Kuwo Mekki

6. Commander Daniel Awet Akot

7. Commander Kuol Manyang Juuk

6. Commander Galerio Modi Horinyang

9. Commander John Kulang Puot

10. Commander Gordon Kong Chol

11. Commander Lual Diing Wuol

12. Commander Vincent Kuany

C. FORMATION OF MILITARY AXIS AND PHASE ONE OF THE CAMPAIGN

In accordance to the Gambela meeting the SPLM/SPLA Politico-Military High Command issued a resolution creating five military axis in War Zone I and War Zone II representing Southern and the Northern Sudan respectively.

The five axis were each commanded by a permanent member of the Politico-Military High Command.

Axis Number I was under the direct command of Colonel Dr. John Garang and assisted by Alternate Commanders, Martin Manyiel, Kuol Manyang Juuk, and Lual Diing Wuol. Additionally, Axis No. 1 was supported by professional officers, some of whom had just returned from Cuba.

Axis Number I covered the areas east of the River Nile, including Kapoeta, Torit, Bor, and Juba districts. This was later on extended to cover Western Equatoria. This important area had direct contact with international borders of Ethiopia, Kenya, Uganda, Congo and Central Africa. Therefore, if many of the towns were captured and occupied by the SPLA, that could send a chilling message to Khartoum.

Axis Number II was created targeting it to Southern Blue Nile mostly areas around Kurmuk, Geissan, and other smaller districts within the vicinity of south of Damazin town. This was equally a strategic axis, mostly to target the Hydroelectric power at Roseiris Dam that supplies most of electricity to Khartoum and the irrigation of the Gezira Scheme.

This area was assigned to Commander Kerubino Kwanyin Bol, Deputy Chairman and Deputy Commander-in-Chief, supported by Alternate Commanders John Kulang Puot and Galerio Modi Horrinyang, and a hoard of young professional officers.

Axis Number III was destined for eastern and northern Upper Nile, including Nasir, Maban, Melut, Renk, Kodok and Malakal. William Nyuon Bany, the Chief of General Staff commanded it and Alternate Commanders Dr. Lam Akol Ajawin, Gordon Kong Chol and other professional officers, some of whom had just arrived from training abroad, assisted him.

Axis Number IV was a military area targeting areas in southern Upper Nile including Pochalla, Pibor and linking up with Axis Number I at Bor military area. It was commanded by Salva Kiir Mayardit, Deputy Chief of Staff for Security and Operations and supported by a number of professional officers involved in reconnoitring missions.

Axis Number V was also a military area. It covered the areas of Ayod, Waat, Akobo and Panjak. It was supposed to support Axis III and IV. Arok Thon Arok, Deputy Chief of General Staff for Logistics and Administration commanded this area. He was assisted by a number of fresh military officers who had just arrived from training in Cuba, and other professional officers.

8.2.3. INDEPENDENT MILITARY COMMAND

In addition to military axis, the Gambela Meeting had also created independent military areas. They were called 'independent military areas' to distinguish them from the military axis. Independent military areas were under zone commanders. They were either members of the permanent PMHC or alternate members. The following were independent military and zonal commands:

1. Bentiu Independent Military Area: Following the discovery of oil in commercial quantities in Bentiu in late 1970s, Western Upper Nile region became an important point of contest between the south and the Arab-Islamic led governments in the north. The tension and tempo was evident in the manner the successive Sudanese governments have been exerting a great deal of efforts to wipe out the natives of the area—as described in the earlier chapters.

However, because of its proximity to southern Kordofan, where the pro-government militias were recruited and trained, Bentiu became an independent military area. The objectives were apparently to protect the oil reserves underground till such a time that the rights and privileges of the south were guaranteed by acceptable constitutional arrangements.

It remained the policy of the SPLA throughout the war that oil should not be exploited because its revenues would help Khartoum prosecute a ruthless war against the south. The protection of the civil population and their properties against the Arab militiamen was emphasised as the main war strategy for creating Bentiu independent military area.

Alternate Commander Dr. Riek Machar Teny Dhurgon was given the charge to realise these objectives. As the zonal commander, he was well staffed with capable officers. This zone included Bentiu, Mayom, Panriang and linking with the Nuba Mountains.

2. The Bahr al-Ghazal Independent Military Area: included the areas bordering western Kordofan and Darfur. These were Gogrial, Aweil, and Abyei. These districts are adjacent to the grazing lands of the Murhaleen or the Arab Misserya militiamen. These Arab groups have historically been responsible for slave raiding in these districts since the times of Zubeir Wad Rahma Mansour. Alternate Commander Daniel Awet Akot was put in charge of this zone and senior commanders; Deng Ajuong, Chol Ayuak Guiny and Bona Baang Dhol, and a number of professional military officers assisted him. This operation was to pass through Yirol, Rumbek, Tonj, Gogrial, Wau, Aweil, Raga and Abyei.

3. The Nuba Mountains Independent Military Area: was an important military campaign in the sense that it proved one of the SPLA's aims of fighting for the whole Sudan. Like the Southern Blue Nile campaign, it was a part of War Zone II (northern Sudan). It was meant to disorient the Khartoumers who stuck to the idea of the 'war in the south.' Now they had to readjust to their understanding of the war brought right to their doors. Nuba Mountains was specifically targeted for SPLA recruitment for future battles in the War Zone II. But more so, to protect the Nuba people from the intensive assimilation campaign and land seizure by the Arab groups who flocked in to grab Nubaland.

This task was given to Alternate and Zonal Commander Yousuf Kuwo Mekki assisted by Commander Abdel Aziz Adam Hellu and a number of professional officers. It was also supposed to link up with the Bentiu independent military area for logistics and tactical support.

4. The Darfur Independent Military Command: was opened to take the war to Western Sudan and to link up with Nuba Mountains. Like the Nuba and Southern Blue Nile, the success of this operation would have confused Khartoum exceedingly. Nevertheless, one of the aims of Darfur command was to recruit in the vicinity, but also linking it up with western Bahr al-Ghazal for tactical support and training. Commander Daud Bolad, surprisingly a long time supporter of the National Islamic Front (NIF), commanded the area. Since his school days, Cdr. Balad had been an executive member of the NIF's Shura (council).

Unfortunately, Darfur Independent Military area was closed quickly as Commander Daud Balad fell and many of his men were captured. Daud was summarily tried and executed under the orders of Brigadier Dr. al-Tayeb Ibrahim Mohamed Kheir, the Military Governor of Darfur. He is popularly known as al-Tayeb Sikh (the iron bar wielder) because of his ruthless behaviour towards those opposed to Islamic orientation.

The closure of the Darfur zonal command was a big blow to the SPLA aims in the Darfur. It perhaps deprived the potential opportunities to challenge the existing authority in the area.

5. The Hadendowa Independent Military Area: Like that of Darfur command, it was hastily created. Mahmoud Bazara commanded it. Considering the difficult terrain, the distance from the supply centres and the difficulty posed by the Darfur experience, this command was merged with the Southern Blue Nile axis until such a time that it would be feasible to open up an independent military zone in the Red Sea coastal areas.

Apart from the aforementioned axis and independent military areas, a guerrilla unit was created to operate in areas where conventional war was not yet planned. Indeed, Raga, Renk, and Pariang were allocated the 'hit and run' guerrilla operations. This unit was under strict orders from the High Command.

Throughout the SPLA military campaign, maximum efforts were exerted with stringent orders given and subsequently were to be maintained. The prime reason of which was the Movement wanted to avoid contradictions that might possibly hamper the smooth conduct of the war at its various axis and independent military zones.

Additionally, the control of various guerrilla units was seen as of paramount importance given the nature of their activities and operations.

In the process, all the military strategies and plans were successfully implemented in areas of operations. Indeed, the military organisational structure described earlier was designed as a prelude to the subsequent launching of the more effective military campaign; thereafter code-named the Bright Star Campaign.

8.3.1. ARREST AND DETENTION OF KERUBINO KUANYIN

While the Movement proceeded well with its elaborate military campaign, it was not immune to other political problems. One of the serious events that almost hampered the smooth progress of the Movement at this early stage of its military campaign was the arrest and detention of Commander Kerubino Kwanyin Bol[9].

Commander Bol was the provocateur and executioner of the Bor Mutiny that triggered off the rebellion in 1983. As the second man in the hierarchy of the Movement, his sudden exit was bound to cause danger to the prosecution of the war.

The reasons and causes that led to the arrest of Kerubino Kwanyin Bol, whatever they were, testified to incoherence in the internal administration of the SPLA. Incoherence, if any, might have been early storms gathering toward the split some years on the road.

On the other hand, since the war commenced in 1983, Kerubino may have taken it for granted that he was a *de facto* leader of the SPLA. And from that perspective, his flamboyant behaviour, which at times embarrassed the SPLA leadership, was to become a point of friction between him and John Garang.

One of the early schisms may have been the rejection of Kerubino's list of NCOs chosen to Alternate Command positions in the PMHC, that Dr. John Garang turned down in favour of highly talented and educated professionals. It was also mentioned that Kerubino had pulled his pistol and threatened to shoot John Garang in one of their scuffles, but William Nyuon intervened. Kerubino had been also accused of systematic human rights violations in the Movement between 1983 and 1987.

For instance, an eyewitness account spoke of Kerubino executing officers who caused some insubordination to him or committing petty crimes. These crimes, perhaps, were committed in the light of his assumption that he was the true leader of the Movement.

It was also from this assumption and believing that he was so powerful that he had wanted to take over the leadership of the Movement. He also assumed that all the commanders would automatically back him up and pledge unconditional support to his leadership. Unfortunately, this was not the case.

The story of Kerubino's arrest started following the battle over the strategic town of Jekou in eastern Upper Nile. The town was contested between the Sudanese army and the SPLA forces in 1986.

In the battle for Jekou, the SPLA incurred substantial losses in terms of men and material before they could finally overrun it. Nevertheless, the government forces equally sustained heavy losses, including the capture of Colonel Said. It was reported that most of the 25 SPLA officers, including Commander Francis Ngor Makiech—the most able and proud military officer—were killed.

After the capture of Jekou, it was natural that Kerubino Bol should carry the blame for the heavy losses. These included his reported insults to Francis Ngor, accusing him of cowardice.

As an overall commander of the operations, Kerubino Bol was said to have become very depressed and sick, affected by the heavy losses. He was asked to remain in Addis Ababa to recuperate from the humiliation. He remained there until 1987.

Jekou town, located strategically on the Sudan-Ethiopian border, is a gateway to the interior of the south and an entry point for many recruits. Commander Kerubino Bol had been made to believe that he was a military genius and therefore invincible; that he was witty and whose military skills and bravery knew no bounds. But now, he was a humiliated man!

In 1987, after the creation of independent commands, Cdr. Kerubino was then assigned the Command of Southern Blue Nile Axis. This assignment, though it marked a new start for him, also marked the beginning of the end of one of the poignant and volatile heroes of the SPLA armed-struggle.

Before he left for Southern Blue Nile, Commander Kerubino Kwanyin Bol sent a team of officers to Itang, the main refugee camp, to collect all the necessary requirements he would need for himself and his men.

Unfortunately, the team could not obtain the necessary supplies from Elijah Malok Alaeng, the man in charge of Itang. Instead of referring this act of insubordination to the Commander-in-Chief, and instead of waiting for reasons which made Elijah Malok not to cooperate and accept the orders from his senior Commander, Kerubino ordered that Commander Malok report to him at once.

Back in 1983, Alaeng had fallen out with Kerubino over the issue of inflating salaries of Bor Battalion (discussed in Chapter 2). Now he was not sure what Kerubino was up to this time around. Malok decided not to go.

Instead Alaeng reported the case to the Commander in Chief Dr. John, stressing that his life would be in danger if he reported to Kerubino's administrative zone. Without delay, John Garang overruled Kerubino's order and permitted Malok to stay put.

Upon hearing that Garang had intervened in the matter and told Malok to stay, Kerubino was reported to have become very angry. He accused John Garang of favouring officers from his hometown Bor. He went on to recount his earlier quarrels with Arok Thon Arok when Garang did not punish Arok for insubordination to the Deputy Chairman in his person. "How could Garang always protect the officers of his own district and tribe Bor?" Look, Dr. John did not intervene on behalf of the officers from Bahr al-Ghazal region like Victor Bol Yool and Kawac Makuei when I ordered for their arrest and detention. How come now that he openly comes out to protect the officers from Bor?" Cdr. Bol Complained bitterly.

The rot has set in. Commander Kwanyin Bol's anger had reached its boiling point. He was reported to have lost his respect for John Garang. From then onward, he was a man of his own empire.

He started dispatching letters to all the area commanders, particularly the officers from Bahr al-Ghazal (his home region) announcing that he had taken over the Movement being the pioneer of Bor Uprising,which heralded the insurrectionist activities in the south. He told his would be supporters and sympathisers that Garang was becoming more arrogant and was undermining his power as the de facto leader of the Movement.

Commander Bol was reported to have telephoned alternate commanders Dr. Lam Akol, Dr. Riek Machar and Lual Diing Wuol to support him in his venture to oust Colonel John Garang. To his disappointment, the three alternate commanders told Kerubino bluntly that they would not support him in his rebellion.

All the same, Commander Bol announced that he had taken over the leadership from Colonel John Garang. He was now the SPLM/SPLA Chairman and Commander-in-Chief.

Having received no positive replies and assuming that the tide would turn against him, Commander Kerubino decided to remain in Southern Blue Nile, seemingly leading an independent splinter group.

All the persuasions and requests for him to report to the General Headquarters where his complaints could be reviewed and possibly reconcile with Colonel John Garang and Alaeeng, as has previously been the case, were fruitless. Kerubino remained belligerent. Personal messages from General Mesfin, the Ethiopian Chief of Staff and plenipotentiary in charge of the SPLA could not induce him to report to Addis Ababa.

It was only when he became sick and was to have an operation at Assossa, a post on the Sudan-Ethiopian border operated by Cuban doctors, that General Mesfin went and persuaded him to go to Addis Ababa in order to meet Chairman Mengistu Haile Mariam. Only then did he go to Addis Ababa.

Meanwhile, security reports had been powering into the Ethiopian and SPLA authorities that Kerubino Kwanyin had sworn to assassinate Dr. Garang and take over the Movement. That the plot had been uncovered and that if the assassination efforts failed he could take over by the use of force. Following these reports, the Politico-Military High Command met and decided to arrest Commander Kerubino Kwanyin Bol.

Such a move could only be affirmed by both the Cuban and the Ethiopian authorities who admired Kerubino's flamboyant but charming character. In addition, he was approvingly a reputably good fighter.

While in Addis Ababa, General Mesfin advised Kerubino that Chairman Mengistu Haile Mariam would want to meet him and to hear his part of the quarrel with Colonel Garang. The Ethiopian and Cuban authorities saw the situation as threatening enough in which case it would have deflected the Movement away from pursuing its objectives.

According to the interviews conducted to ascertain the circumstances and events that brought the quarrel between the Chief and his Deputy, the quarrel was probably more about attitudes and suspicions, not any ideological issues. These could have been easily resolved without the intervention of General Mesfin or the Cubans.

However, while waiting to see Mengistu in Hotel Wabe-Shabella, Kerubino met many officers, prominent among them was Professor Bari Wanji. These officers were reportedly only too happy that Kerubino and Garang had at last broken apart. The group allegedly began to agitate persuading Commander Kerubino Bol not to back down or accept any reconciliation with John Garang.

Professor Bari Wanji, the alleged leader of the group is a veteran politician, anti-Arab, anti-Islam, and a supporter of an independent Southern Sudan. He admired revolutionary movement world-wide and indeed was inclined to socialism. He was a life-long fighter for social justice.

Wanji had just left the Movement after the rumours of his impending arrest accused as one of the notorious progressive officers, and indeed the ringleader. He sought sanctuary in the Cuban Embassy in Addis Ababa.

Reports suggested that Professor Wanji (who then preferred to be known as Captain Wanji, to assert his newly gained military rank as opposed to a mere academic) from his hiding volunteered and prepared a political case for Kerubino against Colonel Garang accusing him of inefficient management of the Movement. The document was so politically charged that it made the possibility of reconciliation remote.

However Kerubino Bol accompanied by Wanji took the letter to Chairman Mengistu Haile Mariam as a means of arguing his case against Colonel John Garang.

Although not much had been reported about the gist of what had happened between Kerubino and Chairman Mengistu, what was evident was that Mengistu advised Kerubino to go back to the hotel and wait there until he got back to him.

Comrade Kerubino Kwanyin Bol retired to his hotel room. For the next few weeks, he was much in limbo, unsure what Chairman Mengistu would say or do to him. After two weeks, Kerubino was asked to meet Colonel Tesfy, the Minister of Interior, who had all along been fond of Commander Kerubino. The meeting at the Ministry of Interior was a quagmire for Kerubino. He realised that he had voluntarily walked into jail.

As he was entering the Ministry, accompanied by Commander Mario Muor Muor, SPLA officers under the Command of Alfred Lado Gore intercepted Commander Bol. He was taken to the Ethiopian Air Force base for detention. He was there for a few months and then taken to Buma Plateau where he languished there until 1992. It was his cohort Commander William Nyuon Bany, who had also defected and joined the anti-Garang groups, who went and stormed the prison and got him out.

Whenever John Garang referred to Nasir coup against his authority in August 1991 as 'theatrical coup,' an isolated case and so forth, the history of anti-Garang struggles within and outside the SPLA had been longer than that. His fall-out with his Deputy, Commander Kerubino Kwanyin Bol, suggests otherwise.

Nevertheless, the arrest of Kerubino and subsequent long detention was the beginning of the end of Kerubino's military and political career as we will discuss later on in Chapter 12.

When Kerubino was arrested, Commander William Nyuon Bany was made Deputy Chairman and Deputy Commander-in-Chief in addition to his post as Chief of General Staff.

Other changes also occurred among the zonal commanders. Commander Martin Manyiel was transferred to the Office of the Chairman in Addis Ababa to be in charge of External Relations that were increasingly becoming very important in SPLA diplomacy. This post was held earlier by Dr. Akol, who became the zonal commander of the newly created Northern Upper Nile Command.

Commander Daniel Awet Akot, who was commander of Bahr al-Ghazal region, was appointed the zone commander of Northern Bahr al-Ghazal. Commander Kuol Manyang Juuk was appointed as Commander of the Central Southern Sudan sector that included southern Upper Nile, eastern Bahr al-Ghazal and eastern Equatoria axis. Galerio Modi assisted him in the Eastern Command and James Wani Igga in the Central Command. Following the reconciliation with Anya-Nya II, Gordon Koang took over the command of eastern Upper Nile from William Nyuon who was sent to the Southern Blue Nile to replace Kerubino.

8.3.2. RISE AND DEMISE OF PROGRESSIVE OFFICERS

One of the factors worth discussing in some detail is the issue of the progressive officers. As mostly college and university graduates, former senior government officials, or university lecturers, the progressive officers were not good military men in a sense of obeying orders, even stupid military orders, Said Commander Dominic Diim Deng, in an interview. Secondly, the Politico-Military High Command, which combined together the political and military aspects of the Movement, was likely to create many contradictions that plagued the Movement since its inception.

Since inception, as indicated in the SPLM/SPLA Manifesto 1983, it was natural that the Movement should adopt a socialist orientation and ideology as enshrined in its core objectives.

It was decided that a Political and War Studies School should establish at Zing in Gambella region. Thousands of recruits that were assembled for training and were put into two categories: a small and educated group, comprising the former government officials, students, and intellectuals were taken to the Political and War Studies School rather than rigorous military training. This was a semblance of Sudan Officer Corps College and, indeed, the graduates provided the SPLA with well-trained cadres as officers and political commissars. The multitude of the recruits, illiterate and semi-illiterate, were only given military training rather than political and ideological training.

If this might have been another way of appeasing the educated classes that joined the Movement, it became clear that this group was to remain more a thorn in the Movement body politick demanding all kinds of reforms as discussed below.

Others resented categorisation of people in the Politico-Military High Command according to educational qualification and ability. While John Garang and Salva Kiir Mayardit favoured such division, William Nyuon Bany, Arok Thon Arok, and Kerubino Kwanyin Bol disapproved. Instead they wanted military merit to determine everything.

Kerubino made it clear that he was opposed to the artificial division of those who would be the custodians of the Revolution and those who would die in defence of the Revolution.

Those who opposed this classification apart of Arok Thon were themselves uneducated or semi-illiterate. They thought that John Garang favoured the educated because he was a PhD holder and wanted to create a special cadre so that when time came, the less educated cadre would be discarded.

Kerubino bluntly asked one of the graduates of this School: 'You people are not made to fight, and when we the combatants are dead, you will come to take over the revolution?' Such was the schism between the educated and the uneducated.

By 1985, when the ideology of the Movement had become clearer, the issue of the so-called Progressive officers, assault officers and the reactionary officers became more pronounced. It became even more serious as more Socialist cadres got the senior and key positions in the Movement. It was now another class struggle in a Movement campaigning to eliminate classes and govern according to the dictates of the proletariat.

According to a report by some of the graduates of the SPLA College it was alleged that the Commander of the Political and War Studies School, Chol Deng Alak favoured most of the graduates of his School in gaining key positions as Socialists. It was also alleged that Commander Amon Mon Wantok did the same when he became the Commander of Itang refugee camp (recruitment centre as well).

According to the report, the Socialists actually behaved like members of the ruling party and the reactionary officers, the followers of the opposition party. The new recruits were caught up between the rivalling factions. Mayom Kuoac, one of the early graduates of the Political and War Studies School, in an interview stated: "Although the Socialist officers were ordered to give the Socialist orientation to the refugee communities, they, unfortunately, went beyond the normal political conscientisation and transformation of society. They instead forced indigent lots to become and behave like Socialists overnight."

The issue became even more disturbing as more officers who had gone abroad for military training came back not only seasoned with military skills, but with a great deal of political philosophy and Marxist-Leninist ideology. This was naturally frightening to the reactionary group in the High Command who were now openly critical and expressed fears about their future in the Movement.

During the appointment of alternate members of the Politico-Military High Command, there was even tension of who should be recommended to the alternate positions. There too, William Nyuon, Kerubino and Arok were clearly opposed to high doses of socialist ideology and increasingly they became more aggressive. Hence, they coined the term 'Progressive Officers' which was created to counter the increasingly popular Socialist cadres in the Movement.

As agitation and wrangling between Progressive and Reactionary officers was heightened day by day, it soon involved the external expertise: the Cubans and the Ethiopians.

For his own personal interests, Arok played William Nyuon and Kerubino Kwanyin Bol against John Garang and Salva Kiir. Arok even became more aggressive than the former two commanders to the point of rebellion and insubordination. Arok Thon ordered arrests at will and even executed officers belonging to the Socialist cadre.

To a lesser extent, Kerubino and William Nyuon were doing the same too, especially at their command levels when they would be in operations far away from other High Command colleagues.

When Commander Kerubino Kwanyin was arrested Arok Thon Arok immediately enlisted William Nyuon Bany to side with him against the Socialists. He finally made a hit list and swore to hit the Progressive Officers with impunity. Arok listed over 110 senior and junior officers he knew were Socialists and apparent supporters of John Garang and Salva Kiir Mayardit. Arok used his experiences in military intelligence with impunity. He was once quoted as saying: "It's either me or I destroy this Movement."

Having collected a number of names for his hit list, Arok began to frame charges that the officers in the list were planning a revolution within the revolution. He charged that the Progressive officers were reportedly holding 'secret meetings' and had formed cells everywhere in areas under the SPLA control. He also urged the security organs to support his list confirming that the officers named were anti-revolution.

While this crafty work was going on, the Ethiopian security had been following him and that would subsequently deliver him over to John Garang.

Finally, Arok and William Nyuon exceeded the threshold of tolerance of their behaviour. They ordered mass arrests in Itang including Commander Chol Deng Alak, the Commander of the Political and War Studies School, his Deputy George Maker Benjamin and his brother Ater Benjamin, and Dr. Amon Mon Wantok and his assistants. Other arrests were also made elsewhere including Michael Manyang, Commander Adhok, and many others.

Those who were also in the list but happened to be with John Garang included Alfred Lado Gore, and Deng Alor. But once Alfred Gore came for operations in Nasir, he was immediately arrested and taken to Buma Plateau where the rest of his comrades were being detained.

Later on, when Arok himself was arrested for these sweeping arrests, there was clamour for the release of all the Progressive Officers. An investigation team formed under Commander Mawien Dut realised that William Nyuon would not be persuaded to have the officers released in accordance to the recommendations of the investigation team. The situation remained cloudy until events at Nasir overtook the Movement in 1991[10].

8.3.3. ARREST AND DETENTION OF AROK THON AROK

The arrest of Arok Thon Arok, Deputy Chief of Staff for Logistics and Administration and the long time friend of John Garang, clearly demonstrated that something was unusually wrong inside the SPLA, and that John Garang was ready to weed out those who posed threat to the Movement.

In turn, this confirmed the persistent fear expressed by the other less educated members of the High Command that John Garang might one day find them expendable in favour of the more educated officers.

The important point to note at this point is that Arok Thon Arok was not part of the Underground Movement we discussed in the early part of the book. Unlike Kerubino who had been instrumental in the preparations preceding the Bor Uprising in 1983 and the execution of the insurgency, Arok only joined John Garang in 1982-83 in Juba (Chapter 2 for detailed accounts).

By then Arok Thon represented the military in the Southern Sudan People's Regional Assembly. During that time it was common knowledge that every southern Sudanese identified himself or herself with one group or the other: a divided south or a unified single south. Arok was in the latter camp supporting one Southern Region. In the event that the government reneged on the Addis Ababa Agreement the south should retake up arms.

With his military intelligence background, he was heading the Assembly's Security Committee, a position which conferred a deputy ministerial status in the south. In that capacity, Arok Thon was induced into politics of the day and was able to throw his security hat in favour of the nationalist one.

It was then that John Garang had a good encounter with Arok and the two worked toward a liberation struggle. He successfully camouflaged Garang's movements in many ways during that time.

Upon the mutiny in Bor, Arok flew to Khartoum under the pretence that he should not be associated with the Bor insurrection. However, he was arrested and detained for a year for allegedly covering up John Garang's clandestine activities between February and May 1983.

Arok's role in Juba should have been to monitor and report all the anti-government activities in the south, to the central government as Chairman of the Security Committee in the Regional Assembly.

As he was released from detention, Arok was enlisted by the members of the Underground Resistance and helped out to leave the country where he went and joined the SPLA in 1984.

As he got to the SPLA, Arok had mistakenly hoped that his valuable experiences in military skills and the role he had played in the months preceding the Bor Uprising could have placed him in a key position—at least as the second man—in the leadership hierarchy.

But this could have been unlikely because the three top positions of Chairman, Deputy Chairman, and Chief of Staff were already filled by equally capable persons.

Arok was apparently not satisfied with being the Deputy Chief of Staff for logistics and Administration, a position that needs a capable person with huge military experiences as he had.

However Arok Thon, yearning for a better position, could have been responsible for his final demise and exit from the Movement. There is no doubt that Arok was a professional and efficient soldier with unmatchable bravery and wit in the war front. However, by 1986 Arok had already begun to demonstrate a negative attitude against his colleagues in the High Command.

In the process, Arok's ambition made him divide the High Command into two groups with him in the centre. On his left was John Garang and Salva Kiir as Communists. On his right were William Nyuon Bany and Kerubino Kwanyin Bol as primitive and uneducated. This was the beginning of the end for Arok.

In Arok's calculation, the contradiction between the two groups would soon come to the surface. If this happened he would provide an alternative leadership.

Such was Arok's attitude during the meetings in the High Command where he would play a passive role, a move that made him ineffective in holding the opposing views in the High Command together. Arok's ambition did not stop at the High Command. He divided the rank and file into communists and democrats[11].

It soon became clear in every conversation and meeting with the rank and file of the Movement. For sometimes it appeared as if the Movement would not react to Arok's controversial position in the Movement.

His contacts with external forces without considering the consequences those contacts would bring to bear on the Movement and his position or personal safety was so apparent beyond doubt that Arok was out for a rough ride. However, the Movement would act while the iron was red-hot.

One of the events that offered opportunity to the SPLA High Command to strike on him was Arok's appointment in 1986 as the SPLA's special representative in the joint SPLA/M-National Alliance Committee that was expected to follow up the Koka Dam Declarations and to liaison with the National Alliance. This was an Adhoc Committee charged with the plans to hold the Constitutional Conference.

In that capacity, Arok became too exposed to many Sudanese delegates from Khartoum, many of whom were members of the Umma Party, SCP, Professionals, and Workers Federation and lecturers from the University of Khartoum.

According to subsequent interviews in the SPLM-SPLA information team (1986), Arok's Thon's contacts and associations with National Alliance delegates was viewed with concern within the rank and file in the Movement. Still no action was taken—even when the SPLA security drew the attention to the High Command.

The first serious accusation against Commander Arok Thon Arok came in July 1986. The Ethiopian security agents had completed an incriminating report against Arok which was handed over to the SPLM-SPLA High Command.

The report disclosed that Arok was dealing directly with the Sudan

Military Intelligence and National Security through individuals via National Alliance. The report also pointed out that Arok was dealing directly with Tiny Rowland, the British Business Tycoon of the London based Lonrho that has wide business interest in Africa.

These reports, though they could not be independently verified or confirmed, streamed to John Garang, but he sat over them. There were new allegations and developments in July 1988, which led to his immediate arrest.

Arok had just lost his wife in difficult childbirth. At the funeral, which was held in Itang, Arok was said to have accused the SPLA leadership of neglecting the critical condition his wife was in. If the Movement had given him money his wife would have been flown to Addis Ababa for an urgent medical operation which could have saved her life.

However after the funeral, Arok was given leave to take his children to his cousin who lived in England. It appeared that just before he took off for London Arok Thon had made some contact with the Sudanese Embassy in Addis Ababa. From Khartoum a large Sudanese delegation followed him.

Upon his arrival in London that night, Arok was informed by the office of Tiny Rowland about the incoming Sudanese delegation that would meet. Earlier on, Arok's brother, a retired Colonel Deng Thon Arok who worked at the military intelligence unit in Khartoum had also arrived to meet his brother.

The Sudanese military delegation headed by Major-General Fadhallah Burma Nasir, Minister of State for Defence, Lieutenant General Abdel Azzim Siddig (Chief of General Staff), security and military intelligence chiefs and a number of security personnel soon got in and requested a peace meeting with Arok[12].

Arok Thon, realising the repercussions of such a sensitive meeting with the enemy delegation, immediately sent an urgent message to Commander Martin Manyiel Ayuel, Director for External Relations in the SPLA Headquarters in Addis Ababa.

Arok asked if he could be given the green light to conduct such a meeting with the Sudanese delegation. He received no reply. Whether it was his commitment to hold talks or angry over the lack of response, Arok Thon nevertheless formed a delegation with some members of the SPLM London Office. The meeting took place in which a number of resolutions were made.

One of the SPLA security members in the London Office had sent a damaging report to the headquarters disclosing that they had held several meetings with the Sudanese government delegation. That Arok had been given a lot of money in order to go and stage a coup against John Garang after which a peace deal would be negotiated with him as the leader of the SPLA/SPLM.

The report allegedly further disclosed that Arok had made a pledge to the

Sudanese delegation that he would bring pressure to bear on John Garang in order to give peace a chance.

And in order to bring pressure to bear on John Garang, the government must do two things: Send a deterrent force to bypass the SPLA position from Malakal to Juba during the dry season. That the areas between the Nile and the Ethiopian borders are always free of SPLA forces during the dry season.

The government army, the report added, would intensify the war. When these two things happened he would put pressure for Garang to give in for peace. But, the report is said to have stressed, "If Garang refused, he (Arok) would therefore stage a coup.

This report was received according to sources, before Arok arrived in Ethiopia. Upon his arrival, he went straight to Itang, the main refugee camp. Before he could brief the High Command about his meetings with the Sudan delegation, Arok picked up a quarrel with the Chief of Staff, William Nyuon Bany. The Chief of Staff ordered him to return to the Headquarters in Addis Ababa.

But Arok insisted that he wanted to meet and brief the High Command of his London meeting with the Sudanese government delegation. He also complained bitterly that his messages had not been replied to.

The quarrel almost led to a shoot-out between William Nyuon and Arok Thon. But Salva Kiir and Martin Manyiel persuaded Arok to leave for Gambella, some 45 miles away from Itang.

As expected, William Nyuon Bany wrote a report to John Garang accusing Arok for gross insubordination, threatening that he would tender his resignation if Arok was not arrested. A week after this, John Garang summoned Salva Kiir and Arok Thon to go to Boma Plateau in the pretext that they were to go hunting.

While in Buma, Commander Salva Kiir produced a document containing 17 charges against Arok. The charges were delivered to Commander Arok Thon Arok. The most serious charges included:

1. Holding an unauthorised meeting with the enemy in London.

2. Insubordination against the Deputy Chairman and Commander-in-Chief and Chief of General Staff.

3. Instigating junior officers to disobey orders from their Chief of Staff.

4. Anti-revolutionary activities and conspiring to overthrow the leadership of the Movement.

After reading the charges, Commander Arok Thon Arok, who had been led to believe that he was the dynamo of the Movement, was securely caged only to re-emerge and sign peace with the Sudanese government in 1997[13].

Despite the arrests of senior members of the Movement, it appeared that SPLA military engagements with the enemy were never interrupted in any way.

Instead, war was actually intensified during this difficult period in which more towns were fell to the SPLA.

Between 1986 and 1988, the SPLA was politically recognised as a national movement whose existence and role in influencing the national political discourse could no longer be ignored.

Even the Sudan government was painstakingly convinced that the Movement had transcended its previous position at inception when it was regarded as a regional rebel force fighting for parochial aims and programs.

Equally, Colonel John Garang was recognised and accepted as a national opposition figure whose war aims can never be ignored when dealing with war and peace in the Sudan. The SPLA leader was therefore recognised as holding the key to the resolution of the country's complex problems, sapping the national resources and energies.

Indeed the SPLA credentials as a national Movement that had come into existence to change the order of things in the country for the better were shown during the Koka Dam Declaration, Addis Ababa and Ambo Accords we discussed earlier. Militarily, the SPLA was visibly holding the centre stage in which it was going to wield that for the much spoken about and expected National Constitutional Conference.

As of 1987, the SPLA had taken military initiative in the battle fronts than in the preceding years, and scored a series of victories capturing in the south as well as in Southern Blue Nile (Kurmuk, Geissan, Dueim Mansour, Shah Fil, Khor Yabus and others). The victories in Southern Blue Nile in particular sent electric shocks to the authorities in Khartoum that the SPLA could possibly strike at Roseiris Hydro-electric Dam near Damazin which supplies electricity to Khartoum and irrigates the Gezira Agricultural Scheme.

In eastern Upper Nile the SPLA Independent Military Command under William Nyuon Bany, who had replaced Kerubino Kwanyin Bol following the arrest of the latter, took grip of the military situation. This was to bring about the capture of Nasir, Jekou, and smaller posts of Maiwut, Adong, Ayod, Waat and the isolation of Malakal.

In the western Upper Nile, Dr Machar, the able zonal commander, had already linked up with Nuba Mountains Independent Command and overrun the oilfields in Bentiu and other posts in Mayom District. The government forces under the Command of Colonel Omar Hassan Ahmed al-Bashir (now the President of Sudan) were forced to evacuate to Muglad in southwest Kordofan.

These victories were repeated in other areas. But the cataclysm of Nasir in August 1991 could be regarded as cumulative effects of various kinds of issues that have been sapping the Movement.

8.3.4. THE BRIGHT STAR CAMPAIGN SENDS SHOCK WAVES TO KHARTOUM

Even though the SPLA was embroiled with its internal power struggles and subterfuges, its impact on the regimes in Khartoum was profound. The victories SPLA inflicted on the NIF were to be responsible for two fundamental changes in the Sudanese politics. First, it ended the Third Liberal Democratic government of Sadig al-Mahdi. The military Ultimatum of February 1989 and the mobilisation of the NIF to seize power were concomitant effects of the Campaign. Second, it provoked a more radical militarism under the NIF whose end is yet to be determined.

After taking stock of the its earlier Campaign the SPLA Politico-Military High Command drew up new strategies and tactics ostensibly aimed at efforts to rectify the shortcomings that may have been experienced in the battle fields. A number of resolutions were drawn up including the retraining of its troops as well as new recruits that were flocking in from all directions[14].

In this regard three divisions, Koryom, Muor Muor and Zalzal were recalled and put back into three main training camps in Bilpam, Itang and Dimma. Also thousands of recruits from the Nuba Mountains, Eastern Equatoria, and Bahr al-Ghazal were distributed to the main camps according to their groupings.

Two professional officers, Colonel Dominic Diim Deng and Colonel Salva Mathok who had defected from the Sudanese Army and had just joined the Movement, were appointed to help train the recruits. The two officers were had been trained at the Sudan Military Academy and had distinguished themselves before defecting to join the SPLA.

More importantly, these officers had been in Anya-Nya One. They were therefore bringing valuable experience into the Movement. They came also at the time when Kerubino Bol and Arok Thon were already thrown in jail at Boma Plateau. The arrival of two experienced officers boosted the moral of the Movement significantly.

The first resolution of the High Command stressed that besides training recruits in military skills and tactics the movement should start to give them political training. They had realised that politicisation of the Southern Sudanese polity was an important and necessary component of the liberation struggle.

The second resolution passed by the High Command was that areas that have demonstrated a great deal of hostility against the SPLA during the first half of the campaign must be brought under its administration. Getting more brave native warriors into the ranks of the SPLA Eastern Equatoria was the chief target.

The leadership of the Movement was too aware that seeds of the South

Sudan liberation struggle were first sown in Eastern Equatoria when the Equatoria Corps mutinied in Torit, August 1955. Hitherto, the feeling that the liberation and the attainment of an independent southern state had seasoned them to the extent that little efforts were needed to let them join the SPLA.

The third resolution concerned the deployment of the Anya-Nya II, which had just become part of the SPLA. Conventional war strategy was also recommended to deploy these forces in the field.

Thus in July 1988, the rejuvenated SPLA assembled a huge force code-named the Bright Star Campaign, and launched it against the Sudan government army.

The Bright Star Campaign was to take the war to Equatoria, an area which had not seriously felt the SPLA presence except for guerrilla groups sent there earlier. The aim this time was to take Kapoeta and Torit and the countryside. If these towns were successfully overrun, the war would then proceed to lay siege around Juba City.

The SPLA was also aware that the war in Equatoria must be backed up by its control of both banks of the River Nile between Juba and Malakal so that the steamers from Khartoum could not easily bring in supplies and reinforcement. William Nyuon Bany was entrusted with that task. For this purpose, Axis II (formerly commanded by Kerubino in Southern Blue Nile) and Axis III were combined under William Nyuon Bany. Axis IV and V were merged together under Salva Kiir. Colonel John Garang maintained Axis I.

Having assembled all the battalions, the Bright Star Campaign was divided into two phases. Each phase assigned specific objective targets to achieve. It would at the same time be able to link up and coordinate its activities with the adjacent independent commands.

In order to confuse the enemy, all the commands were ordered to be on the move. The main thrust to Eastern Equatoria went into action. Kuol Manyang Juuk was ordered to divert the attention of the enemy away from the action in the main military thrust in the east bank of the Nile.

Infijaar' forces, commanded by Cdr. Akec Aciek and Cdr. Dominic Diim Deng occupied Jebel Lado just 15 miles north of Juba City. Juba airport and other installations in the City were continuously shelled. The enemy, expecting more attacks upon the City, naturally started to dig in. The SPLA's objective to tie down the troops inside Juba City was accomplished when the government ordered one brigade of troops that was supposed to relieve Torit back to defend Juba.

Continuous shelling of Juba City was maintained for three months. Work on Kapoeta and Torit was vividly maintained. When these town were captured, the Infijaar forces were divided up into Malek, Kon Anok, Shambe, Bahr al-Naam and Deng Nhial Task Forces.

The Deng Nhial Task Force was ordered to bypass Rumbek and headed for Tonj, putting the enemy into panic, as it thought this was an attempt to link up Tonj with northern Bahr al-Ghazal. Deng Nhial task force was particularly for politicisation and recruitment mission in Tonj, the hometown of one of the earlier leaders of the liberation struggle, late William Deng Nhial.

Meanwhile, Kon Anok Task Force under Chief Kon Anok's great grandson, Isaac Kon Anok, moved into Yirol area for skirmishes and recruitment. Bahr al-Naam forces under Commander Dut Dom Kaoc went to Rumbek area to wait for the main force that would eventually attack Rumbek town.

Also Shambe task force under the Command of Deng Monydit went to Shambe to cut off the Shambe River Port from any possible stealth of government's steamers that might appear from Malakal. Malek task force Commanded by Akec Aciek overran Ngangala, Mongala, Gemeisa and linked up with the Infijaar Brigade base command under Kuol Manyang Juuk, waiting for orders to move to Bor.

8.4. THE IMPACT OF THE FALL OF KAPOETA AND TORIT

With all the arrangements in order, the Bright Start Campaign's main thrust under the direct command of Colonel John Garang assisted by poignant Commanders Oyai Deng Ajak, Bior (Asuat) Ajaang, James Oath, Gieer Cuang Aluaong and Obote Mamur Mete was advancing successfully.

On February 26, 1989 Kapoeta town fell. Infijaar moved swiftly and overran a number of posts including Kiyala, Ikotos, Katire, Parajwok and Magwi. Now Torit was exposed and isolated. The government forces dug in to defend the Town.

But in March 1989, the government troops were uprooted from their trenches and Torit was made the SPLA Headquarters. The SPLA captured a great deal of munitions, big guns, tanks and many prisoners of war including the Commander of Torit garrison.

Nimule was also captured the following day by SPLA forces who were camouflaged in Sudan army uniforms as the government convoy that was expected to deliver suppliers and reinforcements from Juba. The Nimule garrison was disarmed without fighting.

Within a matter of three months, the whole of eastern Equatoria was seized. The humiliation of being easily beaten, the loss of equipment and thousands of captives sent a chilling puzzle to Khartoum.

The national army was naturally demoralised, and General Abdel Majid Ahmed Khalil, the Minister of Defence, was psychologically disturbed that he tendered in his resignation to Sadig al-Mahdi. This humiliation was also responsible for the Military Ultimatum signed by 300 senior military officers addressed to Sadig al-Mahdi's government to either equip the army to enable it face the rebel offensive, or accept the peace overtures under the Koka Dam Declaration and the DUP-SPLA peace accord of 1988.

8.5. THE CAPTURE OF BOR—A MISSED OPPORTUNITY!!

Upon disengaging from Juba, The Bright Star Campaign forces under the command of Kuol Manyang Juuk and Malek Task Force Commanded by Akec Aciek converged and laid a two-month siege around Bor town. The government forces were subjected to starvation to the extent that soldiers had to survive by shooting vultures that landed on the bodies of their dead comrades. Bor was finally attacked and the entire Brigade that had been defending it wiped out. Those who attempted to escape were hunted down and killed by SPLA forces marauding everywhere in the countryside.

According to reports, only 13 soldiers managed to cross over the Nile and reached Terekeka which was still under the government forces. Thus after six years since soldiers of Battalion 105 were dislodged in 1983 by government forces marking the beginning of the second armed struggle in southern Sudan, Bor Town was captured again in May 1989.

It was expected that the SPLA, having taken Bor, should have continued keeping the same momentum it had gained since the beginning of the year. This move, many believed, would have at best enabled the SPLA to take over the entire War Zone One, South Sudan. SPLA would have then turned around to face war zone two, Northern Sudan. But the SPLA decided to declare a unilateral Cease-fire, thereby losing that momentum.

Essentially many people had expected that keeping the momentum, the SPLA Bright Star Campaign would have moved swiftly to liberate Western Equatoria, that was a possible easy target.

Since the launch of the military campaign in 1983, SPLA had never attempted to have presence in that region. It did not even try to win recruits from there until SPLA had trained nationalists and political officers from that region and deployed them among the populace for politicisation, especially in the rural areas of the region. It appeared that the SPLA decision had baffled the authorities to the extent that they began a near hysteria anti SPLA, anti Nilotics propaganda.

Precisely, the government authorities were apparently made to believe, rightly or wrongly, that the populace in Western Equatoria composed mainly of non Nilotics, on the top two nationalities, the Zande and Moru, were law abiding in contrast to the war-like Nilotics and the Nilo Hamites. In that perspective they would exert maximum efforts to keep the Dinka and their cousins out of their territories only if they were properly coached. In that way, both the Equatoria regional authorities and the central government were not worried very much about the security situation in Western Equatoria. The army in that region was ordered to keep low profile in order not to provoke the people's sympathy for the rebels

The liberation of Western Equatoria would have enabled the SPLA to link up with Bahr al Ghazal and reinforce the siege of Wau, the Capital.

The third move would have involved Western Upper Nile, under the Command of Riek Machar, for his forces to move north and capture Kodok, Melut, Maban and Renk. Thereafter Machar's forces would move south to reinforce the siege of Malakal.

Accordingly, the Bright Star Campaign's main thrust from its base at Nimule would move and capture the whole western Equatoria. The Bright Star would then move swiftly to the east and reinforce the Siege of Juba.

The Bright Star Campaign's final assault would involve the capture of Juba, Wau and Malakal, while sending task forces to clear pockets of government forces still resisting.

In order to complete the plan, task forces would reassert hold on northern Bahr al Ghazal, Abyei, the Nuba Mountains Ingessna Hills. SPLA would have brought the whole of Southern Sudan under its control and would then move to face the war zone number two, northern Sudan.

But unfortunately, and in a move that was reminiscent of the arrival of the Christian Crusaders on the Tomb of Salah Eddin Ayyoubi, the SPLA leadership issued a statement on May 9, 1989 declaring a unilateral cease-fire, thereby putting its elaborate war plan on a hold albeit temporarily. SPLA also promised to renew the cease-fire in June if all went well with the peace process.

This was 'unfortunate' and 'non-strategic said some military experts. For the SPLA to have declared a cease-fire at a point of an eminent military victory over a superior force is the biggest blunder ever committed by a guerrilla army. If the SPLA continued with its operations, no doubt Juba City could have been overrun when the iron was still red-hot.

With Juba in SPLA hands, the government in Khartoum would have been brought to its knees and concessions in sharing the national power would have been extracted easily. In a nutshell the capture of Juba would have brought a *de facto* independent South Sudan.

Politically, this would have forced the Sudanese government to speed up preparation and the convening of the long spoken National Constitutional Conference scheduled for September 1989.

More importantly, Perhaps the fall of Juba would have prevented the NIF from seizing power, as it came to power equally weak militarily. Even if the NIF had succeeded to take over power as it did in June, General al-Bashir would, as reported, have been in favour of letting the south secede if that would have ended the war.

Had the SPLA continued with its military operations in all fronts as it did between January and May 1989, and continued throughout the rainy season, a total conquest would have been realised in War Zone I. This would have released the forces for War Zone II operations.

The cease-fire, according to some observers, permitted the Sudanese Army with a breathing space and planning new strategies. In consequence, it was able to take courage, to regroup, and reorganise.

A determined dry season offensive by the Sudanese Army in February 1990, code named the *Jundi al-Wattan al-Wahed* or 'The soldier of one nation' would have not succeeded to neutralise the SPLA victories of the previous eight months and frustrated further SPLA major achievements.

The *'Jundi al-Wattan al-Wahed'* had been assembled since the rainy season of 1989, just as soon as the NIF seized power. The force comprised 500 heavy military trucks, 35 tanks and a number of personnel armoury carriers, anti-aircraft, artillery pieces, and a large quantity of modern weapons of mass destruction which the NIF had canvassed from friendly Arab states like Iraq and Yemen.

Crossing at the canal mouth (Sobat River) and moving discreetly in accordance to the alleged secret plan given to the Sudanese Army by late Commander Arok Thon Arok during their meeting in London in 1988, they managed to avoid all the SPLA positions and passed unnoticed till half way through.

Unprepared and ill equipped to face a huge enemy force, the SPLA attempted to halt it, but was too late to defeat or prevent it from reaching Juba.

Following the fall of Bor, SPLA friends and allies were ready to assist the SPLA initiatives in order to liberate the whole of War Zone I and the Southern Blue Nile and Southern Kordofan. With a massive assortment of modern weaponry provided by friends and allies, the liberation of War Zone II could even have been realised.

This would have enabled the Movement to dictate conditions and terms favourable to its objectives: to halt the war and restore democracy not only to the south but also the whole Sudan.

But the Polico-Military High Command was perhaps aware of danger and repercussions in the event of external forces coming to its aid. The SPLA leadership, apparently anticipating a possible intervention of some Arab-Islamic countries, and Egypt in particular, to rescue the north and fight against the south, declined the prosecution of war in that fashion.

The experiences during the capture of Kurmuk in 1987, when the entire north rallied against the SPLA, were of course still fresh reminders.

Additionally, it was reported that, the second capture of Kurmuk and Geissan had provoked the Egyptian President Hosni Mubarak to make an abrupt visit to Khartoum with his top military advisers who became involved in co-ordinating the recapture of those territories.

The Egyptian leader was too aware that the greater part of the Blue Nile Basins, in the hands of pro-Ethiopia rebels, was going to be outside the Egyptian control.

According to the 1959 Nile Water Agreement, Egypt has the lion's share (estimated at 59.9 milliard) of the Nile water in annual reserves.

The SPLA fears were also founded in that during the capture of Kurmuk, even its supporters and sympathisers from the north protested against the SPLA incursions into the northern territories.

Aid from the Arab-Islamic nations also would pour to Khartoum confirming that they would always come to the aid of the north in efforts to keep the Sudan a united Arab country.

According to the SPLA sources, the cease-fire was basically declared as a peace gesture, a move they expect would enable the peace process that was at its advanced stage to have a chance of success.

But military critics doubt the SPLA's prudence of declaring a cease-fire at the time it had the military advantage over the government forces. The experts added, "...this was 'a missed opportunity,'"

Suffice to state that the SPLA just lost the first chance to liberate, at least, the Southern Sudan—its constituency—in favour of high stakes, objectives, goals and ideals.

However, students and scholars of politics and history would better pass the verdict whether it was a right thing for the SPLM-SPLA to have turned down the offer of friends and allies to liberate the south.

8.6. SPLA TAKES STOCK

As is always the case, there can never be successes without reverses. The SPLA victories described above were counter-balanced by reverses that tilted the military balance on the side of its enemy, the Sudan's army, as it continued with its military campaign.

The reverses that hampered the progress of the SPLA war efforts apparently were:

1. The failure of the SPLA to maintain the upper hand military initiative to the end. The declaration of the cease-fire in May 1989, as we discussed earlier, had been seen as untimely in that it enabled its enemy to regroup its forces, hence were able to make a counter offensive during the dry season of 1989-90 when Khartoum launched the 'Soldier of one Nation' operation.

2. The SPLA failure to consolidate its military victories and its subsequent disregards of the advice of friends and allies during the critical moment when they were ready to stand on the SPLA side. It is common sense that this offer

would have helped the SPLA to conclude the war in 1990 in favour of the marginalised areas.

3. The SPLA's failure to make contingent plans to defend the liberated areas has been one of the weakest of policies ever pursued by a strong guerrilla movement. For instance, a huge force of *'Al-Jundi al-Wattan al-Waheed'* passed from Malakal to Juba through the SPLA-controlled territory met no stiff resistance at all. In fact, the SPLA was taken by surprise.

4. Failure of the SPLA to set up effective civil administration which could have been a buffer backing up to the SPLA soldiers. The soldiers, being bogged down with civil duties which they least knew, could have been released to preoccupy themselves with purely military duties and tasks.

5. SPLA failures to capture Rumbek that could have been used as a springboard to entrench the war effectively in Raga, Aweil, Gogrial and Tonj districts: the effects that would have been the isolation and capture of Wau.

6. SPLA failure to capture Maban and the most of the northern Upper Nile after which all the forces would have converged on Malakal, the capital of the region.

However, although these reverses had apparently weakened the SPLA in a military sense, it did not in the main halt the SPLA from completing the mission of the Bright Star campaign.

Instead it made the government army to forget controlling the whole south and only concentrated its efforts in defending strategic towns like Yei, Kurmuk and Geissan, Juba, Wau, Malakal, Bentiu, Kodok, Renk and Aweil on the railway line between Wau and Northern Sudan.

8.7. THE BRIGHT STAR TAKES FIRM GRIP OF THE SOUTH.

However, despite threats posed by the invigorated Sudan army and the new government decision to declare a unilateral cease-fire and the invitation to discuss ways and means of ending the war, SPLA had continued preparing for the next dry season offensive, to liberate Western Equatoria. This was the Bright Star Campaign phase II.

Throughout the rainy months of June, July, August and September, the SPLA having maintained Eastern Equatoria assembled a huge force for the final push to Western Equatoria. The Bright Star final phase was very crucial for the SPLA to occupy the whole Equatoria in its liberation process because Equatoria borders five African countries of Ethiopia, Kenya, Uganda, Congo, and Central African Republic.

Controlling Equatoria would therefore frustrate Khartoum's plans of ferrying troops to the neighbouring countries to attack the SPLA from the rear. Equatoria also had warrior tribes whose enlistment would provide the forces it needed to the SPLA.

As described earlier that the main strategic objective was to take the war to the whole Equatoria, the Bright Star Campaign's final phase went into action in the beginning of 1990. Moving away from its rear bases in Nimule area, the main SPLA *'Intisar'* Brigade, under the direct command of Colonel John Garang, and deputised by commanders Oyai Deng Ajak, James Oath, Bior Ajaang, Obote Mamur Mete, crossed the Nile and stormed Kajo Keji. It swiftly moved and took the strategic border town of Kaya—where Sudan Congo and Uganda adjoin.

The Instisar Brigade inflicted heavy casualties against the enemy along its trail. Huge military hardware, foods stocks, and medical assortments were captured. These additional supplies helped the SPLA strengthen its positions. It enabled it to overrun a string of towns which included Morobo, Lasu, Tore, Ras Aulu and connected with Lainya. Yei garrison that had just been reinforced by the Sudanese government and was heavily protected was avoided.

After joining forces at Lainya, the Bright Star Campaign task forces proceeded and captured Mundri and Amadi. Rokon post, 40 miles north west of Juba also came under sustained shelling. This shelling alarmed Juba as well, as it was not sure whether the SPLA officers were planning another plucky attack upon the City. Whereas Maridi town in extreme Western Equatoria was bypassed, Iba, a small post between Maridi and Yambio was overrun instead.

By April, the Bright Star Campaign's special task force moved swiftly and captured Yambio, the provincial capital headquarters of Western Equatoria. Yambio surprisingly fell without any serious fight. This suggested a great deal of low morale upon the government's soldiers—despite the government's powering of more resources to keep the region out of the war.

Although the SPLA's did not have a high profile presence in Western Equatoria, it is strongly believed that there had been a great deal of sympathy to the SPLA cause in the region. The fifth columnists under retired ex-Anya Nya officer and the former regional minister of wildlife Brigadier General Samuel Abu-John Kabashi were believed to have done a great deal of homework.

Even while keeping a low profile, Abu-John kept regular contact with police officers, wildlife, and soldiers to the extent that when the SPLA arrived in the area, it swept a large territory with ease.

The government's fateful attempt to rescue Yambio came from Nzara, 12 miles away, under the Command of Brigadier Isaiah Paul. But that force was wiped out and Nzara itself fell, as well as Ezo and Tombura.

In April 1990, the Bright Star task force returned to Maridi. After a fierce battle, the government's troops, under the command of Colonel Henry Akaoon (who surprisingly was an ex-Anya Nya), escaped with few soldiers to Zaire (now Congo).

Precisely, the Bright Star Campaign, which laboured steadfastly, had wonderfully attained most of its target in Equatoria in just four months of campaigning.

Though Juba and Yei were still firmly under the government's hands, the SPLA was able to declare that it had taken firm grip upon the Southern Sudan. It could then move freely and at will using conventional warfare tactics instead of guerrilla activities at the start of the war. Toward the end of 1990, the SPLA had controlled nearly 95 percent of Southern Sudan.

Having paralysed the government efforts to stop the SPLA's incursion into Western Equatoria, the SPLA task forces at last converged and laid a ring around Juba. Thus throughout the middle of 1990 the rebel forces flexed their muscles around the Juba City. This sent a chilling signal to the Sudanese government that Juba was the next target.

The capture of Western Equatoria and many parts of Bahr al-Ghazal brought in thousands of fresh recruits. Most of these were trained locally instead of trekking hundreds of miles to Ethiopia.

By the end of 1990, the SPLA was composed of most of the citizens in War Zone I. This had altered the earlier position where the SPLA was regarded as 'Dinkier' or Nilotic Movement. At this point, the SPLA was expected to enter a D-Day over Juba, Malakal and Wau—hopefully during 1991-92.

Unfortunately, the siege on Juba and other major towns coincided with political problems magnified by the fall of Mengistu's Government in Ethiopia. Hence, it is worth discussing those problems here before we could go further. These problems include the Ethiopian political change, the NIF's military strategy, and the internal SPLA power structure.

8.8. THE ETHIOPIAN POLITICAL SCENE

The collapse of the former Soviet Union, which was the major backer of the Mengistu regime in Addis Ababa since early 1977, and the subsequent wind of change (Perestroika and Glasnost) made satellite states like Ethiopia witness to crushing defeats.

Between 1989-90, Ethiopia's regime was increasingly confronted by an ideological crisis and decreasing foreign support on one hand, and increasing assault by EPLF and EPDRF and other smaller rebel groups (OLF) on the other.

By the beginning of 1990, it was evidently clear that Mengistu was increasingly losing the grip of power. Attempts to conclude a negotiated settlement with the rebel groups was futile.

To the SPLM-SPLA that was a serious blow because it was about to lose a committed friend, which had been ready to carry the SPLA through to success. Essentially, Mengistu Haile Mariam had remained throughout, the only friend that could be relied upon for the political, moral, psychological and most importantly, military support, however meagre that could have been.

The Soviet Union that could help the Socialist regime in Ethiopia in which some few scrums could reach the SPLA was unable to address the liberalisation caused by Perestroika without destroying the Communist system. Even there, the Baltic republics were defiantly seeking for independence from Moscow.

Erick Honecker's East Germany that participated in training the SPLA was also bogged down by similar crisis topped by attempting to prevent its citizens from crossing to West Germany after the collapse of the Berlin Wall. Against such a situation, SPLA's future became very uncertain indeed.

It was against this background and political climate that the SPLM-SPLA was brought to its knees when the revolt in Nasir split the Movement on 28 August 1991 at the crucial time when victory was eminent.

We turn to discuss in the coming chapters, details about the circumstances of the NIF Coup, the split in the SPLM/SPLA, the subsequent fratricidal atrocities in the south and how these twists of events deflected ultimate military victory.

CHAPTER 9
THE ISLAMISTS MILITARY IRON FIST REGIME

9.0. THE SETTING

In the last two chapters we have discussed how the Islamists were responsible for the break up of al Mahdi fourth government. How all the pro peace parties formed the Fifth Coalition Government in three years from March 1989 in order to work for peace in accordance to the Koka Dam and DUP-SPLM peace initiative. The NIF party political line and thinking was thus determined not to allow such a peaceful settlement that would squarely compromise the vital Arab interest in the Sudan.

We also touched on why the NIF was vehemently opposed the SPLM/ SPLA demand for the establishment of non-racial, non-religious and non-ethnic political system in the country; a system that would undoubtedly guarantee equal opportunities to all citizens at all levels of the national life. That was basically why the NIF party summoned all its might and resources to frustrate all the previous plans to attain peace under the Koka Dam Declaration embodied in the SPLM/DUP November 1988 peace initiative.

We also mentioned that as the National Alliance for peace was preparing to work out modalities for convening the National Constitutional Conference, scheduled to start on September 18, 1989, the NIF was at work, urging the army to intensify the war against the rebels in the south. It also kept on trying to convince all the political forces in the north to recognise the looming danger being posed by the African majority in the country against the Arab race dominating the affairs of the country. The NIF as a party was preparing the northern public opinion to mobilise and rally behind its leadership, as the only capable political force in the country alive and active to defend the right of the northern populace's main objectives——to keep the Sudan as Arab—Muslim oriented state.

In this chapter, we shall discuss at greater length, detailed analysis why the NIF took over power and announced the establishment of an Islamic state in the country. How it ran the country the way it did (1989-2002), until external forces were finally forced to come in and impose a negotiated peaceful settlement of the two-decade-old destructive ethnic conflict between the south and the north.

9.1.1. THE REVOLUTION COMMAND COUNCIL SET UP

Following the military take over of power, the coup makers immediately formed a 15-man military junta known as The Revolution's Command Council for National Salvation (RCC).

The Junta was composed of the middle ranking officers: 7 Brigadiers, 5 Colonels, 2 Lt. Colonels and one Major. Brigadier General Omar Hassan Ahmed al-Bashir was nominated as the RCC's Chairman, who immediately promoted himself to the rank of Lieutenant General and Commander-in-Chief of the Sudanese Armed Forces. Brigadier al-Zubeir Mohamed Saleh became Deputy Chairman, promoted to the post of Major General and Deputy Commander-in-Chief.

Lt. General al-Bashir had been known in the army as an Islamic zealot but with inherent ambition to rule. Before taking over power, al-Bashir had been fighting the SPLA in the western Upper Nile oil fields District of Bentiu. He had been forced to transfer his headquarters from western Upper Nile to Muglad in southwest Kordofan.

Al-Bashir was on his way from western Sudan to Egypt when the success of the coup found him in the capital Khartoum. However, within a couple of hours since taking over power, al-Bashir announced the dawn of an Islamic Revolution to the embarrassment of the non-Islamist members of the RCC.

At its initial stages the coup was planned and executed by a coalition of conspirators: Islamists forming one third and non-Islamists the other two thirds.

According to General Hassan Ahmedein[1], a former member of the junta, the non-Islamists had apparently joined the coup in the belief that the coup was being staged to correct the nature of things and the mess made by politicians in their political wrangling in the previous three years.

They had also thought that the coup was staged in accordance with the Army High Command's memorandum to Sadig's government in February 1989. But when they discovered that the coup was being hijacked it was too late to do anything to revert power to them.

Any move intended to snatch power from the Islamists who were already consolidating their power and placing their supporters in sensitive positions, such as security organs, was met with stern warnings.

In the end, non-Islamists found themselves in the periphery of power. In subsequent years they were dismissed one by one. The same thing happened to the soldiers who supported the coup. This practice was later made clear by the late General al-Fathi Mohamed Ali, Commander-in-Chief, at the time of the coup.

On being released from detention, General Fatihi left the country. He later formed a rebel army, the Legitimate Command, whose aim was to fight the junta in order to restore democracy. General Fathi stated:

"Conscious of its light political weight and hence its inability to rule the country, this group (NIF) used deceit, treachery and ruse. The group used the name of the lawfully Military High Command to mislead the soldiers and officers into supporting the coup by claiming that the coup plotters were ordered by the Army High Command to realise the February Move."

But when the soldiers and officers (non-Islamists) realised the trick and were preparing to react against them (Islamist officers) it was too late, even at this early hour. The non-Islamists later became victims of the purges that ran into thousands.

Aldo Ajou, a political advisor to the RCC and later one of the Deputy Speakers of the Transitional Assembly (Parliament1992 and 1994), told the author that the coup was staged by a coalition of conspirators brought together by a marriage of convenience to take over power in order to rule.

Indeed, it was, for every practical purpose, a marriage of convenience between the Islamists who were well organised and with Islamic agenda to implement, and the non-Islamist conspirators who were there to gamble their chances in order to come to power.

Because they were in the mechanised units, armoury and artillery, airforce and signals, once in firm control, the Islamists acted very fast and managed to bring things under the NIF control within a matter of hours. They were therefore able to dictate the direction of the revolution.

The second group of conspirators was composed of military adventurers like Brigadier al-Zubeir Mohamed Saleh who sprang from unknown entity to become the Deputy Chairman of the Revolution Command Council.

Al-Zubeir's name was among the nine top members of the coup makers that mushroomed in the army. At the time of the coup, al-Zubeir was in prison accused of plotting a pro-Nimeiri coup attempt. He was released from jail by the coup plotters and appointed him Deputy Chairman of the RCC. He was later charged with the responsibility to weed out anti-revolution's elements both in the army and in the civil service.

The third group of conspirators was composed of highly educated, trained, and experienced officers whose only aim was to come to power to rule. These officers were in fact the mind behind the coup making.

All the plots and policies were concocted, brewed, and executed by this group. One such officer was Colonel Hassan Ahmedein Suleiman from the artillery unit. He was promoted in 1993 to the rank of Major General and was almost at the centre of all events leading to and after the coup. But he was elbowed out into oblivion when the NIF took over power with all its colours and might.

Nevertheless, because of his high qualifications and training in the military academies, strategy studies and organisational skills, General Hassan Ahmedein was appointed at first as the rapporteur of the RCC for Political Affairs Committee. He was later given the responsibility to organise the National Congress, now the ruling party, where he became its first General Secretary.

Before being trashed into the dustbin of history, the General was appointed Governor of the most remote and newly created state of western Darfur, an area notoriously noted for its perennial tribal feuds between the Arab and African ethnic groups of Darfur, some of which sprawl across into Chad. But when time came for non-Islamists and non-conformists to exit, General Hassan topped the lists.

The fourth group of conspirators in the coup making were politicians in the Umma Party led by Bahri Ahmed Adeel, one of the Umma politicians opposed to the way their leader Sadig al-Mahdi had been handling the affairs of the party.

Bakri, like his mentor Mohamed Ahmed Mahjoub, the former Prime Minister and Umma pleader in the 1960s, was opposed to the idea of combining the affairs of the Ansar al-Mahdi sect with the political affairs of the Umma Party.

According to Aldo Ajou Deng[2], Deputy Prime Minister during Sadig's tenure of office, Bakri had been pestering Umma supporters in the army and security to act first and take over power before others did.

The Umma nominee to lead the group of Umma loyalists in the words of Aldo, was none other than Shams Eddin, the Junta strongman who oversaw the army and security in the capacity of advisor to the President General al-Bashir between 1989 and 2001.

Shams Eddin, according to reports, was a well-known Islamist zealot in the army and a long time member of the NIF underground cells. And, indeed, he headed the NIF's underground Council of Forty. Major Shams Eddin was the officer who took over the GHQs with a tank unit described earlier.

The fifth group was composed of the officers who joined the coup or were drafted into these ventures in the hope that they would manipulate things in the ruling junta in order to correct the mess already made by the politicians such as corruption, nepotism, and favouritism. This group of officers assumed that they would sway the public to their support.

This group included Brigadier Osman Hassan Ahmed who was appointed Political Committee's Chairman, and Brigadier Faisal Ali Abu Saleh who was later appointed Minister of Interior. The two officers were dismissed disgracefully when they protested against the execution of 28 officers alleged to have plotted to overthrow the junta in April 1990.

Besides, there were other professional officers who were brought into the junta because of their respect in their units in the military. There were some that were brought by Islamist colleagues in the regime.

These included: Brigadier Tigani Adam al-Taher; Brigadier Ibrahim Nail Edam; Colonel Faisal Muktar Medani; Colonel Suleiman Mohamed Suleiman; Colonel Salah Eddin Mohamed Ahmed Karrar and Colonel Martin Malual Arop.

Malual had also served in the Artillery Unit with General al-Bashir. Apart from this long relation with the junta leader, it appeared that Malual's appointment was in regard to other political considerations, such as winning over the Dinka ethnic group who comprised the bulk of the SPLM/SPLA. Other two officers from the south taken into the RCC were Brigadier Pio Yukwan Deng and Brigadier Dominic Kassiano Sebit. They were appointed either to represent their regions or mainly because of their clear anti-SPLA stance.

From this background, it would make sense to make an observation that the Islamists were not alone in the coup plot. Rather they simply seized control from an agglomeration of conspirators and successfully ran away with it. The very fact that the Islamists were mainly from the mechanised and security units while other came from various units can give credence to this observation.

The combination of coup plotters with different aims and agendas can explain the reasons why the RCC Chairman General al-Bashir was so evasive and illusive in his first speeches to the army and the nation.

For sometime, al-Bashir continued to deny the involvement of his group of Islamists in the planning and execution of the coup. According to reports, al-Bashir was not sure whether the Islamists were actually in full control of the affairs of the country or not.

Also fearing that perhaps things may go the wrong way to the destruction of the NIF leadership, the Junta decided to arrest the NIF leader Dr. Hassan al-Turabi and two of his deputies; Sheikh Ibrahim al-Sanousi and Ahmed Abdel Rahman Mohamed. These two were also interned in the Kobar Maximum Security Prison along with other political prisoners including Osman al-Mirghani, the spiritual leader of the Khatmi sect and DUP party.

The arrest of Turabi enabled Ali Osman Mohamed Taha (NIF strongman), aided by al-Nafie Ali al-Nafie, a former lecturer in Agriculture, to supervise the coup and direct the NIF in its process to consolidate power smoothly without alerting the Sudanese public that an Islamic fundamentalist regime was being installed.

Dr Kok[3] writes that, since a military takeover seizing power from an elected partisan regime in the Sudan would be most unpopular, the NIF did a lot to mask its involvement in the June 30th coup. Even to the extent of telling the officers and soldiers that the coup was being staged with the authorisation of the Sudanese armed-forces General Command." That by itself vividly explained the nature of the coup. It reflected why General Omar al-Bashir continued throughout the first few days of the coup, reiterating that his political colour was green (simple soldier) a reference to the green uniform of the Sudan Armed Forces (SAF).

Al-Bashir, without noticing that the green colour was also the colour of Islam, was telling the nation that he had no political colour but a simple soldier who has come to power to change the state of affairs in the country.

Having empowered itself as the legitimate authority to appoint and dismiss the officers and officials of the State and government in the country, the coup leaders formed the following members of the Revolution Command Council for National Salvation.

1. Lt. General Omar Hassan Ahmed al-Bashir, Chairman (NIF)
2. Major General al-Zubeir Mohamed Saleh, Deputy Chairman (pro-NIF)
3. Brigadier Faisel Ali Abu Saleh
4. Brigadier Osman Ahmed Hassan
5. Brigadier Ibrahim Nail Edam
6. Brigadier Tigani Adam al-Taher
7. Brigadier Dominic Kassiano Sebit
8. Colonel Pio Yukwan Deng
9. Colonel Salah Eddin Mohamed Ahmed Karrar
10. Colonel Suleiman Mohamed Suleiman
11. Colonel Martin Malual Arop
12. Colonel Faisal Muktar Medani
13. Lt. Colonel Mohamed al-Amin al-Khalifa
14. Lt. Colonel Bakri Hassan Saleh
15. Major Ibrahim Shams Eddin

The following were also appointed to positions of influence:

1. Colonel Abdel Rahim Mohamed Hussein (NIF), rapporteur to the RCC office in the Palace
2. Colonel Hassan Ahmedein Suleiman, rapporteur Political Committee
3. Colonel Kamal Muktar, Security
4. Colonel Pio Yukwan, supervisor for Southern Sudan
5. Dr. al-Tayed (Sikh) Ibrahim Mohamed Kheiri, overseer the Council of Ministers

Ascertaining that it was in total control of affairs in the country and having enfranchised itself the sole supreme law making authority in the country, the military junta began to draw its line of authority by issuing decrees.

9.1.2. THE JUNTA FIRST CONSTITUTIONAL DECREES

Decree Number 1: Under this constitutional decree, the RCC suspended the 1956 Transitional Constitution through which the country was being ruled till the writing of the permanent constitution. This Decree also dissolved the Constituent Assembly (Parliament) and the Council of Ministers and enfranchised the RCC as the supreme constitutional and legal authority.

Decree Number 2: authorised the RCC to dissolve all the political parties and political association, confiscate the assets of the former politicians and political parties; and the arrest of all the politicians and influential persons likely to oppose the introduction of Islamic system of government in the country. Decree Number 2 also ordered for the dissolution of the local and regional governments and trade unions; the withdrawal of licenses of independent newspapers and confiscated their assets. Editors and journalists were also arrested and detained. Some religious and foreign non-governmental organisations, especially the Christian organisations, had their licenses suspended.

Under Decree Number 3: The junta empowered the military regional commanders to take over the authority and administration from the ousted regional governors. This Decree also empowered the under-secretaries in the central government to take over the administration of respective ministries in acting ministerial capacities.

For more immediate and practical purposes, the RCC formed four committees to act as political commissioners and administrative overseers of public affairs. The Committees were to report their activities to the RCC Chairman on a daily basis. These Committees were also empowered to co-opt other members they believed would conform to Islamic orientation being instilled in the general public. The Committees' activities were later extended to the government ministries and at a later stage to villages and cities and suburbs. The main function of the Committees was to act as a vehicle through which the RCC junta would administer the policies that were aimed at efforts to deal with urgent problems arising in the course of time such as security or political threats posed by real or imagined anti-Islamic Revolution elements. The main committees were as follows:

1. **The Security Committee**: This Committee was under the Chairmanship of Major General al-Zubeir Mohamed Saleh, Vice Chairman of the Revolution's Command Council for National Salvation. General al-Zubeir was assisted by hard core Islamists such as Al-Nafie Ali al-Nafie and Colonel Bakiri Hassan Saleh, an RCC Member, and to a lesser extent by Brigadier Nail Edam. Through this Security Committee, the NIF was to settle scores of its account old and new with those who had in one way or the other been responsible for its failure to realise its objectives.

Besides the Head of the Committee and his assistants, a good number of Islamists security organs were lined up behind this Committee basically in order to make the Revolution work. Predictably, this Committee had to recruit some of the former security personnel who were disgracefully dismissed en mass following the collapse of the May Regime in 1985. Also those security officers and men dismissed subsequently by the regime of parties between 1986 and 1989 were also drafted. Understandably, no mercy was expected from these disgruntled security men.

It was on this Committee that the destruction or survival of this nascent regime squarely rested. Hard hit among the junta adversaries were the members of the big sectarian parties (Umma and DUP), the Sudan Communist Party and suspected SPLA sympathisers (pejoratively known as 'Fifth Columnists').

With immediate effect the Security Committee, now divided into several organs, went into activity included: The Revolution Security Organ, Sudan Security Organ, Political Security Organ, Military Intelligence/Security Organ.

In addition, there were scores of groups posing as members of Popular Committees in the places of work and residential areas: numerous unemployed citizens and students found themselves either officially drafted or used as sources or informants. Soon the prisons were full with alleged enemies of the Revolution.

To that effect, private buildings were converted into detention centres which later became known by those who opposed the junta as "Ghost Houses," or torture chambers, which were opened all over the cities of Khartoum, Khartoum North and Omdurman.

2. **The Political Committee:** Brigadier Osman Ahmed Hassan was the Chairman of this committee and Colonel Hassan Ahmedin Suleiman as rapporteur. But because the two officers were non-Islamists by background, the Political Committee was effectively run and managed by a group of hard line Islamists derived mainly from the NIF cadres.

The political Committee, in brief, was placed in the hands of highly educated people from different disciplines. Some of the NIF zealots and bigots had lived in exiles raising money or had been in hiding in various places of work in the country. The future Popular Defence leaders were recruited among such cadres.

3. **The Information Committee:** was under the Chairmanship of Colonel Suleiman Mohamed Suleiman, an RCC Member. This Committee had the most committed members who, for the best two years, preceding the coup had been the main party propagandists or the 'Crusaders for Islamic Revolution.'

The Information Committee was run by journalists/newsmen of the major newspapers: al-Rayah, al-Alwan and al-Sudani. Notorious among them include

Ahmed Kamal Eddin; Amin Hassan Omar and Hussein Khogali and Mohi Edin Teitawi, the former editor of al-Ayaom during the May Regime.

4. **The Economic Committee:** This was chaired by Colonel Salah Eddin Mohamed Ahmed Karrar, an RCC Member but of non-Islamist background. This Committee was run by highly educated and talented NIF cadres, among them, bankers, economists, and financiers. It was this Committee that all economic and monetary policies and planning were designed and directed. Future economic plans were formulated in this Committee.

5. **The Foreign Relations Committee:** This was under Colonel Mohamed al-Amin Khalifa. A team of NIF inner circles cadres such as Dr. Mustafa Osman Ismail assisted him. A notorious NIF zealot Fadl al-Sid Abu Gasseissa ran the Peace Sub-Committee. His role in the Peace Sub-Committee will be discussed later when we discuss the peace prospects. This Sub-Committee later on set up a Peace Forum through which the future negotiation with the SPLA would be handled.

9.1.3. THE MILITARY JUNTA FIRST POLICY STATEMENT

For sometime since its inception, both foreigners and Sudanese public did not comprehend adequately to which way the new regime was driving the country. At one time it appeared as an Islamic regime and at other time as if it was a classical military takeover under the usual pretext that the civilian government overthrown was corrupt.

The use of Islamic slogans did not even prove the point. But as time passed by, it became abundantly clear that the new rulers were not the usual "khaki boys" in dark glasses seizing power to rid the country of socio-economic and political mess created by the civilian rulers. Rather they were the *Mullahs* ready to merchandise religion.

The announcements over Radio Omdurman included; the appointment of Major Younis Mohamoud, a fanatic Islamist whose voice became intertwined with the junta's rhetoric over the years, that: "We have come to get rid of false democracy and to liberate the people...Sudan Pan-Arab interests are appreciated by your Armed Forces...and the Armed Forces' motivation is a Pan-Arab one." This too did not confound nor clarify the situation sufficiently enough.

However, things became clearer only when the Military Junta finally issued a meandering policy statement, just to borrow Dr. Peter Kok's phrase, in which it outlined what the new rulers intentions and motivations were.

For all the practical purposes, the statement was a clear reflection of the National Islamic Front's long established position, a position which spelled out the Islamist's vision dating back to the 1960s when the Islamic Charter Front (ICF) was formed in 1964.

According to this statement, the Junta clearly aimed at efforts to win the

Arab and Muslim countries to come to the junta's aid immediately. The first thing the new rulers promised was the reorganisation and re-equipment of the Sudanese Army which the Junta said, had been humiliated and demoralised by the string of victories scored by the rebels of the Sudan People's Liberation Army (SPLA) in the south, as described in Chapter VII. The intention the statement added was to make the army ready for the next offensives and to regain the lost military ground.

The next move, according to the statement, was to rescue and revitalise the economy, improve foreign relations, especially with the major Arab states of Iraq, Libya, Egypt and Saudi Arabia. These countries were also expected to foot the bill of the new regime in Khartoum.

On the unity of the country, the statement pointed out that the junta would spare no efforts to rescue the country from disintegration. It emphasised the Junta's determination to set up effective security apparatus to combat breaches of activities of foreign security services. The statement also revealed the new rulers' intentions to remove the traces of sectarian, partisan, and racist orientation—a reference to that practice of multi-party democracy would never be permissible thereafter.

On foreign policy, the statement affirmed the new junta's commitment to abide by international conventions. In regards to the war and peace in the Southern Sudan, the statement noted that the new regime would make peace with those carrying arms in the country (SPLA), a priority.

Like the civilian government it has just replaced, the new rulers put the issues of war and peace much at the bottom line of their list of priorities. Even so, the regime indicated that it would pursue the issue of peace, but in accordance to its own terms.

Having outlined its policies, the Junta set up the Council of Ministers in July 1989, which predictably was composed mainly of the NIF hardline cadres in key and sensitive ministries. The following was the first Council of Ministers and Government as of July 1989[4]:

1. Lt. General Omar Hassan Ahmed al-Bashir, Prime Minister and Minister of Defence

2. Major General al-Zubeir Mohamed Saleh; Deputy Prime Minister

3. Colonel al-Tayed Ibrahim Mohamed Kheir; Cabinet Affairs

4. Brigadier Faisal Ali Abu Saleh; Interior

5. Mr. Ali Sahlul, Foreign Affairs

6. Hassan Ismail al-Bili; Justice/Attorney General

7. Ali Mohamed Shommu; Information and Culture

8. Professor Ahmed Ali Geneib; Agriculture

9. Abdalla Deng Nhial; Religious Affairs and Endowments

10. Yagoub Abu Shura; Irrigation

11. Omer Abdalla Mohamed Ahmed; Industry
12. Sayyed Ali Zaki; Finance and National Economy
13. Mahjoub Bedawi; Education
14. Abdel Moneim Khojali; Energy and Mining
15. Farouq al-Bishiri Abdel Gadir; Trade and Supply
16. Mohamed Shoker al-Saraj; Health
17. Mohamed Mamoun al-Mardi; Housing/Public Utilities
18. Peter Orat Ador; Displaced Persons and Relief
19. Ali Ahmed Abdel Rahim; Transport and Communication
20. Fr. George Longokwo Kinga; Labour and Social Insurance
21. Natale Pancrasio; Local Government and Regional Co-ordination
22. Brigadier Nail Edam; Youth and Sports

There were also other ministers of state (mostly NIF cadres) put as overseers in ministries under non-NIF cadres.

9.1.4. SPLA OFFICIAL RESPONSE TO THE JUNTA POLICY STATEMENT

For two months since the June 30, 1989, the Sudan People's Liberation Army (SPLA) position on the new Military Junta was unknown. But on August 10, 1989, Dr. John Garang de Mabior, the SPLM/A Chairman and Commander-in-Chief gave a lengthy speech[5] assessing the new changes of government in Khartoum. Garang outlined the Movement's official reaction to the new regime that had brought the peace process that was at an advanced stage to an abrupt halt. The SPLA Leader summarised the Military Junta's agenda as containing four ridiculous points that:

1. It has declared a cease-fire in the south; offered amnesty to the rebels that were expected to surge out of the jungle in response to the cease-fire.

2. To talk with the SPLM/A on the 'problem of the south.'

Garang dismissed the Junta's appeal describing it as "...shallow and distorted perception of the nature of the central problem confronting the Sudan." He added that the RCC position was a crude and reactionary position that can only bring disaster, not peace, to the country. Garang sarcastically implored the leader of the Junta saying: "Omar thinks that he is the Sudanese nationalist and we in the SPLA are his southerners. Has Brigadier Omar al-Beshir bothered to ask the question as to what makes him the Sudanese and makes Dr. John Garang his southerner?[6]

On peace process, the SPLA leader said that the attainment of peace was possible and would be possible only if the RCC restores democracy and holds the constitutional conference in accordance to the 1986 Koka Dam Declaration with the National Alliance and the 1988 DUP/SPLM peace accord.

But that would mean the establishment of a broad-based National

Government composed of all the political forces in the country including the Sudan Army and the SPLA.

The aim of such national government, Garang explained, would be the drafting of a permanent constitution (prepared by an interim government); free elections and subsequent ratification of such constitution by an interim constituent assembly, and the establishment of a democratic government. Dr. Garang hoped that the RCC would send emissaries to discuss the four-point plan to restore democracy.

On whether the Movement would be ready to discuss peace with the RCC, the SPLA leader stated that: "With respect to whether the Movement will talk with the new Military Junta in Khartoum, the answer is yes. They are the de facto government in Khartoum. Our policy has always been to talk with anyone who claims to be in power in Khartoum."

The Government of Sowar al-Dahab, was a military dictatorship, while the Government of Sadig al-Mahdi was a sectarian dictatorship. Yet we talked with these governments. We will talk with the Junta and will have to brief the Movement as to why they took over power and presumably present their peace programmes. However, we will present the Movement's peace programme in the context of the establishment of a democratic and united Sudan.

The SPLA leader concluded that the Movement would reject "...a Sharia-based system which it believed would prevent progress in substantive talks and would in the end prove that the RCC has a hidden agenda to partition the country." Imposing Sharia would cause the country to disintegrate.

Following John Garang's speech, the Junta responded by sending emissaries to Addis Ababa to meet with the SPLA. This took place between 19 and 20 August 1989. The Junta delegation was led by an RCC member, Colonel Mohamed al-Amin al-Khalifa, and that of the SPLA by Dr. Lam Akol Ajawin.

Although talking to the new regime had taken the peace process many steps backwards, this initial face-to-face meeting between the junta and the SPLA was to reactivate the peace process that was interrupted by the coup. In the meantime, it was apparently clear that the two sides were preparing for the 1990 dry season military offensives than for peace.

9.2. THE JUNTA RADICAL POLICIES

Having asserted effective control over the country within a couple of months, the new regime, now calling itself "the Government of National Salvation Revolution," came out in its full colours and might to implement its radical Islamic policies in line with the National Islamic Front (NIF) *Sudan Charter* of 1987.

The Sudan Charter was a blue print designed to transform the Sudan into a purely Arab-Islamic country. This radical approach worried not only the Sudanese who had expected a government armed with better policies aimed at resolving the then six year war, but also the international observers, especially the neighbouring countries who could be affected by the spill-over of such radical Islamic government activities in the region. The rise of Islamic fundamentalism was expected to meet internal resistance, especially by those who find such Islamic system alien to them.

To make everybody conform to Islamic fundamentalist ideals and above all, making sure that such policies were implemented smoothly and without resistance, the new regime began to impose strict codes of Islamic behaviour and modalities on the whole country, with special emphasis on Northern Sudan, its natural political constituency. Hence, the implementation of Islamisation process unparalleled since the nation came into existence three decades and half before. All the Islamisation processes were to be followed and adhered to in spirit and letter.

Most of the Islamic policies and a range of decrees and ordinances, a programme similar to Iran's Islamic Cultural Revolution, were to be carried through and over the national media (radio and television).

The newspapers, which were already brought under the Government control, were also involved in the daily commentaries and highly charged polemics of Islamisation process, which were intended to re-orient the public into born again Muslims.

Prayers were conducted five times a day over the radio and television and in public parks besieged by the Islamist security to apprehend dissenters and detractors. Such would be whisked away to unknown destinations. The Friday Sermons in various Mosques were also carried on prime time TV and lasted most of the afternoon. No work, but prayer!

To make these policies effective, the Commissioner of Khartoum province, Sayyed Mohamed Osman (one of the coup plotters) with the assistance of another Islamic zealot, Lt. Colonel Yousif Abdel Fatah, made local ordinances by which all the businesses, places of work and public offices were closed during the Friday Sermons.

More so, an edict against women was also imposed. Every woman, Christian or Muslim, must wear a veil and a long black dress reaching to the heels, and anything less was regarded as indecency. The morality police were in the street corners—on the lookout for women wearing indecent clothes. If discovered, they were flogged in the streets or apprehended by the National Youth Association (NIF Youth or Morality Police).

Alcoholic beverages were prohibited, and anyone found drinking would be flogged, put in prison or fined. Social gatherings between men and women were prohibited. The teaching of arts and music in schools was also outlawed.

The reasoning behind all these activities was that the building of a new Islamic society should not be profaned by the encroachment of western cultures. But it was not the Western cultural expressions that were outlawed. Even traditional Sudanese arts and music were also outlawed. It was the end of culture.

In December 1989, combined forces of trade unions, students and lecturers, medical and veterinary doctors, engineers, professionals and technical associations headed by Sudan Bar Association, attempted to challenge the Junta in order to put a halt to this 'Islamic cultural revolution', a pandemonic business that had befallen the country. This attempt was met with unprecedented ruthlessness by the NIF security.

In the process, thousands of arrests were made, and prisons were full to the brim. The main prisons were relieved when detention centres, mostly from commandeered private buildings converting them to detention houses, were set up.

And to frustrate any future attempts to make strikes and demonstrations, the arrested strikers described as non-law abiding members of the public were put on mock trials. Such trial centres were set up everywhere by the state security. Dr. Mamoun, the head of Sudan Medical Association, considered the ringleader, was sentenced to death for organising a strike and unrest.

In the process, the former security personnel during President Nimeiri's time, purged following the collapse of the May Regime, were re-engaged, and in addition with the Islamists security guards. These security forces were responsible for gross human rights violations, including; extra-judicial execution; torture in the Ghost Houses; and other psychological torture such as denying of sleep for days.

By the end of 1990, the country was utterly thrown into confusion, intimidation and fear. Speaking to the author, one of the RCC members stated that the December Trade Union strikes and students' unrest saved the Islamic System in the sense that they all came out at once, and the regime hit them hard once and for all with one stroke. "Had the strikers planned a phase by phase action, the regime, which was still shaky in form and content, would have been overthrown earlier than had been expected," he added. The December strikes the Junta adopted harsh revolutionary methods to weed out anti revolutionary elements in the army, police and public service.

To prevent the general public to react sharply against the harsh treatment being meted against them, as was the case in 1964 and March 1985, the NIF regime immediately preempted that by making massive purges among the members of organised forces and all branches of the public sector.

The Military High Command was the first to feel the purges when over 600 officers (ranging from Brigadier General to Generals, were either retired prematurely or simply thrown out without sufficient reasons. This was followed by mid-ranking and junior officers, suspected of possible sympathy with the public in the event of future clashes between the regime and demonstrators.

By the beginning of 1990, regardless to the intensification of war in the south, 1,500 officers of various ranks had at least been laid off. Hundreds of police and prison officers were also purged.

In the Judiciary, 14 Justices of Supreme Court, 12 Members of Appeal Court, and a tier of 128 judges and legal counsellors from the Attorney General's Chambers were dismissed with immediate effect. All of them were replaced with inexperienced and ill-qualified individuals whose only qualification was being committed Islamists. These were repeated in other departments. Effectively, the corpus of the government, the pivot of the country's civil service, was removed.

In response to this, many highly educated and experienced military and police officers, judges, and many more, resigned in protest rather than wait for humiliation.

In the public service, Dr. al-Tayed Ibrahim Mohamed Khair, nicknamed 'Sikh' or iron-bar wielder, caused a great deal of havoc in his department. Sikh's Islamism has been well known since his school days. And as the Minister of Cabinet Affairs in the Council of Ministers, he was placed in an influential position to strike a deadly blow on his bogey-men.

Within a short period, hundreds of civil servants lost their jobs either on being retired prematurely or purged in 'public interests.' Others were dismissed on the grounds that the government had taken austerity measures in order to revive the economy of the country allegedly destroyed by the previous sectarian parties. Similarly, 150 ambassadors were dismissed in the Foreign Affairs Ministry.

9.3. FORMATION OF POPULAR DEFENCE FORCES

As if the hardness already meted upon the corpus of bureaucracy was not sufficient, the NIF ordered for the revival of the Popular Defence Force, apparently to assist the Sudan Army in the Holy War (jihad) being planned against the south.

Basically popular Defence Force was started by the former Prime Minister Sadig al-Mahdi in 1987. But such a move had been abandoned in 1989 when the National Army opposed the formation of the PDF. The NIF's aim in re-introducing the PDF was to raise a huge army within a short time, a move, expectedly made so that by a certain date (year 2003 by Turabi's accounts), these forces would have successfully replaced the regular Sudan Defence Force. The NIF thus ordered that PDF centres are established all over the country.

To Islamist trainers, the main theme was to instil hard Islamic dialectics in the minds of the trainees so that they embrace the spirit of *Fidaa* (sacrifice), *Shahada* (martyrdom), and Faith (in Islamic religion) against the infidel rebels in the south.

Accordingly, the PDF training camps were set up right from village to national level. The first to go to the PDF were the government's top executives and then followed all the way up to the secretaries. Precisely, all government employees must register in the PDF campsites.

There were five categories: public servants; Islamist Holy Warriors (Mujahideen); Islamist Volunteers; Students and Unemployed Street Boys. Every forty-five days, a batch of PDF was being graduated from any of these categories.

Between 1990 and 1991, nearly every able-bodied man and woman in the country was trained and had become a PDF card holder. Practically all the public banks, public corporations, and commercial banks were given Islamic names. National parastatal and corporations, Islamic relief agencies and many more were also Islamised. Universities and institutions of higher learning also underwent the same fate.

9.4. SEEKING LEGITIMACY AND POPULIST BASE

In pursuance of its policies of Islamisation, the NIF regime adopted politicisation of the populace by adopting the idea that state policies must be derived from popular conferences. It stated that the conferences were vehicles through which it could seek national consensus over its Islamic policies. The resolutions and recommendations of each conference would be taken as a popular endorsement of its policies.

By August 1989, for instance, four conferences had already been envisaged, namely: The National Dialogue Conference; The Diplomacy Conference; The Information Conference and the Inter-Religious Dialogue Conference. The regime stated that the resolutions and recommendations of these conferences would be incorporated into the policy-making process and would be implemented since these grassroots opinions were conducted through the people and for the people.

In October 1989, the National Dialogue Conference was convened in Khartoum. Mohamed al-Amin al-Khalifa, the RCC member and Chairman of Foreign Relations and Peace Committee was appointed the Chairman of the Convention. Professor Ahmed Abdel Halim who had been responsible for formulating policies of the defunct May Regime was also appointed as the rapporteur of the Conference.

After a two-week deliberation, the Conference, which was attended by 104 appointed delegates from the public and private sectors, came out with a number of recommendations which were contained in what became to be known as the regime's 'Pink Book.' Dr. Peter Nyot Kok[7] writes: "The recommendations appeared to have been in line with the NIF Political Charter referred to earlier." Prominent among the recommendations adopted by the Conference (some recommendations which the regime used to issue constitutional decrees), were:

1. The creation of an Islamic State.
2. Federalism as the most suitable system for the Sudan.

The adoption of federalism was probably crucial, as it was frequently emphasised by the regime officials was an answer to the Southern Sudanese demand for federation since 1955. Like the 1947 and 1952 conferences, no mandated Southern Sudanese politicians were consulted over the issues concerned.

From the onset, the regime failed to address the crucial issue that brought about the war they were preparing to settle once and for all. According to a senior member of the Conference, the Southerners were expected to be grateful with the federal offer since federalism had been their long demand.

Of course, the question is: if the regime thought that federalism was the system it could negotiate with the Southerners—inside or outside—why were Southerners not invited to become part of the designing process? They would have naturally discussed about the number of states that must be adopted and the powers that must be conferred upon these states.

Unfortunately, the regime designed its own federal system in closed doors and later started to propagate for its acceptance among the southern populace in the country. "If the Southerners inside the country were to accept federalism, the rebels would have no reasons to continue fighting," so went the NIF argument.

It was from these recommendations that the regime in 1991 divided up the country into 26 mini-states and 66 provinces, and addition to local government councils. Like the previous agreements the federal offer was not attractive enough as bait to end the war.

9.5. THE ISLAMISTS OFFER SECESSION AS BAIT TO WIN THE WAR

The June 30th military Junta in its desperate effort to defeat the SPLA have succeeded and identified a number of means to destroy the SPLA. One of the means it adopted was to sell 'secession' of the south as a mean to break it asunder between the majority secessionists and the few nationalists who desire to reform the whole Sudan.

The idea orchestrated and concluded by the hard-line Islamists in the new regime was reportedly given to Brigadier Pio Yukwan Deng, one of the

Southern Sudanese members in the Revolutionary Command Council (RCC) to sell the secession package to Southerners.

Brigadier Yukwan, well known for his anti-SPLA stance, was in 1990, made the Chairman of Peace Department in the ruling military junta. He apparently started to approach other Southern Sudanese whom he knew would support the separation offer.

In the opinion of the junta, according to Brigadier Dominic Kassiano, [8] the south, during an interim period toward the establishment of a separate state, a moderate Southern Sudanese leader must take charge of its administration. Such an individual was expected not to be hostile against the government in Northern Sudan.

The principal aim was apparently to keep the way open for future reconciliation leading to a possible reunification of the south and the north.

Thus between 1989 and 1990, discreet but frequent visits by a number of so-called 'peace officers' were sent on errand to Addis Ababa possibly to identify possible separatists within the SPLM-SPLA leadership.

The envoys brought news of great joy, as such cadres were not in short supply in the SPLA. The envoys reported:

1. That there was disenchantment and general discontent in the SPLM-SPLA.

2. That most of the commanders and senior officers were against John Garang whom they accused as a dictator. A list of potential anti Garang was made available for the Junta for perusal.

Preparations to win separatists were undertaken in earnest. Ahmed al-Radi Jaber, a born again southern Muslim, and Colonel Gatluak Deng Garang, the Governor of Upper Nile Region, were assigned the task to work on the would be replacements of Dr. John Garang in the SPLA and the home front [9].

The shuttling mission by the junta's envoys to Addis Ababa coincided with general debate among the rank and file of the Movement particularly at Itang main refugee camp. These debates indicated a general clamour for internal restructuring and reorganisation in the SPLM-SPLA leadership echelons.

Proponents for the change and restructuring of the Movement and the main speakers in those debates were reported to have given the Movement the label of a 'one-man show." That Garang dictated on many issues in the Movement without reference to the Politico-Military High Command.

The previous arrest of Kerubino Kuanyin Bol, Arok Thon Arok and members of Progressive officers, were said to have prepared a fertile ground hostile to Colonel John Garang's leadership.

In Khartoum, Fadhl al Asid Abu Gasseissa, a hard-line Islamist and the chief architect of penetrating the SPLA rank and file, was made the paymaster general in the bid to win as many, Southern intelligentsia at home and in the SPLA, as possible.

9.6. SECRET PLANS TO BREAK UP SPLA REVEALED

Following the previous conference, the National Dialogue in October, and in January the Diplomacy one, the most important Conference was held in February 1990. It was called the Conference on Problems and Issues of Information and Governance.

Throughout the previous months, Lt. General Omar Hassan al-Bashir emphasised that the media must reflect the Islamic values, mobilise the public behind the national goals of the regime and protect the Sudan from the western foreign invasion.[10]

This was a clear reference to the SPLA powerful radio station at Naru, outside Addis Ababa, and the international press. Thus it appeared that the main purpose of holding the Information Conference was to enable the regime to brainstorm and re-orient the media Barons and newsmen toward the regime's Islamic agenda and to lead public opinion to that end.

The revolutionary propaganda was intended to achieve the main objective to defeat the rebels in the South considered the main stumbling block on the road to the regime's success. Thus on the last week of February 1990, all the Sudanese newsmen from public to private sectors—including the editors of major journals and newspapers, freelance writers, poets and artists and so forth—were mobilised to attend such a Conference.

The main items on the agenda of the Conference were loosely put: to discuss in general terms the reorganisation of the audio, visual, and print media and the problems of war and peace.

Also according to the Chairman of the Conference, Colonel Suleiman Mohamed Suleiman, he stated that without strong committed media, the policies of the government and the life of the Revolution itself would be at risk of being misunderstood. Hence the need to involve the press community to understand the government political and Islamic orientation and ideology and to impose it on the public.

Before the end of the Conference, all the media men were called to attend a "closed-door" briefing on the issues of war and peace in the Southern Sudan.

Inside the briefing room inside the Friendship Hall, the media men were surprised to note that it was not the usual press briefing in which the interviewers and the interviewees were able to exchange questions and answers for their medium in a roundtable manner. This was not the case. Rather the briefing was to be in camera.

Before the briefing could begin, security guards went round to remove pens, notebooks, recorders and cameras from the attendees. This was to make sure that none of the attending media men should take notes on the briefing.

Suddenly, the lights went off. On the screen was a large map of the Sudan with all its neighbouring states clearly marked. The map of the Southern Sudan was distinctively marked to alert the media that war in the south was subject for the briefing. All was still and tense!

Suddenly, a number of officers appeared at the briefing table: Military Operations Commander; Military Intelligence Officer; Military Strategist Officer; National Security Advisor and External Security Advisors.

Assuming that the media men were properly indoctrinated, given sufficient doses of orientation in the previous week, and were ready now to comprehend the agenda and speaking one by one, the officers analysed first the neighbouring states and their effect and impact on the war in the south.

On the war in the south, the officers disclosed that the SPLA had defeated the Sudanese Army and that the government was only holding 8 main towns in the whole south. It was also disclosed that plans were under way to defeat the SPLA and thus restore the tarnished name of the army and rescue the unity of the country. It was further disclosed that with the help and commitment of all the Muslims and particularly the Muslim press, all would be well.

The speakers blamed the defunct regime for not equipping the army to stand in its role to defend the national territorial integrity that was being threatened by the rebels.

The officers appealed to the media men to carry home this message to the public about the government's plans to defeat the rebels.

The military experts stressed that what was needed was the national will and cooperation in assisting the government to protect the land and the faith. Special emphasis was placed on the need to have effective propaganda machine to defeat the rebels once and for all.

During the course of the briefing, five points were stressed as areas through which the rebels would be defeated. The press appeared to have been convinced and ready to defend the government's Islamic orientation.

On the main strategy, the military strategist expert stated. "In order to defeat an army, the best and effective strategy is to hit the Commander, either by physical elimination or discrediting him." Hence the need to call the SPLM/SPLA "Harakat Garang"—"Garang's Movement" or "Harakat al Tamarud"—"the Rebel Movement." It was stressed that anybody referring to the SPLM/SPLA would be considered a fifth columnist or sympathiser of the rebel movement.

Second, to play up ambition within the SPLA leadership, a move aimed at efforts to cause disagreement among the top members whose end was to split them.

Third, to encourage fake defections from the Army to the SPLA to go and wreck it apart from within the rank and file. Those who defect and join the SPLA would be instructed to make failed attacks on the government forces so that those attacks result in heavy casualties on the rebel side.

Fourth, to play up tribalism within the SPLA rank and file and among the civil population, the aim of which was to deny the SPLA any support and recruitment.

Fifth, launch peace process in accordance to the government's laid down policies to win the civilian population away from the Movement.

And last but not least, a declaration of a Jihad (holy war) on the beleaguered rebel movement.

When the briefing was over, the three Southern journalists who had innocently sneaked into the briefing Hall included Alfred Taban of the British Broadcasting Corporation (BBC), Arop Bagat of Radio Juba and the author [11].

We were soon whisked out by the security, subjected to intensive investigations and finally thrown into jail, February 1990 to May 1991. Our crime seems to have been to listen to all those conspiracies against the south and strategies to defeat the SPLA.

9.7. THE JUNTA'S POLICY ON THE ADMINISTRATION OF THE SOUTH

As stated earlier, the RCC, upon seizing power, assigned three southern members in the Junta to oversee the administration in Southern Sudan. These were Brigadier Pio Yukwan Deng, Upper Nile; Brigadier Dominic Kassiano Sebit, Equatoria; and Colonel Martin Malual Arop for Bahr al-Ghazal.

This was reminiscent to the Nimeiri's policies on taking over power in 1969. He appointed Dr. Toby Maduot Parek, Hillary Paul Logali and Luigi Adwok Bwong for Bahr al-Ghazal, Equatoria and Upper Nile respectively.

In what appeared like the action of General Suwar al-Dahab's TMC when it appointed Major General James Loro Siricio, Chairman of the Provisional High Executive Council (Regional Government) in 1985, the RCC also appointed Brigadier Yukwan as the overall supervisor of the three southern provinces above Kassiano and Martin Arop.

For administrative purposes, Major General Andrew Makur Thaou was appointed Governor of Bahr al-Ghazal; Major General Alison Manani Magaya was appointed Governor of Equtoria; and Lt.Colonel Gatluak Deng Garang was appointed Governor of Upper Nile.

Makur and Alison, being members of 'Underground Movement' discussed in the earlier part of the book, have traversed a long journey to join an extremist Islamic government.

Their appointment should be understood from the humiliating defeats that the Sudanese Army received under the Bright Star Campaigns discussed earlier. So old veterans of the Anya-Nya I war were appointed in the hope that they would make a difference in the battlefields.

Hopes were also raised further when Brigadier Yukwan, assuming that he was empowered to device ways and means that might help the new regime to reverse the war, began contacting southern politicians of various shades of opinion. He asked concerned southern leaders to hold a meeting and to make recommendation that might produce an agenda the regime might use to solve the southern problem.

Of course, the main dispute centred on whether the south would be administered as one region as was the case in 1972-82 period or divided into three regions as was the case in the 1983-89 interlude.

But while these contacts and meetings were still going on among the southern politicians, rumour began circulating that the new regime was working on the possibility to permit the south to secede—as the south has proven a stumbling block for establishment of an Islamic state in the country.

This rumour gave a new impetus to more politicking and hope that Brigadier Yukon's recommendations could herald the beginning of a new era. But as southerners were speculating what line of action the new regime would take toward the realisation of peace in the south, the Junta made an abrupt reshuffle.

It gave no reason why political appointees and the governors were replaced so soon. It only became clearer later that the new appointees were all Muslims, most of who were newly converted Muslims or born-again southern Islamists.

Pio Yukwan, Dominic Kassiano and Martin Malual lost their jobs to Islamists: Ahmed al-Radi Jaber, Amin Ismael Jula and Ali Tamin Fartak respectively. Instead Yukwan was moved to a new place, as Chairman of the RCC Political Committee replacing Brigadier Osman Ahmed Hassan. The latter had been dismissed from the regime following dispute over the execution of 28 officers for their alleged role in the foiled coup attempt in April 1990.

Also in the reshuffle, the new regional governors were appointed. George Kongor Arop, former Brigadier of Police who was retired prematurely for administrative reasons, was reinstated into active service and appointed Governor of Bahr al-Ghazal in the place of Makur who was assigned a new role as Ambassador in the Foreign Ministry.

Brigadier Paul Reth (also of police) was appointed Governor of Upper Nile instead of Gatluak Deng who became minister of Health, and Brigadier Saturnino Arika was appointed Governor of Equatoria replacing Alison Manani Magaya who also became minister of Labour.

The governors in the south were deputised by Islamists, the real power wielders, and a move that raised suspicions about the circumstances behind these appointments. The Deputy Governor of Upper Nile became Mangu Ajak; Abakar Mustafa, Deputy Governor of Bahr al-Ghazal; and Khamis Mursaal, Deputy Governor of Equatoria.

Besides, appointees to the newly created ministries in the south—such as education, culture, religious affairs, youth and social affairs—were all occupied by Islamists.

The appointment of Islamists to key positions in the south for the first time was contrary to the regime's repeated assertion that the south was spared from Islamic Sharia Law.

Appointing Islamists to places of authority made it obvious that, Islamising the government in the south, was only a harbinger to the Islamisation of the south and its public institutions in a top-down fashion.

9.8. THE JUBA PEACE ENCOUNTER AND CONSEQUENCES

Encouraged by the response by Southerners to join the system and in line with the recommendations of the National Dialogue Conference of October 1989, and aware that it was securely in the hands of hard-core Islamists, the regime convened in the regional capital of Juba in 1990. It was chaired by Colonel Mohamed al-Amin al-Khalifa, the Chairman of the RCC Peace Commission.

The government brought together all the pro-government southern members from the three regions. This was despite the fact that the city was under the SPLA siege. At first, it appeared as though the Convention was organised as a challenge or defiance against the SPLA attempt to exert total control over the city.

But in essence, it was an attempt to make the southern politicians to endorse the Islamist policies, a parallel to the Juba Conference of 1947 that brought together northern representatives and the southern chiefs under the auspices of the colonial authorities.

Indeed, the purpose of the Juba Encounter, like the Juba Conference of 1947, was to make the southern politicians endorse the recommendations of the National Dialogue that had recommended the Sudan as a united entity ruled under a federal system.

Most of the southern representatives were hand picked in accordance to their political commitment to the new system. Southern Islamists were notorious in their display of Islamic fervour, including painting the Convention Hall in 'Green' assumed to be the colour of Islam.

During the week long discussion there was a simmering resentment by many conferees about the way in which the proceedings were being manipulated by the Islamists. This resentment was expressed in various ways including shouting down the Chairman. Regardless, a number of recommendations were hammered out at last. The most important were that:

1. The representatives of the south had unanimously adopted the National Dialogue resolution that federalism was the best solution to the problem of Southern Sudan.

2. The three regions should continue to be administered separately as opposed to the 1972 order.

3. The representatives of the south were of the opinion that peaceful settlement of the conflict in the south be based on negotiated settlement between the Sudanese themselves and without any foreign interference.

The proposal for an internal peace settlement, especially that it came from Southerners, was very attractive to the authorities to the extent that it was played out of proportion to let it appear as a total surrender in favour of a lasting unity of the war torn nation.

In brief, the aim of the authorities seemed to have been to "liberate Southern Sudan from the war of SPLA through internal negotiations," just to borrow the words of Matthew Obur, one of the veteran southern politicians.

Back in Khartoum to report to the RCC Chairman, Colonel al-Khalifa brought news of great joy to the Junta that Southerners have endorsed the National Dialogue recommendations on the top, an internal settlement of the southern problem.

From then on all top executives and the mass media were all out campaigning vigorously for an internal negotiated peaceful settlement which came to be popularly known as the "Peace from Within" approach.

Basing its decisions on the Juba Encounter, RCC, without any hesitation, ordered the formation of the Peace Commission charged with the responsibility to formulate policies for the peace from within strategy. Within weeks, the Peace Commission set up its structures and appointed administrative personnel. The peace from within was set rolling to its goal.

9.9. THE ISLAMISTS PEACE FROM WITHIN STRATEGY

Observers of the Sudanese peace process did not seem to agree about the origin of the internal peace process often referred to as the NIF's "Peace from Within" strategy on the war in the south. Many believed that it was the brain child of General Zubeir Mohamed Saleh. Others were of the opinion that it was al Turabi's basic strategy to win the war.

Whatever people say about the origin of "Peace from Within" approach, the consensus is that the junta NIF had, right from the onset, adopted an approach which was different from the approaches used by the previous Khartoum regimes for peace talks with the SPLA.

The earlier strategy was seen as internationalising the problem of the south and must be abandoned in favour of a new policy to win the Southerners from within the country and negotiate peace with them.

The new strategy, as the authorities assumed, would clearly alienate the SPLA from its recruitment bases in the south rendering it weak in the process to the point were it could easily finally collapse if not defeated.

However, while winning the support of the Southerners inside the country through peace gestures, other methods that included political blackmail and direct financial inducements were also being used to include weakening the rebels and perhaps force them to accept the terms of the peace within the regime planned stratagem.

Basically the aim of the "Peace from Within" strategy was to starve the SPLA from the grassroots from which it derived the bulk of its support. In the meantime policies could be formulated to identify suitable and committed southerners that could implement these policies in cooperation with the northern authorities at the back seat supervising and directing the process. Major General Zubeir Mohamed Salih, the Deputy Chairman of the RCC Junta, was appointed to oversee this important mission and to organise the Peace Commission and put the plan to action.

9.10. THE PEACE AND DEVELOPMENT FOUNDATION

The Peace Development Foundation, a political and administrative mechanism that would translate and put the "Peace from Within" strategy into practice was immediately established. Fadl al-Sid Abu-Gasseissa, a hard core Islamist zealot was appointed minister of state and Director General to head of the Peace Foundation.

Musa Sid Ahmed, another Islamist, became his Deputy in addition to number of assistants. These included : Dr. Mubarak Gissm Allah Zaid (who claimed to a southern origin); Brigadier Kamal Muktar (fresh from Talaban Afghanistan); Abdel Salam Suleiman (of Dawa al-Islamiyyah); Ahmed al-Radi Jaber (of southern origin); Mohamed Kheir; Musa Suleiman (Nuba); Ali Tamin Fartak (Southerner) and many members of the NIF security apparatus. At the helm of this apparatus was Colonel Mohamed al-Khalifa, who heads the Peace Commission under the guidance of Zubeir Mohamed Saleh.

The set up of administrative structures in the Peace Foundation meant that cadres had to be appointed to carry out the duties of the jihad state and to open up branches all over the southern regions where they would recruit southern cohorts who meet specific criteria of selection. The rules were strict that any official who served in the Peace Development Foundation must carry one of the following labels at his lap. He has to be a)—anti-SPLA confirmed by words and deeds; b) a confirmed and committed Islamist; or c) a newly-approved Islamist convert.

At first hand, it appeared as if the cadres needed would not be available in the south. But with huge sums of money floating in the Peace Foundation, many southern former government officials and unemployed youth were attracted to choose between two hard choices: the devil and the deep blue sea, death by starvation or survival.

In the Sudan of the NIF, the combination of two conditions (an affirmed anti-SPLA and an approved Islamist) was an added advantage in the job market for southerners. The people who passed the two conditions had no problems but climbed rapidly from one constitutional post to another.

A good example was Arop Acier Akol. As an anti-SPLA he was appointed Regional Minister of Agriculture in Bahr al Ghazal Region. On becoming a professed Islamic convert, he was immediately appointed Governor of Warrap State which combined former Gogrial and Tonj districts in Bahr al-Ghazal region.

When he went on Hajj in Mecca, Arop Acier became so entrenched in the system to the extent that nobody could compete with him in any incentive distribution. Even individuals like Kerubino Kwanyin Bol, former SPLA strongman, could not deter authorities from standing solidly in support of Sheikh Arop Acier whose loyalty could not even match the ethics set in the Holy Quran.

Throughout the war it became a normal practice that southerners who demonstrated their anti-SPLA poster and were Muslims stood the best chances of recruitment, not only in the Peace Foundation, but also, as a general rule, in the public service employment. The next group that benefited from the state's incentives was the new anti-SPLA and converts to Islam. Through the application of Islamic criteria and hatred against the SPLA—of which any bigot could excel in both—the administration in the south was veritably handed over to the novices, inexperience and unskilled manpower. Southern Sudan became a region of no system and no professional ethics.

Most of the southern officials had to choose (in the process) whether to convert and work in the south, leave for northern Sudan or join the SPLA at the first available opportunity or join the system against their conscience. Those who could afford to join the rebels sold whatever property they had and trekked into exile en mass via Egypt.

The bulk of the southern population previously displaced from the south into northern states and who continued to live in squalid conditions were to survive at the skin of their teeth so to speak.

By doing odd jobs such as brewing local beers at the risk of being flogged before Islamic courts after confiscating their brewing utensils or detained in prisons when apprehended by the Islamic police, southern women and children became the main bread winners for the families' survival.

In the northern cities the daily death of friends and relatives became a blessing since their death became means of survival. On hearing of the death of a friend or relative, people would run and converge at the funeral places in order to eat free meals.

As a result of this poverty-charged environment, many elderly politicians who had nothing to live on, though embarrassed by the need to compromise their political beliefs, reluctantly agreed to join the Islamic bandwagon. Others however, managed to survive miraculously though emaciated by malnourished ailments and untreated diseases.

Southerners who went or were already behind the rebel lines of defences were the lucky ones. They could feed on the leaves, wild fruits and roots of plants. Thanks to the mercy of the bushes of southern Sudan, wild fruits and leaves were in abundance.

Nonetheless, few leading politicians from the defunct Union of African Partied USAP despite financial difficulties and assistance they gave to southerners in serious need like the sick and the bereaved, stood their ground and became spokesmen for the southern communities. It was through them that the voice of the south was raised louder. In the end they became the political vanguard for the south throughout the war.

Having set up an effective plan to defeat the SPLA and institutionalised in it in various branches through the Peace Foundation, the next move for the regime was now to implement the anti-SPLA policy to starve the SPLA of any source of support from the grassroots.

As an affirmation of their support for the regime, weaklings among southern politicians were trumped and given handouts to go out and reach tribal chiefs in the rural areas to bring them into the fold. The Chiefs in turn were expected to influence their subjects to support the system or buy them away from the SPLA rank and file.

Money from the Peace Foundation was often channelled through private means to all the chiefs, particularly in Upper Nile and Bahr al-Ghazal. The intention of which was to buy some SPLA commanders in their localities. But such a venture became very risky because those who were identified as being involved in this peace from within business in the SPLA had reportedly paid dearly.

Abu Gasseissa, the Director General of the Peace Foundation, spent most of his time in the plane travelling to and from the south supervising and the implementation of this "Peace from Within" policy.

One such a dramatic example of an attempt to channel money secretly is best demonstrated when Abu Gassaeissa sent a coffin full of money to an SPLA local commander in order to win him away from the SPLA.

According to report, the coffin was expected to contain the body of the

Commander's late father who had died in the north and was being brought home for burial.

Unfortunately, according to reports, the whereabouts of the coffin and the accompanying team headed by the late Chief's son who was living outside the country and who had just been recruited by the Peace Foundation had not been revealed since arriving to the locality. Nor did the SPLA or the Sudanese government bother to talk about the incident.

The third step made by the Peace Foundation was to send a large sum of money to the Islamists who were made Deputy Governors in order to neutralise the mainstream SPLM in their regions.

But this was not practicable in Equatoria, as 98 per cent of the region was kept at bay by the Bright Star Campaign, and in Bahr al-Ghazal where the bulk of the SPLA fighting force was derived. The mission was very successful and effective in Upper Nile for various reasons that are outside the purview of this book.

Suffice it to state that the move to neutralise the SPLA in Upper Nile region is best demonstrated by the Mangu Ajak in a conversation with the author in his office in Khartoum in 1992. Commenting as to how he managed to bring peace into the larger part of Upper Nile, Governor Ajak[12] said:

> "It was not an easy task. It was a co-ordinated effort with the cooperation of the central government and the Peace Development Foundation. On my part, when I received the funding, I ordered according to the laid down plan that the old approach, (whereby the rebels who strayed into the cities were apprehended and handed to the security organs or police), was abandoned and instead a more peaceful and workable approach was adopted. For instance, I divided Malakal into wards. Each ward was well supplied with food provisions and money. And whenever a rebel strayed into a ward in any part of the city, the leader of the ward would entertain the rebel concerned. A celebration (of his return) was held in his honour and when he left the city back to the forest he was given money, food, and relief items for himself and his friends."

Mangu Ajak remarked with a great deal of air of a commander who succeeded luring many enemy troops into his side with nothing but simple non-military tactics. When news reached all the corners of the regions many rebels, in response to our new generosity, poured into the cities. Perhaps rebels tracked to Malakal almost weekly. For instance, about 18 SPLA officers reported to Malakal just before the split in 1991. "That is how we gradually brought peace to our region," Mangu concluded.

The fourth successful mission by the Peace Foundation that almost broke the backbone of the SPLA was launched in Nairobi, one of the main refugee concentration centres in East Africa. This mission was successfully carried through by Musa Ali Suleiman, one of the hard core Islamists who was appointed an emissary for refugee affairs and attached to the Sudanese Embassy in Nairobi.

Upon arrival in Kenya, Suleiman set up relief centres in Nairobi and particularly in areas with large concentration of refugees. Suleiman's operations involved identifying the vulnerable—the sick, the hungry, the bereaved and especially those refugees who had fallen out of favour with the SPLA.

In a conversation with the author, Musa Ali said. "Once I sighted a refugee in great need, I would give him assistance and if he suspected the offer, I assured him that it was a personal gift by a Sudanese to a Sudanese in great need and was entitled to it. Within a short period many sick, hungry and penniless refugees were supplied."

One such good example Musa Suleiman noted was in 1990 when a senior SPLA commander was sick in Nairobi. The SPLA did not have sufficient money to treat this commander. "I released a good sum of money and of course the commander was treated. He also got a substantial amount of money on being discharged. I understand now that that commander is in charge of the SPLA in Kajo Keji area," Musa[13] concluded.

The fifth strategy which appeared on the surface as humanitarian in nature but in essence very humiliating to the displaced people from southern Sudan was the role played by the Islamic Relief Agencies, especially *Dawa al-Islamia* and Islamic African Relief Agency (IARA).

These agencies were veritably government organs advancing the government's Islamic project for the Sudan. This was demonstrated in the fact that both of these agencies were headed outstanding public figures where the former TMC President General Suwar al-Dahab was the Chairman of Dawa al-Islamia while the former Junta Premier, Dr. Gizzouli Dafaalah, was the Chairman of the IARA.

The Islamic Agencies, instead of sending relief items to the displaced people as foreign aid agencies did, adopted a policy that put forward Islamisation as a precondition for receiving such food aid.

So, whenever Dawa al-Islamia and IARA staff moved to the displaced camp with their food, they always required willing converts to come forward, utter some Quranic word such as Allah Akbar (God is great), and then they will receive food while those unyielding starved.

The immorality of tying relief to religious proselytisation defeats the purposes of philanthropy or charity. Charitable organisations are generally supposed to offer a service without hindering prohibitions. But in Islamic Sudan, this is a clear-cut option. Islamise or starve!

The most humiliating practice by the Islamic Relief organisations and particularly *Islamic Muafig al-Kheiri* was a practice carried at Marial Ajiith camps some few miles north east of Wau town and at Obel camp in Upper Nile.

In those camps, the people, even the most elderly men who embraced Islam through food inducements, were expected to undergo the painful ritual of circumcision so as to be a complete Muslim.

The Sudanese Arabs believe that circumcision is an Islamic tradition more than anything to do with hygiene. But some of the natives in South Sudan do not usually practice circumcision in their traditional taboos. So they naturally found this practice veritably alien and humiliating.

Some of the natives who underwent that unacceptable operation at Marial Ajiith in Wau, which were done in unhygienic conditions, suffered serious bleeding and swelling of their organs and some even died.

For the natives involved and their dependants; undergoing circumcision just to receive regular rations of food was such an ordeal to undertake.

Reportedly, many natives who resisted such practice could not receive food, and decided to walk out of those camps into the SPLA controlled territories. Many who left Wau with nothing to eat on the way to the countryside died on the way.

One elder speaking to the author once said: "I better die with dignity than suffer humiliation and indignity in order to live." Indeed, many chose death instead of accepting food in exchange of Islamic faith. It was predictable that the NIF government was out to destroy the south right from the grassroots to the top echelons and then face the SPLA with the fervour of Jihad as discussed below.

9.11. THE JIHAAD WAR IN THE MAKING

In Islam, there are only two conceptions of the cosmos: *Dar al-Islam* (or the abode of Islam) and *Dar al-Harb* (the frontier of war). In the former, peace and Islamic social justice prevails. While in *Dar al-Harb*, the state of war prevails. *Dar al-Harb* is normally a nation under pagan or non-Muslim rule. The entire South Sudan was declared Dar al Harb.

Thus, a Muslim ruler, under holy wrath and obligation, is supposed to wage a Jihad (holy war) upon *Dar al-Harb* nations until the people therein capitulate and sign a *dhimma* (contract of surrender). They must then be made to pay (*jizya*) a tax to an Islamic state in order to; affirm a second class status and obedience to Islamic government until they embrace Islam.

Traditionally, a jihad may be waged to obtain land/territory or to purify society. This is also the context by which the Sudanese Islamists understand and undertake Jihad in the Southern Sudan. They view the south as *Dar al-Harb*, and the North, *Dar al-Islam*.

Northern Sudanese have been seeking desperately and would do anything to keep the Sudan united despite the difficult war situations facing them. They will never allow the Southern Sudan to go its own way to have a separate nation; Hilary Paul Logali said in an interview: "The wealthy always conjure countless tricks in order to stick permanent to power. Therefore the wealthy northern Sudanese elite have, since independence in 1956, been conjuring tricks including the Jihad so as to create a homogeneous Muslim Arab state in which they have the monopoly over the African land and its resources and thereby hold to power permanently." [14]

Perhaps Hilary Logali may have been right and probably so because the successive northern Sudanese rulers have all along used Islam as the weapon against the south, particularly against the SPLA which they saw strong enough to make the dreams of the liberation of the peripheral peoples come true.

The Jihad, to some extent, had also been used by the traditional Islamic parties as a whip against the secular nationalism in Northern Sudan said Hilary Logali.

Apparently, it was against this background that the Islamic Government of the National Salvation declared a Jihad in 1990 in order to defeat the SPLA rebels who by then had exerted firm hold of many parts of Southern Sudan and also made incursions into Northern Sudan. The SPLA was also at the threshold of achieving a complete victory by 1992.

The declaration of *Jihad (1990)* was clearly a pre-emptive move to launch a counter offensive against the SPLA in the next dry season (1992). The intention was apparently to deny the SPLA any opportunity it could have seized to launch their final assault on the remaining parts of the South Sudan which were still in the hands of the government troops. With the south firmly under their control, as discussed earlier, the SPLA could have turned to concentrate their efforts in War Zone II (Northern Sudan).

Before the government could launch its dry season offensives, it was decided that areas in northern Sudan under rebels' control should be recaptured first and then massive military operations in Southern Sudan could be conducted.

Thus in the middle of 1990, the government summoned all the able-bodied men to report to the camps of the Popular Defence Force to be ready for a *Jihad* in the south. Large PDF (the Mujahideen holy warriors) were assembled, (often induced with money as well), which also included the students from the main universities.

The NIF cadres included Senior Ministers, medical/veterinary doctors, engineers, businessmen and others. It was a war of survival of the Arab-Islamic interests in the Sudan that was about to be taken over by the Christians and Africans from the south.

According to reports, all those assembled were told (in no uncertain terms) to fight the war of survival. While still waiting for a final assault, the Mujahideen were also given instructions about what they expected in the south: *"Defending the faith or martyrdom!."*

To the simple village warriors who have been enlisted as Mujahideen, some war poetry (similar to the early wars of Prophet Muhammad) were recited to incite their zeal. The verses[15]:

When the Army of God (Mujahideen) are marching in the south, against the rebels; when birds on the trees see the Mujahideen advancing, they just fly towards the rebel camps…the Mujahideen would then attack and wipe out the rebels without any resistance…God is great, God is great.

And when the monkeys on the trees top see that the Mujahideen are coming to attack the rebels, they (monkeys) would swoop down the roads and sweep the mines. The Mujahideen would then march without difficulty until they reach the rebel camps which they would devastate…God is great God is great.

And when a Mujahid (holy warrior, singular) is wounded and lifted up his eyes, he would then see his allocated seat in Heaven…God is great God is great. The bodies of the fallen martyrs do not decompose but release the Heavenly odour from their bodies…God is great! God is great!

9.12. THE JIHAAD WAR IS FINALLY UNLEASHED

When the jihad was finally unleashed, the forces went on four fronts. The First front marched through the Southern Blue Nile. Within a matter of weeks, Kurmuk, Geissan and other posts under the SPLA were overrun with ease. This jihad, it may be recalled, coincided with political changes in Ethiopia and the crumbling Communist world.

Most serious hit was Ethiopia, it was increasingly battered by various rebel groups fighting the regime in Addis Ababa. The regime was hard pressed by the two main rebels groups of the Ethiopian People's Democratic Revolutionary Front (EPDRF), and the Eritrean People's Liberation Front (EPLF).

The second Jihaad front going along the White Nile also defeated the SPLA in Maban forcing the SPLA retreat to the border zone around Gambella. The SPLA forces in northern Upper Nile (the Melut area) also withdrew to eastern Upper Nile around the Nasir area after a crushing defeat by the government's forces.

Meanwhile, the SPLA forces under William Nyuon Bany clashed with Ethiopian rebels (EPDRF) and retreated to eastern Upper Nile. Nyuon, who was acting also as Chairman (since John Garang was away), had assisted the Ethiopian government in the western front around Assossa area. But he stumbled over a superior force of EPDRF and was forced to flee to eastern Upper Nile. These changes in the military situation in the region were working in favour of the NIF regime.

Acting swiftly, the NIF started giving supplies to the EPDRF and at the same time moving in its forces to occupy the areas vacated by the SPLA in the Sudan-Ethiopian border. In the process a small contingent of SPLA force, under Commander Abu aila Mustafa, finding itself isolated in Southern Blue Nile, decided to surrender to the Sudan government forces. Commander Mustafa had been captured by the SPLA in Kurmuk in 1988 and had joined the SPLA willingly. He became a commander and posted back to Southern Blue Nile.

Nevertheless, Mustafa's surrender was celebrated in Khartoum. He was interviewed every day over Radio Omdurman and TV under a programme "Sahat al-Fida" or the "Fields of Sacrifices." This was a boost to the Mujahideen, who were made to believe that Allah was sanctioning government victories over the rebels.

Another huge front of the jihad offensive was sent to Nuba Mountains. The first target there was Jebel Tulshi, which the attacking forces had assumed was the Headquarters of Commander Yousuf Kuwa Mekki.

Despite intensive attacks and despite being isolated from the main SPLA bases in the south, Commander Kuwa Mekki managed to dig in and concentrated his forces in the south-western parts of Nuba Mountains. There he held firmly entrenched until new consignment of arms and men reached him in 1992.

However, the scale and manner of the jihadyya devastated the Nuba Mountains and Ingessena Hills, northern Bahr al-Ghazal and western Upper Nile can best be demonstrated by the *Fatwah* (Islamic injunction) declared by the Muslim *Ulema* (Islamic scholars) meeting in El-Obeid during the peak of this jihad in 1992/93. The Ulema's injunction stated[16] that the Conference of the Ulema, the Imams of the Mosques and the Sheikhs of the Sufi Sects of Kordofan State held at the People's Committee Hall in El-Obeid, has hereby resolved the following. It issued a fatwah about the imperative of mobilising the people for jihad to fight the rebel forces in Southern Kordofan and in Southern Sudan for the reasons stated here below:

1. The rebels in the southern Kordofan and the Southern Sudan have rebelled against the state. They have waged war against the Muslims with the prime objective, being the killing and massacring of Muslims, the destruction of the Mosques, burning the copies of the Quran and violating the honour and dignity of Muslims.

2. The rebels are being driven and misled by the enemies of Islam from among the Zionists, the Christian crusaders and the forces of arrogance who have been supplying them with food and arms. Therefore the rebels who are Muslims and are fighting against the State are hereby declared apostates of Islam.

3. As for the non-Muslims fighting against the state, they are hereby declared kuffar (infidels) who have been standing up against the efforts of preaching, proselytisation and the spread of Islam into Africa...

4. Islam has justified the fighting and killing of both categories without any hesitation whatsoever with the following Quranic Evidence: Allah says, Oh you who believe, if there is anyone who becomes an apostate from among yourselves away from Islam, Allah will bring about another nation who will love him and loves them of those who are humble towards the believers and proud above the *kuffar,* they will struggle in jihad for the sake of Allah and will not heed any blame which may be levelled against them by any one.

The result of the government's forces and the Mujahideen's massive attacks on the Nuba Mountains was to have everlasting effects on the Nuba people.

According to Human Rights and other international organisations[17] who visited the Nuba Mountains, the attacks on Nuba displaced tens of thousands. Many of the displaced Nuba were driven to the so-called 'peace zones' (similar to the Nazi Concentration Camps) where about 91 camps were set in Um Ruwaba District near El-Obeid town.

The camps were guarded by the PDF (similar to Hitler's SS), while the Islamic relief agencies worked on Islamisation. Professor Lesch writes: "Nuba villages were systematically encircled and destroyed, using helicopter gunships and high-level bombers as well as artillery and foot soldiers.

Terrified civilians were first relocated to North Kordofan, where there were virtually no health or relief services and jobs could be found only in Arab farms and homes. The nine-one special 'peace villages' were established outside the Nuba Mountains, guarded by PDF militiamen".

Those 'villages' contained 167,000 residents by September 1992, 80 percent of who were children. Children attended Quranic schools, women's literacy programs inculcated NIF's version of Islamic beliefs and behaviour, and men were forcibly circumcised.

By the year 1993, 250,000 Nuba people had been displaced—nearly a third of the 800,000 Nuba were displaced in the mountains. The government sold their land to Arab entrepreneurs or handed it over to government and military officers and leaders of Arab militias[18].

Meanwhile, a third prong had moved from Nuba Mountains to Bentiu Oil-fields areas to link up with the Arab Messirya militiamen in south-western

Kordofan. In the event, western and northern Upper Nile was effectively re-occupied.

It was at this juncture, perhaps, that the Anya Nya II warlord, Paulino Matip Nhial, was given a license to own a huge army in order of protecting the oil fields from the rebels in the whole western Upper Nile.

On the Bahr al-Ghazal front, the troops were moved by rail until they linked with Mujhadeen and the Messirya militias mid-way. There, an invasion of northern Bahr al-Ghazal was undertaken. Waves of attacks were launched which caught the SPLA forces in the area almost by surprise, consequently were unable to make any resistance.

It appeared that the Nuba front also marched through Abyei District. The Abyei northern part was completely swept clean and used as a springboard to attack Gogrial District.

The Wau rail-track was another Front used by the Mujihaadeen in collaboration with the Arab Murahaleen. Thus moving in great numbers along both sides of the rail track, others on horse back while others were on foot, the forces swept the country along the rail tracks clean.

According to reports monitored by the author, the trains carried military wares and food, while the militiamen were the vanguard army attacking and destroying the Dinka villages. In the process, granaries and houses were set on fire, cattle and goats were driven away while looting and plundering anything of value including chickens. A chunk of the booty was slaves: mostly women and children. Professor Lesch wrote that the PDF publication specified that, following the Quranic injunction, each foot soldier during those raids should obtain one portion of the booty. And each member of the cavalry should obtain two portions. Furthermore, fighters were encouraged to take women as concubines and when they become pregnant become bounties since the children born by these women would be Arabs and Muslim [19].

The Arabs' militias, the Messirya, had made a devastating attack on the Nuba and Daju villages in the Lagowa county in western Kordofan just some few months before the overall jihad fronts were unleashed.

An incident between the Arabs and the Nuba of Lagowa had taken place when the Arab herd man allowed the cattle to pasture in the farmland and breaking crops of Daju Nuba native. This led to intertribal war.

In the attacks, the Arab militia joined by PDF soldiers with the encouragement of Military Commander massacred 125 Nuba natives, destroying 20 villages, and set fire upon the crops that were yet to be harvested. At least 20,000 Nuba natives were left homeless and displaced.

The Lagowa incident coincided with that in White Nile, December 1989, when the Sabah Arabs went on rampage killing between 600 to 1,000 people belonging to the Southern Sudanese communities: the Shilluk, Burun, Nuer and Dinka.

A Shilluk worker had killed an Arab trader over a dispute to take leave during Christmas holidays. The employer (the Arab businessman) had refused to grant leave. This dispute soon led to a fight. In the scuffle the Arabs in the town, with the support of the army, retaliated. In the massacre, those who took refuge at the police station (91) were never spared.

Thus while the SPLA forces were flexing their muscles in the remaining cities hoping to retake the towns already occupied by the government forces, the government's operations that were discreetly planned and managed hit the SPLA territories starting from the weakest points.

While widening its areas of control in the Southern Blue Nile and Kordofan, the government forces were, in the next dry season of 1992, to carry the war into the SPLA main bases in the deep south.

Nevertheless, looking at the government's activities, the changing international circumstances and geopolitics, it was possible to predict that the SPLA military defeat or victory in 1992 hung on the hinges.

CHAPTER 10
THE NIF STRATAGEM AND SPLIT IN SPLM/SPLA

10.0. THE SETTING

The Bright Star Campaign activities that brought greater part of the south and some parts of the Northern Sudan under SPLA control were supposed to be accelerated in the next dry season of 1991. This was not to be. In fact it was the beginning of a setback in SPLA armed struggle.

The disintegration of the former Soviet Union and other Communist States in Eastern Europe had had political repercussions upon their satellite states in Africa, such as Ethiopia. The regime of Mengistu Haile Mariam, which was the main backer of the SPLA, had collapsed in the spring of 1991 causing great anxiety in the SPLA camp.

The SPLA Politico-Military High Command must meet and assess the situation and draw up new strategies due to the loss of military support and bases in Ethiopia. But while preparation was in progress to hold a meeting in Kapoeta District in Eastern Equatoria, a coup sought to topple Dr. John Garang was announced in Nasir on 28 August 1991.

Three Alternate members of the High Command Dr. Lam Akol Ajawin, Dr. Riek Machar Teny Durghon and Commander Gordon Koang Chol stated that they have overthrown the Chairman and Commander-in-Chief of the SPLM/A.

The three officers in their statement read over the BBC World Service stated their reasons that justified their actions. The reasons were that John Garang was:

1. Ruling the Movement in authoritarian fashion.

2. Forcefully recruiting teenagers into the SPLA.

3. Jailing officers who challenge him and not able to expound differences between the north and the South amicably.

Although Dr. Garang dismissed the move as a theoretical coup, it nonetheless heralded the beginning of split in the Movement into what became known as Torit and Nasir factions that were the headquarters of respective groups.

The SPLA split came at a wrong time, especially after achieving strings of victories in the South Sudan. But the internecine factional conflict that ensued tied each faction to its own adamant position.

Both sides subsequently employed tactics that were designed to defeat the other, This inevitably led to the break-up of the Movement. As a result the NIF forces took control of the areas which had been under the SPLA.

Thus Jomo Kenyatta's adage that: "When two elephants fight, the grass suffers," indeed, became applicable to the two factions in the subsequent years when the people of Southern Sudan, the grass in this case, bore the brunt of the internecine war between the two sides. In this Chapter, I shall discuss the factors that led to the break-up of the Movement.

10.1.1. THE FIRST SIGNS OF CRACK IN THE SPLA/SPLM

Observers of the Southern Sudan second civil war seem to concur on one basic fact that the crack in the SPLA High Command in August 1991 did have far fetching root causes. The activities and methods used by the Sudan government against it and the behaviour and activities of some of the SPLA members were probably instrumental. The latter, as an internal element, is probably more crucial than the former, an outside element.

The behaviour of some SPLA officers was destined to shake the movement almost to its foundation. From this perspective, it would appear that the main problem was the initial composition of the SPLM/SPLA leadership hierarchy itself (discussed in Chapter 8).

From the onset, it was obvious that the composition of the leadership hierarchy was neither homogenous nor did it belong to one politico-ideological orientation as well as military training.

Perhaps some senior members on the top echelon did not ascribe to the agenda contained in the Movement's Manifesto. All five permanent members of the High Command fell into this category. John Garang de Mabior and Salva Kiir Mayardiit had worked together as members of the Underground Revolutionary Movement since the Bussere days in 1973-74 (Chapter 2).

It was the Bussere group that later became the revolutionary group. This group was well versed with what the goals and strategies of the liberation struggle were all about. The revolutionary group was assumed to follow revolutionary principles in spirit and letter. It was not surprising, therefore, that the bulk of the Movement rank and file owed their allegiance and respect to the revolutionary wing.

This group won the respect of the bulk of the fighting men and the refugee community because they were humane and human. Hence, they represented and reflected the ideals the Revolution cherished: to import into the minds and souls of its followers, revolutionary principles and values. Essentially, it was this group that accepted the socialist orientation as a means to an end and not the other way round.[1]

The second group, composed of Commander Kerubino Kwanyin Bol and William Nyuon Bany, were nominal members of the Underground Revolution and became active members between 1981 and 1983. As for Arok Thon Arok, he climbed the bandwagon in 1983-1984. The three were, therefore, regarded as co-opted members of the Movement. This group, however, saw the liberation struggle differently.

To the trio, liberation was an end in itself. They saw the liberation through the power each one of them mustered in the Movement and how South Sudan could be liberated with one of them at the helm of the Movement. This could explain why they had at the initial stage been fighting against Anya II before they staged the Bor and Ayod uprisings.

The magalomaniac manners of Kwanyin, Nyuon and Arok and the torturous and ruthless way in which they dealt with soldiers under their control earned them the label of 'reactionary officers;' a name which offended the trio and made them more brutal against those who appeared to stand in their way to glory.

It was perhaps in this light that the atrocities recorded against the SPLA/SPLM leadership could best be explained. It was also in this light that the struggle between the two groups, which made up the top leadership of the Movement, could be explained and which eventually brought about the break-up.

However, as the Movements proceeded with the liberation struggle, the differences on the top echelon began to widen. The behaviour of the trio became a time bomb, which should be safely defused without making further damage. But that also became more explosive than leaving them in the Movement. To tolerate the trio was as dangerous as getting rid of them.[2]

But a decision had to be made. It was finally made and Kerubino Kwanyin Bol and Arok Thon Arok, who thought there would be no Movement without them, were finally caged to the relief of everybody among the rank and file who had had the share of atrocities meted upon them by them. A major threat to the SPLA split was thus averted albeit temporary and the struggle continued.

Following the arrest of Commanders Kerubino Kwanyin Bol and Arok Thon Arok (1987-1988) it was expected that the Movement had gone through its most difficult period in its five years of continuous liberation struggle. From then on, the Movement would pursue its objectives unperturbed since the elements of reactions have supposedly been eliminated.

Reassuringly, the SPLA Bright Star campaign launched in 1988 had scored victory after victory. By 1991 it had not only brought larger chunk of southern territory under its control, it had substantial presence in the traditional northern Sudan—in the Nuba Mountains and Ingessena Hills. Even so, the arrest of two senior members of the Movement seemed to have left some cancerous marks on the Movement. Sooner than later, some serious signs showing power struggle within the Movement began to show up again here and there.

One of such was the debate and clamour for change and the reorganisation of the Movement's top echelon. This was heard everywhere, especially in the refugee camps and particularly at Itang, the main refugee camp discussed in Chapter 8. According to reports, the debate emanated from letters written by Professor Bari Wanji and orchestrated by elements within the High Command which were not known at first, but which became known as the 'Security Reports' came in to the High Command.

During the arrest of progressive officers in 1987, Captain [Professor] Bari Wanji, apparently the ringleader of the group, had escaped arrest and had, according to reports, sought sanctuary at the Cuban Embassy in Addis Ababa.

From his sanctuary, Captain Wanji is said to have continued writing letters agitating for change in the leadership of the SPLA/SPLM. In the opinion of Wanji the Movement had lost its Socialist oriented ideological track. At first, Professor Bari Wanji allegedly circulated his letters to the Socialist Embassies in Ethiopia urging them to stop their support for the SPLM/SPLA till a total change had been made and the Movement seen to be properly Socialist in its orientation and practice. Wanji later on began to direct his campaign for change to all the SPLA cadres and other non-Socialist Embassies in Ethiopia.

By 1988, Wanji's letters appeared to have gained sympathy from the rank and file of the SPLA and especially among the disgruntled officers and some of the members of the refugee communities who finally took it up against Dr. John Garang.

Wanji's letters were said to have been instrumental in provoking heated debates which eventually went all the way to the bushes of South Sudan. Eventually, some disgruntled members in the High Command were also believed to have approved such demands for change. It was not too long according to reports before the SPLM security named Dr. Lam Akol Ajawin as the prime suspect behind the agitation.

Dr. Peter Nyaba was also a suspect but was apparently spared for being regarded as one of the few revolutionaries who have only been enraged by the megalomaniac and ruthless performances and behaviour of the reactionary elements in the Politico-Military High Command such as extra-judicial executions of simple uneducated liberators.

Dr. Nyaba was particularly angered and disillusioned by the conduct of people like Kerubino Kwanyin Bol, William Nyuon and Arok Thon Arok. He continually referred to the necessity in changing the leadership which the reports said was directly against the person of the Chairman and Commander-in-Chief.

Another issue that directly contributed negatively in the future cohesiveness of the Movement and perhaps ignited the tendency for final break-up of the

Movement was the effect of a letter purportedly to have been written by Dr. Chol Dau Diing[3], a medical officer who worked in England.

Dr. Diing, a staunch supporter of the Movement was, indeed, one of the student pioneers of the armed struggle movement which spearheaded the formation of the SPLM/SPLA chapters in the United Kingdom in the 1980s. Diing later attended the launch of the SPLM/SPLA in Ethiopia in 1983 and consistently remained one of the most active leaders of the Movement in the United Kingdom.

Dr. Diing allegedly had written a personal letter to Dr. John Garang and delivered it to a person travelling to Addis Ababa. Unfortunately, the alleged letter was handed over to Lam Akol, the Director of the SPLM External Relations in Addis Ababa with a promise to hand it over to whom it concerned or to Deng Alor Kuol, the Office Manager in the Chairman's Office.

Perhaps out of curiosity and apparently to know its contents, according to report, Dr. Akol opened the letter and read it. Dr Diing's letter was advising that since victory was certain, it would be better if the officers of his home District of Bor be appointed to sensitive positions in various departments of the Movement's hierarchy.

The letter further advised that the Bor officers must be posted to important positions in foreign countries, ostensibly, to safeguard the continuity of Garang's leadership or perhaps to guarantee the Revolution by committed citizens.

Whichever the letter referred to, the old adage that charity must begin at home was probably the purpose of Dr. Diing's letter. Hence, since Garang comes from Bor District and is the Chairman of the Revolution, social and material benefits must first flow to his home area.

Amused and stunned by the contents of the letter, according to reports, Dr. Akol apparently photocopied the letter, sealed it back in the same envelope and passed it over to Commander Deng Alor in the Chairman's Office.

It had been the SPLA practice that letters to the Office of the Chairman from abroad must be opened for the security of the Chairman, as some mail might contain bombs from the enemy intending to injure the Movement. So all mail had to be opened before it could reach the Chairman. This letter was no exception, and upon receiving it, Deng Alor opened it and of course read it.

Upon reading the letter, he too was amused but also embarrassed by its contents. He jokingly remarked "...what is this charity 'begins at home?' Why don't these people in England come over to fight and to take the war to its logical conclusion?"

With this remark, and unaware that Akol had read it too, Alor passed it over to him to read. Pretentiously, as if he had not seen it before, Akol gave the letter back to Alor without any comment.

When John Garang came into his office and read the letter, according to reports, he too dismissed it outright as rubbish. "These people in Europe are joking. Do they think that this Movement is Anya Nya I or Anya Nya II? This is a people's revolution and people are given assignments according to their revolutionary contributions," Garang is said to have remarked. Although the letter was filed and almost forgotten, it was touchy and perhaps a scoop to Dr. Akol. It was perhaps a time bomb for the Movement as discussed in the subsequent paragraphs.

For sometime, Dr. Akol was reported to have used Dr. Diing's letter very discreetly among his confidants and close associates. However, in order to discredit Dr. Garang it was later seen by other members of the refugee community and most importantly by the disgruntled officers who had fallen out of favour with their leader.

To Akol, Dr. Diing's letter was an article of disrepute, a despicable matter which he felt should be exposed and publicised. While at first it did not have any impact, it was subsequently taken seriously in an underground campaign to oust John Garang rather than to urge him to reform the Movement.

10.1.2. IMMEDIATE CAUSES OF THE SPLIT IN THE SPLM/SPLA

In 1990, another important event presented itself—an event that would accelerate the ultimate cracking up of the Movement. Dr. Garang had just arrived in Addis Ababa ahead of a foreign tour which would take him to many parts of central Africa, Europe and the United States.

Dr. Garang had just given orders to meet his Politico-Military High Command to brief them and for some to accompany him on this trip. Dr. Riek Machar, the zonal Commander of Western Upper Nile, who had been fighting in the field since he was commissioned in 1985, was called to Addis Ababa to join the Chairman's entourage being put together. Commander James Wani Igga, the Zonal Commander of Central Equatoria had also arrived in Addis Ababa to join the mission.

In Addis Ababa, according to reports, Lam Akol and Commander Lual Diing Wuol were at the Headquarters. It was here that Dr. Lam Akol suggested that a meeting be held first with the Chairman to discuss some important and urgent issues (the issues he felt affected the Movement negatively) before the entourage could leave for the planned foreign tour.

Reports suggested that Machar seconded the idea that since there were five members of the High Command in town, it would be appropriate to meet the Chairman. Igga and Lual Diing also accepted Akol's suggestions and John Garang was informed accordingly. He responded positively and invited the four members to meet him.

In the meeting, according to reports, Akol presented three sensitive issues to the meeting, that:

1. Dr. John Garang had been running the Movement alone, making appointments, promotions, or dismissals without delegating authority to the PMHC for collective decision-making.

2. The question of detained prisoners was to be resolved.

3. The war strategy is reviewed; the Movement's goals and structures were to be re-appraised and reset.

Dr. Riek Machar is said to have seconded Akol's demands, commenting further in favour of the proposals. Machar stressed that the issues should be resolved with immediate effect. The other two members, Igga and Lual Diing, are reported to have not commented on the points raised.

John Garang is reported to have responded and informed the meeting that plans to hold a meeting of Politico-Military High Command were underway. Garang is said to have hinted that the meeting would be convened in the Gambella area in Western Ethiopia in June. The Chairman further advised that the issues that were raised in the meeting be re-tabled in their right perspective in the forthcoming meeting. He closed the meeting and he and his entourage left on the planned mission abroad.

In June, the proposed meeting did not convene as scheduled. Instead, general transfers of the zonal commanders and senior commanders were affected.

In the subsequent transfer, Commander Akol was removed from the Headquarters as the Director of SPLM External Relations, and posted to the front line at Maban area in north eastern Upper Nile adjacent to Southern Blue Nile. Dr. Lam may have seen his transfer with suspicion.

Dr. Riek, who seconded Akol's suggestion for reform was also transferred from western Upper Nile zonal command. Machar was ordered to proceed to take charge of a force in Melut area between Malakal and Renk in northern Upper Nile. Machar may have also taken his transfer with suspicion.

After being a zonal commander of western Upper Nile since he was commissioned in 1985 Riek did not appreciate this abrupt transfer and especially the transfer coming after challenging exchanges with the Chairman. In the event the two commanders—like colleagues who were affected by the transfer—grudgingly reported to their new command posts without any protests or complaints.

At his new command post in the north-eastern Upper Nile, Akol was reportedly not too happy with his new assignment, being haunted apparently for having unwittingly exposed himself when he criticised his most senior commander during the Addis Ababa meeting. He may have felt that he could possibly be detained like Kerubino and Arok.

Hence forward, Akol became more open about his disaffection with John Garang's style of running the Movement. Understandably, Akol began writing and circulating letters urging for the removal of John Garang as leader of the Movement. Dr. Diing's letter reportedly was often revealed as further evidence of "why Garang must be removed".

Aware that these letters might have reached John Garang, Akol then wrote an open letter to Garang—where copies were made available to various readers in the Movement and the High Command—against the SPLA rule that, letters to the Commander-in-Chief should not be subject to distribution.

In his open letter, however, Akol demanded that Garang must respond to the three points he had raised in the previous Addis Ababa meeting namely:

a) That Garang was running the Movement alone.

b) The question about the detained colleagues.

c) New war strategies and restructuring power relations. Akol was thus commencing his campaign against John Garang.

By early 1991, it was becoming abundantly clear that the political and military tides were all turning against the regime of Mengistu Haile Mariam in Ethiopia. The demise of Communist and Socialist governments in the former Soviet Union and Eastern Europe discussed above had directly affected Socialist satellite states in the developing world, especially in Africa.

Rebel groups of the Eritrean People's Liberation Front (EPLF), the Ethiopian People's Democratic Revolutionary Front (EPDRF) which combined the Tigrinyan (TPLF), Oromo Liberation Front (OLF), and other smaller ones, were now gaining ascendancy.

In the spring of 1991, Mengistu's regime collapsed, and the chaos that followed included the Sudan government's attempt to maximise the situation by continuous bombing of Sudanese refugees fleeing from the Ethiopian rebels.

The Sudan government had entered to support the EPRDF logistically and tactically when it saw a coalition of rebel groups was likely to push out the Derg's regime. External support was also flowing through Sudan towards that goal, and the EPRDF intensified the war and gained ground day by day.

In order to aid the ailing friend, the SPLA Acting Commander-in-Chief William Nyuon Bany sent an SPLA force to support the Ethiopian Army against the rebels. William Nyuon Bany occupied the Assossa Region and literally halting the Western flank of the EPRDF rebel advance. Unfortunately, the SPLA assistance ended up in a fiasco.

As soon as the SPLA forces were taking positions, they found out that they had been outnumbered and outgunned by the combined Ethiopian rebel forces and the Sudan's army superior fire power.

Without delay, Commander Nyuon Bany acted fast and withdrew his forces not only from Assossa Region but moving away altogether from Western Ethiopia to Eastern Upper Nile.

During this time, Commander Riek Machar, whose forces had earlier scored victory over the Sudanese Army and had chased them out of the area, now found himself hard-pressed once again by a larger enemy force. He decided to withdraw with some of his forces to Nasir in eastern Upper Nile.

On realising that his second in command was a suspect, Akol was forced, according to reports, to abandon his command post at Maban area and with a small force trekked all the way to Itang. Even there, his force was thrown into confusion as a result of the changing circumstances in Ethiopia[4].

Since the SPLA Commander-in-Chief John Garang was away during this time, and all power was left to his Deputy William Nyuon Bany and Salva Kiir Mayardit, the Chief of Operations, the administration was in disarray under the Ethiopian rebel advance to take over the country. However, a hard decision had to be made by the Acting Commander-in-Chief William Nyuon Bany and it was made.

"The tough decision facing the SPLM commanders at that critical moment was how to relocate the SPLA bases along the Ethiopian-Sudanese borders, and how to resettle the large numbers of displaced Sudanese refugees by the raging war taking place between the Ethiopian Government and the EPRDF rebels." [5]

Precisely, the SPLA efforts to put itself together in order to cope up with what appeared as an insurmountable task, the resettlement of thousands of fleeing refugees and the reallocation of its forces amidst the Sudan Government's continued aerial bombardment, was in deed a formidable task for a guerrilla army.

Amidst this bleak confusion, Dr. Lam Akol is reported to have put his ideas together and continued to agitate. He apparently found sympathy among the fleeing refugees and soldiers on the ground. By then, it was already Akol's open campaign against Garang who was his archenemy.

It was also then that Commander Riek was officially co-opted into the venture and accepted to lead the open rebellion against John Garang. Dr. Machar, who had been a warlord unto his own for over five years in the field, may have not been a party to the previous wrangling for power in the headquarters.

According to those who viewed Machar as not the architect of the split, they fathomed that he found himself only a cohort in the plot of which the chief designer was Dr. Lam Akol.

By proximity in northern Upper Nile their coordination efforts between the two was made easier. Reportedly, SPLA security agents kept reporting their tracks and activities to the SPLA Headquarters, regularly.

Dr. Nyaba[6], one of the so-called progressive revolutionaries who had been complaining bitterly against excessive use of power by some senior members in the High Command, was induced into the venture. After he backed away from the Nasir Faction Nyaba he writes:

"The activities of Dr. Machar and Dr. Akol were uncovered and revealed through their publication entitled 'The Need for a New Socio-political and Military Order in the SPLM/SPLA.'"

In essence, the document revealed the magnitude and the extent the political opposition has developed within the SPLA High Command. Additionally, the distribution of this publication was followed by an agitation for change in the SPLM/SPLA leadership.

Having made their position clear and open, Machar and Akol immediately stepped up wider contacts among the SPLA officers and men they believed would give unswerving support to their adventure.

According to Nyaba and confirmed by some of the refugees who were at Itang during those days, the dissidents' mobilisation was at first confined to the Shilluk and Nuer officers and communities.

The SPLM security among the groups contacted obviously passed on the motives of the SPLA dissidents to the SPLA leadership. These reports were given credence because immediately following these agitation and mobilisation, some Shilluk and Nuer officers in the SPLA security network were warned to keep away from the two officers.

However, Machar and Akol contacts outside their immediate tribesmen were apparently not positively received. This may have suggested that the coup making process was not gaining extensive popularity among the senior officers. For instance, Akol's letter to Nyaba said in part that: "Commander Martin Manyiel Ayuel is still in Nairobi and we have not heard from him since 3/7/1991"(Nyaba).

When the agitation within the SPLA seemed to have not exceedingly brought immediate results, according to reports, Machar and Akol broadened the justification for a coup to reach Southern Sudanese leaders inside and outside the country. For instance, when Dr. Peter Adwok Nyaba was visiting Germany, Dr. Akol wrote him a letter whose purpose may have been to disseminate it to the community in Diaspora. The letter in part reads:

As usual, he (Garang) is trying to play tricks. Recently he (Garang) secretly summoned his stooges William Nyuon Bany and Salva Kiir to Nairobi where they held secret meetings. The plan they came up with was to isolate us from our forces and then arrest us (Machar, Gordon Koang and myself). To execute the plan, he (Garang) called for a meeting of the High Command in Kidepo on 21/8/1991 and the three of us are to be picked up by a plane from Nasir to Kapoeta. There they may be arrested, a desperate plan, needless to say, we will not be fooled.

The three of us, and Martin Manyiel, are the members of the so called High Command they identify with the opposition and discontent now simmering in the rank and file. The other point of paramount importance is the question of contacting Lt. Colonel Gatluak Deng, Governor of Upper Nile State. He is said to be in Germany—if he is there, find him out and talk to him frankly in the spirit of this document and tell him that the three of us have asked you to contact him. We know him very well, so do not feel inhibited. Akol added. "I did however send to Dr. Peter Nyot Kok[8] a document entitled: 'Why Garang Must Go' So if you have not yet received a copy, it must be on the way. On your side you can send him a copy of our 'Toward the Organisation of the SPLM.'"

Looking at the above letter the coup plotters may have been tipped off about their impending arrest and detention and therefore were on their guard to ward off the onslaught—the fate of Kwanyin Bol, Arok Thon, Martin Majer and Joseph Oduho.

Whatever reasons that made the two leaders to stage a coup on that fateful day of August 28th 1991, the fear of the unknown may have been the only most appropriate course of action that was left open, especially when it involved the issue of—die or live.

Malek, a former SPLA Captain who was in the epicentre of events in the SPLA Headquarters and watched all these events before he too defected to join the National Islamic Front regime, noted:[9]

"I think the so-called coup of 1991 by the three SPLA commanders was not really planned with the aim to take over the SPLM/SPLA leadership and then restructure it accordingly. It was not even intended to oust Garang. It was actually a preemptive move by the said officers to avoid being arrested and detained like Bol and Arok. Basically, there were obvious signs that these officers would be arrested anytime in order to minimise the serious damage their activities would bring to bear on the Movement as it was entering its most crucial stage of the struggle. In brief, the fear for the known forced Riek and Akol to take drastic action without proper preparations and plans necessary for any military undertaking. Rightly or wrongly, the two considered the August 21 meeting a mere trap set up to arrest them when they would be far away from their forces."

As discussed earlier, Dr. Akol and Dr. Machar had in the previous months widened their contacts in order to muster sufficient support for their coup. For instance, they made full use of some sympathetic personnel of the Presbyterian Church working in eastern Upper Nile and who were apparently supportive to the causes the coup plotters stood for: i.e. the separation of Southern Sudan from the northern Arab Muslims.

A pastor at the Sudan Desk in the Washington D.C. office of the Presbyterian Church (USA) for instance was reported to have availed himself to help campaign in favour of Nasir faction separatism. Thus, through such contacts of Church personnel working in Eastern Upper Nile, the ideology of separatism was spread widely beyond Southern Sudan. The Presbyterian Church has been dominant in the Sobat Valley since the colonial days. The Presbyterian Church naturally has historical connection and sympathy to the natives of eastern Upper Nile.

10.1.3. THE CHURCH ELEMENT IN THE SPLA/SPLM SPLIT

Sudan However, as indicated above the Church networks, was soon to engulf the Council of Churches (SCC), a move that would naturally have reached most Southern Sudanese inside the country to support separation as the chief goal for liberation.

Between 1989 and 1990, Brigadier Pio Yukwan Deng was the Chairman of the Peace Commission in the NIF regime. He was also the Chairman of the proposed Council for the South, an apparent replacement of the defunct High Executive Council, the southern Sudan regional government of 1972-1982.

As the Chair of the proposed Southern Council, Yukwan was tipped that the new regime was considering the possibility of allowing the South Sudan to secede in order to put an end to the long protracted war. That could only happen if the SPLM/SPLA was led by a moderate group of southern officers in the SPLA during a set transitional period.

In that capacity, according to reports, Yukwan began mobilising the southern opinion, beginning first with his colleagues in the Command Council and his close associates about the regime policies toward the south.

General Dominic Kassiano, former member of RCC and Aldo Ajou Deng, former political advisor to the Junta confirmed this assertion in interview with the author in London, 1999 and 2000, stated, categorically that the NIF's generals did not actually view secession as the best way of resolving the Sudanese conflict. Rather, in their view, the Generals were just using secession as a bluff in order to lure Southerners to support the regime against the powerful rebel forces of the SPLA.

In July 1991, the news of the power struggle in the SPLA had filled the air in Khartoum and had apparently reached the SCC that plans were underway to oust Colonel Dr. John Garang de Mabior, the SPLM/A leader, and would be replaced by willing separatists.

It was apparently in that light that Rev. Ezekial Kutjok, the SCC Secretary General, called for an urgent meeting of the SCC Executive Committee in Khartoum so as to brief the Church leaders about the impending changes in the SPLA leadership and the subsequent declaration for a separate south.

Like most Southerners, Rev. Kutjok was an advocator of a genuine independent South Sudan did not entertain establishment of an Arab-Islamic system of governance in the Sudan.

Breaking the news to the stunned Church leaders during the meeting, Rev. Kutjok said,

"The south, I guess, is breaking away (from the north) under a new leadership. But I don't know under whose leadership it will be. The Church must not be left in the cold as it was in May this year when the regime of Mengistu was overthrown without the knowledge of the Churches inside Ethiopia. You as Church leaders must be involved. We must write a position paper to support the separation of the south and the new leadership which we still do not know."

Responding to the news of the breakaway of the South Sudan, the Church leaders received the message with mixed feelings: some in utter outrage and disbelief and others in total embarrassment and shock. Rev. Adam Kuku, President of the Nuba Mountains based, Sudanese Church of Christ asked.

"What would happen to us, the small Churches in the Northern Sudan when the Southern Sudan breaks away with its large Christian population to form a separate entity? What would be our fate we the northern-based Churches? Adam Kuku envisioning a north that would be completely intolerant to existence of Christianity in a purely Islamic State remarked, "We shall definitely be throttled over completely. Perhaps we would be wiped out if not totally assimilated into a vast Muslim population around us. The Churches must not be involved in politics. We must not support separation of the south."

Fr. Hilary Boma, representing the Catholic Church viewpoint, said that the Catholic Church, being a universal Church, would not involve itself in such [political] matters like separation and breakaway of any part or parts. That was not the role of the Church he stressed.

In sum total, the Church leaders overwhelmingly rejected the idea of being involved in political debates which they said have absolutely nothing to do with the Church's vital role to preach the word of God among all nations of the earth irrespective of race or colour. Hence, they refused to become advocates of separatism and instead maintained a neutralist view.

Rev. Fr. Antonius Fakris, SCC Acting Chairman and expressing apparently, the opinion of the Coptic Orthodox Church, closed the meeting with the following remarks. He stated.

"Since all of you, the Church leaders, have expressed your opinion and all of you have rejected the proposal, I move that the matter be closed and dropped completely."

The meeting thus was closed.

10.1.4. THE FINAL SPLIT IN THE SPLM/SPLA

Meanwhile, July 1991 was a difficult month for Riek and Lam. The support they had hoped to receive from the SPLA officers and men from other regions was not forthcoming and the date for holding the Military High Command meeting was approaching.

The two officers were reportedly restive, and there was nothing else they could do than to act in a dramatic way. The zero-hour countdown was finally fixed. But before announcing the coup, they were reported to have made a final consultation with the government authorities in Malakal about the possibilities of getting assurances of support once the coup was announced.

Commander James Biel Jaak was dispatched to Malakal to meet the Lt. Colonel Gatluak Deng Garang, the State Governor. But because Gatluak Deng was away for treatment in Germany, Biel met his Deputy Mangu Ajak, a born again southern Muslim, who for convenience sake took the label of an Islamist hard liner. Mangu Ajak therefore became instrumental in neutralising SPLA forces in Upper Nile through the propaganda by the Peace Foundation (chapter 9).

Deputy Governor Ajak and the Military Commander and the National Security Officers (most of whom were Northerners) were also briefed and told to standby ready for action. Ajak was ordered to release the Anya Nya II militias who were stationed at the Doleib Hill, 15 miles south of Malakal town, to join with the Popular Defence forces to join on the "D Day".

Assurance for full support, apparently, was secured and the authorities in Khartoum were alerted of the impending coup in the making, and the beginning of the long awaited moment to divide the SPLA. Preparations were made and supplies were shipped from Khartoum to Malakal.

Ahmed al-Radi Jaber, the Islamist Political Supervisor of Upper Nile Region also moved his office to monitor events in Malakal. Earlier on, senior government officials led by the First Vice President al-Zubeir Mohamed Saleh—the Chairman of the Peace Commission in the RCC—have been regularly shuttling between Khartoum and Malakal. General al-Bashir had also announced in a press conference that 'peace would soon descend upon the South but first in Malakal.'

In Khartoum, the long awaited time for reckoning and the ramification of the SPLA had come. Immediately, Fadl al-Sid Abu Gasseissa, the chief architect of the Peace and Development Foundation, and his team started preparing a steamer/flotilla to rush the logistics promised to the coup makers once the coup had been announced.

As he was apparently working to put last touches on his plan at Itang, Dr. Akol received instructions to proceed to Cairo and attend, on behalf of the SPLM Chairman, celebrations marking the establishment of the National Democratic Alliance[11] in which the SPLA was a founding member.

This assignment was apparently taken by Dr. Akol as a tactic designed to suggest that he was still in the Chairman's good books. This would make him forget the impending danger and walk into jail. Being confident of his mission, however, Akol attended the Cairo celebration and immediately flew back to Itang to continue with his plans.

After the fall of Mengistu's regime in May 1991, the SPLA ordered that all its bases and the reallocation of refugee camps inside Ethiopia must be evacuated to stable places across the border in eastern Upper Nile and eastern Equatoria. The latter was preferred because Commander Salva Kiir Mayardit, the SPLA Chief of Security, aware apparently of the threat that was already visible in view of the activities of two commanders.

Akol declined to support the relocation of the SPLA bases to eastern Equatoria, insisting that Nasir would be a perfect place. This was probably a matter of proximity for his future plans.

Commander Lual Diing Wuol seconded Kiir's proposal. There was no agreement. So while Kiir was telling everyone to leave for Kapoeta, Akol told them to go directly to Nasir. Akol supporters and forces who were mostly from eastern Upper Nile ended up in Nasir. The rest went to Kapoeta. Captain Wadang Biong Kuol observed :

"It was very clear to everybody in the SPLA that Machar, Akol and Taban Deng were going to cause trouble in Nasir. So nearly everybody agreed to follow Commanders Salva Kiir and Lual Diing to Eastern Equatoria. Those who went to Nasir were fully aware of the impending danger and decided to go at their own risks."

Captain Wadang Kuol was one of the SPLA daring officers who opened up eastern Equatoria amidst formidable odds in 1985. He was present in the hectic evacuation days of Itang camps in August 1991 and hence offers eyewitness accounts of those evil days.

By the beginning of May 1991, it was reported that the Ethiopian rebels of the Ethiopian People's Democratic Revolutionary Front (EPDRF) were closing in on Addis Ababa, the Ethiopian Capital City.

By the middle of May, Mengistu had abdicated power for exile in southern Africa. Soon the Debre Zeit Airport and Addis Ababa City had both fallen to the EPDRF, and the latter was in the process of forming a new government under Meles Zenawi. This new government in Ethiopia was hostile not only to the SPLA (which supported the Mengistu's regime) but also the Southern Sudanese people. Clashes had already been reported between the SPLA forces and the EPDRF forces.

When these chaotic situations were taking place, John Garang was away on a tour. As soon as he got back to Kapoeta, he called for an urgent meeting of the Politico-Military High Command. The meeting was crucial as the Movement needed to assess the political and military situation in the light of the new geopolitical changes and particularly in Ethiopia.

The SPLA had lost its best friend and committed ally in the person of Mengistu Haile Mariam and his government. The loss of bases inside Ethiopia was another terrible blow that the SPLA had to put up with. Hence, ways had to be devised how to continue with the next phase of the war.

External pressure for a negotiated settlement of the war was also in the pipeline and the warring parties must respond to the proposed peace talks in Abuja, Nigeria.

John Garang had ordered that the members of the Politico-Military High Command and all zonal commanders must attend the Kapoeta meeting. Without delay, preparations were made and a plane was sent to collect commanders from distant and isolated command posts—such as Yusuf Kuwo Mekki in Nuba Mountains and commanders in Upper Nile.

But Machar and Akol would not go to Kapoeta. They were marking time. Finally they acted and announced the overthrow of John Garang and the birth of new reconstituted leadership in the Movement. Machar was elevated to the position of SPLM/SPLA Chairman and Commander-in-Chief. Akol became his Deputy and Commissar for External Relations and Peace.

There was no mention of what position Commander Gordon Koang Chol would hold in the new Movement nor was there any mention of other members of in the new politico-military command and its hierarchy.

The first news of the coup was flashed over the British Broadcasting Corporation (BBC) and through radio messages to all commanders and units of the SPLA. There were no immediate reactions from the SPLA units even those who had received the radio message.

Initially, many people were confused and began to speculate that no coup could have been announced unless some dramatic action had taken place such as the arrest or even physical elimination of the SPLA Leader, John Garang and those around him.

As days passed, fears were heightened and tension was rising in the cities where Dr. Garang supporters were preponderant, such as in Bahr al-Ghazal and Southern Upper Nile and Khartoum.

The only response supporting the coup came understandably, according to reports, from western Upper Nile, Dr. Machar's home county and his former command post. Machar had been fighting there since his commissioning in 1985—1990, as zonal commander.

On 31 August 1991, three days after the Nasir Declaration, the SPLM/ SPLA Chairman and Commander-in-Chief Dr. John Garang de Mabior announced from Kapoeta that he was alive and well and still in charge of the Movement. The coup has failed.

Addressing the SPLA units and commands in the war zones, and the Sudanese nation in particular, John Garang described the Nasir Declaration as a 'theoretical coup.' He assured the nation that the Movement was intact.

Though John Garang was euphemistic enough about what had happened, it was apparent that the Movement that had been able to control all sorts of contradictions since 1983 was finally torn apart.

Upon hearing the declaration of a coup, Khartoum moved as per agreement. A relief steamer, with various relief items, was sent from Malakal to Nasir. In the steamer accompanying these relief items was Abu Gasseissa, the Head of the Peace and Development Foundation and Ahmed al-Radi Jaber, the NIF Political Supervisor of Upper Nile and hoards of other Islamic bigots representing their Islamic Relief Agencies.

The Khartoum's delegates and the Nasir SPLA faction, as it came to be known, held a meeting for strategic cooperation against the 'SPLA of John Garang.'

A cease-fire was declared between the Nasir faction and the NIF troops. From documents that were not released to the public, it was clear that the two sides would fight together against their common enemy—John Garang's SPLA. The chapter for internecine factional wars in Upper Nile was thus opened.

Although the three commanders did not succeed to take over the

Movement as planned, yet the split created tremendous crisis not only ripping the Movement into two wings, but within the rank and file of the fighting men and the entire Southern Sudanese population inside and outside the Sudan.

It was natural that the people of Southern Sudan were now forced to identify with either of the two groups. Professor Lesch vividly captures this in her new book *Sudan-Contested Identities*. She notes:

> "The coup had caused acute crisis within Southern Sudan because it destroyed the prospects for a constitutional conference which would provide chances to restructure political life in the country along ethnic pluralistic lines.[12] Ironically, she continued, the Sudan Government benefited substantially from the split inside the SPLA. The government had encouraged the split by sending false signals that it might let the south secede. Once the split occurred, the government developed a four-prong strategy that encouraged the SPLA factions to fight each other. It backed away from offering independence, mounted large scale offensives against Garang's forces and used the disintegration of the SPLA to facilitate its repression of the African people in Southern Kordofan, Darfur and Southern Blue Nile."

However, when the SPLA Polico-Military High Command finally met in Torit the following September 1991, eight senior commanders who remained loyal to John Garang's leadership attended. These were:

1. Commander Dr John Garang de Mabior
2. Commander William Nyuon Bany
3. Commander Salva Kiir Mayardit
4. Commander James Wani Igga
5. Commander Daniel Awet Akot
6. Commander Kuol Manyang Juk
7. Commander Lual Diing Wuol
8. Commander Galerio Modi Horrinyang
9. Commander Martin Manyiel Ayuel, who was sick in Nairobi, sent his support for Dr. John Garang
10. Commander Yousif Kuwo Mekki at his Command Post in the Nuba

Mountains was unable to attend, but also managed and sent a radio message pledging his support for the Dr. John Garang's leadership.

The meeting duly convened and passed a resolution condemning the split as a set back to liberation, a delay for peace and was in the interest of no one. Besides condemning the coup the Torit meeting passed a number of resolutions in which the commanders outlined new plans and strategies for the next phase of the campaign. The Movement was at last prone to changes previously called for by the coup makers.

The most important resolution concerned the proposed peace talks in Abuja mediated by General Ibrahim Babangida's government. Since then, fighting and talking became the official strategy of the SPLA.

The SPLA interest to send a delegation for peace talks won the SPLA international respect that it was not usual for a guerrilla force but a well-intentioned Movement with set goals and strategies for peace in their country.

The government's previous effort to discredit the SPLA in the eye of international community, that it was not interested in peace and would not therefore attend the peace talk was simply disproved as unfounded. Other rumours also circulated by the regime included that if the SPLA attended the Abuja for peace talks it would demonstrate its weakness was also laid to rest.

Apart from the peace Conference, the Torit meeting set up committees charged with various responsibilities to review the basic issues connected with invigoration of the Movement. The

outstanding responsibilities were to include:

1. Control and accountability within the Movement—a clear response to the previous charges heaped upon the SPLM/SPLA leadership by the breakaway group of officers.

2. Setting up effective civil administration in order to relieve the officers to attend only to military issues in the war front.

3. Reviewing cases of the detained SPLA Commanders and senior officers.

Although these resolutions could have been done earlier before the split to preempt claims built by those who broke the Movement, yet these outstanding resolutions of the Torit meeting set clear direction in which the SPLA goals contained in the Manifesto of July 1983 were modified.

Additionally, the Torit meeting proposed four options the Movement would present to the peace conference scheduled to convene in Abuja, the Nigerian capital city. The four options were:

1. The maintenance of the SPLA demand for a united secular democratic state.

2. Confederation between the north and the south.

3. Association of sovereign states.

4. During the referendum the people of the marginalised regions shall choose between unity and secession.

The last option was the most significant departure from the first one because it was the first time that the SPLM/SPLA in its eighth year of armed struggle was able to give signal that the South Sudan could possibly secede if the government of the Sudan maintained its centralised and unitary Arab-Islamic state in the country (Lesch 1998).

10.1.5. PUBLIC REACTIONS TO THE SPLIT

Dr. Peter Adwok Nyaba[13] writes:

"August 28 will go down in the history of the Southern Sudan as the most important single day when the people's aspirations for freedom and justice suffered a serious blow at the hands of their own sons. This was so because some of the ablest sons of the nation were up for power struggle at the time the movement was at its weakest but also there were no preparations for an effective transfer of power."

Nyaba was simply making an honest statement which ultimately, I suppose, originated from those bitter experiences which demanded a sincere re-examination of conscience.

Reflecting on Nyaba's statement one could say that August 28, 1991 would have gone down in the annals of Southern Sudan's turbulent history only if they had steadfastly stuck to the goals and ideals they had expressed in their statements to the Southern Sudanese people in that somber day that they had taken over power from John Garang in order to liberate the people of Southern Sudan from the continued Arab domination so that they could gain their statehood.

Unfortunately, the leaders of the Nasir faction instead consolidated their position and concentrated all their efforts and resources to win public support in order, perhaps, to realise their own personal glory. Mayom K Malek said in an interview:

"There is no wonder that they would have witnessed many nationalists defecting from the SPLA to join the Nasir faction en masse had they faced the enemy. They would be kings of Southern Sudan today said one southern nationalist shortly after the announcement that the Nasir leaders were cooperating and collaborating with the enemy. However, instead of making use of the huge war machine at their disposal then, some of which was abandoned by Mengistu's fleeing soldiers, they invited the NIF to claim all these. Furthermore, their prime objective became the fight for survival and endless agitation against the SPLA. Thus, the people they claimed to be fighting for were unnecessarily split and misused—as they were thrown from one leader to another but without any sign of liberation. Additionally, the Nasir faction did not only fight the SPLA, but actually turned their guns against the Dinka officers who were amongst them. The Dinka officers were picked and lynched or were extra-judicially executed before their colleagues on the suspicion that they may not be obedient supporters to the venture the Nasir faction leaders were about to embark on."

The execution of the Dinka officers became so embarrassing to the extent that some Dinka politicians, like Professor Isaac Cuir Riak and Justice Dhol Acuil, who had supported the Nasir coup, were forced to resign."

The activities of the Nasir faction, as we have traced its development in this chapter, may have marked the beginning of its end as the People's Movement. Because, apart from the execution of the Dinka officers within its ranks, the Nasir faction's invasion of Bor District in 1991/92 and the crimes committed, simply tilted away public sympathy and the human rights groups were also quick to magnify the devastation meted upon the civilians in particular.

Subsequent statements by the Nasir leaders to explain away those atrocities and further attempts to justify their existence only felt into logical contradictions.

In his assessment as to why the people contacted did not respond before or after the coup, Dr. Nyaba revealed the following facts:

"First the radio message sent out to all the SPLA units on the morning of August 28 was done without a full knowledge or consent of the targeted units.

Second, the message was sent out in the hope that those who were assumed as against Garang's leadership would rise automatically and joined the coup. This was a funny way of executing a military coup leave alone the fact that the SPLA despite of its growth and strength still is a guerrilla force without a permanent base or seat to be captured like in a conventional military coup.

Third, the coup also came at a time when many SPLA officers and men were still going to their new areas of deployment. And even if there were officers and men who might have supported the Nasir faction leaders in the preparatory days, there was no way they could have participated because they were either still fresh in their new location or had not arrived.

Fourth, as to why the Nasir faction endured despite its lack of popular support outside their immediate region, it endured more due to external factors than internal support.' For instance, the relief planes and personnel flying in and out of Nasir became the mailbag for the coup leaders. Also Dr. Machar's marriage to a British woman, Emma, who worked as a relief worker (but allegedly reported by many sources as working for the British Intelligence), was also calculated to use her service for influence in the relief community. This indeed bore immediate fruits."

As regards to the other fronts which had received the radio message regarding the coup, either in the preparatory stage or during its execution stage, the reactions were as follows.

On September 4, 1991 Captain Marconi Okuch Aba stormed and took over the Command from Captain Akuoch Mayom at Agworo, the SPLA headquarters in north Western Upper Nile zone. Whether he was apparently receiving the instructions from the High Command in Eastern Equatoria or acting alone was not immediately known, said Captain Mayom who was inclined towards the Nasir coup.

Meanwhile, in the Maban area which was under the direct Command of Dr. Lam Akol, many officers and men there refused to take orders from their commander as they did not agrre with the breakup of the Movement. Instead they withdrew to the Shilluk area where they waited for further instructions apparently from the SPLA High Command.

In Panaru-pariang and Melut areas, which were under Dr. Machar, the officers and men who had shown signs for supporting the coup were simply arrested by Captain Mayik Jaw.

SPLA forces in the Lau Nuer area and southern Nuer areas of Waat and Akobo were grudgingly reported to have pledged their support and came under the coup between September 10 and 15, 1991. This may have been due to tribal sentimental appeal made by Machar after the coup.

The forces in Ngok Dinka, Bailiet area, under Captain George Athor defied the coup leaders' appeal and managed to fight on and held the area till help came later from the main SPLA.

In the Southern Blue Nile area, Commander Abul Aila Mustafa finding himself isolated and refusing to join the Nasir forces decided to surrender with all his forces to the government-held garrison at Damazin. In the Nuba Mountains, Commander Yousif Kuwo Mekki refused to co-operate with the Nasir forces.

To win him over to the government's side, Colonel Mohamed al-Amin al-Khalifa, the Chairman of the Government's Peace Commission, sent an emotional letter[14] heavily charged with Islamic fervour and sentiments to Commander Kuwo. He was persuading Kuwo to distance himself from the southern infidels and return to join the 'Nation of Islam.'

Commander Kuwo, in reply to al-Khalifa, stated, "I do not know to whom the letter was addressed. But since it was addressed to a brother Yousif, and since my name incidentally is a Yousif, I shall reply. Kuwo then replied in a non-committal language where he literally dodged the regime until he linked up his forces with Pariang and later on with Abyei and Gogrial forces of the SPLA.

Summing up, Mayom Kuoc stated that the Nasir Faction survived for some time—despite lack of popular support from the officers and men in the SPLA for three reasons.

First, because of its cooperation with the Sudan government, it was not short of resources.

Second, Dr. Lam Akol was very successful in mobilising international public opinion to support the Nasir venture. And third, there was foreign interest and support, especially among the relief agencies operating in the Sobat Valley, many of which had flocked to help the refugees fleeing from Ethiopia.

The international assistance to the coup leaders was very vital for their survival without which the coup would have died a natural death at its infancy.[15]

10.1.6. ATTEMPTS TO PATCH UP THE SPLIT

While the Nasir leaders were grappling and desperately exerting themselves as genuine leaders, many individuals who were very sympathetic to the cause of the people of Southern Sudan for racial or religious reasons intervened in attempts to bring both sides together and possibly reconcile them.

Archbishop Desmond Tutu of South Africa, a Nobel Prize Winner whose advocacy dismantled Apartheid, Mr. Bethuel Kiplagat, the Permanent Secretary in Foreign Affairs Ministry in Kenya, the New Sudan Council of Churches, the National Council of Churches of Kenya, the People for Peace in Africa and other religious organisations based in Nairobi/Kenya joined various international groups to try to bring the two sides together but with no success.

They noted that while there might have been genuine reasons that led to the break up of the Movement, the break up itself was not the solution. Southern Sudanese leaders who met and issued the Adare Declaration the same time the coup was made, were also able to think along these lines.

Thus, the leaders of the two factions (Nasir and Torit factions) were invited to send their representative to Nairobi for peace and reconciliation talks. Unfortunately, a number of things contributed to the delay of convening such an urgent meeting.

The first reason for the delay of reconciliation was that SPLA Torit faction was at this time busy in reorganising itself and trying at the same time to keep out the combined offensives of the Nasir faction and the Sudan government. Until the end of November 1991, Torit faction did not send its representative.

The delay gave the Nasir faction an advantage to poise as a peacemaker while depicting Torit faction warmonger. This theory was confirmed especially when Torit's faction forces under Commander William Nyuon Bany attacked and occupied Adok and Leer in western Upper Nile an area was considered by Nasir faction as their area (Nyaba).

The second reason that worked against the reconciliation early on was the arrival of Dr. Lam Akol to Nairobi/Kenya. Dr. Akol, while seemingly talking for peace and reconciliation, was actually working for the survival of their faction.

In order to ward of imminent assaults by the Torit faction, Dr. Akol was aware that unless his group obtained logistics and funding, their survival was in jeopardy. It was this reality that made him maintain contacts with the Sudan government which was, indeed, standing by to offer any assistance that the Nasir faction may need.

Concurrently, Tiny Rowland, a British Millionaire whose business interests in Africa and a long time friend of the SPLA, was also available to offer assistance where and when possible. He was interested in reconciliation efforts, but his naivety may have actually worked negatively against any hope for reconciliation.

The third and perhaps the most damaging attempt against reconciliation was the arrival of Sudan government's delegation led by Ali al-Hajj Mohammed to hold talks with the Nasir faction inside Nairobi. Thus between October and November 1991, the two-sides met. While the Sudanese delegation was headed by Dr. al-Hajj was composed mostly of the Sudan security officers and hard core Islamists, in addition to the officials in the Sudan Embassy in Nairobi, the Nasir faction was led by Dr. Akol himself and a number of officers.

At the end of the meeting, the two sides agreed, among other things, on the following:

1. Strategic alliance.

2. That the Government of Sudan should commit itself to giving continual military and financial support to the Nasir group.

3. That Alternate Commander Taban Deng Gai be dispatched immediately to Khartoum to work out details of the kind of assistance and size that would be given to the Nasir faction as contained in their agreement.

4. That Taban Gai would shuttle between Khartoum and Ethiopia from time to time in order to coordinate the sending of the military assistance to their forces in Upper Nile region.

5. That the venue for the next meeting would be in Frankfurt, Germany......

By the end of the year it appeared that the more efforts were being exerted toward reconciliation the more these efforts became counterproductive.

All the same efforts for reconciliation were ceaseless with the Khartoum based Sudan Council of Churches playing the internal role while the New Sudan Council of Churches (Nairobi based) were acting as a go between trying to connect the two groups.

In brief the collapse of the Nairobi reconciliation talks in February 1992 described above created "a de facto recognition and existence of two factions in the SPLA: the Nasir faction and Torit factions."

10.2. BOR-KONGOR INVASIONS AND CONSEQUENCES

The hardening of positions in the Nairobi peace talks owed much to tangible pledges the Khartoum government made to the Nasir faction. Taban Gai Deng's visit to Khartoum, indeed, supplied the Nasir faction with what it needed most: military logistics.

Having obtained enough logistics and financial support an Antonov bomber was made available to ferry the goods from Khartoum to Malakal. When these logistics were obtained, Nasir started operations against the Torit faction in conjunction with the Sudanese army there.

From his base in Malakal, Taban, using the plane at his disposal, began dropping ammunitions, food and money to their forces in western Upper Nile. With these weapons, the Nasir forces began attacking the mainstream position in Leer, Duar and Adok, the Towns previously overrun by Commander William Nyuon Bany.

Within a couple of days, Leer, Adok, Duar and nearly the whole south western Upper Nile was brought under full control of Nasir after defeating the mainstream forces that immediately retreated to Yirol area in Bahr al-Ghazal.

Using long range radio communications Taban was in constant contact with Dr. Riek Machar at his tactical headquarters at Ketkek, 3 miles east of Nasir town where he had been maintaining communications with all his forces. At Ketkek, Commander Machar began directing Taban Deng's plane to supply troops on the ground on various locations under his control.

Apparently encouraged by successes of his forces and with assurances from the NIF regime that it would let the south secede if he could defeat Torit faction and bring the whole Southern Sudan under his control, with his newly supplemented forces and equipment Commander, Machar invaded Kongor and Bor Districts.

Bor is the hometown of Dr. John Garang, the SPLA/SPLM leader. The liberation of Kongor and Bor Districts, mostly inhabited by Dinka ethnic group, would indeed bring the whole of Upper Nile practically under his control.

In interviews at the Green Village Hotel with various ex-SPLA members of Nasir faction in Khartoum, 1997, they disclosed that the Nasir strategy was to occupy Bor and Kongor Districts. Then, proceed to capture the Headquarters

Torit, where John Garang had been issuing instructions to all his forces in the region.

After capturing Torit, the Nasir forces would advance and clear remnants of Garang forces away from the borders with Uganda and Kenya.

With that strategy apparently in mind, Machar is reported to have contacted the governor of Upper Nile and the Commander of Upper Nile Military Administrative Area in order to give the necessary support agreed before the coup between the Government and Machar's envoy in Malakal Commander James Biel Jok.

Eventually, a huge force that had been put together in the previous months October 1991 and January-February 1992 was unleashed to undertake the Kongor-Bor expedition. Thus the largely Nuer forces of Nasir faction, joined by thousands of the Anya Nya II and Nuer tribesmen, trooped into a devastating destruction of the Dinka villages and crops in the area.

In the process, the merciless tribal marauders in hundreds of thousands seized cattle, children and women, many of which were taken as war booty. Some of the cattle were sold in the markets of Malakal, Kosti and even as far as Khartoum (Nyaba). In late 1991 alone 200,000 Twic Dinka fled their homes in Kongor and Bor Districts retaining only 50,000 out of 400,000 herds of cattle (Lesch, p.158).

Captain Malek, who had sympathised with the Nasir faction but resigned following these atrocities, gave a vivid account of these activities. He said, "5,000 lives were lost during the four-month operation. In addition to thousands of cattle looted, most of the victims in the Bor-Kongor operations were poor elderly men, women, and children".

> "In September 1991 when Ayod, Waat, and Akobo came under his control, Riek Machar ordered a large contingent of Nasir troops, elements of Anya-Nya Two from Doleib Hills and heavily armed Nuer civilians—Jiech Mabor (white army) mainly Lou and Gawer— to invade Bor and Kongor Districts. In the thinking of Dr. Riek Machar, Garang could be defeated either by destroying his home area or destroying his SPLA troops. Initially, the involvement of armed civilians was due to the fact that he did not have enough forces. He therefore intended to wet the appetite of his armed civilians for wealth of Dinka cattle, women, and child captives," Nyaba observed:

The use of Jiech Mabor for operations against the SPLA in Bor area had serious difficulties. After this looting spree, there now arose the need to take home the loot. And since they obeyed no military orders, the marauding forces returned to central Nuer, falling short of pursuing Machar's objective of capturing Torit, the presumed Headquarters of John Garang (Nyaba).

The results of the unprecedented invasion of Dinkaland[16]that had no parallel in the long history of the two people in addition to Dr. Machar's continued struggle to defeat the mainstream SPLM/SPLA on behalf of the Sudan government, was so embarrassing to many Southern Sudanese who had expected him to liberate Southern Sudan (Nyaba).

It was more embarrassing to his Nuer tribesmen who saw no reasons to participate in the destruction of the entire Dinka population and their wealth when such destruction and wrath could have been directed against the known enemy the government of the Sudan[17].

Reacting apparently to the embarrassing atrocities inflicted upon the Dinka in Bor, the public outcry throughout the South Sudan and the international condemnation and blame brought against him by his own tribesmen, who questioned the logic behind the Bor-Kongor invasion, Dr. Machar decided to launch a face-saving device. This he carried out with great skill without calculating the end results of such a move.

Borrowing Dr. Nyaba's words, Dr. Machar had to bluff the people of South Sudan by pretending that he was mobilising the Nuer population for the capture of Malakal from Jallaba Arabs. Dr. Machar without delay laid down a strategy aimed at efforts to divert the Nuer wrath against him. If the plan succeeded, the Nuer might consider him a genuine Nuer leader who took over in order to restore their hegemony under which they would not only be the rulers of an independent south, but benefit a great deal from it.

With the above apparently in mind, Dr. Machar was reported to have concocted a fake plan to capture Malakal. The plan was that his forces, with the assistance and cooperation of the Southern Sudanese in the Army, the police, prisons, and wildlife warders, it would be easy to capture Malakal. The Nuers were reportedly told that their son, Lt. Col. Gatluak Deng, the State Governor, was sympathetic to their cause and would definitely cooperate thereby making it easier for the eventual capture of the town.

In order to win large numbers of Nuer to join his venture, the Nuer spiritual leader Gatkek Kutnyang was allegedly involved in the fake military preparations for the capture of Malakal. A date was apparently fixed to be in July during the rainy season. But July came and passed. But there were no further orders to execute the plan to capture Malakal.

The spiritual leader Mr. Gatkek Wutnyang with a large armed force consisting largely of Nuer tribesmen with no military skills or tactical training invaded Malakal. Catching the army, the police, prisons warders and wildlife guards by surprise the invaders captured the army Headquarters and occupied a large chunk of the Town of Malakal.

Realising that the invaders were not military people but civilians, as demonstrated by the way they gave orders in Nuer language, that they were not able to operate heavy war machines such as tanks and artillery pieces, the Sudanese army regrouped and launched a well coordinated action against the invaders. Before dawn, law and order was restored in Malakal.

Like the Bor-Kongor invasion, the Malakal incident ended in a fiasco, adding to more embarrassment to the engineer turned over night politico-military commander.

However, having chased out the Nuer civilian invaders, it was the turn of the Government headed by Deputy Governor Mangu Ajak who, cooperating with the army and security, made it be known that all the innocent Nuer town-dwellers were Fifth Columnists. The PDF and Arab Mujahideen were, therefore, unleashed and the Nuer in Malakal had their fair share of atrocities.

The Dinka displaced during the Bor-Kongor invasion and who had sought sanctuary in Malakal were given the golden chance to exact their revenge by settling accounts with the people who had had nothing to do with their own tragedy in the Bor affair.

As if that was not enough, the Government authorities unleashed a former SPLA battalion (Abu Shok), consisting of Ngok Dinka of Bailiet to participate in the cleansing of Malakal town of any remnants of the Nuer invaders. At the heat of the split, Abu Shok Battalion refused to join the Nasir venture and had surrendered to the Sudan government forces in Malakal.

However, for several days, Malakal and its suburbs were dreadful scenes of killing and torture of innocent Nuer city dwellers. According to eyewitness accounts, it was enough to carry Nuer like tribal marks or utter some words in Nuer language and you were as good as dead.

Failing to capture Malakal, the same spiritual Nuer leader Gatkek Kutnyang led another expedition. This time the attack was against an isolated government relief centre at Obel, south of Malakal.

After escaping from Malakal, according to reports, Chief Kutnyang had gone and assembled a large force of armed Nuer tribesmen and invaded the Obel relief centre: Looting and killing all its contents including the entire staff of *Al-Mawafag al-Kheiri*, an Islamic Relief Agency.

The government forces, with the Malakal venture in mind, moved fast and within few days, the area was turned into a ghostland. This time it was the government forces which went on a looting and killing spree. Those who were captured underwent indignities. Women were raped; men were circumcised after converting to Islam. This time it was the government forces that went back to Malakal with their loot consisting of women, children and cattle.

Adding together the Bor-Kongor invasion and the Malakal-Obel fiascos, it was becoming abundantly clear day by day that it would be a matter of time that the Southern Sudan would be completely devastated and the Nasir faction, in particular, would finally be dragged into the ruins of their making.

However, with many of its officers resigning in protest and the international condemnation about the disaster that the Nasir venture had brought on their people, the best hope for the leadership at least for their own survival was to double up and move faster to the government side. Even this road was full of thorns as discussed below.

Cooperating with the NIF government with some of the cohorts resisting such a move, it soon became clearer and predictable that the Nasir Faction was on a winding road to more splits and further splits into many ineffective and insignificant militias, each threatening to do away with the other in their attempts to survive.

10.3. THE SPLINTERING OF NASIR FACTION

Since its emergence in 1991, the Nasir faction appeared to have started on a wrong note so to speak. From the onset, the faction underwent factional struggles in its own camp including the mysterious death of Mr. Joseph H. Oduho, the veteran politician who was attracted by a secessionist programme of this group that had been his dream throughout his political life (1958-1992). Further splits continued until factionalism weakened their resolve to stand as credible armies.

By 1997, six fronts mostly derived from the Nasir faction submitted themselves to the NIF through the April 21, 1997 agreement. This sort of truce would soon commit the Nasir Faction into an Ian Smith-Abel Muzorewa type of internal settlement.

Though the Nasir leaders had started their venture in a bloodless manner on the morning of August 28, 1991, it soon became not only bloodier, but more destructive even to those who launched it. The main reason, according to former Nasir SPLA insider, was due to the manner and way in which their leadership had handled their wing of the Movement just right from the start.

Paul Anade Othow who had been an SPLA representative in Washington DC before he joined the Nasir venture (he died when SPLA captured Fashalla 1998) told the author in an interview soon after his arrival in Khartoum to join the internal peace settlement. He remarked:

"The Nasir faction collapsed because it was taken away from Dr. Akol, whom he said planned and orchestrated it and handed over to Dr. Machar who began to steer the ship away from its right course to the embarrassment of his shipmates (grinning). Any attempt to persuade him to bring the ship back to the right course ended up in utter frustration." He went on: "The crew, seeing the ship going the wrong way, revolted and in the struggle the ship began rapidly to sink. I took a raft and safely paddled my way to this Reef Island," he concluded with a sense of alacrity.

Commenting on the demise of the Nasir Faction in an interview, Captain Mayom Malek gave a number of reasons to this author as to why the Nasir section could not survive long. His views:

<Begin excerpting here>

" First the unscrupulous, hectic and haphazard approach to issues of peace and war, and more importantly, the liberation struggle, were responsible for the final demise of this faction of the SPLA.

Second, the "policies of the Nasir faction were so jumbled up to the extent that it became very difficult to follow what the leaders of this faction were up to."[18]

Third, the Nasir faction collapsed because its leaders differed as to how they should command the faction right from the onset. They disagreed precisely on all that they had wanted to do or plan to do. For instance, they differed on matters of general policies and in everything that came before them for discussion, even in ideas not yet put on the papers.

Fourth, the Nasir leadership did not have clear vision as to how they should proceed once they had declared themselves a separate Movement. For example, when Dr. Akol proposed something, Dr. Machar would outright reject that proposal. He was at times non-committal on the issue being proposed for discussion. On the other hand, when Akol began to relent or show some sign that he could concur on the cancellation of the issue under discussion, Machar would accept it. And in the process, handled that issue in a style that was so outrageous and embarrassing to the whole Nasir leadership. Another good example was that at the start of the Nasir Declaration, Dr. Riek Machar had proposed that the Nasir Faction should drop the name SPLM-SPLA altogether and adopt a new name. This proposal was immediately rejected by Akol; arguing that the name SPLM-SPLA had been developed and had won international recognition as a synonym to the revolutionary struggle of the disadvantaged Sudanese people. Such a popular revolutionary name should not be left to Garang alone. It must be maintained. In response, Dr. Machar gave in, albeit temporarily.

Fifth, another thing which brought up sharp disagreement between the two top leaders of the Nasir faction, and which contributed to the final break up of Nasir, was the question of where the nascent faction would get its logistics and financial assistance in order to stand as a viable Movement.

"When Akol proposed that the movement should obtain financial and logistical assistance from the government of Sudan, Machar turned down the proposal. Instead, he counter proposed that in order to protect them from Torit faction of the SPLA, they should approach the new Ethiopian government or Eritrea' so that they could receive some supplies. In all the proposals and counter proposals, Dr. Akol would always prevail over his boss," Mayom remarked.[19]

Sixth, another important aspect of differences between the two leaders was the conduct of peace talks with the Sudan government delegation led by Dr. Ali al-Hajj Mohamed who had arrived suddenly from Khartoum specifically to hold talks with the Nasir faction.

Without any clearance or consultation with Dr. Machar, Akol held several meetings with the Government delegation in which numerous items were included in an agreement. According to Malek, one of the items in the agreement was the arrangement for further talks regarding future relations between Khartoum and Nasir. The venue and date for next talks was then fixed to be in Frankfurt (Germany). But when the news was flashed to Dr. Machar, he admitted that he was not kept in picture about what his second in command was discussing with the Sudanese government delegation. However, Machar's remark did not stop Akol from holding further talks with the government delegation. Akol in the end concluded the meeting successfully regardless of Machar's complaints.

Following the military set back after the Bor-Kongor invasion, Machar surprisingly confirmed the Nairobi meetings between his faction and the government of Sudan delegation. Dr. Machar also said that the proposed Frankfurt meeting should go ahead and ordered the formation of the Nasir faction delegation to the meeting. The following were members of the Nasir's delegation to the Frankfurt meeting:

1. Commander Dr Lam Akol Ajawin, Head
2. Alternate Commander Deng Tiel Awien, Deputy Head
3. Alternate Commander Telar Deng Ring Takpiny, Member
4. Commander John Luk Jok, Member
5. Alternate Commander Taban Deng Gai, Member (joined from inside Sudan)

On 25 January 1992, however, a meeting was held at Frankfurt as scheduled between the government of Sudan and the Nasir faction. Dr. Ali al-Hajj Mohamed led the government of Sudan delegation flanked by a number of Islamists and security personnel.

Dr. Akol was quoted to have disclosed that, Dr. al-Hajj had assured him that his government would let the south secede in which the Nasir faction had in return received the government's financial and military support including airdrops of ammunition and military supplies to the SPLA Nasir outposts [21].

Essentially, the Frankfurt meeting discussed a number of issues including:

First, the recognition that the ongoing Sudanese conflict could be resolved peacefully.

Second, both sides agreed that the Government would give military and financial supplies to the Nasir section. This would also enable Nasir forces to fight alongside the National Army in order to crush and defeat the Torit faction (main SPLA) which was enemy number one to both sides.

Third, the future system of rule in the Sudan after attainment of peace was deferred to a later discussion.

Fourth, the future of the south within the United Sudan was discussed. The Nasir delegation proposed that a referendum be agreed upon, a choice that would offer an opportunity for the Southern Sudanese people to determine their own political future.

While the talks were in process, it was alleged that the protocols governing the Frankfurt meeting were worked out secretly by Cdr. Dr. Akol and Alternate Cdr. Taban Deng Gai without any prior knowledge of the other members of the delegation.

This point was reported to have brought friction between Dr. Akol and his colleagues in the delegation who argued that the protocol agreed upon weighted heavily in favour of the Sudan government.

So when the details of the said protocols emerged, two members of the Nasir delegation, Telar Deng Ring Takpiny and Tiel Deng Awien, resigned in protest. They also resigned from the Nasir faction altogether and walked back to join the main SPLA (Torit faction) under John Garang.

When the results of the Frankfurt meetings reached Machar, he reacted unfavourably to the protocol but remained passive and silent about it. This made many observers to believe that he was actually acquiescing to what he was against. But necessity made him embrace the Frankfurt deal, concluded Mayom Malek.

Launched as a movement to oust the SPLM/SPLA leader Dr. John Garang, Nasir leadership was delaying the liberation and whose removal would accelerate the liberation struggle fell into disarray in the process of doing just that. Consequently, the Movement that was already closer to attaining its objectives at the latest in 1992 was suddenly turned into a bloody shooting spree in the subsequent years.

In a matter of years after its launch some of the ablest members of the Movement ended up either in the Presidential Palace in Khartoum or in Khartoum graveyards. The dead, like Arok Thon Arok who died in a plane crush, did not even receive the credit and honour they might have deserved as martyrs in recognition of their participation and contribution to the struggle for the liberty of their people.

Nevertheless, suffice it to state that after failing to topple Dr. John Garang, the Nasir faction disintegrated with more rapid intervals than its leaders had anticipated. By 1995, the Nasir faction had splintered into six main factions.

Surprisingly, each of these factions felt privileged to wear the SPLA emblem on its lap by its own right: owning the Movement while at the same time supporting and collaborating with the very enemy, the government of Sudan, which the SPLA insurrection rose to overthrow.

10.4. NASIR FACTION BECOMES SPLM/SPLA—UNITED

Two years after the split, the Nasir SPLA-SPLM underwent a series of splinterings that are worth discussing in some more details. In 1992, two important events happened which were instrumental in the abandonment of the Nasir faction in favour of 'SPLM/SPLA United.'

First some of the commanders who had been detained at various stages and times (previously discussed) escaped from prison. These included Cdr. Arok Thon Arok, Cdr. Chol Deng Alak and Dr. Amon Mon Wantok. They appeared in Kampala and Nairobi, the epicentres of regional politics.

In Kampala, the escapees began to make contacts with all the disgruntled groups and other dissidents in the SPLA roaming about in these cities. These groups converged to make an anti-Garang lobby aimed at ousting him and re-unite the Movement.

The second event was equally epic; the defection of the SPLA Chief of Staff Cdr. William Nyuon Bany. In fact it was the defection of Cdr. William Nyuon that soon accelerated the escape of other prisoners as well as attempts to oust John Garang and re-unify the movement.

However, following Nyuon's defection, he erected his station near the government's garrison outside Juba City. He also made it known to his coterie, the anti-Garang coalition, that he was part and parcel of the group. Indeed the defection of Nyuon Bany actually boosted the morale of the anti-Garang groups. It emboldened them in their subsequent propaganda campaign.

These two events, in addition to a general feeling among the SPLA dissidents against John Garang's 'alleged autocratic style of rule,' were instrumental in wrecking the future plans of the SPLA. The dissidents had erroneously assumed that the SPLA had become weaker and it could easily be overwhelmed militarily. If that happened, reunification of the Movement could come about. Concerted efforts were needed to coordinate military assaults on Garang's remaining SPLA forces.

To crown their efforts, a meeting of all the anti-Garang coalition was hastily called to convene in Kongor District, home and birth place of Dr. John Garang and Arok Thon Arok.

Following the Bor-Kongor invasion described earlier, the area and the Jonglei areas in general had been deserted by the SPLA mainstream. This lured the dissidents into making a miscalculation that the Kongor area was conducive for such a meeting. It was indeed a miscalculation as discussed in the following paragraphs.

The meeting of anti-Garang coalition was convened at last and in Kongor Town. The meeting was attended by :

1. Dr Riek Machar
2. Dr Lam Akol
3. Cdr. Kerubino Kwanyin
4. Cdr. William Nyuon Bany
5. Cdr. Arok Thon Arok
6. Cdr. Chol Deng Alak
7. Alt. Cdr. Faustino Atem Gualdit
8. Cdr. Amon Mon Wantok
9. Justice Dhol Acuil Aleu
10. The veteran politician Mr. Joseph Haworu Oduho
11. Cdr. George Maker Benjamin Bil
12. Cdr.Ater Benjamin Bil

and a number of senior dissident officers

The meeting adopted that the name of the Nasir faction be dropped and replaced with the "SPLM-SPLA-United" to counter balance the weight of the mainstream under John Garang. This was also a tactic to encourage those supporting Garang to defect and join the united group.

The spite and bitterness emanating from previous arrest and long years of detention made some of the comrades in the coalition feel rather uneasy with the late dissenters like William Nyuon. But the realisation that their success depended on forgiving and forgetting the past, the united faction strove to find its way within the SPLM/SPLA-United.

Unfortunately, before the meeting could wind up and celebrations could have ensued, the meeting was stormed by surprise by the SPLA squadron under Commander Kuol Manyang Juuk, who many in the meeting knew that he was a lion-hearted being and merciless devil who could wipe them all out.

Through the confusion, the Kongor Assembly and all the forces guarding them scattered in disarray with heavy casualties left on the ground. Over 60 people, including the veteran politician Joseph Oduho, were killed.[22]

Oduho was one of the founding members of the SPLM/A, and a founding member of the Sudan Africa National Union Party in the 1960s during the Anya-Nya civil war. He was also among the first Southern Sudanese members of parliament who was also instrumental in the session leading to a walk out of southern members in the parliament of 1958 against the draft Islamic constitution on the floor of the House for debate. The elderly southern statesman regrettably lost his life in mysterious circumstances.

Uncle Oduho was mourned all over the south. The rest fled in disarray toward Nasir town. It was the first time that the SPLA entered the district since the Bor-Kongor invasion by the Nasir faction.

After dispersing the anti-Garang meeting in Kongor, the SPLA ransacked and devastated Ayod, Waat, and Yuay Districts. The scale and destruction meted upon these areas and other activities elsewhere attracted condemnation from the international community [23].

What the relief agencies called the "Death Triangle," was applied to the man-made misery of cruel death and starvation in the Kongor-Waat-Ayod Districts. But the activities of the SPLA mainstream in the area forced the SPLA-United group to relocate its Headquarters in Nasir.

10.5. THE FINAL BREAK UP OF SPLM/SPLA—UNITED

By 1994, six months since the launch of the SPLA United, some sharp differences began to crop up within its leadership. What was apparent, according to observers and some insiders, was that apart from differing over general policies, clashes of personalities began to take the upper hand, making it extremely difficult for them to cooperate in whatever they wish to do.

The most complicating issue that brought SPLA-United to a downward spiralling ending was perhaps the fact that some senior members of the new movement were members of the SPLM-SPLA Politico-Military High Command they had deserted.

Commander Kerubino Kwanyin Bol, for instance, was the Deputy Chairman and Deputy Commander in Chief in the former hierarchy before he was arrested and detained. William Nyuon, likewise, was the Chief of Staff. The two had wanted to maintain their previous ranks. Arok Thon Arok also former Deputy Chief of Staff for Logistics and Administration in the High Command was campaigning that he was the ablest to lead the united faction.

In such a state of affairs, there was little room for compromise, and much lobbying was needed in order to break the leadership stalemate. In the end, it was made clear to them that it was Riek Machar and Lam Akol who launched the new revolution and therefore had the right to the top posts of this movement. But even this explanation could not sway Kwanyin Bol or Arok Thon Arok away from their claim. The commanders present at the Kongor Assembly were reportedly ready to compromise and grant leadership to Joseph Oduho as Chair of the Political Wing. The military posts could then be apportioned among the most senior commanders. But the sudden attack by the SPLA mainstream left this issue unresolved.

It was apparently the issue over the compromise discussed above that may have mistakenly led to the speculation that, in order to deprive him of the leadership of the new united front, Oduho might have been killed or left to his fate by his own group (the Nasir group). However, this theory had never been proven nor substantiated by those who advanced it.

Members present in the Kongor Assembly and later interviewed on the circumstances leading to the death of uncle Oduho on that fateful day had different stories to tell as to how he really died. Others were simply evasive and non-committal.

Back in Nairobi, Kenya, the political squabbling and wrangling over who should lead the new group resumed. And although the group differed over politics, it appeared unanimous over one main thing, cooperation with the Paymaster General, the Sudan Government.

Even while agreeing to work together for the viability of their faction, and also cooperating with the government, apparently for material and strategic reasons, the group continued condemning it and referring to it as the 'enemy.' This move was seen by many as a clever way of maintaining respect and support among the refugee community in Kenya.

But as simmering in the SPLA-United over the leadership was continuing and the differences widening, Dr. Machar and Dr. Garang were invited to visit Washington in 1993, apparently for a conciliatory conference.

In Washington, Garang and Machar were made to sign an accord in which the two pledged they would work together as a team in order to stop bloodshed among their people.

In the accord, the two leaders pledged that they would jointly confront the Sudan Government, their common enemy. The accord, which became known as the Washington Declaration, also provided that Garang and Machar were to consult with their respective supporters on the possibility of reconciling the two factions after which they would agree to reunite the movement, thereby bringing to an end the internecine fighting.

During a brief stopover in London en route to Nairobi, Dr. Machar held a meeting with the Southern Sudanese community and briefed them about the Washington Declaration. In the briefing, which was attended by the supporters of the two factions, Machar announced the good news about the possibility and efforts being exerted by the friends of South Sudan to reunite the movement.

In his brief statement, which was punctuated by outbursts of applause, Machar said he regretted that the resultant division among the southerners caused by the split in the Movement in 1991, had indeed brought untold suffering. Hence there was a need to abandon their differences and reunite in order to save the situation.

But he pointed out, "...the split had also brought us what we intended to achieve, democratisation of the Movement." "Now," Dr. Machar added, "we can criticise ourselves starting from the grassroots up to the leadership at the top."

Dr. Machar concluded his briefing by admitting that the 1991 split had benefited the enemy more than necessary because the government had made more military gains and had therefore become very arrogant in its negotiations with the SPLA/SPLM Factions.

After arriving in Nairobi to brief the leadership of the SPLA-United, Dr. Machar was met with rebuke by those who were aspiring for the top job in the Faction. Reportedly, Dr. Akol and Cdr. William Nyuon criticised the Washington Accord and continued to attack the SPLM/SPLA mainstream positions.

Soon after, Commander Kerubino Kuanyin Bol and Cdr. William Nyuon Bany met and declared that they, as the rightful leaders of the movement and the founding fathers of the SPLM/SPLA, had dismissed Dr. Riek Machar Teny from his position as Chairman and Commander-in-Chief of the SPLA-United. The two cohorts accused Machar of mishandling the affairs of their Faction.

As if this was what he had wanted, Machar reciprocated and announced that he too had dismissed Cdr. Kerubino Kuanyin Bol and Cdr. William Nyuon Bany from the SPLM/SPLA-United, stating that he had fully assumed the power as the overall Chairman and Commander-in-Chief of the SPLM/SPLA-United.

Dr. Machar, against the advice that he must not dismiss Bol and Bany, and that instead of dismissing them, he should proceed to implement the Washington Accord, decided to continue with his plan to launch his new movement.

Furthermore, Machar had also the guts to announce that he had also dismissed the architect of the Nasir Conspiracy, Dr. Lam, from the Movement for his continued cooperation with the enemy, the Government of the Sudan.

Reacting against his dismissal, Dr. Akol issued and circulated a document in which he apparently hinted that he was not alone in that cooperation. In the document, Akol was very euphemistic when he said. "Who could be more royal in the King's Court than the King himself!" A clear reference to the fact that Dr. Machar, as the Chairman of the SPLM/SPLA-United, might have been aware of whatever was going on in their movement's collaboration with the Sudan Government.

Dr. Akol told the author that the King was quite aware of what his Majesty's Counsellor was doing. Akol disclosed that he was prepared to have the two factions reconciled and even with Garang as the overall leader of the reunited SPLM/SPLA.

Dr. Akol later held true to his statement when he negotiated his way back to the Movement on time before the signing of the comprehensive peace agreement.

Since his return to the rejuvenated Movement Akol had become once more one of the main pillars on which the SPLM could depend on for its survival. War tactics were replaced by politics in which Akol could play an effective role to win national and international support but only if he used his organisational skills to make the SPLM a broad based polital party.

However, dismayed by the endless squabbling and wrangling, some members of the SPLA-United, led by Justice Dhol Acuil Aleu, former SPLM/SPLA representative in Rome, who had joined the Nasir venture, resigned their positions and trekked back and rejoined the SPLM/SPLA mainstream.

10.6. THE BIRTH OF SOUTH SUDAN INDEPENDENT MOVEMENT/ARMY

For some time it would appear as if Machar would continue as the overall leader of the SPLA-United after dismissing Bol, Bany and Akol. But following the resignation of scores of his officers, Machar suddenly assembled his supporters, mostly from the Nuer nationality, and announced that he had abandoned the name of the SPLM/SPLA-United. He launched in its place a new movement called the Southern Sudan Independent Movement and its military wing, the Southern Sudan Independent Army SSIM/SSIA.

After the launch of SSIM/SSIA, Dr. Machar also pulled his supporters out of the Humanitarian Wing of the SPLM/SPLA, the Sudan Relief and Rehabilitation Association (SRRA) and formed the Relief Agency of the South Sudan (RASS).

For the first time in five years Dr. Machar appeared positive about what he intended to do. In some of his speeches he hinted that SSIM was a genuine Liberation Movement and would do what the Nasir Faction had failed to do.

Immediately, southern separatists from different regions including those disgruntled with the SPLM/SPLA announced their intention to join SSIM. Being the only dissident officer with a large following, it was not difficult for Machar to reorganise his forces into a seemingly effective Liberation Movement.

Forthwith, Dr. Machar appointed himself Chairman and Commander-in-Chief of the new movement—SSIM/SSIA. Machar's new move made some friends of the Southern Sudan suggest that the time was ripe for the reunification of the southern rebel movement in all their factions and wings. Committees would then be available for reconciliation missions.

But while the public was waiting to see SSIM/SSIA proving its worth on the ground, it became an open secret that SSIM/SSIA leaders were still on the payroll of the Government of Sudan.

Softly, softly, many genuine southern Separatists who had made their position clear for joining SSIM/SSIA, began to shy away from the new movement.

However, Machar's continuing contact and association with the Government of Sudan was very embarrassing to many people in the South and particularly Machar's great foreign supporters.

The apparent cooperation of Machar's movement with the Government of the Sudan openly made one of his admirers, Mr. William O. Lowrey of the U.S. Presbyterian to take a bold step by writing a lengthy analytical article in which he lamented Machar's precarious military situation.

In his letter Lowrey appealed to the U.S. Government and others not to supply the SPLM/SPLA mainstream as this would widen the gap between the two southern movements, the SPLM/SPLA and SSIM/SSIA, something that would make it difficult to reconcile the two.

Mr. Lowrey further advised, "If Machar could be helped with logistics and sufficient finances and adequate zone to launch his movement, (e.g. Ethiopia) Machar could still become a genuine liberator.

And Rev. Ezekial Kutjok, an all time southern separatist, went all the way and contacted the Deputy Chief of the U.S. Mission in Khartoum and appealed to him so that he asked his government not to give Garang SPLA *any assistance*. That according to him would widen the gap of reconciliation between the two factions of the SPLA.

Rev Kutjok moved that pressure must be brought to bear on Garang to accept reconciling with Machar[24]. He further advised the Diplomat that maximum efforts be exerted to prevent Machar and his team from joining the peace from within ploy.

However, as we all know, neither Lowrey, Kutjok, nor anyone else could dissuade Machar from his well-established cooperation with the Government as discussed in chapter 13.

Apparently encouraged by Machar's abandonment of the SPLM/SPLA-United, it was up to the others to make their position clearer, whether to join Machar's SSIM, return to the SPLM/SPLA mainstream or form their own separate movements. Many of the dissident commanders were soon to act—and they acted fast.

Summing up this chapter, what befell the SPLA-United or Nasir Faction, it would be instructive to name some of the factions into which it proliferated, each with its own entity and political structures. And all but one of them stuck the label of SPLM/SPLA on its Lap as a matter of expedience and convenience.

Following were the factions or off-springs of the SPLA-United and their fateful end:

1. The Southern Sudan Independent Movement (SSIM) Political Wing and Southern Sudan Independent Army (SSIA) Military Wing. Its Chairman and Commander-in-Chief was Dr. Riek Machar Teny Dhurgon. Most of its fighters hailed from Nuer Nationality. Its area of operations: Bentiu Area in Western Upper Nile and Nasir-Fangak-Akobo triangle in Central and Eastern Upper Nile. SSIM signed the Khartoum Agreement and its leader became assistant president. He re-defected and negotiated his way back to the main rebel group, the SPLM/SPLA. He became second Vice President to John Garang the man he had unsuccessfully tried to oust in 1991.

2. The SPLA-United: This faction had a sizeable force but also hailed from Shilluk Nationality. Its overall leader, Chairman and Commander-in-Chief, was Dr Lam Akol Ajawin. Its area of operation: northern and southern Shilluk Rethdom. His forces continued for sometime launching some skirmishes against the Government Forces. He signed what became known as the Fashoda Agreement with the Sudan Government in 1997. Following genuine clamour to unite all the S\southern rebel ranks before the signing of the Naivasha Peace Deal between the south and the North, the SPLA-United and the main SPLA were finally reunited. Its leader Dr Akol was back in the New Reunited SPLA/SPLM from where he had defected in 1991.

3. SPLA-Unity Groups: The third significant faction, also with a sizeable force, was the one headed by Cdr. William Nyuon Bany, former SPLA/SPLM Chief of Staff (1983-1992) and Deputy Chairman (1988-1992). His forces consisted of Nuer and some from Equatoria Region who fell out of favour with the SPLM/SPLA following the defection of Cdr. Galerio Modi, former Commander of Eastern Equatoria who died a natural death in 1994. Area of operations: Eastern Equatoria and particularly Torit District. Nyuon was assassinated apparently by SSIM forces in Eastern Upper Nile in 1995.

4. SPLA-Bahr al Ghazal Group: The fourth group, the Bahr al Ghazal SPLM/SPLA Group was created by Cdr. Kerubino Kuanyin Bol, the man believed to have helped ignite the rebellion in Bor in 1983. He claimed he was the rightful leader of the Movement. Bol was a number two in the movement till his arrest and long detention. He was the Deputy Chairman and Deputy C in C 1983-1987. He fled from prison in 1992, assisted by the defection of his friend William Nyuon Bany. His forces, which numbered some scores of soldiers, crossed over to Western Upper Nile where he aligned himself with an Anya Nya Two War Lord Paulino Matip Nhial. With the support of Cdr. Matip Kuanyin crossed over to his hometown Gogrial, later on to Wunrok where he wreaked havoc on his own people without remorse or regret. While collaborating with the Sudanese Army and the Nuer militias, Bol devastated the

area, creating in the process severe hunger which hit Northern Bahr al Ghazal in 1997-1998, in which over 70,000 people were reported dead. He re-defected to the SPLM/SPLA in 1998 and re-defected once more to the Government side and went back to Bentiu, where he was killed in mysterious circumstances but apparently by the NIF iron-willed-strong man, Colonel Ibrahim Shams Eddin in October 1999.

5. SPLA-Bor Group: The fifth group was composed of Bor dissidents who left the Movement following the death of Judge Martin Majer Gai, former Secretary of SPLM/SPLA Legal Affairs Department. Judge Majer died shortly after he was allegedly tortured by one of his guards following scuffles and subsequent escaped of detained prisoners from the rebel camp in 1994 mentioned elsewhere in the book. The leader of the Bor SPLM/SPLA Group was Cdr. Arok Thon Arok. Cdr. Arok Thon was the SPLM/SPLA Deputy Chief of Staff for Logistics and Administration (1984-1988). Though with few forces, Cdr. Arok Thon established his command post in Bor Town under the protection of the Sudanese Army Garrison. Cdr. Arok joined the Khartoum Agreement in 1996-1998. He was very effective in his opposition against the SPLM/SPLA Leader, Dr. John Garang, and was much welcomed by his former colleagues in the Sudanese Army and Security as the only southern rebel they could do business with. His fluency in Arabic and fair knowledge of the Quran, Islamic history and Arabic culture put him in the limelight for NIF favour better than those who had gone to Khartoum with or before him. After the Khartoum Peace Agreement Arok was reinstated into the army with full honours and promoted to the rank of Brigadier General. Arok died on February 12, 1998 in a plane crush that killed, among others, the First Vice President al Zubeir Mohamed Saleh and top Islamist hard-liners in Nasir Town where the fruits of the Khartoum Agreement were first sown. For unexplained reasons, Arok Thon was much mourned by the regime as much as declaring him an Islamic Martyr.

6. The sixth group was the Equatoria Defence Force led by Cdr. Theophilous Ochand. This force, small as it was and had its command post in Torit under the Sudan Government Army protection. The force continued to operate against the SPLA mainstream until their Commander left for Khartoum in 1997 where he joined the signing of the Khartoum Agreement. Commander Theophilous was later appointed Minister of State for Health in the Southern Sudan Co-ordinating Council. Dr. Theopolous rejoined the SPLM/SPLA in 2004.

7. The seventh group, which appeared suddenly but dissolved itself when its leader trekked back and joined the SPLM/SPLA, was the one created by Dr Richard K. Mulla, former SPLA Commander and its official spokesman. Dr. Mulla fell out of SPLM/SPLA favour following the Abuja 1 Peace Talks in which the two factions unexpectedly decided to merge their two delegations

into one. Dr. Richard Mulla's Faction appeared under the name of Southern Sudan Freedom Fighters Front.

8. The eighth and last significant group, which did not effectively take off the ground, apparently due to lack of logistics and finances and which was a genuine liberation movement, indeed a separatist movement, was the Southern Sudan Patriotic Liberation Front. This Front which, theoretically, remained active throughout the war without contacting or connecting with the enemy was led by two former SPLA senior officers, Cdr Alfred Lado Gore, SPLA ideologue (1983-1988) and Captain/Professor Bari Wanji (see arrest of Cdr Kerubino 1987).

The dissident groups continued to exist separately (except the last one) though bitterly criticising one another policies and performance towards the liberation struggle. Yet they at least concurred on one important and vital point necessary for their very survival—the acquisition of logistics and financial support from the Government of Sudan coffers.

Despite having technically surrendered to the Government, the groups had the nerve to constantly remind Southern Sudanese, their supposed constituents, that they would some day reunite as one formidable front capable of fighting the 'enemy, the Arab dominated Khartoum government.' They would do that only after they had ousted Dr. Garang and democratised the SPLM/SPLA'. Regardless of what they were saying, the groups continued to receive assistance from the Government of Sudan via the Sudanese Embassies abroad and through clandestine frequent visits by some of their comrades as envoys (1991-1995). These operations were halted when the groups signed the Peace Agreement with the Government of Sudan in 1997 as discussed in Chapter 13.

CHAPTER 11
NIF LAUNCHES OPERATION' SEIF OBUUR AGAINST SPLA

11.0. THE SETTING

In September 1991, barely a month after the Nasir Declaration, the Government representative Fad al Sid Abu Gasses and the SPLA dissident Leader Dr. Rick Machar, signed a protocol in which the Government and the dissidents would work together by coordinating their military operations against the SPLA Torit Faction.

This protocol allowed the dissidents to post some of their officers in Malakal City in the hope that it would lead to improved cooperation between the two sides. As a result, 18 dissident officers under Alternate Commander Awad Jago were moved to Malakal, the Capital of Upper Nile Region. The main function of these officers, among others, was to receive financial and military assistance from the government authorities in the city on behalf of their group.

The presence of the dissident officers in the city under government control was said to have worked beautifully in favour of the Sudan Government authorities that began in earnest, to put together plans of how to crush the rebellion once and for all.

The 18 officers were now the ones to direct the government forces and to hit the SPLA's (Torit) weakest positions on the ground. It was also reported that the SPLA dissident officers might have given valuable information to the authorities about the Torit SPLA plans, military strategies and resources.

11.1. SEIF AL OBUUR CAPTURES FOSHALLA, PIBOR AND BOR

Whether it was for fresh information solicited from the dissidents about the SPLA mainstream positions and apparent weaknesses, it was time to launch its perennial concerted dry season military operations or for both reasons, the Military High Command in Khartoum, launched in January 1992, its biggest ever military offensive. The military operations were directed against the SPLA at all fronts throughout South Sudan including areas with the rebel presence in the Northern Sudan.

Having completed its preparations and assembling Troops ready to strike, the rmy began moving its heavy military hardwares and other essential supplies for the operations from Khartoum to Kosti and then to Malakal, the tactical Headquarters for the impending operations.

Assured that preparations for the start of the Campaign completed the Sudanese Army in February 1992, launched massive military operations code-named 'Hemlat Seif al Obuur' or the dry season campaign.

The Operation Dry Season, with a force of 80,000 strong, mostly new recruits and Mujihadeen, the Holy Warriors finally went into action, starting with the Torit SPLA weakest positions and easy targets.

Perhaps because of its precarious military situation in Upper Nile Region and the areas adjacent to Northern Sudan, the SPLA had decided earlier to vacate its forces from easy target positions such as Nuer Counties in the Eastern and Western Fronts, as well as northern Upper Nile.

Specifically, the SPLA continued to have presence in Eastern and Western Equatoria in addition to larger areas in Bahr al Ghazal.

As discussed, the operation 'Seif Al Obuur' was launched on a phase by phase strategy. Phase one would make a concerted attack on Bor, Pibor and Foshalla Districts.

Having brought the three Districts under the government control, the Operation would then reinforce Juba City before it ventured further afield to attack Torit, the main rebel Command Post. From Juba City the Campaign would also reinforce Yei in the west, and Kapoeta in the east and Nimule in the south of Torit. Basing its experiences on the previous military expeditions like "Operation the Soldier of One Nation" discussed in Chapter 9, the Army General High Command in Khartoum in February 1992 ordered the Campaign into action.

According to the plan, the Seif al Obuur was directed to move on a four pronged front. The first was ordered to attack and capture an SPLA isolated garrison town of Fasholla on the Sudan-Ethiopian border south of Akobo. To that effect, one contingent was unleashed immediately. It began moving discreetly from Southern Blue Nile, via northern and eastern Upper Nile.

After making several detours across the Ethiopian borders (according to Dr. al Turabi in an interview with the BBC) and taking the SPLA Forces by surprise, this task force attacked and occupied Fasholla town without a fight.

The loss of Fasholla sent a demoralising signal to the SPLA High Command not because it was a rear base, but its only outlet to the outside world through Ethiopia in the east. From then on, SPLA became aware that more surprises were coming in droves.

The second prong which was directed at the Bahr al Ghazal Front moved swiftly in gunboats from Malakal, fought its way through, attacked and occupied Shambe Port, a gateway for the control of Bahr al Ghazal from the East.

After taking Shambe, the Task Force went and occupied Yirol Town, 45 miles to the west. According to SPLA reports, Yirol was occupied without resistance because it was only an administrative centre taking care of civilian populations. Apparently most of the forces in Yirol were withdrawn in order to reinforce and defend Western Equatoria, said a source who was in the area during the attack.

Whatever the reasons were behind the fiasco, it would appear that, in the light of those circumstances, the SPLA decision to withdraw its forces orderly from remote and non-strategic positions long before the enemy attack might have been based on Yirol, Shambe and Fasholla experiences. With the capture of Shambe and Yirol Towns, all the big cities of Bahr al Ghazal Region were effectively brought under the government control.

The third prong, and perhaps the biggest, the main thrust apparently intended to make a break through the rebel defences without difficulties, was then unleashed from Army tactical Headquarters in Malakal City. This massive contingent left Malakal moving on two fronts, the land and the river flanks.

Moving steadily in a large number of convoys including heavy artillery weapons, the land force passed through with little resistance, from Khor Fulus, the assembling point, Ayod, Duk Payuel, Duk Padiet, Kongor and headed for Bor Town.

Meanwhile, the River Flank had moved swiftly without apparent resistance through Shambe and also headed for Bor.

At last, the land and the river forces converged at a given point. It then attacked and captured the town from which the first bullet that set the country ablaze, was shot in 1983, Bor.

The fourth contingent, in the meantime, was given instructions to move from Nasir and Akobo Towns in the east and with the tacit assistance and cooperation with the dissident units trekked all the way and occupied Pibor almost without a serious fight.

By the end of April 1992, the entire Upper Nile Region's big towns were either in the hands of the Nasir Faction of the rebel movement or effectively under the government control. This would mean that the Seif al Obuur or Dry Season Operation was now ready to carry the war further afield to complete its objectives.

With the whole Upper Nile and big towns of Bahr al Ghazal Regions brought, effectively, under government control, Seif al Obuur' Campaign undertook to capture Eastern and Western Equatoria Regions. A contingent plan was immediately made available.

11.2. SEIF AL OBUUR TAKES KAPOETA AND TORIT

According to the plan revealed to the author by an officer who was apparently present at the time the plan was put together, a large force was to be assembled and ordered to proceed to capture Buma Plateau, the presumed SPLA biggest tactical headquarters.

The purpose of that plan was to deceive the SPLA that its biggest station was under threat. It would then pull large forces out of Kapoeta, Torit and Juba, in order to defend Buma. This would make these cities vulnerable to government attack. If that happened, the government's large forces would move in immediately to capture Kapoeta and other SPLA strategic rear bases in the area.

When the plan was put into action, two government detachments were employed. One task force left Bor and the second left Pibor. The two at last converged midway in the desert before attacking the Buma plateau, SPLA Main Base.

Predictably, the SPLA deployed large forces in order to defend Buma. But while the SPLA was expecting attack, the two government task forces were detected withdrawing—back to Bor and Pibor posts respectively. This move surprisingly confused the SPLA about the government's actual plan.

However, as the SPLA Forces were preparing their defences for the onslaught, one government Division, aided and directed by local Toposa tribal militiamen, had gone unnoticed, bypassing the SPLA defences and surprising the SPLA Forces, invading from the rear, occupied Kapoeta, inflicting heavy casualties on the retreating defenders.

Besides the great human and material losses, the SPLA was reported to have lost most of its wealth that included large quantities of gold, arsenals left behind during the sudden withdrawal from the town.

Encouraged by the fall of Kapoeta and a string of victories in the previous months, the Government Army which had been preparing to march on Torit since February 1992, decided to undertake the capture of this Southern Sudan historical City the rebels had made their headquarters.

The capture of Torit was very vital for the government because it was in Torit that the first liberation struggle in the South Sudan erupted in 1955 just four months before Sudan obtained its independence in 1956.

Thus in March, one Division commanded by a major general and assisted by the Commander of the First Infantry Division stationed in Juba, stormed out of Juba and began attacking the SPLA built up along the entire Juba-Torit road. Just 27 miles outside Juba, at the Ngangala gorges, the Sudanese Army had its first engagement with the SPLA Forces.

For the first time since the conflict started in 1983, the SPLA and the Government Troops were engaged in direct military confrontation using conventional warfare, watched and witnessed by the public and the world at large through wire media. For the next three months, March—June, a ferocious war was fought in which all sorts of modern weapons were used.

According to reports, over 10,000 casualties of the government's total losses of 20,000 in the five month operations were lost between Juba and Torit and before Torit was finally taken by the government forces.

In June 1992, as the world was to learn, the SPLA Forces defending Torit, finding themselves outnumbered and outgunned by the huge invading forces, decided to withdraw all its forces orderly and almost with all its war machine intact long before the enemy forces entered the city. After withdrawing from Torit, the SPLA reallocated its new defences along the Imatong ranges of mountains south of Torit.

The decision to withdraw our forces orderly from Torit was meant to keep the morale of our forces very high in preparedness for the next round of fighting[1]. "And indeed we managed to take out our war machine intact from the City before the arrival of the enemy force," said Cdr. Diim. "We are a guerrilla Army. Therefore withdrawing our forces before the arrival of the enemy force was a part of guerrilla tactics, that was why our losses were very minimal compared to that of the government that wanted to take our headquarters using human death waves," concluded Diim.

The fall of the headquarters of the rebels was considered a tremendous achievement for the government. It was celebrated in Khartoum and in almost all over the big cities in northern Sudan.

The rebel forces had held the nation hostage for a number of years and the government had been looking for a face-saving device in the face of huge losses the army and the government had incurred since the intensification of the war (1990-1992).

The fall of Torit, while it was an important event for the regime, it was a morale—boosting event for the army forces who had been longing for such an occasion so as to prove its salt.

Like the capture of Kurmuk and Geissan in 1987 and 1989, five years to the day, the capture of Torit became a national occasion that the entire people in Northern Sudan had to observe as a grand event.

During the celebration marking the fall of Torit, one western diplomat in Khartoum remarked, "The occasion does indeed have some great significance in the sense that it was in Torit that hundreds of northern soldiers and civilians lost their lives when the southern troops mutinied in August 1955 which ignited the first 17 years old war ending in 1972."

The withdrawal of the SPLA to the Ugandan Kenyan borders following the Seif al Obuur offensive, fitted beautifully with the prophetic statement by the former Prime Minister Sadig al Mahdi in an interview with this author in 1987, when he described the SPLA war as 'Garang border war.'

For the next three years it became a true border war but a tough one because the Sudanese Army despite its huge forces and arsenals could not succeed to wipe out the SPLA Forces completely from the borders' trenches.

Dug in its defences at the border, the SPLA planned new strategies that enabled it in the end to stage a come back in a big way when it seized new military initiative (1995-1998). This initiative will be the basis for discussion in the next chapter.

11.3. OPERATION JUNGLE STORM COUNTERS SEIF AL OBUUR CAMPAIGN

After the abandonment of Torit in June and as the government forces were preparing to take firm hold on this historical town, the SPLA Military High Command decided to strike a deadly blow on Juba City, the political capital of Southern Sudan and headquarters of the First Sudanese Infantry Division.

Since the start of military offensive in 1992, the Sudanese authorities had made sure that Juba was well defended and equipped with modern and heavy war machinery, that had just been provided for by the Arab Gulf States and their Islamic allies so as rescue their Islamic regime in Khartoum.

According to reports the numbers of government troops and paramilitary forces like the popular defence forces, the tribal militiamen and the Mujhadeen (holy warriors) in Juba, in 1992 were corresponding to the civilian population in the city by 1:3 (one in three).

Captain Malek[2] in an interview told the author. "The SPLA decision to take Juba at this particular difficult time was twofold. First, to occupy the city effectively and, if successful, to announce the birth of the New Sudan State in accordance to the SPLM/SPLA manifesto."

It would have also been easy to dictate terms of agreement between the SPLM and the government on the position of the marginalised areas in the new Sudan. It too would negotiate with the Islamic government and the NDA the type of political system that the SPLM and its allies intend to create in the country—secular system versus Islamic system.

If, on the other hand, the attempt to take Juba failed due to the heavy government defences, such an attempt would have left a psychological impact and demoralising effect on the Islamic regime in general and the Sudanese army in particular.

Such an attempt would continue to haunt the Sudanese authorities and the army, reminding them that the SPLA meant business and that any further urge for the continuation of the war was not going to be a smooth-running affair.

Thus the SPLA forces, while fighting against the massive government offensive (Feb—June 1992) and the subsequent battle for Torit, managed to assemble a formidable force code-named 'the Jungle Storm' which had been flexing its muscle around Juba ready to move in, once orders were given to strike.

According to interviews with former members of SPLA who witnessed the operation, the Jungle Storm task force was to invade Juba from west of the River Nile.

In accordance to the plan, the task force was expected to take Lologo, a government military outpost, south of the Army General Headquarters, a post which was formerly a base for former Anya Nya absorbed Forces of Battalion 116.

After taking Lologo successfully, according to the plan without alerting the Army General Headquarters and its security organs that dotted the City, the SPLA Task Force of the Jungle Storm would then attack Juba on two fronts.

One detachment would move quickly, while bypassing government defences in order to occupy the bridgehead on the River Nile, east of the City. The presence of the SPLA Task Force would have automatically isolated Juba City from the East Bank, denying it in the process any chance of getting reinforcement coming across from the large Government Army forces in the area.

With the assistance of the SPLA internal cells, comprising the Southern Sudanese soldiers in the Army, Police Force, prison warders and wildlife guards and paramilitary units, the main rebel thrust was poised to invade the city. It would then move in and occupy the Army General Headquarters and using it as springboard to occupy the whole city more quickly.

The General Army Headquarters and security organs firmly in the hands of the Jungle Storm, the SPLA Mechanised Unit would then surge out of the jungle and reinforce the rebels' hold on the City, including the Artillery and Armoury Units north of Juba.

It was in this light that the SPLA Jungle Storm Campaign under the overall command of the Commander-in-Chief, Dr. John Garang and the operational command of Cdr. Oyai Deng Ajak invaded Juba in June 1992 just as its forces were just pulling out of Torit.

11.4. THE BATTLE FOR JUBA CITY

Breaking in through the government defences without alerting the defenders, the SPLA Task Force swiftly moved in disarmed all the government sentries of the Lologo Camp (Unit) and occupied it without any resistance from the defenders.

According to accounts by soldiers who escaped the onslaught, most of the government soldiers of Lologo Unit were caught unaware and most were killed in their beds without struggle.

Having succeeded to take Lologo Post, the Jungle Storm Task Force divided up into two detachments. The first detachment went very swiftly bypassing the enemy positions and, in accordance to the plan, occupied the bridgehead on the River Nile thereby sealing off effectively the coming of any reinforcements in order to relieve the City from the Eastern Bank.

After taking control of the bridgehead, the Task Force began shelling government positions from the East. These positions included the mechanised unit and support units as well as the artillery base at the airport.

Other government positions hit by the invaders included the Headquarters of the notorious National Security Bureau which Human Rights Watch accused of the disappearance, murder and torture of tens of thousands of Juba civilians suspected as rebels of the SPLA or their mere sympathisers.

The second task force had moved out of Lologo heading to capture the White House, residence of Colonel Ibrahim Shams Eddin, the Islamic Regime strongman then stationed in Juba to oversee the execution of the war and the headquarters of the First Infantry Division.

Colonel Ibrahim Shams Eddin's White House was also notorious for the torture of suspected Juba town dwellers for their alleged sympathy with the SPLA and hundreds of innocent citizens are known to have either been murdered or maimed through torturing there.

But before the SPLA task force could overwhelm the White House and the Military General Headquarters, it transpired that one SPLA commando had gone and set ablaze the main military petrol station making such an explosion that alerted not only the army generals in their sleep, but the whole city.

Colonel Ibrahim Shams Eddin and officer commanding First Infantry Division and a number of officers who lived at various points away from the army barracks, seeing that their headquarters was apparently in the hands of invaders, made their way to the airport that was heavily guarded by artillery division.

North of the airport was indeed well defended by a number of military defences. It was therefore natural that Colonel Shams Eddin and his commanders took over the airport and started organising how to respond to the onslaught.

Within a matter of hours since the start of the attack, SPLA forces of the Jungle Storm Campaign were already in effective control not only of the Army General Headquarters, but most of the town's residential areas as well as small army units scattered in the city. In the attack only the artillery and mechanised divisions were not taken over by invaders.

Having occupied most parts of the city and particularly strategic areas, the SPLA support units and the mechanised divisions were expected to move in from their sanctuaries so as to consolidate the effective control of Juba.

Unfortunately for the invaders, the mechanised unit failed to turn up in time because, according to reports, it went into a quagmire and was held up at Khor Ramlla, scores of miles south of the Army General Headquarters[3.]

As the Government Army Artillery and mechanised divisions were regrouping and began attacking the areas suspected to be under the control of the invaders and realising that further attempt to lend support to the forces in the City was not feasible, the SPLA High Command apparently called off the operations.

In the morning following the invasion, the SPLA invading forces had to fight their way out of Juba and along with them some of the internal cells that had effectively participated in the invasion.

One of these forces was Major Thomas Cyrillo from the artillery unit stationed at the airport who, after unsuccessfully attempting to overwhelm his unit and having killed his commander and some of his colleagues, with a hand full of soldiers deserted and joined the retreating rebels force.

The first attempt to take Juba failed. Major Thomas Cyrillo was, at the time the final Peace Agreement was signed (2004), was one of the most able SPLA commanders that for a long time had laid effective siege on Juba City.

The reason for the failure to take over Juba, according to eye-witness account, was that the internal cells, though aware of an imminent assault on the city, were not told of the final time of the operation.

It would also appear that there had not been well-established coordination between the fifth columnists and the invaders. Indeed this mistake plus others was directly responsible for the failure to take over the city.

Few hours after the withdrawal of the invading forces, President al Beshir, as Commander-in Chief of Sudanese Armed Forces, flew down to Juba partly for morale boosting of his troops and partly to reassure the stunned nation that Juba was still under the control of their gallant forces.

Al Bashir apparently went to Juba in the belief that his presence in the beleaguered city following its alleged fall to the hands of the rebels, would be a proof that the rumour was a naked lie, concocted by the world media.

Regardless, his presence in Juba could not obscure the truth that something nasty had befallen the City, that a disaster had occurred was soon revealed. On being briefed that a number of his senior commanders and hundreds of soldiers had their throats slit while sleeping in their residences at the military barracks and at the officers messes, General al Bashir could not control himself, but shed tears at the glare of the national television camera.

Encouraged by the visit of their President and Commander-in-Chief, and after getting fresh reinforcements of men and materials from Khartoum over night, the army immediately took concerted action and launched a massive indiscriminate pugnacious attack not only on the retreating rebel forces but on the whole City. Juba City was condemned.

For hours on end nothing could be heard in Juba but the thundering of heavy artillery guns, shells pounding everywhere on anything whether or not it had anything to do with the rebels' attack. For days Juba was nothing but the smell of gunsmoke and dead bodies littering every corner of the city.

As the rebels were pulling out with their dead and the wounded, the Army launched a massive house to house operation in all the suburbs, mainly on the civilians' settlements, allegedly in search of rebel soldiers who, the army said, had been hiding inside the City. During these operations tens of thousands of innocent civilians were reported killed and buried in mass graves outside the city by the Security Forces.

Reporting in the wake of Juba invasion on September 29, 1993, Amnesty International stated, "The Government Forces responded [to the invasion] by extra-judicially executing civilians and the captured SPLA soldiers during the house to house search operations and arresting, at the same time, over 230 soldiers, police, prison guards and wildlife forces in addition to the paramilitary personnel', mostly Southern Sudanese citizens."

"In addition," Amnesty International added, "prominent politicians like Major General Peter Cyrilo, former Governor of Equatoria (1986-1988) and public figures like Fr. David Tombe of the Roman Catholic Archdiocese of Juba were arrested and detained."

Amnesty International further reported that very few arrested civilians, soldiers or politicians had escaped death from the hands of the Sudanese Army and Security Forces during these operations.

At Lologo, the report disclosed the densely populated residential area through which the rebels staged the invasion was razed to the ground. Consequently thousands of its dwellers that escaped death were displaced.

The reason, according to accounts, confirmed by Amnesty International[4] and by NGOs in the area, the government wanted to create a free-fire zone—thereby displacing tens of thousands who spent weeks without food and shelter at the height of the wet season (May—October).

The government was quoted as saying that the people who showed resistance and young adult men suspected of being SPLA soldiers were taken out and shot dead during the subsequent mobbing operations.

The later defection of a number of soldiers and members of other forces who joined the SPLA for fear of being killed out of suspicion in the days following the attack heightened the government suspicion.

The attempt to capture Juba City unfortunately ended in a fiasco not only to the invaders but also to the defenders whose highly trained officers were slaughtered in their beds, a move that was demoralising to the extent that many officers forced to retire from services prematurely.

One month later, the SPLA launched another daredevil incursion into

Juba, this time more successful than the first one, but also ended in a fiasco both for the invaders and the defenders.

Although the SPLA assaulted Juba in Mid-1992 and succeeded in controlling the military headquarters for several hours, nearly 40 per cent of the SPLA fighters were either wounded or died in the operations.

"Many SPLA commanders criticised the unacceptably high casualties and predictably heavy government reprisals inside Juba," Anna Mosely Lesch writes[5].

11.5. THE SPLA PULL FORCES TO THE BORDERS

Provoked, apparently by SPLA two attacks on Juba City and the heavy casualties inflicted on its troops, and as if looking for a face-saving device about the rebels' showdown, the government ordered a mobbing operation throughout the Ssuth to rout out what military spokesman called "pockets of rebels resistance" With immediate effect the army launched a massive military offensive against the rebels forces already on retreat.

Moving on three fronts, the new military offensive was finally unleashed against the rebel positions. The Torit Front was the first to go into action. This front was supposed to attack the SPLA positions south of Torit and then moved toward the Acholi land across the Imatong ranges of mountains. But due to the difficult terrain and even despite the defection of the SPLA Chief of Staff, who had joined the government side, this front could not make any headway.

A breakthrough was made in 1993 but only when another SPLA senior commander, Galerio Modi Horinyang and scores of his tribesmen defected to fight on the government side.

Because Cd. Galerio and his tough Lotuko Warriors knew every aspect of the area and the local conditions, they enabled the government forces to make a breakthrough and went right into the SPLA territory in the deep south.

In 1993 the Government Forces Torit Flank managed to take over a string of SPLA posts which included Ikatos, Magui, Parajwok and finally the former Anya-Nya One headquarters, Owing Kibul. The loss of these posts brought most of Eastern Equatoria under the effective control of the Sudan Government's Forces. Professor Ann Mosely Lesch states: "The loss of control over Eastern Equatoria hurt the SPLA mainstream severely, since that dominated the land routes to Kenya and Uganda and provided income from gold mining, tea plantations and teak forests."

11.6. THE JUBA—NIMULE FRONT

After receiving heavy military support, the government forces, composed almost overwhelmingly of the Islamist Zealots—the Mujhadeen, led by the top leaders of the NIF hard core, went into action. Between 1992 and 1993 these forces inched their way fighting desperately and using human waves against the SPLA positions all along the Juba-Nimule Route. Professor Lesch writes: "Fighting between SPLA and the government forces remained at stand off during the winter of 1993, the army used a human waves tactic to try to capture territories south of Juba. But immense casualties, difficulty of re-provisioning garrisons and the inability to pay soldiers hampered its operations."

With a loss of tens of thousands soldiers on the way, mostly the ill-trained Mujahideen, the Government Forces finally succeeded in taking a number of SPLA positions. These included the SPLA tactical headquarters at Pageri, a few miles from River Aswa and just barely 18 miles from Nimule, the last post on the Sudan Uganda Frontier.

The future attempt to push on to Nimule was to prove more disastrous for the government battles against the SPLA since the start of the offensive in 1992.

According to an interview with soldiers who witnessed this onslaught, it was during this battle on Nimule that some of the government ministers, public figures, engineers, medical and veterinary doctors from the Mujhadeen contingent lost their lives, all but a few on River Aswa.

Future attempts to get on to Nimule all ended in disasters till it was finally abandoned with the government forces making Pageri its tactical headquarters.

The battle for Nimule, a town just 18 miles away from the battle front proved even more difficult than had been expected by the regime whose intention was to announce the end of the rebellion in the south after its capture in 1995 as the latest date.

This was not to be because of the difficult hilly terrain overlooking Nimule. The SPLA, knowing this natural barrier, broke the Aswa Bridge, thereby effectively warding off the Mujhadeen, who were attacking in human waves, from crossing over the river to Nimule.

11.7. THE JUBA—YEI FRONT

The third column, and perhaps the most important one, left Juba as soon as it received orders to move. The mission of this flank was to reinforce Yei Town, the most heavily defended of all the towns in the Southern Sudan and which had remained under government control since the war erupted in 1983.

Yei Town, besides its military strategic importance, is also important both to the army generals in Juba and Khartoum and to the merchant class in Juba and in the Northern Sudan for the following reasons.

To the generals in Khartoum and their cohorts in the war zones in the south, Yei had been a source of wealth to the extent that those who had had access to Yei during the war years have opted to retire early in order to start their own business. The reason for the love of Yei by the generals is simple. Most of the smuggled goods from Congo including hashish that sold like hot cakes in the northern cities came through Yei.

According to observers, the Yei business had contributed immensely to the delay in the conclusion of the war and the generals knew this.

To the merchant class in Northern Sudan, Yei District was synonymous with the oil-rich Arab Gulf States. A common question posed by some northern traders, who had themselves become richer than their colleagues in the north was: "Why go to Saudi Arabia or the Gulf States when you can get richer and do business so faster in Yei or Kaya?"

Essentially, Yei was also important for its potential agricultural produce. Yei District with its fertile arable land and equatorial rain forests is home to tea, coffee and tobacco plantations in addition to timber, available in commercial quantities, to say the least.

Fighting desperately for months, the government reinforcements reached Yei at long last. And from Yei a huge force was sent out to clear the way to Kaya, another important trading centre situated where Uganda, Sudan and the Republic of Congo adjoin. The Task Force finally attacked and captured Morobo and Kaya thus effectively isolating the SPLA controlled region of Western Equatoria within a short space of time.

By 1993 and 1994 the military situation in the Southern Sudan was effectively altered and tilted in favour of the Sudan Government. Precisely, the Sudan Government was virtually in control of most of the Southern Sudan if not a large chunk of its territory for the first time in ten years.

Nonetheless, the SPLA was now only in control of the entire countryside of Bahr al Ghazal, the whole of Western Equatoria Region, a foothold in the Nuba Mountains and the strip of land extending right along the Kenyan, Ugandan and the Democratic of Congo borders.

Having consolidated its position in Yei and Kaya, the Government Forces were ordered to capture the SPLA tactical headquarters in Kaji Keji after which they would, without difficulty (so it was assumed), capture the last SPLA stronghold, Nimule.

On July 11, 1995 despite a four month cease-fire, negotiated by former U.S. President Jimmy Carter, the Government Forces moved in and seized the SPLA headquarters in Kaji, Keji.

As a consequence to the loss of Yei, Kaya and now Kaji Keji, hundreds of thousands of civilians were displaced from this fertile region where they were fending for themselves into Uganda and Kenya where they continued to live in squalor throughout the war time period.

Encouraged by victories in Central Equatoria, in addition to the capture of the strategic towns of Kaji Keji and Yei, the government, with the massive military and financial support from its Arab allies, launched an effective propaganda ploy. It was telling the Sudan public and its allies that, at long last, its forces had broken the backbone of the rebellion in the southern part of the country.

Preparations for the capture of what the government called the last rebel hold, Nimule, were made, in earnest after which the government would announce the end of the war. To that effect, the timetable was set for the capture of Nimule and the remaining towns still in the rebels-controlled Western Equatoria. Programmes for the rehabilitation and redevelopment of the war-ravaged southern states were also being envisaged.

In conjunction with this propaganda, Uganda was singled out as the only obstacle that would frustrate the efforts being worked out in order to regain the last territories and to reestablish a lasting peace in the country. Uganda, the reports said, was still harbouring pockets of the rebel movement.

To remove this obstacle, Ugandan border towns like Moyo were subjected to aerial raids and border skirmishes, a move which the authorities said was undertaken in hot pursuit of the rebels made frequent incursion into the Sudan from across the borders in Uganda. The Ugandan rebels of the Lord Resistance Army under Joseph Kony[6] were immediately enlisted and began not only to fight the Ugandan Army but the SPLA alongside the Sudanese Army.

To prevent SPLA rebels from invading the country with the help of the Ugandan Allies, the Government started mobilising former Idi Amin's soldiers, intelligence and security personnel, who were given orders to infiltrate into the rank and file of the SPLA as well as striking deep into the Ugandan Army.

According to confidential information, former Amin soldiers[7] were being used by the NIF regime. The source added that some of them were based in the Sudanese Embassy in Kampala for the reconnoitring mission and others in Juba and Khartoum for information gathering.

Sudan also began bribing government officials in the former Zaire, the Democratic Republic of Congo and the Central African Republic. The move, according to reports, was to allow the Sudanese forces to invade SPLA positions in Western Equatoria from the rear. Additionally, the Sudan government also managed to set up a base at Dungu inside Zaire (Congo) from which Idi Amin rebels of the West Nile Bank Front raided northwestern Uganda.

To frighten the Ugandan Army from assisting the SPLA rebels, the Sudanese Air Force was ordered to make constant aerial bombardment on Ugandan positions suspected of collaborating with the SPLA rebels and suspected potential SPLA training camps inside the Ugandan territories.

That was the military situation on the ground when the SPLA seized once more new military initiative in October 1995 marking the start of a long drawn out military campaign that would determine the fate of the war as discussed in Chapter 12.

CHAPTER 12
THE SPLA SEIZES NEW MILITARY OFFENSIVE

12.0. THE SETTING:

After losing military initiative in addition to loss of most of its territories and failing to take over Juba City (discussed in Chapter 11), the SPLA, like most guerrilla forces, suddenly pushed against the wall by a mightiest force, withdrew tactfully and orderly all its forces nearer to international borders. There it re-established new defences further south (See chapter 10).

Therefore with all of its equipment and war machine intact and the morale among its commanders and troops apparently still high, the SPLA High Command reorganised and retrained its forces for the next round of fighting.

The SPLA also revised its military tactics, strategies as well as policies in the diplomatic front, a move that was seen as matching the new situations on the ground. Soon after, the High Command seized a new military initiative.

It also decided to undertake new steps not only to regain the territories it had lost to the Government Forces, but also to try once more to take over Juba, its prime and ultimate target for the Campaign.

Without losing much time, the rejuvenated SPLA put together a huge force in readiness for the second phase of the fighting, which the commanders were describing as the last push to Juba, the capital of the expected New Sudan.

It was in this light that while the government was busying with war rhetoric about the possibility of wiping out the last pockets of the rebels' resistance and the media propaganda against Uganda, SPLA decided to reassert its previous position to take control of War Zone One—Southern Sudan. It would then move on to take control of War Zone Two—Northern Sudan.

The SPLA, in October 1995, launched a four-prong campaign conducted in a phase by phase operation, each operation with specific objectives and targets to pursue (described below).

Phases one, two and three were apparently targeted toward War Zone One with a final push on to capture Juba, establishing it as a springboard where it would complete the revolutionary main objective of creating a new Sudan. Phase four was to take the war to War Zone Two—Northern Sudan.

12.1. SPLA TAKES NEW MILITARY OFFENSIVE

Thus surging out of its tactical headquarters in October (1995) the SPLA phase one axis, bypassing the large government forces concentrations at Pageri and River Aswa, swiftly attacked and captured 13 government garrisons between Nimule and Juba within seven days period.

These garrisons included the former Anya Nya One Headquarters Owing Kibul, Magwi, Ikatos, Parajwok, Opari, Loa and Palotaka.

In November, SPLA, after capturing Obbo, Panyikwara, Ame, Moli, Loa and advancing toward Kit, the SPLA Task Force was set to move swiftly and capture Juba.

Frightened by sudden upsurge in the fighting; and aware that the SPLA forces intended to capture Juba, the government forces in what Professor Lesch described as 'human waves tactics,' moved out from Juba and broke Kit River Bridge, 36 miles south, stopping effectively, SPLA advance to Juba. Throughout the war, the Kit Bridge became known, as mile 36, the last government southern line of defence.

Having been halted, the SPLA turned and laid siege on Pageri that the government had made its tactical headquarters to protect SPLA from crossing Aswa River.

After clearing all the government army garrisons south of Juba, SPLA attacked Pageri and Aswa. According to reports, the 15,000 strong government forces at Pageri assigned for the capture of Nimule were finally annihilated. Again like what had happened to Bor garrisons (discussed in Chapter 8) neither the government nor the SPLA had ever mentioned anything that had befallen the Pageri defenders.

The second phase of the new campaign was put into action. Moving out of its tactical headquarters in the bushes of Eastern Equatoria, in October 1995, the rejuvenated SPLA mobile unit under the direct command of Dr. John Garang de Mabior overwhelmed and captured Kaji Keji just three months after it was taken over by the government forces (Chapter 11).

From Kaji Keji the SPLA moved quickly and captured a number of government outposts including the commercial border posts of Kaya and Morobo. Bypassing the government well-defended town of Yei, the SPLA task force went straight and captured Lainya 60 miles west of Juba.

The government, with the previous experience of battle between its forces and the SPLA, when it broke the Kit Bridge at Mile 36, stopping the SPLA advance, moved its forces immediately in human waves and sealed off the SPLA advance to Juba from the west.

In pitched battles that followed, the government forces broke the Bungu River Bridge, 40 miles west of Juba on the Juba-Yei Road so as to prevent SPLA reaching Juba. The Bungu Bridge also became mile 40 up to the end of the war. The Bungu battle was reported to have raged for several days, costing the government thousands in human lives, mostly the ill-trained Islamic Mujihadeen.

With the SPLA dug in at Bungu mile 40 on Yei—Kaji Keji Road and mile 36 on the Juba Nimule Road, the City of Juba was fully besieged. It remained so till the time of signing the final Peace Agreement between the GOS and SPLM/SPLA (2004) with the SPLA holding the upper hand.

Having sealed off Juba from all sides, from the east, the SPLA main thrust moved out of Kaya and circled Yei. After a fierce battle lasting several hours, Yei with a huge force, numbering up to about 15,000 strong (SPLA estimates), was stormed and captured.

Reportedly, about 1,500 were taken prisoners of war[1], a large number killed and the rest scattered in the bushes of the equatorial jungles. Neither the SPLA nor the government of Sudan had ever given details about the exact casualties of the battle of Yei. What is clear was that the recapture of Yei in 1995 was a real human disaster for the government. To the SPLA it was the start of the beginning to end the war.

General Fathi Mohamed Ali, the former Sudanese Commander-in-Chief, then Commander of the Opposition Legitimate Command forces in eastern Sudan during a visit to Yei soon after it fell to the SPLA, was reported to have suffered a serious stroke on being shown the results of the battle. He died later in Egypt where he was immediately taken for treatment. According to the SPLA, the Yei prisoners of war were later released.

While some of the POWs went back to Khartoum, the majority of them decided to join the newly formed SPLA/NDA United Armed Forces and the New Sudan Brigade which was conducting the war in Eastern Sudan against the Khartoum Islamic Regime before the signing the final comprehensive peace agreement.

In December 1995 the SPLA attempt to recapture the government controlled towns of Kapoeta and Torit was thwarted. In 2002 following the Machakos Protocol and the signing of temporary cease-fire (October 2003), the two towns were finally recaptured.

But though Kapoeta had remained in the hand of the SPLA, Torit was later retaken by the Government following the intervention by the International cease fire monitors. Although the SPLA relinquished Torit to the government, it remained effectively besieged till 2004 when the final peace agreement was signed.

Following the first SPLM national convention in 1994, which formulated the setting up of civil administrations in the liberated areas, the SPLA reactivated its activities in most of the Southern Sudan, especially in Bahr al Ghazal that continued throughout the campaign under the SPLA control. Commanders were appointed to speed up the separation of civil administration from the military control thereby reversing the practice of the previous years.

In Bahr al Ghazal the appointment of Cdr. Nhial Deng Nhial, the son of the murdered southern leader William Deng Nhial, as governor of the region, was received with relief by the civil population who, for the previous seven years, had been subjected to maltreatment by regional war lords. Consequently large numbers of SPLA fighters had abandoned fighting and began fending for themselves.

With the appointment of Cdr. Nhial Deng, SPLA activities were reactivated throughout the region. These included cutting off the government communications routes between Juba and Wau and reopening link with the SPLA units that had been isolated in the Nuba Mountains, since 1991.

The reopening up of routes with the Nuba Mountains was a vital move and Cdr. Yousif Kuwa Meki had the opportunity to go back to take over his new post as governor of Southern Kordofan.

The SPLA after the Convention sent a political mobilisation team headed by Cdr. Joseph Kuol Amuom and in membership of Cdr. Dominic Diim Deng, Cdr. Deng Alor Kuol and Justice Ambrose Riiny Thiik to Bahr al Ghazal. The main mission of the mobilisation team was to win back hundreds of SPLA officers and men back to the movement.

The appointment of Cdr. Joseph Kuol Amuom, a veteran commander of Anya Nya One Campaign in the region (1964-1972) had great significance and a morale boosting indeed and many of the soldiers, mostly from the first Anya Nya war, reported back to their SPLA units.

The other mission undertaken by the team was to assure the civilian population of the good news about the setting up of civil administration in collaboration with the natives' administration.

It was through SPLM team recommendations[2] that the formation of a nucleus of the civil local militias was envisaged. The plan was then laid. A force which later became known as Tiit-Weng or Gel-Weng militia was put together and ordered to counter the perennial threats poised by the government sponsored Arab Murhaleen militia forces that had been a cause of anguish to the civilian population in the region.

12.2. SPLA REASSERTS CONTROL OVER EASTERN UPPER NILE

In accordance to its new strategy and encouraged by its recent string of scores of victories over the government forces everywhere, the SPLA in 1996 opened up a new front along the Sudan Ethiopian border.

This was in part made possible by the SPLA/NDA coordination and cooperation in the military activities, and when Dr. John Garang, the SPLA leader and SPLA Commander-in-Chief became the commander of the opposition joint command following the Asmara Declaration in 1995. It was indeed a morale boosting to the SPLA fighting capacity.

In March 1996 a new force was assembled named the New Sudan Brigade under the Command of Cdr. Malik Agar, leader of the Ingessna Front. On April 4, 1996 the New Sudan Brigade ambushed and seized 1,000 government soldiers when it captured Khor Yabus in Southern Blue Nile.

The New Sudan Brigade, renamed the Joint Armed Forces, in January 1996 seized the government garrisons of Kurmuk, Geissan, Shali, Dueim Mansour and negotiated the surrender of a number of government outposts in the area.

Thereafter, Agar immediately consolidated the SPLM control of the province with the exception of the provincial capital Damazin and the adjacent important hydro-electric centre at the Roseiries Dam west of the city, a centre which supplies most of the capital Khartoum with much of its electricity demand. Roseiries also supplies the vital Gezira scheme with much of its power demand.

Malik Agar's hold on Southern Blue Nile was enhanced by the NDA forces which captured much of the northern part of this Blue Nile State in a closely coordinated operation in the spring of that year.

In the same month January 1996, the SPLA forces, in a surprise move which shook Khartoum authorities, attacked and recaptured the garrison post of Fasholla on the Ethiopian border in Eastern Upper Nile Region. The capture of this strategic post was made easy by two important factors.

First the government had assumed that Fasholla was securely in the control of the Anyuak local militia commanded and led by former SPLA/SPLM spokesman in the USA, Cdr. Paul Anade Othow, a former government regional minister, and supported by Philip Obang Otway and Simon Mori Didumo, former regional ministers. Brigadier (rtd) Stephen Ogut, a veteran Anya Nya One officer newly drafted was also there supervising the formation of local Annuak Militias.

Second, the government had also taken it for granted that this vital post was being protected by the forces of the Southern Sudan Independent Movement led by Dr. Riek Machar who had just signed a political charter with the Khartoum regime.

When it became abundantly clear that the town faced eminent attack from the SPLA which was already flexing its muscle across the border with Ethiopia, the Annuak intellectuals in the Town went into an emergency session in order to decide the course of action that would save the Town.

In the meeting, one militia faction, supported by Brigadier Stephen Ogut, who became an SPLA commander, and Philip Obang, one of the SPLM leaders, suggested that the militia should negotiate the surrender of the town with the SPLA rebels because the fall of the town was very apparent.

The other faction, supported by Cdr. Paul Anade Othow and Simon Mori

Didumo, opposed the idea insisting that the militia must not surrender, but sided with the government army in order to protect the town.

The next day when the SPLA forces overran the Town, Stephen Ogut and Philip Obang led their faction out before the town fell and joined the invading forces. In the attack Paul Anade Othow was fatally wounded. He died later according to reports, while his cohort Simon Mori trekked a distance of 75 miles in two days and safely reached the government controlled post of Pibor [3].

The capture of Kurmuk, however, like its capture in 1987 and 1988, received wild and hysterical reactions in Khartoum and elsewhere in the Northern Sudan. It provided the enormous political and moral support that the government badly needed. Henceforth it gave the army impetus and morale to fight in order to crush the rebellion that was apparently on the threshold of success.

The immediate initial reaction about the capture of Foshalla was that the government accused Ethiopian authorities not only for masterminding the invasion, but executing the plan. No mention was made of the SPLA as the prime attacker, but only that the rebel movement was being used by a foreign backers (Ethiopia), posing as mercenaries in order to destabilise "our own country."

The sudden attack and recaptured of Kurmuk and Geisan, in particular, made the authorities in Khartoum order the governor of the Blue Nile State, Colonel Dr. Babiker Jaber Kabelo, to take charge of a hastily assembled two divisions to expel the foreign invaders—the Ethiopians.

The two brigades were ordered; one to proceed and recapture Kurmuk, and the other Geissan. In addition, tens of thousands of soldiers, popular defence forces, Islamic volunteers and Mujhadeen (Holy Warriors), paramilitary and auxiliary forces were being ferried by the hour to Damazin, Capital of the State to join the war in order to resist the invasion.

Senior ministers and top Islamist and businessmen led the government forces unleashed against the invaders. These included NIF leader Dr. Hassan al Turabi. All converged at Damazin Town in order to give moral courage to their forces as they faced the enemies of God, as the slogans displayed everywhere in the City of Damazin depicted.

But when the two brigades were put into action, the Kurmuk bound force was taken out of action just forty miles outside Damazin. The casualties included a colonel, the force commander.

The second force sent out to recapture Geissan was immediately ordered to recoil toward Damazin. For unexplained reasons, the force commander, Colonel Mario Kuol Monyluak Dak, a southerner, was given orders to transfer back to Medani Capital of Gezira State, with immediate effect.

Following presidential orders for general mobilisation for the war of "prestige and survival," all schools and universities were closed indefinitely. The students, teachers and lecturers were forced to sign up in Damazin ready to join the war.

Subsequent attempts to move the forces further afield in efforts to repulse the invaders ended in fiascos. On one such attempt, the State Governor, Colonel Dr. Babiker Jaber Kabelo's car was blown up by a land mine wounding him seriously and killing his bodyguards.

But as the days became weeks and weeks turned into months, all became quiet again and many of the non-combatants who went to Blue Nile to join the war walked back to where they came one by one. No doubt the area had been abandoned for the time being at least, or perhaps forever.

And Cdr. Malik Agar, widening up his area of control inch by inch, was reported (2004) to be in control of most of the Southern Blue Nile except Geissan (retaken by government), Damazin and the Roseiries hydroelectric dam.

The government's further efforts to relieve Southern Blue Nile from the rebels control was soon abandoned when it became crystal clear that the intention of the rebels was not only to control Kurmuk and Geissan; they could extend the war far north to include the grain-rich province of Gedarif, Kassala. They could even take it to the Red Sea coasts[4].

Months after the fall of Kurmuk and Geissan, the Combined Forces of SPLA United Armed Forces (UAF), Sudan Alliance Forces (SAF) and the Beja Congress Front opened up a fourth front in April 1996, on the Eritrea-Sudan border extending from Gedarif, Kassala up to the Red Sea regions.

The major operation, which sent electric shock to Khartoum, that the combined opposition forces meant business, was the destruction of a railway bridge on the main route linking up Port Sudan (main Port) on the Red Sea and Khartoum in July 1996.

Other operations which were continuing up to the time the temporary cease fire was imposed in September 2003, include sending constantly, raids into the grain producing Kassala and Gedarif regions, and the main route that links the Capital Khartoum with the only national in the east, Port Sudan.

While the government had been mobilising the army and the local populace in to frustrate the rebels advance to the Red Sea area, this was abandoned when one Army Commander defected and joined the rebel Sudan Alliance Forces loyal to Brig. (rtd) Abbdel Aziz Khalid in 1997.

This incident forced the government to back down from mobilising the public for war when it became increasingly unsure about the allegiance of its own armed forces in the region. As a result of this mistrust, only the Mujhadeen and the PDF forces were the ones used by the government to control this outstretched front with the rebels of the National Democratic Alliance (NDA).

12.3. SPLA RE-ENTERS BAHR AL GHAZAL

In 1997, the SPLA, using the time honoured military game of deception and surprise, undertook its biggest ever military expedition into Bahr al Ghazal Region, the first since the start of the conflict in 1983.

Before attacking Bahr al Ghazal, the SPLA High Command, following the previous examples (1995-1996, had unleashed a task force apparently to send signal to the Army Generals in Khartoum that it was time to take Juba.

To that effect, the task force came out of Mundiri and captured Amadi and Rokon west of Juba.

Predictably, the government moved swiftly, but it could only save Rokon. As for Amadi, it only became throughout a tactical the SPLA springboard for warding off government attempts to send further reinforcements into Bahr al Ghazal.

Aware that the Generals in Khartoum were apparently planning how to evict the NDA allied forces from Eastern Sudan, and fully confident that all routes from Equatoria for any possible encroachment to Bahr al Ghazal were cut off; the SPLA main contingent, in May, decide to enter Bahr al Ghazal.

Moving out of Maridi and with rare mobility, the task force stormed and occupied Rumbek, the capital of the Lakes State with ease, capturing large quantities of various arsenals and other essential supplies.

Having taken firm hold on Rumbek, the task force moved fast capturing Thiet and Warrap, the capital of the Warrap State within a matter of days.

As government forces were preparing to move troops out of Tonj, which had just received a large number of vehicles with varied provisions ranging from military and non military (40 vehicles), bound for Rumbek, the SPLA immediately stormed and occupied the town without a serious fight.

According to reports from people who ran out of Tonj during the attack, the SPLA captured large quantities of army personnel carriers and tanks as well as a number of civilian vehicles intact, earmarked for Rumbek.

Ramzi Monyping Cier, the Governor of Lakes State who was on his way to Rumbek, was wounded and captured by the SPLA forces. The government troops that survived the raid and the local officials of Tonj who did not want to join the rebel administration trekked in disarray and reported to Wau one by one from different directions.

The authorities were helplessly watching this sudden turn of events and wondered what this huge SPLA mobile force operation would involve; could it possibly continue and advance to capture Wau, which was certainly the SPLA next target? Would it lay siege to the town?

While this speculation was going on, the SPLA for unexplained reasons called off the attack on the town.

Instead the mobile task force left suddenly and attacked Gogrial, 62 miles north of Wau where it seized natives' stolen cattle in the town, cattle which were taken during the army raid on a nearby village on May 23, 1997[5].

According to reports, Wau would have fallen with ease had the SPLA task force ventured to take it. The SPLA's halt to occupy Wau had since then been widely criticised.

But, according the SPLA sources, the decision was strategic and administrative. The SPLA High Command did not apparently intend to overstretch its resources as it had other objectives behind the decision, as it soon became clearer.

As the authorities were speculating about the rebels' next move, SPLA forces were asked to ease their hold on Gogrial. This move apparently encouraged the government forces that had reassembled west of the Town and eventually reoccupied it.

The sudden appearance of dissident Commander Kerubino Kuanyin Bol, who had been flown down to the area from Khartoum where he had, together with other dissident commanders, just signed a peace agreement with the government (see chapter 13) made it easier for the government troops to achieve success.

Following abandonment of Gogrial, SPLA unleashed another task force from Rumbek to capture Yirol, which it overran without difficulties.

After taking firm hold on Yirol, the SPLA once again sent a contingent trailing the River Nile southward and attempt to take Juba this time from the north.

Within a couple of days the SPLA moved from Yirol and re-captured Shambe River post (see chapter 10). It then moved quickly and overran Tali post and Tindilo 60 miles north of Juba.

The government army command afraid that the SPLA forces intended to attack Juba, sent large forces to Terekeka 50 miles north apparently to defend this strategic river post whose capture would have made Juba in general and the airport in particular, very vulnerable for attack.

The capture of Juba Airport would have been disastrous to the authorities given the fact that this is the only vital supplies route from Khartoum to the City.

Although the SPLA's previous operations did not achieve its prime objective, the capture of Juba had a damaging psychological blow on the Sudan Army inside the city, especially when it became apparent that the City was besieged from all directions—Torit, Nimule, Yei, and Terekeka roads.

12.4. THE RE-DEFECTION OF KERUBINO KUANYIN

While the authorities were coming to terms with the events of the previous months in Bahr al Ghazal when it lost two states and a number of small stations, the SPLA made another surprising move which baffled not only the regional authorities in Wau but the Islamic regime in Khartoum.

The move was the sudden incursion of SPLA officers and men into Wau Town without prior warning of their coming in 1997, a move which was going to frustrate and undermine the government internal peace settlement as discussed below.

In early December 1997, the rebels purporting to belong to the main rebel group, the SPLA suddenly flocked to Wau City. According to Charles Julu Kpoyo,[5]

> "They also entered other towns like Aweil with all their weapons and in non-combat gear. They claimed they were coming to the cities in response to the peace appeal made earlier by the former SPLA deputy leader, Commander Kerubino Kuanyin Bol, within the context of the Khartoum peace agreement signed in April 1997, who were then part of the government. But while efforts were being made to attend to their needs and to understand the reasons for their abrupt incursions to the government controlled cities, a fight suddenly erupted at midnight, at the Grinti military base, between the government troops and the rebel force, the alleged peace respondents. The fight started a little before midnight January 28th ending in the morning of January 29, 1998, when the rebels were repulsed."

The story of Commander Kerubino Kuanyin Bol's re-defection started when, after being disappointed by the Khartoum regime's refusal to give him the top job in the coordinating council for southern states, under the peace agreement (discussed in Chapter 15) he suddenly left for Wau.

On arrival, Bol apparently decided to negotiate his possible return to the rebel movement he had deserted after he stormed out of the SPLA prison (1992) and joined the government five years later (1996).

But as the authorities were battling with the task of winning him back, Bol decided to move his militia forces out of the City and camped 15 miles north of Wau where he was joined by thousands of the SPLA rebels.

At his new base at Marialbai, Bol began to behave in a strange way that baffled the authorities. But as time went by and delegate after delegate from Khartoum was pouring to Marialbai to find out what Kerubino was up to, signals indicating that he was attempting to put pressure on the government to recognise his might, began to appear.

According to members of authorities who met Kerubino, his behaviour was apparently aimed at one thing. To persuade the government to relent, and therefore give him the post of president of the coordinating council, a rubber stamp administration set up under the Khartoum agreement in order to appease the former rebel groups. But even this did not offer significant explanation about Commander Bol's sudden strange behaviour. For example he was sending signals to Khartoum indicating that he would cooperate with the government but in reality doing the opposite

However, in an attempt to win Kerubino, the authorities in Khartoum took immediate action and promoted him to the post of major general and appointing him at the same time Deputy Administrator General and minister responsible for security and local government administration in the new Coordinating Council for Southern Sudan.

But while these efforts were going on, it soon became abundantly clear through security reports that Commander Bol was in an advanced stage of planning to overwhelm Wau under illusions and pretext that he wanted to restore peace in the region with the assistance of the SPLA.

It was in this light that the government took a preemptive action against, Kerubino and his alleged peace respondents, move to take over the City. At this point it became apparent that the alleged peace respondents were already in effective control of most of the sensitive and strategic positions in the city.

The rebel plan to take over the city was thwarted when the government secretly brought a force from Kuarjena, 23 miles east of Wau, to Grinti, army base. But surprisingly the rebels acted fast and instead took over control of the army headquarters and most of the other key positions in the city before the Kuarjena force[6] could overwhelm them.

After regrouping at Jebel Kheir, west of Wau, the army made a counter attack and regained control of Wau on January 29, 1998, when they repulsed the rebels' alleged peace respondents from the city.

In the fight, the rebels peace respondents fought their way out of the city retreating to Marialbai and joined their Commander Kerubino Kuanyin Bol, who once more became part of the rebel movement he helped launch in 1983.

12.5. ARMY REPRISALS ON INNOCENT CIVILIANS IN WAU

Having taken over firm control of the Wau from the rebels in the morning of January 29, 1998, the Army launched a punitive attack on the townships that were inhabited by Dinka and Luo nationalities allegedly accused of sympathising and harbouring the rebels.

Thus normal civilian town dwellers that had nothing to do with Kuanyin Bol action or the rebels' incursion into the City became soft touch target for the army and security indiscriminate attacks.

As these punitive attacks were not enough, the government army also unleashed the government sponsored Popular Defence Force (PDF), the Ferit tribal militia and the Mujihadeen Forces whose number had been increased in the city since the start of those tragic events.

The Combined Forces of the Army and the aligned militias rampaging everywhere in Wau, landed mainly on the Dinka and Luo Townships of Nazareth in the south and Hilat Dinka to the north, razing them to the ground. Other prime townships inhabited by Dinka citizens from Lakes and Warap[7] States were also devastated.

For days Wau became but a pan-demonic scene of killings and looting sprees. Any area suspected as having collaborated or sympathised with the SPLA rebels peace respondents had their fair share of atrocities.

The inhabitants of the Dinka and Luo Township, according to reports, were either killed or displaced. For fear of their lives the survivors left the city in droves and sought protection behind the SPLA line of defences.

Aware of the repercussions that would follow those punitive attacks and with the Juba incident of 1992 experience still fresh in their minds, most government officials, large civilian population and members of the army (southerners), police, prisons and wildlife forces deserted Wau as the rebels were fighting their way out.

Speaking with this author in Khartoum months after these sad events, the governor of western Bahr al Ghazal, Charles Julu Kpoyo, denied that any mass killing had occurred. He described what had happened as an isolated incident involving the rebel peace respondents and the members of the army at the Army General Headquarters in Grinti, north of Wau.

However Julu confirmed that fighting was indeed confined to Nazareth and Hilat Dinka which were razed to the ground adding that between 10,000 and 15,000 inhabitants in these townships were displaced. These areas had been completely destroyed and properties looted by a combined force of gangsters who took advantage of the confusion in the wake of the attack.

With regard to civil servants and members of police, prisons and wildlife forces, the governor said most of them had left Wau earlier, acting on the rumours that had been circulating in the city for some time that the SPLA was planning to take over the City. Adding that, many citizens had taken their families out of the City before the actual fighting erupted for fear of being caught in the cross fire that would ensue, one force attacking and the other one defending the city.

On the claim that the attack on Wau, January 28, 1997 was the work of the SPLA in collaboration with its internal cells, Governor Charles Julu said: "If the attack on Wau was launched by a combined force, involving the SPLA, the Police, Prison Warders, Wildlife and the Southerners in the Army joining the rebels, the situation would have been far worst. Wau would have been subjected to heavy shelling and counter bombardment that would have resulted in casualties much higher than the official and unofficial numbers recorded so far".

If the re-defection of Commander Kerubino Kuanyin Bol to the SPLA was described by many as a boost to its fighting capability, it was a serious setback and indeed a ruin to the regime peace from within programme and as discussed below.

As soon as re-defection of Cdr. Bol became public knowledge, the government immediately sent three high level delegations to the three Southern Regions in order to explain the circumstances that led to Cdr. Bol's abandonment of peace from within agenda. The delegates were expected to reassure the populace there that the government peace process had not been affected in any way.

Unfortunately, the leader of the peace commission, First Vice President, al Zubeir Salih, died when the plane carrying him and members of his entourage plunged into River Sobat near Nasir Town, Eastern Upper Nile. It was there that al Zubeir and the leader of the main dissident group Dr. Machar had initiated a peace accord in 1995.

Among those who perished with General al Zubeir included top leading members of the peace commission include:

1. Musa Sid Ahmed, Director General of the Peace Development Foundation

2. Abdel Salam Suleiman, Director General of the Islamic Relief Agency al Dawa al Islamia

3. Cdr. Arok Thon Arok, former SPLA Deputy Chief of Staff and the man the Regime had depended on very much for the success of its peace from within agenda

4. The new governor of Upper Nile, Timothy Tongyik Tut Lam

Dr. Lam Akol Ajawin, leader of SPLA-United, who had belatedly joined the internal peace package, sustained head injury.

If there were hopes for the Regime that the attainment of peace within its internal peace settlement was within reach, those hopes were apparently dashed to the ground.

This was because all but one of the top cadre of the peace commission, Fadl al Sid Abu Gasseissa, Musa Sid Ahmed, Musa Ali Suleman, Ahmed al Radi Jaber, Abdel Salam Suleiman, Mubarak Gismallah Zaid, Brig. Kamal Mukhtar, died fighting in the south.

It may have, apparently, been due to the death of the above committed members of the peace team that the government immediately turned the commission into a council for peace.

The Council for peace was headed by Mohamed al Amin al Khalifa, who then became the Regime peace chief negotiator with the SPLM rebels for some time (1989 to 1994 before he was jailed with his boss Dr. Hassan Abdallah Al Turabi.)

In the light of the misfortunes that had befallen the supposed Nation of Islam (discussed above) namely:

1. Loss of military initiative on the ground in the Southern Sudan to the main rebels group, the SPLA, in conjunction with their Allied Forces of the Northern opposition parties in Eastern Sudan Front (1995-1999).

2. Loss of its ablest Islamic hard-line cadres who were committed to the total eradication of the rebellion in the Southern Sudan.

3. The 1997 Khartoum Peace Agreement with the former rebels groups apparently falling apart.

4. The NIF no longer a cohesive power as it started before it split into two antagonistic factions; the regime was expected to change its strategies.

Thus while it was coming to terms with these misfortunes and looking forward to finding new committed cadre to redesign its peace aegis, to put together new strategies for a new start, the Islamic Regime staged a walk back to the IGAD peace negotiation in 1994, albeit grudgingly.

From 1994, the Peace within had almost been abandoned in favour of the Peace from without external peace negotiations with the SPLM under the auspices of the Intergovernmental Authority for Development (IGAD), the process of which is going to be the central theme in our discussion in chapter 14.

CHAPTER 13
THE MAKING AND RAMIFICATION OF KHARTOUM AGREEMENT

13.0. THE SETTING:

The Peace Agreement concluded between the Khartoum Islamic Government and six former rebels of the SPLA on April 21, 1997, was one of the many desperate attempts made by successive northern Arab governments (1956-1996) to win the African Christians in the Southern Sudan. That agreement was aimed at effort to strike a compromise in their long drawn out struggle to achieve justice and equality in the country.

The first of such attempts was made in 1972 when the then President Jaafar Mohamed Nimeiri signed an accord with the southern rebels of the Southern Sudan Liberation Movement and its military wing, the Anya Nya Armed Forces. Though that attempt succeeded, albeit temporarily, it was considered a good gesture and could have put an end to the crisis of national identity and sped up establishment of a permanent peace and stability in the country.

Paradoxically, the same Nimeiri who signed peace abrogated it with a stroke of a pen and the two parts went back to war in 1983 (chapter 3), a war which has now become polarised, protracted and more destructive in terms of property and human lives than the first one.

The Islamic Regime that had sworn to crush the rebellion militarily may have decided to try the two approaches simultaneously. A coercing approach and a coaxing approach, in the hope that one or the other would work to create homogeneity in which Arabism and Islamism would predominate in an otherwise multi-racial, multi-ethnic and multi-religious society.

This was precisely what the Islamic Regime in Khartoum had tried to do when it came to power in 1989. First it tried to crush the rebellion militarily (see chapter 9), but when this did not work, it resorted to implementing its Orwellian peace from within approach discussed in chapter 9.

However, between 1991 when the SPLM/SPLA broke up into factions and the time it signed a peace agreement with the dissident groups, the Islamic Regime did try to move heaven and earth to outwit the southern rebels by making several desperate attempts to let their own agenda go through. Such desperate attempts are the subject of discussion as we approach the end of the

SPLM/SPLA story of creating a new Sudan. The way out of this dreary and out-of-the-way method will also be discussed.

The first attempt was, when the regime delegation, headed by Dr. Ali al Hajj Mohamed, an African by birth and complexion and an Arab by upbringing and mentality, signed an accord with Dr. Lam Akol Ajawin, the representative of the SPLA breakaway group, in Frankfurt, Germany.

By all accounts and descriptions, the Frankfurt accord gave a hint to the SPLA dissidents that the Regime was willing to make concession without compromising its Islamic ideology and agenda it had sworn to implement, come what may.

Precisely, the Frankfurt Accord, dubious as it appeared, was a clear sign that the regime was seeking grounds for a search for cheap peace. Sadly, this accord was brushed aside soonest and was never referred to or cited, at least for expediencies.

As it moved to discuss issues of peace and war at different situations and fora with the SPLA main rebel group (Abuja One, 1992, and Abuja Two, 1993) under the auspices of the Nigerian Head of State (chapter 11), the Frankfurt accord was overshadowed by the regime's double standards. Precisely, the Frankfurt accord was placed in limbo when the Khartoum Islamic Regime carried a peace file to the Kenyan President Daniel arap Moi in 1994.

Under the auspices of the IGAD the Peace Process became very elusive given the regime's haphazard and cunning approach by hunting for possible fora apparently to divert peace rather than sticking to the previous serious fora whose efforts have reached an advanced stage like the IGAD (FOUR) Peace Process.

So, while the Regime was looking forward to hold discussions with the mainstream SPLM/SPLA, it had to continue, regardless, to woo the SPLA dissidents, telling them that it, and it alone, was their darling and that it would not forget its promise to sign peace with them. But in accordance with peace from within formula that was being put on the table each time they show some sign of relenting.

The Islamic Regime's second desperate effort to achieve peace was when in early 1993, the Director General of the Peace Foundation Development, the Islamic die-hard, Fadhl al Sid Abu Gasseissa (discussed in chapter nine), and a team of Islamists and security members, left for Fashoda in north-western, Upper Nile Region. Abu Gasseissa was expected to discuss with the SPLA dissident commanders the issues of peace and war.

Abu Gasseissa and his team managed to meet Dr. Lam Akol representing the dissidents group and his delegation in the presence of the Shilluk Reth (King) at his residence in Fashoda Village. The two delegations were reported to have discussed the possibility of signing a peace accord.

The third attempt by the Islamic authorities to win the dissidents was when Abu Gasseissa in August 1993 with his team of Islamists left for Bentiu to discuss the peace from within approach with two of the main rebel factional leaders, Dr. Riek Machar and Commander Kerubino Kuanyin Bol.

But while Machar and Bol were waiting to receive their guests, the plane which was carrying the Government peace delegation exploded in mid-air over the Rubkona Airstrip in Bentiu, the former Headquarters of the American Oil Company Chevron, killing all on board. Those who perished in the Rubkona fiasco included prominent senior officials of the Government sponsored Peace Commission:

1. Fadhl al Sid Abu Gasseissa, the chief architect of the Peace from Within Approach, Minister and Director General of the Peace Development Foundation

2. Ahmed al Radi Jaber, the Islamist Supervisor General for Southern Sudan

3. Musa Ali Suleiman, (Nuba) Commissioner for peace and special envoy for refugees affairs in Eastern Africa

4. Brigadier-General Kamal Mukhtar, NIF special chief security advisor for war and peace affairs in the Peace Commission

5. Brigadier General of Police, Paul Reth, governor of Upper Nile

Despite this tragic incident, another delegation was soon sent to Bentiu without delay. More discussions on the possibility of signing an internal peace settlement as opposed to the IGAD's peace forum were held with Dr. Machar and Cdr. Kerubino K. Bol. Though the two delegations were reported to have discussed the issues of internal peace settlement, not much was released in specific terms, to the general public.

Regardless to the peace discussions between the Government and the mainstream SPLM/SPLA at IGAD (described in chapter 12) and in spite of constant contacts between the Government and the leaders of various dissident groups, peace continued for some time a remote possibility.

In June 1995, the NDA held its first convention in Asmara, Eritrea. The Asmara resolutions, among others, provided a basis through which the NDA called for the removal of the Islamic Regime from power in Khartoum (chapter 12), using all methods available including popular uprisings in the cities all over the Sudan, political and diplomatic offensives, the Government began panicking.

Responding to the threats posed by the NDA, the Government apparently drew up urgent plans aimed at defusing these threats. It would appear that a decision was made for the Government to align itself immediately with the southern dissidents which were already mushrooming—especially following the break-up of the SPLA-United, discussed in chapter 10.

13.1. THE KHARTOUM POLITICAL CHARTER

When the Opposition Joint Military High Command extended its military activities, which included the rich grain-producing areas of Gedarif and Kassala and up to the Red Sea Hills, it sent electric waves to Khartoum that the NDA meant business and therefore must be confronted with vigour.

In 1996 the SPLA, in collaboration with the other NDA Forces, captured the whole of Southern Blue Nile and threatened to move on to Damazin Town, which housed the Hydro-Electric plant that supplies the capital Khartoum and the Gezira agricultural schemes with much of its power.

After the capture of Southern Blue Nile, it became imperative for the Islamic Regime in Khartoum to resort to the old adage that your enemy's enemy is your friend.

Vice President al Zubeir Mohammed Salih, the Regime's Strongman, appealed to the southern dissidents to send some of their forces to the east to join the thousands of troops, popular defence forces and Islamic Mujahideen already parading in Damazin Town in a state of total preparedness to confront the invaders.

The dissident commanders were told in no uncertain terms that they their forces should evict their fellow southern rebels from Kurmuk and the entire area they had occupied in accordance with the previous accord of understanding and mutual cooperation.

But when this did not materialise, Vice President al Zubeir flew down to Nasir Town in Eastern Upper Nile where he met and discussed the possibility of an internal peace settlement with Dr. Riek Machar, leader of the Movement for the Independence of the Southern Sudan (MISS or SSIM).

It was there, according to reports[1], that a document outlining the basis for future discussion for an internal peaceful settlement between the Islamic Regime and the SPLA breakaway groups was first initialled. From there on, things appeared to work favourably for the Government peace deal.

The Nasir meeting between al Zubeir and Machar coincided with the defeat of the SSIM forces in Eastern Upper Nile and Eastern Equatoria, a move which made many SSIM commanders move closer to Khartoum authorities waiting for the time to sign the peace accord with the Regime.

The assassination[2] in December 1995 of Commander William Nyuon Bany, who had just rejoined the mainstream SPLA and who was there at the time, coordinating and mobilising forces in the area in order to reunite the two embattled factions of the movement, spurred the dissidents to move towards Khartoum.

Commander Nyuon Bany's assassins have not yet been identified; nonetheless accusing fingers were being pointed at SSIM Forces. William

Nyuon's assassination contributed to SSIM closing ranks with the Islamic Khartoum Regime sooner.

Whether it was in response to the combined scenarios described above, or just the right time for the concerned parties to sign the much expected agreement, it became very urgent for the Government to sign a charter with its cohorts in the Internal Peace Programme.

However, when the time was ripe, First Vice President Al Zubeir Mohamed Salih in his capacity as the chair of the Peace Commission brought together the six dissident groups that had arrived in Khartoum for the purpose of signing the Internal Peace Settlement with the Government.

Thus on April 21, 1996 the six former rebel groups and the Government signed a political charter, which observers said was nothing short of a declaration of principles through which the concerned parties committed themselves to negotiate an internal peace deal. Below are the names of the six rebel groups that signed the political charter:

1. The South Sudan Independent Movement (SSIM). Leader, Dr Riek Machar.

2. The SPLM/SPLA Bahr al Ghazal Group. Leader Cdr Kerubino Kuanyin Bol.

3. The SPLM/SPLA Bor Group. Leader Cdr Arok Thon Arok.

4. The SPLM/SPLA Independent Group (Aweil Group). Leader Cdr Kawac Makuei.

5. The Equatoria Defence Force. Leader, Dr Theophilous Ochan.

6. The Union of African Parties (USAP). Leader Samuel Aru Bol.

But as the groups were expecting to be called upon to discuss peace in accordance to the political charter they had just initialled, they were asked to abandon their previous titles and positions in the Bush. They were further told in no uncertain terms that unless they adopt a new name which would bring all of them under one organisation and under one leadership, they might not sit to talk peace with the authorities.

Seeing the writing on the wall, the former rebel groups agreed to drop their old names and titles. It was not clear who suggested the new name, but obviously the groups met and adopted a new name—The United Democratic Salvation Front, UDSF. Their fighting men were called the United Democratic Force for the Defence of Southern Sudan or the UDSSF.

But as the UDSF/UDSSF were coming to terms with their new situations, they were further instructed that the UDSF must go out to mobilise the whole Southern Sudan in order to accept peace settlement in accordance with the Government Programme of Action, the Peace from within Programme.

The UDSSF were also given instructions they might have not expected, the task of going to purge the entire Bushes of Southern Sudan from John

Garang's rebels, a reference to the mainstream SPLM/SPLA which the groups had defected from. The UDSF were told further that they might discuss peace with the authorities but only when their effectiveness on the ground was felt in the south.

While the UDSF leaders were waiting to hear when UDSF and the Government would convene a meeting to discuss the terms of the possible peace agreement, they received a circular from the Minister of Peace, Mohamed al Amin al Khalifa. The circular contained the news about the impending formation of a coordinating council for Southern Sudan, the administration that was expected to coordinate, not to rule, the work of the ten States Governments in the Southern Sudan.

The Minister's letter was inviting not the UDSF, as expected, but all the southern intellectuals and politicians from the Southern Sudan in Khartoum to make consultations among themselves and to make suggestions and recommendations on the chairman and number of ministers who would form the coordinating council.

On receiving the Minister's circular, Southerners in general and the leaders of the UDSF were immediately thrown into confusion. 'What comes first,' the UDSF leaders queried, 'the signing of a peace accord or the formation of a government for the south?'

Clearing the air about the confusion that had ensued from his circular, Mohamed Amin Khalifa made a press statement in which he said it would only be through the coordinating council that peace would be negotiated and signed.

Supporting Mr. al Khalifa's statement, Jwong Twoch, the Chairman of Peace Committee in the National Assembly (a Southerner), told pressmen[3] that the ten southern states would continue to enjoy their autonomy embodied in the Presidential Decree No. 12 which regulates the function of Institutions under the Islamic Federal System.

The coordinating council being proposed, Mr. Jwong Twoch pointed out, would mainly be dealing with issues of peace. The sudden news about the formation of the coordinating council was received within the southern communities in Khartoum with mixed reactions.

The mainstream of former SSIM members received the news with some relief since the public in the south was pestering the SSIM leadership to tell them whether there was going to be a peace agreement at all or not. To this section of SSIM, there was something in the right direction, at least for the time being.

As for the members of the radical wing of the former SSIM, they told one another that the move was the typical Northern Sudanese Arabs' way of undoing with impunity whatever they have already agreed to give to the South, in politics at least. "The move is clearly to lure us, the fighting Southerners out of the Bushes," said Peter Riir[4] sarcastically.

In 1972, the Anya Nya rebels abandoned the struggle suddenly at the mention of a regional autonomy and the formation of the High Executive Council for the South. 'Is history repeating itself?' queried another non-conformist member of former SSIM.

The reaction of the Southerners inside the country in general and those who were opposed to the internal peace deal with the dissident commanders was clearly expressed by late Hilary Paul Logali representing his group (USAP) when he said, "Our general view on the matter is that there should be a comprehensive peace agreement signed by all Sudanese political leaders representing the main political forces in the country and sitting in a national constitutional conference.

Mr. al Khalifa's move and the policy of the NIF regime is just a wasted exercise meant to buy time to enable the Regime to deal with the war situation in Eastern and Southern Sudan,' said late Logali to this author.

The meeting with the southern politicians and intellectuals with Mr. al Khalifa later in the Friendship Hall in Khartoum revealed two opposing viewpoints on the formation of the council and who would lead the proposed council.

The former rebel groups' signatories to the political charter instead of insisting on their agenda that they should sign peace first before talking of forming a council, made it clear that their man would be the one to lead the council.

On the other hand, Southerners in the Government headed by Vice President George Kongor and supported by Angelo Beda, Minister of Labour, claimed that they were the right group who should lead the council. 'We have never revolted and have been working for internal peace settlement. How come the credit should go to the rebels or the returnees?' said the Minister.

The post of the President of the Council should automatically go to the Internal Front that had been working for peace, not the rebels, said Arop Acier Akol, Governor of Warrap State, a theoretical Islamist convert and a staunch anti-SPLA lobby of the Internal Front for Peace.

In a statement to the press intended to defuse the controversy, Mr. Jwong Twoch assured the meeting saying that there was nothing to fear or quarrel about since there were no visible contradictions in the positions both members of the groups held on the internal peace matters.

Mr. Jwong Twoch further made it clear that the proposed council was an interim authority set up for a purpose and which will automatically disappear after the results of the referendum for the south and self-determination were announced.

Meanwhile, President al Bashir added fuel to the controversy when he told the public that whatever agreement would be reached with those who signed the political charter on the resolution of the Southern problem would not tamper with the current federal set up or the Islamic orientation of the state. "This is in fact the official position of the Government and nobody needs to be reminded about it," the President and members of his cabinet continued telling the public in their daily utterances.

13.2. SSIM PRESENTS A LEGAL FRAMEWORK FOR PEACE

As the Government continued with its daily rhetoric and slogans that 'the time has come to sign peace, a lasting peace,' SSIM National Liberation Council had been working in consultation with some of its internal experts to write its position paper on peace.

In the end SSIM presented a working paper it called the Legal Framework, the Blue Print[4] through which peace could be negotiated. The SSIM Blueprint, according to experts, was an excellent and elaborate masterpiece. Indeed the articles in the SSIM Legal Framework apparently contained more powers for the proposed Southern Government than in the 1972 Self-Government Act.

Save for those attractive articles, the SSIM Blue Print, observed one western diplomat in Khartoum, was full of loopholes and weak points which each of the parties to the proposed settlement could exploit to its advantage, as was the case of the 1972 Act. 'The writers of the Legal Framework do not appear clear about what they need to extract from the Government,' said an African diplomat in Khartoum to this author.

In the final analysis, the SSIM Document, as it appeared, was not very clear as to how the escalating war that had been sapping all the national resources could be halted. In addition, the document did not attempt to highlight the options the Southerners would choose from them in the event that they were asked to carry out the proposed referendum in their part of the country.

Precisely the paper did not say whether the southern people would have the option to choose between the Government's unconditional unity of the country or form a separate independent state.

Dr. Ali al Hajj Mohamed, minister responsible for the Federal Affairs and one of the chief negotiators with the rebel groups in a speech in a public rally during one of his visits to the Northern Region said: "In the Sudan there are three levels of government recognised in our federal setup: at the bottom is the local government: the state government is in the middle and the federal government is at the top. As for the proposed coordinating council for the ten southern states, it is just an administrative deal made for a purpose and when that purpose is achieved, that council will disappear."

Dr. Ali Hajj was apparently commenting on the slogans raised during the rally that the Southerners who have been responsible for the state of instability and economic woes in the country were being given more than their fair share of the national cake.

Such was indeed the political environment prevailing when the Peace Agreement was signed with the rebels in 1997, discussed in the subsequent paragraphs.

13.3. THE MAKING OF KHARTOUM AGREEMENT

While Southerners were squabbling over who would head the proposed council for the south discussed earlier, the Government was also marking time on how and when it would sign peace with the former southern rebels, the military situation had been changing on the ground very rapidly.

In the south the SPLA had re-entered the Region of Bahr al Ghazal in a massive manner for the first time since the war erupted in 1983 and was threatening to take over the whole region.

To the government it was very apparent that if the SPLA took Bahr al Ghazal and linked up with its isolated forces in Southern Kordofan, it would be a disaster for the Government to fight in the East and the West.

In the Eastern Sudan the SPLA in coordination and collaboration with the Forces of the opposition political parties, and particularly the Sudan Alliance Forces under Brigadier Abdel Aziz Khalid, had carried its activities from Southern Blue Nile Region up to the fringes of Red Sea Hills (chapter 11).

Thus as the SPLA and the Alliance Forces were pulling the noose around the neck of the Government Troops in the East and the South, it became abundantly clear that the Government's plans might be overtaken by events. Furthermore the wide diplomatic and political pressures that the NDA was bringing to bear on the Regime was more than it could bear. It has to act and act very promptly to bring the southern dissidents on its side.

It was in the light of this analysis that the First Vice President of the Junta, Major-General al Zubeir Mohamed Salih brought the leaders of the six former rebel dissident groups together and told them that it was just time to sign the Peace Agreement with them.

On April 21, 1997, one year to the day, in the Presidential Palace Gardens in the cool air of that April evening amid a lavish celebration air—live over TV and radio listened to and viewed by the whole nation, the Khartoum Agreement was signed.

Despite the fact that the ceremonies in the Palace had very little to do with the descent of a genuine peace, the mere presence of Major Kerubino Kuanyin Bol, the officer, who fired the first shot in 1983 that started the second civil war in 1983, was a real consolation. Indeed it was at least to those who had lost beloved ones as well as those maimed by it. For the general public that had been yearning for peace it was a welcome move.

In signing the Khartoum Peace Agreement, the First Vice President al Zubeir Mohamed Salih signed on behalf of the Regime while Dr. Riek Machar Teny and Commander Kerubino Kuanyin Bol signed on behalf of the six groups. 'Allah u Akber! Allah u Akber! God is great! God is great! God is great!' The crowd in the Palace Gardens who had been brought from the cross sections of the capital's population, thundered when the two former rebel leaders put their signatures to the Peace Accord.

Some weeks after the endorsement of the Peace Accord, it was enacted into the law of the land by a Presidential Decree No. 14 that was immediately passed by overwhelming majority in the Rubber Stamp Assembly (Parliament). Thus, while the war was escalating, the Regime in Khartoum had something to celebrate for the time being, forgetting the scourge of the war.

The Peace Agreement concluded in April 1997 (discussed in chapter 12), can be said to have come at the wrong time, if not at the most inappropriate time, for the Islamic Regime for the following reasons:

First, the agreement was signed at the time that the war which the regime had wanted to win in the previous years (1992-1995) was just beginning to escalate, apparently, with the Forces of the SPLA and the Northern opposition political parties taking the upper hand on the ground.

By this time the SPLA had taken over 90 per cent of the entire length of the River Nile starting from Kaji Keji on the Ugandan border up to the border with western and southern Kordofan. This excluded Northern Bentiu where the Government forces had been digging in to protect the oil fields.

The SPLA thus was in control of four of the southern Sudan states, namely Western Equatoria, Lakes, Warap and Bahr al Jebel with Juba and Terekeka under effective siege. In the East Bank of the Nile, the SPLA took firm hold of the rural areas while laying effective siege on Torit and Kapoeta, Bor and Pibor, up to Ayod, with Fangak, Waat and Akobo at the northern fringes of its control.

Meanwhile in the Eastern Sudan which the SPLA referred to as the war zone two (Northern Sudan) the SPLA forces in collaboration with its NDA Allied Forces, had taken over (1999) sizeable territories stretching along the Ethiopian-Eritrean borders up to the Red Sea Hills.

The above areas included Southern Blue Nile, east of the grain-rich Gedarif and Kassala states. Effectively, the loss of the Eastern and the Southern Sudan to the rebels meant that the Sudan Government had lost contact with the outside world from its southern and eastern frontiers.

The second reason was that the agreement was concluded at the time the Regime was at the verge of implementing its brand of Islamic constitution which was not only at variance with the Khartoum Peace Agreement but had adopted a federal system of governance.

According to the new constitution, Sudan was divided up into 26 states carved out of the former nine provinces (1956-1976): 88 provinces from former districts and several hundreds localities and principalities, carved out of the old rural and town councils, with the Federal Authority sitting on their top.

Due to these circumstances and administrative proliferation in a country as vast and underdeveloped as Sudan, the creation of another Local Authority like the coordinating council over and above the ten southern states would present a formidable problem to a regime fighting a war in the south and the east. This meant that the new Authority being proposed would fall outside the new federal structure.

Equally important was that any move aimed at imposing a unifying authority over the recently created ten southern states, like the 1972-1982 One Regional Authority, was expected to present the Federal Authorities with a formidable task. It would demand that the ten states accept the curtailment of their God-given autonomy in favour of one region that was rejected by Equatoria in 1983.

Even assuming that the states in former Upper Nile and Bahr al Ghazal were to relent on the proposal to reintroduce One Regional Authority in the Southern Sudan, it was expected to be rejected outright by the Equatorian States.

The third problem which cropped up while the Central Authorities were speculating as to whether to institute the proposed coordinating council as demanded by the former rebels was what powers were to be vested in the new Southern Umbrella Authority. Obviously this would need immediate amendment of the new Federal Constitution that was already before the Assembly for enactment into the Law of the Land.

When time came for the Southerners to consult among themselves as to who was to take charge of the Council stewardship and to nominate candidates to fill the posts of ministers before forming the Council, this immediately threw them into utter confusion because they could not agree on one candidate.

As the squabbling over the chairmanship of the Coordinating Council was raging, it soon became clear that the Southerners who had extracted themselves from what the SPLM/SPLA stood for were divided up into three main categories.

Category one consisted of the mainstream Southern Islamists. The leaders were Ali Tamim Fartak (Bahr al Ghazal), Mangu Ajak (Upper Nile) and Amin Ismael Jula (Equatoria). This group, as expected, stood for the Islamisation of the South before anything else could be done.

Category two was composed of ex-Government officials who were wearing anti-rebel slogans on their laps. Its leaders were: Vice President Kongor Arop (Bahr al Ghazal), Anjelo Beda (Equatoria) and Colonel Gatluak Deng Garang (Upper Nile). This category identified itself with the Islamic Regime from the first day it came into existence. In short this group considered itself the real peace respondent and accused others as double dealers.

Category three was composed of the former rebel leaders who had signed the Khartoum Peace Agreement and who thought they had the absolute unquestionable right to be the authority to form the Coordinating Council. Thus, with the later birth of the United Democratic Salvation Front (UDSF), an amalgam of the former six rebel groups described in chapter 12, Southern Sudan had three internal distinctive antagonistic political groupings, each presenting itself as the most loved one over the other groups. Essentially the big three political groupings were:

1. The Southern Islamist Front
2. The Internal Peace Front for Unity
3. The United Democratic Salvation Front

As described previously, the three groups clashed ferociously over the formation of the Coordinating Council. Attempts made by Colonel Mohamed al Amin al Khalifa, the Regime minister of peace and its chief negotiator with the rebels only added fuel to the jockeying for the control of the Umbrella Southern Council.

Further attempts made by President al Bashir could not make any of these groups relinquish its position on the claim that it was the real representative of the Southern Sudan.

It was only after the intervention of Sheikh Dr. Hassan Abdallah al Turabi, the country's 'Ayotullah Khomeini,' that the three southern antagonistic groups agreed to cooperate and to share whatever crumbs were left on the table for the Southern Sudan.

According to reports solicited by this author from the parties concerned, Sheikh al Turabi had assured the groups that they had no reason to quarrel, claiming ascendancy over the others since they were under one system, the Shura or the Islamic Consultation Model.

In short it was after Sheikh al Turabi had had separate brunches with each of the three groups at his prestigious Khartoum East suburban Manshie Mansion that the groups established a working relationship. Consulting among themselves thus began in earnest about the formation of the Co-ordinating Council.

After two months of arm-twisting consultations, the Southern Islamist Front (Branch of NIF) and the Southern Internal Front for Peace were persuaded to give way for the returnee rebel groups, the United Democratic Salvation Front, which had signed peace with the Regime to form the Co-ordination

Council. Precisely the two Fronts were told that they were already represented in the system.

Once the two fronts had been convinced to give up the Coordinating Council, the UDSF members were asked to recommend one of their numbers to the President of the Republic for appointment to fill the post of the Council Chairman. They were also asked to nominate people for ministers in the council in accordance with the terms agreed upon by the three fronts discussed above.

But as the consultation was beginning, the ten states objected to being brought under the new umbrella authority being put together. This new move would have wrecked the formation of the council. This was averted when the authorities in the ten southern states were told categorically that the Coordinating Council would have no power over them.

They were further assured that the council would not broker for their interests with the Federal Authorities (Central Government).

According to the new Federal Constitution, the relations between the 26 states and the Federal Authority were being regulated under the Presidential Decree No. 12, with Federal Government on the top and states at the bottom line.

The Southern Council, on the other hand, was to be governed in accordance to the provision of the Khartoum Agreement recently enacted. The issue having been resolved, the UDSF was ordered to name a candidate for the chair of the Council and its ministers.

But while the consultation was going on within the UDSF members and other political forces, as discussed earlier, a new controversy arose over who was to chair the Council from among the six former rebel groups which composed the UDSF.

As it soon turned out, the issue was that each of the members in the UDSF began to claim his seniority in the SPLM/SPLA before they defected. This became very contentious indeed.

While it was apparent that Dr. Machar was the leader of the majority faction within the UDSF, Cdr. Kerubino Kuanyin Bol began to claim his seniority. He was the number two leader in the SPLM/SPLA movement; Hence the most senior of the group to head the Council.

On the other hand, Cdr. Arok Thon Arok who, as described earlier, considered himself the most capable of the groups using his previous credentials in the Sudanese Army also put himself forward as the candidate for the Council's top post.

Seeing that the controversy would wreck not only the peace accord but throws the country into worse confusion; the Federal Authorities were forced to intervene.

The groups were told that the faction with substantial forces in the

UDSF would take the chair. Even with this clear statement from the Federal Authorities, Cdr. Kerubino Bol would not back down from his claim. Instead he threatened to kill everybody in the meeting unless he was allowed to take the chair of the Council.

In order to ward off the crisis, the Federal Authorities told the groups in no uncertain terms that the three Southern Political Fronts have to share the posts that were given to the South in accordance with the three Southern Provinces (1956) of Bahr al Ghazal, Equatoria and Upper Nile.

Thus the most senior posts earmarked for the south were distributed as follows. That since the post of the Second Vice President of the Republic was occupied by George Kongor Arop from Bahr al Ghazal, the post of the Chairman of the Coordination Council (upgraded to the position of Assistant President of the Republic) would go to Upper Nile.

The post of the Deputy Chairman of the Coordinating Council was accordingly given to Equatoria. Automatically, the Chair of the Council was given to Riek Machar, being the leader of the majority faction in the UDSF and from Upper Nile. The post of the Council Deputy Chairman was given to Angelo Beda (Internal Front for Peace) from Equatoria.

On being told that he would be just a minister and a member of the Council and not a number one or a deputy to the chair, Cdr. Bol almost went berserk. He drew his pistol and threatened to shoot down whoever would cross him in the process in the meeting rooms where the posts were being allocated.

However, the Federal Authorities, using all methods of diplomacy, escorted Cdr. Bol out of the meeting while assuring him that his position would be reviewed and given full consideration.

In order to soothe Cdr. Bol, he was reinstated back into the Army he deserted when he led the Bor Mutiny in 1983 and promoted to the rank of Major General.

Three other officers who had also deserted the Army at different times and in different places were reinstalled to the Army and promoted. Cdr. Arok Thon Arok and Cdr. Nicanora Magar Aciek were promoted to the rank of Brigadier Generals while Cdr. Faustino Atem Gualdit was promoted to Full Colonel.

Despite these promotions, Cdr. Kerubino Kuanyin and Faustino Atem Gualdit left for Wau where they started negotiating their way back to the SPLM/SPLA. Cdr. Bol later pulled his forces out of Wau to Marialbai, 15 miles away (discussed in chapter 12). He later re-defected to the SPLA/SPLM.

In August 1997, three months after the signing of the Agreement, Dr. Riek Machar Teny was appointed Assistant President of the Republic and Chairman of the Southern Coordinating Council in addition to his posts of Chairman of

UDSF and Commander-in-chief of Southern Sudan Defence Force, SSDF. The following were appointed members of the Co-ordinating Council:

1. Dr. Riek Machar Teny, Assistant President of the Republic and Chairman of the Coordinating Council (Upper Nile—UDSF-SSIM)

2. Angelo Beda, Deputy Chairman and Minister responsible for Police, Prisons and Local Administration (Equatoria—Internal Front for Peace)

3. Sheikh Beech, Minister of Finance (Upper Nile—Southern Islamist Front)

4. Joseph Nyok Abiel Ayom, Minister for Political Mobilisation and Peace (Upper Nile—UDSF)

5. Dr. Theophilous Ochan, Minister of Health (Equatoria—Equatoria Defence Force-UDSF)

6. James Mabor Gatkuoth, Minister for Humanitarian Affairs (Upper Nile—Pro-UDSF)

7. Akile Deng Acuil, Minister for Legal Affairs (Bahr al Ghazal—Pro-Internal Front for Peace)

8. General Albino Akol Akol, Minister for Engineering Affairs (Bahr al Ghazal—Internal Front for Peace)

9. Paul Mabior Ayom, Minister of Information and Culture (Bahr al Ghazal—UDSF—He did not take up the post for unknown reasons and continued to remain in exile in London.

10. Minister of Education—vacant

11. Minister for Wildlife (UDSF)

12. Alakiir Malwal Chol, Women's Affairs (Upper Nile—UDSF)

13. Kongder Dut Ngong, Minister of Public Service and Manpower Development

14. General Gismallaha Abdallah Rassass, Security Adviser (Pro Internal Front for Peace)

15. Justice Wilson Aryamba, Political and Legal Adviser (Independent)

Despite the fact that the Coordinating council was appointed, it was quite obvious that many of those who signed the Khartoum Agreement were not there to make it work because they had been forced into it for tactical reasons. Considering also the political wrangling and experiences that preceded its formation, not much was expected from it.

It would just be a matter of time before it followed the natural course taken by the ones signed before it, ending in the dustbin of history and the council members were apparently aware of that.

Following the swearing in ceremony of Chairman and members of the Council, given the status of federal ministers, a presidential decree No. 14 was issued spelling out the terms and functions of the Council in relation to other constitutional institutions embodied in the newly enacted federal system. Specifically, the presidential guidelines directed that the council would:

First, receive orders from the presidential palace where it would also be supervised. This in theory would mean that the council chairman would hold the label of assistant president of the republic, a position that did not exist in the Islamic federal set up and line of protocols in force. But in practice, for all intent and purposes, one of the organs of the giant Federal Ministry headed by Dr. Ali al Hajj Mohamed who actually controlled and coordinated the affairs of the state governments and local councils throughout the country.

Second, mobilise the southern Sudan masses in order to win them away from the rebel SPLA Movement and support the Khartoum Agreement.

Third, organise the security network throughout the South, aimed principally for the attainment of peace and stability in the ten southern states.

Fourth, embark, with immediate aim, upon repatriation, resettlement and rehabilitation of Southern citizens expected to surge out of the jungles behind the rebel lines of defences and from the neighbouring countries. There was no mention of repatriating the large number of the internal displaced southern citizens in the north back to their original homes in the south. In this connection, it was assumed that these citizens have permanently settled in the Northern Sudan.

Fifth, use available resources for planning socio-economic development in the southern states.

Sixth, train manpower needed for the efficient running of administration of social services in the southern states.

Seventh, terminate its life span after four years subject to extension depending on how soon peace was achieved

Eighth, end the transitional period following the holding of the expected plebiscite in the South and the announcement of its results.

Ninth, propose that in the said plebiscite, all citizens both southerners and northerners resident in the ten southern states in addition to southern citizens residing outside the country and the southern region, would have the right to vote in the said referendum.

13.4. RAMIFICATION OF KHARTOUM AGREEMENT

While the members of the coordination council began enjoying their ministerial incentives, they were soon to learn that their council was not intended to be a government, but a peace ministry, a component of the peace Commission (discussed in chapter 9).

But as they were coming to terms with these new twists of events, news began circulating that the SPLA main rebel force had seized once again a new military initiative in the South. It was reported that the SPLA had captured

13 towns and military garrisons in Bahr al Ghazal and Central Equatoria (discussed in chapter 11).

Faced with the new military impasse in the south and in the east and assuming that he had brought peace to his beleaguered country through the peace agreement he had just signed with the southern break away factions, President al Bashir launched his high ground diplomatic visit. This took him first to Europe, the Middle East and America. He later visited to eastern and southern Africa.

On the last leg of his interstate visit to eastern and southern Africa, and for reasons only known to him, al Bashir took along with him, the new Assistant President and Chairman of the new Southern Coordination Council, Dr. Riek Machar. Al Bashir move according to analysts was seen as an attempt to persuade the regional leaders that he has at last managed to bring peace to the South Sudan.

In a meeting with the South Africa leader Nelson Mandela, al Bashir stated that the leader of the rebel movement John Garang had no more reason to continue fighting the government since peace had already been restored to the south. He asked Mandela to arrange a meeting with Garang apparently to persuade him also to sign another peace agreement.

Regardless to the SPLA new military offensive, al Bashir told President Moi, in the latter capacity as the Chair of IGAD mediation team, that there was no more reason for the continuation of mediation with the SPLA since peace has already been signed between his government and six rebel factions.

13.5.1. GUBERNATORIAL ELECTIONS IN SOUTHERN STATES

Back in Khartoum after this showpiece tour of southern and eastern Africa, the President, Dr. Machar, ordered that elections of governors in the ten southern states be held with immediate effect in order to complete the formation of the Coordination Council.

According to the Khartoum Agreement, the southern state governors by virtue of their offices were members with equal rights like other ministers of the Council.

Although the elections of the state governors were complementary to the formation of the co-ordination council, it unfortunately became the coup d'grace to the Agreement as well as a catalyst as discussed below.

According to the presidential decree No. 12, an act which governed the gubernatorial elections throughout the country, each state must elect first the members of the state assembly through one man one vote adult suffrage. Once elected, the assembly members would in turn elect the state governor.

In the south it was more difficult to follow such procedures due to the prevailing state of insecurity caused by the war in the region.

It was therefore ruled that all the political forces in each state in consultations among themselves and in proportion to political weight each party muster in the region, should agree and recommend by consensus a list of candidates to the President of the Republic for appointment. They would therefore be declared as duly elected members to the state assembly. These members would in turn elect the state governor.

Thus in consultation with the federal authorities, the three main contending political forces in the South: the United Democratic Salvation Front (UDSF), the Internal Front for Peace (IFP) and the Southern Islamic Salvation Front (SISF), Dr. Riek Machar ordered that elections for state governors be held accordingly.

Having received orders, the three Southern political groupings supportive to the regime put in their lists of nominees. And after hard bargaining, the lists of the candidates for governors in the ten southern states were announced and presented to the state assemblies for election.

So in October 1997, just as the war between the government and the rebels was escalating day by day, the Southern State Assemblies were asked to elect their governors.

13.5.2. EQUATORIAL STATES

In Equatoria elections in the three states Eastern and Western Equatoria proceeded seemingly with few difficulties. In Bahr al Jebel, Colonel (rtd) Henry Jada who had tacitly indicated his anti SPLA fervour and his Islamism was elected governor. Abdalla Kafelo, a born again Muslim, was elected governor of Eastern Equatoria.

And in Western Equatoria, Major General Isaiah Paul a former Anya Nya veteran and who had proven beyond doubt his anti-SPLA stance was elected governor.

Soon after his election and the formation of his state government, General Paul declared that he and his entire cabinet had embraced Islam. But as that was not enough, the general took half of the state budget as incentive to himself and his ministers.

The other half he donated it to the Jihaad-holy war against the SPLA rebels. Thus the governors of Equatoria were elected through Islamic tickets.

13.5.3. BAHR AL GHAZAL STATE

Elections in the four states of Greater Bahr al Ghazal region were somewhat democratic and fairer than those in neighbouring states of Greater Equatoria region in the sense that candidates in the three Equatoria regions were groomed and financed by Islamist paymaster in the central government.

Whereas candidates in all the Bahr al ghazal states were nominated by their political organisations, namely: UDSF, IFP and SISF.

But even so, heavy hand of the central authorities was visibly seen behind advising and directing the election staff as to what they should do and what they should not do in the nomination process throughout the whole campaign.

The three contending parties nonetheless where given chances and adequate time to reach relative consensus and compromise only on the candidates for post of governors and other constitutional posts available for grab in their respective states.

The most fair and democratic election to note was that of the Western Bahr al Ghazal where the former Director of Sudan National Security, Charles Kpoyo (IFP) beat his arch rival Ali Tamim Fartak, the outgoing state governor (SISF).

As an Insider in the NIF hierarchy, Tamim, at the time of election, was the de facto administrator general and the political overseer of the southern states in the name of the central government.

To have allowed Tamim Fartak to contest in the unsafe seat in western Bahr al Ghazal would appear a genuine move by central authorities to tell the world that elections in Southern Sudan, where the war had engulfed the entire countryside, were being conducted in a democratic atmosphere.

However in the elections that followed Julu Kpoyo beat his opponent Tamim by collecting 90 percent of the votes in the assembly that was overwhelmingly Christian. Julu also collected the votes of the southern Muslims who did not ascribe to the Salvation regime.

For fairness sake Fartak conceded defeat and left for Khartoum where he was appointed a senior advisor and supervisor general for the ten southern states at the headquarters of the ruling Congress Party.

In the Lakes State, which comprised the Districts of Yirol and Rumbek, a rather showpiece election was staged. In the contest for state governor, a former SPLA Commander, Nicanora Magar Aciek (UDSF) and another former SPLM Official, Chagai Matet (also UDSF).

After conceding defeat to his contender, Matet left for Khartoum where he, on arrival, and in order to survive, declared his Islamism. But when that did not win him sufficient incentives to keep up with the increasingly skyrocketing living conditions in Khartoum, and to prove the point, Matet went on pilgrimage to the Holy of the Holiest Islamic Shrine in Mecca City.

In Northern Bahr al Ghazal, ex Aweil District, a fairer election was also allowed between an Anya Nya One veteran and former SPLA Commander Kawac Makuei Mayar (UDSF) and his chief contender, the outgoing state governor Joseph Ajuong (IFP).

On conceding defeat Ajuong also left for Khartoum where he was appointed state minister in the central ministry of Finance and Economic Planning.

Though elected comfortably, Governor Makuei Mayar was forced by a combination of circumstances to administer his state by remote control in Khartoum as discussed here below.

The story has it that following his election Makuei went to Khartoum and attended the official swearing in ceremony before the President of the Republic, al Bashir.

After taking the constitutional oath of allegiance, governor Makuei was expected to have returned to Aweil Town, the seat of his government in order to take up his official duties. But before leaving Khartoum, Kawac was warned that he would be killed on arrival at Aweil airstrip. He was not specifically told who was planning to kill him. But the message was crystal clear to Mayar.

Puzzled by this death threat, Makuei Mayar immediately reported the matter to the President. But instead of investigating the truth and giving him advice and necessary protection, the President dismissed the death threat describing it as ridiculous, a naked rumour.

The President ordered Mayar to proceed and take up normal official duties in Aweil. The message was clear. It was left for Mayar to risk going to Aweil or else resign.

Governor Kawac Mayar hired a plane and took off with his ministers for Aweil. At Khartoum Airport Kawac decided at the last minute to remain behind and the plane took off for Aweil without him.

Before the plane could touch down and assuming that the governor was in the plane, gunmen rushed to the governor's official residence ransacked it and killed all its occupants, including Kawac security guards and members of Household.

Despite Makuei protests and his accusing hand at the Vice President George Kongor complicity in the killings to the Chairman of the Coordination Council, Riek Machar and his repeated requests for thorough investigation to bring the culprits to book, no efforts have so far been made to trace the culprits.

Repeatedly governor Kawac was ordered to go to the seat of his government in Aweil, and repeatedly he disobeyed the orders and stayed put preparing to administer his state by remote control from Khartoum. Makuei was finally relieved of his duties as governor.

To prevent him apparently from possible defection to rejoin the rebellion, Kawac Makuei was appointed minister in the Coordination Council in Juba.

The hottest seat for grab in greater Bahr al Ghazal Region that shook Khartoum Agreement almost to its foundation was that of Warap State, the combined District of Tonj and Gogrial previously known as the Jur River District.

In the contest, the outgoing state governor Arop Acier Akol was opposed by two candidates: Moses Machar Aciek (IFP) and Brigadier General Faustino Atem Gualdit a former SPLA Commander and the nominee of Major general Kerubino Kuanyin Bol.

By the time the contest was open, it became an open secret that Kerubino Bol and Atem Gualdit were reportedly in contact with the main rebel group the SPLA, apparently renegotiating their way back to the Movement they had defected from earlier on.

Before election could begin, Moses Machar stepped down apparently for Atem Gualdit. But it appeared later, his supporters ironically voted for Acier, the out going governor.

However in the contest that ensued, Arop Acier Akol's position, perhaps enhanced by the presence of his cousin Vice President Kongor Arop Akol, defeated Atem Gualdit. The rot had set in.

The defeat of Atem Gualdit, his official candidate, only added injury to Kuanyin Bol and accelerated his apparent re-defection back to the SPLA rebels. Soon after the Warap State elections both Bol and Gualdit his deputy, without delay, moved their militias out of Wau to a nearby Marialbai Village 12 miles to the North where they rejoined the main rebel group during the Wau incident on January 28th 1998.

Although Cdr. Kerubino Kuanyin Bol died in mysterious circumstances in Western Upper Nile (1999) after defecting once again from the SPLA to the Government side, Atem Gualdit stayed on as one of SPLA senior commanders.

13.5.4. UPPER NILE STATES

Generally, elections in Greater Upper Nile Region also followed the same pattern as that in the other two regions. Though they appeared reasonably fair on the surface, behind the scenes they were jealously guarded, closely monitored and effectively manipulated by authorities in favour of pro-government candidates.

It was in that light that elections for governors in the three Upper Nile States were conducted in a manner that would bring final ruin to the Agreement in the later years as discussed subsequently.

Elections in the Jonglei State went through smoothly with few security problems. The reasons, according to reports, were that the four nationalities of Dinka, Nuer, Anyuak and the Murle who inhabit the state, had reached amicably, consensus on the proportional representation in accordance to the political weight each of the four have before the elections.

Thus in the process two candidates from the Nuer and Dinka were nominated and asked to compete over the post of governor. In the contest the Nuer candidate Riek Gai (UDSF) defeated his Dinka rival Colonel of police, Riak Akon (IFP).

After winning the post of Governor, Dr. Riek Gai, apparently in accordance to a previous agreed arrangement, appointed his former opponent Colonel Akon his Deputy. The rest of the constitutional posts in the state executive and assembly were also distributed by proportional representation among the four nationalities.

In Upper Nile State four candidates were nominated by their respective political organisations: Timothy Tongyiik Tut Lam (UDSF), Amos Agook, the outgoing Governor (IFP), Mangu Ajak, out going Deputy Governor (SISF) and Lam Akol Ajawin Chairman and Commander in Chief of the united SPLM/ SPLA.

Dr. Akol joined the race against the advice of his aides and friends for a post in the central government soon after he had signed what became known as the Fashoda Agreement making him the seventh of the rebel factions in the Internal peace settlement.

After some behind the scenes arm-twisting manoeuvres and arrangements, Ajak and Agook[5] were asked by the central authorities to make way for two contenders: Timothy Tongyiik (UDSF) and Cdr./Dr. Lam Akol (SPLA-United). In the contest Tongyiik was elected governor.

Dr. Akol conceded defeat and left for Khartoum where he was appointed Federal Minister of Transport. But when governor Tongyiik Tut Lam died in a plane crush that also killed First Vice President al Zubeir Mohamed Saleh in eastern Upper Nile on February 12, 1998, his Deputy Governor Mangu Ajak replaced him.

However, the most contentious of all the gubernatorial contests in the ten southern states was that of the oil rich Unity State in Western Upper Nile (WUN) which the central authorities had been guarding jealously against the rebels encroachment since the start of the war in 1983. The central government would also not guard it against the grab by former rebels.

Unity State was considered the safest seat for the UDSF, being Dr. Riek Machar's birthplace and Machar's former command post. This was not to be, understandably, because of the oil dispute. The central government authorities would like the Unity State therefore administered by a person they seriously trust. It would appear that the central government authorities in the area had goaded the militia warlord, Paulino Matip Nhial, to oppose the UDSF Candidate at all cost.

General Matip, apparently with the connivance of the central government who believed himself the real peace respondent made it known that he or his representative should take the post of the governor of the oil rich Unity State.

Except for a brief period when his Anya Nya Two militias were incorporated into SPLA (1986—1988), Matip had always been fighting protecting the oil fields against the rebels under no other person than Dr. Riek Machar since the start of the war in 1983.

Since then Matip had been given limitless resources and a license by the central government to own a huge army composed mainly of village warriors in order to guard the WUN oil fields. He was therefore a match for the volatile and uncertain former SPLA Commanders the central government authorities believe were forced by circumstances to sign peace agreement with them.

Earlier on fighting had erupted between the UDSF and Matip Forces in which many casualties were reported without the intervention of the government army stationed in the area. The Army could not stop the fight nor resolve the dispute that brought the crisis.

Machar was very disappointed by the central government's obvious reluctance to end the crisis between him and Matip. Machar had expected the central government to persuade Matip to give up the post of governor to the UDSF candidate. For the time being,, Machar managed to brush aside his disappointment with the central government, but it was not forgotten.

It was in this confused environment that elections were carried out in the most sensitive oil rich Unity State for the post of governor. Bol Loth General Matip's nominee opposed UDSF candidate, Taban Deng Gai.

In the contest, the members of the state assembly voted overwhelmingly for the UDSF candidate Taban Deng Gai. Taban Deng was therefore declared the winner of the post of governor.

General Matip, instead of encouraging his candidate to concede defeat for the sake of peace, mobilised his forces and with tacit approval of the central government and support of the government army began fighting Machar's UDSF forces on all fronts in effort to push them out of the WUN. Matip forces managed to evict the UDSF forces first out of Bentiu area and then later out of the oil fields territory.

Because of the infighting in the area, governor Taban Deng Gai could not succeed to take up his post as governor of the Unity State.

Afraid for his dear life and like his colleague, Governor Kawac Makuei of Northern Bahr al Ghazal, Taban Deng left for Khartoum where he and his Boss Machar began to appeal helplessly and hopelessly to the central government to resolve the crisis.

Regardless of Dr. Machar's repeated appeal to President al Bashir to order Matip's forces not to fight UDSF forces and to allow Deng Gai to move to Bentiu the Headquarters of the seat of his government, no efforts were exerted in that direction. Instead, the factions fighting between the two rivalling forces UDSF Machar and the Unity Forces vigorously intensified and continued unabated.

Having apparently received heavy military assistance from the government army in the area, General Matip now promoted to the post of Major General mobilised his forces and declared total war on the UDSF forces.

This was the start for the devastation of the entire WUN area resulting in the displacement of the civil population caught up between the battles of the warring factions. The international oil prospecting companies just came in later and completed the cleansing of the entire area in the later years.

Soon it became abundantly clear that the Islamic regime was siding with Matip's forces against Machar's UDSF forces understandably to clear the area in order to secure the oil exploitation.

The UDSF commanders in 1998, one year after the signing of the Khartoum Agreement began to urge Machar and his allies to denounce the Khartoum Agreement. The Commanders further urged him further for the resumption of armed struggle and immediate hostilities against the Northern Arabs for dishonouring the Agreement.

But when Dr. Machar hesitated to respond to their appeal, UDSF splintered. One faction led by Cdr. Tho Biel defected and began fighting against Matip's forces and the national army in the area. For some time it would appear as if the central government authorities would intervene and resolve the crisis.

But as the fighting between Biel and Matip forces intensified, the army general Headquarters in Khartoum sent heavy reinforcement in men and materials to Matips forces. Thus a fight which had started as a dispute over the post of state governor set the sensitive area ablaze.

Outnumbered and outgunned and without support or reinforcements even from the forces still loyal to Machar, Tito Biel's forces were finally evicted from Bentiu area. They were later pushed southward to Leer, the headquarters of Machar SSIM/SSIA.

Having received further reinforcement from Khartoum, Matip forces pursued them. And after a fierce fighting pushed Biel forces out of Leer and ransacked Machar headquarters.

Faced with the concerted constant attack by combined forces of Matip and the government troops, Biel was forced to retreat further south and to the SPLA controlled Town of Yirol in eastern Bahr al Ghazal region where he apparently obtained some military assistance.

After regrouping his forces Biel desperately fought Matip's and his allies back to Bentiu and reasserted his control on most part of Western Upper Nile (WUN).

In October 1999, Matip's Deputy Peter Gadet surprisingly took over control of Matip's well-equipped headquarters at Mankien Village west of Bentiu.

It was during this sudden takeover of Mankien from Matip's forces that Commander Kerubino Kwanyin Bol, who had been held hostage by the government forces at Matips Headquarters since his second re-defection to the government side in 1999, lost his life in mysterious circumstances[6].

However after taking effective control of Mankien, many Nuer militias joined him. With the latest military materials, Gadet made it known and announced that his forces would fight alongside the SPLA against the government forces in the area in order to protect the southern oilfields from the Arab exploitation. Cdr. Gadet eventually announced that his forces had joined the SPLA forces where he had defected from since the 1991 split.

The SPLA General Command immediately announced that it had welcomed Commander Gadet back into the fold. Immediately Gadet and his forces were incorporated into the Movement.

The SPLA thereafter appointed Gadet as Commander of the Western Upper Nile (WUN) an area covering most of the oil rich region and extending to eastern Bahr al Ghazal and up to the Nuba Mountains in Southern Kordofan in the north.

While Khartoum was coming to term with the defection of Peter Gadet and the mysterious death of Kerubino Kuanyin Bol, 19 commanders of Riek Machar UDSF headed by Peter Bol Kaong UDSSF Deputy Chief of Staff, announced that they had abandoned their Boss, Machar and the Khartoum Peace Agreement.

The officers further declared the formation of an independent Movement in Easter Upper Nile called the Upper Nile Provisional Government (UPNPG).

Dr. Michael Wal Duany who has been shuttling between Nairobi and Khartoum in effort to persuade Machar to de-link himself from the Khartoum Peace Agreement also stated that the 19 officers had launched an independent Movement under his leadership in Eastern Upper Nile.

Dr. Duany claimed that the New Movement would be called the Southern Sudan Liberation Movement (SSLM) the name of the defunct Movement that signed the 1972 Peace Agreement with Khartoum.

Without reference to Wal Duany or the South Sudan Liberation Movement, Commander Peter Bol Kaong said in a statement that his forces have de-linked themselves from UDSF/UDSSF and the Khartoum peace Agreement.

A few days later Commander Bol Kaong said he and his forces had nothing to do with Wal Duany; adding that his forces would support armed struggle for the independence of South Sudan from Arab domination. Bol added that his forces would fight alongside the SPLA.

In a sudden but expected move Riek Machar, in December 1999, left

Khartoum for Germany where he was expected to review the situation there with his friends and supporters before going back to Sudan.

From Germany Dr. Machar instead went straight to Nairobi where he, on arrival, announced that he had resigned from all the posts he was holding in the Islamic regime in Khartoum.

In a letter he sent to President al Bashir dated 31 January 2000, Machar declared that he had resigned from all the posts as Assistant President of the Republic, Chairman of the Coordination Council, President of the UDSF and Commander In Chief of UDSSF.

Giving the reason for his resignation Machar accused the Islamic regime for failing to implement the 1997 Khartoum Peace Agreement which he said had made him join President al Bashir's regime. He further blamed al Bashir for dishonouring the Agreement. Machar did not say whether the Khartoum Agreement had collapsed.

Reacting to Machar's abandonment of the Islamic regime, Dr. Hassan Abdalla al Turabi, the Islamic regime power broker, confirmed in a press statement that al Bashir had failed to implement the 1997 Agreement, a move which signalled a serious crack in the Islamic regime.

While Khartoum had continued to claim the validity of the Khartoum showpiece agreement for the solution of the chronic South-North conflict, it became apparent that its demise had put the government effort for an internal peace settlement in bad light for the southern public to trust.

Thus, the agreement that was laboriously worked out as an alternative or substitute to the external peace process that was being negotiated between the regime and the main rebel group, the SPLM/SPLA, was just brushed aside into the dustbin of history without the usual courtesy of announcing its obituary.

Predictably, the demise of the Khartoum Peace Agreement has only scored one vital point to note and that is, it has validated and updated Abel Alier's Book: *Too Many Agreements Dishonoured*.

With the Khartoum Peace Agreement dishonoured; hence the end of the internal peaceful settlement to the conflict, the Islamic authorities were only expected as a better resort to give the external peace process a try (Chapter 14).

CHAPTER 14
THE GOVERNMENT STRATEGY OF PEACE FROM WITHOUT

14.0. THE SETTING

As soon as it came to power in June 1989, the Islamist new military Junta, despite having scrapped all the previous attempts to resolve the conflict that had bedevilled the country for a decade, immediately launched its own peace initiative well tailored to suit its Islamic objectives.

Thus in July, the Junta sent two non-Arab members of the Revolutionary Command Council, Lt. Colonel Mohamed al Amin al Khalifa and Colonel Martin Malual Arop, to Addis Ababa with the message to the SPLM/SPLA leaders. The message proposed that the new authorities in Khartoum were willing to hold talks with them.

But perhaps the new authorities had not yet made their agenda objectives clear as to how they intended to approach the issues of war and peace the two RCC envoys were not able to meet with the SPLM officials. Nonetheless, they managed to meet the Ethiopian President Mengistu Haile Mariam and some Ethiopian diplomats.

Obviously, the two envoys might have asked President Mengistu to mediate in the Sudanese conflict. Having handed over a letter inviting the SPLM/SPLA leader for talks to the Ethiopian authorities, al Khalifa and Malual returned to Khartoum to brief the Revolution Command Council (RCC) about their mission.

14.1. SPLM-NIF FIRST PEACE ENCOUNTER

The second attempt to meet with the SPLM officials was successful. The two parties held a meeting in Addis Ababa, August 19-20, 1989. The junta side was led by Colonel Mohamed al Amin al Khalifa, an NIF officer who took part in the coup and the SPLM by Secretary for Peace and External Relations, Dr. Lam Akol Ajawin.

During the talks each side stated its position unequivocally. The SPLM delegation started the talks by accusing the new regime of deflecting the peace process by scrapping the previous peace accords it believed might have resolved the conflict. The scrapped accords included the Koka Dam Declaration (1986) and the DUP/SPLM Sudan Peace Initiative (1988), which were being used as basis through which a lasting solution might have been struck.

The SPLM delegation further suggested that any prospects for peace rested on the condition that the new regime revived the Koka Dam and SPLM/DUP accords it had scrapped since all the political forces in the country had endorsed them.

Responding to the SPLM charges and proposal, the government delegation rejected them stressing that there was no going back to the pre-June 30, 1989 agendas. Colonel al Khalifa said that the previous peace accords (Kaka Dam/SPLM/DUP) had already become irrelevant and outdated. He then presented the regime's vision based apparently on the proposals which the regime expected would be endorsed by the National Dialogue Conference about to convene.

Predictably, as it did not discuss serious issues of war and peace and how to resolve the conflict, the meeting was adjourned with the two sides pledging to meet again.

With the recommendations of the proposed National Dialogue Conference in mind, which could be used in any future substantive discussions, the regime leader announced that each side must go back to meet its various constituents in order to achieve the desired results.

In December 1989, nearly two months after the regime's much publicised Conference of the National Dialogue was held, the second meeting between the new regime and the rebel SPLM under the auspices of the former American President Jimmy Carter was convened in Nairobi.

Against the backlash of demonstrations in Khartoum by anti-junta coalition of trade unions, civil disobedience and student unrest in addition to the government military offensive against the rebels in the south, the Nairobi talks, predictably, did not produce any good results.

Instead of placing useful proposals on the table for discussion, the two sides confronted each other heaping charges and counter charges; blaming the opposite number for lack of political will, lack of progress in the talks and the deterioration of political and military situations in the country.

Whereas in the SPLM side in the meeting asked for adoption of Koka Dam and SPLM/DUP peace proposals as basis for talks, the regime again rejected the pre-June 1989 accords and recommendations for the talks. It instead counter proposed that the regime's Final Report of the National Dialogue as basis for discussion

At the end of the meeting the SPLM delegation hinted that the regime Report could be used for future consultations between the two parties. But Colonel al Khalifa, commenting on the meeting called it a success since the SPLM had unwittingly accepted that the Regime Final Report could be discussed, as basis for further negotiations.

On the December 1989 Nairobi talks, Professor Lesch writes: "Each side came [to the meeting] geared for confrontation not compromise. The government side during this second meeting, presented as its peace plan the final report of the National Dialogue Conference. The report endorsed an Islamic federal system in which regions with non-Muslim majority could exempt themselves from certain aspects of Huddud (Islamic punishments)[1]".

The Final Report of the National Dialogue Conference contained in the Regime Pink Book was intended by the regime to replace the Koka Dam and DUP/SPLM accords.

When President Jimmy Carter suggested that there should be a three-month cease-fire and that Sharia could be suspended during the cease-fire, Colonel al Khalifa accused him of bias and rejected his further mediation.

The talks thus ended without achieving anything, and the two parties rushed back to base to mobilise their forces for the next round of the fighting which was already in progress (chapter 11).

14.2. THE HERMAN COHEN BLUE PRINT FOR PEACE

Assuming that he had read the position of the two parties correctly and that he had brought them closer to a common understanding, basing his assessments on the SPLM remark that it would study the Government Final Report, President Jimmy Carter presented an optimistic report to the U.S. State Department.

In response to Carter's Report, the U.S. Government sent unofficial envoys to Khartoum to gauge the real government intention and plans for ending the war in the southern part of the country.

Again misreading the Sudanese government position on the policies of war and peace in the south, the envoys apparently reported that the new regime considered the war as quagmire. That it was considering the possibility of letting the south secede given the military situation on the ground which was already tilting in favour of the SPLA rebels.

In view of the envoys' report and perhaps assured by the RCC, Chairman Omar Hassan Ahmed al Bashir's willingness that he welcomed the American initiative, the State Department proposed that in order to reverse the situation in the south, the Khartoum authorities should do the following:

1. The Sudan Government should evacuate all its forces from the Southern Sudan.

2. Hold a constitutional conference.

3. Conduct general fair free elections in order to restore democracy.

Responding to the American offer to mediate in the Sudanese conflict, the Military Junta rejected the American goodwill initiative outright on the following grounds:

1. Withdrawing its forces from the south was unacceptable since that would create a *de facto* independent territory there.

2. Restoring the democracy that the regime has just scrapped was ridiculous. What would have been the point of staging a coup and scrapping democracy and then restoring it the next day? This would contradict their objective of crushing the rebellion in the south to instal one Islamic-oriented-party system in the country which would promote Arabicisation and Islamisation in Africa, south of the Sahara? This was the government specific rhetoric which was echoed everywhere in the country through its Islamic media.

While President al Beshir was rejecting the American peace package, he accepted two points, cease-fire and safe havens in the south. Surprisingly, it was the first time since it came to power in June 1989 that the regime had shown its true Islamic colours.

However the regime for some time hesitated on whether to accept or reject the American initiative. On the other hand the SPLA/SPLM appeared to have endorsed the American initiative to mediate in the Sudanese conflict, though with some specific reservations and observations.

Despite the Military Junta's inherent reluctance to accept wholeheartedly the U.S. initiative, the U.S. State Department asked the Assistant Secretary of State for African Affairs, Herman Cohen, to put together a plan, the mechanism through which the Sudanese conflict could best be resolved as soon as possible.

Thus in 1990, Herman Cohen drew up a plan which then became known as the Cohen Blueprint. According to the Cohen Blueprint, peace would have been imposed on the warring parties in the following order:

1. A cease-fire must be imposed on the Sudan Government to be followed by an internationally supervised disengagement of the forces to the conflict.

The previous U.S. proposal to evacuate its forces from the Southern Sudan, was replaced with the phrase; to thin down its forces to a mere 20,000 officers and men to be stationed at four specific positions, in Juba, Malakal, Wau and other strategic towns that the warring parties may agree.

2. In case of a contested town, the two forces were to pull their forces out to a distance of 25 kilometres.

3. The SPLA forces were to occupy the areas south of Kiir River, (Bahr al Arab), Bahr al Ghazal and the Sobat Rivers.

4. The Southern Kordofan and the Southern Blue Nile were to be declared demilitarised zones. In this regard both sides were to pull their forces away from the areas concerned back to their areas of occupation.

5. Station international peace keeping forces in Juba.

6. Install an interim administration in Juba to administer the Southern Sudan.

7. The demilitarised zones to be administered jointly.

8. Convene the National Constitutional Conference, etc.

But before the Herman Cohen blueprint could be operational, two important events occurred which were to hinder further action on this plan. The first was eruption of the Gulf War in January 1991 which led to the deterioration of relations between U.S.A. (pro-Kuwait) and Sudan (pro-Iraq).

The second reason was the U.S. Presidential election which ushered in the Democrats with new policies on the Sudan. With the exit of Herman Cohen, the U.S.A. package was stalled, at least temporarily. Thus the first external peace overture was grounded to a halt.

14.3. THE JUNTA PEACE FROM WITHOUT STRATEGY

Predictably, the coming in of the Americans to impose a solution frightened the regime. It began to look at alternative ways and means of keeping them (the Americans) out of Sudanese affairs.

Colonel Mohamed al Amin al Khalifa, the Regime chief negotiator, could not mince his words when he publicly stated 'since the conflict was between truth and falsehood,' the government (Sudan Government) would impose peace by force.

In order to keep the U.S. government out of the Islamic Sudanese affairs one of the ways the regime resorted to was the policy of defeating the SPLA through Internal peaceful settlement (discussed in Chapter 9) or external diplomacy (peace from without)

The peace from without was in fact a euphemistic approach, often referred to by Dr. Garang as NIF "Global Tottering Shopping For Peace Initiatives" going around the world while intensifying war to defeat the SPLA after which there would be no need for peace negotiations.

President Jimmy Carter, however, was once again sought to take up the mediation process in the Sudanese conflict. But, as expected, Carter could not readily accept the offer since the previous experience might have still been haunting him.

But as the war was intensifying and escalating by the hour, the regime desperately began to knock on every door seeking possible mediators. Luckily, chance presented itself during the African Heads of State meeting marking Namibia's independence in Windhoek 1991.

During the meeting, President al Bashir approached the Nigerian Head of State General Ibrahim Babangida, the OAU incumbent chairman. He appealed to Babangida to take over the mediation process in order to keep the Americans away from the Sudanese affairs. Africans are capable of solving their own internal problems without the aid of external players, al Bashir emphasised.

As the chairman of the OAU and President of a neighbouring state with identical problems Between the two countries, General Babangida accepted the offer and approached the U.S. Government to allow Africans' initiative to have a chance.

Accordingly the Americans called off the Herman Cohen Peace Initiative but told Babangida, to return the Sudan mediation file to the Americans once he failed to resolve the issue at stake. General Babangida immediately approached the parties to the conflict. Thus between 1991 and 1992 preparations were made to convene the first Nigerian sponsored peace conference.

It was in this light that General Babangida obtained the Sudan mediation file from the Americans apparently with a pledge to bring it back once it proved difficult for the Nigerians to resolve the issue at stake. The conference was thereby held in the Nigerian new capital Abuja in May 1992 (Abuja 1 Conference).

When the news reached Khartoum that Nigeria had taken over the mediation file from the Americans, it was received with relief. Clearly there were reasons for joy in this achievement. It would keep away foreign direct intervention in what was properly, an internal affair. Other reasons for the celebrations were apparent.

First, the NIF authorities had a belief that Nigeria might not agree to preside over a conference it believed could lead to a break-up of an OAU member state. This would contravene the OAU 1963 charter which provides the maintenance of the state boundaries left behind by the colonial administration.

Second, General Babangida was the incumbent Chairman of the OAU, the authorities in Khartoum had hoped he might not countenance the rebels' call for self-determination for the people of Southern Sudan.

The third reason for joy by the Khartoum Islamic authorities' preference for Nigerian mediation than others might have also been based on the ethno-demographic similarities in the two states where both have a large Muslim population in the north and Christians in the south. The problems in both countries were therefore identical.

The other probability for preferring the Nigerian mediation might perhaps have been the experiment of the defunct Biafran, which bore some semblance to the civil war in the Southern Sudan.

With this analysis probably in mind, the Islamic authorities assumed that chance for a solution within a United Sudan was a possibility.

14.4. THE FIRST ABUJA CONFERENCE

After a year of making contacts and preparations to hold Peace Talks, the parties to the dispute were invited by the Conference Chairman General Ibrahim Babangida to send their delegations to the new Nigerian capital Abuja.

But before discussing the issues raised in the meeting halls, it would be instructive to outline the circumstances and the environments in which the talks were held since such environments did have direct bearing and impact on the expected results of the meeting itself.

The first episode was that the Conference was held amid the intensification of war which had already started in February. Thus while the conference was in progress, the government forces were advancing deep into the SPLA held territories and the SPLA forces were retreating toward the Kenyan-Ugandan borders. The intensity of the war was even felt inside the meeting hall.

For instance, news of the capture of Kapoeta, the SPLA's second biggest city in Eastern Equatoria, by government forces was reported to the Sudan delegation during the meeting, a move which embarrassed not only the SPLA but the mediators.

The news about the fall of Kapoeta in addition to report that the SPLA headquarters Torit was under the threat of falling any time shook the Conference and nearly led to a halt of the discussions.

The second episode was that towards the beginning of the year the regime had held a separate meeting in Germany with the Nasir Faction and had agreed to work together in accordance to the terms the two parties had agreed between themselves.

It was therefore predictable that the Nasir Faction and government delegations were aware of each other's positions on a number of sensitive issues that might be raised in the Conference. This was expected to undermine the SPLM/Torit position immensely since the talks would appear to be the government and Nasir delegations versus the SPLM-Torit delegation.

Perhaps more worrying to the SPLM/Torit was the presence of the architects of the Frankfurt Accord, Dr. Ali al Hajj (who led the government side) and Dr. Lam Akol (leader of Nasir Faction). This factor was expected to have a negative effect on the conference being convened because they had a hidden agenda.

The third event worth mentioning was the position of the Head of the SPLM-Torit Faction delegation, Commander William Nyuon Bany. Commander William Nyuon Bany, SPLM-Torit Deputy Chairman and its Chief of Staff had been an easy prime target by the Nasir Faction since the split. There was an apparent plot to win him away from the Torit-SPLM to other side. In the plot, Nasir officers pledged that Nyuon was sufficiently alienated from his group.

Between 1991 and 1992, Nasir officers have been working on Nyuon Bany to join their bandwagon. Indeed some of them had been quoted as counting on William Nyuon as their man in the Torit Camp.

Therefore to win William Nyuon, he was repeatedly told of SPLM-Torit sensitive misdeeds. For instance the alleged execution of the Nuer officers in Eastern and Central Equatoria by Torit-SPLA commanders, perhaps in revenge on the Dinka officers killed by the Nasir group (Nuer) following the Coup of 1991. They made it clear to Nyuon that Garang's next target would be him (Nyuon). The choice of Cdr. William Nyuon Bany to lead the SPLM-Torit delegation was bound to have a negative effect and impact on the peace talks.

The fourth episode, perhaps the most damaging effect, was the Islamic Regime stratagem. The Government, aware of the vulnerability of the SPLM-Torit delegation and its leader, had selected a Nuer Team composed of people committed to the policy of peace from within (see chapter eleven) headed by the Commissioner of Nasir Province, Peter Challemagne. Peter Challemagne's team was apparently well supplied and instructed about its operations.

Once in Abuja, most members of Challemagne's team melted into the Nyuon Suite in the hotel. It was not very surprising that throughout the peace talk period, southerners who came from Khartoum, and the members of the two SPLM delegations were mixing freely and 'speaking Arabic' as if they had gone to Abuja for family or friendly reunion ceremonies. Such environments outside the official talks were bound to affect the proceedings of the Conference[2].

It was against this background that the Abuja Conference convened in May 1992 under the chairmanship of the Nigerian President, General Ibrahim Babangida, and attended by the Sudan Government and the SPLM-Two Factions' delegations.

At the onset, General Babangida, proposed that the Conference should discuss the security issues, cease-fire and disengagement of the forces in the conflict, stationing of foreign monitors, adoptions of confidence building measures between the warring parties and stoppage of negative propaganda against each other for the interest of peace.

In response to the Chairman's proposals, the head of the Government delegation, Colonel Mohamed al Amin al Khalifa, apparently aware of the military situation on the ground in favour of the government forces discussed earlier, told the Conference that there was no need to discuss such issues.

According to al Khalifa, security issues (issues of war) were internal matters which the Sudanese themselves could handle. He emphasised that there was no dire need for non-Sudanese (Nigerian mediators) interfering in their affairs. Instead, al Khalifa proposed the issues like respect for religious, linguistic and cultural diversities in the Sudan could be discussed.

Reacting to the Government delegation's speech, the two SPLM Factions, though delivering their official statements separately and despite their differences in the field, rejected the Government delegation's position paper in totality. The two Factions urged the Conference that multi-ethnic essence of the Sudan must be upheld only by a secular democratic system based on the principle of equality and justice before the law of the land.

Despite the Frankfurt accord of understanding between the government and Nasir faction, Dr. Lam Akol speaking for his faction stated that since the effort to create a system based on equality and justice had failed and the aspirations of the north and the south were proving irreconcilable, the two sides in the Sudan conflict should stop trying to retain their artificial unity.

At most, Dr. Akol went on, a loose confederation would give a chance for the two sides of the Sudan to institute the legal system of their choice.

On the sixth day of fruitless discussions, amidst advice and caution by the mediators, the Conference was surprised by the arrival to the Conference Hall of the SPLM Factions as one delegation instead of two.

Perhaps the extreme uncompromising positions taken by the Government delegations throughout the previous days or other behind-the-scenes arm-twisting arrangements or both, the two once hostile SPLM Factions decided to merge as one delegation and, surprisingly, with one common agenda.

But while the merger of the two SPLM Factions was welcomed in the interest of permanent peace by the Southern populace being affected by war and as it has delayed possible attainment of peace in their war torn zone, it created immense problems for the mediators. It also created suspicion in the Government circles and especially of those who had signed peace with the SPLM-Nasir.

The merger of the two factions, for instance, had put self-determination for the Southern Sudan at the top of the agenda for subsequent discussion, a move that the Nigerian mediators would not countenance.

Secondly SPLM-Torit leadership, a move which brought problems within its leadership, did not initially endorse the merger of the two factions. It subsequently led to the defection of the head of the Torit SPLM delegation, Cdr. William Nyuon Bany and Spokesman Dr. Richard K. Mulla. The two officers thereafter formed a Unity SPLM/SPLA group. Commenting on the inclusion of self-determination of the Abuja Conference, Professor Lesch[3] writes: "the issue of self-determination was contentious, since the Sudan Government and Nigerian mediators had deliberately excluded it from the agenda. Given Nigeria's suppression of Biafran secessionists, the mediators stressed that they would not preside over a Conference that advocated the dismemberment of the Sudan".

In the subsequent discussions and regardless of the inclusion of the self-determination issue on the rebels' agenda, the Government side, in an effort to show the mediators the government was interested in the end of the war, stated that it would accept self-determination.

But only if the referendum in the Southern Sudan could be based on the Government Islamic Federal System contained in the Government 'Pink Book' on the deliberations and recommendations of the National Dialogue

Conference of October 1989, adding 'but not the referendum that would include secession'.

Reacting to the Government position, Dr. Lam Akol, Deputy Leader of the Combined SPLM negotiation team, said: The South would insist with its demand for self-determination since it was included in the Frankfurt Accord.

Colonel al Khalifa, presenting the Government's official final position on the issue at stake, said emphatically that separation should come, "but only at the mouth of the gun". With Dr. Lam Akol's and Colonel al Khalifa's remarks representing the final position of each side, the talks were doomed to failure.

Whatever efforts the Mediators exerted in order to salvage the talks or try to broker a cease-fire and disengagement of the warring forces and an interim arrangement as prelude to further discussions to end the conflict, the Sudan Government delegation would not back down.

Left with no alternative in the face of the clear breakdown of the talks and not wishing to announce that the talks had collapsed, the Nigerian Leader in his capacity as an honest broker adjourned the talks.

The Sudan delegation, having frustrated the talks in the hope that it would soon defeat the SPLA, left for Khartoum. The war was thereafter intensified.

14.5. THE DEFECTION OF SPLA CHIEF OF STAFF

While Commander William Nyuon was still at Abuja attending the Conference, a number of events happened in the field in the Southern Sudan, events that would affect adversely not only Commander Nyuon, but also the whole SPLA movement, as discussed below.

One such event was a report emanating from Cdr. Nyuon's command post informing him that a number of officers had been summarily executed by the acting area commander, apparently on suspicion that they were planning mass defection to the Nasir Faction of SPLA. Incidentally, most of the executed officers were from Cdr. Nyuon's tribe, Nuer.

According to information reaching Cdr. Nyuon at Abuja, it was reported that some of his officers were executed—apparently in retaliation of some Dinka officers who were murdered by the Nasir Faction on suspicion that those Dinka officers might resist the coup discussed earlier, in Chapter 10.

Other rumours suggested that the Nuer officers who were killed in Eastern Equatoria had to do with revenge on the lives of many Dinka killed during the Kongor-Bor Invasion, also discussed in Chapter 10.

These reports[4] apparently did not please Cdr. Nyuon Bany and perhaps had affected him immensely while the talks were going on between the two united SPLA delegations and that of the Sudan Government.

As a consequence to the above rumours, Cdr. William Nyuon, who hailed from the Nuer Nationality that made up over ninety per cent of the Nasir

Faction, affected the SPLM leader to the extent that he began to question his future position in the SPLM mainstream.

Cdr. Nyuon was reported soliloquising throughout the peace talks that, if the Nuer officers could summarily be executed for crimes committed by their fellow Nuers, what would prevent him from being summarily assassinated in cold blood? [5] That was the mood Cdr. Nyuon was in when the SPLA-SPLM two delegations left Nigeria to return to Nairobi, Kenya, in July 1992.

Commander Nyuon, instead of reporting straight to his command post at Pageri, Eastern Equatoria, waited for the appropriate time when he and his delegation would be called upon to brief the SPLM leadership about the peace talks, and for unexplained reasons decided to stay in Nairobi for a couple of weeks.

Meanwhile two senior members of Cdr. Nyuon's delegation had gone straight to meet the SPLM/SPLA Chairman Dr Garang without their head. Commander Nyuon Bany, suspecting and speculating that those two members might have gone to give adverse reports about his apparent mishandling of the issues of peace during the talks, especially about the merger of the two embattled factions, was outraged.

Nyuon apparently considered such a move was a disregard and disrespect to his personality and his position as the head of the delegation to the peace talks. Cdr. William Nyuon finally reported to his command post and resumed his normal duties as the Deputy Chairman and its Chief-of-Staff.

But before leaving Nairobi for Pageri, Cdr. Nyuon had been seen in constant contact, probably consulting, with leaders of Nasir Venture, Dr. Machar and Dr. Akol. This had perhaps been reported by the SPLM/SPLA Security to the leadership.

Other reports suggested that Cdr. William left Nairobi already agitated for fear that his activities in Nairobi, such as his contacts with diplomats in Western Embassies, a clear contravention of the SPLM/SPLA protocols, might have been reported to the SPLM/SPLA Chairman and Commander-in-Chief. If this had happened, it may lead to his probable arrest.

Additionally, in Nairobi, reports disclosed that the Nasir Faction had been working on Cdr. Nyuon, reminding him about the circumstances that had led to the arrest of some senior officers like Cdr. Kerubino K. Bol and Cdr. Arok Thon.

However, at his command post at Pageri, Cdr. William Nyuon was received by a group of his agitated officers who told him that he was already earmarked for arrest. Cdr. Nyuon was particularly reminded about his personal safety and further deaths of some of the surviving Nuer officers in the mainstream SPLM.

The above combined reports had apparently worked effectively on

Commander Nyuon Bany, who in his agitated mood immediately began to behave suspiciously, taking all possible precautionary measures aimed at warding off any attempts to arrest him.

At long last Cdr. William Nyuon was summoned together with members of his official and full delegation to Abuja for briefing. Nonetheless Cdr. Nyuon Bany attended the briefing against the advice given to him by his lieutenants, who feared that it might be a trap prepared for his eventual arrest.

When Cdr. Nyuon Bany went to the SPLM/SPLA Headquarters for the scheduled briefings, he discovered that the Chairman and Commander-in-Chief, Dr. Garang, was still away, where he had gone to attend the Pan-Africa Conference in Entebbe, Uganda, August 1992.

At the SPLA General Command Headquarters, Cdr. Nyuon, instead of attending to his normal duties or retreating to his command post until he would be called upon for briefing, for unexplained reasons, announced that he had assumed power as SPLA Commander-in-Chief and SPLM Chairman of the reunited Peoples' Revolution.

In that capacity William Nyuon began issuing orders to all officers and men in all the units under the mainstream control.

Nyuon Bany's sudden assumption of power, embarrassing as it was shocking, brought him immediate clash with Commander Kuol Manyang Juuk, who was at the Headquarters ostensibly to keep an eye on his activities.

To avoid the situation getting out of hand as tension began to mount between the two officers, which may have involved their supporters, Cdr. Lual Diing Wuol, who happened to be third in seniority at the Headquarters, ordered that the two beleaguered commanders should be separated.

The situation was contained with the sudden arrival of Cdr. Salva Kiir Mayardit, Deputy Chief-of-Staff for Security to the Headquarters. Commander Kiir began the disengagement process of the supporters of the two commanders.

As the separation of the two forces was in process, the SPLM/SPLA Chairman and Commander-in-Chief arrived suddenly at the General Headquarters from Kampala in Uganda and assumed power immediately. He immediately called for the convening of the SPLM/SPLA Political Military High Command in order to look into the causes that brought about the misunderstanding between the two commanders.

The Commander—in—Chief advised that ways and methods of resolving such a conflict amicably be devised since the quarrel between the two officers was threatening a further split in the movement.

Speaking to the members of the PMHC, Cdr. William Nyuon stated that the misunderstanding was brought by the wanton behaviour of Commander Juuk, who he accused among other things of insubordination.

The PMHC meeting, according to reports,[6] decided to reconcile the two embattled commanders who were each ordered to leave at one and return to his command post.

The meeting over, a statement was issued. The statement was said to have absolved Nyuon of all the reports about his alleged misdeeds and rumours connected with his handling of the Abuja Talks.

Nyuon was further assured that whatever might have occurred by way of errors or omissions, nothing would be held against him as an individual but against the Movement, as he was acting on behalf of the Movement.

Having been reassured that nothing would be done to him, Nyuon was told to go back to his command post and resume his normal duties as the Movement Deputy Leader and Deputy Commander-in-Chief. Terribly hurt and very agitated, Cdr. William Nyuon left for his command post at Pageri.

At his command post and surrounded by his close aides and with troops overwhelmingly hailing from Nuer Nationality, Cdr. Nyuon's anger and suspicion was re-heightened and shored up to breaking point. Nyuon aides warned that if he did not leave the SPLM/SPLA mainstream without further delay, he would be killed in cold blood.

Whether it was from the advice given him by his aides, or pre-conceived decision or both, Cdr. Nyuon Bany put all his forces on maximum alert with stern orders not to allow anybody to leave or enter his post.

On the night of September 27, 1992, Cdr. Nyuon Bany Deng ordered his troops to pack all that they could carry along with them. In the morning of September 28, Cdr. Nyuon left the camp in a convoy of cars. He had defected[6] to join the government side.

William Nyuon Bany, one of the five founding members of the SPLM/SPLA and the number three and later number two in the hierarchy, abandoned the movement he had helped to establish and lead for the previous nine years.

On his way, apparently heading for the Government controlled city of Torit, Cdr. Nyuon and his forces were intercepted by an SPLA detachment and attacked. Without much resistance, Nyuon and his troops abandoned all that they had brought along with them, including cars and heavy weapons, and trekked towards Juba. He arrived at Mogiri, a military outpost 18 miles from the City of Juba.

Aware of atrocities he had committed at Ayod in 1983 when he rebelled and joined the rebellion (Chapter3); conscious that he had been dragged into defection through black mailing (Chapter 13), Nyuon Bany could not go to Juba where he was expected to join the Peace from Within strategy.

He remained at Mogri until in 1995, when he tricked the authority and allowed him to lead attack on the SPLA. It was there that Nyuon changed side and rejoined the SPLA main stream once more in order to finish the job he had left undone through black mail described earlier, the liberation of the South.

During his liberation struggle, Late Nyuon Bany would often stress when he wanted to raise the morale of his forces in battles: "I have killed enough of my jallabas. The jallabas who are still occupying the mother land, the South Sudan, are the jallaba of other Southerners who are still hiding behind the slogan of the struggle."

Paradoxically, Nyuon Bany was slain in an ambush in December 1995 while trying to reunite the SPLA forces at Ayod in eastern Upper Nile by none other than the people he described as "other Southerners who are hiding behind the liberation struggle," the forces loyal to Dr, Machar SSIM[9].

CHAPTER 15
WAR INTENSIFYING AMIDST INTERNATIONAL PRESSURE FOR PEACE

15.0. THE SETTING

Following a year long period of internecine fighting and considering the immense destruction of properties and human disasters in the wake of the fighting, it was natural that the international communities could no longer stand aloof, but made efforts to stop the human carnage.

In 1993, the United Nations, the Vatican, the European Union and United States, called upon the Sudan Government and the SPLA/SPLM mainstream, to stop fighting and negotiate a peaceful settlement of their conflict in order to relieve the civil population caught up in the fighting.

As a consequence of international intervention, against the huge human rights violations and sufferings caused by government intensification of the war against the rebels (1992-1993), the United Nations Commissions for Human Rights on March 10, 1993, appointed Caspar Biro as its special Rapporteur on the Sudan.

The appointment of a special Rapporteur by the UN coincided with the U.S. Congressional hearings on the possibility of humanitarian intervention in order to establish safe havens in the war-ravaged Southern Sudan. The later visit of His Grace George Carey, the Archbishop of Canterbury, to the SPLA-controlled Southern Sudan in January 1993 brought the international attention through the media coverage for the first time since the start of the war about the true situation.

The reaction of Khartoum against the visit of the Archbishop to the rebel-controlled territories resulted in a diplomatic row between Britain and Sudan and speeded up the need for the International Communities to exert more pressure and urge for a swift, peaceful resolution to the conflict.

Whether it was for fear of possible international military intervention; its forces were over-stretched to fight an effective war in the south; or mere tactic to buy time; or for both reasons, the Sudan Government called for the resumption of Abuja peace talks curtailed in June of the previous year.

However, after brief preparations, the second round of the Abuja Conference was convened between April 26 and May 18, 1993.

15.1. THE SECOND ABUJA PEACE CONFERENCE

The second Abuja meeting was held between the delegations of the Government of the Sudan and the main rebel group, the SPLM/SPLA chaired by Ibrahim Babangida, this time not as President of Nigeria but Chairman of the OAU.

The Government side was led by its chief negotiator, Colonel Mohamed al Amin al Khalifa, and deputised by Dr. Ali al Hajj Mohamed (both black Northerners). The members of the government delegation included a team of selected Southern Sudanese who had apparently been selected by virtue of their commitment to the Government policies of peace from within approach.

According to reports southern members in the Government delegation were expected to work on their fellow southerners in the rebel delegation to relent or not to take a hard line position during the negotiations.

The SPLM delegation, on the other hand, was led by Commander Salva Kiir Mayardit, then number two in the Movement and deputised by Cdr. Yousif Kuwa Meki, the Nuba Mountains leader and the number four in the SPLM political and military hierarchy.

In addition, the SPLM delegation was composed of highly experienced members, some of who had held high position in the Sudan Government's public service or in academies.

Most prominent members in the SPLM delegation included: Dr. Peter Nyot Kok, former Lecturer of Law, University of Khartoum. Justice Ambrose R Thiik, former member of the Sudan Court of Appeal and former Regional Minister, Dr. Justin Yaac, former Regional Minister, Nhial Deng Nhial, former Legal Counsellor in the Sudan Attorney General's chambers, and a number of highly qualified experts and advisors.

Presenting the Government position paper during the opening session of the peace talks, Colonel al Khalifa, instead of outlining the Government's position on the issues discussed at the time the talks were stalled, began to reiterate the Government Final Report of the National Dialogue Conference[1]. Precisely al Khalifa's speech centred:

1. Power sharing between the Centre and the states in accordance with the Government Pink Book within the context of a United Sudan

2. Balance development in the socio-economic matters giving priority apparently to the most backward areas in Sudan which included the south

3. Application of Sharia in Sudan without mentioning the thorny issue of separation of state and religion

Commander Kiir presenting SPLM position paper stated that the objective of his movement since it was launched in 1983 had always been and continued to be the creation of a New Sudan. "This," Cdr. Salva Kiir stressed, "is still our preferred and principled objective—a democratic non-sectarian Sudanese commonality that transcends race, tribe, language and religion."

Cdr. Salva Kiir explained further that since the subsequent regimes in Khartoum continued to refuse our vision and as long as their objectives exclude the marginalised peoples, those peoples (the marginalised) would have the right to self-determination.

Kiir warned that if the Khartoum regimes continued with their Islamisation and Arabicisation agenda, the South must demand its independence, even if that be achieved after a great deal of bloodshed and loss of life and misery.

The SPLM, 'considered confederation between the North and the marginalised peoples: of South Sudan, Nuba Mountains and the Ingessna Hills in Southern Blue Nile, as the best way to solve the problem of relationship between state and religion the sharing of wealth and power,' the SPLM chief delegate disclosed.

'Khartoum's Federal system,' Cdr. Salva continued, 'did not and does not share power, but rather it increases the domination of the Central Government as it has always done to Islamise all: the public, economic, cultural and social life in the country.

The SPLM Leader emphasised that in a confederation, each confederate state would be sovereign in its laws and security arrangements. After the interim period following the cessation of hostilities, the marginalised peoples would conduct an internationally supervised referendum to choose between confederation and independence. Over time, a healthy Union could be built voluntarily between the two parts of the country and the New Sudan would then come into being.

Following his speech, Commander Salva Kiir presented to the Conference the SPLM's 'Three-Model Legal Framework'[2] Model One: Unitary state. Model Two: Confederation state. Model Three: Complete separation.

The 'Three-Model Legal Framework' had remained, up to the time of writing, a guiding principle for SPLM to do business, not only with the Khartoum Islamic Regime, but also with the northern political parties that compose the opposition National Democratic Alliance (NDA).

According to political observers of the second Nigeria-sponsored peace talks, it was the first time since contacts for peaceful reconciliation by external players started in 1990 that both sides have come out explicitly with what each of the parties considered the best way out of war.

However, after three weeks of heated debates, mediation, recommendations, proposals and counter proposals including those of the experts, the talks were called off when it became apparent that they had reached a deadlock.

As the two sides failed to agree to issue a joint communiqué to mark the usual end of any negotiations, the Nigerian mediators issued a press statement.

The statement clearly spelled out what the mediators called the fundamental differences which they said were responsible for the failure of the Abuja Two peace talks.

Commenting on Abuja two conferences, Professor Lesch writes: "...the negotiations illustrated the pitfalls of negotiating in a polarised political context, in which talks heightened mistrust rather than bridged differences".

Pleased that the talks had failed and that its political and diplomatic stratagem had worked, the Government launched in July/August 1993 what it called 'the last operation to rout out the remaining pockets of rebel resistance' (discussed in chapter 11).

The second Abuja Talks thus ended with the Government and the SPLA sharply disagreeing over the issue of religion and the state.

The failure of Abuja Two later led to a new joint initiative proposal which became known as the Declaration Of Principles (DOP) [3] discuss at IGAD Four Talks by the countries affected by the war namely; Eritrea, Ethiopia, Kenya and Uganda among the IGAD partners.

15.2. DISAGREEMENTS OVER SECOND ABUJA TALKS

1. RELIGION AND STATE
a) THE SPLM
The SPLM insisted that a unitary system should separate religion from state. In a Confederation the north could institute Sharia except in the shared capital city of Khartoum, where secular laws must apply.

b) THE GOVERNMENT OF SUDAN
The Government insisted that Sharia should remain the supreme public law in a Unified Sudan. Huddud would not apply to the citizens of the south but would apply to non-Muslims in the north. The word 'Islamic' would be removed from the official name of the country in deference to non-Muslims.

c) NIGERIA
Nigeria Proposed suspending Sharia during the interim period except as applied to individual Muslims for personal status issues, as was the case before 1983. The Government totally rejected that proposal.

2. POLITICAL SYSTEM DURING THE INTERIM PERIOD
a) THE SPLM
A Confederation was proposed with each state establishing its own legal system and foreign policy. Supreme authority would lie with the head of state in Khartoum and the Commander-in-Chief of the SPLA (head of the Southern Sudan Government) who would oversee matters of mutual interest, including shared infrastructure.

b) THE GOVERNMENT OF SUDAN
The Government of Sudan rejected Confederation and insisted on

its current Federal formula, the South's division into several states and the exclusion of Nuba and Ingessna from the South.

c) NIGERIA

Nigeria proposed that the South have an Independent Judiciary, its own Security Forces and enhanced administrative jurisdiction within a Federal formula that accorded more authority to the states than Khartoum's plan. But retained key economic powers at the centre and proposed dividing the entire country into many small states to reduce the power of regional blocs.

3. SOCIO-ECONOMIC POLICIES

a) THE SPLM

The SPLM argued that the Southern Confederate State would control petroleum exploration and development policy, including import-export trade, banking, mining, agriculture and international agreements. Each state would control education and religious affairs.

b) THE GOVERNMENT OF SUDAN

The Government of Sudan insisted that the Central Government control socio-economic, educational and religious policies and negotiate international agreements. Since natural resources were common to all Sudanese, the Central Government should control them.

c) NIGERIA

Nigeria reserved curriculum development, commerce and industry and fishing to the States. It gained the parties' acceptance of a Commission on the allocation of national revenue, as had already been agreed at Abuja One, but they disagreed on the Commission's composition and the constitutional authority.

4. SECURITY ARRANGEMENT DURING THE INTERIM PERIOD

a) THE SPLM

The SPLM wanted the Government Troops withdrawn from the South, leaving the SPLA in control, with foreign observers to monitor the cease-fire and the disengagement process. It was wary of Nigeria's proposal to leave the Army within the South and integrate the SPLA into the National Army.

b) THE GOVERNMENT OF SUDAN

The initial government delegation led by Dr. Ali al Hajj accepted the idea of a cease-fire commission without foreign observers. When the High delegation, headed by al Khalifa, arrived, it overruled al Hajj's position and emphasised that the current cease-fire was merely temporary, and insisted that the composition of a cease fire commission could not be discussed until political issues were resolved.

c) NIGERIA

Nigeria proposed gradual separation of Forces leading to demobilisation or encampment and the creation of a cease-fire commission (including a Nigerian member) with detailed instructions for guaranteeing implementation of the accord.

5. REFERENDUM ON SELF-DETERMINATION
a) THE SPLM

The SPLM proposed that each state hold a referendum during the interim period to choose between confederation and independence.

b) THE GOVERNMENT OF SUDAN

The Government of Sudan insisted that a referendum not allow the South to secede and not include marginalised peoples living in the North. It could decide only on the preferred form of union.

c) NIGERIA

Nigeria wanted the SPLM to drop its demand for a referendum since it strongly opposed secession. The National Constitutional Conference could substitute for that referendum[2].

15.3. FROM ABUJA TO IGAD PEACE OVERTURES

Encouraged by the successes of the Armed Forces against the southern rebels; and vaingloriously assured that the rebellion was being crushed, President al Bashir ordered the Islamic Peace Commission to carry out a number of activities that would assist the Armed Forces' on the ground. These activities included:

1. Stepping up highly charged propaganda that the rebellion was coming to an end.

2. Sending large sums of money to the capitals of southern states and to the neighbouring countries with large concentrations of refugees, e.g. Nairobi, Kenya to induce them to come back home.

3. That when giving money to the refugees and the SPLM/SPLA officers and men, and particularly those that have just fallen out of favour with the rebel movement, they should be told that the rebels were being defeated. That peace was on the horizon.

4. The period for repatriation, resettlement and rehabilitation had just begun.

The Government's Peace Commission work was made easier by the schism in the SPLM/SPLA United when the splinter factions, each on its own initiative, began contacting this government agency to give them financial and material support.

Consequently, many refugees and some former SPLM/SPLA United commanders contacted and supplied left for Khartoum. The Khartoum suburban hotel 'The Green Village' was given up to accommodate the southern rebel returnees.

Invigorated by his Government's propaganda rhetoric about the advent of peace among the refugees and that rebels were returning to the country in droves, President al Bashir went on diplomatic offensive. He immediately began to look everywhere to find an affluent new mediator. Al Bashir's efforts were made easier by the following factors:

First, the Eastern African member states in the organisation of the Inter-Governmental Authority on Desertification and Drought (IGADD), aware and concerned about the destabilising impact the intra-Sudanese conflict would bring to bear on its neighbours, had in September 1993 established a standing committee on peace in Sudan. This committee was charged with the responsibility to assist in the mediation efforts by negotiating the end of the civil war.

To this effect President Moi of Kenya, in his capacity as Chair of the IGADD Peace Committee, had begun contacting the warring parties to accept the IGADD mediation.

Secondly, the SPLA factions fighting after the 1991 split had made the American public concerned about the untold suffering of the Sudanese civilian population caught up in fighting.

So in 1993 the U.S. State Department invited the two factional leaders, Dr. John Garang and Dr. Riek Machar to Washington for possible reconciliation which culminated in the August 1993 Washington Declaration.

In the Declaration, the two leaders pledged to reconcile and reunite their factions in order to fight the Khartoum Government.

Thirdly, in the wake of the government's massive military offensive against the SPLA rebels in 1992-1993, the American Congress passed a number of resolutions criticising and condemning the Sudan Government of its huge human rights violations against the civilian population in the southern Sudan.

Fourthly, during the Ethiopian Civil Wars, the Sudan Government had assisted the Ethiopian rebels, which resulted in the creation of two separate states in Ethiopia. The Sudan Government could expect a tit for tat policy in its dealings with Ethiopian and Eritrean presidents Meles Zenawi and Isais Afrewerki.

15.4. THE IGADD ONE PEACE PROCESS

Contrasting IGADD with U.S.A. and assuming that it would find the sympathy it deserved from the Eritrean and Ethiopian leaders, al Bashir contacted the IGADD chairman, Daniel Arap Moi, during the IGADD meeting in Djibouti in 1993 requesting him to mediate in the Sudan civil war instead of Babangida.

Al Bashir's request for Moi's mediation was personal. According to reports, al Bashir appealed, as he did to Babangida, to Moi's great leadership qualities in the Horn, urging him to take up the mediation in the Sudan civil war.

With immediate effect, President Moi, in his capacity as chair to the IGADD Peace Committee, and while misreading al Bashir's real Orwellian intentions, accepted to mediate and set the ball of peace rolling.

It was in this light that the First IGADD Peace Conference was convened in May 1994, chaired by President Moi and attended by the Sudan President al Bashir and the SPLM/SPLA factional leaders Dr. John Garang and Dr. Riek Machar.

Meanwhile, President al Bashir, who had at first wanted to hold bilateral talks with the leader of the main rebel group, Dr. Garang, declined to do so at the last moment.

The latest attempt by IGADD mediators to bring al Bashir and Garang to meet face to face thus ended in failure. In her book *The Contested Identities in Sudan* Professor Lesch writes: "Al Bashir refused to meet Garang or even be in the same room when they signed the joint press statement launching the talks".

Leaving his foreign minister to represent him in the official talks, al Bashir left for Khartoum half an hour before the opening ceremony began, apparently to go and oversee the government offensive being launched from Juba to capture the last SPLA border posts. After attending the ceremony, Dr. Garang left for the Southern Sudan the same evening to counter the army raids against his forces.

When the official talks were held, the IGADD mediators put forward a proposal that the discussion centre on the last issues tackled at the Abuja Two Conference, namely 1) interim arrangements and 2) the constitutional principle underlying the resolution of the civil war.

The head of the Sudan delegation, Dr. Ali al Hajj Mohamed, warned that, while agreeing that the conference discuss only the interim period as discussed at Abuja Two, he would leave the meeting if self-determination was included among the items the meeting was to discuss.

The SPLM-United delegation, despite previous agreement with the SPLM Mainstream to make self-determination the principal issue during the discussion, sided with the Government's delegation on a number of issues. As a result of this impasse the main agenda was not discussed at all. Hence the meeting was adjourned to reconvene in July 1994.

The SPLM head of delegation, Cdr. Salva Kiir Mayardit, stated 'the lack of substantive discussion is an indication that there would be no basis for future talks between us and the Sudan Government.'

In Khartoum President al Bashir, apparently reflecting on the Government victories over the SPLA, stated that "the (recent) military victories has made the SPLA irrelevant[3]," adding that, "in the second round of talks his delegation would attend only for four days."

Al Bashir was signifying that the SPLA by then would have been defeated. Implicitly his delegation's presence at the next talks would just be a formality. However, despite the failure of the talks the mediators managed to extract some agreement from the parties to the conflict.

The mediators succeeded and set up a subcommittee on relief aid to open air corridors to seventy-three sites, create five land passages, and immunise children living in the war zone.

The adjournment of the meeting gave the Government a breathing space to launch further operations against the SPLA. During the period between IGADD One and IGAD Two, the Government Army was able to capture additional SPLA territories including its tactical head quarters—on the Sudan Ugandan border—Kaji Keji. (It should be noted that also during this period IGADD was renamed the Inter-Governmental Authority on Development—IGAD.)

15.5. IGAD TWO PEACE CONFERENCE

The second meeting under IGAD mediation was expected to convene in May 1994. But before it convened, the Sudan Air Force was reported to have bombed the Chukudum airstrip where the SPLM official delegation was expected to embark the plane.

During the opening session of IGAD Two peace talks, the Kenyan Minister of Foreign Affairs made an emotional appeal to the parties to the conflict to take the African (IGAD) initiative seriously. He asked the two delegations to present position papers that would 'display restraint and sensitivity to the negotiation partners' (Wondu 15-24).

Presenting the Government's official position paper Colonel Mohamed al Amin al Khalifa told the meeting that Sudan must remain united and Sharia and custom must be the two main sources of legislation.

He states, 'The Sudanese states with predominantly non-Muslim population, where Sharia laws will not apply, can adopt alternative laws.' According to him, practice and constitution would be silent on the issue of official religion.

Al Khalifa argued further that all citizens were equal and that there was freedom of religious practice. In the interim period the time span must be long enough for the authorities to restore confidence, set up governing and administrative institutions and to undertake rehabilitation and reconstruction, a clear reference that the rebels were being defeated and that the rebellion was coming to an end.

Presenting it official position, The SPLM delegation, while supporting a peaceful resolution of the conflict and the right to self-determination by the people of the south, the Nuba Mountains and the Ingessna Hills, recommended a two-year interim period in which there would be two confederate states in the Sudan. That period would lead to an internationally supervised referendum. But as the warring parties stuck to the Abuja's two positions, the meeting adjourned again without any substantive discussion of the papers presented.

Before the conference could break up, the IGAD mediators surprised the two delegates to the conflict by handing them their own Declaration of Principles (DOP), a mechanism through which the discussion to resolve the conflict would be evolved (Lesch). The DOP, as it became widely known, ordered that the parties to the conflict examine 'confidentially' the DOP document, pointing out that the delegates' remarks and comments would provide a basis for discussion at the third round of talks in July 1994.

According to the DOP document, the parties to the conflict were to commit themselves to a peaceful and just political solution under scrutiny. Declaration of Principles emphasised that the unity of the country must be given priority, 'provided that:

First, social and political system is based on a secular and democratic state with legal guarantees and political and social equalities of all people in Sudan.

Second, extensive rights of self-administration to be given to the various peoples in the Sudan.

Third, a need for the separation of state and religion and

Fourth, appropriate fair sharing of wealth, the incorporation of human rights principles into the constitution and

Fifthly, the independence of judiciary.

In the absence of agreement on the above principles, the respective peoples will have the option to determine their future including independence through a referendum, a clear reference to the peoples of Southern Sudan, Nuba and Ingessna and Ngok Dinka of Abyei.

Responding to the DOP document, the Government Chief Delegate Mohamed al Amin al Khalifa pointed out. "We have no option (now) except to continue the war to its finality. The chief delegate accused the IGAD mediators of bias in favour of the SPLM.

The SPLM delegation, on the other hand, supported the DOP document, considering it a pleasant surprise to them. The SPLM delegation disclosed that their newly elected National Executive Council (NEC) has fully endorsed the document as a basis for the future negotiations with the Khartoum Regime.

15.6. THE IGAD THREE CONFERENCE

In July, exactly three months after the issuing of the DOP document, the IGAD mediators called the convening of the third round of negotiation between the warring parties. On July 18, the third meeting went into session in the Kenyan capital Nairobi, chaired by President Moi and attended by all the parties to the conflict.

In his keynote address to the conference, President Moi called for a cease-fire and the implementation of the agreement to distribute relief supplies in accordance to the provisions of the previous accord reached earlier by the parties concerned. President Moi also requested responses from the warring parties on the DOP document.

The Government Chief Delegate al Khalifa, who arrived in Nairobi on July 22, four days after the session commenced, presented a written statement to the conference in which he outlined his government's response to the DOP document. "His government," he said, "had rejected the DOP document in its entirety on the ground that the mediators should not have stated their preferred agenda".

The government's statement indicated in no uncertain terms that the issues of religion and state, secularism, self-determination and secession of the South were outside the IGAD's scope. The statement stressed that the government delegation was only prepared to discuss the following issues:

Concerning the interim period, al Khalifa said, should be based on the Regime's current federal arrangement, focusing on how wealth and power were to be shared within the Southern Sudan.

On self-determination, al Khalifa told the conference his delegation would not sanction the dismembering of the Sudan and warns, 'If you (IGAD) want to separate the south from the north, it will be done through the barrel of the gun.'

Regarding the DOP document as the basis for negotiation with the rebels, al Khalifa pointed out that the Government would negotiate its own agenda and that they would reluctantly accept a three-phased programme without an international monitoring team.

Al Khalifa explained that in the first referendum, apparently with all the Sudanese citizens voting, at the end of the interim period, should be based on the current federal system. In the said referendum the voters would accept or reject federalism. If the voters rejected federalism, al Khalofa went on, a second referendum would select among alternative forms of union. A third referendum would include secession as one of the options al Khalifa pointed out.

The SPLM-mainstream delegation, which was later joined by the SPLM-United delegation (SSIM), while endorsing the DOP document, expressed full confidence in IGAD mediators.

Their statements to the Conference said that they (SPLM/SSIM) supported the unity of Sudan if it was based within the context of a secular constitution, insisting that a referendum that would be carried out in the Southern Sudan at the end of the interim period should uphold the principle of self-determination.

On July 27, 1994, the IGAD mediators formed a tripartite committee charged with responsibility to thrash out points of agreement and disagreement based on difficulties and differences they encountered during the nine days of serious negotiations.

But while the parties to the conflict were speculating what role the tripartite committee would actually play, on the next day, July 28, the IGAD mediators, to everyone's surprise, issued a six point non-paper document on self-determination.

The IGAD requested the warring parties to respond to all the six points affirming their commitment to them. In the six point non-paper document the IGAD asserted the inalienable right of the people of South-Sudan to freely determine their destiny by means of an internationally supervised referendum by the end of the interim period.

During that time they shall freely choose from all options, including independence. The interim arrangements shall be within the framework of a United Sudan.

While welcoming the IGAD non-paper document, the SPLM delegation added that the right of self-determination should also apply to the Nuba Mountains and the Ingessna Hills.

As for the Sudan, Government delegation rejected the words 'inalienable' and 'self-determination,' adding that the government would only accept the phrase 'the people of the South would freely determine their future status within the United Sudan through an internationally supervised referendum. With these good notes the mediators adjourned the conference for two months.

Back home the government blamed top members of the delegation (both Black Muslims of African origins) for accepting even that limited concession on self-determination. Khartoum immediately rebuked the two delegates and removed them from the list of future delegates to IGAD conferences.

15.7. IGAD FOUR CONFERENCE

When the fourth conference convened on September 5-7, 1994, the government sent a new team headed by long-time Islamist zealot, Ghazi Salah Eddin Atabani and Islamic bigot al Nafie Ali Nafie. Apart from few hand-picked anti-SPLA/SPLM Southerners, the Sudan delegation membership was composed of white Arabs.

In his opening address to the conference on September 5, 1994, the Sudanese representative Ghazi Salah Eddin Atabani criticised the IGAD mediation team for issuing, after all, the DOP document saying 'My Government [delegation] would not discuss self-determination and secularism.'

On the problem of the war in the south, Salah Eddin remarked, 'the problem in the Southern Sudan was bred and nurtured by the British

Colonialists.' He then blamed IGAD for encouraging the SPLM to raise the issue of self-determination, a concept that, Salah Eddin said, 'lacked any legal or moral basis.'

On the prospect for peace, the Government chief delegate made it clear that Sudan would establish a permanent cease-fire, once unity was ensured by force. Sharia, he stressed, is irreplaceable and partial exemption for non-Muslims in the south was a voluntary concession, not a right. "In fact," he went on, "my Government's duty is to Islamise the whole of Africa since that task had been interrupted by the European Colonialism".

The SPLM team were embarrassed by the Government chief delegate's sudden outbursts emphasising that the government was not only planning to assimilate and Islamise the Africans in the Southern Sudan but to extend that mission beyond Sudan's borders. That particular disclosure of the Sudan Government's strategy on Africa as a whole, by a senior government member, the IGAD Chair abruptly ended the session even before the SPLM delegation could deliver its opening address to the conference.

Despite the deadlock of the talks, President Daniel Arap Moi pledged that he would continue to chair the IGAD Peace Committee and the mediation process. Soon after the closing down of the fourth session of the IGAD Peace Initiative, President Moi called for an urgent meeting of IGAD summit apparently to brief the IGAD Heads of State about the stalled peace talks (The IGAD member states comprising the Sudan, Djibouti, Eritrea, Ethiopia, Kenya and Uganda. Somalia would join after the restoration of peace).

Before the summit, President al Bashir, for undisclosed reasons, had sent the Sudan Islamist strongman Dr. Hassan Abdalla al Turabi to meet President Moi. Moi and al Turabi met on 17 September 1994.

Later al Turabi was reported to have told Moi during the meeting that he, the de facto leader of the Islamic regime, rejected any compromise on Sharia and self—determination. Al Turabi told Moi further that the government version of federation was sufficient for the South and especially that the SPLA was apparently being defeated militarily.

President al Bashir, who met President Moi briefly before the summit, also stated his intention of not altering the Government's position on Islamic law and rejecting the self-determination for Southern Sudan.

Al Bashir wanted President Moi to mediate alone in his personal capacity. Al Bashir had approached the Nigerian leader Babangida in the same manner in 1990. Professor Lesch, writes: al Bashir was asking President Moi to broker a bilateral peace deal between him and the SPLM leader John Garang instead of through an international forum. This approach did betray al Bashir's stratagem before the summit was convened.

Contrary to what he had told President Moi, and apparently for diplomatic purposes, President al Bashir affirmed his Government's commitment to the DOP document, which the Government delegation had earlier rejected.

Before the summit al Bashir had emphasised that the DOP document provided a valid basis for talks, even though a deadlock had already been reached by the two sides on the vital issues of separation of state and religion and the self-determination for the Southern Sudan. Concluding his speech, al Bashir told the summit that since the talks between his Government and the SPLM rebels' delegations have reached a dead end; there would be no need for President Moi to continue with further efforts to restart the negotiations. After all, al Bashir added, the rebels were being defeated militarily.

Confident that the rebellion would soon be over, President al Bashir did not apparently have any reason to worry any longer about war and peace issues but only to attend to his government's vital policies at home and abroad.

Thus, upon his return to Khartoum, al Bashir started, with immediate effect, marathon tours which took him to Europe, America and some parts of Africa looking for funds for possible rehabilitation purposes and also seeking another forum as he believed IGAD mediation had come to an end.

15.8. SPLA TAKES NEW MILITARY INITIATIVE

But as al Bashir's Government was expecting to hear that the rebels' last strong hold on the Sudan-Ugandan border, Nimule had been taken by his Forces, an apparent scoop for a national celebration, the SPLA, in October 1995, seized, once more, the military initiative it had lost since February 1992.

Essentially it was this initiative that enabled the SPLA to join ranks with the NDA Forces on the Eritrean Front in Eastern Sudan, which led to the formation of the SPLA-NDA Forces Joint High Command.

One year after the military take over discussed earlier; and in line with its strategy to fight and talk, SPLM began with immediate effect to talk with the Islamic regime being the de facto power in Khartoum (chapter six). The SPLM also stepped up contacts with the northern main opposition political parties of the National Democratic Alliance (NDA). The aim of this coalition, which many described by observers as a 'marriage of convenience,' was to oust the Islamic (or NIF) regime in Khartoum, which, they said, had usurped powers through a military coup.

So, in 1990 the SPLM and the UMMA Party (the majority party whose government was overthrown) pledged that they would work together with their colleagues in the National Democratic Alliance (an amalgam of all political opposition forces) in order to accelerate the overthrow of the military Islamic Regime in Khartoum.

In their pledge, SPLM and UMMA Party called for the convening of the long-awaited National Constitutional Conference in accordance to the Koka

Dam Declarations and DUP/SPLM 1988 Addis Ababa Peace Initiative. The two parties also called for the establishment of a democratic government with the active participation of all the NDA members in it.

The SPLM, as a sign of good will and as an encouragement for future cordial cooperation, allowed the UMMA opposition to use SPLA Clandestine Radio to address the nation and its supporters. The meeting and pledge were immediately endorsed by the UMMA President, Sadig al Mahdi inside the country and under strict security surveillance.

It was also endorsed by legitimate high command, under the former Commander-in-chief General Fathi Mohamed Ali and his two deputies, General Abdel Rahman Said, former chief of staff for operations, and Major General al Hadi Bushra, former chief of intelligence, as soon as it was formed.

On March 4, 1990, the SPLM and the NDA signed an accord in which the two organisations reaffirmed their previous commitment to unite and coordinate their efforts in order to speed up the overthrow of the Islamic Regime. After which they would work for the restoration of democracy, and the convening of the National Constitutional Conference.

February/March 1991, the NDA held a summit in Addis Ababa and affirmed their commitment to work jointly and tirelessly together. They would use all available resources so as to achieve their main objective, the removal of the Islamic Regime from power and to restore democratic processes including elections and the convening of the Constitutional Conference.

However, neither the SPLM/UMMA communiqué nor the NDA summit resolutions had specified the contents of the future constitution, which has been the cause of the political instability since independence in 1956.

In September 1991 the NDA held an urgent conference in Cairo, despite the SPLM/SPLA schism. In the Cairo Conference, key issues such, as the resolution of the Southern Sudan problem and the SPLM conditional unity—on the basis of separation between the state and religion—were resolved.

Regardless, the Cairo Conference failed to support a secular constitution since UMMA/DUP feared a backlash from their supporters and power Islamic bases inside the Sudan in case they agreed to annul the Islamic laws that had been in force since 1983.

It was that spirit that subsequently led to the London Conference in 1992 when the NDA managed to complete a 260-article constitution. Even so, the Conference failed to agree on articles 8 and 9 which concern the sources of legislation in the Sudan.

At the insistence of DUP, and perhaps with the tacit support of the UMMA Party, the debate on the two articles was delayed till the NDA would assume power in Khartoum. This aspect raised fears and suspicion among the SPLM members that once in power, the two parties might go and start all over the old game of deceit and surprise, the business as usual.

With that apparent experience in his mind, the SPLM leader, John Garang had often emphasised that. "Although SPLM would actively work to strengthen the NDA in order to bring about peace within the context of a united secular democratic Sudan, SPLM believed that, confederation, association of sovereign states, or self-determination were legitimate alternatives.

Again, these remarks led the secularists among the northern opposition to believe that partition of the country would strengthen the NIF. Hence they (secularists) therefore went for a secular constitution and started their effective co-operation with the SPLM so as to counterbalance the Islamist members in the NDA.

On October 28, 1992 the NDA held a summit again in Cairo, Egypt. At the end of that conference, a collective statement was issued which was considered by all the NDA members as a breakthrough which would make it possible to resolve the key issues in the relationship of the NDA partners.

After deploring the dangers posed by the Islamist Regime which at that time was trying to transform the civil war into a Jihad (holy war), the NDA Cairo conference issued a statement summarised below. That the Cairo Conference pledges its full commitment to the establishment of democratic Sudan:

1. Based on recognition of cultural and religious multiplicity and respect for religious beliefs.

2. Based on the respect for the rule of law and independence of the judiciary.

3. Based on the respect for human rights and where no legislation or enactment inconsistent with these principles can be based.

4. Where religion cannot be abused for political expediency; in which religion is a divine concept between God and the individuals.

5. For all citizens and which does not accept a theocratic state.

Even though, the reactions of the two religiously based parties were contradictory. UMMA, for instance, had refused to sign the statement, while the DUP expressed some reservation on the wording of the statement, a move which almost broke up the coalition. However, the very urgency to find a suitable and acceptable formula to satisfy both the secularists and the opposite shade of opinion was a breakthrough for both sides in the NDA.

Conference which rejuvenated the NDA was held in the Kenyan Capital, Nairobi, in April 1993. In this conference, the leader of the SPLM/SPLA John Garang reiterated his movement's firm position and vision of a united secular democratic Sudan.

In what appeared as a reference to the solution of the southern problem, Garang reminded his audience once again that the right to self-determination was one of the basic components of democracy and human rights principles that the NDA must uphold.

"Failure to endorse the right of self-determination (would) place the NDA on the same plane as the Sudan Government," said the SPLM leader. Furthermore, Garang said, "if one group dominates others, those peoples cannot be blamed for seceding."

After lengthy debates, the NDA Conference, in spite of the participants' political differences, on April 13, 1993, unanimously endorsed the principles of equal rights and non-discrimination. In the Declaration thereof, NDA resolved that:

1. International and regional human rights instruments and covenants shall be integral parts of the laws of Sudan and any laws contrary thereto shall be considered null and void and unconstitutional.

2. Laws in the Sudan shall guarantee full equality of citizens on the basis of citizenship, respect for religious beliefs and traditions and, without discrimination on grounds of religion, race, gender or culture. Any law or laws contrary to the foregoing stipulation shall be null and void and unconstitutional.

For the second time in a row the two religiously based parties, the DUP and the UMMA, renewed their support for the move to reach a consensus on issuing resolutions on the issue of religion and state from which passages were incorporated into the final Declaration.

Naturally, the SPLM leader John Garang hailed the resolutions of the Nairobi April NDA Conference as a victory for a Unified Sudan[4]. The DUP and UMMA Party also concurred with the SPLM on the view of conditional unity.

15.9. SPLM/UMMA CHUKUDUM ACCORD

The most important development in the strenuous relations within the various groups of the NDA worthy to note in their previous five years' activities (1990-1994) was the UMMA-SPLM meeting held in the SPLA controlled town of Chukudum in Eastern Equatoria, southern Sudan, in December 1994.

The Chukudum conference as described by political observers was a watershed in the history of SPLM's long endeavour to let the northern political parties, recognise it as a genuine liberation movement, a movement with clear-cut national agenda rather than a regional one with a parochial plan.

On December 12, 1994, after almost a year of contacts and discussion, the SPLM and the Umma Party concluded an accord which became known as the SPLM/UMMA Chukudum Accord 1994. The Chukudum Accord was signed by the General Secretary Omar Nur al Daim for the UMMA, and by Commander Salva Kiir Mayardit for the SPLM.

In a statement after the signing ceremony, Dr. Omar al Daim said, 'the meeting was important because the northern Sudanese political party leaders could take a risk to enter the southern Sudan in search of avenues for a possible compromise and cooperation between the two embattled parts of the Sudan.'

The General Secretary of the UMMA Party stressed that the coming of the northern political leaders to the south would actually remove the psychological barriers between the two peoples, and that this would strengthen mutual confidence.

Dr. Nur al Daim concluded that the coming of the UMMA Party leaders in particular here [south] will be a boost for the ongoing search for peace in our country.'

Essentially the Chukudum Accord stipulated that the two sides to the agreement endorsed following terms:

1. Conditional unity, which will only arise as a result of free choice of the people concerned but not unity, based on force

2. The NDA Nairobi 1993 Declaration

3. The IGAD Declaration of Principles (DOP) 1994

4. Creation of a pluralist democracy based on federation or confederation

5. Recognise the right of self-determination for people of Southern Sudan which shall be decided by a referendum during the interim period of two or four years

On the SPLM proposal that the right of self-determination be extended to the peoples of Abyei, Nuba Mountains and the Ngessna Hills, the UMMA side opposed it but the two sides agreed to defer the issue since the representatives of the areas concerned were not represented in the meeting.

Only days after the signing of the Chukudum Accord, the UMMA Party leader and former Prime Minister al Sadig al Mahdi, who was still in the country, said in a speech marking the Ramadan festival that he has also endorsed the Chukudum Accord signed between his party and the SPLM. The UMMA Party leader added, 'if the southerners vote for independence [during the referendum], the northerners should not maintain unity by force.'

Since the Chukudum meeting, self-determination as a right not to be tampered with has figured in subsequent IGAD meetings. It also figured in the bilateral discussions among the various political forces in northern Sudan subject to the IGAD Forum.

15.10. THE ASMARA DECLARATION MAKES NDA, A GOVERNMENT IN WAITING

After the Chukudum meeting described above, it became abundantly clear that consensus over what to do about the peace process on the one hand, and how to overthrow the Islamic Regime in Khartoum on the other, was becoming very urgent. Precisely this would demand that the NDA must act as a cohesive body charged with responsibility to rescue the beleaguered nation.

In that sense, the NDA was expected to make a thorough review of its policies, spelling out guidelines about how the peace process as a whole and the restoration of democracy and the convening of the National Constitutional Conference in particular should be handled.

In cognisance to its declared national commitments and despite the government's backlash against its activities in and out of the country, the NDA in December 1994 held an urgent meeting in the Eritrean capital Asmara. The principal aim of that meeting, according to reports, was to draw up comprehensive policies and strategies which would guide its future political and military activities in its expected confrontation with the Islamic Regime in Khartoum.

During the meeting, which was attended by all leading members of the organisation representing the various factions that it was composed of, it was emphasised that the future political system in the Sudan must reflect the multi-racial, multi-ethnic and multi-religious character of the Sudanese society.

The meeting further emphasised the future non-use of religion in politics and the need to give the south the right to self-determination to be decided in a referendum whose options would include independence.

This particular aspect apparently raised tension that almost hampered consensus on the final document of the meeting. In her book *Contested Identities* Lesch states: "the call for non-use of religion in politics and the endorsement by the meeting of self-determination (for south) caused tension' in the discussions leading to the writing up of the final document inside the DUP and the UMMA parties (Lesch 195).

This tension may have triggered the issuing of an unsigned critique (apparently by DUP al Hindi Wing) on January 28, 1995, suggesting that the two religiously based parties (DUP and UMMA) were favouring instead the inclusion of a clause of unconditional unity in the final document.

According to reports, the DUP Leader Mohamed Osman al Mirghani may have been reluctant to sign the Declaration, but realising that his action might, perhaps, anger the southerners and might disincline them from cooperating, he relented and accepted the inclusion of conditional unity and self-determination in the final document.

Everything having been completed, on December 27, 1994, the NDA meeting issued its final document, the *Asmara Declaration,* which observers described as the NDA Manifesto.

The Asmara Declaration was signed by:

1. NDA Chairman Mohamed Osman al Mirghani, representing his party, DUP

2. Cdr. Dr. John Garang de Mabior, the Leader of the SPLM/SPLA

3. Dr. Omar Nur al Daim of the UMMA Party

4. Brigadier Abdel Aziz Khalid Osman, the head of the New Sudanese Allied Forces (SAF) representing the secular northern politicians and intellectuals previously associated with the National Alliance of the Trade Union Congress as well as military officers.

Six months following the Asmara Declaration, the NDA in June 1995 held its convention again in the Eritrean capital Asmara. The conference, which many attendees called 'a national constitutional conference,' was indeed convened to address the future constitution for the Sudan in case the NDA were to take over power in the country after overthrowing the Islamic Regime in Khartoum.

The Asmara Convention, which was attended by leaders and representatives of all the political forces and trade union members of the NDA, convened and continued in session from June 17-23, 1995.

At the end of a week of deliberations, the NDA Convention agreed to endorse the Chukudum Accord and the Asmara Declaration of 1994. It also agreed that the future political system in the Sudan must be based on democracy and religious pluralism.

The convention called for adoption of a confederate arrangement for the Sudan an arrangement, which the participants said would devolve most of the powers on the two regions (South and North). The Central Government, the participants of the convention stressed, would coordinate defence and foreign policies.

According to this agreement, the South would be allowed to conduct a referendum at the end of the two or four years. In the meantime the South could continue to maintain its own army, at least during the interim period, the convention's resolution maintained.

According to analysts, the inclusion of confederation, the NDA members, were committing themselves to respect the decisions arrived at during this convention.

They wanted also to make an honest gesture in the hope of trying to win the SPLM, that had already begun to assume that the convention was basing its recommendations and proposals on the SPLM Legal Framework it had presented previously to the Abuja (1993) and Nairobi (1994) meetings.

For the SPLM, the Asmara Convention resolution was to some extent a fulfilment of the SPLM/SPLA Manifesto (1983) which at that time was a nightmare as they had then no confidence that it would succeed.

On June 23, the Asmara Convention issued its resolutions that called for the following:

1. Future political systems in the Sudan must be based on democracy and pluralism (not secularism).

2. The international and regional human rights conventions and covenants must be observed in the Sudan's future constitution.

3. A call for the abolition of the Islamic Laws of 1983, affirmed 1989.

4. A call for the prohibition to form political parties in the Sudan on religious grounds

5. The people of Ngok Dinka of Abyei shall be given the right to conduct a referendum on the option whether to join Bahr al Ghazal Region or continue to be administered in Kordofan.

6. After the results of a referendum on Abyei are announced, (if they are in favour of joining Bahr al Ghazal), then Bahr al Ghazal, Equatoria and Upper Nile shall be given the right to conduct a referendum to decide their political future on the options that will include independence. This should be conducted at or before the end of the transitional period of two to four years.

7. The peoples of Nuba Mountains and Ingessna Hills should be given the right to decide their political future during the interim period.

Additionally, to the above resolutions, there were secret annexes dealing with security programmes that included a pledge to topple the Islamic Regime (NIF) in Khartoum viz. militarily, by means of popular uprisings inside the Sudanese cities, or via civil disobedience against the incumbent regime.[5]

It was on the strength of these secret annexes that the NDA formed its joint military command, comprising all the armed factions of various opposition groupings that were opposed to the Khartoum regime.

The joint Command was put under Commander-in-Chief of the SPLA Dr. John Garang. This command until the time of writing (2004), was conducting the joint military campaign in the Eastern Sudan and Southern Sudan.

Speaking after the Asmara Convention, June 1995, the representative of the UMMA Party, Mubarak al Fadhil al Mahdi stated that self-determination had been proposed in order to end forty years of southern suspicion of the north. The South could exercise the right to secede. if the Central Government failed to abide by the agreed upon programme.

Summing up this Chapter, the Asmara Convention's 1994 resolution and Declaration of 1995 can be said to have placed the NDA opposition and its joint military wing as an alternative credible political force to the Islamic military regime in Khartoum that was becoming more alarmed by the day.

As it appeared between 1999 and 2004, NIF was beginning simmering inside its ranks threatened by the new developments apparently set to blow it out of power sooner or later or dismantling itself voluntarily in effort to accommodate others in a pluralistic state.

From 1995 it became crystal clear that any future combined attack by the opposition forces from the east and from the south, in conjunction with popular uprising and civil disobedience in the cities, could predictably be the coup de grace for Islamic authorities in Khartoum.

For the last two decades (1992—2002), it had been circumventing such a move by using all the intrigues and tricks at their disposal in order to avoid such a drama. The drama if happened could bring ruin not only to the Islamist incumbent regime but the entire Islamic movement in the Sudan.

The developments posed by the NDA coalition between 1994 and 2002 had brought it into the limelight, making optimists predict that ruling out the usual disasters politicians bring upon themselves, and given the political simmering and schism in the Islamic regime in Khartoum, it was veritable a Government-in-waiting.

The Sudan Peoples Liberation Movement was then in a position to tell the world that the agenda for the creation of a new Sudan contained in its manifesto of July 1983 was not only working, but also achievable. A successful outcome was now in sight as discussed in the concluding Chapter.

CHAPTER 16
CONCLUSION: FINAL ROAD TO PEACE

16.0. THE SETTING :

In the previous chapters of the Book, I have discussed at length the genesis of the SPLM/SPLA, how it gestated and launched, and its war aims and objectives. The SPLA/SPLM strategies and the tactics it adopted and employed were also illuminated and emphasised. These were mainly 'talking and fighting' approaches, styles that made the Movement outmanoeuvre the military junta under General Suwar al-Dhahab, the subsequent Sadig al-Mahdi's government, the NIF Junta and the northern political parties in the NDA coalition.

This strategy was basically the damaging effects of the SPLA military campaign had in crippling successive governments in Khartoum. The government stratagem in dividing up the SPLM/SPLA rank and file through the peace from within and the peace from without was too, highlighted.

I have also narrated how the SPLM/SPLA matured steadily and finally galvanised into a full-fledged national movement while at the same time maintaining its regional character and catering for its interests. The later polarisation in the conflict where the grand coalition of Northern Opposition parties and the SPLM/SPLA were fighting as a group against the Government in alignment with the SPLA dissidents was extensively discussed.

The last part of the Book essentially describes briefly the intensification of the war amidst international pressures for peace. This move finally brought the two warring parties to the negotiating table at Abuja and the IGAD peace processes, resulting in the signing of Machakos and Naivasha Protocols.

In this concluding Chapter I intend to discuss the failure of the northern opposition groups in the NDA to mobilise the masses in the north to join the war effectively. This failure brought the previous polarity to a halt turning the hand of the clock back to where it began the south versus the north. I will, in addition, throw some light on how a peaceful settlement of the long elusive problem of the South Sudan was achieved at last in Nairobi on January 9, 2005.

I will conclude the book with a summary of what some Sudanese political thinkers and academics see is the endgame of their long drawn out conflict and the road to permanent peace. Adding to it will be a final note to the Sudanese public of what they expect after the conclusion of the period of interim unity.

16.1. POLARISATION AND CONTRADICTIONS

The new polarisation in the Sudanese conflict which followed the National Democratic Alliance (NDA) convention and the subsequent Asmara Declaration in 1995, which overshadowed, *albeit temporarily*, the traditional north south political divide, has been described by observers as a watershed in the Sudan political history.

In the process, the old polarity in which the Arab Muslim North had been fighting against the Christian animist South (1955-1972) was abandoned in favour of a national agenda aimed at effort to remove the military regime from power in Khartoum.

From 1995 onward, the war took a different shape. The government and the southern dissident groups fought as one bloc against the grand coalition of the National Democratic Alliance (NDA), consisting of the northern Opposition political parties and the main southern rebel force, the SPLM/SPLA.

This important political development, the government versus the NDA opposition, marked a new start of military confrontation with the Khartoum regime. It also accelerated the SPLA war effort making it poised as a national movement with a national agenda rather than a movement fighting for the southern region.

Precisely, from 1995 onward, the SPLA was no longer a rebel force fighting against an established government, but a part of a strong united opposition alliance against the brutal military regime that had usurped power from an elected regime.

With the subsequent formation of the Joint NDA Military Command under the overall command of the SPLA Commander in Chief, John Garang, the military coordination among the NDA components became more effective on the ground (discussed in Chapter 14) as it sent threatening signals to authorities in Khartoum.

But as the NDA Forces were fighting the NIF army in the eastern front, capturing many government outposts and towns including the holy shrine of Homesh Koreib, there arose a number of contradictions that hampered its success as an alternative opposition bent to topple the Military regime in Khartoum. Hence the need to make a brief outline of these contradictions before proceeding to conclude the book.

The basic factor of these contradictions was the apparent weakness of Mohamed Osman al Mighani's leadership. At the onset it appeared as if he would lead the grand coalition effectively given the power support his party has mustered in the Sudan since independence and historical relation of his DUP party with Egypt. Had he used this position effectively; according to analysts, NDA would have achieved its goal of toppling the NIF regime in Khartoum much earlier.

With this hindsight (as leader of a grass-root party and ally to Egypt) however, al Mirghani was expected to turn the NDA into an effective opposition politically and militarily. This important position would have enabled him to muster enough power and sufficient money in order to make NDA establish itself as an alternative democratic body to the military junta it was trying to replace in Khartoum.

Under his effective leadership, NDA would have organised alternative military and civic institutions ready to move in and take over power once the monster in Khartoum was removed. NDA would have also embarked on a mass mobilisation at home and abroad.

As Chair of this august body, al Mirghani was too, expected to mobilise the international community beginning with Egypt the traditional ally of his party in order to support the Opposition to topple the Islamic theocratic regime and restored in its place, liberal democracy in the Sudan.

Another missed opportunity was when al Mirghani turned down the American invitation for him to visit Washington where he was expected to win U.S. support and recognition of NDA as the alternative to the brutal government in Khartoum. This would have enabled him to discuss the possibility of NDA joining the peace negotiations along with the SPLA at IGAD peace process.

Disappointingly, al Mirghani parochial outlook and partisan tendencies became apparent as he concentrated more on his DUP party to the disadvantage of other members of the coalition. Even so he could not win over his own DUP supporters to come out of the country en masse in order to have a sizeable force in the NDA political and military structures.

Worse still, al Mirghani distanced himself from the military operations in the East. For instance, when the NDA forces captured Kassala and the surrounding government garrisons, al Mirghani denied having the knowledge of such a plan to invade the town. He could not even visit Homesh Koreib the holy shrine of his religious sect when captured by the NDA allied forces.

Consequently, the NDA found itself redundant in Cairo and Asmara: Money was not forthcoming; Weapons were in short supply; and more importantly there was no recruitment to the NDA joint rebel army. Instead the SPLA forces that were sent to the east in order to train the Northern Opposition troops became the standing opposition NDA army.

As time went by, however, and the NDA becoming ineffective day by day, the regime became more defiant and ruthless against any sign of opposition coming from any direction. Hence the government could not hold peace talks with an opposition that posed no threat to its power.

The NDA as an opposition was thus made toothless by the weakness of its own leadership qualities. In the long run it became nothing more than a public relations agency. But for the sake of holding the coalition together, al Mirghani was allowed to continue leading the Opposition, ineffective as he was.

The escape of Sadig al Mahdi in December 1995 and his joining the NDA bandwagon was welcome because of his supposed leadership qualities and experience. Twice as an elected Prime Minister, al Mahdi was expected to make up for the leadership vacuum in the organisation that lacked everything.

Expectedly and rightly, al Mahdi was the legal leader whose elected government had been overthrown by the regime. Added to this, he was a leader of the biggest grass-root party, the UMMA vis a vis the DUP, and the great grand son of the historical Mahdi. These qualities would have made the NDA a formidable challenge to the NIF regime.

More depressingly, NDA made one vital mistake. It failed to hand over its leadership to al Mahdi as the ousted democratically elected prime minister, who with the presence of the Legitimate command[1] in the NDA, would have undoubtedly won the support of the international community in assisting the restoration of democracy in the Sudan.

Upon joining the NDA, al Mahdi as the legal leader of the Sudan undertook extensive tour of Arab Islamic states as well as many African countries; seeking diplomatic and political recognition and financial and military support in order to remove the military dictatorship and restore in its place democratic institutions.

Initially al Mahdi's physical presence in the NDA enhanced the Grand Opposition Alliance more than when he was opposing the regime from inside the country1995 and 1999.

However, having visited all the countries and assured of the international assistance al Mahdi called on the youth from inside the country to abandon the military junta and join the salvation army en masse so as to form an effective army. He also made repeated emotional appeals, particularly to his Ansaar militias that had notoriously been active against the Nimeiri regime (1969-1985) to surge out and join their Spiritual Leader.

When al Mahdi's appeal received no positive response as expected and, realising that his party was rapidly losing power base at home in favour of the ruling congress party, adding to reluctance to have him taken over its leadership, al Mahdi abandoned the NDA and went back to the Sudan. But even there he was not effective as to undo the well-entrenched NIF military establishment.

Al Mahdi thus put himself and his UMMA party in Limbo. It was only a matter of time and the NIF would eat into his party and finally split it into two factions, with his cousin Mubarak al Fadhil al Mahdi wing joining the regime that had usurped power from them.

Deprived of effective leadership and a dwindling financial and military support and depending very much only on the SPLA that was too bogged down with its own problems and contradictions in the South, the NDA from 1999 became a nominal organisation.

Another important factor to examine closely before concluding this chapter was the effect and impact of the increasingly conflicting regional and international interests on the NDA Opposition as a political organisation and on the war that was already intensifying.

16.2. EFFECTS OF THE REGIONAL DIMENSION IN THE PEACE PROCESS

On the regional front, Egypt and Libya for instance, which have historical interest in the Sudan, instead of giving effective and substantial support to the NDA to remove the army from power, suppressed their own interests as well as discarding their differences and began courting the regime in Khartoum.

The two countries were apparently worried about IGAD mediators being too pro SPLM in their approach and strategy. Egypt in particular and Libya, to a lesser extent, were more concerned about the possibility that a split of the Sudan into two separate states might encourage the Islamic fundamentalists in their countries. Such threats posed by the regime in Khartoum against their systems like the failed attempt on the life of President Hosni Mubarak in 1995 were brushed aside if not totally forgotten.

Precisely, Egypt and Libya were more concerned about finding a solution that may make it easier for the South not to break away forming an independent entity, which was more alarming to them than the threat poised by Islamic Fundamentalism to their respective countries.

Hysterical about the unity of the Sudan and the Arab World, Egypt and Libya finally tabled their own peace agenda intended to undermine the efforts of the IGAD mediation team that the two countries accused was assisting the south to secede. Hence, the birth of the Egyptian-Libyan Initiative (ELI).

The ELI, as it became known, was aimed principally at trying to reconcile the northern opposition members in the NDA with the Khartoum Regime regardless of the intensification of the war and its outcome in the South.

Designed as an attempt to bring peace to the Sudan, ELI became more of a real problem. While the northern members in the NDA were very happy and accepted it because it did not contain the self-determination that they feared would make the south break away which was the main demand of the South, the SPLA rejected it outright.

As expected Egyptian-Libyan Initiative put the SPLM in bad light as it began wavering between accepting it, and lose the South, its constituency, or rejecting it out right and lose both NDA and the necessary Egyptian-Libyan support for the solution of the Southern problem its main concern.

The silence of ELI on self determination, was not only intended to weaken IGAD resolve to make peace process work, it was aimed at effort to bring the reconciliation between the Northern Opposition and Khartoum regime so that they get back to power cheaply. Thus to secure the support of Egyptian and Libyan for their return back to power, most of the NDA members played up Arab unity agenda to the dismay of the SPLA partner.

As for Sudan two eastern neighbours, Ethiopia and Eritrea that had been very supportive of the SPLA in the IGAD mediation since 1990s, they could not, albeit for the time being, be relied upon for the success of peace process because they were ferociously at war against one another.

Until their war was over and their differences resolved, the two countries became less effective in pushing the IGAD mediation to any meaningful end as each began to court the Khartoum regime to support its own agenda.

On the other end of the scenario, Uganda, the only regional neighbour that had consistently been supportive of the IGAD mediation peace process and a backer of the SPLA agenda, at least politically and diplomatically, was too engaged in the Rwanda and the Congo civil wars. Not to mention its civil war in the north bordering South Sudan.

Though not doing business with the Khartoum regime, its involvement in the neighbouring civil wars in addition to its internal problems like fighting against Joseph Kony Lord Resistance Movement in the north, Uganda endeavours in the IGAD mediation was less effective.

16.3. IMPACT OF MULTINATIONAL INTERESTS IN SUDAN OIL

Frustrated by apparent deadlock in IGAD peace process, the European partners, particularly Germany, France and Britain, which had been effective players right from the start, were, between 1995 and 2000, becoming increasingly more interested in oil exploitation than assisting to bring the war to an end. Rather they began to do business with the NIF regime on the so-called peaceful engagement with Islam.

The Europeans could not therefore be relied upon to bring pressure to bear on the Islamic regime so as to respond positively to negotiate with the rebels in good faith. Rather it made it easier for the Islamic regime, to shun political initiative that would accelerate the peace process to a successful end.

Through skillful diplomacy, the once rogue regime managed to calm down the criticism of European diplomats in Khartoum against the regime bad human rights records and made them praise the regime for making political changes insignificant as they were.

Since it took over power in 1989 Sudan had been firmly under lock and key in solitary confinement, besieged by its neighbours, attacked by increasingly confident rebels in the South of the country, the target of United Nations sanctions for sponsoring terrorism and a part of a few friendless rogue states[2].

Despite international outcry and appeal to divest in the oil sector in the Sudan as the use of oil revenues was fuelling the war, European and foreign oil Companies continued competing over prospecting the oil to their own advantage.

Such Companies include The Chinese National Petroleum Company, the Malaysia Petronas, Lundin of Sweden, OMV of Austria and the Canadian Talisman among others.

Following the development and the exploitation of oil in Western Upper Nile Sudan became officially an oil exporter. Using the oil revenues, it bought huge heavy military arsenals from Russia and China, a move that added fuel to the protracted war.

Having acquired the high altitude Russian built antonov planes, the regime started bombarding the SPLA positions at random. These aerial attacks targeted mainly at massive destruction of the entire infrastructures in the south and the indiscriminate killing of its innocent civilians, invoked international out cry and condemnation.

The use of oil as a weapon in the war by the Khartoum at the time SPLA and allied forces were on the offensive rolling back the government armies from the areas they had previously taken from them became worrying to an extent that it demanded international intervention.

Helped by the international outcry against the indiscriminate killing of innocent civilian population and military successes in the south and in the east, the war was no longer pitting the Arab Muslim North against the Christian and animist Southern Sudan. It was now the marginalised regions against Khartoum.

The continued lack of progress in the peace process as Europeans were competing among themselves investing in the Sudan oil industry, in addition to the increasingly threat from Egypt and Libya, the hand of the Sudanese peace process began to turn full cycle back to square one.

By 2001, the war was once again being fought in the traditional manner, the south against the north, thereby making it a vicious circle.

The Sudan People Liberation Army, though it continued to remain part of the NDA, officially adopted the South as it main constituency. It was therefore natural for the people of the South Sudan, Southern Blue Nile and the Nuba Mountains, regions that had directly been affected by the war to mandate the SPLM leadership to negotiate, on their behalf, the end of the war during their respective regional conventions. This regional mandate boosted the SPLM negotiating position that has been weakened by the NDA inability to put full weight behind the SPLM in the IGAD peace process being their partner.

16.4. SIMMERING AND SCHISM IN NIF LEADERSHIP AND THE PEACE PROCESS

Besides the contradictions in the NDA discussed above, the continuous simmering and schism within the Ruling National Islamic Regime in Khartoum became another worrying factor that made the attainment of peace very elusive indeed.

Despite inherent political struggle in the top leadership since 1989, NIF was a cohesive formidable force to challenge. But even so it was not too easy to do business with them as a government that could be blamed for lack of peace or made to accept and cooperate in the peace making process.

However, divided up into alleged two hostile camps; General al Bashir's versus Dr. al Turabi's, it became extremely difficult for Sudanese public to make sense of the schism in the NIF and its government, let alone peace process and the debilitating war in the South Sudan.

But as time passed by the schism became more pronounced. Instead of working together for consolidating their power in order to resist all the forces both national and international that were working to put it out of existence, NIF leadership split into two hostile camps each threatening to do away with the other. The quest for peace became a secondary issue to both factions as discussed below.

According to NIF watchers, the Islamists schism first came into the open in 1998, when President al Bashir urged the Islamic Islamic Consultative Council (Shurra) to elect Dr. Hassan Abdalla Al Turabi to the post of Secretary General of the ruling National Congress.

This move was seen by al Turabi supporters as being intended to take their leader away from the post of Speaker of the National Assembly (Parliament) where he had constantly been accused for waging constitutional war against al Bashir. Nonetheless, in February the National Congress elected al Turabi to the post of the General Secretary.

Three days following his election to the new post, an incident occurred that accelerated the course of events in the NIF hierarchy. The death of the First Vice President al Zubeir Mohamed Saleh in a plane crush in the South gave al Bashir the necessary opportunity to hit al Turabi right on the face.

In accordance to its basic rules, the National Congress recommended three people to President al Bashir to appoint one of them to fill the vacant post of First Vice President: Dr. Hassan al Turabi, Mr.Ali Osman Mohamed Taha and Dr.Ali Al Hajj Mohamed.

Instead of appointing Dr. Al Turabi, the Khomeini of the Islamic Movement, al Bashir appointed Ali Osman Mohamed Taha to the post of the First Vice President.

Grudgingly, al Turabi accepted the post of the general secretary since that would allow him to organise the party and use it as a political mechanism which would enable it to push his Islamic programme through. He also maintained the post of Speaker of the National Assembly in order to push those programmes through constitutional processes.

In December 1998, ten leading members of the NIF leadership and Shura (Islamic Council) sent a memo to al Bashir condemning al Turabi Hegemony both in the party and in the parliament. The Ten members, Dr. Ibrahim Ahmed Omer, Dr. Ghazi Salah Eddin Atabani, Nafie Ali Nafie, Saeed al Kateeb and Hamad Ali Torein, among others, who wrote the memo, asked President al Bashir to curb al Turabi extensive powers.

Though angered by the memo, there was no immediate reaction from al Turabi and his close supporters.

Surprisingly, al Turabi in December resigned from the post of speaker of the House. Three days later, his supporters in Parliament re-elected him and he resumed his post of Speaker.

Encouraged by his re-election, al Turabi decided to declare an all out war on al Bashir inside and outside Parliament. From than on he was seen touring all the states not only as the speaker of the National Assembly but the actual power broker of the Islamic system.

During the National Congress meeting in October 1999, al Turabi mobilised his supporters and went into direct confrontation with al Bashir.

As the general secretary of the party, he dismissed all the members who wrote the memo against him from leading positions within the party. On the top of the list was Professor Ibrahim Ahmed Omer.

Concurrently inside the Assembly, al Turabi's supporters moved a motion amending the constitution. In the proposed amendment the governors of the states were to be elected directly by one-man one vote instead of appointment by the President.

In the proposed amendment the post of prime minister was revived so that all powers enjoyed hitherto by President al Bashir were transferred to the Prime Minster who could necessary be al Turabi himself or his appointee. Supporters of President al Bashir were also removed from key positions in Parliament.

On December 12, 1999, President al Bashir responded with impunity. He issued a number of presidential orders that became known as the Ramadan Resolutions. In one of the resolutions, al Turabi was stripped of all his functions both in the party and in the Parliament.

In order to get rid of the last vestiges of al Turabi influence, President al Bashir accused al Turabi for working clandestinely to instigate the army to take over power by force.

Thus in May 2000 al Bashir dissolved the Congress secretariat headed by al Turabi. Al Bashir also dissolved the Assembly, froze the amended clauses in the constitution and gave himself the absolute power to appoint the state governors.

All the attempts made by Turabi to object to al Bashir decrees through the constitutional court failed to go through.

Furthermore in July 2000, Al Bashir reinstituted the Congress secretariat and appointed Dr. Ibrahim Ahmed Omer to the post of the general secretary.

By the end of the 2000, the NIF had become, technically speaking, two factions: the National Congress chaired by Al Bashir and the Popular Congress headed by al Turabi.

In Al Bashir's Congress, Al Turabi who was the Khomeini of the Islamic Movement was replaced by Ahmed Ali Imam, the Khomeini in the Palace to advise Omer al Bashir, the Waali of the Faithfull.

According to one insider nothing goes in the Palace unless endorsed by Ali Ahmed Imam, the Khomeini. As discussed elsewhere in the book, since the split, each of the two factions had begun planning its own agenda as how to negotiate peace with the SPLA rebels.

Besides its internal squabbling, which had apparently weakened its resolve, the regime was confronted further by a much more serious blow that was bound to have long term damaging consequences for the very survival of the Islamic system in the country as discussed below.

In 1996 the Clinton Administration put pressure on the NIF to expel its financial sponsor, the Saudi millionaire Osama Bin Laden, who it accused among others as one of the sponsors of international terrorism. Sudan was then listed as a rogue state harbouring international terrorism along with Iran, Iraq, Syria, Yemen, Libya and North Korea.

Despite strong opposition from the hardliners, the regime was finally forced to expel Bin Laden from the Sudan in 1996. The exit of Bin laden from the country was a serious blow because it effectively denied the NIF as a party and as a government, the necessary financial resources it badly needed in order to hold to power and implement its Islamic agenda in spirit and letter as previously designed.

It soon became abundantly clear that the Americans would not only work to overthrow their Islamic fundamentalist regime, but wipe out its entire leadership. Reports indicated that in order to avert the impending danger at their very doorsteps, the NIF inner circles met and divided themselves up into anti-peace and pro-peace. Turabi and his team were allegedly labelled as the extremist wing of the Movement just to divert the Americans away from their track.

Although the split within the hierarchy is believed to have been staged in order to survive the looming storm that al Majless al Shura (Islamic Consultative

Council) was renamed the Conciliator Council would continue to remain a riddle, and indeed a suspect in the minds of NIF watchers.

Regardless of what others said about the split (that the two factions could not see eye to eye on major issues such as the fundamentalist Islamic agenda and the attainment of permanent peace in the south) it was apparent that something was seriously wrong in the NIF party.

The split became apparent when the al Turabi faction, the Popular Congress, contacted the SPLM and issued a Memorandum of Understanding (MOU) in Geneva. While his faction the National Congress was continuing negotiating with the SPLM at the IGAD Forum, Al Bashir accused al Turabi of high treason for contacting the rebels. Al Turabi and his top supporters were then whisked away into a maximum security prison.

Dr Turabi and his followers were released in July 2005 under the new interim constitution which stipulated that all political prisoners be released.

16.5. BUSH ADMINISTRATION PUTS SUDAN ON TOP OF ITS AGENDA

The intensification of the war, fuelled by multinational oil companies discussed above, which reached its zenith between 2000 and 2002 and resulted in untold destruction in the entire infrastructure and ethnic cleansing in the oil fields area, coincided with the change of Administration in the United States.

The U.S. presidential elections of November 2001 had brought the Republicans to office. President Bill Clinton, a Democrat, was then replaced by George Walker Bush. The change of administration in Washington also brought a new dimension in the serious quest for peace in the Sudan. President Bush made the quest for peace in Sudan, his top priority in Africa.

Bush policy on the Sudan may have been brought about apparently by the mounting pressure from religious groups and Black Caucuses who had supported him in his election campaign to the White House.

The constant activities of religious groups, appalled by continued persecution of Christians and that of Black Caucuses in the American Congress, accelerated by the continued slavery practice, following the report of the Eminent Persons Group in May 2001, may have influenced the Bush Administration into taking immediate action on the Sudan.

Five days before the September 11 attack on the World Trade Centre and the Pentagon in Washington, Bush appointed as his special peace envoy in the Sudan a former Senator from Missouri, John Danforth.

Danforth took his mission seriously. He made a number of field visits to Sudan where he met and discussed with both the government officials in Khartoum and the leaders of the SPLM/SPLA in Rumbek. He also held talks with IGAD Chairman Daniel Arap Moi and other members of peace negotiation team in Nairobi Kenya.

Back in Washington, Danforth, apparently touched by the unbearable sufferings of the people in the South Sudan, recommended that the Bush Administration should bring pressure to bear on the warring parties to speed up peace process. He later described what he saw in the south in a staement: "One of my most memorable experiences was an open air service near a bombed Episcopal Church in the small southern town of Rumbek".

After several visits to the Sudan, however, Danforth gave his first hand report to President Bush in which he expounded his vision about the possibility of speeding up the peace mediation in order to rectify the human catastrophe in South Sudan.

Danforth's other vital achievement was the conclusion of agreement signed in Geneva on January 19th 2002 between the Government of Sudan and the Sudan Peoples Liberation Movement on cessation of hostilities in the Nuba Mountains where the entire population had been threatened to near extinction by the war.

Senator Danforth acknowledged the IGAD Declaration of Principles (DOP) on which the mediation had been pegged and which recognises the right of self determination for the people of South Sudan in accordance to international law that gives right to a people to determine their social, economic and political destinies. He also recommended that the U.S. government should continue to play pivotal role in convincing the warring parties the benefits for accepting a negotiated peace settlement.

The U.S. envoy visit to the Sudan was followed by a series of high level U.S. visitors including Assistant secretary of state for African Affairs Walter Kansteiner and counter-terrorism co-ordinator Francis Taylor, who gave positive encouraging reports for accelerating the mediation process.

The convergent of domestic and foreign interests in the United States in the Sudan conflict brought about by activities of the leaders of Christians Lobby and Black Caucuses did apparently play a greater role in pushing the Bush Administration to put pressure on the warring parties to accept peace finally.

The later terrorist attacks on September 11 gave the U.S. government further incentive to take up the peace process in the Sudan more vigorously and seriously as a part of fighting international terrorism in which Sudan was on the list of countries harbouring and sponsoring terrorism.

This was followed by the U.S. Congress Sudan Peace initiative, which was later endorsed into law by the President, used as a stick to pressure the warring parties to abandon war in favour of peace.

According to the Congress Sudan Peace Initiative, the U.S. would give a sum of 100 million dollars for the development of the Southern Sudan for three successive years if it was proved that it was the government to blame for the failure to achieve peace. Likewise, U.S. government would put sanctions against the SPLA if it were blamed for the failure of the peace process. Reading the message on the wall, the warring parties began to cooperate in earnest. From then on a peaceful solution of the long elusive conflict was made possible.

It was against this background that the American strategic Centre for International Studies (SCIS) a Think Tank Studies[3] group came up with a paper spelling out how the U.S. new administration should bring the war in the Sudan to a speedy end. After a detailed study, SCIS issued recommendations and proposals as to how the Sudanese conflict could be resolved.

The SCIS document which appeared to be a revised version of the Herman Cohen Blue Print of 1990 was urging the Bush Administration to exercise leadership on the Sudan. Basically the SCIS document recommended that the new administration should:

1. Concentrate U.S. policy on the single overriding objective of ending the war in Sudan.

2. Actively join the UK, Norway and Sudan neighbouring countries in establishing an international nucleus to press forth for serious and sustained talks between Khartoum and southern opposition.

3. Build this new extra regional initiative by Sudanese government and the opposition on the Declaration of Principles as the basis for any negotiations.

4. Seek first to reach agreement on the creation of an interim arrangement "One Sudan and Two Systems Formula" that preserves the unity of the Sudan with two viable self-governing democratic regions, north and south.

5. Devise enhanced multilateral inducements and pressure that would move both sides to participate in peace negotiations in good faith.

6. Catalyse the launch of a high-level international plan for a viable self-governing south.

7. Assign top priority in negotiations in early confidence building measures.

8. Resume full operations of U.S. embassy in Khartoum with the appointment of a top level Diplomat as Ambassador to Sudan.

16.6. THE NAIVASHA COMPREHENSIVE PEACE AGREEMENT

In May 2002, intensive and extensive international pressure to bring war to a quick end brought together U.S., UK, Norway and Italy. This was the start of the serious work.

By June the Sudan Government and the Sudan People Liberation Movement were finally brought to the negotiation table at the Kenyan Town of Machakos under the auspices of the IGAD Team headed By President Moi of Kenyan.

On July 20th, following five intensive weeks of soul-searching negotiations in which emotions and tensions often ran high, the Machakos Protocol was signed. This provided a framework through which a peace deal could be hammered out.

After nearly twenty years of destructive war in which an estimated number of over two million people were killed and much property destroyed, bringing the country to the verge of total collapse as a nation state, Sudan was at last at the threshold of peace.

Despite the subsequent intensification of the war in which the SPLA took two strategic towns of Kapoeta and Torit, the two antagonistic parties were grudgingly forced to sign a temporary cease-fire, which came into effect on October 25, 2002, renewable every three months.

Through international pressure, Ali Osman Mohamed Taha, the NIF stakeholder in the NIF regime was brought together to negotiate directly with the Leader of the SPLA, Dr. John Garang de Mabior.

The presence of the two stakeholders on both sides gave hopes that the negotiations that had been dragging on for years may after all bear fruit.

Nonetheless, after dragging on for several months of serious soul searching negotiations another landmark agreement, the Security Arrangement Protocol was signed on September 25, in 2003.

On January 7, 2004, the two parties scored another positive step toward the realisation of the peace when they signed the wealth sharing Protocol that divided the two billion dollars annual oil revenue from the country oil industry on a fifty-fifty basis. Additionally, the non-oil national revenue in the south was also to be shared equally.

Following another four months of arm twisting negotiations, the two chief negotiators signed, at the Kenyan Lakeside Town of Naivasha, a historic peace accord on power sharing and the future of the Three Disputed Areas of Nuba Mountains, Southern Blue Nile and Abyei, on May 26, 2004

Prominent in the power sharing protocol was Islamic Sharia law, which almost led to the break down of peace talks. It was agreed that it should continue to prevail in the capital Khartoum provided that Christians and other non-Muslims were exempted from its codes and legislation.

It was also agreed that in the divisions of seats in the future parliament and the executive, the Ruling National Congress, would get fifty two per cent, SPLA, 28 percent, northern opposition 14 percent and the southern opposition parties six percent.

The signing ceremony was attended and witnessed by the foreign ministers of IGAD, local and international dignitaries that included U.S. Assistant Secretary of State for Africa, Charles Snyder and Hilda Johnstone, Norwegian Minister of International Development.

Commenting on the protocols on the comprehensive peace agreement in one of his speeches, the leader of the Sudan People Liberation Movement, and the architect of the creation of a new Sudan, Dr John Garang de Mabior said:

> "We suggest that the most viable solution is to have a confederation during an interim period as a form of interim unity to solve the problem of Religion and State (Sharia). This will be followed by exercise of the right of self-determination to choose between maintaining the confederate union, or full independence. In the confederate union there will be two constitutions, one for each state, and a third for the confederate Authority."

On June 6th 2004, the five protocols were put together and initialled as the Naivasha Draft Peace Agreement at the State House in Nairobi Kenya witnessed by the Kenyan President Mwai Kibaki in his capacity as Chair of the IGAD mediation countries. This was followed by another six months of painful wait.

On January 9th, 2005, amidst lavish celebrations and attended by seven heads of state, Ambassadors and diplomats accredited to Kenya, human rights and humanitarian organisations and thousands of Sudanese from both sides of the Sudan political spectrum, the Sudan's First Vice President, Ali Osman Mohamed Taha and SPLM/SPLA leader, John Garang de Mabior, finally signed a comprehensive peace agreement[4] thereby bringing to a dead end, Sudan's Painful Road to peace.

The Comprehensive Peace Agreement was witnessed by President Mwai Kibaki of Kenya whose country has hosted the peace negotiation for nearly two decades and President Yoweri Museveni of Uganda Chair of the Eastern Africa regional Grouping IGAD and Daniel Arap Moi former President of Kenya and Chair of IGAD (1993-2003). It was also witnessed by regional and international bodies; among them UN Secretary General representative Jan Pronk, US Secretary of State, Colin Powell, Amr Musa, Secretary General of the Arab League and Alpha Konari, Secretary General of African Unity.

The Agreement has now effectively brought to a final halt the five decade old ruthless war with an alarming cost of over two million people killed, four million displaced, much property destroyed and the fabric of the Sudan as a nation state threatened. There were genuine reasons indeed for Sudanese in both north and the south to celebrate except that the agreement had yet to be implemented in letter and spirit.

Asked what the guarantees were for the CPA to survive and whether the United Nations could be the best guarantor for the CPA, Garang told the author:

" The UN is never a guarantor because Southern Sudanese as aggrieved citizens are not subject to the UN Charter. In the event of any violation of the Peace Agreement by the Sudan Government, the UN could only apply sanctions against her. But that will take time before those sanctions can effectively bring pressure to bear on a rogue state. Our guarentee is organic. The fact that Southern Sudan will have its own separate army during the interim unity in addition to the integrated forces and other security forces, is the only fundamental guarantor and indeed the cornerstone for the survival of the Comprehensive Peace Agreement".

On his message to Southerners, now that the future of the south is to be decided through a referendum in accordance with the Comprehensive Peace Agreement and not through the barrel of a gun as was the case during the war, John Garang stated:

"While I am and remain a convinced believer in a united secular Sudan on a new basis, a Sudan where no stronger clever persons can cheat their weaker compatriots, I cannot impose my will on the people of South Sudan. The people of South Sudan should use the democratic processes given to them by the CPA in order to get their rights. It will be up to them to choose and decide during the refendum what each and everyone of them think or believe is the best interest for the survival of Southern Sudan. Of course the talk of total unity of the Sudan is now out of the question in face of the new realities after the signing of the Comprehensive Peace Agreement. In the referendum there will be two options for the Southerners to choose from: to maintain the interim unity establisghed by the CPA or to have a separate state of their own. My only message to them is to make up their minds now as to what their best interests are and not what others tell them. We should all make sure that the Comprehensive Peace Agreement is implemented in its entirety."

Asked about whether the two areas of the Southern Blue Nile and Southern Kordofan would not drag the south back into war if their agreement was dishonoured, Dr Garang said:

"The people of the two areas came and joined the liberation struggle in order to create a new Sudan where everybody enjoys his rights to freedom and equality and the CPA has given them just that, the right for consultation within their legislature. The two areas have been given the right to decide their future in their legislative assembly. They should try to educate their constituents that it will be in their interest not to lose sight of this right. They should not be naïve and abandon their freedom as the Eritreans did in the past when they abandoned federation with Ethiopia in favour of unity. It took the Eritreans thirty years to get back that right but with a cost of untold suffering and the loss of millions of lives. The leadership in these two areas should use their consultation rights wisely and effectively in order to achieve their final objective."

16.7 PUBLIC REACTIONS TO THE PEACE AGREEMENT

The news about the descent of peace on the Sudan unexpectedly was received with mixed reactions both in the South and the North.

Whereas the majority of the people accepted the peace deal as a means to an end, the northern political leaders, particularly the old guard politicians who have been holding power in the country and those waiting on the wing amid political bickering among themselves, were very elusive in their response. They neither accepted it, in totality, nor rejected it altogether.

But after hesitating for some time they warned that in order for the Naivasha peace to succeed, it must be inclusive. Without being specific of what they actually wanted, the northern political leaders including prominent members in the NDA demanded that there was a dire need for all and sundry to be included in the peace agreement if it was to work smoothly.

And the leader of the Umma Party, Sadig al Mahdi, in his daily public utterances said repeatedly that the Six protocols contained in the peace agreement would be endorsed by his party, but only during the constitutional conference that shall be attended by all Sudanese political parties. By implication his part would have nothing to do with the Machakos Protocols in the meantime.

Since the signing of the Machakos Protocol (2002) the guarded response from the northern politicians had sent immediate early warning signal to the Southerners. The north has yet to fully commit itself and accept the terms of the peace agreement that gives the South the right to determine its political future.

It soon became crystal clear that majority of politicians in the north would accept self-determination for the south as a process that will only bring about voluntary unity in a devolved Sudan but not that that would enable the south to secede.

According to political analysts, the elusiveness by the North about the peace agreement is indeed a worrying factor that may derail the peace agreement in the long run if nothing is done to bring the northern political parties and northern public opinion effectively on board. Until that has been done southerners have genuine reasons to worry given the bitter experiences of the past five decades in which many agreements have been put in the dustbin of history.

To harmonise the implementation of the peace agreement in spirit and letter and to make unity attractive to the south, northern leaders must first resolve their differences, take a unified stand and accept the peace agreement in totality. If not, attainment of a permanent peace in a united Sudan which is the north's choice number one just becomes a mere elusive war game; a nightmare.

As attainment of permanent peace in the Sudan will need concerted efforts and serious thinking during the interim period, it is extremely instructive to sound out what some Sudanese politicians and academics have already advanced in that direction in order to prevent the country from drifting into total abyss. Their views:

Abdullahi an Naim, a legal scholar. During the NDA convention in Asmara, Eritrea in 1995 An Naim agreed that the responsibility lay with northerners to prove to southerners that they would be secured within a united Sudan; otherwise he went on, the south should be allowed to secede.

Faroug Abu Eisa Sudan former Foreign Minister in the defunct Nimeiri regime and a leading member of the NDA. He argued, "The top priority for the National Democratic Alliance would be for all the opposition groups, to cooperate to remove the incumbent Islamic regime in Khartoum. If at the end of an interim period the north and the south found that they could not live together, then the south could secede."

Dr Taiseer Mohamed Ahmed Ali, political scientist, a key mediator between the SPLM and the Sudan Government in the 1980s, and at the time of writing a member of Sudan Alliance Forces (SAF) maintained that "secession would be the easy way out. Dr. Taiser concludes" it would be more challenging and ultimately more rewarding for each side to yield to the other in order to establish a common non religious state."

Dr Francis Mading Deng, former minister, legal scholar, diplomat and writer. In his book, *War of Visions*, Dr. Deng discusses elaborately on the subject under scrutiny. He writes. "The bitter history of broken promises and dishonoured agreements, the elusiveness of peace suggest that no option can be ruled out." But, he continues, the best guarantee for unity is for the leadership especially at the national levels; to rise above factionalism and to offer vision that would inspire a cross-sectional majority of the Sudanese people irrespective of race, ethnicity, region or religion; to identify with the nation and to stand together in collective pursuits of their common destiny. "Only through mutual recognition, respect and harmonious interaction among African and Arab populations throughout the country, can the Sudan achieve and ensure a just and lasting peace and live up to its role as a true microcosm of Africa and a dynamic link between the Continent and the Middle East.

Dr. Peter Nyot Kok, Lecturer in constitutional law. In his book, *Governance and Conflict in the Sudan,* has this to say. "The challenges which the broader Sudanese opposition should brace and is bracing itself to meet are the liquidation of the NIF-state...and more importantly, the putting in place of a system of governance based on justice, freedom, sustainable prosperity and respect for fundamental human rights.

Dr. Mansour Khalid, Former foreign minister also in the Nimeiri Regime, legal scholar, thinker and writer, states. "Sudan can still come out of its present mire, but only through a genuinely national leadership capable of achieving an unfeigned historical compromise. Such a historical event cannot be realised by mere change of guard. Nor by the decisions of one group, however earnest they may be."

Late Hilary Paul Logali, Former minister, politician and thinker in an interview with this author stated (1995), " In the light of the given circumstances of endless war and political bickering, Sudan can only survive if the Sudanese young generation of leaders supposedly now holding the reins of power in Khartoum and those waiting on the wings to take over power of the state in the event of any changes taking place, if these leaders can only draw useful lessons from the problems and the experiences of the past eventful period, it is still possible to build a strong beautiful rich and united Sudan in diversity but not in entity.

Dr. Abdel Wahab El Effendi[5] in "Southern Sudanese Dilemmas For Islam In Africa states:

"It is thus unlikely in the given circumstances that the conflicting demands of the two major camps (South and North) could eventually be satisfied within one state." El Effendi goes on,"The emergence of the Sharia laws as a key issue in the dispute only hides deeper divisions that predate and will survive the issue..." he concludes. "Illusions that a strong authoritarian modernising regime could enforce a national homogeneity in the long run must now be abandoned in the light of the emerging realities about such entities in former Yugoslavia, Bulgaria and the former Soviet Republics."

Arnold Toynbee a specialist on the Sudan was proven right on January 9, 2005. He had earlier remarked: "Sudan, a microcosm of Africa, holds Africa's destiny in her hands. It is a heavy burden that the modestly educated, inexperienced first generation Sudanese nationalists neither sought nor were equipped to shoulder. Their successors are much bolder and are more forthcoming with grand designs. One day they may hear about the virtue of modesty."

16.8. THE END-GAME

Regardless, however, of what political thinkers and academics are saying about attainment of permanent peace in the Sudan, the best way, in the opinion of this author, will be for the north to create an amicably conducive environment in the run up to the referendum. This may enable southerners to make educated choice between interim unity and secession. And Dr. Francis Deng has already explicitly emphasised in his famous Book, *War of Vision,* about the real alternative options left open for Southerners. He states.

"Besides, the song of unity in a new Sudan has been sung long enough for many, especially in the leadership (of SPLA), to enjoy the tune." Deng continues, "At the same time, however, it is becoming increasingly clear, even to the leadership of the movement that the country, far from making headway in that direction, is indeed regressing. Even if the creation of the new Sudan were possible in the long run, many observers, including black Africans, are beginning to wonder whether the massive loss of human lives, destruction of property and retardation of development are worth that long term vision. Since Southerners have always understood the position of the Movement as a pragmatic strategy to maximize support for the struggle rather than an unqualified commitment to unity, this changing perspective is welcome to them. Recent adjustments in the position of the movement, which now considers confederation and even self-determination as alternatives to a united democratic secular Sudan underscore the point."

So in a nutshell, as we start the interim period, it becomes extremely important and instructive for Sudanese to look back into the past overview about the political history of their country. They must do so and see if important lessons have been learned, lessons that could be used as catalyst for the restructuring of their country whether it shall remain united or split up into more states. If, indeed, important lessons have been learned, such lessons could guide the leadership in the South and the North and prepare them to make up their mind to accept the results of the referendum in effort to avert another relapse to long drawn out civil wars. The lessons that the north and the south should examine are enumerated here below:

(a) TO NORTHERNERS

The main stumbling block in the smooth relation between the north and the South has all along been the northern Arab Muslim self aggrandisement, the lack of political will and commitment to resolve the Southern demand for special status. This self-aggrandisement and lack of political will for change on the part of the north, if not discarded, will continue as the main cause of the country political predicament.

Indeed, the period of fifty years (1955-2005) is a long time for a nation to have grown to maturity in all aspects of national life. During those difficult years of continued civil strife, Northerners who have been holding power should have learned enough lessons from the experiences in the north-south conflict that have been characterised by broken promises and suspicions.

If leaders of successive northern regimes that took over power from the colonial administrators had learned important lessons as they moved through to face the conflict between the North and the South, those lessons could have provided them with useful guidelines and the war could have been avoided. Unfortunately the post successive regimes both democratic and military appeared to have not given thought to the issues which are enumerated here below:

First, Northerners failed to make proper prognosis and identify the real problem that had brought about the war in the first place. If they did that, they would have found out that, the country they were inheriting at independence was not a homogenous one. Therefore, a suitable form of political system and governance should have been first priority as soon as they took over power from the colonial administration.

Second, they should have learned from history that war had never solved problem of racial and ethnic nature. As such, the southern demand for a special status within a united Sudan since 1956 should have immediately been addressed thereby averting the troubles that have brought ruins to the country.

Third, Northerners should have also recognised that, writing a religious constitution and for that matter an Islamic one, could have not permitted national integration they wanted let alone national consensus necessary for the making of a nation state. A workable form of a constitution that accommodated all the existing diversities in the country could have saved them from the predicament of fighting ceaseless destructive wars.

Fourth, the North should have not taken the South for granted as a region inhabited by a misled group of people who could, with the passage of time, be won over by force of arms and thereafter, re-orient and integrate them into the Nation of Islam.

Fifth, throughout the past five decades, the political and socio-economic developments should have been distributed evenly all over the country. This aspect would have consolidated the desired national unity.

Sixth, Northerners should have realised that the intention of the south had all along been to be a part of the Sudan on equal basis.

Seventh, they should not have taken the south as an appendage that could only be given a portion of the national cake in the form of autonomy like the Addis Ababa Accord of 1972. In this respect they should have realised that the south would have liked the power of state broaden at the centre, giving various regions the right to manage their local affairs.

Eighth, the northern leaders, who have now inherited the reins of power from their predecessors, do still think the same way. Power is theirs and the south can only in time be given the crumbs that fall from their high tables, as they are not full participants in the process of forging a nation state.

Ninth, since independence, the power in the Sudan had, on and off, been revolving around northern two religious Sects: The Mirghanists and the Mahdists. And now on the stage, are the Turabists/Tahaists. Obviously the Turabists, who have all along been hiding behind the shields of the Mirghanists and the Mahdists pretending to be non-sectarian otherwise progressive, have now come out in their full colours to lead not only the north but the whole country. They are doing this instead of their previous position of manipulating things in the background, as was the case during Jaafar al Nimeiri Era. The three sheikhs: al Mirghani, 68, al Mahdi, 67 and al Turabi, 72, are not thinking that power should pass out to their young followers let alone the peripheral southern, western and eastern Sudanese. To hold the country together will demand that northerners must necessarily dispense with their sectarian leadership.

Tenth, Northerners and particularly those who have been led to believe that it is their God given privilege to keep the southerners, westerners and easterners always at bay, by giving them empty promises through continuous conjuring of tricks must now read the message on the wall. The marginalised people of the rural Sudan have now refused pariah position. They have now taken up arms to fight in order to obtain their fair share of the national cake. They would otherwise opt out of the Old Sudan.

Eleventh, Northerners must abandon their long held view where they consider the South as a cultural vacuum; hence a fertile ground for Islamic proselytization and Arabicisation.

Twelfth, they must realise that the war of a racial nature can never be won by force of arms not even by continuous conjuring of tricks in order to hold to power and maintain artificial unity.

Finally, to enable Southerners to make an unprejudiced choice in a referendum that shall be held after the interim unity, northern leaders must become less parochial but nationalistic enough and change their traditional attitudes and mentality that have been the basic cause of disharmony and predicament. But as the traditional Islamic parties continued to remain in control of the affairs of thecountry, such abrupt and drastic change is unlikely.

(b) TO SOUTHERNERS

Emerging from the protracted destructive war, handicapped by generations of hardships and scarce opportunities for education and socio-economic development, Southerners have been stating their case for equality of treatment from a position of disadvantage. Here is now golden opportunity to state their case for equal treatment through democratic processes. To do that Southerners must take note of the following:

First, they should now realise that, South Sudan has now graduated from their previous weaker position in which they have been fighting to separate out rightly through armed struggle, to that of giving the unity a chance and to get their rights through peaceful and democratic processes.

Second, during the interim unity Southerners must genuinely and objectively try to jointly own the Sudan with the Northerners seriously and on new basis and for mutual benefit. Here is a golden opportunity for them to put the northerners to test by acting as equal partners in the history that is being made.

Third, Southerners must also realise that the great nation-states of the world today were founded on the ruins left behind by racial, ethnic and religious wars. Could Sudan be one of them!

Fourth, Southerners should also take note of the existance of the poverty-stricken black majority, that has recently risen in soldarity against all forms of injustice, as opposed to the rich Arab Muslim minority. Hence there is now a chance more than ever before in favour of black majority rule in a decentralised Sudan.

Fifth, Southerners must further recognise that during the interim period, the conflict will no longer be between the geographic north and the traditional south. It will be between those who have continuously been locked out of power, the people of the long neglected rural Sudan, vis a vis those who would like to perpetually enjoy the power they had benefited from since independence; the urban dwellers of the central and the geographic northern Sudan.

Sixth, Southerners must take serious note that with the Darfur Region now up in arms and the east ill at ease, a new threat is already at the doorsteps of the Arab North. Give them only the rope and they will hang themselves.

Seventh, needless to remind Southerners that the enemy from within, throughout the five decades of war, has all along been the northern merchant class—*the jalaba*—living in the south. They have done what they could to frustrate the Southerners' age long demand to have a separate state of their own. They have secretly reported potential leaders to the army barracks and they were immediately liquidated and thousands of southern nationalist and patriotic politicians have perished in that way; branded as separatists or rebels.

Eighth, during the interim period, the northern merchant class will still dominate the private sector in the South. Using all its previous skills the northern merchant class will work relentlessly to destroy the budding potential southern businesses. To avoid this happening to the Government of Southern Sudan must make the south economically viable by promoting private enterprises and encouraging cooperative movements and the establishment of public corporations. This should be the top of its priorities as the way to compete with the northern merchant class.

Ninth, to enable the internal displaced people, the diaspora and the refugee communities to come home as soon as possible the Government of South Sudan must make Southern Sudan attractive. To do this the GOSS must provide adequate health and education services and address any weakness and vulnerability that might make a Southerner prone to bribery, political blackmail and social manipulation, as happened in the past. Failing to do this will discourage these communities from going home; a move that will negatively affect the results of the referendum in six years time in favour of a free South Sudan.

Tenth, in order to avoid disillusionment and loss of confidence in the system, so that Southerners feel free vote in favour of an independent country of their own in the anticipated referendum without prejudice and frustration, the GOSS must provide for the population, good governance, food security, adequate shelters, maximum employment free from discrimination, guaranteed transparency in public administration, fair land distribution and vocational training for skilled workers during the interim unity period. The GOSS must make the system work. Making the South attractive will mean one thing: the entire population of South Sudan will make an unprejudiced choice when they finally vote in the referendum in 2011.

16.9. FINAL NOTE

TO SOUTHERNERS: They should stop being vague about what they stand for. This is their last chance to have a state of their own. They must now begin in earnest to make up their mind and decide on one of the two options offered to them by the Comprehensive Peace Agreement in the referendum in 2011: a united confederate democratic secular New Sudan or an independent southern African state.

TO NORTHERNERS: This is their only chance to win the south. They must stop their time-honoured tradition of using deceptive methods of maintaining artificial unity for their own interests. They must seriously take note that the continued existence of Sudan as *a nation state* in its present form will continue to be at risk. Unless the northern political leadership realises the looming danger and comes down to earth and accepts the reality of the situation—unless they can genuinely be adaptable and humbly embrace the South African experiment and experience when the white minority regime willingly discarded apartheid in favour of the black majority rule—unless they can readily evolve the country into confederate states before it is too late—the end result will be anyone's guess. The Sudan, this African giant could splinter into several fully fledged independent states. Unfortunately all indications are that it may already be moving in that direction.

EPILOGUE AND EULOGY
JOHN GARANG: THE REBEL LEADER TURNED STATESMAN

THE SETTING

After signing the Comprehensive Peace Agreement in Kenya between the government of Sudan and the Sudan People Liberation Movement which ended Africa's longest civil strife, it was expected that the peace deal that had taken so much to achieve would have been implemented in spirit and letter and with immediate effect.

But as it turned out its implementation became so sticky to the extent that international communities began to express fears that it might unravel. They therefore stressed the need to bring extra effort and pressure to bear on the government of the Sudan, the chief player, and the new SPLM leadership to live up to their commitment to the CPA.

As described in the Book, the government of the Sudan and its former foe, the SPLM/SPLA, were grudgingly ushered into the peace process because the war they had been fighting for two decades would not be won through the barrel of a gun.

There was therefore a dire need for them to accept peace and to move the country towards sustainable socio-economic development that had been held up by the war for so long.

The Islamic regime in particular was persuaded to abandon its Islamic path and accept the principle of creating a Sudan that would accommodate all its diversities.

The SPLM, the other player, was also pressured into accepting the peace deal given the fact that the war had brought much destruction to the entire Southern Sudan causing untold suffering to its people. The SPLM was thus forced to become pragmatic and to readjust its regional policies and strategies in favour of the national one.

But to implement fully the articles of the peace agreement in spirit and letter was going to be a very difficult task.

The first difficulty was how to put pressure on the Khartoum Islamic regime, which had earned billions of dollars from the Islamic world over the years to spread Islam, not only to Southern Sudan but deep into the heart of Africa. Persuading them to implement the peace agreement became another tortuous war that needed hard work. This demanded that the peace mediators and international communities exert extra efforts to convince the government that implementing the peace deal was in its own interest. They also needed to convince all the Islamic hard liners in the North of the country in particular, and the Arab Islamic World in general, that they had a lot to lose if they did not accept the changes brought about by the CPA.

For the Comprehensive Peace Agreement to be successfully implemented, the first thing the Sudan Government and the SPLM needed to do was to start establishing political mechanisms and fora through which the two parties could meet and discuss problems arising. These mechanisms were to include the formation of various institutions and commissions provided in the CPA six protocols. The top priority, in this connection, was the urgent creation of political and civil institutions in the South where all infrastructures had been destroyed by the war. This would speed up the repatriation, resettlement and rehabilitation of the people who were internally displaced by war as well as refugees coming from neighbouring countries. Adequate funding was therefore much needed from the donor countries and other willing non-governmental international communities. These efforts would help the returnees allowing them to resettle in their original homes.

The second priority was to sustain and implement the comprehensive cease fire. This would involve the disengagement and demobilisation of the former combatants and organising them into a peacetime national army before the end of the six months of the pre-interim period.

The third priority, characterising the actual implementation of the CPA, was the writing of the interim constitutions for the whole country and for the government of South Sudan.

Unfortunately six months of the pre-interim period came and went with little to show that the two parties to the agreement were serious. For instance, apart from the formation of the presidency and the enactment of the interim constitution into the interim law of the land, the political Commission that would oversee the comprehensive cease-fire between Khartoum troops and the SPLA forces was not even set up. This mechanism was meant to provide a forum through which the two parties could meet and assess how far the agreement was being implemented. This simple lack of progress was indeed worrying as it signalled lack of political will and invited speculation that the CPA might not be implemented at all.

Between April and May however, the two parties took some bold steps when they set up committees to write the interim constitution. But even so it took much time and energy before the draft constitution was ready for endorsement by the Sudan National Assembly and the SPLM Liberation Council.

It was only in the last week of June that the National Assembly and the

SPLM Liberation Council approved the interim constitution paving the way for the formation of the three man presidency just in time to swear in its three members on July 9, 2005.

On July 8, Garang arrived in Khartoum and was given a rapturous welcome by an estimated crowd of six million Sudanese of all social and political backgrounds and religious persuasions. Unfortunately he could not address these enthusiastic citizens who had come to welcome him as an apostle of peace. The loudspeakers had apparently been damaged by a 'system' that may not have liked a former rebel leader to address such an unprecedentedly large gathering. Garang climbed on the roof of the lodge where he could only respond to the standing ovation of the crowd by throwing kisses in the air. This situation was most embarrassing to the man who had expected to be welcomed by the other partner of the Peace Agreement. Even when Garang later managed to address the nation during the swearing in ceremony on July 9 his speech was given poor coverage by the nation's television. The public listened to his speech without seeing his face because the camera was not properly focussed on him.

Before the arrival of the SPLM/SPLA leader in Khartoum it was expected that an SPLA advance contingent of 1,500 officers and men would be brought to Khartoum on July 5 for confidence building purposes in accordance to the CPA.

But when this contingent began moving on its way from Eastern Sudan to Khartoum, armed with 200 tanks and other essential military equipment they were met with rebuff.

The Sudanese Army General Headquarters gave counter instruction that the SPLA detachment should not continue advancing toward Khartoum by land. Because moving such a well supplied force by land would make it appear like an invading force. This was unacceptable to the army which had been fighting those rebels. The SPLA officials were advised in no uncertain terms that they should bring their forces to Khartoum by air carrying with them only light weapons.

This had been a prerequisite designed to encourage the SPLM delegation to come to Khartoum. Stopping the SPLA detachment created a crisis between the government and the SPLM. Unless that crisis was resolved, the SPLM Chairman would not come to Khartoum on time to be sworn in as a member of the Presidency on July 9, 2005, a move that would be the start of the interim period.

This crisis was averted when it was decided that the question of SPLA troops would be looked into after July 9 when the interim period has started. This would later be handled by Dr Garang and Ali Osman, the two chiefs of the Naivasha Peace Negotiation Team. In the meantime the SPLA Khartoum detachment should remain stationed in Gedarif in Eastern Sudan till further notice.

Another important event, which could also have caused a crisis, as the country started its interim period, was the Abyei boundary Issue. On July 13, 2005, the Abyei Boundary Commission (ABC) of international experts presented its finding to the nascent presidency. According to the CPA, the ABC finding would be final and binding. The Misseriyia, one of the parties to the border dispute, rejected the ABC report outright.

Instead of accepting the report in a spirit of goodwill, President Bashir and his Vice President Ali Osman were quoted as saying that the ABC report would not be acceptable to the Misseryia. They alleged that the experts did not adhere to its terms of reference when writing the report. This was not true. According to the Commission's terms of reference, the report once presented would be final and binding on the two parties to the Comprehensive Peace Agreement.

However, Dr John Garang, the third member of the presidency, did not have time to respond to Bashir, Ali Osman or the Misseryia concerning their negative reaction to the report. His only remark was that the Abyei Area must not be turned into an area of ethnic tension and a hot spot for confrontation as that would wreck the Peace Agreement. Rather the two neighbours, the Dinka Ngok and the Misseryia Homr people, should be encouraged to coexist peacefully.

International peace monitors and keepers had not arrived before the start of the interim period in July 2005. More worrying was the fact that from January 9 to the start of the interim period the salaries of the former rebels had not yet reached them.

As discussed above, lack of progress led the International Crisis Group based in Brussels to send a stern warning that pressure should be brought to bear on the government of Khartoum to start implementing the Comprehensive Peace Agreement.

Although some articles of the CPA had been implemented, such as the enactment into law of the interim constitution and the appointment of John Garang as First Vice President and President of the Southern Sudan, ninety per cent of the CPA had still not been implemented by July 9.

However in order to show his nation and the world that things were going smoothly, President Omar al Bashir using his new power given him by the new interim constitution dissolved the national government and parliament and set up a caretaker administration. He also dissolved state governments and state assemblies.

Reciprocating, while still in Khartoum, John Garang dissolved all the SPLM institutions including the Liberation Council, the National Executive

Committee and the SPLA staff command structures. Garang went further by appointing a Southern Sudan caretaker government headed by nine of his most senior commanders. He also appointed his long time deputy Commander Salva Kiir Mayardit as Deputy President of the government of South Sudan.

While some commanders welcomed Garang's action in Khartoum as a first positive step in the right direction toward the implementation of the much expected peace agreement, a sizeable number of his commanders in Rumbek received the news with utter anger and outrage. They thought that Garang should have come back to the seat of his government in the south and consulted his aides before forming his government. Rumours began to abound particularly as the northern press began signalling that there were already rifts in the SPLM/SPLA and that there was rebellion against Garang's latest action.

Apparently worried about these rumours, Garang left for Rumbek partly to explain his action in Khartoum and partly to start consultations with his senior commanders and aides on the formation of the government of Southern Sudan. He would also name members to join the interim government of national unity administration in Khartoum as provided for in the Comprehensive Peace Agreement.

After a few days in Rumbek where he held a public rally and explained his plan of action, he went to New Site, the former administrative headquarters of the Guerrilla Army just on the Sudan Uganda border. There he was apparently expected to put the finishing touches to his government to be announced on August 9.

On Friday, July 29 John Garang left suddenly for Kampala to meet Uganda's President Yoweri Museveni, apparently to thank him for having given sanctuary to the SPLA throughout the armed struggle in Southern Sudan. He may have gone to meet the Ugandan President to discuss the continued existence of the Ugandan northern rebels of the Lord's Resistance Movement in the South Sudan. This is likely bearing in mind the comment made by the International Crisis Group about Garang's important role in resolving issues in the region. According to the International Crisis Group, Garang was not only the key to ending the war between Khartoum and Darfur and Eastern Sudanese rebels, he was also key to a strategy of ending the nineteen year old insurgency of the Ugandan Lord's Resistance Army which continued to use southern Sudan as a rear base for launching attacks in northern Uganda. Through his personal relationships he played an important role in preventing a renewed war between Eritrea and Ethiopia.

It was in this light that on July 30 after meeting Museveni, Garang left Entebe Airport at 4.45 pm aboard a Ugandan presidential helicopter on his fateful journey back to base at New Site in Southern Sudan.

On July 31 his helicopter was reported missing. On Monday August

1, 2005 it was reported that Garang and 13 others had died in a helicopter crash on the Sudan Uganda border. The whole world was stunned to hear of the sudden tragic death of Dr John Garang, the person on whom all hopes about the survival of the Comprehensive Peace Agreement and its successful implementation were pinned.

The news of his death was received with utter devastation as it sent shock waves across the country both in the southern cities and in the capital Khartoum when angry Southerners attacked Northerners and their properties. The Northerners responded and in the street violence that ensued several hundreds of innocent people were killed or missing and large unknown numbers wounded. The violence thus provoked further fears that the peace deal might unravel in the absence of a charismatic leader to guide the people through during the inherent turbulent times ahead.

According to international press reports, the death of such a strong charismatic leader was a big blow to peace as it left a immediate vacuum at the heart of the Southern Sudan leadership that would take time to fill as it faced an uncertain future.

On August 6, 2005, John Garang's remains and those who died with him in the tragic incident were interred at a site near the Legislative Assembly in Juba. Heads of state and governments attending Garang's funeral included: President Thabo Mbeki of South Africa, President Mwai Kibaki of Kenya, former Kenyan President Daniel arap Moi under whose auspices the first part of the peace process was negotiated, President Paul Kagame of Rwanda, Prime Minister of Ethiopia, Deputy President of Nigeria. Amr Mousa of the Arab League and representatives of many countries including the UN and the IGAD Troika countries (USA, UK and Norway) also attended the funeral.

In the funeral procession, wailing, praying and grieving Southern Sudanese thronged to Garang's tomb in their thousands, as they bade farewell to their fallen leader. The man who had led them through two decades of war before he made a landmark peace deal with Khartoum, which gave them the right to determine their political future.

As Garang's leading role in Sudan's tortuous journey to peace is adequately described in the book, only a brief account about the colourful life he led and the popular reaction to his tragic death is needed. This will enable readers to judge for themselves what the future holds for Sudan after the man it was thought would hold its people together, at least for six more years, is no longer on the scene.

EULOGY TO GARANG 1945-2005

This tragedy ocurred just three weeks after his triumphant return to Khartoum where he was sworn in as First Vice President of the Republic and just six months after he skilfully negotiated a peace package that had promised independence for his long impoverished war ravaged people of Southern Sudan and other marginalised areas in the Sudan. He was the undisputed energetic visionary leader who moulded a huge guerrilla army of volunteers into a formidable political military machine that withstood the prowess of the mighty fanatic Islamic fundamentalist Army for 22 years. He was the dynamic leader that many Sudanese took as a symbol of national unity and described by others as a green hope for the marginalised people of his country. John Garang de Mabior met his fate, in violent mysterious circumstances yet to be uncovered, just as he was returning from Uganda to his home base in Southern Sudan to put together a government for his people who had never tasted the fruits of peace and good governance. His charismatic leadership will be missed by all.

In the words of SPLM Secretary UK Chapter, Comas Wani, John Garang, was an unassuming man who knew his roots, an entertainer with a good sense of humour who would keep his listeners engaged for hours in an effort to persuade them. A man of extraordinary energy and strength of character and an excellent communicator who will be missed by Southern Sudan, the Sudan and the World at large.

Born to a farmer, Mabior Atem Aruai, Garang was born and raised in Kongor District, in Jonglei Province in Upper Nile Region. He went to Tonj Primary School in 1954 and Bussere Intermediate School, both in Bahr al Ghazal Province, in 1958. He was then accepted in the first year at Rumbek Secondary School in 1962.

When the schools in the South closed down indefinitely because of student unrest that heralded the start of the Anya Nya war in 1963, John Garang went to Northern Sudan where he worked for some time as a messenger as he waited for the reopening of schools in South Sudan. He expected to go back to Rumbek in order to complete his secondary education. But as fate would have it, schools in the South never opened as the war escalated.

Young Garang, like thousands of other Southern Sudanese school children of his age, had the choice of either joining the increasing Anya Nya insurgency in the South or crossing over the border into exile. Garang therefore left Northern Sudan and trekked all the way to Uganda. But finding Uganda unsympathetic to the cause of Southern Sudan, Garang proceeded to Kenya. Even there, life became so difficult to the extent that he was forced to work at a restaurant in Nairobi to get money, for his onward journey into the world in search of security and further studies. In Kenya at the dawn of independence the young republic did not want to alienate the Sudan government by helping Sudanese refugees, and for other reasons beyond the scope of this book, Garang found life extremely intolerable.

After earning sufficient money for his journey, Garang travelled to Tanzania where his future political career as a revolutionary leader was shaped.

In Tanzania, Garang de Mabior Atem was able to resume his secondary school studies. He soon completed his secondary school education along with Yoweri Museveni, Paul Kagami and Laurent Kabila who both became revolutionary leaders and presidents in their respective countries.

It was during his studies in Tanzania that Garang de Mabior Atem became seasoned with revolutionary fervour and took Mwalimu Julius Nyerere as his mentor and icon for success.

It was in Tanzania that Garang took the brand of African socialism seriously and became a Pan-African socialist whose goal was to transform life in rural Africa as a whole. It was also in Tanzania that Garang's vision about his country and the world at large was apparently widened as he continued to search for academic excellence.

It was there too that Garang's vision as how best to address the problem of South Sudan in relation to the North Sudan was developed. According to him the so called problem of Southern Sudan could be resolved but only in conjunction with the struggle of the other marginalisied people of the Sudan. As his long time friend Ugandan President Yoweri Museveni said during the funeral service: "Vision is a scarce commodity in Africa and Garang was a visionary Pan-Africanist leader who could not compromise the destiny of his country the Sudan for anything". Museveni added that he met Garang for the first time in 1967 and during their first encounter, Garang had told him that the Sudanese conflict was not about the Northern Sudan versus the Southern Sudan. Rather the struggle was about religious bigotry and sectarianism. Even the Black Muslims were discriminated in the Arab dominated North, he confided to Museveni.

It will be most appropriate at this juncture to point at out that as a teenager Garang's political perceptions might also have been influenced by the uncertainty of the politics of liberation of Southern Sudan as far back as 1965 when politics took firm shape in South Sudan.

It was apparently in that light that on reaching political maturity Garang may have conceived his political agenda as how best to approach the solution of Southern Sudan based on the previous approaches made earlier by Southern Sudanese leaders of the time.

It must be recalled that after the failure to reach a negotiated peace settlement between the North and the South at the Round Table Conference in 1965 for instance, four shades of opinion had emerged about Southern Sudan's future relations with the Arab Muslim north.

An extreme shade of opinion was held by Aggrey Jaden, Joseph Oduho, Dominic Muorwel Malou, Marco Rume and Elia Lupe, and other leaders of SANU Party then operating outside the country, who stood for total independence for Southern Sudan, which could be achieved through protracted armed struggle.

At the other extreme was Santino Deng Teng of the Sudan Unity Party, advocating local government for the South within a united Sudan.

In the middle ground were two moderate views. The leaders of the Southern Front Party Clement Mboro, Gordon Muortat, Hilary Paul Logali, Abel Alier and Bona Malwal among others were advocating self determination as an inalienable right that might be exercised by the people of Southern Sudan. The leaders of the Southern Front held that Southerners were not involved in the politics which led to the so-called independence of the Sudan from the colonial power in 1956. Therefore Southerners must be given the right to determine their political future in a referendum, to be carried out in that region and supervised and monitored internationally.

The other moderate vision advocated by William Deng Nhial leader of the SANU Party inside the country was to broaden the power base in Khartoum in a federal set up which would give more power to the regions leaving less at the centre.

Deng's view immediately gave rise to the formation of an African regional grouping that became known as the Congress for New forces. The Congress was composed of SANU, Darfur Front, the Beja Congress and the General Union of Nuba Mountains. The South, in Deng's view, could enjoy a federal status within a united secular Sudan.

It was perhaps from these experiences that Garang, on reaching political maturity, combined the two moderate views: Deng's Congress for New Forces and the Southern Front's self-determination into the vision of creating a new Sudan that would accommodate other marginalised areas.

Seasoned with vision about the future of his country and desirous of pursuing his further studies, Garang left Tanzania for the United States where he worked and studied. He later went to Grinell College at Iowa. After obtaining his first degree Garang came back to Southern Sudan and joined the Anya Nya Movement in 1970 at the time the insurgency was growing in strength and numbers.

After intensive training, along with forty other young men, by Israelis military experts about guerrilla warfare, Garang was commissioned as an officer with the rank of Captain. Having received a huge amount of military hardware from Israel following the Arab Israeli Six Day War, the Anya Nya movement and its political wing, the Southern Sudan Liberation Movement became a formidable fighting force.

It was at this juncture that the May regime, that had taken over power in a military coup d'etat, decided to solve the southern problem. Contacts were made in an effort to reach an agreement with Anya Nya rebels.

On hearing about peace overtures, in January 1972, Garang wrote a letter to his Commander Joseph Lagu advising him not to enter into any peace negotiation with the military regime until the Anya Nya movement had become strong enough in the battlefield. The Anya could then negotiate with the Sudan government in the position of strength.

As we all know Garang's advice was not heeded. Instead, more efforts were exerted and the Addis Ababa Accord was signed on February 27, 1972.

Unable to prevent the peace agreement, Garang and the Anya Nya group of officers mostly from Bahr al Ghazal described in Chapters 1 and 2, decided to be absorbed into the Sudan Army. They would wait till such time that they could launch the people's revolution. Garang and his group of conspirators were soon detected and plans were made as to how Garang could be kept away from the country. In 1974 Garang was transferred away from Bussere in Bahr al Ghazal where he was a threat to Khartoum. To remove him from the scene, where he would have great influence on the former Any Nya personnel in the Sudanese Army that might have led to the resumption of war that had just ended, Garang was given a scholarship to Fort Genning, Georgia in the United States where he later graduated with a Master's Degree in Military Science.

Upon his return to Sudan which coincided with political turmoil in the South (created by border and Jonglei crises described in Chapters 2 and 3 of this book) the security reported that Garang was having intimate interaction with most of the former Anya Nya absorbed forces.

So in 1977, Garang was given a further scholarship to Iowa state University where he obtained his Doctor's Degree in agricultural economy in 1981. The subject of his thesis was "The economics of the Jonglei Canal Project".

Back home, Dr John Garang, now promoted to the rank of Colonel, was posted to the Army General Headquarters in Khartoum and appointed to the position of Deputy Director for Military Research. He was at the same time teaching agricultural economy at the University of Khartoum's Faculty of Agriculture. It was during this time (1981 to 1983) that John Garang planned the launch of his revolution (Chapter 3).

While planning his revolution in Khartoum, Garang's main point of contact with former Anya Nya absorbed forces in the south (Battalions 104, 105, 110, 111, 116 and 117) was a young Captain, Salva Kiir Mayardit who became in the later years the SPLA/SPLM's most loved and respected strongman. It was those Battalions (as discussed in Chapters 2 and 3) that later ignited the famous Bor and Ayod uprisings and which formed the bulk of the Sudan People Liberation Army.

During the initial formation of the first SPLM/SPLA politico-military high command in 1983, Salva Kiir Mayardit was named Deputy Chief of Staff for security and operations, a post he held until he became Chief of Staff upon the exit of Kerubino, Nyuon and Arok.

During the most difficult days, when the SPL/SPLM was shaken almost to its foundation following the split in 1991, Kiir held close to Garang from beginning to end. Following the tragic death of his leader Kiir became the SPLM/SPLA's number one man. A strong professional military man, following in the footsteps of his charismatic leader, the man he had fought side by side with for twenty-two years, Kiir is expected to steer South Sudan successfully through the turbulent storms ahead.

POPULAR REACTIONS TO GARANG'S TRAGIC DEATH

*Deputy President of Southern Sudan, Salva Kiir Mayardit on hearing the tragic news about the death of his leader said: "South Sudan and indeed the whole of Sudan has lost its beloved son, Dr John Garang de Mabior, the first vice president of the Republic and President of South Sudan. I take this opportunity to assure the Southern Sudanese in particular and the Sudanese in general that we in the SPLM/SPLA leadership will continue the vision and the objectives of the movement that John Garang de Mabior has moulded and articulated and hoped to implement. He called upon all members of the SPLM and the entire Sudanese nation to remain calm and vigilant. Southern Sudanese community leaders were also quick to call for his legacy to be continued."

*The UK Chapter stated: "Dr John Garang de Mabior was a great visionary leader who stood for what he believed in, a fighter and a great peacemaker who died on a mission of peace. We urge all our people to unite, at this difficult time and work towards reconciliation and forgiveness. Let us work together to implement the Comprehensive Peace Agreement as it is the only real gift we could offer to honour the memory of the late leader."

*UN Secretary General, Kofi Annan described Garang as larger than life and rather charismatic. Annan called his inauguration in Khartoum as Vice President of the Sudan three weeks before his death, a moment of hope saying: "Here is a man who has lived and fought for peace and one united Sudan. And just as he was on the verge of achieving what he had lived and fought for, he is taken away from us. What is important is that the Sudanese continue with the process of reconciliation and the process of peace. I hope his legacy will stay with all the people of Sudan. They should make peace irreversible. Let us move ahead with the peace process in the north and the south, in the west and in the east. We should all do whatever we can to ensure that it does not unravel."

*African Union Commission Chief, Alpha Aumar Konare warned: "Garang's death comes at the critical time for the north-south peace agreement. In this short three weeks, he has indeed taken remarkably bold decisions to restructure the SPLM and no less bold steps to reach out for reconciliation and cooperation with his erstwhile adversaries. While Dr Garang has left behind a great and enduring legacy, his death has also left an enormous vacuum amidst efforts to fundamentally reconstruct the social, political and economic landscape of the Sudan."

*Peter Moszynsky, a veteran journalist and a friend of Sudan explained: "The power vacuum left by the death of Dr Garang goes right up to the highest levels of Government in the South and is one that Salva Kiir (Garang's successor) is unlikely to overcome by merely taking up the reins of his former comrade in arms. One reason that everyone is so nervous is because Garang was one of the few southern leaders who actually believed in Sudan's unity and whatever the exact composition of the new interim leadership, it is clearly likely to be far more separatist in character. As Sudan's tortuous road to peace hits one of the biggest road blocks it has encountered (death of Garang, the peace driver) the country faces an unknown future."

*John Prendergast, special adviser to the President of the International Crisis Group writing in Nairobi for the Wall Street Journal, August 5 stated: "The reverberations from the death of John Garang will be felt throughout the Horn of Africa for decades to come. A Soviet backed Marxist rebel leader 20 years ago, Mr Garang became a pragmatic peacemaker who charmed Western statesmen as easily as he navigated village meetings under southern Sudanese acacia trees." Prendergast described the helicopter crash that killed Garang as a cruel twist of fate and that Garang's passing puts at risk peace efforts in the entire region.

*Jacob Jeiel Akol, a veteran Sudanese journalist stated: "Garang's death will also hit very hard the marginalised peoples of the Nuba Mountains and southern Blue Niles whose armed forces have been part of the SPLM/SPLA all the 22 years of armed struggle against Khartoum based governments. They saw him as a symbol for the oppressed, now in leadership in Khartoum for the first time. His absence from the newly formed Presidency, heading the government of national unity, will be felt by those marginalised peoples of Darfur and eastern Sudan, the man who could articulate their dream of a new Sudan. And for the lost boys and lost girls (in North America), John Garang has remained in their minds the 'invincible liberator of the Motherland' and it is heart rendering to read their weeping words on the website. To them he has become a legend, no longer an ordinary man to be pronounced dead by mortals."

*Finally it would be instructive to read two quotations from the speeches John Garang gave at the signing ceremony of the Southern Sudanese peace deal in Nairobi and at the ceremony when he took his oath of office as Sudan's First Vice President and President of Southern Sudan in Khartoum...The two quotations are expected to give the reader a glimpse of the true character of the man who had sacrificed so much in order to achieve peace and dignity and freedom for his people and who fate had taken away before he could see through the fruits of its successful implementation.

"Peace will bless us once more with hearing the happy giggling of children and the enchanting ululation of women who are excited in happiness for one reason or another." January 9, 2005.

"My presence here today in Khartoum and coming with my family including my little daughter Atong, is a true signal that the war is over." July 9, 2005.

BIBLIOGRAPHY

Most of the information contained in this book was obtained through personal interviews with chief players in the Sudanese South North conflict. And also from personal experiences as a participant and an observer of the two Liberation Movements in the Southern Sudan in the first war Anya Nya war (1962 to 1972), Regional Self Rule (1972-1982) and in the second SPLA war (1982-2002). This information is constantly referred to in the book as well as indicated in the end notes which follow.

But to understand fully the story of the two Movements and what actually went wrong, it would be advisable for the reader to read the following selected works from most distinguished experienced people from whom I have learned much of the knowledge that has made the book what it is. The selected references are:

*Alier, Abel, Southern Sudan, Too Many Agreements Dishonoured. (ITHACA PRESS, EXETER 1990)

*Albino, Oliver Battali, The Sudan, A Southern View Point (London: Oxford University Press)

*Beshir, Mohamed Omer, Southern Sudan Regionalism and Religion, (Khartoum, Graduate College, University of Khartoum, 1984) The Southern Sudan, Background to Conflict (London C Hurst 1968)

*Daly M.W., and A.A. Sikaibga (eds) Civil War in the Sudan (London, British Academic Press 1993)

*Deng, Francis Mading, War of Visions (Washington DC, The Brookings Institution, 1995)

*Johnson, Douglas, H. The Root Causes of Sudan's Civil War, (International African Institute/ James Curry, 73 Botley Road Oxford, Fountain Publishers, Kampala, Indiana University Press, Bloomington, 2003; the Southern Sudan and South—North issues)

*Khalid, Dr Mansour, (The Government They Deserve, (Kegan Paul International, London and New York)

*Khalid, Dr Mansour, John Garang Speaks, Nimeiri and the Revolution of Dismay (London Kegan Paul International, 1986)

*Kasfir, N. Southern Sudanese Politics since the Addis Ababa Agreement (African Affairs 76 (1977)

*Kok, Peter Nyot Governance and Conflict in Sudan (Deutsches Orient Institut, Hamburg-Hamburg Dt. Orient-Inst. 1996)

*Kulisika, Simon Hajj, The Southern Sudan.

*Leek Mawut, Why Back to Arms (Khartoum University Press)

*Lesch, Ann Mosely; Sudan, Contested National Identities

*Madut-Arop, Arop, Addis Ababa Agreement, A Ten Year Experiment in Coexistence in Sudan, What went Wrong; City University of London MA Thesis 1985)

*Malwal, Bona, People and Power in Sudan, (London Ithaca Press 1981) The Sudan; the Second Challenge to Nationahood ((NY Thorton Books1985) Mom, Kou Arou and B.Yongo-Bure, North-South Relations in Sudan, Since the Addis Ababa Agreement (Khartoum Institute of African and Asian Studies, University of Khartoum 1988)

*Nyaba, Peter Adwok The Politics of Liberation in South Sudan Fountain Publishers, First Edition 1997, second edition 2000.

*Nyibil, Thaan, Experiences in the Resistance Movement, Vantage Press New York. Los Angeles 1990

*Oduho, Joseph H. and Deng, William, The Problem of Southern Sudan (London: Oxford University Press for the Institute of Race Relation) 1963)

*Said, Beshir Mohamed, The Sudan, Crossroads of Africa, (London: Bodley Head 1985)

*Wai, D A, The African-Arab Conflict In the Sudan, (NY Africana Publishing Co., 1981)

*Wakoson, Elias Nyamlell, The Politics of Southern Self Government, 1972-1983), The Southern Sudan, the Political Leadership of the Anya Nya Movement, (H.Dickinson ed 1980)

*Woodward, Professor Peter, Badal, Hardallo, Sudan Since Independence (Aldershot; Gower); and Sudan after Nimeiri (Routledge 1991)

REFERENCES AND NOTES

CHAPTER 1

[1] In Bahr al Ghazal, the Districts of: Aweil, Gogrial, Wau, Raga and Tonj, a part of Rumbek and Yirol were under the Roman Catholic Church influence. Part of Rumbek and Yirol were under the Church Missionary Societies. In Equatoria; the District of Tombura and a part of Yambio were Roman Catholic. Half of Yambio, Maridi and Mundri were under the Church Missionary Society. The District of Torit and Kapoeta were Roman Catholic. Yei was shared by the Catholic and CMS. In Upper Nile the Catholic Church, controlled Western Upper Nile(Bentiu) and Kodok. The CMS controlled Bor, Akobo and Pibor and Renk. While the Presbyterian controlled eastern Upper Niles

[2] William Deng was the Secretary General of the Sudan African National Union (SANU) since its inception in 1962. He was on a tour in Europe in 1964 when a convention was held and was dismissed from his post. Deng apparently took his dismissal as humiliation. However following the restoration of the second democratic experiment in 1964 Deng thought it was better to work inside the country. He was assassinated while contesting elections in the South in 1968

[3] Owiny Kibul means in Acholi language beating the drum to alert people for war

[4] Bahr al Ghazal command post at Teet Adol was Muortat political backyard, hence the fear that it would not support Lagu leadership

[5] Muortat disclosed to this author in London 1999

[6] the arms sent to Samuel Abu John camps in western Equatoria were intercepted and taken by the Government forces between Maridi and Yambio

[7] see Heritage Weekly Newspaper, Khartoum November 1987

[8] the said letter was taken to the South by this author, unaware of the its adverse contents

[9] the three politicians later joined the SPLM/SPLA and both died in the South

[10] The secret letter originated from the Army General HQs in Khartoum tacitly intended for the benefit of the senior Northern Officers stationed in the South

[11] Gismalla Abdalla Rassass from Fertit tribe in western Bahr el-Ghazal, converted to Islam and dropped his Christian name, Bartholomew, following

a wedding to a Muslim woman from the North whom he met while in the army

[12] Makur was permanently kept out of the South as long as the rebellion raged by being given political assignment after another

[13] According to the 1980 Act the Northern Sudan was supposed to be divided up into regions in accordance the existing six provinces in 1956

CHAPTER 2

[1] A Monthly periodical published in Khartoum by the Ministry Of Culture and Information

[2] See Dr Khalid in the Government They Deserved 1991

[3] The author was a member of Abyei Central Committee

[4] An interview with Arok Thon, Addis Ababa, December 1986

[5] Albino Akol was one of the leaders of the underground cells

[6] See Elijah Malok letter to Dr Amon Mon Wantok in 1991

[7] An exclusive interview published in Heritage Newspaper Khartoum November 1987

[8] See letter of Elijah Malok to Dr Amon Wantok, 1991

[9] See Heritage Newspaper, November 1987

CHAPTER 3

[1] Interview with Elia Duang Arop and Gordon Muortant, London 1984

[2] Albino Akol denied the charge in an interview with the author in London 2003

[3] The author remained in Juba watching the situation (1983-1984); hence gives an eye witness account

[4] He later became Ethiopian Ambassador to Khartoum 1989/1991 and gave this information to the author in an interview

[5] The author was arrested and detained along with the rest, January to May 1983

[6] Interview by author, "Colonel Dr. Garang Speaks to Heritage on War and Peace in Sudan" *Heritage Newspaper,* Monday 9 November 1987, pp.4-6. For further details see SPLA/SPLM Manifesto July 1983

CHAPTER FOUR

[1] Interview with Laal Longo, one of the surviving recruits, Addis Ababa December, 1986

[2] Interview with Cdr Lual Diing, Addis Ababa December, 1986

[3] Interview with Kerubino Kuanyin Bol, Addis Ababa, December 1986

[5] Cdr Dim's interview, London 2000

[6] Personal conversation with the author in his house, Khartoum 1987

[7] Deng Alor became one of the chief negotiators in the peace negotiations that ended with the signing of the Naivasha Comprehensive Peace Agreement, 2005

[8] Chol Deng Alak studied marine engineering in the former Soviet Republic of Ukraine

[9] Published in Heritage Newspaper November 9, 1987

[10] Cdr Lual Diing disclosed to this author in an interview, Addis Ababa, December 1987

[11] Nyaba: Politics of Liberation page 35, 1997

[12] M K Malek was one of the so called progressive officers at SPLA/SPLM Bonga military and political school in Western Ethiopia

[13] See Garang Speaks 1987; edited by Dr Mansour Khalid, SPLM Political Adviser

CHAPTER 5

[1] See Dr Khalid, The Government They Deserve, Kegan Paul International, 1991

[2] See Dr Khalid, Garang Speaks p12 1992

[3] See Dr Khalid in the Government They Deserve 1991 p330 and Amnesty International 1994

[4] ibid

[5] See Dr Khalid, in Garang Speaks p9, 1992

[6] See Dr Khalid in Garang Speaks p9, 1992

[7] ibid

[8] Ngor Ayuel Kuocgoor, a Dinka trader married to an Equatoria stayed in Juba throughout this difficult period and gave an eyewitness account to the author in an interview 1989

[9] See Heritage Newspaper, Khartoum, November 1987

[10] See Dr Khalid in Garang Speaks p28, 1992

[11] See Nyaba, Peter Adwok, in Politics of Liberation, 1997

CHAPTER 6

[1] Dr Mansour Khalid's They Government They Deserved p342, 1991

[2] See Dr Khalid 1991

[3] See Garang Speaks edited 3by Dr Khalid 1992

[4] ibid

[5] Khalid in the Government They Deserved, p393, 1991

[6] ibid

[7] Dr Mansour Khalid 1991

[8] Dr Turabi's Challenger won because the other parties withdrew their candidates in order to defeat Dr Turabi. This may explain why al Turabi put all his weight in favour of NIF military take over

[9] See Kok. Governance and Conflict in Sudan, 1996

CHAPTER 7

[1] Kok: Governance and Conflict in Sudan 1996

[2] The author attended this session of parliament

[3] Ann M Lesch in Sudan: Contested National Identities 1998

[4] ibid

[5] Dr Khalid, The Government They Deserved, 1991

[6] Heritage Newspaper Khartoum, November 1987

[7] Heritage Khartoum 1987 and Africa Events, London 1987

[8] ibid

[9] Dr Kok. Governance and Conflict in Sudan 1996

[10] Mansour Khalid. The Government They Deserve 1991

[11] ibid

[12] Kok. Governance and Conflict in Sudan 1996

[13] Heritage Newspaper, Khartoum, November 1987

[14] For more details, see pamphlet written by two prominent Khartoum University Lecturers; Dr Suleiman Ali Baldo and Dr Mahmoud Ushari 1987

[15] Dr Khalid. Government They Deserve, 1991

[16] Abdel Wahab El Effendi.The NIF Discovering the South: South Sudan Dilemma for Islam in Africa

[17] Heritage Newspaper, Khartoum November 1987

[18] ibid

[19] Dr Kok. Governance and Conflict.1996

[20] Dr Khalid. Government They Deserve 1991

[21] ibid

[22] Professor Lesch 1998 and Dr Kok 1996

[23] Dr Kok. Governance and Conflict in Sudan 1996

[24] Dr Khalid: The Government They Deserve 1991

[25] Heritage Newspaper, Khartoum 1987

[26] Dr Kok. Governance and conflict in Sudan 1996

[27] Dr Khalid. The Government They Deserve 1991

[28] Dr Kok. Governance and Conflict 1996

[29] ibid

[30] Heritage Newspaper Khartoum 1987

[31] Dr Khalid.. the Government They Deserve, 1991

[32] Funding was made through Faisal Islamic Banks in Sudan.

CHAPTER 8

[1]This analysis was obtained in an interview with M K Malek a former member of SPLM political school at Bonga, Ethiopia

[2] ibid

[3] ibid

[4] Dr Peter Nyaba. The Politics of Liberation, 1997

[5] Mayaom kuaoc in an interview with the author Birmingham 2000

[6] Heritage Newspaper, Khartoum, January 1987

[7] The detailed analysis was given by Mayaom Kuaoc; who was at the centre of events in the SPLA, in an Interview with author in Birmingham 2002

[8] ibid

[9] The circumstances surrounding the arrest and detention of Kerubino Kuanyin Bol was related by three prominent members of SPLA Commander Lual Diing Wuol, Commander Dominic Dim Deng, Captain Mayaom K Malek and Sergeant Laal Longo who was Kerubino Driver.

[10] The rise and demise of progressive officers was vividly related to the author by Mayaom K Malek, one of the early graduates of the SPLA Bonga Political School and who was himself, one of the progressive officers.

11 ibid

[12] Interview with Major General Burma Nasir in Khartoum, 1988

[13] Arok Thon Arok died in 1998 at Nasir, eastern Upper Nile, in a plane crash that also killed Vice President al Zubeir Mohammed Saleh, who was leading the peace mission to the region. The aim of the mission was apparently to explain the circumstances that led to the re-redefection of Cdr Kerubino Kuanyin Bol to the SPLA on January 29, 1998

[14] Sources: Interview with Dominic Dim in London 2000. Cdr Dim was one of the field commanders during the Bright Star Campaign. For more detailed information see Dr Khalid in Garang Speaks, Kegan Paul, 1987

CHAPTER 9

[1] Most of the information published here was obtained through official and unofficial interviews with members of the Junta and on the top General Hassan Ahmedein Suleiman, one of the coup plotters

[2] Aldo Ajou was a political adviser to the Revolution Command Council and later, deputy speaker of the National Assembly before he defected and joined the SPLM in December 1993

[3] See Dr Kok in the Governance and Conflict in Sudan, 1996

[4] Sources: Sudan News Agency and Professor Lesch's Contested National Identies

[5] ibid

[6] ibid

[7] Kok Governance and Conflict in Sudan, 1996

[8] Brigadier Dominic Kassiano, former member of RCC in an interview with the author in London 2000

[9] Interview Ahmed al Radi Jaber in his Omdurman residence before he died in plane crash over Bentiu in 1993

[10] A M Lesch: Contested National Identities, 1998

[11] The author was detained at New Halfa in Eastern Sudan. Arop Bagat in Kassala, also in eastern Sudan and Alfred Taban in Kober Maximum Security Prison, in Khartoum

[12] Interview with Governor, Mangu Ajak in his office in Khartoum.1992

[13] Interview with Musa Ali Suleiman in the Parliament Building in Omdurman shortly before he died in a plane crush over Rubkona, Bentiu in August 1993

[14] Interview with Logali published in Heritage Newspaper Khartoum 1987

[15] Reported by one of southern Sudanese Christian trainee recruits in the "FAROUQ FOUR BATCH" Popular Defence Force Training camp " at Qatheina County, South of Khartoum, 1992

[16] Fatuah was published by Alex de Waal in Africa Watch and the Cotholic Bishops Conference Bulletin August-July 1993

[17] Alex de Waal, in the Nuba people of Sudan Facing Genocide

[18] See A M Lesch in, Contested National Identities pp 1962-1963, 1998

[19] ibid

CHAPTER 10

[1] Interview with Mayom Malek in Birmingham, 2000

[2] ibid

[3] ibid

[4] Interview with Wadang Biong, Birmingham

[5] Dr Nyaba in the Politics of Liberation

[6] The document was a clandestine literature being circulated discreetly by the group to selected readers

7 ibid

[8] Dr. Peter Nyot Kok was a senior member of Dr. Akol's Khartoum-based Sudan African Congress Party in 1985-89 period

[9] Interview with Malek Birmingham 2002

[10] The author was the Director of SCC Advocacy and Communications Desk, hence a rapporteur of the meeting

[11] National Democratic Alliance (NDA) is the main opposition group in the North that had come into being following the 1989 Islamist military coup d'tat. The SPLA/SPLM joined NDA officially in 1995

[12] Lesch, Ann M. 1998. *The Sudan: Contested National Identities*. Oxford, James Currey

[13] Dr. Nyaba was sympathetic to the Nasir faction. But when it became clear that nationalists had been dragged unwittingly into the Arab camp, he simply retracted and rejoined the SPLA main wing

[14] The letter was delivered to the author by a representative of the Nuba Mountain secret cells in Khartoum, 1991

[15] Interview with Malek, Birmingham 2000

[16] Since time immemorial, the Dinka and the Nuer have been living together. Additionally they are the most integrated and intermarried among the southern tribes

[17] See Nyaba politics of Liberation

[18] Interview with Commander Paul Anade Othow at the Hotel Green Village in Khartoum, 1997

[19] ibid

[21] A M Lesh in Contested National Identities

[22] Simon al Hajj Kulisika and A M Lesch

[23] See Human Rights Watch/Africa. 1994. *Civilian Devastation: Abuses by All parties in the War in Southern Sudan.* New York, Human Rights Press

[24] The Meeting occurred at the US Embassy on July 21, 1993. It was attended by the author. in his capacity as SCC Director of Advocacy

CHAPTER 11

[1] Cdr Dim was one of the field commanders during Seif al Obuur offensive. Hence offers eyewitness account

[2] Malek was at the SPLA tactical headquarters and had watched the events unfolding

[3] the SPLA commander of the mechanised task force failed to move into the city on time because according to reports, he was sympathetic with the Nasir SPLA

[4] Amnesty International Report September 1992

[5] Anna Mosely Lesch—Contested National Identity 1996

[6] According to interview with the Editor of The Referendum Magazine, (a local Southern Sudanese magazine published in Nairobi), Nhial Bol Akaen , Joseph Kony stated that he was introduced to the Sudanese authorities by Commander William Nyuon Bant after defecting form the SPLA and joined the Government side under the Khartoum peace agreement. It was after that the Lord Resistance Army became an allied militia to the Sudanese Army

[7] Interview with a former Amin intelligent officer Abdel Hameed Baramatali at his residence at Soba West, Khartoum in 1993. Baramatali was captured and detained by Ugandan Authorities accused of spying for Sudanese intelligence before he escaped and came and settled in Khartoum. Several times the Sudanese security tried to reengage him but he refused

CHAPTER 12

[1] Interview with various SPLA field commanders and government security personnel in private capacity

[2] Source: SPLA Ad hoc committee recommendation to the SPLA/SPLM Leadership Council 1994

[3] Interview with Paul Anade and Simon Mori Didumo at the Green Village Hotel in Khartoum 1997

[4] Kassala was later attacked and occupied temporarily by NDA forces. The war was also extended to eastern Sudan including the holy shrine of Homesh Koreib

[5] Sudanow Magazine: interview with Charles Julu , Governor of Western Bahr al Ghazal, February 1998

[6] The commander of Kuarjena force was killed when he tried to overwhelm the rebels force at Girinti, Wau

[7] Warrap state (combining the Districts of Tonj and Gogrial) was captured by the SPLA in 1997 when it re-enters Bahr al Ghazal

CHAPTER 13

[1] Interview with Ahmed al Radi Jaber in his house in Omdurman 1992

[2] Accusing fingers are pointed at SSIM Forces for Cdr Nyuon Bany assassination. No investigation has so far been carried out

[3] The author attended this press conference

[4] Peter Riir, disclosed this to the author in an interview at the Peace Commission Head Quarters in Khartoum 1993

[4] See the SPLA Legal Frame Work itself for more details

[5] According to reports, Ajak and Agook were asked to withdraw from the contest in effort to defeat Dr Akol. who had just signed the Fashoda Accord. According to security personnel monitoring the dissident returnees groups, the authorities were not convinced that Akol was a genuine peace respondent. He could not therefore be trusted. to take charge of the position of governor of the sensitive region of Upper Nile

[6] Although Peter Gadet claimed that he killed Kerubino Kuanyin, there is a strong belief that he was killed by orders of Colonel Ibrahim Shams Eddin, the regime strongman who was then in total control of the security operations in the South

CHAPTER 14

[1] Sudan, the contested national identities pp171 1996

[2] Interview with Dr R.K. Mulla in London 1999. Dr Mulla was the SPLM Main Stream Spokesman during the Abuja One Peace Talks

[3] See Sudan: Contested National Identity, 1996

[4] Interview with Dr Richard Mulla, Spokesman of Torit Faction at the Abuja One Conference

[5] Interview with one of the southerners who was in the government delegation at Abuja One Talks

[6] Interview with Cdr Dominic Dim who sent a detachment that attempted to intercept Cdr Nyuon

[7] Interview with Bishop Paride Taban at the White Fathers Residence in Rome September 1994

[8] According to reports, William Nyuon chose and went to Eastern Upper Nile on a specific mission. To meet his old friend Cdr Kerubino Kuanyin Bol. He would then persuade him to accept the reunification of the SPLM/SPLA under John Garang. Unfortunately Nyuon died before meeting his friend Kerubino

CHAPTER 15

[1] See Lesch Contested National Identities, 1996

[2] See SPLA Four Model Legal Frame Work for the solution of the Sudanese conflict

[3] With the capture of Kaji keji by the government forces in August1995, only Maridi, Yambio, Tombura and Nimule were left in the hands of the SPLA.. Whereas before the split the SPLA held most of the major towns in the South. except Renk, Kodok, Raga, Bentiu, Yei, Fangak, Aweil and of course the three regional Capitals of Juba, Malakal and Wau

[4] See Lesch. Sudan; Contested National Identities, 1998

[5] Reminiscent of October 1964 and March/April 1985 when the incumbent military regimes were overthrown by popular uprisings

CHAPTER 16

[1] The legitimate Command was composed of: General Fathi Mohamed Ali former Commander in Chief, General Abdel Rahman Said, former Deputy Chief of Staff for Operations and General Al Hadi Bushra, former Deputy Chief of Staff for Security

[2] the Economist: London, June 12th1999

[3] for more details see the SCIS document 2001

[4] Other heads of government and state that attended the signing ceremony include, Algerian President, Abdel Aziz Bouteflicka, Paul Kagami of Rwanda, President Omar al Bashir of Sudan, Meles Zenawi, Prime Minister of Ethiopia, Former Presidents of Sudan, Jaafar Mohamed Nimeiri and Abdel Rahman Mohamed Hassan Sowar al Dahab. The countries that facilitated the peace process: Norway was represented by Hilda Johnstone, Minister for International Development. USA, UK and Italy were represented by their respective Ambassadors. Human Rights Organizations and international civil societies attended. Additionally an estimated of 30,000 Sudanese citizens led by prominent persons attended this historic day of peace in their country after 49 years of war and instability

[5] Abdel Wahab al Effendi is a Sudanese scholar and author of the Turabi Revolution, a prophetic prediction about the fateful end of Sudan as one country

[6] John Garang the leader of the SPLM/SPLA said on January 13, in a press statement in Rumbek, temporary capital of the now autonomous Southern Sudan

INDEX

A

B

C

D

H

J

K

O

Q

R

(Footnotes)

300142

Made in the USA